THE SWORD AND THE STYLUS

THE SWORD AND THE STYLUS

An Introduction to Wisdom in the Age of Empires

Leo G. Perdue

WILLIAM B. EERDMANS PUBLISHING COMPANY
GRAND RAPIDS, MICHIGAN / CAMBRIDGE, U.K.

Published 2008 by

Wm. B. Eerdmans Publishing Co.

2140 Oak Industrial Drive N.E., Grand Rapids, Michigan 49505 /

P.O. Box 163, Cambridge CB3 9PU U.K.

Printed in the United States of America

13 12 11 10 09 08   7 6 5 4 3 2 1

Library of Congress Cataloging-in-Publication Data

Perdue, Leo G.

   The sword and the stylus: an introduction to wisdom in the age of empires /

   Leo G. Perdue.

      p.   cm.

   Includes bibliographical references (p.   ).

   ISBN 978-0-8028-6245-7 (pbk.: alk. paper)

   1. Wisdom literature — Criticism, interpretation, etc.   I. Title.

BS1455.P38   2008

223'.06 — dc22

                             2008003709

www.eerdmans.com

Contents

Abbreviations

AASOR	Annual of the American Schools of Oriental Research
AB	Anchor Bible
ABD	*Anchor Bible Dictionary*
ABRL	Anchor Bible Reference Library
ActSum	*Acta Sumeriologica*
AfO	*Archiv für Orientforschung*
AGAJU	Arbeiten zur Geschichte des antiken Judentums und des Urchristentums
AnBib	*Analecta Biblica*
ANET	*Ancient Near Eastern Texts*
ANETS	*Ancient Near Eastern Texts and Studies*
AnOr	Analecta Orientalia
ANRW	*Aufstieg und Niedergang der römischen Welt*
AnSt	*Anatolian Studies*
AOAT	Alter Orient und Altes Testament
AS	*Assyriological Studies*
ATD	Das Alte Testament Deutsch
BASOR	*Bulletin of the American Schools of Oriental Research*
BBB	Bonner Biblische Beiträge
BDB	Brown-Driver-Briggs, *Hebrew and English Lexicon of the Old Testament*
BETL	Bibliotheca ephemeridum theologicarum lovaniensium
Bib	*Biblica*
BibOr	Bibliotheca Orientalis
BIFAO	*Bulletin de l'Institut Français d'archéologie orientale*

BJS	Brown Judaic Studies
BKAT	Biblischer Kommentar: Altes Testament
BO	*Bibliotheca orientalis*
BZ	*Biblische Zeitschrift*
BZAW	Beihefte zur Zeitschrift für die Alttestamentliche Wissenschaft
BZNW	Beihefte zur Zeitschrift für die Neutestamentliche Wissenschaft
CAH	*Cambridge Ancient History*
CANE	*Civilizations of the Ancient Near East*
CBQ	*Catholic Biblical Quarterly*
CBQMS	Catholic Biblical Quarterly Monograph Series
CJTh	*Canadian Journal of Theology*
ConBOT	Coniectanea Biblica, Old Testament
CR:BS	*Currents in Research: Biblical Studies*
CRINT	Compendia rerum iudaicarum ad Novum Testamentum
DJD	Discoveries in the Judaean Desert
DSD	*Dead Sea Scrolls Discoveries*
EncJud	*Encyclopedia Judaica*
FAT	Forschungen zum Alten Testament
FOTL	Forms of Old Testament Literature
FRLANT	Forschungen zur Religion und Literatur des Alten und Neuen Testaments
GBS	Guides to Biblical Scholarship
HAT	Handbuch zum Alten Testament
HAW	Handbuch der Altertumswissenschaft
HdO	Handbuch der Orientalistik
HSM	Harvard Semitic Monographs
HThR	*Harvard Theological Review*
HUCA	*Hebrew Union College Annual*
IB	*Interpreter's Bible*
IEJ	*Israel Exploration Journal*
Interp	*Interpretation*
JAAR	*Journal of the American Academy of Religion*
JAOS	*Journal of the American Oriental Society*
JBL	*Journal of Biblical Literature*
JCS	*Journal of Cuneiform Studies*
JEA	*Journal of Egyptian Archaeology*
JEOL	*Jaarbuch van het Vooraziatisch-Egyptisch Gezelschap*
JJS	*Journal of Jewish Studies*
JNES	*Journal of Near Eastern Studies*
JNSL	*Journal of Northwest Semitic Languages*

JPS	Jewish Publication Society
JQR	*Jewish Quarterly Review*
JSJ	*Journal for the Study of Judaism in the Persian, Hellenistic, and Roman Periods*
JSNT	*Journal for the Study of the New Testament*
JSOT	*Journal for the Study of the Old Testament*
JSOTSup	Journal for the Study of the Old Testament Supplements
JSP	*Journal for the Study of the Pseudepigrapha*
JSPSup	Journal for the Study of the Pseudepigrapha: Supplement Studies
JSS	*Journal of Semitic Studies*
JTS	*Journal of Theological Studies*
KAT	Kommentar zum Alten Testament
LÄ	*Lexikon der Ägyptologie*
LBS	Library of Biblical Studies
LCL	Loeb Classicla Library
LD	Lectio divina
LEC	Library of Early Christianity
LSJ	Liddell-Scott-Jones, *Greek-English Lexicon*
NIB	New Interpreter's Bible
NovTSup	Novum Testamentum Supplement
NTS	*New Testament Studies*
OBO	Orbis biblicus et orientalis
OCD	*Oxford Classical Dictionary*
OLA	Orientalia lovaniensia acta
OLZ	*Orientalistische Literaturzeitung*
Or	*Orientalia (NS)*
OrAnt	*Oriens antiquus*
OTE	*Old Testament Essays*
OTL	Old Testament Library
OTP	*The Old Testament Pseudepigrapha* 1 and 2
OTS	*Oudtestamentische Studiën*
PRU	*Le palais royal d'Ugarit*
PTMS	Pittsburgh Theological Monograph Series
RB	*Revue Biblique*
REJ	*Revue des études juives*
RevQ	*Revue de Qumran*
RHR	*Revue de l'histoire des religions*
RSR	*Recherches de science religieuse*
RTL	*Revue théologique de Louvain*

SBAW	*Sitzungsberichte der bayerischen Akademie der Wissenschaften*
SBLDS	Society of Biblical Literature Dissertation Series
SBLEJL	Society of Biblical Literature Early Judaism and Its Literature
SBLMS	Society of Biblical Literature Monograph Series
SBLSCS	Society of Biblical Literature Septuagint and Cognate Studies
SBLSP	*Society of Biblical Literature Seminar Papers*
SBLSymS	Society of Biblical Literature Symposium Series
SBLTT	Society of Biblical Literature Texts and Translations
SBS	Stuttgarter Bibelstudien
SBT	Studies in Biblical Theology
SCHNT	Studia ad corpus hellenisticum Novi Testamenti
SCS	Septuagint and Cognate Studies
SJLA	Studies in Judaism in Late Antiquity
SJOT	*Scandinavian Journal of Old Testament*
SJTh	*Scottish Journal of Theology*
STDJ	Studies on the Texts of the Desert of Judah
SUNT	Studien zur Umwelt des Neuen Testaments
SVTP	Studia in Veteris Testamenti pseudepigraphica
TB	*Tyndale Bulletin*
TDNT	*Theological Dictionary of the New Testament*
TDOT	*Theological Dictionary of the Old Testament*
TLZ	*Theologische Literaturzeitung*
TSAJ	Texte und Studien zum antiken Judentum
TUAT	Texte aus der Umwelt des Alten Testaments
TynBul	*Tyndale Bulletin*
UF	*Ugarit Forschung*
UTB	Uni-Taschenbücher
VT	*Vetus Testamentum*
VTSup	Vetus Testamentum Supplements
WdF	Wege der Forschung
WMANT	Wissenschaftliche Monographien zum Alten und Neuen Testament
WO	*Die Welt des Orients*
WUNT	Wissenschaftliche Untersuchungen zum Neuen Testament
ZA	*Zeitschrift für Assyriologie*
ZÄS	*Zeitschrift für ägyptische Sprache und Altertumskunde*
ZAW	*Zeitschrift für die alttestamentliche Wissenschaft*
ZBK	Zürcher Bibelkommentar
ZNW	*Zeitschrift für die neutestamentliche Wissenschaft*
ZThK	*Zeitschrift für Theologie und Kirche*

1. A Prolegomenon to Wisdom in the Empires

Wisdom, History, and the Empires

Wisdom and Historiography

In this introduction I begin and end with the general view that the wisdom tradition cannot be understood apart from the larger social history of the cultures in which it took root and flourished and the more particular position that the understandings and roles of sages assumed their shape and changed within different social locations over the centuries. Wisdom was a product of the empires, which required savants to write court annals, teachings of moral virtues to the elite and professionals who held important posts, texts on astrology, cosmology, religion and the gods, nature, science, music, architecture, engineering, and mathematics, and a crafted ideology that provided the legitimation of reigning kings and dynasties. In this volume I move away from the stranglehold of idealism, which has dominated most research concerning wisdom for the past century. Idealism understands the teachings of the sages as disconnected ideas that are seen as eternal thoughts the savants understood to be true. Consequently, I begin this introduction with a brief review of historiography and history, before proceeding into the literary data and material culture that together form the social and historical matrix for understanding the sages, their roles, and their worldviews.

Historiography involves three major concerns.[1] The first is to discover the

1. In general see Edward H. Carl, *What Is History?* with a new introduction by Richard J. Ev-

material and cultural data of past civilizations and to reconstruct the human thought and behavior that produced them in particular times and places. The second is to examine the ways that the various pasts of these civilizations have been reconstructed and interpreted by later historians from antiquity to the present. The third is the focused effort of the modern historian to interpret the peoples and events of civilizations in order to understand their past experiences and preeminent understandings and events by current theories that shape the histories of the contemporary period.

Contemporary historiography is grounded in a number of different philosophical orientations. Positivistic history continues to emerge in some form in most modern histories, whether the focus is on historical forces that shape people and events, great people who have had an important role in directing the course of human existence in a particular civilization, the response of cultures to significant crises that confront a people, a dialectic of opposites that leads to synthesis, the importance of struggle, the geographical and environmental terrain in which a civilization exists, or the formulation of new ideas that reorder human lives within a past culture. Historiography is, in part, the application of historical-critical and archaeological methods to the existing material and written data in order to reconstruct and describe the development, continuation, and end of human cultures, which include a collage of sequential events, interactive and distinct ideologies, and temporal and spatial locations. Historiography seeks to record and interpret the society, culture, religion, politics, and major ideologies of a people in the past within the matrix of psychological, geophysical, anthropological, sociological, and philosophical theories.[2] Data, of course, do not interpret themselves, and regardless of the methodology or orientation of an historian, his/her imagination is drawn on to shape a collage of images that, taken together, constitute the history of a past culture. Due to the limits of the data and the varieties and subtleties which these elements may represent, the most a historian can usually hope to attain is plausibility, on occasion even probability, but not certainty.

We can no longer be content simply to reconstruct, translate, and interpret the texts of the scribes outside the domain of social history. Otherwise, we run

---

ans (Basingstoke, Eng.: Palgrave, 2001); and Mark T. Gilderhus, *History and Historians: A Historiographical Introduction* (5th ed.; Englewood Cliffs, NJ: Prentice-Hall, 2002).

2. See Seth Schwartz, *Imperialism and Jewish Society, 200 B.C.E. to 640 C.E.* (Princeton: Princeton University Press, 2001) 2-3. Also see John Huizinga, "A Definition of the Concept of History," in *Philosophy and History: Essays Presented to Ernst Cassirer,* ed. Raymond Klibansky and H. J. Paton (New York: Harper & Row, 1963) 1-10; Edgar Krentz, *The Historical-Critical Method* (GBS: OT; Philadelphia: Fortress, 1975); John Van Seters, *In Search of History: Historiography in the Ancient World and the History of the Bible* (Winona Lake, IN: Eisenbrauns, 1997).

the risk of oversimplifying the ideas that often reflect our own interests and understandings. To place the sages within the historical matrix of the ancient Near East and the larger eastern Mediterranean world along with the formation and development of their institutions is a significant challenge, but to avoid it constricts, hinders, and even distorts much of the interpretive task.

The proper understanding of wisdom literature requires one to move out of the realm of philosophical idealism and into the realistic dimensions of history and social construction. The literature of the sages did not transcend its historical and social setting, but rather was located in a variety of historical events and social circumstances of an evolving nation and its subgroups that reflect different and changing epistemologies, moral systems, views of God, comprehensions of human nature, and religious understandings. Earlier understandings entered into the stream of a people's tradition that shaped their identity and provided insights for the reconstitution of the self-understandings of later generations. The disregard of historical and social contexts leads to the distortion of the literature and deposits it into an impenetrable isolation. Even today, too many interpreters have often made the teachings of the wise impervious to history and immune to the roles and institutions of social life.[3]

In addition to the evidence of the literary tradition of the sages, the material culture yields relevant epigraphic, symbolic, artistic, and architectural evidence for the reconstruction of the sociohistorical location of the sapiential literature and the social institutions in which the sages and scribes carried out their professional activities. In addition, the material data provided by archaeological excavations in the other cultures of the eastern Mediterranean world provide important evidence for consideration, due to the expansive cross-fertilization brought about by conquest and commerce. Written materials in the form of manuscripts, ostraca, scarabs, stelae, cuneiform tablets, artifacts of various kinds, the dating and reconstruction of the history of sites, and the portrayals in sculpture, friezes, and frescoes give expression to the larger cultural context for the interpretation of classical and even ordinary compositions and

---

3. In 1990 John G. Gammie and I edited a collection of essays that had as its objective the presentation of the social locations and roles of the sages not only in ancient Israel but also in the larger ancient Near East (*The Sage in Israel and the Ancient Near East* [Winona Lake, IN: Eisenbrauns, 1990]). I am continuing this project in a new volume, *Scribes, Sages, and Seers: The Social Roles of the Wise in Israel and the Eastern Mediterranean World,* ed. Leo G. Perdue (FRLANT 219; Göttingen: Vandenhoeck & Ruprecht, forthcoming). This volume will address new texts and studies that have appeared since the previous volume, fill in the gaps of the previous volume, and examine the roles of sages as teachers and composers, scribes as writers of legal materials and correspondence, copyists and redactors of literature, recorders and archivists, and seers as recipients and conveyors of esoteric wisdom.

epigraphic writings and often demonstrate that scribes were conversant with a wide variety of other cultures, languages, and literary traditions.

The construct of history in its written expression, which is based on a chosen philosophical theory, is an act of the imagination.[4] The data from history consist of written, epigraphic, artistic, and archaeological evidence placed within a matrix of time and space. Most contemporary historians point to earlier interpretations of events as secondary evidence for their own interpretation of events, while quick to realize the ideological character of interpretation, past and present.[5] The way of processing this information and placing it into a system of meaning begins with the imagination of the historian and continues through empirical analysis and rational reconstruction of events, cultures, and people within their particular sociohistorical settings in order to shape a synthesis of a social history. However, it is impossible for any historian to avoid the influence of his/her own ideological views shaped within his/her own social and cultural settings.

Wisdom and Imagination

In one sense, "wisdom literature," like the writing of history, is an act of the imagination. This refers to the ability of the sage to construe through his/her inventiveness the existence and character of God, the nature of reality, and the moral character of sapiential life that lead to well-being and the constitution of the larger orders of reality in both society and the cosmos. For the sages, the observation of animate and inanimate objects led them to imagine an interrelated reality that betrayed the typical, the consistent, and the predictable. The objective of these observations by the sages, which are expressed in the sapiential literature and narrative descriptions of wisdom, was primarily to set forth moral instruction that incorporated proper ways of living and acting in concert with the divine paradigm for cosmic and social construction. This order of reality was not a law of science, but rather a human fabrication given a moral quality. Thus the order that permeated creation, society, and human character was named "justice" (mišpāṭ) or "righteousness" (ṣĕdāqâ). All things, including hu-

4. See R. G. Collingwood, History as Imagination (rev. ed.; Oxford: Oxford University Press, 1994). Also see Paul Ricoeur, "Biblical Hermeneutics," Semeia 4 (1975) 129-46; idem, "The Narrative Function," Semeia 4 (1975) 177-202; and Hayden White, Metahistory: The Historical Imagination in Nineteenth-Century Europe (Baltimore: Johns Hopkins University Press, 1987).

5. Stephen Crites, "Unfinished Figure: On Theology and Imagination," in Unfinished . . . : Essays in Honor of Ray Hart, ed. Mark C. Taylor (JAAR Thematic Studies; Chico, CA: Scholars Press, 1981) 155-84.

mans, existed within a reality of order in which its constituent parts related to one another in ways that were considered to be congruent and transparent.

Thus one may say that the sapiential imagination shaped a cosmology and a social world that were theologically coherent, aesthetically attractive, and morally compelling. Through their imagination the sages depicted a world of beauty, insight, and bounty in which they invited their protégés to enter, take up residence, and dwell. This world was incarnated microcosmically in human nature and existence and in a larger way within the constituent makeup of social institutions, while the sages possessed the insight to appreciate and understand the inherent related features of cosmos and society. The imagination of the wise moved from the perception and arrangement of images, to the description of their nature, to an interconnectedness, and ultimately to an order of creation associated together in a larger system of reality. The sages posited that humans are drawn to the pursuit of wisdom as much as they are by the allure of sight, sounds, smells, tastes, and touch. Through the attainment of wisdom they pursued the rational intricacies of profound ideas and varied experiences. They moved beyond a hidebound Aristotelian logic and empirical testing to the aesthetic description and expression of the real, which led, among other things, to the creation of a language that combined logic with beauty. They also used the senses to gain an appreciation of what exists and may be experienced. Thus these images and other products of the human senses were shaped into compelling and meaning-laden metaphors that resided at the center of sapiential thinking and its common discourse. This discourse was not cold abstraction or the deductions of principles obtained by pure logic, but rather an aesthetically nuanced set of rhetorical devices that included the experience and enticement of things that affect the senses and thus attract the student to sagacious teaching. What was learned was derived from the engagement of content and the beholding of beauty and then tested in the arena of personal experience to authenticate its veracity within an unfolding tradition of sapiential insights.

Imagination involves a number of features, the first of which may be called "tradition and memory." The sages revered their ancestors and learned from their teachings, which were handed down through the generations (Job 15:17-19). By means of corporate memory, the teachings of the wise and their observations expressed in forms of sapiential rhetoric their understandings, which merged and were passed down through the centuries in order to assist new generations of sages to continue to construct worlds of knowledge and the moral life for their successors. While these ancient sages and their insights were honored, they were not inevitably and unconsciously embraced and affirmed uncritically. Rather, sages felt compelled to assess the validity and sagacity of these earlier teachings through reasoned analysis, present experience, and aesthetic consciousness residing deeply within the human person. They thus rejected, endorsed, or reshaped ancestral teachings in the effort to form their own cosmic and social constructions and understandings that would enable them to exist in an ever new and changing world.

When setting forth a worldview that was based on cosmic and societal order, the sages were concerned not simply with origins (Prov. 3:19-20), but also with providence, which continued to vitalize the forces of life and give shape to the continuing structures of life. At the same time, the sages believed that all humans were judged by God through the process of retributive justice. Behavior and speech that were in accord with the tested wisdom teachings based on order led to blessings in a variety of senses, ranging from a long life, to joy and contentment, to honor, and even to the accoutrements of pleasure and economic benefit. Improper behavior and language contravened cosmic and social order and led to loss in a variety of ways, ranging from pain, to the forfeiture of honor, to destitution, to death. Their understanding of retribution did not represent some infallible system that was inevitably true, but rather enveloped expectations of well-being and fulfillment or their opposite. Through wise behavior and the aesthesis of imaginative and instructive language the sages spoke and lived this world into being.

Yahweh (or Elohim), the creator, judge, director of the cosmos, and bestower of wisdom and life, was the center of sapiential imagination, reflection, and teaching. Wisdom is based on the "fear of God" *(yir'at ĕlōhîm),* and assumes the theology of a righteousness that permeates creation and social institutions and becomes the goal for human embodiment through discipline and action. The central affirmation of the sages is the declaration, "the fear of Yahweh (God) is the beginning of wisdom." The word "beginning" *(rē'šît)* conveys the understanding that the "fear of Yahweh," that is, trust in and reverence for God, participates in sustaining the world and becomes the basis for the validity and nomic character of the sapiential tradition. God used his wisdom (metaphorically portrayed on occasion as his divine consort or daughter) in shaping the cosmos and human society. This "fear" is wonder evoked by the marvelous acts of creation and providence that awakens human mimesis and allegiance.

God also is the benevolent giver of wisdom to those who would follow divine instruction enfolded in the teachings of the sages. God is viewed as transcendent and does not take up residence even in the temple, for he exists beyond the constrictions of time and space. Personified divine Wisdom embodied God's active presence in the world, and divine teaching was eventually made available to humans through the gift of the Torah. Thus divine revelation came

6

through the order of creation and the writings of the sages in their teachings, which came eventually to be identified with the Torah. God was known through nature and sapiential insight emerging from imagination. Presented through the canons of prosaic discourse, revelation was viewed as an intellectual eros or the alluring incarnation of divine Wisdom, who, like an entrancing and intelligent woman teacher, called the simple to embrace her, to learn from her the pathways to life, and to obtain ultimately knowledge of the creator and how to live within God's domains of creation and society. Of course, other sages (e.g., Agur and Qoheleth) eventually denied the possibility of penetrating the veil of divine mystery to know and understand the character and activity of God. God remained hidden within the darkened cloud of impenetrable mystery that denied human ability to move to an awareness of the divine. Even the insight of the wisest sage could not penetrate this darkness to grasp a divine transparency of who God is and what he does.

The sages also admitted that there were limits to their understanding of God. While quick to affirm divine and human freedom, they nevertheless argued that God oversees human existence and behavior, judges both the righteous and the wicked, and blesses and punishes accordingly. In this respect, God generates and forms life in the womb, brings the newborn under divine guidance and protection, and gives humans knowledge and the tools of the senses and reason to understand divine teachings and to live lives of righteous behavior. He is neither the eschatological God who draws history to its culmination nor the Lord of Israel's salvation history. He is not even specifically Israelite and Jewish in character. Rather he is the universal God of life, guidance, and justice for all. Perhaps to deal with contingency and mystery, "wisdom" in apocalyptic literature (e.g., the Enoch tradition and Daniel) and in Gnosticism became esoteric knowledge, obtained through dreams, visions, heavenly journeys, and enlightenment. There is a step toward this understanding in the Wisdom of Solomon and 1 Baruch, but it remains to be fully developed in the Jewish apocalypses and Gnostic systems of primitive Christianity.

"Wisdom" connotes a body of knowledge that includes written and oral texts, traditions, and teachings that are transmitted through a variety of channels of human discourse. This body of knowledge was placed within literary genres largely characteristic of their oral and literary teachings: sayings (proverb, beatitude, question, riddle, numerical saying, prohibition, and admonition), instructions, didactic narratives, disputations, and learned poems that included psalms of praise or panegyrics. Knowledge moved beyond the static understanding of data to an active force that defined human behavior. By actualizing virtue in their character and in their behavior, the sages taught that they participated in the sustaining of social order that was the basis of communal life. This enabled both the sage and the larger human society to exist in harmony with the cosmic order. Indeed, even the stability of the world was dependent in part on the result of wise behavior formed by Yahweh's teachings in sapiential instruction and ultimately located in the Torah.

"Wisdom" was a discipline that fashions human character, ranging from thinking critically to disciplined study, to spiritual meditation, to ethical behavior. Wisdom (ḥokmâ) was discipline (mûsār), that is, a structured type of existence that led to the formation of character, routinized a regimen of study, and devised a curriculum to be studied, mastered, and learned that enabled one to become a sage. Character was forged through study, reflection, and the actualization of virtue in both discourse and action. This embodiment of moral virtue led to a mode of being and a way of existence that gave issue to the integrity of the sages and enabled them to live in harmony with the cosmos, society, and the creator. Sapiential existence produced a sphere of well-being that included both internal peace and contentment and the aura of honor, respect, integrity, and dignity. Coveted blessings included long life, prosperity, and joy resulting from wise discourse and virtuous actions.

Finally, wisdom literature includes the canonical and deuterocanonical texts that were produced by a professional group of scribes and sages who were teachers and royal administrators in the court during the First Temple and then in the temple, in colonial administration, and in the internal governing and legal authority in the Second Temple. These writings continued through the Hellenistic and into the early Imperial Roman periods in the form of pseudepigraphal and Qumran texts. The three canonical books (Proverbs, Job, and Qoheleth) and the two deuterocanonical texts (Ben Sira and Wisdom of Solomon) share a common epistemology in affirming the superiority of reason and experience in determining what is true, a common language (literary structure, forms, and vocabulary), and equivalent content. These texts emerged out of eastern Mediterranean cultures that included numerous literary parallels in Egyptian (hieroglyphics, hieratic, and demotic), cuneiform (Sumerian, Assyrian, and Babylonian), Ugaritic, Aramaic, Greek, Latin, Syriac, and Hebrew, and that comprised comparable social groups who wrote and transmitted these respective traditions, while sharing both a common epistemology and cosmology.

Jewish pseudepigraphal texts include Pseudo-Phocylides, Aristobulus, and Sentences of the Wise Menander,[6] while the Qumran sapiential texts include 4QInstruction (1Q26, 4Q15-18, 423), the Book of Mysteries (1Q27, 4Q299-301),

---

6. Max Küchler, *Frühjüdische Weisheitstraditionen: Zum Fortgang weisheitlichen Denkens im Bereich des frühjüdische Jahweglaubens* (Göttingen: Vandenhoeck & Ruprecht, 1979).

4QWiles of the Wicked Woman (4Q184), 4QSapiential Work (4Q185), 4QWords of the Maśkil (4Q298), 4QWays of Righteousness (4Q420-21), 4QInstruction-like Composition B (4Q424), and 4QBeatitudes (4Q525).[7] Finally, early rabbinic texts (Tannaitic/Amoraic) that resemble earlier sapiential writings include tractate *'Abot (Fathers)* and *'Abot de Rabbi Nathan*.[8]

Wisdom also has to do with aesthetics. Intrinsic to the literary and spoken formation of sapiential language are the eloquence of form and clarity of thought. Aesthesis combines the attraction of beauty with the order and assuagement occasioned by harmony. Through the eloquence of speech, the cogency of logic, and the rhetorical elegance of written language, the sages invite their hearers to enter and dwell in a world viewed as one of beauty, harmony, reason, and order. Within this living space, the sages pursue lives of knowledge and artistry in which well-being and meaning are achieved.

The Definition of Wisdom and the Language of the Israelite and Jewish Sage

The formal and ideational character of wisdom (Heb. *ḥokmâ;* Gk. *sophia*) in the Hebrew Bible, the Apocrypha, and the Pseudepigrapha comprises numerous features. The Hebrew word *ḥokmâ* has a variety of synonyms used in parallel lines and half lines in poetic discourse.[9] Frequent synonyms of the stative verb *ḥākam* ("to be wise") are *bîn* ("to perceive"), *yāda'* ("to know"), and *śākal* ("to be prudent"). *Ḥākam* ("to be wise") refers to one who embodies and acts upon the basis of insight and knowledge. Likewise, the noun *ḥokmâ* ("wisdom") and its shorter form *ḥākām* have several synonyms, including *bînâ* ("perception/insight" = *tĕbûnâ, nābôn*), *da'at* ("knowledge"), *dābār* ("word"), *'ēmer* ("saying," "word"), *māšāl* ("saying," "proverb"), *'ormâ* ("shrewdness"), *mĕzimmâ* ("planning"), *tûšîyâ* ("practical wisdom"), *kišrôn* ("success," "skill"), and *taḥbūlôt* ("words of wisdom"). The abstract plural of wisdom, *ḥokmôt*, refers to Woman Wisdom (Prov. 1:20; 9:1), as does, on occasion, the singular *ḥokmâ* (8:1). The noun *ḥākām* refers to both a wise person or sage (Jer. 18:18; Prov. 22:17; 24:23) and a variety of abstract nouns: sagacity, intelligence, rational and critical insight, acuity, rationality, common sense, shrewdness, judiciousness, judgment, prudence, circumspection, logic, soundness, advisability,

---

7. Matthew J. Goff, *Discerning Wisdom: The Sapiential Literature of the Dead Sea Scrolls* (VTSup 116; Leiden: Brill, 2007).

8. Günter Stemberger, "Sages, Scribes, and Seers in Rabbinic Judaism," in *Scribes, Sages, and Seers* (forthcoming).

9. See H.-P. Müller and M. Krause, "חכם," *TDOT* 4 (1980) 364-85.

mastery, expertise, skill, proficiency, expertness, accomplishment, adeptness, capacity, and capability.[10] Related terms for the sage (*ḥākām*) are *mēbîn* ("one who has understanding," "teacher"), *maśkîl* ("prudent, intelligent one"), and *mĕlammēd* ("teacher").

Often associated with the term "wisdom" are a number of words that point to teaching and instruction: *leqaḥ* ("instruction," indicating that the sage is one who educates students), *mûsār* ("teaching," "discipline"), *tōkaḥat* ("argument," "dialogue," "debate"), *tôrâ* ("instruction"), *miṣwâ* ("commandment"), and *ʿēṣâ* ("counsel"). These nouns have verbal forms: *yākaḥ* ("argue," "debate," "reprove," "rebuke," with words and blows), *yārâ* ("cast"), *ṣāwâ* ("command"), *yāsar* ("discipline"), and *yāʿaṣ* ("advise," "counsel"). Other common verbs identified or associated with wisdom are *yādaʿ* ("know"), *lāmad* ("teach," "learn"), *bîn* ("perceive," "discern," "observe"), *śākal* ("observe," "give attention to," "consider," "be prudent"), *dābar* ("speak"), *ʾāmar* ("say"), *ʿāram* ("acquire wisdom," "be cunning, crafty"), *ʾālap* ("teach," "learn"), *šāmaʿ* ("hear," "obey," "understand"), *šît lēb* ("pay attention to"), *lāqaḥ mûsār* ("receive/take instruction"), *māšal* ("utter a proverb, be like"), *ḥāqar* ("seek out, search"), *bāqaš* ("seek"), and *kātab* ("write"). Skill of writing, a primary activity of scribes, is *sāpar* ("to write," "to record"), while the noun for the scribe is *sōpēr*.

Finally, various parts of the body were involved in the reception, depositing, and understanding of wisdom. Most important is the *lēb* ("heart"), considered by the sages to be the part of the human anatomy that is the receptacle for wisdom and knowledge in order to understand, reason, and act according to virtue (cf. 1 Kgs. 3:12; Prov. 10:8). Other parts of the body that involved wisdom and its acquisition are *ʾōzen* ("ear," which allows instruction and speech to be heard and understood), *lāšôn* ("tongue" for speaking wisely, "speech"), *peh* ("mouth" used for "speaking," "speech"), *śāpâ* ("lip," "speech"), and on occasion *beṭen* ("belly" as the "receptacle of thought and emotion").

Words for those to whom instruction is offered include *naʿar* ("youth"), *petî* ("simple," "uninstructed"), *ḥăsar lēb* ("lacking intelligence"), *bēn* ("son," "student"), and *kĕsîl* ("fool," one who usually avoids or does not have the capacity to learn), while the teacher is *ʾāb* ("father"), *ʾēm* ("mother"), and *môreh* ("instructor"). Verbs for learning include *šāmaʿ* ("hear," "obey"), *qānâ* ("acquire," "obtain"), *nāṣar* ("keep," "observe"), *ṣāpan* ("treasure up"), *šāmar* ("keep"), and *ḥāzaq* ("seize," "grasp"). Physical and mental discipline were used in teaching. Students who were lazy or poor performers were "beaten" (*nākâ*) with a "rod" (*šēbeṭ*) and issued verbal "reproof" (*tôkaḥat*).

10. Leo G. Perdue, "Wisdom in the Book of Job," in *In Search of Wisdom: Essays in Memory of John G. Gammie*, ed. Leo G. Perdue, et al. (Louisville: Westminster/John Knox, 1993) 73-80.

"Wisdom" denotes several meanings that may be summarized as follows. First, the concept refers to the acquiring of knowledge through empirical experience, rational thought, and comparative analysis, which enable one to reach studied conclusions and to act accordingly. Thus "wisdom" is an epistemology, that is, it is understood as knowledge that is derived from the study of things that may be empirically assayed by the human senses (hearing, seeing, touching, tasting, and smelling), characterized as the organs of understanding or perception, and, through rational analysis, may be placed into the configurations of definition and understanding. In addition, the sages, convinced of the connectedness of the world, sought to find associations between various elements of reality. This required a type of comparative thinking that allowed the sage to observe links between two or more objects. These links were often not obvious to the casual observer. If reality reflected a cosmic and social systematization, however, then these connections were to be discovered in order to detect the underlying cosmic order that provided the foundation for all that exists. The senses and the capacity to know and understand were divine gifts that allowed humans to understand the world of everyday existence. The organ of reason and intelligence was the "heart" *(lēb)*, also shaped by the creator in the making of humanity. The objects of study, analysis, and reflection were creation, the components of the world, human society and behavior, and the teachings of sages (both past and present), which were presented in oral and written forms. The sages taught that wisdom was not only a divine gift but also a human acquisition obtained through rigorous thinking, arduous study, and disciplined reflection and action. What God bestowed upon the sages was neither esoteric nor universal knowledge, but rather the capacity to learn, study, compare, classify, analyze, and reflect on the objects of reality engaged by human experience through the senses and then to move into rational formulation of their nature and relationships. Additionally, the sages sought out linkages between things they understood that reflected the symmetry of reality. Thus things decidedly different were scrutinized in order to discover some underlying common feature or features. Different objects of observation, having no seemingly obvious connection, were examined to find an intrinsic order or pattern that linked them in some way.

This knowledge was not merely theoretical, but also was to be used constructively in ordering the world, establishing justice, and acting and speaking correctly and righteously. Knowledge provided the basis for behavior of virtue and sagacious speech. Thus wisdom contained a system of moral discernment and behavior.[11] What the sages learned came to them through "discipline"

---

11. The language of ethics, involving moral discernment, virtues, and vices, encompassing

(mûsār), that is, the study and routinized actualizing of the tradition and the objects of knowledge in creation and society in canons of knowledge and human embodiment. The sages came into possession of wisdom by study and reflection on the insights encapsulated in the instructions of the wise and, during the Second Temple, the divine gift of the Torah with which wisdom was identified. Thus all wisdom ultimately came from God in the form of divine gifts, those of wisdom and finally the Torah, which became the object of study and meditation.

Wisdom was also distinguished by its quest for "order" in creation, society, and human thought and behavior. Thus it had its own distinctive cosmology, sociology, and anthropology, which, taken together, formed the three tiers of its moral system. The sages believed that God created a righteous order *(ṣĕdāqâ)* as the foundation of reality that shaped and permeated all that exists. Consequently, society was to be based upon righteousness *(ṣĕdāqâ)* so that its institutions and collective existence and activities came into harmony with the cosmos. Finally, the wise person *(ḥākām)* was one whose behavior and speech were to be shaped by that same just order of world and society so that he/she could not only live in concert with reality, but also could sustain the vitality and organizing character of its features. The wise called this person the *ṣaddîq.* Wisdom, as practiced by the sages, sustained the order of life inherent in the cosmos and human society as well as that actualized in human beings. By contrast, the "fool" *(kĕsîl,* Qoh. 7:25), who rejected or was not educated in wisdom, and the "wicked" *(rāšaʿ),* who knowingly and unknowingly created chaos in both the world and society, accompanied each other to their destruction.[12]

---

both actions and dispositions, includes the following. In addition to crimes and sins prohibited by social and cultic laws, the vices *(rāšaʿ)* in wisdom literature include *šeqer* ("falsehood"), *ʿāṣēl* ("lazy," "idle"), *kāzāb* ("lie," "liar"), *rĕmîyâ* ("deceit," "cunning behavior"), *mirmâ* ("deceit"), *tôʿēbâ* ("abomination"), *ʾawwâ* ("desire" in a bad sense, "lust"), *ham/ḥēmâ* ("heated person," ruled by the passions, emotions; "heated," "passionate"), *mādôn* ("cause strife"), *qĕṣer rûaḥ* ("short-tempered"), *rāgal* ("slander" and "idle gossip"), *bāzâ* ("belittle" and "hold in contempt"), *nĕbālâ* ("folly," "loquaciousness," and the "rejection of, turning away from, abandoning of, instruction"). Virtues *(ṭōb)* include *ʾĕmet* ("truth"), *ṣedeq/ṣĕdāqâ* ("righteous/righteousness"), *mišpāṭ* ("justice"), *ʾawwâ* ("desire" in a good sense), *qar-rûaḥ* ("cool of spirit" = the control of the passions), *ḥārēš* ("be silent" in the sense of moderation and restraint in speech, and an avoidance of garrulous talk, especially that harms others; cf. other terms for "being silent," *šātaq* and *šāqāṭ*), *ʾārak ʾappayîm* ("slow to anger"), *šāpēl rûaḥ, ṣānûaʿ, ʾănāwâ* ("humility" and "modesty"), and *šāmaʿ* ("reception of," "being attentive to," "receiving," and "accepting" instruction).

12. Other terms for fool include *ʾĕwîl, ʾiwwelet* ("foolish one," i.e., one who commits "folly"), *lēṣ* ("mocker"), *baʿar* ("brutish," "stupid"), *nābāl* ("senseless one," usually of inferior social status), *sākāl* ("fool" who has achieved often illicitly high social prominence), and *hôlēlût* ("madman"). See Nili Shupak, *Where Can Wisdom Be Found? The Sage's Language in the Bible and in Ancient Egyptian Literature* (OBO 130; Göttingen: Vandenhoeck & Ruprecht, 1993) 200-211.

Finally wisdom often came into the service of institutions of wealth and power, in particular monarchies and temples. Serving as sages within the empires of the eastern Mediterranean world, many of the poet-scribes shaped an ideology of beneficent order and divine legitimation that supported rulers and dynasties. Indeed, the important components of sapiential doctrines of justifying kings and their rule included what one finds in later Western European political systems: the rule by divine right in which rulers and dynasties were chosen by the nation's supreme deity, the political order that was based on sacred and revealed law, the extraordinary virtues possessed by the king (justice, beneficence, strength, glory, charity, wisdom, and mercy), and the incomparable intelligence of chosen kings such as Solomon and Ashurbanipal. The wisdom of the wise was used to advise and counsel the king to effective and successful rule, while the writings of the sages supported royal entitlement to the throne and recounted rulers' deeds in often glowing expressions, even achieving on occasion an air of hymnic adoration.

Defining the Cultural Boundaries of Wisdom in the Age of Empires

The sages and other writers of Israelite and early Jewish literature recognized that wisdom was international in scope and transcended the national boundaries of the peoples residing in Egypt and the Levant (1 Kgs. 4:30-31; cf. Jer. 49:7; Obad. 8-9). The cultures long considered superior due to knowledge, paideia,[13] and conquest were often thought to have a more highly developed intellectual tradition than their neighbors in Syria-Israel and consequently strongly influenced the sapiential tradition of Israel and later Judah. But this does not mean that the smaller nations and colonies could not exert their influence on the empires' understanding of the world of the gods, the cosmos, the development of history, and aesthetic expressions. To accomplish this cross-fertilization required a lingua franca and the education of sages in some of the ancient Near Eastern languages, ranging from Egyptian (hieroglyphics, hieratic, and demotic) to Sumerian, Akkadian, Aramaic, Greek, and Latin. The knowledge of these languages and some familiarity with their cultures and social organizations was necessary in a variety of areas, including composition of literature, communication, trade, and diplomacy.

---

13. Paideia refers to two related features: the process of education that enabled a youth eventually to take his place in society and the state of the educated person.

Egypt

Introduction

The land of Egypt achieved an advanced civilization when Menes (Narmer?) united Upper and Lower Egypt into a single nation. The major cities were located along the Nile, which produced a thin strip of land in the Libyan desert for some five hundred miles and provided the arable soil needed for farming. The mythological understanding that provided the political and social character of Egypt was the group of nine major deities, the Ennead, ruled by different sun deities (Amon, Re, and Ptah). Numerous other gods were part of an expansive pantheon that included the reigning pharaoh (the incarnation of Horus) and the ruler of the underworld (Osiris), who was the symbiosis of deceased kings who had joined the afterlife. This theological view of the worship of the sun god, who brought the gifts of life, fertility, and order *(ma'at)* to the land blessed by the gods that was threatened by chaos in the form of desert, invaders, and internal evil, and the Osiris-Horus complex provided the twin axes of Egyptian self-understanding for some three thousand years.

The material culture as well as the documentary evidence from the Bible and Egyptian literature, annals, monuments, and epigraphic data point to substantial interaction of Syria-Israel with Egypt beginning with early prestate Israel and increasing through the periods of the Israelite and Judahite monarchies, especially from the latter part of the Egyptian Eighth Dynasty until the fall of Jerusalem in 587 B.C.E. This engagement of cultures reappeared especially during the Hellenistic and the early Roman periods. The sages from the land of the Nile taught in Egyptian schools and worked as scribes in the burgeoning administrations of the Egyptian court, provinces, and cities throughout the kingdom and in foreign cities in the territories over which they ruled during imperial expansions. The genres they used included didactic psalms and poems; panegyrics to wise kings, ancestral sages, and the gods of wisdom; instructions; sayings; and grave biographies. Papyri, monumental inscriptions, statues, wooden tablets, and frescoes on tomb walls were the materials on which their writings and artistic representations were placed. Some of their wisdom writings directly influenced the sapiential literature of ancient Israel and Judah. The best-known example is "The Instruction of Amenemope," which was used as the primary source for one of the collections of the book of Proverbs (22:17–24:22).[14]

---

14. Harold C. Washington, *Wealth and Poverty in the Instruction of Amenemope and the Hebrew Proverbs* (SBLDS 142; Atlanta: Scholars Press, 1994).

The terms used for wisdom and its associated activities and features, which include nouns, adjectives, and verbs in hieroglyphics, are found especially in the classical texts that follow.[15] The terms are *sb3* ("to teach"), *sb3y.t* ("instruction"), *mtr(t)* ("to reprove," "reproof"), *shr* ("counsel"), *ʿrḳ* ("be proficient," "wise," "wisdom"), *wḥʿ* ("explain," "resolve"), *rdi ib, rdi m ib, rdi ḥ3.ty r* ("put in the heart," "give the heart to"), *šsp* (+ *md.t* and synonyms as an object, "to take," "to accept"), *ty sbʿ.t* ("to grasp instruction"), *wni* (+ "instruction" is "to neglect," "abandon"), (s)ʿd3 ("to lie"), *grg* ("falsehood"), *ʿwn ib* ("greedy"), *skn* ("be greedy"), *ḥnt* ("be greedy"), *ḥnty* ("greed"), *štm* ("be angry"), *ṯṯṯt* (to quarrel"), *t3w* ("heat" = "anger"), *šmm, šmw* ("anger," "quick tempered"), *gr* ("to be silent"), *grw* ("silent man"), *grw m3ʿ* ("truly silent man"), *ḥm* ("simpleton"), *wḫ3* ("fool"), *iw.ty ḥ3.ty* ("stupid"), *ḫn* ("fool"), *swg* ("stupid"), *ḫn* ("fool"), *lḫ* ("fool"), *swg* ("stupid"), *ḫn* ("fool"), *gwš* ("crooked"), *rḫ* ("to know," "knowledge"), *rḫ iḫ.t* ("wise man"), *ḥmww* ("skilled," "artisan"), *s33* ("be wise," "wisdom"), *si3* ("wisdom"), *ḫn* ("speech," "saying"), *ṯs* ("well-constructed saying," "maxim"), *md.t nfr.t* ("good speech"), and *mnḫ ḏd/ṯsw* ("excellent saying").

The Texts of Egyptian Wisdom

Prolegomenon

These texts, ranging from the Old Kingdom (the Early Bronze Age) to the end of dynastic Egypt with the conquest of Alexander, followed by the Hellenistic and early Roman periods, include especially instructions, although other forms also gave literary expression to the teaching of the wise.[16] The major wisdom texts, in chronological order, include "The Instruction of Prince Hordjedef" (twenty-seventh century B.C.E.), "The Instruction for Kagemni" (late Old Kingdom?), "The Instruction of a Man for His Son" (1985-1773 B.C.E.), "The Instruction of Ptahhotep" (2450 B.C.E.), "The Instruction for Merikare" (twenty-second century B.C.E.), "The Instruction of Amenemhet" (a ruler who died c. 1960 B.C.E.), "The Instruction of Kheti, the Son of Duauf" (between 2150 and 1750 B.C.E.), "The Instuction of Sehetepibre" (a hymnic tribute to King Nimaat-Re, nineteenth-eighteenth century B.C.E.), "The Prophecies of Neferti" (Middle Kingdom), the "Instruction of Ani" (c. 1500 B.C.E.), the "Instruction of Amennakhte" (New Kingdom), "The Instruction of Amenemope" (thirteenth

---

15. See Shupak, *Where Can Wisdom Be Found?* 340-42.

16. Antonio Loprieno, ed., *Ancient Egyptian Literature: History and Forms* (Leiden: Brill, 1996).

century B.C.E.), "The Instruction of Ankhsheshonqy" (fifth or fourth century B.C.E.), "The Instruction of Papyrus Insinger" (third century B.C.E.), the "Tale of the Eloquent Peasant" (early Middle Kingdom), the "Discourses of Sisobek" (Middle Kingdom), the "Papyrus Lansing" (manuscript dates from the Twentieth Dynasty), and the "Satirical Letter: P. Anastasi I" (end of thirteenth century B.C.E.; Ramesses II?).

Two of the better known disputations are "The Dialogue of a Man Tired of Life with His *Ba*" (end of the third millennium B.C.E. during the First Intermediate Period) and "The Admonitions of an Egyptian Sage" (c. 2000 B.C.E.), which appeared as Egypt emerged from the devastation of the First Intermediate Period. Likewise, the Harper's Song, written during the reign of one of the Intef kings (c. 2000 B.C.E.), emphasizes the joys of human life and expresses skepticism concerning a future existence. The "Lament of Khakheperre-sonbe" from the Nineteenth Dynasty of the Middle Kingdom during the reign of Senusert II or perhaps his successor also speaks of the distress of a priest who had endured the chaos of life.

During the Middle and New Kingdoms the panegyrics "The Loyalist Instruction" (early Middle Kingdom) and "In Praise of Learned Scribes" (c. 1300 B.C.E.) speak, respectively, of the divine attributes of the ruling king, thus serving as a text of court propaganda, and the celebration of the greatness of the noble sages of the past whose writings provided them immortality.[17]

While there are several genres of sapiential texts (instructions, royal testaments, autobiographies, sayings, fables, laments, and panegyric hymns),[18] the primary Egyptian wisdom genre is the instruction or teaching *(sbōyet)* written to educate the Egyptian youth, who in the Old Kingdom were children of the aristocracy and sought to succeed their fathers in the social and political positions they held.[19] Less prominent youth who came from the scribal classes were

17. For translations see Günther Burkard, et al., eds., *Texte aus der Umwelt des Alten Testaments* (hereafter *TUAT*), vol. 3: *Weisheitstexte*, 2 (Gütersloh: Gerd Mohn, 1991); Miriam Lichtheim, *Ancient Egyptian Literature* (hereafter *AEL*) (3 vols.; Berkeley: University of California Press, 1973-1980); idem, *Late Egyptian Wisdom Literature in the International Context* (OBO 52; Göttingen: Vandenhoeck & Ruprecht, 1983); William H. Hallo and K. Lawson Younger Jr., *The Context of Scripture* (hereafter *COS*), vol. 1 (Leiden: Brill, 2003); J. B. Pritchard, *Ancient Near Eastern Texts* (hereafter *ANET*) (3rd ed.; Princeton: Princeton University Press, 1969). For German translations see also Hellmut Brunner, *Die Weisheitsbücher der Ägypter: Lehren für das Leben* (Zurich: Artimus & Winkler, 1998).

18. Ronald J. Williams, "Egyptian Wisdom Literature," *ABD* 2:395-99. For a comparable analysis of wisdom literature, see Miriam Lichtheim, "Didactic Literature," in *Ancient Egyptian Literature*, ed. Loprieno, 243-62.

19. See Jan Bergman, "Discours d'adieu. Testament, Discours posthume. Testaments juifs et enseignements égyptiens," in *Sagesse et religion: [actes du] colloque de Strasbourg, octobre 1976*

trained to succeed their fathers in the administration as scribes and lower officials, so that texts reflecting their instruction appear as early as the New Kingdom. Literary texts that became classics (i.e., continued to be copied and edited
by successive generations, usually over many centuries) were written largely by
honored sages of legendary fame possessing high social rank, while in the New
Kingdom several came from sages in lower administrative circles of the Egyptian bureaucracy. Instructions assumed two major forms.[20] The earlier, classic
form possessed a title consisting of the name of the type of writing (an instruction) and the titular and personal names of the teacher. A list of admonitions
and exhortations followed, with occasional proverbs inserted and the voice of
the teacher in the first person interrupting to tell of his own experiences and insights.[21] The conclusion consisted of either an epilogue or an exordium in
which the "author" spoke of the nature of his text and his own life. The second
form is an expansion made up of a narrative introduction to the teaching.

The Old Kingdom

The uniting of the land of the Nile (Upper and Lower Egypt) by Menes
(Narmer?) at the end of the fourth millennium launched the period in which
Egypt reached its cultural apex, established its traditional cultural and religious
forms, formulated hieroglyphics into classical expression, and launched a
golden era in the history of the kingdom/empire of order founded on divine
ma'at that regulated cosmic and social departments of reality (including the
first two dynasties through the eighth, 3100-2130 B.C.E.). Rebellion against this
order in any form, internal revolts, invasion, and unrighteous living could result only in chaos. Thus the monarchy and its divine expression became the
center for the maintenance of order in both nature and history. The oldest
Egyptian instruction of which there is literary evidence is "The Instruction of
Hordjedef,"[22] attributed to a son of the Fourth Dynasty ruler Khufu. While the
text mentions the earlier instruction of the great Egyptian sage Imhotep, vizier
of Djoser (2667-2648 B.C.E.), which is not preserved, Hordjedef originates from
a later sage of the Fifth Dynasty who presents himself in the fictional role of a

---

(Bibliothèque des centres d'études supérieures specialisé d'histoire des religions de Strasbourg;
Paris: Presses Universitaires de France, 1979) 21-50.

20. Hellmut Brunner, "Die Weisheitsliteratur," in *Ägyptologie* (HdO 1; Leiden: Brill, 1952) 90-
110.

21. See Kenneth A. Kitchen, "The Basic Literary Forms and Formulations of Ancient Instructional Writings in Egypt and Western Asia," in *Studien zu altägyptischen Lebenslehren,* ed. Erik
Hornung and Othmar Keel (OBO 28; Göttingen: Vandenhoeck & Ruprecht, 1979) 235-82.

22. See Lichtheim, *AEL* 1:58-59; Brunner, *Weisheitsbücher der Ägypter,* 101-3.

son of an earlier pharaoh.[23] He offers to his infant son Au-ib-Re an instruction of living as an adult in the high class of the Egyptian court. Topics include refraining from boasting, marrying a wife and fathering a son, building his "house," making preparations for his life in the city of the dead, and honoring the dead through mortuary rituals.[24]

The only surviving part of "The Instruction of Kagemni" is the conclusion.[25] In this literary fiction, the vizier who is presented as Kagemni offers his counsel to a person who serves as vizier to King Huni of the Fourth Dynasty. Self-control is the dominant thesis of this fragmentary text, warning the recipient against boasting, overindulgence in eating, and the babbling of a fool.

"The Instruction of Ptahhotep" dates from the Sixth Dynasty and portrays an aged vizier of the Fifth Dynasty (2494-2343 B.C.E.) instructing his son on serving the king.[26] Common sapiential virtues taught include etiquette, self-control, obedience, patience, generosity, truthfulness, honesty, and justice. Most important, however, is loyalty to the king, the reward for which is participation in the afterlife.[27] Ma'at (justice, truth, righteousness) is the order of divine creation that is sustained by the rule of the divine king.

The First Intermediate Period and the Middle Kingdom

The First Intermediate Period (2130-1940 B.C.E.) occurred during a disruptive time that engulfed Egypt briefly, but continued among some of the various dynasties at different times during these two centuries. As regards instructions, the royal testaments make up a subgenre. Sages active as officials in the royal administration and loyal supporters of the monarchy were responsible for these texts to defend kings against political intrigues at court and revolutions in different regions of the kingdom and to provide apologies for particular rulers ascending the throne.[28] These appeared during the period of transition from the

---

23. Adelheid Schlott, *Schrift und Schreiber im Alten Ägypten* (Munich: Beck, 1989) 146-47.

24. *ANET,* 419 and n. 4.

25. See Lichtheim, *AEL* 1:59-61; Brunner, *Weisheitsbücher der Ägypter,* 133-36; Schlott, *Schrift und Schreiber,* 197.

26. In general see Lichtheim, *AEL* 1:61-80; Brunner, *Weisheitsbücher der Ägypter,* 104-32; Schlott, *Schrift und Schreiber,* 197-99; Burkard, *TUAT* 3: *Weisheitstexte,* 2:195-221. Also see Dieter Kurth, *Maximen für Manager: Die Lehre des Ptahhotep* (Darmstadt: Primus, 1999); Friedrich Junge, *Die Lehre Ptahhoteps und die Tugenden der ägyptischen Welt* (OBO 193; Göttingen: Vandenhoeck & Ruprecht, 2003). On the date see Lichtheim, *AEL* 1:62.

27. *ANET,* 414. See Gerhard Fect, *Der Habgierige und die Maat in der Lehre des Ptahhotep* (Mitteilungen des Deutschen archäologischen Instituts 1; Glückstadt: Augustin, 1958).

28. Georges Posener, *Littérature et politique dans l'Égypte de la XIIe dynastie* (Bibliothèque de l'École des Hautes Études 307; Paris: Librairie Ancienne Honoré Champion, 1956); Aksel Volten,

disruptive forces of the First Intermediate Period to the more stable Middle Kingdom. "The Instruction for King Merikare" and "The Instruction of Amenemhet" are two examples in which deceased rulers offer counsel from the afterlife for their successors during the transition of royal rule during contested reigns.[29]

Possibly written by the famous sage Kheti, "The Instruction of King Amenemhet," the deceased pharaoh (the founder of the Twelfth Dynasty, 1985-1956 B.C.E.), instructs his son (Senusert I, 1971-1928 B.C.E.) at the time he "appeared as a god" (likely his coronation).[30] The dead king not only relates his successes but also tells of the court intrigue that led to his assassination. Thus the son is to withhold his trust from any court official and remove those who oppose his reign. This reflects the final stages of the First Intermediate Period and the beginning of the more secure and enduring security of the Twelfth Dynasty that initiated the Middle Kingdom.

The First Intermediate Period witnessed different types of natural and historical catastrophes afflicting at different times the various dynasties ruling different areas. The First Intermediate text, "The Instruction for King Merikare," is an instruction by the dead father of the last ruler of the Herakleopolitan dynasty that ended by 2125 B.C.E.[31] The instruction gives directions to Merikare on how to rule the kingdom in order to achieve harmony and political order.[32] His rule is to realize *ma'at* in both the cosmos and the social world that reflects it through means of wisdom.[33] The teaching also includes a hymn in praise of the

---

Zwei altägyptische politische Schriften (Analecta Ägyptiaca 4; Copenhagen: Einar Munksgaard, 1945); R. J. Williams, "Literature as a Medium of Political Propaganda in Ancient Egypt," in *The Seed of Wisdom: Essays in Honour of T. J. Meek,* ed. W. S. McCullough (Toronto: University of Toronto Press, 1964) 14-30.

29. See Leo G. Perdue, "The Testament of David and Egyptian Royal Instructions," in *Scripture in Context,* vol. 2, ed. William W. Hallo, James M. Moyer, and Leo G. Perdue (Winona Lake, IN: Eisenbrauns, 1983) 79-96.

30. In general see Lichtheim, *AEL* 1:135-39; Wolfgang Helck, *Der Text der Lehre Amenemhets I. für seinen Sohn* (2nd ed.; Kleine Ägyptische Texte 1; Wiesbaden: Harrassowitz, 1988); *COS* 1:66-68.

31. The author may have been the legendary sage Kheti. For the translation of the text, see *ANET,* 414-18; *COS* 1:59-66. Important studies include Volten, *Zwei altägyptische politische Schriften;* Siegfried Herrmann, *Untersuchungen zur Überlieferungsgestalt Mittelägyptischer Literaturwerke* (Deutsche Akademie der Wissenschaften zu Berlin Institute für Orientforschung 33; Berlin: Akademie, 1957); Schlott, *Schrift und Schreiber,* 199-201; J. F. Quack, *Studien zur Lehre für Merikare* (Göttinger Orientforschungen Reihe 4, Aegypten 23; Wiesbaden: Harrassowitz, 1992).

32. Alexander Scharff, *Der historische Abschnitt der Lehre für König Merikarê* (Sitzungsberichte der Bayerischen Akademie der Wissenschaften 8; Munich: Beck, 1936).

33. Siegfried Herrmann, "Die Naturlehre des Schöpfungsberichtes," *TLZ* 86 (1961) 413-23. See Solomon in 1 Kgs. 3:9-14.

creator who made the world and maintains its order. Under the beneficent oversight of the creator, the humans he made continue to flourish.[34]

Written during the First Intermediate Period and later placed on the wall of the royal tomb of one of the Intef kings of the early Eleventh Dynasty, the "Harper's Song" belongs to a genre of texts that depicts a minstrel entertaining the guests at a meal in celebration of the recently departed loved one (who also may be present). In the best known of these,[35] this harper is skeptical about any future life, the effectiveness of mortuary religion, and the possibility of returning from the dead (strophe 1). Instead, he suggests to his hearers that they enjoy their present life (strophe 2) and "make holiday, and weary not therein!" Indeed, for this harper there is no one who has entered into the West who ever returned. The harper even refers to two legendary sages of the distant past, Imhotep and Hordjedef, and observes that their tombs now lay in ruins.

"The Dispute of a Man with His *Ba*,"[36] also composed during the First Intermediate Period, points to the perception of the growing limits of mortuary religion.[37] A man engages in a debate with his *ba* (vital forces) over the necessity of tomb preparations, priestly actions, and rituals of death for participation in the afterlife. While the man maintains the importance of mortuary planning, the *ba* indicates the obvious shortcomings of this expensive activity and instead points to himself as the means by which his lord may continue into the future life.[38] While the *ba* remains skeptical, he finally consents to stay with the man even during this period of personal ordeals in order to give the man opportunity to insure his future through the now challenged necessity of mortuary religion. The *ba* admonishes the man, in the meantime, to turn his thoughts to the experience of joy. The dispute appears to end with the *ba* reassuring the man he will not leave him prior to death. If this occurred, then the man would forfeit his one realistic chance to participate in the next life.

The panegyric text from the early Middle Kingdom called "The Loyalist In-

34. Elke Blumenthal, "Die Literarische Verarbeitung der Übergangszeit zwischen Altem und Mittlerem Reich," in *Ancient Egyptian Literature: History and Forms*, ed. Antonio Loprieno (Leiden: Brill, 1996) 105-35.

35. *ANET*, 467-69.

36. In general see Lichtheim, *AEL* 1:163-69. Also see Émile Suys, "Le dialogue du désespéré avec son âme," *Or* 1 (1932) 57-74; Alfred Hermann, "Das Gespräch eines Lebensmüden mit seiner Seele," *OLZ* 34 (1939) 345-51; Emma Brunner-Traut, "Der Lebensmüde und sein Ba," *ZÄS* 77 (1944) 18-29; Raymond Weill, "Le livre du 'Désespéré,'" *BIFAO* 45 (1947) 89-154; R. O. Faulkner, "The Man Who Was Tired of Life," *JEA* 42 (1956) 21-40; Hans Goedicke, *The Report about the Dispute of a Man with His Ba* (Baltimore: Johns Hopkins University Press, 1970).

37. See Winfried Barta, "Die Erste Zwischenzeit im Spiegel der pessimistischen Literatur," *JEOL* 24 (1975/76) 50-61.

38. Louis Žabkar, "Ba," *LÄ* 1 (1973) 588-98.

struction" is written to extol the divine king (Horus) who sits on the Egyptian throne.[39] The divine qualities he incorporates are drawn from a variety of major Egyptian deities (Re, Khnum, Bastet, and Sekmet). The reward of loyal sages is eternal life.[40] This is obviously a piece of royal propaganda to exalt the divinity of the reigning king.

Similarly, the so-called "Prophecies of Neferti,"[41] written by a lector priest active during the reign of the Fourth Dynasty ruler Snefru (2613-2494 B.C.E.), "predicts" the righteous results of the future rule of "Ameny" (Amenemhet I, 1985-1956 B.C.E.). This ruler, the dynasty's founder, will bring to an end the chaos of the First Intermediate Period. This piece is written to support the claim of the founder of the Twelfth Dynasty and to argue that he is the divine choice for ending the chaos of the First Intermediate Period.

Also probably written during the Twelfth Dynasty of the Middle Kingdom (1985-1773 B.C.E.), "The Instruction of a Man for His Son" is introduced by a narrative and then presents the instruction proper.[42] The virtue extolled is that of loyalty to the reigning king. Students who are preparing to enter the royal administration as scribes are to be loyal, reliable, hardworking, attentive, honest, and "silent" (i.e., control their speech and passions).[43] Blessings and prosperity come to those who are faithful to the king.[44]

While many have attributed the "Satire on the Trades" to the scribe Kheti in the early Twelfth Dynasty, this text is likely the creation of a pseudonymous scribal official during the Middle Kingdom. A father, Kheti, son of Duaf, takes his young son Pepy to the Residence City in order to put him into its school. He instructs him in the responsibilities of the scribe and tells him of the rewards

39. See William Kelly Simpson, ed., *The Literature of Ancient Egypt: An Anthology of Stories, Instructions, Stelae, Autobiographies, and Poetry* (3rd ed.; New Haven: Yale University Press, 2003) 198-200; Antonio Loprieno, "Loyalistic Instructions," in *Ancient Egyptian Literature: History and Forms*, 403-14.

40. See Georges Posener, *L'enseignement loyaliste: Sagesse égyptienne du Moyen Empire* (Hautes Études Orientales 5; Geneva: Droz, 1976); more recently, Hans-Werner Fischer-Elpert, *Die Lehre eines Mannes für seinen Sohn: Eine Etappe auf dem 'Gottesweg' des loyalen und solidarischen Beamten des Mittelerens Reiches* (Ägyptologische Abhandlungen 60; Wiesbaden: Harrassowitz, 1999). An abbreviated copy of the text was inscribed on the stele of Sehetepibre, who served Amenemhet III (1831-1786 B.C.E.) as a highly placed official.

41. See Lichtheim, *AEL* 1:139-45; *COS* 1:106-10.

42. See Hans Goedicke, "Die Lehre eines Mannes für seinen Sohn," *ZÄS* 94 (1967) 62-71; Kenneth A. Kitchen, "Studies in Egyptian Wisdom Literature — I: The Instruction by a Man for His Son," *OrAnt* 8 (1969) 189-208.

43. See Williams, "Literature as a Medium," esp. 27.

44. Brunner adds an introduction and conclusion to a fragmentary manuscript of the Middle Kingdom he entitles "The Sayings of the Papyrus of Ramesses II" (*Weisheitsbücher der Ägypter*, 193-95).

that accrue from this profession, in contrast to odious occupations that involve hard work. The sages and service in the royal administration are coveted roles in a stable political order.

The Second Intermediate Period

The end of the security achieved by the Twelfth Dynasty led to the decline of political order in Egypt. Rival dynasties and even foreign conquest (the Hyksos) led to internal hostilities weakening the political and economic power of the nation. "The Admonitions of Ipuwer,"[45] likely written toward the end of the Thirteenth Dynasty (1773 B.C.E. until just after 1650 B.C.E.) or more likely during the Second Intermediate Period,[46] is a dialogue between the wise man Ipuwer and the creator.[47] The sage accuses both the creator and the ruler for failing to maintain justice and cosmic order.[48] The consequence is social and natural chaos: crime, social upheaval, loss of arable land, diminishing food, decrease in children, foreign invasion, revolution, and disobedience of servants and slaves. In a damning indictment of Re, the sun god, for failing to perceive human wickedness, the creator is condemned for failing to maintain cosmic order, for fashioning humans to be evil, and for failing to punish the wicked. The king is also roundly condemned.

45. See Lichtheim, *AEL* 1:149-63; *COS* 1:93-98. Also see Eberhard Otto, "Weltanschauliche und politische Tendenzschriften," in *Ägyptologie*, 111-18; R. O. Faulkner, "The Admonitions of an Egyptian Sage," *JEA* 51 (1965) 53-62; Gerhard Fecht, *Der Vorwurf an Gott in den 'Mahnworten des Ipuwer'* (Abhandlungen der Heidelberger Akademie der Wissenschaften, Philosophisch-Historische Klasse; Heidelberg: C. Winter, 1972); Friedrich Junge, "Die Welt der Klagen," in *Fragen an die altägyptische Literatur*, ed. Jan Assmann, Erika Feucht, and Reinhard Grieshammer (Wiesbaden: Reichert, 1977) 275-76.

46. See John Van Seters, "A Date for the 'Admonitions' in the Second Intermediate Period," *JEA* 50 (1964) 13-23.

47. The literary genre of this piece of literature has been seen as prophecy (*ANET*, 441), wisdom (Sir Alan Henderson Gardiner, *The Admonitions of an Egyptian Sage* [Leipzig: Hinrichs, 1909]; Herrmann, *Untersuchungen zur Überlieferungsgestalt*); and, more specifically, disputation (Eberhard Otto, *Der Vorwurf an Gott: Zur Entstehung der ägyptischen Auseinandersetzungsliteratur* [Vorträge der orientalistischen Tagung im Marburg, Fachgruppe: Ägyptologie; Hildesheim: Gerstenberg, 1951]).

48. See esp. Otto, *Vorwurf an Gott*; Dorthea Sitzler, *Vorwurf gegen Gott: Ein religiöses Motiv im Alten Orient (Ägypten und Mesopotamien)* (Studies in Oriental Religions 32; Wiesbaden: Harrassowitz, 1995); Winfried Barta, "Das Gespräch des Ipuwer mit dem Schöpfer Gott," in *Studien zur altägyptischen Kultur*, vol. 1 (Hamburg: H. Buske, 1974) 19-33. Elke Blumenthal's survey of wisdom texts during the First Intermediate Period points to the appearance of disputations, pessimistic literature, and laments that question traditional teachings of justice and the afterlife ("Die Literarische Verarbeitung der Übergangszeit zwischen Altem und Mittlerem Reich," in *Ancient Egyptian Literature: History and Forms*, 105-35).

The sage contrasts the present chaos with the social accord of previous periods and hopes that the future holds the possibility of the renewal of order and justice.

The New Kingdom

With the driving out of the "rulers of foreign lands" (Hyksos), native Egyptian dynasties moved the kingdom into an aggressive empire that was to last for 350 years. Egypt expanded its western empire until it shared with the Hittites control over this part of southwestern Asia. One of the wisdom compositions probably originating in the Eighteenth Dynasty (1550-1295 B.C.E.) of the New Kingdom, "The Instruction of Ani," has thirty maxims framed by a prologue and an epilogue.[49] The narrative frame describes a disputation between Ani, a minor official of a temple administration, and his son over the ability of hearers to understand sapiential instruction. The son is encouraged to be diligent and faithful to his god, who will reward him with success and other blessings. While avoiding pantheism, the teacher notes that the true god is the "sun, which is on the horizon." Interesting is that the son dares to argue with his more learned father, before finally acquiescing to the older savant's superior wisdom.

Another New Kingdom text, "The Instruction of Amennakhte,"[50] is issued by a scribe of the "House of Life" to his apprentice, Harmin, who is to enter a wisdom school and pursue the career of a scribe.[51] The young man is exhorted in the virtues of the successful scribe: obedience to the instruction, patience, reticence in speaking, and actualization of these and other virtues of the wise man.

A royal scribe and chief overseer of the cattle of Amon-Re, king of the gods, Nebmare-nakht, addresses his apprentice, the scribe Wenemdi-amun, in "The Papyrus Lansing," which has features of a manual for scribal students, an instruction, a eulogy, and a dialogue.[52] Topics include the veneration of the scribal profession, admiration for the teacher, the praise of the scribal career (cf. "Satire on the Trades"), rebuke of the indolent student, and the virtue of application to studies. The grateful student responds that he will reward his teacher with a house, trees, grain, fruit, vegetables, and domesticated animal herds.

Also from the New Kingdom, as it neared its end (thirteenth century), is

---

49. See Lichtheim, *AEL* 2:135-46; *COS* 1:110-15. Also see J. F. Quack, *Die Lehren des Ani: Ein neuägyptischer Weisheitstext in seinem kulturellen Umfeld* (OBO 141; Göttingen: Vandenhoeck & Ruprecht, 1994).

50. See Simpson, *Literature of Ancient Egypt*, 341-42; Susanne Bickel and Bernard Mathieu, "L'écrivain Amennakht et son Enseignement," *BIFAO* 93 (1993) 31-51.

51. A. H. Gardiner has made this connection in *Hieratic Papyri in the British Museum*, 1, 3rd series (London: British Museum, 1935).

52. See Lichtheim, *AEL* 2:168-75.

"The Instruction of Amenemope," which serves as the exemplar for the sapiential "book" in Proverbs (22:17–23:14).[53] The literary structure consists of a prologue and thirty chapters, the last of which is an epilogue. We know from the text that the teacher was a highly placed administrative official who attended to royal estates. He addresses his "son," Horemmaakheru, who is a young scribe serving in the temple administration of a temple dedicated to Min (a fertility god). Sapiential virtues include piety, charity, honesty, and the control of the passions (the "silent man" contrasted to the "heated person," i.e., the one who was tempestuous and misguided by a range of emotions and lusts). While behavior leads to punishment or reward, the deity is not constrained by the principle of retribution.

As one might expect from this period of military expansion and empire building, one wisdom text, "A Satirical Letter," is a "scribal controversy" from the New Kingdom, perhaps written during the lengthy reign of Ramesses II.[54] A military scribe ridicules his opponent in regard to a variety of topics, in particular mathematics, military logistics, and geography.

The Persian Period

The Achaemenid rulers of Persia established control over Egypt with only a half-century interruption from 525 B.C.E. to the time of Alexander's conquest in 332 B.C.E. "The Instruction of Ankhsheshonqy" is also enfolded into a narrative introduction and conclusion.[55] Dating from the fifth to the third century B.C.E.,[56] this text undertakes to instruct students in the virtues of the scribe. Important moral themes, often presented in antitheses, include the contrast between wise and foolish, good and evil women, and wealth and poverty. Also praised or emphasized are the family/household, friends, landlords, neighbors,

53. See ibid., 2:146-63; Irene Shirun Grumach, "Die Lehre des Amenemope," *TUAT* 3: *Weisheitstexte*, 2:222-50; *COS* 1:115-22.

54. See Adolf Erman, *The Literature of the Ancient Egyptians* (London: Methuen, 1927) 214-34.

55. Lichtheim, *AEL* 3:159-84; idem, *Late Egyptian Wisdom Literature*, 13-92. Also see Heinz-Josef Thissen, *Die Lehre des Anchscheschonqi* (P.BM 10508) (Papyrologische Texte und Abhandlungen 32; Bonn: Habelt, 1984); Burkard, *TUAT* 3: *Weisheitstexte*, 2:222-50, 251-77; Brunner, *Weisheitsbücher der Ägypter*, 257-91; S. R. K. Glanville, "The Instructions of 'Onchsheshonqy," in *Catalogue of Demotic Papyri in the British Museum*, 2 (London: Printed by the Order of the Trustees, 1939-1955); Thissen, *Lehre des Anchscheschonqi*.

56. Williams, "Egyptian Wisdom Literature," 397; Glanville dates the text to the fifth or fourth century B.C.E. ("The Instructions of 'Onchsheshonqy," XII), while B. Gemser agrees it is not prior to the fifth century ("The Instructions of 'Onkhsheshonqy and Biblical Wisdom Literature," in *Congress Volume: Oxford, 1959* [VTSup 7; Leiden: Brill, 1960] 106). For the dating of the text in the Saite dynasty, see B. H. Stricker, "De Wijsheid van Anchsjesjonqy," *JEOL* 15 (1933) 11-33.

religious obligations, the relationship between cause and effect in the process of retribution, and two differing versions of the Golden Rule. The narrative describes Ankhsheshonqy's imprisonment due to the false charge of engaging in a plot to murder the king. Thus the teacher offers this counsel from prison to teach his son, who is preparing to enter his father's profession.[57]

The Hellenistic Period

During the Hellenistic period, Egyptian wisdom primarily emanated from the class of scribes who did not share in the imperial power of the Ptolemies. The scribe who writes "The Teaching of Pordjel" in the period of Ptolemaic rule directs his instruction to his "beloved son."[58] Among the counsels offered are controlling the passions, avoiding sexual intimacy with a married woman, keeping good company, honoring the god and the master, providing them what is their due, and teaching the son.

The range of Egyptian wisdom literature included other types of texts, among these didactic legends, proverbs[59] inserted into letters and other types of literature, onomastica, and reliefs. In addition, among the epigraphic materials, there are countless numbers of scarabs that point to the offices and names of scribes in the Egyptian administration and occasionally include a proverb as well as ostraca of various subjects written by common scribes.[60] Originating and used extensively in the period of the New Kingdom, the "Kemyt" is a manual for instructing youth to acquire the scribal arts.[61] It likely included formulae for epistles, a model letter, and sentences incorporating correct syntax. The introductory narrative tells of a young graduate who returns home. The profession of the scribe is admired, thus providing the young readers with the motivation to study hard to achieve the coveted life of the sage.

Important Themes

The major themes of Egyptian literature included natural and social order (*ma'at,* also understood as justice, discipline, and truth) that originated in primordial times during the acts of divine creation and continued through provi-

---

57. Lichtheim (*Late Egyptian Wisdom Literature,* 24-28) demonstrates that this text is not directed to Egyptian farmers and peasants and thus is not a popular wisdom text.

58. See ibid., 93-106. Also see Burkard, *TUAT* 3: *Weisheitstexte,* 2:277-80 (note the bibliography).

59. Shupak, *Where Can Wisdom Be Found?*; Lichtheim, *Late Egyptian Wisdom Literature.*

60. Brunner, *Weisheitsbücher der Ägypter,* 421-24.

61. See Winfried Barta, "Das Schulbuch Kemit," *ZÄS* 105 (1978) 6-7.

dential guidance of history and nature. Central to this regularity and continuation that led to harmony, well-being, and sustenance was the role of the king. As Horus, he sat upon the throne and ruled not simply the Egyptian kingdom but also the entire world in its natural and social expressions. As Osiris, he ruled the underworld and the land of the dead. Through the king's relationship to the gods and to humans, the divine order of creation continued, especially emphasized in cultic ritual, political rule, and management of the kingdom. This order was personified as the daughter of Re who bore the name Maʿat.[62] The creator and the divine king established and maintained a beneficent order. This does not mean, however, that attacks on divine justice and the failures of rulers did not occur during periods of great distress and chaotic disturbance. Even the creator and the king received the brunt of strong criticism on occasion, especially during the First Intermediate Period. And, like a great deal of Hellenistic literature, Egyptian wisdom texts and grave inscriptions reveal an intrinsic pessimism especially regarding the question of a future life.

Also among the important constructs was the use of the generic term *ntr*, "god," or sometimes "the god."[63] This does not necessarily connote Egyptian monotheism,[64] but rather the changing deities who held the position of creator and ruler in the pantheon. Then too this term on occasion referred to the patron deity on whom sages depended for their needs to be met and their ambitions to be realized.[65]

Another important theme is the anthropology of the sages who saw humans as made by the gods and provided with the means of understanding, especially through the heart, which was conceived to be the seat of knowledge and the rational and aesthetic dimensions of human nature. Thus the contrast between the "passionate/heated" person and the "cool" individual is based on this view. The former refers to the fool, who is controlled by his passions and unbearably loquacious, while the latter is the rational, intelligent, and knowledgeable wise person, whose intellect is the primary means of thinking, judging, and acting and controlling his tongue.

---

62. Joachim Spiegel, *Das Werden der altägyptischen Hochkultur* (Heidelberg: Kerle, 1953) 464.

63. Brunner, *Weisheitsbücher der Ägypter*, 11-45.

64. Siegfried Morenz considers "the god" in wisdom texts to refer to the *Urgott* (*Egyptian Religion*, trans. Ann E. Keep [Ithaca: Cornell University Press, 1973] 27). Joseph Vergote has argued that there were monotheistic tendencies in Egyptian wisdom ("La notion de dieu dans les livres de sagesse égyptien," in *Les Sagesses du Proche-Orient Ancien* [Bibliothèque des Centres d'Études supérieures spécialisés; Paris: Presses Universitaires de France, 1963] 159-90), as did Eberhard Otto earlier: "Monotheistische Tendenzen in der ägyptischen Religion," *WO* 2/2 (1955) 99-110.

65. Merikare, 11.131-32; *ANET*, 417. See Winfried Barta, "Der anonyme Gott der Lebenslehren," *ZÄS* 103 (1976) 79-89.

Eschatology was the final theme of the sages. The necessity of mortuary religion and of the rites that allowed passage to the next world is found in Old Kingdom texts that limit living into the future world to the pharaoh, his family, and important officials. Beginning with the First Intermediate Period, however, the elaborate mortuary religion reserved only for the very wealthy was supplemented by the understanding of eternal life through the *ba* and made less expensive the means for the future life. Through democratization eventually even the lower class could hope to make their way into the West and live forever. Yet the later Hellenistic wisdom corpus and grave biographies elicit a deeply entrenched pessimism concerning life beyond death.

Summation

The instructions from the Old Kingdom were private teachings offered by highly placed officials and given to their sons who would succeed them. Not only were they advised on how to live successfully, they were also to preserve and extend the justice of *ma'at* that brought life and order to Egypt through their wise behavior and teaching. The Middle Kingdom teachings, however, focused primarily on the kings and often bore the character of propaganda in which sages were admonished to serve the rulers faithfully. This is especially apparent in the so-called "Loyalist Instruction."[66] This propaganda developed in the aftermath of the chaotic First Intermediate Period and provided a strong authoritarian antidote to the difficult turmoil that had engulfed Egypt for a century. In the New Kingdom, instructions moved into the personal sphere of the instructed. Instructions were no longer the exclusive domain of the upper class of officials, but came to include also the social stratum of lower-positioned scribes who were to seek inner satisfaction and security. The divine will was no longer connected to *ma'at*, but it was now out of individual piety and love of a god that the sage acted righteously. Finally, in the demotic instructions abstract formulations became emphasized, while there was no role for the monarch. Righteous deeds were a reward in and of themselves, requiring no additional motivation based on retribution. Thus it is accurate to conclude that wisdom literature in Egypt interacted with the social history of the kingdom/empire through the three thousand years of its existence.

---

66. See Simpson, *Literature of Ancient Egypt,* 198-200. Now see the 3rd ed.: William Kelly Simpson, ed., *The Literature of Ancient Egypt: An Anthology of Stories, Instructions, Stelae, Autobiographies, and Poetry* (New Haven: Yale University Press, 2003).

Mesopotamia

Introduction

By the mid-fourth millennium B.C.E. the Sumerians established a civilization in southern Mesopotamia that in its classical form consisted of approximately two dozen independent city-states, each of which had its major sanctuary and deity and was headed by a *lugal* ("Great man"). The cities and their populations were viewed as the extended households of the divine pantheon, ruled by Enlil and his family of a spouse and children. This period lasted until the conquest of the Amorites under Sargon around 2300 B.C.E., although there was a brief renaissance in the Third Dynasty of Ur (twenty-first–twentieth centuries B.C.E.). Later Akkadian dynasties, beginning with Hammurabi (1810-1750 B.C.E.), moved to unification, a process that ended only with the conquest by the Persians in the sixth century B.C.E. Sumero-Akkadian cultures in Mesopotamia produced sapiential literature that helped define the world in which Israel and Judah lived.[67] The influence of Assyrians and Babylonians on ancient Israel and Judah was substantial, beginning with their incorporation into the empires that their northern neighbors established. The sages in the sixth-century B.C.E. exile were likely knowledgeable of Babylonian wisdom literature and may have even interacted with the court and administrators involved in the ruling and managing of that significant empire.

While defining "wisdom" in Mesopotamian circles, especially in Akkadian texts, has been problematic, there are numerous correlations between sages and sapiential literature in Israelite and Akkadian texts. Genre,[68] epistemology,[69]

---

67. Due to the lack of a single, specific term in Sumerian and Assyriological literature for wisdom, most scholars have concentrated on genre as the key to identifying the texts of the sages. However, E. I. Gordon emphasizes subject matter, especially life and nature that provide insight into life ("A New Look at the Wisdom of Sumer and Akkad," *BO* 17 [1960] 122-52). Giorgio Buccellati identifies wisdom as "a cultural tradition." This includes themes, embodiments in texts, the settings (schools and popular tradition), and temporal points of history ("Wisdom and Not: The Case of Mesopotamia," *JAOS* 101 [1981] 35-47).

68. S. N. Kramer, "Sumerian Wisdom Literature: A Preliminary Survey," *BASOR* 122 (1951) 28-31; J. J. A. van Dijk, *La sagesse suméro-accadienne* (Leiden: Brill, 1953); Gordon, "New Look," 122-52; Manfried Dietrich, "Babylonian Literary Texts from Western Libraries," in *Verse in Ancient Near Eastern Prose*, ed. J. C. de Moor, et al. (Neukirchen-Vluyn: Neukirchener Verlag, 1993) 41-67. Sara Denning-Bolle resists attempting a comprehensive definition (*Wisdom in Akkadian Literature. Expression, Instruction, Dialogue* [Mededelingen en Verhandelingen van het Vooraziatisch-Egyptisch Genootschap "Ex Oriente Lux" 28; Leiden: Ex Orient Lux, 1992] 30). Also see idem, "The Notion of Wisdom in Ancient Mesopotamia," *Epochē* 8 (1980) 80-90.

69. Gordon, "New Look."

and cultural tradition[70] have been used to point to Akkadian wisdom's identifying marks. Even W. G. Lambert acquiesces to the convenience of the term in referring to common and recurring characteristics of a social world, profession, epistemology, themes, and genres that compare to those found in the biblical wisdom texts.[71]

The terms for wisdom, including nouns, adjectives, and verbs, are bountiful, pointing to a rich language developed in literary circles in which the sages participated.[72] The nouns are *apkallu,* "wise man, expert, (a mythological) sage, priest, or exorcist"; *emqu,* "wise person"; *igigallu,* "wise person, wisdom"; *mār ummâni,* "a member of the *ummānu* class, craftsman, expert"; *mūdû,* adjective used as a substantive for "wise"; *ummānu,* "surveyor, craftsman, artist, scholar, expert, moneylender." Adjectives include *ḫāsisu,* "intelligent, clever"; *assu,* "intelligent, clever"; *itpēsû,* "wise, expert"; *lē'û,* "able, capable, skilled"; *naklu,* "ingenious, clever, artistic"; *palkû,* "full of knowledge"; *tele'û,* "able, exceedingly competent." Finally, substantives meaning "wisdom" are *asīsu,* "aperture of the ear, ear, hearing, understanding"; *issatu,* "intelligence, understanding"; *igigallu,* "wise person, wisdom"; *igigallūtu,* "wisdom"; *inû,* "knowledge, technical knowledge of a craft"; *kabattu* (variant *kabittu*), "inside (liver?), emotions, thoughts, mind, spirit"; *karšu,* "stomach, belly, womb, body, mind, heart, plan, desire"; *libbu,* "heart, abdomen, mind, thought, intention, courage, wish, desire, choice, preference"; *mērešu,* "knowledge, wisdom"; *nēmequ,* "knowledge, experience, wisdom"; *nikiltu,* "ingenuity, skillful work, ingenious or clever idea, trick, cunning, deception"; *pakku,* "consideration"; *pīt asīsi,* "wisdom"; *tašīmtu,* "insight, understanding"; *tēmu,* "ability to plan, the power to make decisions, understanding, direction, advice"; *ummânūtu,* "artistic craft, teaching ability"; *uršu,* "desire"; and *uznu,* "ear, wisdom, understanding." Finally, a key verb is *asāsu,* "to think of, give heed to a deity, be pious, be intelligent or understanding."

Thus among the most important Akkadian words are *nēmequ* ("wisdom"), *mērešu* ("knowledge"), *uznu* ("ear"), *emqu, mudū, eršu, itpēšum,* and *assu* ("wise").[73] It is important to note, however, that in Akkadian the term "wisdom" connotes not only practical advice and ethical decision making, but also magic

70. Buccellati, "Wisdom and Not," esp. 35.

71. See W. G. Lambert, "The Development of Thought and Literature in Ancient Mesopotamia," in *Babylonian Wisdom Literature* (repr. Winona Lake, IN: Eisenbrauns, 1996), 1 (hereafter = *BWL*).

72. Ronald F. G. Sweet, "The Sage in Akkadian Literature: A Philological Study," in *Sage in Israel,* 45-65. Also see idem, "The Sage in Mesopotamian Palaces and Royal Courts," in *Sage in Israel,* 99-107.

73. Hannes D. Galter, "Die Wörter für 'Weisheit' im Akkadischen," in *Megor Hajjim: Festschrift für Georg Molin* (Graz: University of Graz Press, 1983) 89-105.

and cultic skill or knowledge.[74] Yet there is a second source of wisdom that moves outside the areas of experience, rational analysis, and acts of the imagination — divination, which provided the initiated with esoteric knowledge of the gods and their divine actions in creation and history. In addition to the words used within a sapiential cultural tradition, these terms also refer more generally to "knowledge," "craft," "intelligence," "skill," and "shrewdness."[75]

Sumero-Akkadian Wisdom Literature

Wisdom literature in Sumer and Akkad is especially a distillation of the knowledge of the natural world, the gods, religion, the sciences, and moral living.[76] Yet this literature understands that it is not only reason, but also feelings and the imagination that come into play in the formulation of the sapiential worldview and the obtaining and articulation of understanding about the various facets of human life.[77] At the same time, this literature serves especially to educate youth in the task of seeking to prepare for a scribal profession in the administration of the state and in the temple through learning the scribal arts, proper behavior (including etiquette), and disciplined study and reflection. Wisdom becomes the search for an order in the cosmos and society and the desire to instill within that order both a harmony of creation and life and a synthesis of all that is experienced by the human senses and intelligence and shaped by the imagination.

Texts of Wisdom

The Sumero-Akkadian wisdom literature includes texts from the third millennium (c. 2800 B.C.E.), and especially the Third Dynasty of Ur (c. 2112-2004 B.C.E.), to the end of the Neo-Babylonian period.[78] The classical texts, not to mention the substantial number of sayings,[79] include disputations: "The Baby-

---

74. *BWL*, 1.

75. Denning-Bolle (*Wisdom in Akkadian Literature*, 34-39) sets forth a list of terms for wisdom.

76. Gordon, "New Look," 123.

77. See the emphasis on the aesthetic features of wisdom by van Dijk, *Sagesse suméro-accadienne*, 3.

78. Gordon, "New Look," 122-52.

79. E. I. Gordon, *Sumerian Proverbs* (Philadelphia: University of Pennsylvania Press, 1959); Bendt Alster, *Studies in Sumerian Proverbs* (Mesopotamica 3; Copenhagen: Academisk Forlag, 1975); idem, *Proverbs of Ancient Sumer: The World's Earliest Proverb Collection* (Bethesda, MD: CDL, 1997); idem, *Wisdom of Ancient Sumer* (Bethesda, MD: CDL, 2005).

lonian Theodicy" (Kassite period); "The Dialogue of Pessimism" (twelfth century B.C.E.); instructions: "Instructions of Šuruppak" (mid-third millennium B.C.E.); the "Counsels of Wisdom" (Kassite period); the "Counsels of a Pessimist" (Kassite period); the "Advice to a Prince" (1000-700 B.C.E.); and psalms: the bilingual "Hymn to Ninurta" (Middle Assyrian period), "The Šamaš Hymn" (perhaps Middle Babylonian), and "The Poem of the Righteous Sufferer" (*Ludlul bēl nēmeqi*, Kassite period). These texts, produced during periods of empire by both the conquerors and the conquered, responded to the social and historical circumstances of their respective ages.

As is true elsewhere in the cultures of the ancient Near East, the wisdom literature is generically composed of proverbs, instructions, didactic poems, and disputations. Yet Akkadian sapiential literature also delved into the esoteric knowledge of divination and incantation more than was the case elsewhere. This magical and secretive lore obtained by priests and seers was a component of an esoteric wisdom that developed in Judah particularly under the guise of apocalyptic.[80]

Of the surviving sapiential literary forms in the Mesopotamian traditions, the most frequent one is the proverb. As is true elsewhere in the ancient Near East, the proverb is a short, pithy saying that incorporated within itself an observation of the cosmic and social world that provided insight into human nature and nature.[81] One finds many of these interspersed in a variety of written materials as well as in personal names, which provide a vast array of examples.

Instructions, less frequent than their Egyptian counterparts, were largely second person admonitions and prohibitions given by a teacher to his "son" (in Akkadian, *mārī*, "my son"), that is, student, for moral edification.[82] Formally, there are monologues that are the distillation of a sage's or group of sages' insights into reality and the moral life. The best-known texts are "The Instructions of Šuruppak," "The Counsels of Wisdom," "Advice to a Prince," and "The Counsels of a Pessimist."[83] These teachings are primarily ethical and social in content, addressing moral behavior, decorum, and responsibilities of the wise person to the family and the oppressed.

In "The Instructions of Šuruppak" a prediluvian sage and protégé of Ea (the god of wisdom) named Šuruppak instructs his son, Ziusudra, who escapes the deluge of the primordial flood.[84] This Sumerian teaching deals with

---

80. Hans-Peter Müller, "Mantische Weisheit und Apokalyptik," in *Congress Volume: Uppsala, 1971* (VTSup 22; Leiden: Brill, 1972) 268-93.

81. Gordon, *Sumerian Proverbs*; Alster, *Proverbs of Ancient Sumer*; *COS* 1:561-68.

82. Denning-Bolle, *Wisdom in Akkadian Literature*, 124-29.

83. *BWL*, 107-9; Denning-Bolle, *Wisdom in Akkadian Literature*, 126-28.

84. See *BWL*, 96-107; B. Alster, "Shuruppak," *COS* 1:569-70; Denning-Bolle, *Wisdom in Akka-*

a variety of topics, including the household, agriculture, herding of flocks, human associations, and sexual morality. What is missing is interesting, for there are no teachings that pertain to the gods, worship, and political leadership. Important, however, is the mythological location of wisdom before and immediately following the flood in this version, one of several flood accounts in ancient Mesopotamia.

"The Counsels of Wisdom" is a well-structured collection of more than 160 lines that offers moral exhortations to a student.[85] Dating is problematic, but Lambert points to the Kassite period as the time of origin. The Kassites were possibly Indo-Europeans who, perhaps from the Zagros Mountains, came into the area just north of Babylonia in the eighteenth century B.C.E., and eventually established the Second Dynasty of Babylon. This Akkadian text covers topics including avoiding foolish and evil associates, learning to speak wisely, charity, avoiding confrontations with enemies, shunning prostitutes and rejecting women slaves as suitable wives, offering worship to the patron deity, and taking care against deception, especially of companions. This was likely a manual of instruction given to Babylonian youth who would enter the service of the colonial government subject to the Kassite rulers.

Another Akkadian text focuses on the rights of the citizens of Nippur, Sippar, and Babylon by limiting a ruler's authority in assuring that he may not engage in taxing them (at least to impose excessive taxes), misappropriating their land, and in forcing them to engage in compulsory labor. "The Advice to a Prince" is an Akkadian instruction possibly deriving from Babylon in the tenth to the seventh centuries B.C.E., when Babylon was again ruled by native rulers.[86] It sets forth the responsibilities and duties of kingship. If the ruler establishes justice by emulating the work of Ea, the gods will reward his rule, while a failure to do so results in divine retribution. This caution legally and theologically warns rulers to recognize the limits of their power.

"The Counsels of a Pessimist" also is difficult to date, for it may originate

---

dian Literature, 126-28. For the translation of "The Instruction of Shuruppak," see COS 1:569-70; Bendt Alster, The Instructions of Šuruppak: A Sumerian Proverb Collection (Mesopotamia 2, Copenhagen Studies in Assyriology 2; Copenhagen: Akademisk Forlag, 1974).

85. BWL, 96-107.

86. See BWL, 110-15; TUAT 3: Weisheitstexte, 1:170-73; I. M. Diakonoff, "A Babylonian Political Pamphlet from about 700 B.C.E.," in Studies in Honor of Benno Landsberger, AS 16 (Chicago: University of Chicago Press, 1965) 343-49; Erica Reiner, "The Babylonian Fürstenspiegel in Practice," in Societies and Languages of the Ancient Near East: Studies in Honour of I. M. Diakonoff (Warminster: Aris & Phillips, 1982) 320-26; Bendt Alster and H. L. J. Vanstiphout, "Lahar and Ashnan: Presentation and Analysis of a Sumerian Disputation," ActSum 9 (1987) 1-43; Denning-Bolle, Wisdom in Akkadian Literature, 125-26.

anywhere from the dynasty established by Hammurabi to the Assyrian ruler Ashurbanipal.[87] This Akkadian instruction offers admonitions concerning life, but with a pall of pessimism hanging over the teachings. This is due to the recognition of how short life is and how brief in their duration are the exploits one is able to accomplish that have any important consequences. Nevertheless, the teacher's son *(mārī)* is to follow the prescribed counsels offered him.

Three other genres found in Sumerian and Akkadian wisdom literature are laments, disputations, and dialogues.[88] The dialogue assumes the form of *adaman-dug₄-gad* ("contest literature").[89] Dialogues present a disagreement between two or more parties. These texts include the Sumerian "A Man and His God," the Akkadian *Ludlul bēl nēmeqi*, "The Dialogue of Pessimism," "The Babylonian Theodicy," "The Dialogue between Two Gods," and "The Dialogue between a Teacher and His Student." The literary form of dialogues contains the following features, although few texts possess all of them:

1. a mythological-etiological introduction that places the topic(s) debated within the cosmic order and articulates the lines of disagreement between adversaries
2. the body of the disputation that outlines the positions taken by the two or more opponents
3. a divine judgment leading to the correct position once the debate concludes
4. and an emphasis on reconciliation between the disputants[90]

Written at the end of the Kassite period, "I Will Praise the Lord of Wisdom" is similar to the lament of the individual.[91] The sufferer, a feudal lord, who is possibly a ruler of Babylon, describes his sufferings, which he attributes to the responsibility of his lord and protector, Marduk.[92] His plight drives him to raise questions about his theology and the validity of cultic observance. Marduk

---

87. *BWL*, 107-9.

88. See Denning-Bolle, *Wisdom in Akkadian Literature*, 85-175; idem, "Wisdom and Dialogue in the Ancient Near East," *Numen* 34 (1987) 214-34. In addition, see W. H. Ph. Römer, "Aus einem Schulstreitgespräche," *UF* 20 (1988) 233-45; William W. Hallo, "Lamentations and Prayers in Sumer and Akkad," *CANE* 3:1876-81.

89. See van Dijk, *Sagesse suméro-accadienne*, 31-85.

90. Ibid., 39-42.

91. See *BWL*, 21-62; *COS* 1:486-92; D. J. Wiseman, "A New Text of the Babylonian Poem of the Righteous Sufferer," *AnSt* 30 (1980) 101-7; Denning-Bolle, *Wisdom in Akkadian Literature*, 129-33.

92. Jacob Klein, "'Personal God' and Individualized Prayer in Sumerian Religion," *AfO Beiheft* 19 (1982) 295-306.

sends him three revelatory dreams that promise purification and redemption from his tribulations.[93] After his deliverance, he comes to Esagila (the temple of Marduk in Babylon) to offer thanksgiving and sacrifices to this ruler of the gods and his consort.

Laments and lament-like compositions are found in various ancient Near Eastern wisdom texts, including the Sumerian "A Man and His God."[94] This dialogue portrays a young sage who belongs to the aristocracy of Sumerian society and undergoes great suffering, including the displeasure of his ruler.[95] Speaking in the first person, the man proclaims his innocence and even accuses his god of afflicting him with evil.[96] Even so, he continues with his lament to ask his god to deliver him from this undeserved suffering. In the concluding episode, the voice of a third person narrator intrudes to describe the young man's deliverance. Continuing to plead his case, the protagonist is finally redeemed by his deity.

An Akkadian text perhaps written at the end of Kassite dominance of Babylonia, "The Dialogue of Pessimism" involves a conversation between a lord and his slave.[97] If the conversation is serious, it leads to an emphatic denial of all meaning. If read as a dour or humorous satire, it still denies the possibility of finding the proper course of action that makes life worthwhile. Repeatedly the lord announces his decision to pursue a particular activity, only to change his mind almost immediately. His slave, the real wise man in the story, supports both decisions. Finally, having exhausted his efforts to find meaningful action, the lord asks the slave, "What, then, is good?" To this the slave responds: "To have my neck and your neck broken and to be thrown into the river is good." Since all actions are ultimately futile, the slave concludes there is nothing worthwhile in human living. Thus the only recourse is suicide. The lord, wish-

---

93. See A. Leo Oppenheim, *The Interpretation of Dreams in the Ancient Near East* (Philadelphia: American Philosophical Society, 1956); idem, "Mantic Dreams in the Ancient Near East," in *The Dream and Human Societies*, ed. Gustave Edmund von Grünebaum and Roger Caillois (Berkeley: University of California Press, 1966) 341-50.

94. S. N. Kramer, "'Man and His God': A Sumerian Variation on the 'Job' Motif," in *Wisdom in Israel and in the Ancient Near East*, ed. M. Noth and D. Winton Thomas (VTSup 3; Leiden: Brill, 1955) 170-82; Klein, "Personal God." Klein had available eight more duplicates than Kramer.

95. *ANET*, 589-91; *TUAT* 3: *Weisheitstexte*, 1:102-9; *COS* 1:485. For three school dialogues see *COS* 1:589-93.

96. A. Leo Oppenheim, *Ancient Mesopotamia: Portrait of a Dead Civilization*, ed. Erica Reiner (rev. ed.; Chicago: University of Chicago Press, 1996). See the essay by William W. Hallo, "The Limits of Skepticism," *JAOS* 110 (1990) 187-99.

97. Lambert stresses not the humor but rather the seriousness of the dialogue (*BWL*, 139-49). By contrast, E. A. Speiser views the text as satire ("The Case of the Obliging Servant," *JCS* 8 [1954] 98-105).

ing to test the sincerity of his slave's counsel, states he first will execute his slave. The slave replies that, even if the master does so, he would see that his slave is correct in his position of the meaninglessness of life and would choose to end his own life within three days.

"The Babylonian Theodicy" is an acrostic composition, consisting of twenty-seven stanzas, each composed of eleven lines.[98] Originating in Babylonia during the Kassite period,[99] two sages, a sufferer and his friend, debate the issue of human torment. Through the interchange of speeches, the dispute centers on the greatest liability of human living, that is, the divine decree of death. While the friend urges the sufferer to look to divine deliverance from his plight by offering worship to his god, the one afflicted complains of the abandonment and disregard of his patron deity. For him social injustice proves that cultic religion, faithfully followed, does not lead to a righteous redress by the gods. Finally, the friend is won over to the position of the complainant by affirming that the gods are responsible for the corruption of human nature. The sufferer continues to affirm his innocence and to plead to his patron god and goddess for mercy and deliverance.

Themes

One of the significant themes appearing in sapiential literature from Sumer and Akkad is the mythological location of wisdom's origin, knowledge which is provided to the seven *apkallu*s prior to the cosmic deluge and to those who came immediately after to a new group of hoary sages. These latter wise men were the ones who provided the arts of civilization to the "black-headed" people, as the inhabitants of Mesopotamia were called. Especially important is the wisdom of the friend of humanity, Ea, the god of wisdom, who provides Šuruppak (= Utnapishtim) the warning of the great flood planned by Enlil and supplies him with instructions on building a vessel to escape the approaching destruction. Justice is another important theme, especially attributed to the god Shamash, who in his journey across the heavens as the sun disk surveys the doings among humans and then judges the righteous and the wicked according to the principle of retribution. The issue of theodicy nevertheless emerges, espe-

---

98. Wolfram von Soden, *TUAT* 3: *Weisheitstexte*, 1:143-57; Hallo, *COS* 1:492-95. Also see Georgio Buccellati, "Tre saggi sulla sapienza mesopotamica, III. La teodicea: condanna dell'abulia politica," *OrAnt* 11 (1972) 161-78. For a list of Akkadian acrostics, see Denning-Bolle, *Wisdom in Akkadian Literature*, 136-37. In the case of this text, it spells the name and provides a brief description of the author, "Saggil-kinam-ubbib, an incantation priest, worshiper of God and king."

99. Lambert (*BWL*, 63-64) dates it c. 1000 B.C.E. Also see idem, "Ancestors, Authors, and Canonicity," *JCS* 11 (1957) 11.

cially during the Kassite period when complaints against Marduk the Babylonian high god are issued, while pessimism over the futility of life is expressed during this time of the bitter rule of foreign conquerors. Virtues for wise rule and loyal service, and vices to avoid, common to wisdom texts, abound in the instructions and the sayings that exist among this important tradition. Kings were instructed in the teachings of the counselors to rule their kingdoms in justice and with insight.

Conclusions

Mesopotamian wisdom in its classical formation developed first in Sumer and then continued in Babylon during Amorite rule until the end of the Kassite conquest and the emergence of Babylonia as an independent state at the end of the second millennium B.C.E. These classical texts continued into the stream of later tradition, but we do not find their like in Neo-Assyrian and Neo-Babylonian periods of the later first millennium. This does not mean the wisdom tradition ceased to exist, for there continued to be scribes active in temple and palace circles who operated schools, advised kings, and used the classics to educate students. Sayings of a sapiential nature abound, but the great texts were the ones that continued to shape and form new generations of sages.

Ugarit

A Syrian coastal city of the Late Bronze Age provides an important religious and socioeconomic understanding of the later Canaanites encountered by early Israel in the Iron Age. This urban area encompassed a commercial seaport at modern Ras Shamra, known in antiquity as Ugarit. The city had significant commercial connections with Cyprus and Minoa in the eastern Mediterranean, and also established political and trading relationships with Mesopotamia to the northwest, and south to Egypt and its mighty rulers of the New Kingdom. This made Ugarit one of the important Late Bronze Age coastal cities of this eastern shore of the Mediterranean.

Ugarit flourished between 1450 and 1200 B.C.E., when it was likely destroyed by the invading Sea Peoples. A cosmopolitan city, its sages wrote and stored tablets involving the knowledge and use of Ugaritic and several additional languages, including Egyptian, Luwian, Cypro-Minoan, Sumerian, Akkadian, and Hurrian.

The Sociopolitical and Religious Constitution of Ugarit

Ugarit's libraries (two private, one in the temple, and another archive being pieced together) illustrate in their expansive collections the activity of scribes who, in composing various types of literature, copied a small number of wisdom texts of sages who likely taught in royal and temple schools and served in the court.[100] These sapiential texts were written in Sumerian, Akkadian, and Hurrian; some were bilingual but most were not in Ugaritic cuneiform. This is likely due to the fact that these languages were the international means of communication and writing of the nations and scholars of the ancient Near East during the Late Bronze Age. The Ugaritic wisdom texts include a righteous sufferer poem, a lament of a sufferer to Marduk, fragments of the Gilgamesh Epic, proverbs, and an instruction.

The important compositions of wisdom at Ugarit include the following:

1. RS 15.10 is a bilingual Akkadian-Hurrian text that consists of sayings.[101]
2. RS 25.460 (= Text 162) in Akkadian presents the suffering of a person that those skilled in exorcism and incantation cannot help.[102] Marduk eventually restores the man to health.[103]
3. RS 22.439 (= Text 163) is an Akkadian text of admonitions whose sage, Šubê-awīlim, may be equated with Šuruppak, presenting thus the posture

---

100. See J. P. J. Olivier, "Schools and Wisdom Literature," *JNSL* 4 (1975) 49-60; Manfried Dietrich, Oswald Loretz, and Joaquin Sanmartín, eds., *Die keilalphabetischen Texte aus Ugarit* (hereafter *KTU*) (AOAT 24; Neukirchen-Vluyn: Neukirchener Verlag, 1976) nos. 402-7; W. J. Horwitz, "The Ugaritic Scribe," *UF* 11 (1979) 389-94; D. Arnaud and D. Kennedy, "Les texts en cuneiform syllabiques découverts en 1977 à Ibn Hani," *Syria* 56 (1979) 319-24; Loren R. Mack-Fisher, "A Survey and Reading Guide to the Didactic Literature of Ugarit: Prolegomenon to a Study on the Sage," in *Sage in Israel*, 67-80; idem, "The Scribe (and Sage) in the Royal Court at Ugarit," in *Sage in Israel*, 109-15; Manfried Dietrich, "'Ein Leben ohne Freude . . .': Studie über eine Weisheitskomposition aus den Gelehrtenbibliotheken von Emar und Ugarit," *UF* 24 (1993) 9-29. Now see Ignacio Márquez Rowe, "Scribes, Sages, and Seers in Ugarit," in *Scribes, Sages, and Seers,* forthcoming.

101. Jean Nougayrol, "Tablette bilingue accado-hourite," *PRU* 3 (1955) 311-24. He also published the first of the "school texts" on pp. 211-14. Among his articles on wisdom texts at Ugarit, consult "L'influence babylonienne à Ugarit, d'après les textes en cunéiformes classiques," *Syria* (1962) 28-35.

102. Jean Nougayrol, "(Juste) Souffrant," *Ugaritica* 5, ed. C. F. A. Schaeffer (Mission de Ras Shamra 16; Paris: Imprimerie Nationale, 1968) 265-73.

103. See also Benjamin J. Foster, "A Sufferer's Salvation," *COS* 1:486, which derives from Ugarit (see Nougayrol, *Ugaritica* 5:435, no. 162). According to W. W. Hallo, "scribal schools adopted and adapted the Mesopotamian curriculum in the Late Bronze Age" (*COS* 1:486).

of primordial wisdom.[104] It also is translated into Hittite. Šubê-awīlim was perhaps the greatest Ugaritic sage.

Scribes and sages served a variety of roles, from copyists, to lawyers, to notaries (Šapšumalku), to teachers (e.g., Attēnu, the instructor of Ilimilku), to viziers. It is likely that the famous scribe Ilimilku was an advisor, even vizier *(tāʿiyu)*, of the king of Ugarit around 1200 B.C.E.

Themes

One of the important themes found in the Ugaritic corpus is the wisdom of El (Ilu). Anat praises El: "Your decisions, Ilu, are wise, / you are wise for eternity, / a life of good fortune is your decision" (*KTU* 1.3 v 30-31 and 1.4 iv. 41-43, words echoed later by his wife, Asherah [Atiratu]). Another is the importance placed on counsel and wisdom in the "Admonitions of Šubê-awīlim to His Son," the opening lines of which begin: "Hear the counsel of Šubê-awīlim on whom Enlilbanda (Ea) bestowed understanding, / the wise counsel of Šubê-awīlim whom Enlilbanda endowed with wisdom" (RS 22.439).[105] Third, the patron gods Nabû and Nisaba are mentioned in the colophons of six students' textbooks.[106]

---

104. Nougayrol, "Sagesse," *Ugaritica* 5:273-90 = "The Counsels of Shubeʾawilum." Also see the discussion by Duane E. Smith, "Wisdom Genres in RS22.439," *Ugaritica* 2:215-47; John Khanjian, "Wisdom" in *Ras Shamra Parallels*, ed. L. R. Fisher (AnOr 50; Rome: Pontifical Biblical Institute, 1975) 371-400.

105. RS 25.460 was published by J. Nougayrol in *Ugaritica* 5, no. 162. The manuscripts of the "Poem of Early Rulers" were also published by J. Nougayrol in *Ugaritica* 5, nos. 164-66. More recent studies have been written by M. Dietrich, "'Ein Leben ohne Freude . . .': Studie über Weisheitskomposition aus den Gelehrtenbibliotheken von Emar und Ugarit," *UF* 24 (1992) 9-29; J. Klein, "'The Ballad About Early Rulers' in Eastern and Western Traditions," in *Languages and Cultures in Contact: At the Crossroads of Civilizations in the Syro-Mesopotamian Realm*, ed. K. van Lerberghe and G. Voet (OLA 96; Leuven: Peeters, 1999) 203-16. RS 15.10 was published by J. Nougayrol (the Akkadian text) and E. Laroche (the Hurrian text) in *PRU* 3:311-24; Lambert reexamined the Akkadian text in *BWL*, 116; the Hurrian text has been dealt with by M. Dijkstra, "The Akkado-Hurrian Bilingual Wisdom-Text RS 15.010 Reconsidered," *UF* 25 (1993) 163-71. RS 22.439 was also published by J. Nougayrol in *Ugaritica* 5, no. 163; also studied by M. Dietrich, "Der Dialog zwischen Supe-ameli und seinem 'Vater'. Die Tradition babylonischer Weisheitssprüche im Westen," *UF* 23 (1991) 33-68. Because fables are conventionally included under the category of wisdom literature, one should refer here to two fragmentary tablets, RS 25.526A written in Akkadian (so far unpublished), and RS 86.2210[A] with three columns (Sumerian, syllabic Sumerian, and Akkadian, the last lost) published by D. Arnaud in RSOu 14, no. 29.

106. Márquez Rowe, "Sages, Scribes, and Seers in Ugarit."

Conclusion

From this small group of texts, it becomes obvious that the Ugaritic sages, whose specific names and writings are sparsely attested, drew from the sapiential tradition in Mesopotamia, indicating that the cultures of Sumer and Akkad were the intellectual centers from which learning extended into northern Syria. From the languages used and the themes present (especially those of the righteous sufferer), Ugarit was clearly dependent on the wisdom tradition that preceded it in Mesopotamia and used it as the classical source for the education of their native scribes. Ugaritic wisdom texts also demonstrate the antiquity of the tradition in Syria-Israel prior to Israel's state formation. This at least allows for the plausibility of the view that there was a viable Syrian tradition that likely would have continued into the First Temple and that the sages of the two cultures would have interacted.

Aram

While the dominant colonial powers and their claims for superior civilization including religion, culture, and knowledge arose in the two geographical extremes of the ancient Near East (Mesopotamia and Egypt), the regions in Syria-Israel still established their own localized cultural identities. Beginning in the mid-ninth century B.C.E., Aram became a powerful state in the central region of the Levant, so powerful that the Syrian ruler, Adad-idri (= Hadad-'idri), leading the small states in the area against the invasion of Assyrian forces under Shalmaneser III, stopped the Assyrian advance at Qarqar in 853. The coalition under the same leadership fended off several later forays by Shalmaneser III. However, Tiglath-pileser III defeated the coalition in 732 B.C.E., so that these small states fell under the sway of Assyrian power.

The Sayings of Ahiqar

From Aram or ancient Syria the best-known sapiential text is "The Sayings of Ahiqar,"[107] which eventually made its way to ancient Uruk (Warqa) in the

---

107. Ingo Kottsieper, *Die Sprache der Ahiqarsprüche* (BZAW 194; Berlin: de Gruyter, 1990); idem, "Die Geschichte und die Sprüche des weisen Achiqar," *TUAT* 3: *Weisheitstexte*, 1:320-47; idem, "The Aramaic Tradition: Ahikar," in *Scribes, Sages, and Seers,* forthcoming. Also see Michael Weigl, "Compositional Strategies in the Aramaic Sayings of Ahikar: Columns 6-8," in *The World of the Aramaeans*, vol. 3: *Studies in Language and Literature in Honour of Paul-Eugène Dion*, ed. P. M. Michèle Daviau, John W. Wevers, and Michael Weigl (JSOTSup 326; Sheffield: Sheffield Academic

Seleucid period as well as to Elephantine in Egypt as early as the fifth century B.C.E. The text combines sayings with a narrative, both originating in different periods. The narrative, written in Imperial Aramaic in the sixth century B.C.E., describes the betrayal of the wise scribe Ahiqar, who served as vizier originally in the court of Sennacherib and then in the court of his successor, Esarhaddon. Composed in the first-person style of an omniscient narrator, the sage asks the "king of Assyria" that he be allowed to instruct his nephew Nadin to succeed him to the office of the vizier. Betrayed by Nadin, who accuses him of disloyalty, Ahiqar is imprisoned in the house of Nabusumiskun, a high official of the king who directed him to execute Ahiqar. However, he heeds the request of Ahiqar to live, kills in his place an Ethiopian slave, and hides the endangered sage in his house. While hidden in the house of his savior, Ahiqar composes his sayings, and then is released and restored. Nadin is reprimanded for his treachery and ultimately dies.

The sayings date no later than the early seventh century B.C.E.[108] and consist of nine columns of proverbs that have survived in fragmentary form. A variety of themes was covered: proper decorum, moral behavior, appropriate and wise speech, rejecting slander, avoiding marriage to a prostitute or a sacred priestess of Ishtar, loyalty to the prince, giving alms, withholding retribution against an enemy, piety to the patron deity, long life, fulfilling one's promises, and acting in ways pleasing to Shamash, the god of justice and wisdom.

Conclusion

The themes of wisdom are perhaps not always clearly attested, due to the significant damage to the admonitions and prohibitions found in the sayings. The narrative's emphasis on loyalty and the rescue of the innocent just man, while not complete, presents the thesis of a highly placed sage, a major counselor to Esarhaddon, who is loyal to his ruler even though falsely accused. The narrative depicts Ahiqar as the father and counselor to all of Assyria or its army. The court as the center of wisdom is duly depicted, as is the role of the sage as a royal vizier and counselor to the king and instructor of his successor. Loyalty to the ruler, likely the subjected Syrian king who led a colony in the greater Assyr-

Press, 2001) 22-82; Bezalel Porten and Ada Yardeni, *Textbook of Aramaic Documents from Ancient Egypt*, vol. 3: *Literature, Accounts, Lists* (Jerusalem: Hebrew University Press, 1993); James M. Lindenberger, *The Aramaic Proverbs of Ahiqar* (Baltimore: Johns Hopkins University Press, 1983); M. H. Goshen-Gottstein, *The Wisdom of Ahiqar: Syriac and Aramaic* (Jerusalem: Hebrew University of Jerusalem, 1965).

108. See Kottsieper, "Geschichte und Sprüche"; cf. Lindenberger, *Aramaic Proverbs of Ahiqar*, 20.

ian and then Babylonian Empire, is suggestive of the local court for both narrative and sayings. The sayings, however, dating from the seventh century B.C.E., point to the court as only one of their social milieus and suggest a more middle-class social setting than that of powerful aristocrats. At the same time, the original introduction of the proverbs depicts Ahiqar as the counselor of the king, working in his court as a scribe in the royal service and acting as the bearer of the his seal (I 3 [3], II 3 [19]). And it is only the king who relies on his advice. The Jewish sages' interaction with this text in the colony at Elephantine would suggest a much traveled text that made its way into Syrian-Israelite circles at an earlier time and even into Hellenistic Mesopotamian wisdom in the Seleucid period. The imprisonment and liberation of Joseph in the narrative of this patriarch in Gen. 37–50 points to a general typos in Israel and Aram in the First Temple period.

Greece

Introduction

After the death of Aristotle, among whose students was Alexander the Great during his youth, the classical age of ancient Greek city-states came to an end, to be replaced by smaller Greek kingdoms and then larger empires in the eastern Mediterranean world, the latter fomented by the massive empire of Aristotle's student, Alexander of Macedon. With assimilation of Eastern cultures due to hellenization, the blending of Greek and indigenous cultures, which was promoted largely though the paideia of the schools, led to a Hellenistic culture that included a variety of areas: religion, philosophy, language, and sociopolitical structures. During the Hellenistic period, the philosophers, sophists, rhetors, gods, and religions of Greco-Roman culture also significantly influenced Hellenistic Judaism and its wisdom traditions.

The substantial variety of Greek terms associated with wisdom, philosophy, and teaching make it impossible in this brief review to be complete, but I will mention some of the key ones based on the LXX's Wisdom of Solomon and the parts of Ben Sira available in Greek. A number of terms are important to note. The Greek noun *sophia* ("wisdom") refers to a quality, not an activity, and means theoretical and practical knowledge.[109] Especially in the LXX and the NT, the term is an all-embracing one to include general knowledge, knowledge of the natural world, knowledge imparted by God, divine wisdom, and a

---

109. Georg Fohrer, "σοφία," *TDNT* 7 (1971) 465-526.

goddess (a consort of God or a personification of a divine virtue).[110] *Sophos* is both an adjective that denotes "wise," "skillful," "clever," "learned," and a noun used to signify "wise one" or "sage." *Sophizō* is the verb that means "to make wise," "teach," "instruct," and "to reason." Other important words of the Greek vocabulary for "wisdom" and "knowledge," along with their verbal and nominative forms, include *gnōmē* ("saying," "intention," "opinion," "consent," and "declaration"), *gnōsis* ("knowledge," sometimes in the sense of esoteric, revealed insight), *synesis* ("comprehension," "insight," and "intelligence"), *mathēma* ("knowledge" and "teaching"), *epistēmē* ("understanding" and "knowledge"), *logos* ("word," "reason"), and *akouō* ("hear" and "understand"). Wisdom was a significant human attribute, indeed a prized virtue in moral philosophy, and was a seminal characteristic of heroes, philosophers, orators, and statesmen.

Gymnasia and schools of rhetoric flourished in the Hellenistic period. The literature studied in the curriculum included the following genres.[111] Teachers used handbooks (*Hermeneumata* or *Colloquia*) that contained rules for learning to speak and write. These were to be memorized and applied by students seeking to receive an education that was appropriate for their social status and to enter a variety of occupations in public life. Handbooks had four sections: a general glossary, a topical glossary, vignettes of common life, and finally moral pieces consisting of brief stories, fables, and sayings.[112] The literary classics also were studied for their insights into life and the elegance of their literary style. These texts included writings of Homer, Hesiod, Euripides, Aeschylus, and Sophocles. Historians like Herodotus were read for their understanding of history and the major events and personages of the Greek past. The writings of the important philosophers were also read and studied in order to learn from a variety of categories of knowledge important in Greek thought. These philosophers included Socrates, Plato, Aristotle, Zeno, and Epicurus, while the subjects covered included metaphysics, physics, epistemology, morality (virtues and vices), and rhetoric.

The *gnōmē* was a proverb or saying that frequented the literary and oratory works of Greeks from the earliest period into the first centuries of the hege-

110. William F. Arndt and F. Wilbur Gingrich, *A Greek-English Lexicon of the New Testament and Other Early Christian Literature* (Chicago: University of Chicago Press, 1957) 766-67.

111. Edward P. J. Corbett, *Classical Rhetoric for the Modern Student* (4th ed.; Oxford: Oxford University Press, 1999); Richard A. Lanham, *A Handlist of Rhetorical Terms* (2nd ed.; Berkeley: University of California Press, 1991); and Heinrich Lausberg, *Handbook of Literary Rhetoric: Foundation for Literary Study* (Leiden: Brill, 1998).

112. Rafaella Cribiore, *Gymnastics of the Mind* (Princeton: Princeton University Press, 2001) 15.

mony of Imperial Rome.[113] These sayings expressed a truth about existence or captured some insight into moral behavior.

Gnomologia were collections of sayings (*gnōmē*) used in teaching students and by orators and composers to support their arguments, demonstrate their personal learned character, and to enhance their speeches and texts. In the latter part of the Classical Age, gnomologia became a recognized category of rhetoric. They were used to support an argument as well as to express simply a truism readily recognized in the larger culture.

A *paroimia* is a proverb or saying, while a *chreia* is a saying used to state a general observation.[114] Both became a means of teaching rhetoric and ethics to students in the schools.

Used especially by rhetoricians, the *progymnasma* was an exercise used in the education of students in the schools of rhetoric.[115] The genres covered in these texts included myth, fable, narrative, *gnōmē, chreia*, topos (i.e., commonplace), refutation and confirmation, speeches of various types, description, question, and legal introduction. These were learned and then used in legal debate and interpretation, epideictic oratory, and historiography.

The *eulogia* ("eulogy") was a specific type of speech of praise offered in remembrance of the glorious dead, their accomplishments, and virtues, and normally delivered at the funeral of the deceased.

The panegyric is the term used to refer to a formal oration, verse, and narrative of praise regarding a person, virtue, event, city, state, or deity.[116] Derived from the word *panēgyrikos* ("for an assembly"), this praise is not intended to be critical, but rather laudatory in nature. It was a term used to refer to public speeches during formal occasions that extolled the qualities and virtues of a person or thing. One type of panegyric was the public oration given at the games in Athens in which the assembly of athletes and spectators were exhorted to emulate the examples of their esteemed "ancestors."

Rhetors taught their students the exercises of impersonation (or formation of character) and praise (*ēthopoiia* and *encomium*).[117] The first consisted of declamation in which a student assumed the role of significant figures (histori-

113. Michael S. Silk, "Gnome," *OCD*, 640.
114. Kenneth James Dover, "Chreia," *OCD*, 324-25. Ronald F. Hock and Edward N. O'Neil, *The Chreia in Ancient Rhetoric*, vol. 1: *The Progymnasmata* (Atlanta: Scholars Press, 1986); idem, *The Chreia and Ancient Rhetoric: Classroom Exercises* (Atlanta: Society of Biblical Literature, 2002).
115. Donald Andrew Frank Moore Russell, "Progymnasmata," *OCD*, 1253; G. A. Kennedy, *Greek Rhetoric under Christian Emperors* (Princeton: Princeton University Press, 1983) 52-73.
116. See D. A. Russell and N. G. Wilson, eds., *Menander Rhetor* (Oxford: Clarendon, 1981). Menander made use of panegyrics in his treatises.
117. Cribiore, *Gymnastics of the Mind*, 228.

cal, mythical, literary, and heroic) and chose the literary form that was appropriate for the occasion. These impersonations gave students the opportunity to develop the figure's arguments within the context of the speech. The student usually selected the literary pattern appropriate for a particular occasion (e.g., exhortation and the request for forgiveness). At times, the speech of the personage was simply memorized and presented. The second is a prose or poetic panegyric designed to praise a person, thing, or idea (see Aristotle, *Rhet.* 2.20, 1393a23-1394a18). On occasion this included the recounting of the past through the praise of ancestors, gods, and cities.

During the Hellenistic period, four important schools of philosophy appeared and influenced significantly the culture and thought of the eastern Mediterranean world: Stoicism, Epicureanism, Neopythagoreanism, and Skepticism. These came to influence to a degree Hellenistic Judaism in both Judea and the Diaspora.

Stoicism

The reputed founder of Stoicism was Zeno, who came to Athens in the latter part of the fourth century B.C.E. and established his school.[118] Many of its most famous adherents participated in public life (e.g., the Romans Seneca and Cicero). In their epistemology, the Stoics were empiricists who spoke of the sense impressions that objects made on the human mind. Some of these could not be considered false, although every area of knowledge required proper and detailed principles of explanation. Stoic physics held that the world was both materialistic and deterministic and that the fundamental element that produces everything is fire. Objects in the world operate according to laws to which there are no exceptions. These interactions of things are not random, but rather are teleological, that is, fate providentially guides human beings to their destiny. The cosmology of Stoicism centers on the divine Logos or reason, which permeated reality and ordered its component parts, thus establishing the rules of existence for each element, living and inanimate. This same Logos dwelt within human beings in the form of reason. Stoic ethics held firmly to the view that only virtue is good. Virtue was defined as the correct purpose and use of a thing. The fundamental virtues were based on self-control so that knowledge consists of proper choice, resilience, and justice in the fair distribution of

---

118. Julia Annas, "Stoicism," *OCD*, 1446; John M. Rist, *Stoic Philosophy* (Cambridge: Cambridge University Press, 1977); idem, ed., *The Stoics* (Berkeley: University of California Press, 1978); Brad Inwood, *Ethics and Human Action in Early Stoicism* (Oxford: Clarendon, 1985); idem, *Cambridge Companion to the Stoics* (Cambridge: Cambridge University Press, 2003).

goods. For the Stoics, the only significant possession in life was virtue, meaning that all other things, ranging from possessions to health to death, were of no significant consequence. In contrast to the virtues are uncontrolled passions, which lead to all things that are evil. Humans are to live according to reason, which is intrinsic to human nature and its most important and noblest element. The goal of human life, then, was to live in harmony with the Logos and to experience well-being. Acting in ways contrary to the divine Logos led to harm and even destruction of the self. While there are necessities for existence, nothing, including pain and poor health, could detract from the happiness of the truly wise person. Indeed, true wisdom that led to happiness consisted of living in agreement with oneself and with nature.

Epicureanism

A second Greek school of philosophy developing in the Hellenistic period was Epicureanism.[119] Epicurus (341-270 B.C.E.) came to Athens and developed a philosophy that in many areas was directly opposed to Stoicism.[120] Epicurus made pleasure, understood as simple and moderate in its character, the fundamental and natural goal of a happy life. Shunning public life, Epicurus lived in his garden, cultivating intimate friendships with his adherents, practicing an austere existence, and warning against participation in public life. Eschewing social differentiations, Epicurus had among his friends and followers women and slaves. While the Stoics believed in divine providence in the form of fate, Epicurus taught that the gods, while perfect, pay no attention whatsoever to human beings and live in a state of perpetual bliss, the same goal of human existence. His objective was to liberate humans from their fear of the gods, since they neither reward nor punish people. One seeks a balance between pleasure, the goal of life, and pain, which is to be avoided. The goal of life is *ataraxia,* freedom from disturbance, and *aponia,* freedom from pain. Pleasure is not sensual, although it was popularly misunderstood to be the primary teaching of Epicureanism, but rather it is undisturbed joy. Moderation, not hedonism, is the key to the good life. His epistemology was also radically empirical, for it is the perceptions of the senses, he affirmed, that gave rise to all knowledge. While the appearance of objects to the senses is not false, it is possible to form incorrect views about them. For Epicurus, cosmology was centered in the belief in

119. James Warren, *Facing Death: Epicurus and His Critics* (Oxford: Clarendon, 2004); idem, *Epicurus and Democritean Ethics: An Archaeology of Ataraxia* (Cambridge: Cambridge University Press, 2002).

120. See esp. Lucretius, *De rerum natura,* for a description of the life and teachings of Epicurus.

chance, not providential fate. The world came into existence through the chance collision of atoms, and it one day will disintegrate. As for physics, all things are composed of atoms, even human nature and thought, so that at death the atoms are dispersed and connect to others in the formation of new objects. Change is simply the new arrangement of atoms, which themselves are unalterable and eternal. Death was simply viewed as the reformulation of the deceased's atoms.

Neopythagoreanism

A third school of importance was Neopythagoreanism.[121] Pythagoras, who established the school of Pythagoreanism in Athens in the sixth century B.C.E., taught that he was associated with the god Apollo and could even call to mind his own former lives. His philosophy also taught "the kinship of all beings," based on speculation on numbers in seeking out the harmony that exists among all things.[122] A resurgence of this school in the form of Neopythagoreanism occurred in the first century B.C.E.[123]

Skepticism

A fourth school that became influential during the Hellenistic period was Skepticism.[124] The father of Greek Skepticism was Pyrrho of Elis (c. 365-272 B.C.E.), who taught that no one can know anything for certain. This is true even of the objects perceived by the senses, for there is no proof that they are real and not illusory. This meant that equal arguments could be made on either side of a proposition. Humans are to suspend judgment on the reliability of sense impressions and to learn to view reality as it appears, not necessarily as it is. Things-in-themselves cannot be known by either rational deduction or empirical experience. This being true, humans ought to suspend judgment about the

121. John Dillon, *The Middle Platonists. 80 B.C. to A.D. 220* (rev. ed.; Ithaca: Cornell University Press, 1996); Holger Thesleff, *An Introduction to the Pythagorean Writings of the Hellenistic Period* (Åbo: Åbo Academi, 1961).

122. For a brief summary see *OCD*, 1035-36. Major philosophers of this school who lived in Alexandria in the first century C.E. were Apollonius of Tyana, who considered himself the reincarnation of Pythagoras (see Philostratus, *Life of Apollonius*), and Moderatus of Gades.

123. See Dillon, *Middle Platonists*, 117-21.

124. For an introduction to and summary of Hellenistic skepticism, see A. A. Long, *Hellenistic Philosophy: Stoics, Epicureans, Sceptics* (2nd ed.; Berkeley: University of California Press, 1986); Keimpe Algra, et al., *The Cambridge History of Hellenistic Philosophy* (Cambridge: Cambridge University Press, 1999).

world. While common sense can and should give direction to choice, there is no certainty about the world, moral values, or the existence of God.

During the early Hellenistic period (from c. 269 to the mid-first century B.C.E.), the Academy of Plato was dominated by a series of highly regarded Skeptics.[125] The philosophical orientation of the New Academy flourished under the leadership of Archelaus, Carneades, and Clitomachus.[126] For these philosophers, Plato may be understood only through the lens of skepticism. The conflict with the Stoics was largely stimulated by differences in epistemology. Stoics taught that sense perception, which was stimulated by an experience of something, was to be logically and accurately defined, thus providing the basis for affirmations that are reasonably true. Skeptics of course denied this foundational basis. Instead, they taught what was known as *akatalēpsia*, the idea that absolute knowledge or truth was impossible to obtain, for there were no criteria for establishing what was unquestionably true. Thus the only reasonable conclusion is the suspension of judgment, or *epochē*, about any and all affirmations.[127] According to Cicero, Carneades engaged in a methodological criticism of all doctrines. He espoused the important notion of the "plausible" *(pithanon)*, a theory that a proposition could be affirmed but still be contested. Even so, the "plausible" was not a certain guide to what was true. Convincing arguments could be made against any conclusion. Thus Carneades adhered to the fundamental Hellenistic rejection of assertion based on "mere" opinion. Nevertheless, his student Clitomachus held that moral doctrines may be used to provide guidance in life, even though they cannot be anything other than unproven opinions.

Rhetoric

Public speaking or rhetoric was a cultivated skill in Classical and Hellenistic Greece and was especially important in philosophical debate, legal settings,

---

125. See Malcolm Schofield, "Academic Epistemology," in *Cambridge History of Hellenistic Philosophy*, 323-51.

126. John Glucker, *Antiochus and the Late Academy* (Hypomnemata, Untersuchungen zur Antike und zu ihrem Nachleben 56; Göttingen: Vandenhoeck & Ruprecht, 1978); Martin Ostwald and John P. Lynch, "The Growth of Schools and the Advance of Knowledge," *Cambridge Ancient History* (hereafter *CAH*), vol. 6: *The Fourth Century B.C.*, ed. D. M. Lewis, et al. (2nd ed.; Cambridge: Cambridge University Press, 1994) 592-633.

127. Schofield summarizes the three significant arguments of Arcesilaus against Stoic epistemology: (1) "there is no true impression such that there could not be a false impression indistinguishable from it. From this he further argued (2) that in that case if the wise person assents, what he will be holding is an opinion — since cognition is impossible. And he held (3) that it is necessary for the wise person not to hold opinions, and so not to assent" ("Academic Epistemology," 334).

teaching, and public address.[128] Plato defined rhetoric as the art of persuasion (Plato, *Gorg.* 453a2). Thus it is not simply the craft of skilled and ornamental speech, but also a speech that seeks to convince others of the correctness of the position articulated. Important types of rhetoric were deliberative (persuasion to follow a course of action), judicial (argue points of law in a specific case), and demonstrative (revealing the good or bad features of a particular subject under discussion).[129] In addition, the elegant shaping of the language was a cultivated skill of rhetoricians. Due to the emphasis on proper speaking, the moral character of the speaker, and the themes that are addressed, rhetoric may be compared to the wisdom traditions of the ancient Near East. In addition to the explication of the features of eloquence, the topics discussed included criticism of the morality of the times; the condemnation of adultery; the rejection of luxury; praise of a variety of things (e.g., a city, marriage, and childbearing); denunciation of a city; lamentation on the brevity of life, injustice, and the capriciousness of fortune; and the censuring of lying, rumor mongering, and false witnesses. Rhetors taught their students the polished skills of speaking, while some even wrote speeches for use by others on public occasions. Some of the more famous and highly sought out rhetors established schools to teach students in public speaking. The earliest surviving handbook on rhetoric is the *Rhetorica ad Alexandrum,* written by Anaximenes of Lampsacus (c. 380-320 B.C.E.).

Conclusion

While there was significant variety among philosophers, rhetors, and composers in the Hellenistic period, what united these diverse views was the quest to find something intrinsic to the world and to life that allowed a person to transcend the vagaries and insecurities of human existence. To discover the goal of living and the meaning of life, various areas were examined that included diverse views of cosmology, physics, ethics, and religion. Behind each of these was a particular type of epistemology or esoteric knowledge that led to the possibility of understanding. Only the Skeptics rejected the possibility of this discovery

128. Donald Andrew Frank Moore Russell, "Rhetoric, Greek," *OCD,* 1312-14; G. A. Kennedy, *A New History of Classical Rhetoric* (Princeton: Princeton University Press, 1994); idem, "Historical Survey of Rhetoric," in *Handbook of Classical Rhetoric in the Hellenistic Period. 330 B.C.–A.D. 400,* ed. Stanley E. Porter (Boston: Brill, 2001) 3-43; Thomas Habinek, *Ancient Rhetoric and Oratory* (Blackwell Introductions to the Classical World; Oxford: Blackwell, 2005). Quintilian noted that the rhetor is not simply a person whose language is elegant and persuasive, but also one who is moral (*Inst.* 2.15.34).

129. Habinek, *Ancient Rhetoric and Oratory,* 102-3.

and contented themselves with the recognition that nothing could be found about which there was universal and provable consent. Their views moved into the dark chasm of meaninglessness and the nonsensical that was to reappear in a variety of philosophical forms, including the current infatuation of some intellectuals with postmodernism.

The Social Character of Wisdom and the Roles of the Sages in the Empires

Israel and Judah

Introduction

The scribes and sages of ancient Israel and Judah existed in a nation surrounded by different countries that possessed their own sapiential traditions.[130] The wise of Israel and Judah acknowledged the existence and value of several of these traditions, even though they claimed their wisdom was superior. For example, the Deuteronomistic History in 1 Kgs. 5:9-14 (4:29 34) compares favorably Solomon, the legendary patron of the wise, to the notable sages of the people of the East and of Egypt and even calls four of them by name: Ethan the Ezrahite, and Heman, Calcol, and Darda, the sons of Mahol. Israel's and Judah's indebtedness to the wisdom traditions of the ancient Near East and finally the philosophies and rhetoric of the Greeks during the Hellenistic period is illustrated by the appropriation of "The Instruction of Amenemope" by the editor of Prov. 22:17–24:22; "The Sayings of Agur" (Prov. 30), which appears to draw on the *apkallu* tradition in Akkadian wisdom; the Edomite identities of Job and his opponents (Job 1–2); the instruction given by the Arabic queen mother to her son, Lemuel of Massa, in Prov. 31:1-9; and popular Stoicism. These are examples of influence occasionally recognized even by the Israelite and Jewish sages themselves. Furthermore, scribes were necessary for Israel's and Judah's national life in the internal and international contexts of Israel and Judah, the ancient Near East, and the later Hellenistic and early Imperial Roman worlds. These scribes were not only required to perform their administrative and written tasks inside their own countries, but at least some had to develop the skills to read, write, and speak the different languages that served as the international mode of communication in the

---

130. In general see Gammie and Perdue, *Sage in Ancient Israel;* Perdue, *Scribes, Sages, and Seers,* forthcoming.

larger eastern Mediterranean world: Akkadian, followed by Aramaic, and then Greek.

Scribes and Sages in the Courts of Israel and Judah

With the rise of the Israelite monarchy, sages and scribes became an important professional class in both the royal administration and that of the temple.[131] One important role was that of serving as a wise counselor *(yō'ēṣ)* to kings and other people of power (Prov. 11:14; 15:22; 24:6; 25:15; Isa. 19:11-12). The task of the counselor was to formulate plans to assist both rulers to succeed in their efforts to rule wisely and well and others to experience well-being (Deut. 32:28-29; Isa. 16:3; 41:28-29; see Ahithophel, 2 Sam. 16:20; Hushai, 2 Sam. 17:6-14). Wise counselors also included women, for example, the wise woman of Tekoa (2 Sam. 14) and the wise woman of Abel of Beth-maacah (2 Sam. 20). Indeed, in the early cabinets of the monarch, *hassōpēr* ("the scribe" = "the secretary") became one of the most important officials in the royal bureaucracy, for he served as chief advisor to the king and the chief officer of the political administration. His duties paralleled those of the vizier in ancient Egypt. Other scribes served in the bureaucracies of the state and the Jerusalem temple, from powerful positions to lowly ones of copyists and recorders. In the Deuteronomistic History Shaphan is our best example of a First Temple sage. He held the powerful post of secretary ("the scribe") in Josiah's cabinet (2 Kgs. 22:3, 8). He and his descendants in the Deuteronomistic History are depicted as Deuteronomic sages having significant political positions. Other portraits include: the description of Qoheleth in 12:9-14, Baruch (Jer. 36; 45:1-5; and the later Baruch tradition, esp. 1 Baruch), and Ben Sira (38:34b–39:11).

By the reign of Omri in the ninth century B.C.E. in the north, and in the south by the reign of Hezekiah in the latter part of the eighth and early years of the seventh century, important and powerful kingships required a substantial number of scribes and highly placed sages to carry out the duties and responsibilities of their kingdoms.[132] The dynastic monarchial system, which began

---

131. See Keith Whiteland, *The Just King: Monarchical Judicial Authority in Ancient Israel* (JSOTSup 8; Sheffield: JSOT Press, 1979); G. W. Ahlström, *Royal Administration and National Religion in Ancient Palestine* (Leiden: Brill, 1982); Marvin L. Chaney, "Systemic Study of the Israelite Monarchy," *Semeia* 37 (1986) 53-76; E. Lipiński, "Royal and State Scribes in Ancient Jerusalem," in *Congress Volume: Jerusalem, 1986,* ed. J. A. Emerton (VTSup 40; Leiden: Brill, 1988) 157-64.

132. See Israel Finkelstein and Nadav Na'aman, eds., *From Nomadism to Monarchy: Archaeological and Historical Aspects of Early Israel* (Jerusalem: Israel Exploration Society, 1994). For a full-ranging discussion of sociological data and theories, see Volkmar Fritz and Philip R. Davies, eds., *The Origins of the Ancient Israelite States* (JSOTSup 228; Sheffield: Sheffield Academic, 1996).

with Saul, David, and Solomon, originated for several reasons: advances in technology with the manufacture of tools and weapons from iron for more productive farming,[133] the building of strong and powerful armies that mastered the use of chariots, and the dramatic increase in Israelite/Judahite urbanism that included strategically located military fortifications.[134] However, it was not until the ninth and eighth centuries that sophisticated administrations emerged that provided the context in which sages and scribes in large numbers were needed for more advanced administrations.

Not coincidentally, the proverbial collection assembled by "the men of Hezekiah" (25:1–29:27) outlines a royal ideology constructed by court sages that includes the knowledge, wisdom, and justice of sages and kings, the exalted status of the king, and the behavior expected of the wise men who served as royal officials in positions of power (e.g., proper speech, honor, caring for the rights of the poor, knowing proper court etiquette, impartiality in judgment, husbandry of flocks and care for productive fields, a reminder to rulers of the transitory nature of wealth and crown, and obedience to the law [likely the civil law of the monarchic state]).

Deuteronomy 17:2-13 and 2 Chron. 19:4-11 suggest that there existed a national system of courts in which a law code developed and was administered by scribes and sages. The king was ideally the supreme judge in ancient Israel and Judah, and sages served as judges and lawyers. They were the writers and codifiers of civil laws. Subsequently, among the specialties in the royal schools would have been the study of civil (Jer. 8:8) and religious legislation (Jer. 18:18).

The administration of the state would have included also the mustering, outfitting, and location of a professional military to maintain order within the state, to protect it against invaders and raiders from the outside as well as outlaws within the nation's boundaries, the collection of taxes, the building of an infrastructure (roads, military installations, water collection, and irrigation), mercantile and trade networks, diplomacy, and the building and maintenance of a royal cultus. These activities were placed under the leadership of the king and a royal cabinet. The cabinet, as noted above, included the priest, the scribe and diplomat, the commander, the supervisor of the governors and city leaders, the friend of the king,[135] one over the house/palace (palace administrator), and the overseer of forced laborers. Additional offices are "the king's son" (successor

---

133. See Israel Finkelstein, *The Archaeology of the Israelite Settlement* (Jerusalem: Israel Exploration Society, 1988) 330-35.

134. See Israel Finkelstein, "The Emergence of the Monarchy in Israel: The Environmental and Socioeconomic Aspects," *JSOT* 44 (1989) 43-74.

135. Herbert Donner, "Der 'Freund des Königs,'" *ZAW* 73 (1961) 269-77.

designate?), "the king's servant," and the "ruler of the city" (cf. 1 Kgs. 22:26; 2 Kgs. 23:8; 2 Chron. 34:8).

Within the progression of generations during Iron Age II, there are a steady development of centralization, the increasing power of the monarchs, an expanding population, and escalating urbanization.[136] However, with Assyrian domination, beginning as early as 734 B.C.E., the decline of the two kingdoms was dramatic. The Assyrian invasion of Israel culminated finally in the destruction of the capital Samaria in 722 B.C.E. coupled with the massive devastation of the north along with the depletion of its civil service and leaders. Judah initially acquiesced to Assyrian domination, and it was only later that Hezekiah's failed attempt to remove the colony from imperial domination almost led to the dissolution of the south as well.

The increasing complexity in society, in the period of more than a century prior to Assyrian domination, is evident from the correlation with archaeological data.[137] This may be seen in the hierarchy of settlements: a small number of large cities, a growth in the number of towns, and a very significant number of villages. In addition, later Iron II witnesses the substantial increase in monumental architecture and the numerous types of forms, ranging from large public buildings, including administrative palaces, temples, storage facilities, and stables, to the building of large fortifications, colonnaded buildings, walls, and gates, to public works including water tunnels and roads, to the variations in size and quality of private quarters, and to the multiplicity of industrial workshops. In some sites, large aristocratic homes and small houses of the lower classes were built in urban sites, pointing to significant social stratification. Luxury items increased, including ivory inlays in furniture and stunning jewels (precious and semiprecious). Yet, at the same time, there were small village settlements with a few private houses, normally four-room structures, several of which shared a courtyard, and perhaps a few industrial sites like wine and olive presses and small storage pits. The urban center provided the administrative, economic, and military location for nearby settlements within its orb of control that constituted a socioeconomic network of farms, villages, and towns. Even tombs point to social stratification, with the wealthy being interred in large tombs often built for several or more people together with accompanying grave offerings, including luxury goods, terra-cotta figurines, and inscriptions. The

136. See Ephraim Stern, *Archaeology of the Land of the Bible*, vol. 2: *The Assyrian, Babylonian, and Persian Periods, 732-332 BCE* (New York: Doubleday, 2001); William Dever, "Social Structure in Palestine in the Iron II Period on the Eve of Destruction," in *The Archaeology of Society in the Holy Land*, ed. Thomas E. Levy (New York: Facts on File, 1995) 416-31.

137. Paula M. McNutt, *Reconstructing the Society of Ancient Israel* (Library of Ancient Israel; Louisville: Westminster John Knox, 1999) 148.

bureaucracy, temple, and the royal court were dependent on taxes, gifts to the temple, tools, and occasional tribute from conquered nations and tribes. While criticisms were directed against the monarchies of north and south, the relationship between city and village was not always necessarily one of opposition, but also of social, military, and economic interdependence.

In the area of literary culture, the evidence for the expansion of written materials (largely in the form of ostraca, seals, bullae, stamped jar handles, and inscriptions) throughout Israel appeared in significant numbers prior to the end of the kingdom of Judah.[138] This supports the argument that scribalism developed significantly in the late First Temple period as a consequence of the expansion of royal power and administrative control exerted through a large bureaucracy interconnecting various regions and cities. This would require additional schools for the education of the increasing numbers of scribes needed for the work of the royal administration. Some cultural evidence exists in the form of abecedaries used to teach students the rudiments of reading and writing in the schools.[139] Some of the literature of court scribes supported rulers by means of royal propaganda (e.g., 2 Sam. 7, the "Promise to David," related to Ps. 89; and the court narratives, e.g., the "Solomonic History" in 1 Kgs. 3–11). Another text, the so-called Succession Narrative (2 Sam. 9–1 Kgs. 2), portrays the roles of numerous sages in the court and in the smaller cities. These include Ahithophel, Hushai, the wise woman of Tekoa, and the wise woman of Abel of Beth-maacah.

In the Second Temple period, the role of the sage as interpreter of the law, especially the Torah, became a significant new development (cf. Ezra). This type of learned sage is best represented by Ben Sira, a noted teacher of considerable wealth and social standing. However, now his major role and that of sages with whom he worked and who were to follow was to be the interpreter of Scripture, since this was beginning to develop in its tripartite form. The understanding of the scribe as the authoritative and inspired interpreter of the Torah and the larger canon may be cautiously followed in Chronicles and Ezra–Nehemiah. Ezra, the scribe and priest of God Most High, was the second Moses and the Zadokite priest who enfolded within his office the scribal and priestly structures of localized power in the Jewish community. Indeed, Ezra became so

---

138. André Lemaire, *Inscriptions hébraïques/introduction, traduction, commentaire* (Littératures anciennes du Proche-Orient 9; Paris: Cerf, 1977); idem, *Les écoles et la formation de la Bible dans l'ancien Israël* (OBO 39; Göttingen: Vandenhoeck & Ruprecht, 1981); Menahem Haran, "On the Diffusion of Literacy and Schools in Ancient Israel," in *Congress Volume: Jerusalem, 1986*, ed. Emerton, 81-95.

139. The "abcedary" was a primer for learning an alphabet. See André Lemaire, "Abécédaires et exercices d'écolier en épigraphie nord-ouest sémitique," *Journal asiatique* 266 (1978) 222-35.

prominent a source of authority that he was appropriated as the paragon of mantic wisdom in apocalyptic circles (cf. 1 Enoch). Ben Sira and his sapiential colleagues were not only teachers of aspiring scribes and sages, but also cosmopolitan men of the world who served in important roles and offered their "inspired" teachings" (Sir. 39:1-11). The "scribal" community of Qumran represents a similar, albeit sectarian approach to Scripture, and its members continued, as did Ben Sira, to write their own literature, which took on an eschatological dimension. With Ben Sira and the Qumran community, the age of the sage dawned in early Judaism; it reached its apogee in the rabbinic office in the Tannaitic period.

The sages of note belonged to the elite, as indicated by a number of factors. First, only the well-to-do possessed the time to study and learn. Second, the cultivation of the arts and behavior of sages, including proper decorum in the royal court and later the governor's office, points to individuals of high position who interacted with powerful officials. Third, charity, an important virtue taught by the sages, was the providing of gifts to sustain the life of the poor and could come only from those with excess wealth. Indeed, the elite were responsible for the sustenance of the poor and were expected to pay fairly their laborers. Fourth, affluence was praised, even though wisdom was more highly prized, and was possible to accumulate only by the social elite. Fifth, only the wealthy and those of high position would have the means and opportunity to receive an education in the schools that would have taught them to read, write, and speak according to the skills of rhetoric. Sixth, the social stratification present in the texts points to the respect for and importance of the wealthy.

Among the seers (*ḥākām, ḥōzeh,* and *rō'eh*) were mantic sages who acquired their knowledge through esoteric means. These avenues to knowledge included especially dreams or visions, while other methods of divination were normally rejected in Israel and Judah (consultation of the dead, augury, extispicy, and divine oracles). Mantic seers included Joseph, Enoch, and Daniel. Even Eliphaz claims this type of special knowledge (Job 4:12-21). Eventually, these seers developed into the writers of apocalyptic and were founders and/or participants of apocalyptic movements and groups, which formed their own traditions and communities. The seer is thus an initiate into this type of secretive lore.[140] He learns not only from his esoteric experiences and the teachings of the ancestors, but also from the revelation of divine knowledge that comes from the gods and priests who endowed him with these special understandings through special revelation, ranging from flights into heaven, to conversations with divine messengers, to dreams and visions.

---

140. *BWL*, 1.

While a great deal of wisdom resided beyond human understanding, the "sages" engaged in persistent efforts to know empirically and rationally the natural and social world that they encountered. They did speculate through their imagination about matters, including the world of the divine, the historical past, and the future that was yet to occur, all of which transcended their own immediate experience. But most did not lay claim to any special revelation in their speculations. As supporters of the kings and later the hierarchical high priests, the sages participated in the efforts to establish the authority and legitimacy of their masters who sought to create and sustain a righteous order in the society through their own justice and the institutions they led.

The Family Household (Mišpāḥâ)

The family household *(mišpāḥâ)*, the different roles that existed in this institution, and moral instruction about behavior and responsibilities are regarded as important, related themes in the wisdom tradition. However, this does not mean that this was the social setting for the origin and shaping of the various literary genres and collections in the Bible. Rather, these references simply indicate that the family was one of the social contexts in which sages and their students carried on their lives and about which instruction was issued and sayings reflect common understandings.[141] The conventional values of the agricultural villages, including charity, a social network of support, a familial kinship structure, established tasks, defined social roles, and shared resources (property, cisterns, wells, walls, fields, houses, and tools) were central to communal life and based on familial solidarity. God was a family deity who protected the household and was worshiped by its members. Larger festivals were seasonal, following agricultural harvests, and celebrated by gathered clans at local sanctuaries. These values and religious practices did not easily fit the urban society and political system of an authoritarian monarchy that stressed loyalty and service to the king in which there was royal control of the judicial system, the standing army, gathering taxes, carrying out commerce, and overseeing land resources. It is this system of royal authority expressed through administrative control of people and resources in which the sages whom we know from literary sources operated. State formation led to a stratified society, individual ownership of property, and professional groups that functioned with their own professional ethics. Religion was centered on the understanding of God as the patron deity of the king and the royal state. His primary cultic worship was centered in the state capital with the chief priest

---

141. See Leo G. Perdue, et al., *Families in Ancient Israel* (Louisville: Westminster John Knox, 1997).

a member of the royal cabinet and a subject of the ruler. The festivals were also seasonal and involved pilgrimages to Jerusalem, with perhaps the most important being the New Year's Festival during the autumn, following the harvest of the vineyards. In this festival God was the creator of the earth and the one who provided the fruits of fertility to the worshipers and the monarch. The sages and scribes of Israel carried out their tasks in the institutions of the monarchy's administration and that of the temple, which centered its rites on the worship of the creator and protector of the chosen monarchy. Scribes and sages, who functioned in the administrations of the state and temple, interpreted the authority of the monarchy as supreme. The collapse of the monarchy reoriented the sages and scribes locally to service to the priesthood and eventually the Torah and externally to the colonial governments of empires. The sages and scribes became shapers and interpreters of the Torah in particular and the other socioreligious traditions that continued to develop.

The Sage in Schools in Israel and Judah

The major social locations reflected in wisdom literature were the city and the household, in which scribes, sages, and their students carried on their daily lives. The city, not the village, was especially the place where sages lived and engaged in their professional activities. It is true that the family received substantial consideration in regard to social ethics and responsibilities: marriage, family, children, and inheritance, but this does not mean that the household was the context for the creation of wisdom texts and oral traditions. The social titles of the family were adopted by the sages in their teachings: "father," "mother," and "son(s)." Evidence of schools (associated with the court) is implied in Proverbs (5:13-14; 25:1; 31:1), the references to the king (court, esp. 16:10-15), and the virtues taught (discipline, study, diligence, and concerted effort to gain wisdom). Students are described as young, naïve, simple, and untutored in insight and are collectively called the *pĕtā'îm* (see 1:4, 22; 8:5, *petî*). The purpose of this literature, largely moral in nature, was to teach students to value, cultivate, and learn sapiential values and understandings. This ethic formed the character of their professional lives in their roles as scribes and sages.

The existing knowledge of schools and curricula in the eastern Mediterranean world (see esp. Qumran, the Mishnah, Philo, the wisdom sources of the ancient Near East, and Greek gymnasia and schools of rhetoric) provides important insights into those of Israel and Judah in the First and Second Temple periods. Israelite and later Jewish students in the schools learned reading, writing and composition, logic, and debate. It is also plausible that the wider curriculum moved beyond the fields of ethics and the scribal arts to include the knowledge of calculation, astronomy and astrology, interpretation of the law, music, architecture, and diplomacy. Proverbs and Ben Sira were likely manuals of instruction in professional ethics for young students. External sources suggest that in Israel and Judah there were also stages of education, ranging from elementary to advanced, with at least some of the best students going into the more advanced level to study for a variety of careers.

Egypt

The ordinary scribe was not only a copyist and clerk, but also a bureaucratic official in the Egyptian administration of the courts and temples. Like their counterparts in Israel, scribes were responsible for the development and transmission of Egyptian culture, including literature, monumental histories and inscriptions, tomb frescoes and texts, and ordinary administrative texts. Since most Egyptians were illiterate, only the elite and upper class of society had ample opportunity to study at scribal schools and to enter administrative and temple service. Lower-class scribes could learn to master the elements of literacy, but had no real opportunity to advance in social standing. The wisdom literature of ancient Egypt indicates the profession and social status of sages and scribes were quite desirable.[142] The conclusion of the book of the *Kemyt,* the manual of education from the Middle Kingdom, reads: "As for the scribe in whatever position he has at the Residence [school associated with the temple], he can never become miserable in it." "The Satire on the Trades" adds: "There is nothing which surpasses writing. . . . Moreover, it is greater than any (other) office; there is not its like in the land."[143] Some sages themselves belonged to the elite, especially the king and the royal family members, while the scribes of higher placed officials had access to the powerful rich and possessed a limited opportunity to advance in position. Famous sages held in continued esteem were assured of immortality through their writings even when their tombs had

---

142. The tomb of another son of Khufu, Kawab, also has been discovered. It contained statues made out of diorite and granite. Three are of scribes in a seated position with a papyrus scroll on their laps, indicating the prominence of the profession in the Old Kingdom (Schlott, *Schrift und Schreiber,* 148). The high level of prestige obtained by those in the scribal profession is also indicated by the mastaba of a scribal official, Hysyra (c. 2660 b.c.e.). After the New Kingdom, however, the role of the scribe was more frequently a type of skilled laborer than a prestigious position held only by members of aristocratic families (Schlott, *Schrift und Schreiber,* 149). Still, sages of noble rank, including officials and honored wise men, continued to maintain the highest status among the scribes and in the kingdom.

143. *ANET,* 432.

disintegrated and mortuary services ceased. Thus "their names are (still) pronounced because of their books which they made, since they were good and the memory of him who made them (lasts) to the limits of eternity."[144] Some eight are named in this text ("In Praise of Learned Scribes"), six of whom are known from the copies of their writings that have survived through the centuries, and four of whom are depicted on a Ramesside tomb chapel at Saqqara. Some scribes accrued wealth and even could afford expensive tombs and mortuary preparations for their family and themselves. Scribes helped to create and preserve the classical tradition, and sages contributed their own writings.

During the Old Kingdom, some sages were highly placed officials and even royalty who held positions in the scribal ranks, although the writings may have been pseudonymous. During the First Intermediate Period, scribes wrote literature that reflected the uncertainty of the age, while in the Middle Kingdom sages sought to establish the authority and credibility of the early rulers.[145] The New Kingdom and later saw scribes functioning in various areas of administration of the kingdom and temple in order to manage a kingdom that on occasion developed into a large empire. The literature was not written only by the elite, but also came from sages of the lower social class.[146]

Sumer and Akkad

Scribes and sages belonged to professions that required a particular type of knowledge or expertise: craftsmen, architects and builders, soldiers, priests, diviners, musicians, physicians, counselors, and teachers.[147] However, only a few references are made to requesting counsel from the sage.[148] Kramer summarizes the roles and professions of the Sumerian sage under the two categories of educator and humanist.[149] And this also would be true of the later Akkadian scribes. Some sages taught in the schools (Sum. *edubba* and Akk. *bīt ṭuppi*) of the courts and temples. Proverbial literature and other types of sapiential texts were com-

144. "In Praise of Learned Scribes," *ANET*, 431-32.

145. See Schlott, *Schrift und Schreiber*, 179-208. These texts include "The Prophecy of Neferti" (see Wolfgang Helck, *Die Prophezeiung des Nfr.tj* [Kleine ägyptische Texte; Wiesbaden: Harrassowitz, 1970]), "The Admonitions of Ipuwer" (Lichtheim, *AEL* 1:149-63), "The Dialogue between a Man and His Ba" (see Erik Hornung, *Meisterwerke altägyptischer Dichtung* [Zurich: Artemis, 1978] 77-78), and "The Instruction of Amenemhet" (Lichtheim, *AEL* 1:135-39).

146. Brunner, *Weisheitsbücher der Ägypter*, 11-94.

147. Jean Bottéro, Clarisse Herrenschmidt, and Jean-Pierre Veernant, *L'Orient ancien et nous: L'écriture, la raison, les dieux* (Bibliothèque Albin Michel; Paris: Albin Michel, 1996).

148. Sweet, "Sage in Akkadian Literature," 45-65.

149. Samuel N. Kramer, "The Sage in Sumerian Literature," in *Sage in Israel*, 32-37.

posed and transmitted in the schools, primarily for teaching morality, religion, cosmology, and the scribal arts.[150] Rhetorical features of the language were studied by advanced students. Scribes did not limit their study to wisdom literature, as they also wrote, transmitted, and taught a variety of poems, disputations, myths, epics, hymns, laments, and prayers. In the sapiential writings, the instructors introduced their students to the complexities of life, the theological understanding of the world, the doctrine of the fate of the individual in the hands of the gods, and the critical issues of theodicy, ambiguity, and divine justice.

In Mesopotamia scribes also were ordinary copyists and clerks as well as intellectuals greatly honored.[151] They consisted of administrators, composers of texts, and scholars.[152] As possessors of knowledge, they were known as "the wise" (Sum. *ABGAL* or *UM.ME.A*; Akk. *apkallu, igigallu, ummānu,* and *nēmequ*).[153] The students who were from the upper echelons of Sumerian and later Assyro-Babylonian societies entered the schools to train for a profession in the upper ranks of government, temple, and military life. Others, not so highly placed, studied to serve as low-placed scribes in the bureaucracies of the state and its temples. A few of the elite became noted sages, like Šaggil-kinam-ubbib ("Saggil-kinam-ubbib, an incantation priest, worshiper of God and king"), who is considered the author of an acrostic text that approaches the issue of theodicy ("The Babylonian Theodicy").[154] Some were teachers, called the *ummānu*.[155]

Ugarit and Aram

The libraries and archives of Ugarit suggest the presence of significant numbers of scribes who performed the varied tasks of composition, copying, and

---

150. Bendt Alster, "Proverbs from Ancient Mesopotamia: Their History and Social Implications," *Proverbium. Yearbook of International Proverb Scholarship* (University of Vermont) 10 (1993) 1-19.

151. A. Leo Oppenheim, "The Position of the Intellectual in Mesopotamian Society," *Daedalus* 104 (1975) 37-46. For an examination of women sages, see Rivkah Harris, "The Female 'Sage' in Mesopotamian Literature," in *Sage in Israel,* 3-17.

152. Oppenheim, "Position of the Intellectual."

153. Hartmut Waetzoldt, "Der Schreiber als Lehrer in Mesopotamien," in *Schreiber, Magister, Lehrer,* ed. J. G. Prinz von Hohenzollern and Max Liedtke (Bad Heilbrunn: Kinkhardt, 1989) 33-50. Also see Yvonne Rosengarten, "Le nom et la function de 'sage' dans les practiques religieuses de Sumer et d'Akkad," *RHR* 162 (1962) 133-46.

154. John F. Brug, "Biblical Acrostics and Their Religionship to Other Ancient Near Eastern Acrostics," in *The Bible in the Light of Cuneiform Literature,* ed. William W. Hallo, et al. (Scripture in Context 3; Ancient Near Eastern Texts and Studies 8; Lewiston, NY: Mellen, 1990) 293.

155. See Waetzoldt, "Schreiber als Lehrer."

recording of different types of records and literature.[156] Since most of the wisdom texts were written in Akkadian and in bilingual texts that included Hurrian and Sumerian or Akkadian, Hallo indicates that the schools of Ugarit incorporated a multilingual curriculum.[157] Mack-Fisher also recognizes that sages and scribes were quite similar to those in ancient Mesopotamia.[158] Prediluvian sages included Adapa and Šuruppak in Sumer-Akkad, and Šube'awilum in Ugarit, while the sages who experienced the flood and represented the transition from the primordial *apkallu* to the postdiluvian *apkallu* were Ziusdra, Atra-ḫasīs, and Utnapishtim in the Sumero-Akkadian tradition and Zurranku at Ugarit. Postflood sages were Gilgamesh in Mesopotamia and Dan'el in Ugarit. In an essay Mack-Fisher also lists many of the Ugaritic scribes in a chart.[159] He contends that while there were hundreds of scribes at Ugarit, only a very few were revered as great sages. If any historical scribe was honored as a sage, then, according to Mack-Fisher, the best candidate would be Na'amrašap. He was a scribe and counselor during the reigns of three kings whose name appears in the colophon of the flood tradition in text 167 (*Ugaritica* V).[160]

The Elephantine library contains the Aramaic version of Ahiqar in which this scribe is called a *sāpar ḥakkîm māhîr* who gave "advice/counsel" (*'ātâ*).[161] The legend presents him as a chief counselor to Esarhaddon, thus positioning this sage in the royal court. Most of the sayings are directed to rural freedmen of a conservative middle class in southern Syria in the eighth century B.C.E., indicating that the family was the social matrix for these proverbs. However, the topic of service to the king in other sayings indicates that the editors or collectors of these sayings shaped them to fit the context of a royal court.[162]

---

156. See esp. the essays by Jean Nougayrol, *PRU* 3 (1955) xxxvi-xl; 4 (1956); 6 (1970); idem, "Textes suméro-accadiens des archives et bibliothèques privées d'Ugarit," *Ugaritica* V, ch. 1; Anson Rainey, "The Scribe at Ugarit: His Position and Influence," *Proceedings of the Israel Academy of Sciences and Humanities* 3 (1969) 126-46.

157. *COS* 1:486.

158. Manfred Dietrich and Oswald Loretz, "Die Weisheit des ugaritischen Gottes El im Kontext der altorientalischen Weisheit," *UF* 24 (1993) 31-38.

159. Mack-Fisher, "Scribe (and Sage)," 111-12.

160. Jean Nougayrol, et al., *Ugaritica V: nouveaux textes accadiens, hourrites et ugaritiques des archives et bibliothèques privées d'Ugarit. Commentaires des textes historiques (première partie)* (Paris: Imprimerie nationale; Librairie orientaliste Paul Guethner, 1968).

161. See esp. Kottsieper, *Sprache der Ahiqarsprüche*. Also see the earlier study of Goshen-Gottstein, *Wisdom of Ahiqar*.

162. Kottsieper, "The Aramaic Tradition: Ahikar," in *Scribes, Sages, and Seers*, forthcoming.

Greco-Roman Culture

The extensive number of texts, ranging from literary, to administrative, to inscriptional writings, that were composed during the Hellenistic and early Roman periods of the Republic and Empire required a very large number of scribes who knew the arts of language and culture. Of course, there were well-known philosophers, rhetors, poets, sophists, and historians who composed a vast number of writings.

Among the philosophies of the Hellenistic period, those that significantly influenced Hellenistic Judaism were the schools of Stoicism, Middle Platonism, and Skepticism, originally centered in Athens, although many of its significant representatives and teachers came from the larger Hellenic and Hellenistic world: Zeno from Citium of Cyprus; and from Asia Minor, Cleanthes of Assos and Chrysippus of Soli. Stoicism, which appeared in the late fourth century B.C.E., was more of a tradition than a physical school comparable to those of the Academy and the Lyceum. The later Stoics, including Seneca, Epictetus, Cicero, and Marcus Aurelius, were, of course, Romans. Due to its prominence in the Hellenistic and early Roman worlds, Stoicism exerted the greatest influence on Judaism during these periods.

While variety characterized this philosophical tradition, the most prominent tenet included the concept of a world soul or rational capacity that permeated the cosmos and the human soul. Humans participated in this world of indwelling reason as evidenced by their rational capacity. Thus epistemologically speaking, rationalism dominated Stoicism's understanding of the proper act of knowing. Stoic logic, essentially propositional, may be divided into two major features: the theory of arguments and assertions.[163] In general an "assertible" is a proposition that is true or false in and of itself at a particular moment and in a distinct place. Arguments consist of premises leading to a conclusion. Thus something is true or valid if it is built on certain verifiable premises and results in a correct conclusion.

Nature is a key theme, and it includes both the cosmos and humanity that are entwined. A cosmic soul (Logos or reason) that permeates the world also is found in human nature. Human nature is entwined with the composition of nature and thus is part of the whole. Humans therefore share in the pervasive Logos that unites the various components of reality. For the Stoics, virtue and the desire for its actualization in living are centered in human nature. Simply stated, ethical behavior is rational. While the constitution of the self is commit-

---

163. See Suzanne Bobzien and Mario Mignucci, "Logic III: The Stoics," in *Cambridge History of Hellenistic Philosophy,* 92-176.

ted from birth to self-preservation and self-love, this constitution develops through life, especially in education, to evolve into a commitment to virtue that extends beyond the self (prudence and self-control) to include altruism, in particular the distribution of justice.[164] This adult constitution of self does not replace the one that exists since infancy, but rather is a more developed one. The commitment to self and to others is regarded by the Stoics as natural and based on the same understanding of human nature. What is "good" is understood as virtue and completion. What unites virtue and completion in a rational being is consistency. This extends to self-love and to altruism; both are consistent with the constitution of human nature that essentially is rational. Reason is to be the dominant force in human nature and behavior and should be actualized by moral human beings to control the passions and to follow consistently the ordered world presupposed by virtue. The goal *(telos)* of life is understood as that for which everything is done. Yet for the Stoics this goal is completion, the perfect culmination *(teleios)* of life in regard to virtue, and the avoidance of conflict with the rational principle that is inveterate in human nature. Thus the goal of life is to live in harmony with nature, both in the cosmos and the human self, for together they form an inextricable unity. The virtuous action in life is therefore appropriate when it conforms to the natural order. The life of virtue will be one of contentment, because it is orderly, harmonious, and joyful. It dispels conflict with reason, which permeates everything. From this single feature, all other virtues derive: wisdom, pleasure, harmony, prudence, and so on. What is considered to be "good" benefits the agent. Since humans are part of a larger reality that is imbued with and activated by reason, then the good is that which is perfect or complete for the rational being, and thus the quest for the good profits not only the self but also the whole.

Yet nature also includes the cosmos. There is in the fabric of the cosmos a world soul or Logos that guides providentially both existence and the ongoing animation and direction of nature. This means nature or God is involved in the world. Reason is at the heart of nature, because it would not be logical to create a world with its creatures and then to abandon them to struggle on their own. The unity of the world is central to understanding the Stoic conception of cosmic nature, unity being a fundamental affirmation in their philosophical presentation. By the observation of cosmic nature, humans may learn a great deal about virtue and responsible ethical behavior. Since the world is considered to be rational, orderly, consistent, and well structured, so is human nature. Thus through the will the moral person lives by means of reason, order, consistency, and structure. Moral improvement comes through the exercise of reason in hu-

---

164. Brad Inwood, "Stoic Ethics," *Cambridge History of Hellenistic Philosophy,* 680.

man behavior to make the proper choices.[165] Formation through study produces the correct opinions that are reached through reason, embodied in human character, and actualized in choices. This person becomes the sage who is the embodiment of wisdom, for he/she knows the proper virtues and the correct opinions and lives accordingly.

The important Middle Platonists were Plutarch of Chaeronea (c. 46-120 C.E.) and two other second-century thinkers, Albinus and Apuleius. An earlier form provided the philosophical system at the basis of Philo's thought and was presented in a less erudite fashion by the composer of the Wisdom of Solomon. This philosophy became prominent beginning in the first century C.E., allowing the impress of other philosophies, especially Stoicism and Neopythagoreanism, to be incorporated into traditional Platonism. Leading ideas included the prototypical forms of what exists, the hierarchy of divine principles, the supreme principle or the "One," the separation of the soul or mind from the body, the ascent of the human mind to union with the divine *nous,* and the concern with the problem of evil.

By the mid-fifth century B.C.E., higher education was taken over by the Sophists, itinerant teachers traveling throughout the Greek world, lecturing on a range of topics, and introducing their students to numerous philosophies.[166] In Athens the Sophists were in charge of all education. Kerferd notes that there were three changes as a result of this development. First, there were teachers in the circles of higher education that included the schools of the Academy, the Lyceum, and the rhetoricians. Second, the sage became identified with a particular school of philosophy that was especially concerned with epistemology or the philosopher's knowledge of truth, that is, what he knows, and how this knowledge is known. Third, the virtuous man becomes the model or ideal for humans to emulate.[167] The sage was especially the one who acquired knowledge of grammar, rhetoric, semantics, literary criticism, philosophies, mathematics, anthropology, cosmology, nature, and geography.

Rhetoric was the art of persuasion (Plato, *Gorg.* 453a2), learned and used by lawyers, public orators, and teachers to present their arguments in cogent and compelling ways in order to convince their audience of the veracity and convincing nature of their positions.[168] Rhetoric *(rhētorikē)* is also the "art of dis-

---

165. Ibid., 690.

166. See *OCD,* 1422; G. B. Kerferd, *The Sophistic Movement* (Cambridge: Cambridge University Press, 1981).

167. Kerferd, "The Sage in Hellenistic Philosophical Literature," in *Sage in Israel,* 319-28; A. A. Long and D. N. Sedley, *The Hellenistic Philosophers* (2 vols.; New York: Cambridge University Press, 1987).

168. Kennedy, "Historical Survey of Rhetoric," 3-43. Kennedy notes that rhetors were "workers of persuasion" (see Plato, *Gorg.* 453a2).

course" *(technē)*, although it was extended to include composition. The more educated student spent five to six years in rhetorical schools in order to cultivate the finer skills of language, although very few had the time and resources required for this achievement. The schools of rhetoric and more general ones that taught this art regarded declamation and its composition as the quintessential task of education and its crowning achievement. The student began with the *progymnasmata,* the preliminary rhetorical exercises that taught students the basic techniques of writing and how to select themes to develop.[169] Exercises of impersonation (*ēthopoiia,* "imitation, mimesis") and praise *(enkōmion)* were also common.[170] The first type of exercise involved declamations that allowed students to play the roles of mythological, heroic, or literary figures (see the fifth- and early-fourth-century B.C.E. orator Lysias, particularly orations 1, 7, 9, and 21). These impersonations gave students the opportunity to develop the figure's arguments within the context of a speech. The student usually selected the pattern appropriate for the occasion, ranging from exhortation to the request for forgiveness, although the same type of speech in the writing was often simply imitation. The second is a prose or poetic panegyric that praises a significant person, thing, or idea.[171] This was occasionally combined with the historical recounting of the past through the praise of ancestors, gods, and cities (encomium).

Rhetoric was one of the key features of education in Greece and Rome, in both formal gymnasia, schools of rhetoric, and the lecturing and tutoring of Sophists. The teachers of rhetoric were normally Sophists, philosophers, and instructors in schools. The art of rhetoric was a much desired skill in many arenas of life, especially among the wealthy (see the treatise on public speaking by Dio Chrysostom, *Dic exercit. = Or.* 18). The Sophists especially placed rhetoric at the center of paideia. Indeed, it was viewed as the culmination of the *enkyklios paideia.*[172] Rhetoric became a necessary skill of teachers and philosophers in their arguments about a variety of issues in trying to persuade those who heard them of the truthfulness of their position. Rhetorical understanding is given formal analysis by Aristotle *(Rhetorica),* who speaks not only of skills of public speaking and persuasion but also of the power of language to convince

169. Cribiore, *Gymnastics of the Mind,* 222.

170. Ibid., 228.

171. Aristotle, *Rhet.* 2.20, 1393a23-1394a18. See Thomas R. Lee, *Studies in the Form of Sirach 44–50* (SBLDS 75; Atlanta: Scholars Press, 1986), esp. 91-95; Burton Mack, *Wisdom and the Hebrew Epic: Ben Sira's Praise of the Fathers* (Chicago Studies in the History of Judaism; Chicago: University of Chicago Press, 1985), esp. 128-37. Cf. Wis. 10:1-11:1.

172. Teresa Morgan, *Literate Education in the Hellenistic and Roman Worlds* (Cambridge Classical Studies; Cambridge: Cambridge University Press, 1998) 190-239.

and convict. In his view, however, rhetoric was neither a body nor an element of knowledge. Rather it encompassed several types of argument. He identified these types of rhetoric: the forensic (legal), the deliberative, the epideictic, and the persuasive. Rhetoric included the characteristics of what was ethical and true, what appealed to move the emotions or passions, and what was the logical development of the argument. Rhetoric developed from being limited to public speaking to include written composition that made use of its major features in persuasive literature: veracity, argumentation, skilled and artistic language, and the appeal to logic and the emotions, all of which were guided by reason.[173] Rhetors were required to learn a body of truths *(logoi)* and commit them to memory in order to draw on them in the construction of argumentation.[174] The complaints of Plato and Aristotle about rhetors are that they present a finished product for imitation and are not capable of describing the craft and the steps necessary to produce a compelling speech or text. Aristotle's simile is that the rhetor is like the cobbler who gives his students a pair of shoes to imitate in making rather than providing instructions on how to craft the material into a finished product.

Rhetorical schools were established in the eastern Mediterranean world likely in congruence with hellenization, although the curriculum varied from one school to another. However, the common elements appear as follows. Upon the conclusion of formal education in Greek grammar (from around the age of seven until twelve to fourteen), a student who moved into the second level then entered into a rhetorical school to study theory, lectures, and the declamation of his/her teacher.[175] The practice of various types of declamation and their composition continued for the most advanced students seeking to master language.

It is important to recall that the "audience" of educated hearers was surpassed by literate readers, perhaps as early as 300 B.C.E., so that rhetoric was no longer limited to public speaking. Rather it was embodied in texts, including especially the classics, which were read and appreciated for their literary elegance and persuasive qualities by educated people who had access to them.[176] The classics of Greek literature, along with lesser known works, were copied, sold, and borrowed by teachers and students who could access them. In addition, students and teachers in prominent cities had the opportunity to read the manuscripts archived in libraries. This was certainly true in the Museion of Al-

---

173. Plato (esp. *Phaedrus*) considered rhetors to be superficial.

174. Hock and O'Neil, *Chreia in Ancient Rhetoric;* idem, *Chreia and Ancient Rhetoric: Classroom Exercises.*

175. Kennedy, "Historical Survey of Rhetoric," 18-19.

176. Thomas Cole, *The Origins of Rhetoric in Ancient Greece* (Ancient Society and History; Baltimore: Johns Hopkins University Press, 1991).

exandria, where scholars from all over the eastern Mediterranean world gathered to study and teach. This does not suggest the demise of oratory or that the written text replaced the spoken word. Indeed, texts that were composed often incorporated the speech or speeches of the rhetors. Thus while there was the movement from the artistic craft *(technē)* of speaking to the literary reading of educated people, oratory remained a prominent skill. The *technē* was not a list of rules for composing or speaking artfully in persuasive ways, but rather an exemplary text that comprised the features of skilled writing/speaking, rhetorical and elegant turns of phrases and arguments, and cogent argumentation. Speeches and texts are presented to be imitated by students learning to speak or to write texts of artful persuasion that, as Aristotle would say (*Rhet.* 1.1), serve as verbal embodiments of the rhetor's argument.[177] The Wisdom of Solomon was not intended for the common masses of uneducated Jews who lacked the resources and thus the time to study and learn.

The Social Institutions of Scribes and Sages

The Court

The major social location for the activity of scribes and sages of Israel and Judah in the First Temple period was the royal administration, which was hierarchical in nature. The people who served in the bureaucracy were the aristocratic elite, consisting of kings, officers, sages, and counselors, and the scribes who carried out a myriad of tasks in running the kingdom. The sapiential texts did not engage in a critical judgment against kings and misrule, but rather affirmed the monarchy as responsible for establishing justice in society and continuing it through the activities of royal rule, military engagement, and judgment. The counselors are reminiscent of those met in the Succession Narrative and the cabinets of David and Solomon, although these materials are likely composed after the so-called united monarchy. Royal officials or "secretaries" *(sōpěrîm)* to kings included Seraiah in 2 Sam. 8:17 and in another listing, Sheva, in the cabinet of David (2 Sam. 20:25). Solomon's list of officials has two secretaries, Elihoreph and Ahijah, indicating a larger bureaucracy (1 Kgs. 4:1-6). However, the number returns to a single secretary in later lists. Shebnah is the secretary in the cabinet of Hezekiah (2 Kgs. 18:18-19; Isa. 36:3; cf. 22:15), while Shaphan was the secretary of Josiah (2 Kgs. 22:8-10). The secretary operated the vast administration of the kingdom. In addition to the *sōpēr*, there is the "re-

177. Ibid., 27.

corder" *(mazkîr)*. These included Jehoshaphat in David's cabinet (2 Sam. 8:16), Ahilud in Solomon's (1 Kgs. 4:3), and Joah in Hezekiah's (2 Kgs. 18:18, 37). The responsibility of the recorder was likely to write and archive official documents to and from the king, which were sealed with the monarch's stamp. Other cabinet officials included "the one over the household" (*'ăšer 'al-habbayyit,* the overseer of the palace administration, Gen. 43:19; 44:1, 4; 1 Kgs. 4:6; 16:9; 18:3; 2 Kgs. 10:5; 15:5; Isa. 22:15; 36:3) and the king's "friend," who was the chief servant to the monarch to carry out his bidding with legal authority (*rē'eh,* 2 Sam. 15:37; 16:16; 1 Kgs. 4:5). Even if these are anachronistic, they still reflect the fact that the royal courts eventually established cabinets that included scribes who advanced in the two administrations of kingdom and palace.

The royal courts and administrative bureaucracies of Egypt were similar. Some of the sapiential texts are attributed to royal viziers or prime ministers and to the kings themselves. Kagemni of the Fourth Dynasty is instructed by his father in the duties and virtues of serving the king as a wise vizier. Ptahhotep, a vizier of the Fifth Dynasty, teaches his son and successor ways to become a loyal servant to the king. "In Praise of Learned Scribes" lists a number of famous sages who continued to be remembered: Hordjedef, Imhotep, Neferti, Kheti, Ptahem-Djedhuti, Kakkheper-(Re)-seneb, Ptahhotep, and Kairis. In this New Kingdom text, these honored and high-placed sages who served as viziers, even though their tombs crumbled and turned to dust, will continue to survive through the memory of later generations. Another important text for understanding the social roles of the sages is the Papyrus Lansing, a Twelfth Dynasty instruction composed by Nebmare-nakht, a royal scribe and chief overseer of the cattle of Amon-Re, king of the gods. His apprentice, the scribe Wenemdiamun, who is the recipient of the teaching, responds that he will provide gifts of great value to his teacher. This sage's bipartite role demonstrates the king was the titular head of the kingdom and the court's major temple dedicated to the head of the pantheon. Kings themselves were sages whose wisdom allowed them to rule the kingdom according to the dictates of order. Two royal instructions, "The Instruction for Merikare" (First Intermediate Period) and "The Instruction of Amenemhet" (the first ruler of the Twelfth Dynasty), are designed to instruct the kings in the traditions of justice with a view to actualize the order of creation and to preserve both their reigns and their kingdoms. In "The Satire on the Trades," probably written by an unknown scribal official during the Middle Kingdom, Kheti, son of Duaf, takes his son Pepi to the Residence City to study in its royal school in order to become a scribe. He teaches him about the duties of the office and indicates that his rewards will be wealth and honor.

The royal court and its extensive administration that connected to the major centers of conquered nations were the major settings for the cultivation of the arts of wisdom in Mesopotamia.[178] Some of this is due to the requirement that the ruler be exceedingly adept in ruling a kingdom and engaging in such activities as the promulgation of laws and the construction and renovations of cities and temples. Sages who served in the palace of the ruler developed an ideology of kingship that gave this institution the highest human authority in the city-state, second only to the city's deity. Like the Akkadians who were to follow, the Sumerians believed that kingship was handed down from heaven, both before and after the cosmic upheaval of the flood, in order to govern humans. The king's *me* (norms, regulations) included the laws of royal authority, the role of intermediary between the gods and humans, and his regalia and insignia.[179] Wisdom in the court is also important in the administrative duties of officials who carry out the manifold tasks of royal rule, both domestic and foreign. Thus professionals said to require wisdom included scribes to write correspondence, to keep records, and to maintain financial accounts; architects, builders, and craftsmen for construction projects; managers to oversee the smooth operation of city life and the larger kingdom; diplomats; technocrats; and scientists. The king was wise due to his own education and divine endowment. This personal wisdom was enhanced by the skills and knowledge of those who served him, not simply in the palace but also in the larger court and the royal bureaucracy. Crown princes, and possibly others, also learned their wisdom in the settings of the court, thus pointing to the existence of royal schools for educating the children of the king, especially the crown prince, and of the aristocracy.

Palace scribes (see Sum. *dur-sar-é-gal*) were at the center of power and largely managed the kingdom under the direction of the ruler and his vizier (*sukkalmaḫ*). The ruler's scribe (*dub-sar-lugal*) was likely his chief secretary who gave counsel and carried his seal, the indication of legitimacy and authority, while many other scribes were responsible for royal inscriptions, accounting for donations to the temple, and the composition of texts that included king lists and eventually even chronicles. Palace scribes would have composed the hymns in praise of a ruler, legal texts, and possibly the wisdom texts, epic legends, and myths.[180] The diviner (*bārû*) in Akkadian courts who communicated with the gods also served under the ruler. Sweet refers especially to Neo-Assyrian letters as the best attestation to the existence of sages in the courts of Mesopotamia.[181]

---

178. Sweet, "Sage in Mesopotamian Palaces," 99-107.

179. Kramer, "Sage in Sumerian Literature," 40-44.

180. Sweet, "Sage in Mesopotamian Palaces," 103-4.

181. Sweet, "Sage in Mesopotamian Palaces," 105-7. See also Simo Parpola, *Letters from Assyrian Scholars to the Kings Esarhaddon and Assurbanipal* (2 vols.; AOAT 5; Neukirchen-Vluyn: Neukirchener Verlag, 1970-1983).

According to Kramer, the portrait of the ideal king in Sumerian royal hymns speaks of him as the offspring of the gods and the recipient of blessings, especially from Enlil.[182] The ruler brought blessing and well-being to his people, and he was a graduate of the *edubba,* making him literate, wise, and knowledgeable in the scribal crafts. He was the perfect man who was courageous, wise, pious, just, and powerful. Šulgi was especially the one who spoke of his education and knowledge of the scribal arts, was a diviner, and served as a wise counselor. Through his sacred marriage to Inanna, he made the land, animals, and population fertile. He may have ascended into the heavens as a god at death (see Dumuzi in the myth of "Inanna's Descent into the Underworld," who is given immortality for half the annual year).[183]

Several kings claimed not only to be wise but also to be master scribes, including Šulgi, Lipit-Ishtar, and in particular Ashurbanipal.[184] The ruler was the ideal sage.[185] The personal name Šarru-mūda ("the king is wise") is attested in the early Sargonic period (twenty-fourth century B.C.E.). This wisdom was a divine endowment. For example, five centuries later, Kudurmabug of Zamutbal, father of Rim-Sin of Larsa, proclaims that the god had given him "wise understanding" *(uzun igigallim)* to build a temple of baked brick.[186] Hammurabi (1792-1750 B.C.E.) also attests to his reception of divinely given wisdom in the prologue to his law code. He is "a wise man *(emqum)* who gets things done, one who has attained all wisdom *(uršum).*" Similar claims to royal wisdom are present in the period of the Sargonid dynasty, especially those made by Sargon II. Also Merodach-baladan II (721-703 B.C.E.) claimed not only the throne of Babylon but also the aura of being a wise ruler. Sennacherib (704-681 B.C.E.) also prided himself with being a wise king and a recipient of divine wisdom, especially in regard to his building projects. Esarhaddon (680-669 B.C.E.) spoke of his wisdom when building temples and fashioning cultic projects. The ruler who especially extolled his own wisdom was Ashurbanipal (668-627 B.C.E.). He stated that while he was still living in the crown prince's quarters, he learned the divine wisdom *(nemequ)* of Nabû. He told of later receiving understanding

---

182. Kramer, "Sage in Sumerian Literature," 40-44.

183. See *ANET,* 52-57.

184. Denning-Bolle, *Wisdom in Akkadian Literature;* Benno Landsberger, "Babylonian Scribal Craft and Its Terminology," *Abstract in the Proceedings of the 23rd Congress of Orientalists* (Cambridge: Cambridge University Press, 1954) 123-26; idem, "Scribal Concepts of Education," in *City Invincible: A Symposion on Urbanization and Cultural Development in the Ancient Near East Held at the Oriental Institute of the University of Chicago, December 4-7, 1958,* ed. Carl H. Kraeling and Robert M. Adams (Chicago: University of Chicago Press, 1960) 94-123.

185. Sweet, "Sage in Akkadian Literature," 65.

186. Quoted by Sweet, ibid., 51.

(uznu) and intelligence *(ḫasīsu)* from Marduk and the scribal craft of Nabû. He spoke of having learned the art of the sage, *apkallu,* that of Adapa, and, being the possessor of all scribal learning, he could, among other things, read inscriptions from the time prior to the flood.[187] Neo-Babylonian kings also spoke of their divine wisdom and said they were wise and learned (see Nabopolasar, Nebuchadnezzar II, and Nabonidus).[188] The wisdom of kings was based on their devotion to the gods, which was the beginning of wisdom. These deeds of religious devotion included the construction of temples and their equipping for cultic service.

The School in Ancient Israel

One of the primary social locations of wisdom was the schools,[189] although these assumed a variety of forms.[190] Intimations of royal schools are present in 1 Kgs. 12:8, 10; 2 Kgs. 10:1, 5-6; 2 Chron. 17:7-9; temple schools (or at least priestly teachers) in 2 Kings 12:3[2] and Jer. 18:18; and even prophetic "schools" in 2 Kgs. 6:1-2; Isa. 8:16; 28:9; and 50:4-9. Proverbs 5:13 (at least teachers and instructors are named), 15:31 ("lodging among the wise"), and 17:16 (tuition) suggest the existence of scribal schools, as do the paraenetic invitations teachers extended to the unlearned to come and learn from them (e.g., 1:20-33; 8:1-11). In addition, the existence of schools and the growth of the scribal profession are indicated by the significant increase in epigraphic material, beginning in the eighth century B.C.E.[191]

Schools would have been located in the home of the teacher, the gate or marketplace, or perhaps even in a separate building; they consisted of private tutors and larger staffs, and possessed a variety of curricula that depended on

187. See ibid., 55.

188. Ibid., 56-57.

189. See esp. James L. Crenshaw, *Education in Ancient Israel* (ABRL; New York: Doubleday, 1998); David M. Carr, *Writing on the Tablet of the Heart: Origins of Scripture and Literature* (New York: Oxford University Press, 2004).

190. The existence of schools in ancient Israel is supported only by a little documental evidence and few remains from material culture.

191. See H. J. Hermisson, *Studien zur israelitischen Spruchweisheit* (WMANT 28; Neukirchen-Vluyn: Neukirchener Verlag, 1968) 97-136; Lemaire, *Écoles;* Bernhard Lang, "Schule und Unterricht im alten Israel," in *La Sagesse de l'Ancien Testament,* ed. Maurice Gilbert (rev. ed.; BETL 51; Leuven: Peeters, 1990) 186-201. Pottery sherds of schoolboy exercises have been identified in several locations (Gezer, Lachish, Arad, Kadesh-barnea, and Kuntillet Ajrud) that begin to appear in the twelfth century. For a criticism of the hypothesis of Israelite schools, see Friedemann Golka, *The Leopard's Spots: Biblical and African Wisdom in Proverbs* (Edinburgh: T&T Clark, 1994).

the nature of the education given (administrative, legal, and scribal). While textual evidence indicates the subjects taught were largely compositions of moral instruction, material culture points to a variety of written and epigraphic sources, ranging from cuneiform tablets, to papyri, to scarabs, to bullae, to stamped jar handles, to mortuary inscriptions. One may imagine that among the subjects taught in various types of schools were mathematics, architecture, engineering, reading and writing, literary forms, the written classics of myths, legends, and poetry, music, ancient Near Eastern languages, and later Greek.[192]

As noted above, there are numerous references to fathers (occasionally mothers) instructing their sons. This could refer to a sage who undertakes to teach either his/her child or his/her student who would enter the ranks of the scribes, master the scribal arts, learn the sapiential tradition, and instill a professional code of ethics in order to be prepared for scribal careers (Job 8:8; 15:18). Familial terms are commonly used to refer to teachers, tutors, and students in the wisdom literatures of the ancient Near East. Of course, there were wise women who may have taught in the schools. At least there are two politically important women sages who are mentioned in the Succession Narrative ("the wise woman of Tekoa," 2 Sam. 14:1-24; and the "wise woman of Abel of Beth-maacah," 2 Sam. 20:16-22).

Some teachers may have been hired to tutor the children of elite families in their own residences. This was the case in Greek education, and could have been a possible location for instruction in Israel and Judah. Another setting for a school in Judah is a boarding school (Prov. 15:31) or lodging in the home of the sage (Sir. 51:23-28). The text in Ben Sira is capable of both understandings. This lodging would be necessary for students who lived at some distance from the residence of their teachers. Cities had marketplaces and gates where instruction would have been offered, both by teachers educating their students and by sages issuing invitations to come and study under their guidance. In Prov. 8:2 the reference to the "house of paths" *(bêt nĕtîbôt)* may be a metaphor for a school to describe the place where instruction is offered that leads the students in the paths of life, since later in the chapter the teacher, in this case Wisdom, stands at her house's gates and beside her doors to invite the unlearned to hear her instruction (8:33-34). Royal schools and teachers are implied in 1 Kgs.

192. For a more recent assessment, see Crenshaw, *Education in Ancient Israel*, 85-113. In his view the epigraphic evidence is sufficient to support the existence of schools at least as early as the eighth century B.C.E. He concludes that guilds and schools educated scribes prior to the collapse of the monarchy. Also see Gunther Wanke, "Der Lehrer im alten Israel," in *Schreiber, Magister, Lehrer,* 51-59; G. I. Davies, "Were There Schools in Ancient Israel?" in *Wisdom in Ancient Israel*, ed. John Day, et al. (Cambridge: Cambridge University Press, 1995) 199-211; E. W. Heaton, *The School Tradition of the Old Testament* (Oxford: Oxford University Press, 1994).

12:8, 10; 2 Kgs. 10:1, 5-6; and 2 Chron. 17:7-9. The first passage, 1 Kgs. 12:8, 10, points to the common instruction received by Rehoboam and his fellow students; the second makes reference to the guardians of Ahab's seventy sons charged with their upbringing, which may have included instruction; and the third refers to priests, and presumably the Levites, commissioned by King Jehoshaphat to teach the people the Torah in their traveling to the towns and villages of the country.

The temple in Jerusalem and perhaps other sanctuaries had schools in which scribes were educated to carry out their activities in managing the sacred places and gifts offered by worshipers. This in part may be inferred from cultic and scribal literature of Jerusalem, which legitimated the state and the monarchy and even pointed to the mythical view of Jerusalem as the center of the cosmos from which God as creator providentially ruled history, revitalized creation, and gave direction to the elements of nature (see Pss. 46 and 48). The economic importance of the temple also became significant, since its revenues and facilities for housing national and private wealth were important to the monarchy.[193] Due to their service in the cultic administrations, the sages even made use of the temple as a metaphor in describing the origins and rule of goddess Wisdom in her contest with the fertility goddess, likely Asherah, who is identified with personified Folly (see Prov. 9).

The term *liškâ* refers to an ancillary building or a part of a building, including a room, chamber, and hall, most often found in Ezekiel (23 times) and Jeremiah (8 times). The term in Jer. 36:10, 12, 20-21 is used to refer to the office or building of Gemariah, the son of the scribe Shaphan (v. 10), located in the upper court of the new gate, and to the room or building of the scribe Elishama (who was of royal descent, 2 Kgs. 25:25), adjacent to the royal palace. Shaphan was the secretary during the reign of Josiah (2 Kgs. 22:3, 8), whom the Deuteronomistic History presents as involved in informing the king of the discovery of the law book during the renovation of the temple. This law book, an earlier form of Deuteronomy, was likely produced by temple scribes, possibly in the building called the *liškâ*. This would be the likely reason why Baruch read the first scroll of Jeremiah's prophecies there (Jer. 36). Among the officials of the temple, Gemariah was the one who instructed his son to go to the royal court and read the scroll of Baruch to the king. The specific functions of these two buildings/rooms mentioned in ch. 36 is not clear, but the differentiation be-

---

193. The economic function of the temple should receive more significant attention in research (Marty E. Stevens, *Temples, Tithes, and Taxes* [Peabody, MA: Hendrickson, 2006]). For the example of the temple of Artemis functioning also as a bank, see Paul Trebilco, *The Early Christians in Ephesus from Paul to Ignatius* (WUNT 166; Tübingen: Mohr Siebeck, 2004) 25-30.

tween the two intimates that there were two groups of scribes (priestly and royal) located in two similar buildings in the temple complex, adjacent to the palace. Thus even following the destruction of the monarchy and Jerusalem, the rebuilt temple would likely have had similar buildings/rooms for the major scribal administrators serving both the governor and the priesthood.

While Jerusalem was the location of the central temple of the united monarchy and then Judah, other important temples were located in the northern kingdom, particularly the ancient sanctuaries of Dan and Bethel that were the important shrines of the northern kingdom following the division of Israel into two kingdoms in the latter part of the tenth century B.C.E. There were also regional holy sites that were located elsewhere during the Iron Age: Megiddo, Lachish, Taanakh, Beth-Shean, Tel Qasile, Tel Amal, Arad, Beersheba, Tel Qedesh, Tell es-Sa-'ideyeh, and Kuntillet Ajrud. These sanctuaries would have been served by priests and perhaps even cult prophets and scribes. The scribes of temples would have managed, written, and archived commercial and ritual documents and kept records of gifts. The secretary, for example, Shaphan, secretary of King Josiah, was responsible for such things as oversight of the temple renovation in Jerusalem, the payment of laborers from the sanctuary treasury, and reading documents (in this case the Torah discovered in the temple; 2 Kgs. 22). These scribes and priests would have been educated in local schools, whether in a public location, a private household, or a tutorial setting. Kings and their local administrators, consisting of officials and scribes, would have had some regulatory power over these shrines. During the First Temple period, the chief priest who had responsibility for the operation of the temple in Jerusalem was a member of the cabinet as well as the king's secretary.

During the Second Temple period, Levites and priests instructed the people in the meaning of the Torah, a task that, along with translation into Aramaic, occurs in Ezra and Nehemiah. In Prov. 9:1-6 a cultic festival occurs to celebrate the completion of Woman Wisdom's building of her "house" (temple or school). She issues her protreptic through her maidens to invite the simple to come and eat of the banquet she has prepared. Coming to the banquet involves leaving simpleness behind in order to feast on her teaching. A possible interpretation of this metaphorical text is the establishment of the wisdom tradition and its formulation and transmission in a school. There are references to temple instruction by priests (e.g., 2 Kgs. 12:3[2]; Jer. 18:18). In the first instance, the chief priest Jehoiada instructed Jehoash the king, while in the second case the priests are those who offer instruction.

Ben Sira considered himself to be a teacher of wisdom, and as a learned sage he possessed knowledge of the ancestral tradition, particularly the emerging tripartite canon, parables, and proverbs. What he stressed in his teaching was reflection on the commandments, pious behavior, proper speech and etiquette, and the skills of diplomacy (Sir. 38:34–39:10). Yet, based on some of his themes and his use of literary forms, we can surmise that he was familiar with some of the sources of Greek philosophy (esp. Stoicism) and rhetoric that he could adapt to Jewish wisdom and literary sources. Ben Sira invited youths to come, take up residence, and study in his *bêt midrāš*, likely a boarding school housing students that may have been under the direction and authority of the Zadokite priesthood.

Greek paideia infiltrated Hellenistic and Roman Jewish schools of the Diaspora.[194] Paideia involves two related understandings: the process of education that culminates in a young man's eventually taking his place in society, and the character of the educated person.[195] This state of the "cultivated mind" enables a person to become virtuous and civilized. But this quest is lifelong and does not end at the conclusion of education in the gymnasium or even the *ephebeion*. Our knowledge of Hellenistic Jewish schools is more extensive than of earlier periods, even though there are major gaps. From the Hellenistic and Roman period, our best Jewish sources are Philo, Qumran, and Josephus.

Based on his command of Greek and his knowledge of Hellenic culture, it is clear that Philo Judaeus, who belonged to an aristocratic and extremely prominent Jewish family in Egypt, may have studied in a Hellenistic gymnasium in Alexandria, even though gymnasia were under the patronage of pagan gods. This attendance would have meant that he enjoyed Alexandrian citizenship. In addition, his knowledge of Judaism, including the LXX, demonstrates that he was tutored by Hellenistic Jewish teachers (*Spec.* 1.314) and educated in the tradition handed down by the "elders of the nation" (*Mos.* 1.4). He also was acquainted with Palestinian Judaism's haggadah and halakah.[196] In his essay *On the Preliminary Studies,* he describes in detail Greek paideia and refers to the

194. Robert Doran, "The High Cost of a Good Education," in *Hellenism in the Land of Israel,* ed. John J. Collins and Gregory E. Sterling (Christianity and Judaism in Antiquity 13; Notre Dame: University of Notre Dame Press, 2001) 94-115. Also see Martin P. Nilsson, *Die hellenistische Schule* (Munich: Beck, 1955); H. I. Marrou, *A History of Education in Antiquity* (New York: Sheed & Ward, 1956); Daniel Kah and Peter Scholz, *Das hellenistische Gymnasion* (Wissenskultur und gesellschaftlicher Wandel 8; Oldenbourg: Akademie, 2004). Also see Jean Delorme, *Gymnasion. Étude sur les Monuments consacrés à L'Éducation en Grèce (dès origines à l'Empire romain)* (Paris: Boccard, 1960) 253-315; Chrysis Pélékidis, *Histoire de l'Éphebie Attique des Origines à 31 avant Jésus Christ* (Paris: Boccard, 1962); Stephen G. Miller, ed., *Arete: Ancient Writers, Papyri, and Inscriptions on the History and Ideals of Greek Athletics and Games* (3rd ed.; Berkeley: University of California Press, 2004).

195. Alan Mendelson, *Secular Education in Philo of Alexandria* (Cincinnati: Hebrew Union College Press, 1982) 1.

196. See Jacob Neusner, *Early Rabbinic Judaism* (Leiden: Brill, 1975) 100-136.

curriculum that included philosophy, grammar, geometry, and music. Only philosophy was the "lawful wife" (*Congr.* 74-76), while other areas of study served her as "handmaidens." The areas of philosophy studied included ethics, and physics (esp. cosmology), topics commonly pursued in the Hellenistic schools.[197]

Philo spoke of the education ("encyclical training") of students from wealthy families in *Spec.* 2.230, *Prob.* 2.44-46, and *Congr.* 74-76. His *enkyklios paideia* includes both the liberal arts and the sciences.[198] In regard to Jewish religious schools, Philo does speak of "Sabbath schools," where the population was taught a variety of virtues: good sense, temperance, courage, justice, and so on (*Spec.* 2.62). He notes that Sabbath schools are in every city (*Mos.* 2.216). His comparison of synagogues to schools suggests that the two activities were carried out in the same location, a house of prayer to which a house of study was connected. Indeed, the people devoted their Sabbaths to philosophy in order to improve their character and to examine their consciences (*Opif.* 128). He notes in *Spec.* 2.63-64 that the faithful on the Sabbath study both duty to God and duty to others. Thus it may be that the *enkyklia* were studied on weekends, and moral responsibilities were examined particularly on the Sabbaths.

In *Vita* 7–12 Flavius Josephus describes his intellectual development, which included such a high degree of personal wisdom that even sages sought out his counsel. He began at the age of sixteen to study the major Jewish schools of his time, including the Pharisees, Sadducees, and Essenes. This was followed by three years of study as a disciple to Bannus, who was an ascetic residing in the Wilderness of Judea. Josephus borrowed the conventions of the accomplishments and character of famous men. Thus like the Greek and Roman notables prior to him, he also asserted that he was a child prodigy, a person committed to the simplicity of life, a student of a rigorous teacher, and a person committed to philosophy for practical living.

In Egypt scribes were needed to carry out the fundamental activities of administration, law, and related pursuits.[199] These scribes learned to read,

---

197. Kah and Scholz, *Hellenistische Gymnasion.*

198. J. M. G. Barclay, *Jews in the Mediterranean Diaspora from Alexander to Trajan (323 BCE–117 CE)* (Edinburgh: T&T Clark, 1996) 161.

199. In general see Eberhard Otto, "Bildung und Ausbildung in Alten Ägypten," *ZÄS* 8 (1956) 41-48; Hellmut Brunner, *Altägyptische Erziehung* (Wiesbaden: Harrassowitz, 1957). On scribes in particular see Ronald J. Williams, "Scribal Training in Ancient Egypt," *JAOS* 92 (1972) 214-21; idem, "The Sages in Ancient Egypt," *JAOS* 101 (1981) 1-19; Ursula Kaplony-Heckel, "Schüler und Schulwesen in der ägyptischen Spätzeit," in *Studien zur altägyptischen Kultur* 1 (Hamburg: H. Buske, 1974) 227-46. The high status of the scribes is set forth in the "Satire on the Trades" of the Twelfth Dynasty (*ANET,* 432-34) and the *Miscellanies* in the New Kingdom (Lichtheim, *AEL* 2:167-

write, speak correctly, keep records, and maintain archival records. Officials engaged in strategic planning, supervising building structures, and organizing and equipping a military. In educating youth in the scribal arts to enter into varied professions, sages composed wisdom literature in the form of moral instruction and taught this material in the schools. Education was pursued in two related ways: an official tutored his "son" to follow him in his profession, and schools known as "houses of life" were attached to temples. The first process prevailed during the Old Kingdom. The "son" might have been either a biological descendant or a novice in a guild. Daughters do not seem to have received a formal, literary education.[200] In the Middle Kingdom, schools were established for the education of scribes and officials.[201] Students learned how to master languages, write reports, practice accounting, and read literature that enabled them to enhance their literary skills, to become familiar with the major features of culture, and to shape their behavior according to the rules and virtues of propriety. They also learned to emulate the compositions of their teachers that included a variety of wisdom writings, including especially instructions.

The most important Egyptian schools ("the houses of life") were located in the capital cities and associated with the major temples. These schools were staffed with administrators and teachers, some of whom also served as officials of the kingdom and as highly placed priests of the cult.[202] The royal residence close to Memphis was the location for the major school to educate children of

78). See Hermann Te Velde, "Scribes and Literacy in Egypt," in *Scripta Signa Vocis: Studies about Scripts, Scriptures, Scribes, and Languages in the Near East, presented to J. H. Hospers,* ed. H. L. J. Vanstiphout, et al. (Groningen: E. Forsten, 1986) 253-63; Schlott, *Schrift und Schreiber;* Leonhard H. Lesko, "Some Comments on Ancient Egyptian Literacy and Literati," in *Studies in Egyptology Presented to Miriam Lichtheim,* ed. Sarah Israelit-Groll (2nd ed.; 2 vols.; Jerusalem: Magnes, 1990) 2:656-67; and R. B. Parkinson, "Teachings, Discourses and Tales from the Middle Kingdom," in *Middle Kingdom Studies,* ed. Stephen Quirke (New Malden, Surrey: SIA, 1991).

200. Gay Robins, *Women in Ancient Egypt* (London: British Museum, 1993) 111-14; Annette Delpha, "Women in Ancient Egyptian Wisdom Literature," in *Women in Ancient Societies,* ed. Léonie J. Archer, Susan Fischler, and Maria Wyke (London: Macmillan, 1994) 24-52. While women and female images are frequent topics in Egyptian literature, only a very small percentage seem to have received a formal education. Letters attributed to women are found from the New Kingdom, although male scribes could have written them (see Deborah Sweeney, "Women's Correspondence from Deir el-Medinah," in *Sesto Congresso Internazionale di Egittologia,* Atti 2 [Turin: International Association of Egyptologists, 1993] 523-29).

201. Papyrus Anastasi V, 22-23. See Ricardo Augusto Caminos, *Late-Egyptian Miscellanies* (London: Oxford University Press, 1954) 262-63.

202. A. G. McDowell, "Teachers and Students at Deir el-Medina," in *Deir el-Medina in the Third Millennium AD: A Tribute to Jac. J. Janssen,* ed. R. J. Demarée and A. Egberts (Leiden: Nederlands Instituut voor het Nabije Oosten, 2000) 217-33.

the aristocracy and officials for administrating the kingdom.[203] Other schools would have been attached to administrative centers in major cities. This educational system continued through the dynastic period. In their elementary education, students studied not only the classics of culture written in the Old and Middle Kingdoms, but also a collection of various writings called the "Miscellanies." Much of the literature of ancient Egypt survived as schoolchildren's copies. Following the completion of the first level of education, some students then entered into more advanced training that was essentially vocational. For those who were preparing for the priesthood, the place of education was called the "House of Life," which served as a scriptorium for the copying of older texts and the writing of newer ones and was attached to each of the important temples in the kingdom.

The sages of Sumer and Akkad believed that the gods provided them with wisdom, yet at the same time they pursued its cultivation, beginning as students in the "tablet house" (Sum. *edubba* and Akk. *bīt ṭuppi*) in which instruction was provided them.[204] We know something of the administration of the *edubba*, which included the principal; the major *ummia*, who established the curriculum and taught with colleagues; and the "big brother" responsible for mentoring younger students.[205] In the theocracy of Sumer, each city-state had a patron deity and an *edubba* that was a link to both the temple and the political administration. The Akkadians established a dynastic kingdom so that the schools were directly connected to the monarchy and the royal administration.[206] The *edubba* and the later Akkadian *bīt ṭuppi* were a type of university where knowledge of every field was cultivated and taught, including music,

203. Edward Wente, "The Scribes of Ancient Egypt," *CANE* 4:2211-21.

204. The *bīt ṭuppi* was the Old Babylonian term not only for school, but also for archive, thus indicating that writing, copying, and archiving texts were activities performed in the tablet house. From the first millennium, the term comes to refer specifically to the temple school. Berossus, a Babylonian priest and historian, wrote in the first half of the third century B.C.E. He mentions the disciplines that students studied (S. M. Burstein, *The Babyloniaca of Berossus* [Malibu: Undena, 1978]). For schools in Sumer and Akkad, see C. J. Gadd, *Teachers and Students in the Oldest Schools* (London: School of Oriental and African Studies, 1956). Also see D. E. Weisberg, *Guild Structure and Political Allegiance in Early Achaemenid Mesopotamia* (Baltimore: Johns Hopkins University Press, 1967); A. W. Sjöberg, "The Old Babylonian Edubba," in *Sumerological Studies in Honor of Thorkild Jacobsen on His Seventieth Birthday* (AS 20; Chicago: University of Chicago Press, 1975) 159-79; H. L. J. Vanstiphout, "How Did They Learn Sumerian?" *JCS* 31 (1979) 118-26; Miguel Civil, "Sur les 'livres d'écolier' à l'époque paléo-babylonienne," in *Miscellanea Babylonica. Mélanges offerts à Maurice Birot,* ed. J.-M. Durand and J. R. Kupper (Paris: Éditions Recherche sur les Civilisations, 1985) 67-78; Petra Gesche, *Schulunterricht in Babylonien im ersten Jahrtausend v. Chr.* (AOAT 275; Münster: Ugarit-Verlag, 2001).

205. Kramer, "Sage in Sumerian Literature," 32.

206. Van Dijk, *Sagesse suméro-accadienne,* 22.

morality, religion, language, history (annals), lexicography, dialects, poetry, and the composition and telling of narratives.[207]

Some of the priests in Mesopotamia appear to have attended the scribal schools ("tablet houses"). Finishing their time in these schools, they were then introduced to the sacred lore and rituals reserved for cultic personnel. Some also were taught how to obtain esoteric knowledge through extispicy and augury and to exorcise demons. Some of these schools were likely associated with the temple. Kramer has contended that the temple high priest/priestess *(en)* and administrator *(sanga)* were likely educated in the *edubba* or by a tutor or *ummia*.[208] This would help to clarify the close connection between temple and school theology and thought. Akkadian legend refers to Adapa as a priest who knew the mind of the Anunnaki. Indeed, these priests, like other sages of the schools and court, traced their knowledge of esoteric wisdom and rituals to the prediluvian *apkallus*. Administration of the temple, along with the keeping of records and the producing and transmission of liturgical texts and other associated literature, would have been the task of educated scribes.

Hellenization in the East, which was largely effectuated through paideia,[209] led to the establishment of Greek schools for the education of scribes and officials. Schools were of three types: the gymnasium, limited to citizens of the polis; schools of rhetoric; and the tutoring of Sophists. The three stages in Greek education included, first, teaching young boys from the age of seven until ten or eleven the basic skills of reading and writing as well as the composing of letters to syllables to sentences to short poetic passages.[210] Students then entered secondary schools for more advanced language study that comprised learning to compose complicated texts and mastering grammar. Especially important was the study of the classics. The third stage had the purpose of shaping an ideal person advanced in knowledge of different areas, physically fit from participation in sports, and guided by important virtues. Students entered the third stage at fifteen and studied in a school or with a tutor. Included in their studies were exer-

207. See H. L. J. Vanstiphout, "The Dialogue between an Examiner and a Student," *COS* 1:592-93; idem, "Remarks on 'Supervisor and Scribe' (or Dialogue 4, or Eduba C)," *NABU* (1996) 1:1-2; idem, "The Dialogue between a Supervisor and a Scribe," *COS* 1:590-92; idem, "The Dialogue between Two Scribes," *COS* 1:588-90.

208. Kramer, "Sage in Sumerian Literature."

209. See Ronald F. Hock, "Paul and Graeco-Roman Education," in *Paul in the Graeco-Roman World: A Handbook,* ed. J. Paul Sampley (Harrisburg: Trinity Press International, 2003) 198-227; Rafaella Cribiore, *Writing, Teachers, and Students in Graeco-Roman Egypt* (American Studies in Papyrology 36; Atlanta: Scholars Press, 1996); idem, *Gymnastics of the Mind;* Morgan, *Literate Education;* and Kah and Scholz, *Hellenistische Gymnasion.*

210. In general see Hock, "Paul and Graeco-Roman Education."

cises *(progymnasmata)* that taught style and argumentation. At the completion of their studies students were well educated and suited for a number of different social and professional roles. One would expect that a similar process occurred for the few Hellenistic Jews who were citizens of the poleis.

Superior students in the gymnasia would then attend *ephebeia,* which were professional schools, to become military officers, teachers, and high-ranking officials that required specialized education. Schoolbooks from the third century B.C.E. point to the reading of Homer, Hesiod, Euripides, Aeschylus, and Sophocles for their literary quality, teachings about life, and elegant Greek style. Philosophers were also read, including Socrates, Plato, Aristotle, Zeno, and Epicurus. Subjects included metaphysics, ethics, art, science, geography, mathematics, and rhetoric.

From the third century B.C.E., Alexandria became the primary center of Hellenistic education until its incorporation in the later part of the first century B.C.E. into the expanding Roman Empire. Some Jews of privilege who were citizens of the poleis attended some of their gymnasia.[211] Attendance in these schools, along with participation in other aspects of Greek and Roman cultural life, including the games[212] and the theater, opened highly educated Jews, who would have had to hold the status of citizen, to a new world that was not seen as inhibiting at least the more liberal practice of their religion. Many Jewish texts were written in Greek during the Hellenistic period, and even the sacred Torah was translated into Greek. Many Hellenistic Jews merged Jewish religious ideals with the Greek world, including Greek religion.[213]

Writing in the latter part of the first century and the early second century C.E., Plutarch (46-119 C.E.) goes into some detail about Roman education for the wealthy in four tractates (in *Moralia*): "The Education of Children," "On Music," "How to Study Poetry," and "On Listening to Lectures." He argues for the value of education, ranking it above the status of birth, wealth, reputation, beauty, health, and strength. He gives counsel to parents about instilling proper virtues in their children during their early, formative years while tutored at home. In the schools the study of the poetry of the classics, Homer, Hesiod, Pindar, Theognis, Aeschylus, Sophocles, Euripides, and Menander is combined with understanding philosophy, thus producing an ethical and cultivated person who would have been considered learned in Roman society. He, like many

211. Louis Robert, "Un Corpus des Inscriptions Juives," *REJ* 101 (1937) 73-86.

212. H. A. Harris, *Greek Athletics and the Jews* (Cardiff: University of Wales, 1976). He notes that there is no evidence that even orthodox Jews refused to attend the games, once they were established in Jerusalem in association with Jason's gymnasium.

213. See Victor Tcherikover, *Hellenistic Civilization and the Jews* (New York: Athenaeum, 1970) 352.

philosophers and teachers, achieved an envied and honored position. Thus, while our major source for Jewish understanding of the gymnasium is Philo of Alexandria,[214] Plutarch presents us with the features of education of the upper crust of Roman society. Of course, education, particularly of a formal nature, was inevitably a luxury offered only to the socially prominent. A general education, in the family and in the synagogues, was available to lower classes, but not a more formal, advanced one.

The Rhetoric of Wisdom Literature in Israel and Judah

Introduction

Elegant speech and discernment of the appropriate time to utter insight joined with the artistry of language to form the foundational adroitness of sapiential skills and insight. This adeptness embodied the wisdom of the sages, which consisted of the veracity of knowledge gained from the study of tradition and culture, and the observation of nature and the social world. Some sages even claimed the gift of divine wisdom. Together, the content of understanding and the artistry of spoken and written language configured a reality of beauty, order, and joy where the sage resided and invited others to dwell and participate. This world contained the components of knowledge, social decorum, and moral living. Most of the rhetorical genres of wisdom reveal artistic quality for the expression of their understanding. Meaning was created by the content of the language and the elegant locution of its expression, both gracefully combined into an aesthesis of meaning.

Rhetorical features of sapiential language include repetition, parallelism of poetic lines, the fashioning and knitting together of strophes by such devices as chiasms and acrostics, anaphora (the repetition of an initial word or words of several clauses, lines, or strophes), alliteration, assonance, refrains, interweaving words or phrases (*mots crochets*), and inclusios. Reading and hearing with deftness leading to understanding involves the slow and reflective savoring of both the reasonableness of the insight and the beauty and symmetry of expression.

Literary Forms of Wisdom

The sages of Israel and Judah, like their neighbors in adjacent cultures, developed and utilized a variety of rhetorical forms, which they categorized under the

---

214. Mendelson, *Secular Education.*

general heading of *māšāl* (Prov. 1:6; 26:7, 9): "sayings" (Ezek. 12:22-23; 18:2-3), wisdom psalms (Pss. 49:5; 78:2), didactic poems (Isa. 14:4-10), parables (Ezek. 17:2; 21:5; 24:3), and lists (Job 38–42). The verbal form, *māšal*, signifies "to rule" (Qal, Prov. 16:32; 17:2; 19:10; 22:7), "to be like" (Niphal, Isa. 14:10; Pss. 28:1; 143:7), or "to compare or liken" (Hiphil, Isa. 46:5). The first meaning suggests the effort of the wise person to master life — to know the proper place and time to act and to speak, what to say, and to control the situation in order to achieve success. The second and third meanings result from the sapiential understanding of "order" in the cosmos and society that combines the various components of reality into a harmonious whole. Through observing these various elements, the wise sought to understand their relationality to the world in which they existed.

The wisdom sayings included the proverb, the comparison (comparative sayings sometimes are formed with the technique of *a minore ad majus:* "if this, then how much more this"; see, e.g., Prov. 15:11), the beatitude (*'ašrê*, 16:20; 28:14; 29:18), the better saying ("better than," *tôb min*, 15:16, 17; 16:8; 19:1), the "abomination" *(tō'ēbâ)* that condemns destructive behavior and language (3:32; 8:7; 11:1, 20; 12:22; 13:10; 15:8, 26; 16:5; 17:15; 20:10, 23; 21:27; 24:9; 28:9; 29:27), and the numerical saying (pointing to the best or the worst of a list of three to seven items, 30:15-16, 18-19, 21-23, 24-28, 29-31). Each of these sayings was crafted into a minute aesthesis that gave form and elegance to the content of the understanding derived from observation, reason, experience, and the imagination.

The question *lāmâ* or *maddūa'*, "why," often introduced by the interrogative *hă*, and the interrogative pronouns (*mî*, "who," and *mâ*, "what") and the riddle are also succinct expressions. The question may be a true interrogative, rhetorical in the understanding that what is asked has an obvious answer, and catechetical in teaching students precise answers to particular questions. Additionally, there is the "impossible question" that has no answer. The riddle (*ḥîdâ*, "dark or hard saying") was used by the sages (Prov. 1:6; Ps. 49:5[4]; 1 Kgs. 10:1 = 2 Chron. 9:1), although none exists in the wisdom literature save for Ps. 49 (see Judg. 14:12-18; also Num. 12:8). The riddle is veiled in mystery, not clarity, and conceals the subject of the sage's statement, although one or more clues may be given. The intent of the sage who hears the riddle is to detect accurately the answer (1 Kgs. 10:1-3).

The second principal wisdom genre is the "teaching/instruction" (*mûsār, tôrâ;* see Prov. 1:3; 8:10, 33; 24:32). The teaching/instruction seeks to inculcate within its audience moral behavior. Its structure consists of the following:

1. The introduction: the teacher ("father," *'āb;* rarely "mother," *'ēm*) addresses the student/s ("son," *bēn;* and "child," *yeled*) and invites him/them to listen to his/her instruction.

2. The teaching proper: the teacher issues imperatives, admonitions, and prohibitions, coupled with one or more clauses (result, motive, conditional,
   and causal), and exhorting them to act or speak according to particular
   sapiential values, or to avoid certain occasions, people, actions, and man-
   ners of speaking.

3. The conclusion: the teacher usually ends with a characterization of the results of certain types of speech or behavior, with a saying that summarizes
   the teaching, or with an inclusio that points back to the beginning.

Examples include Prov. 1:8-19; 2:1-22; 3:1-12, 21-35.

An admonition exhorts or seeks to persuade, rather than simply command,
the hearer/reader to act or speak wisely according to known virtues (Prov. 4:23-
26; 5:1; 8:10). Prohibitions are admonitions plus a negative ("no," "not") that en-
joins or attempts to persuade the hearer/reader to avoid foolish or evil behavior
or people and potentially compromising situations (3:28-31). These were considered as intrinsically authoritative, since they are based on the insight of a
recognized sage and/or the veracity of the sapiential tradition. Even so, the admonition and prohibition may be coupled with one or more clauses (result,
motive, conditional, purpose, and causal) to buttress the authenticity of what is
exhorted or prohibited.

The sages also wrote a variety of aesthetically compelling poems and
psalms. These included wisdom psalms used in worship in the sanctuaries and
perhaps originally in schools in praise of wisdom, the Torah, and, at least implicitly, the creator and divine judge (Pss. 1, 19, 32, 34, 37, 49, 73, 111, 112, 119, 127).
Didactic poems are crafted into strophes connected by the cardinal features of
Hebrew poetry. Among the best in regard to beauty and content are those that
depict Woman Wisdom as a teacher or goddess who dispenses life to those who
accept her invitation to become her students (Prov. 1:20-33; 8:1-31; 9:1-6; Job 28;
Sir. 24).

Dialogues, often placed in the form of disputations, involve two or more
sages who debate opposing sides of an issue, including such topics as the justice
of God. The best known are the speeches of Job and his three opponents that
are framed by the issue of innocent suffering. At the end one or the other position prevails or is resolved by a theophany in which the divine judge renders a
verdict about the authenticity of one position over against the other.

An important genre of wisdom literature is the collection (mišlê, "sayings
of," dibrê, "words of"), in which a variety of sayings are listed, occasionally according to theme or rhetorical device (Prov. 1:1; 10:1; 25:1; Qoh. 12:11). The book
of Proverbs contains seven collections, and is concluded by a didactic poem.
Each of the collections is introduced by a title or superscription. Collections

unite a number of sayings, normally by means of similarities of poetic devices, and rarely by thematic coherence. Many longer ones are broken down into smaller units that are shaped into the larger whole. Other collections include the Coptic Gospel of Thomas and tractate *'Abot.*

Narratives of model sages were common in the biblical and postbiblical wisdom texts. These include Joseph (Gen. 37–50), Baruch (Jer. 36; 45; 1 Baruch), Job (the prologue and epilogue), and Ezra (a story that formed one of the bases of the larger corpus of the Chronicler's History). These narratives of honored sages were examples for students to emulate.[215] This genre, told from the perspective of a third person, consists of an omniscient narrator who relates the story of a wise man whose behavior incorporates important wisdom virtues. The legend focuses on the hero's undeserved misfortune, which is occasioned by the protagonist. The typical flow of the plot involves the movement from distress to successful resolution, due to the virtues of the hero. In the conclusion of the narrative, the heroic sage often regains his lost social stature, prestige, possessions, and/or family, while his antagonist, by contrast, is punished or even dies as a result. Mythological allusions in some of the introductions are important in setting the stage for the dramatic enactment of the story (e.g., the "council of God" in Job 1–2).[216]

Finally, lists were a literary form in wisdom literature, found in Israel and in other cultures of the ancient Near East.[217] These comprised a register or catalogue of related phenomena ranging from cosmological elements in the heavens (Job 38–39) to animals (Job 40–41) to characteristics and virtues of wisdom (Wis. 7:21-23). These were used in cataloguing a variety of different things that provided a ready reference for consultation and pointed to the order inherent in reality.

The rhetoric of wisdom contains not only a variety of forms specific to wisdom, themes incorporated in the wisdom tradition, and rhetorical features of sapiential poetry, but also key words and their synonyms that aided the meaning by giving the tradition a common vocabulary. These key sapiential words included "way" *(derek)*, "wisdom" *(ḥokmâ)*, "teach/learn" *(lāmad)*, "listen" *(šāmaʿ)*, "speak" *(dābar)*, and "understand/know" *(yādaʿ)*. These terms, and many others, served to focus and then heighten the mean-

---

215. There also are people who are fools and sinners, whose behavior is to be avoided. See the one enticed by the "strange woman" (Prov. 7:1-27).

216. See Hans-Peter Müller, "Die weisheitliche Lehrerzählung im Alten Testament und seiner Umwelt," *WO* 9 (1977) 77-98.

217. For example, see Gerhard von Rad, "Job XXXVIII and Ancient Egyptian Wisdom," repr. in *Studies in Ancient Israelite Wisdom*, ed. James L. Crenshaw (Library of Biblical Studies; New York: Ktav, 1976) 267-91.

ing of the text.[218] The abomination *(tôʿēbâ)* is the final type of literary proverb and reflects the sapiential adaptation of priestly language. In a two-line literary saying, one line refers to the detestable action or attitude, while the other normally contrasts it with what is acceptable (e.g., Prov. 21:27; 28:9).

At times verse is used in the telling of a narrative.[219] A didactic narrative that makes use of verse is the tale of Woman Wisdom in Prov. 7. The tale is told by an imaginary witness, a narrator, presumably Woman Wisdom, who observes the seduction of a youth by a prostitute or a promiscuous wife. This narrative of verse develops the common sapiential teaching of the "way," only in this case the path leads to destruction (7:8, 27). Thus the poetic narrative illustrates a key teaching of the wise: the moral course to sagehood and the achievement of the embodiment of wisdom are obstructed by a youth's unbridled lust for the strange woman.[220]

The most complicated question is how specifically sapiential the rhetoric of the sages is in comparison to features of the Hebrew language in general and Hebrew poetry in particular. Features unique to sapiential rhetoric include literary forms specific to or especially common in the wisdom literature, frequent themes, and key terms. Creation theology that becomes the foundation for moral instruction and enactment is expressed in these teachings or at least provides the basis for the articulation of others. The rhetoric of wisdom points to a social group of sages who compiled and transmitted a developing sapiential tradition.[221]

218. Shupak notes that the vocabulary of wisdom may be placed into two categories: terms that occur only in wisdom texts and words that have a higher distribution in sapiential literature than in other types of canonical writings *(Where Can Wisdom be Found?).*

219. Robert Alter, *The Art of Biblical Poetry* (New York: Basic Books, 1985) 27-61.

220. For recent discussions of the "strange woman," see Christl Maier, *Die 'fremde Frau' in Proverbien 1–9* (OBO 144; Göttingen: Vandenhoeck & Ruprecht, 1995); Claudia Camp, *Wise, Strange and Holy: The Strange Woman and the Making of the Bible* (JSOTSup 320; Sheffield: Sheffield Academic Press, 2000).

221. James L. Crenshaw, "Wisdom and Authority: Sapiential Rhetoric and Its Warrants," in *Congress Volume: Vienna, 1980,* ed. J. A. Emerton (VTSup 32; Leiden: Brill, 1981) 10-29; Philip J. Nel, "Authority in the Wisdom Admonitions," *ZAW* 93 (1981) 418-26.

2. Wisdom during the Kingdoms of Israel and Judah: The Book of Proverbs

General Introduction

The book of Proverbs consists of collections of sayings, instructions, and poems by unnamed sages of ancient Israel. The foundational theme of the entire book is the "fear of God/Yahweh," best understood as both a theological construct and a religious virtue underlying sapiential speech and behavior. Theologically interpreted, the "fear of God" refers to the conviction that God is both the creator of the world and the judge who oversees, tries, and decides the proper response of punishment or reward for human behavior. In addition, this affirmation perceives God to be the one who imparts wisdom to guide those receptive to divine teaching in directing their lives toward the achievement of well-being, honor, and justice. As a religious virtue, the "fear of God" is pious devotion to the God of creation and wisdom, reflection on the world and the social reality that this deity created, and the behavior consisting of ethical decisions and conduct. Wisdom was even imagined as a divine voice instructing the simple, the daughter of God, and the "Queen of Heaven," who, as the consort of God, chose rulers and offered instruction through the sages to those who responded affirmatively to her invitation.

Proverbs is one of the thirteen books of the "Writings" *(kĕtûbîm)*, the third and final section of the Tanakh that also includes the "Law" *(tôrâ)* and the "Prophets" *(nĕbî'îm)* (cf. the Prologue to Ben Sira; Josephus, *C. Ap.* 1.8; *B. Bat.* 14b-15a; 4 Ezra 14:18-48; Philo, *Contempl.* 25; Luke 24:44). This section contains a collection of various literary forms and contents: "historical" writings, psalms, legends, wisdom texts, and apocalypses. While the texts in the "Writings" bear the characteristic features and temporal indications of the later Second Temple period, the one exception is several of the collections in the book of Proverbs. Indeed, the lateness of this third section of texts is attested by the different order of the books held in common by the Masoretic text and the Septuagint and the additional texts in the Greek translation. Further, the location of the wisdom texts in the Second Temple period as indicated by their placement in the third division of the Tanakh and the addition of several didactic texts, Ben Sira (Ecclesiasticus), the Wisdom of Solomon *(Sapientia Solomonis)*, Baruch, and those that combine wisdom and apocalyptic (1 Enoch and Daniel), point to the fact that the influence of the sages and scribes grew exponentially in the Persian and Hellenistic periods.

Date and Historical Context

Establishing the dates of the collections and the concluding poem of the book as well as the time of its final editing represents an imposing challenge, due to the lack of specific criteria on which to make concrete judgments. These criteria, often missing from Proverbs, include the specificity of social groups active during a particular period, references to historical events, and linguistic features, not simply of the Hebrew but also of the influences of other languages, including especially Aramaic and Greek. One other factor complicates the dating of the collections and redaction of Proverbs: the difference between the time of the origin of a particular passage (a proverb, instruction, or poem) and its inclusion in the collection and the establishment of the final canonical form of the volume. For example, while the concluding poem on the "Woman of Virtue" appears, on redactional grounds, to be the last text added to Proverbs, this does not necessarily mean that the poem was written in the period when this redaction occurred. Due to the lack of precise evidence, it is not surprising to find considerable variation in scholarly dating of both the collections and the final redaction of the book.

The following scholars represent a few select examples of the variety of positions on dating. According to the view of Grintz, the three "Solomonic Collections" point to the time of the united monarchy.[1] Snell argues that, due to

---

1. For the English translation of the Hebrew essay by Jehoshua M. Grintz, see "'The Proverbs of Solomon': Clarifications on the Question of the Relation between the Three Collections in the Book of Proverbs Attributed to Solomon" (trans. Daniel C. Snell), in Snell, *Twice-Told Proverbs and the Composition of the Book of Proverbs* (Winona Lake, IN: Eisenbrauns, 1993) 87-114.

the reference to rulers in the superscriptions and the mentioning of kings in some of the collections, much of Proverbs dates from the monarchy, with some collections assembled even before the divided kingdom.[2] Fox has suggested that the references to Solomon are untenable, although the mentioning of kings may suggest that some of the materials originated during the First Temple period.[3] While he dates the collection in chs. 1–9 to the final stage of redaction due to its serving as an introduction to the other collections, he thinks that the final edition of the volume originates in the Persian or Hellenistic period and is no later than Ben Sira (early second century B.C.E.), who was familiar with the book. Requiring more evidence than the collections themselves allow, however, Scott argues that one cannot hope to date any of them with precision, although he, like most scholars, is convinced that the legendary association with Solomon lacks historical veracity.[4]

In spite of these imposing hurdles to overcome in constructing a plausible chronological sequence of the collections, it is still important to their interpretation to attempt to identify the general historical periods in which they occurred. This chronology provides the interpreter with a historical matrix for understanding Proverbs. To regard the book as originating in the Second Temple period has led some interpreters to associate the book with an emphasis on Torah. The unsupportable and misleading argument in earlier generations of Christian scholarship that this is the time of intrinsic, unbending legalism has had as its consequence the association of wisdom, in particular Proverbs, with this contested view of the religious climate of the period of Ezra and the emergence of early Judaism. Thus, in this inappropriate characterization of Judaism, it should come as no surprise that wisdom, in particular the book of Proverbs, has been dismissed in a substantial body of earlier Christian scholarship. I would agree with Snell and Fox that some of the materials included in several collections indicate they should be assigned to the preexilic period, although there is no compelling textual and archaeological evidence, aside from the legendary Solomon narrative, to suggest a royal court with sages existed prior to the eighth century B.C.E. and the reign of Hezekiah. While a literary tradition incorporated into the Deuteronomistic History about Solomon's great wisdom developed in Israel as early as the sixth century B.C.E. (1 Kgs. 4:29-34 [MT 5:9-14]), it is largely legendary (see the late texts of Qoheleth and the Wisdom of Solomon). Solomon ruled from about 961 to 922 B.C.E. It is doubtful that he was personally responsible for any of the extant wisdom materials, but the Sol-

2. Snell, *Twice-Told Proverbs.*

3. Michael Fox, *Proverbs 1–9* (AB; New York: Doubleday, 2000) 6.

4. R. B. Y. Scott, *Proverbs, Ecclesiastes* (AB; Garden City, NY: Doubleday, 1965).

omon narrative in 1 Kgs. 3–11, composed by the Deuteronomistic Historians and completed no later than the Babylonian exile, identifies him as the paragon of the wise ruler.[5] This legend of Solomonic wisdom at the very least suggests that the Deuteronomistic History writers in the sixth century B.C.E. understood that wisdom was an intellectual activity of sages in the First Temple period. The variations of arrangement of the collections offered by the LXX intimate that it followed an earlier Hebrew redaction than the final one preserved in the MT. This indicates that the continuation of the formation of Proverbs moved into the Hellenistic period. In my judgment, the final editing of the volume was concluded in the Ptolemaic period.

However, the materials collected in Proverbs do not militate against an earlier date for some of the sayings and brief collections. My argument for a monarchic dating for some of these texts depends on the superscriptions and the social content of some of the sayings. The form of the superscription is best understood to be a dedication that parallels the Egyptian sapiential instructions' titles and scribal colophons. In addition, the "men of Hezekiah" and the mother of Lemuel may suggest collections appropriate for Israel during its monarchic political history, although foreign rulers during the successive imperial periods could be referenced in the sayings about the king. However, the exaltation of the king would appear unlikely to come from Israelite and Jewish sages speaking of non-Israelite rulers.

My own historical sequencing of the collections and growth of the book, which is based on very limited evidence, unfolds as follows. The three "Solomonic Collections" formed the first collections of sapiential materials assembled in the First Temple period, perhaps during the kingship of Hezekiah (25:1). To this first formulation, the three non-Israelite collections (Agur and Lemuel) and 22:17–24:34 (influenced by Amenemope) were eventually added, also dating from the late First Temple period. These collections suggest interaction with non-Israelite sages and the ability also to read Egyptian (likely hieratic), Arabic, Aramaic, and possibly Akkadian. The general introduction in 1:2-7 and the poem on "The Woman of Worth," which frame the collections, were added in the final, major redaction of the book, although their composition prior to the Ptolemaic period is probable. The book of Proverbs continued to be tweaked, as evidenced by differences between the LXX and Masoretic consonantal text.

On a larger historical scale, one may view the collections of the book of

---

5. Contra Richard J. Clifford, *Proverbs: A Commentary* (OTL; Louisville: Westminster John Knox, 1999) 3. He suggests that Solomon may have "collected, sponsored, or possibly even written, various kinds of writing, including wisdom literature."

Proverbs, which were composed during the First Temple and Second Temple periods, as an example of international wisdom in which Israel's and Judah's sages participated. They were especially influenced by the social setting (the school and the royal and temple administrations), the literary forms, and the moral and theological teachings of ancient Egypt with whom their state had extensive commercial, diplomatic, and hostile interactions from the end of the Late Bronze Age to the first century C.E. Knowledge of the Egyptian, Aramaic, Arabic, Canaanite, Akkadian, and Old Persian literary traditions and languages would have been learned in the schools, particularly the royal schools established in the capitals of Jerusalem and Samaria for the education of scribes, sages, teachers, officials, and others whose occupations required them to become literate. Contact with Egyptian and other kingdoms, noted by historical records, narratives presumably based on earlier annals, and evidence of material culture, would have compelled at least some of the scribes to possess a more detailed knowledge of Akkadian, the international language during the First and early Second Temple periods, Canaanite, likely Egyptian, including particularly hieratic and demotic scripts, and eventually Aramaic, Old Persian, Arabic, and Greek. From Assyrian times, Royal Aramaic would have been required for diplomacy, travel to and residence in foreign courts, and correspondence. In a tiny nation that was often part of the Egyptian *Kulturkreis,* especially since the New Kingdom, it would be unimaginable that Canaan and then Judah would not have been influenced significantly by their imposing neighbor to its south. The same is the case with Assyria, Babylonia, Persia, and the Hellenistic kingdoms of the Ptolemies and Seleucids.

This interaction between these nations and Israel/Judah demonstrates from its inception the multinational character of wisdom. For the sages of Proverbs, the international scope of wisdom pointed to the acceptance of knowledge and insight from the sages of other nations living outside the national boundaries of Israel/Judah.

Rhetoric (Literary Structure and Form)

Proverbs consists of seven collections *(měšālîm)* of sayings, instructions, and poems. The final redactors provide a general introduction at the beginning of the book and conclude it with a poem. Its redaction reveals the artistry of skilled sages and teachers who likely compiled the book as a developing manual for instruction in rhetoric and moral virtue for youth studying in the schools. By means of this manual, they learned to compose literary forms, use elegant language, engage in proper speech, and incorporate principles of behavior to guide them in life in general and in the performance of their professional roles at the conclusion of their education. It is unlikely that the book was composed originally for the general population. The suitability of Proverbs for general reading was later debated (cf. tractate *'Abot*).[6]

Rhetorical Structure

The seven collections of Proverbs and their superscriptions are:

I.   1:1   "The Proverbs of Solomon, the Son of David, King of Israel" (*mišlê šĕlōmōh*)

II. 10:1   "The Proverbs of Solomon" (*mišlê šĕlōmōh*)

III. 22:17   "The Words of the Wise" (*dibrê ḥăkāmîm*)

IV. 24:23   "These Also Are (the Words) of the Wise" (*gam-'ēlleh [dibrê] ḥăkāmîm*)

V.   25:1   "These Also Are the Proverbs of Solomon, Which the Men of Hezekiah, King of Judah, Edited" (*gam-'ēlleh mišlê šĕlōmōh 'ăšer he'tîqû 'anšê ḥezqîyâ melek-yĕhûdâ*)

VI. 30:1   "The Words of Agur" (*dibrê 'āgûr*)

VII. 31:1   "The Words of Lemuel, King of Massa, Which His Mother Taught Him" (*dibrê lĕmû'ēl melek maśśā' 'ăšer-yissĕrattû 'immô*)

Lacking any superscription, a poem on the "Woman of Virtue" (*'ēšet ḥayil*, 31:10-31) brings the book to its conclusion.

Introduction to the Book of Proverbs: 1:2-7

The superscription in 1:1 is the title for both the initial collection (chs. 1–9) and the entire book. This is followed by an introduction in 1:2-7, which also inaugurates the first collection as well as the whole of the book. These early verses of the introduction include infinitive clauses (vv. 2-6) that are similar to those of Ptahhotep (ll. 40-50, *ANET*, 412) and Amenemope (I, 1-12, *ANET*, 421). This introduction lists not only the important social roles of the sages in the seven collections (teacher, counselor, jurist, scribe, and administrator), but also identifies the major sapiential synonyms for "wisdom": "to know" (*lāda'at*), "wisdom" (*ḥokmâ*), "discipline/instruction/curriculum" (*mûsār*), "to under-

---

6. See the discussion of this issue in Fox, *Proverbs*, 6-12.

stand" *(lěhābîn),* "words" *('imrê),* "insight"/"cleverness" *(haśkēl),* "cunning" *('ŏrmâ),* "shrewdness" *(mězimmâ),* "learning" *(leqaḥ),* and "counsel" *(taḥbūlâ).* Moreover, the three foremost nouns having to do with justice or order, which serves as a major theme in the book, also are present in this introduction, specifically in v. 3b, *ṣedeq* ("righteous"), *mišpāṭ* ("justice"), and *mēšārîm* ("righteousness," "justice," and "equity"). Several important literary forms of wisdom literature are given, the first in v. 1, and the other two in v. 6 ("proverb," *māšāl;* "figure," *mělîṣâ;* "riddle," *ḥîdâ).* The audience consists of two often related social groups: the "simple/unlearned" *(pětā'yim),* and "youth" *(ně'ārîm).* Furthermore, even older sages honored for their wisdom are encouraged to add to their "learning." This "learning" includes the skills of the scribe, the knowledge of the sages, and the "received tradition" of the ancestral wise (Job 11:4; Prov. 9:9; 16:21). Finally, the "fear of the Lord is the beginning of wisdom" is a frequent theme (9:10; 15:33; Ps. 111:10; Job 28:28) and serves as the closure for both the introduction and the entire book (Prov. 1:7; 31:30).

The First Solomonic Collection: 1:8–9:18

The first collection of Proverbs presents a series of instructions of "sons" (students) in significant sapiential values. The purpose of this collection is the education of wealthy youth who are taught moral virtues appropriate for their class and position in society. There are thirteen instructions (complete or partial) in the following locations: 1:8-19; 2:1-22 (acrostic = 22 lines, *'alep, lamed*); 3:1-12, 21-35; 4:1-9, 10-27; 5:1-23; 6:1-11, 20-22 (partial); 7:1-5 (partial), 24-27 (partial); 8:32-36 (partial); and 9:7-12 (partial).

The collection also contains four wisdom poems: 1:20-33; 3:13-20; 8:1-36; and 9:1-6 + 13-18. Woman Wisdom is at the center of these four poems, even as she is in an instruction in 4:1-9. Wisdom is the goddess of the sages, perhaps early on a divine consort of Yahweh, but then is understood at times metaphorically as the teacher and personification of the wisdom tradition. These poems present her as the divine force at work in creation and the maintenance of the cosmos, the incarnation of the voice of God, the embodiment of social justice, and the divine lover of the wise who, like an ancient Near Eastern fertility goddess, offers her paramours life and wealth. Her rival, the "Strange Woman," is the adulteress, fertility goddess, and personification of folly.

The Solomonic Collection: Proverbs 1–9

The first collection is closely related to Egyptian wisdom literature, in particular the dominant place given to instructions and the importance of the aretologies of Woman Wisdom.[7] The thirteen instructions and partial instructions in this initial collection resonate well with the Egyptian predilection for this sapiential form. Even more significant, however, are the parallels of Prov. 1:20-33; 8:1-31; 9:1-6 with the hymns of self-praise in Egyptian religion, especially those of two goddesses, Maat and Isis.[8] These suggest possible Egyptian influence on Woman Wisdom in the hymnic strophes in chs. 8–9.[9] Instead of a speech of a goddess, the first person hymn in 1:20-33 depicts Woman Wisdom as a peripatetic teacher who takes to the streets, stands at the gates, and cries out from the squares of the city to issue invitations to become her disciples and to warn sternly of the dire consequences that await those who spurn her call.

Panegyrics are first person hymnic speeches of gods and goddesses that originated in the First Intermediate Period of Egypt and continued into the early Roman Empire.[10] They were usually uttered by lesser-known deities seeking to establish their divine credentials and cultic worship by extolling their own glory and greatness. In Proverbs these hymns also have the objective of revealing the mysterious God of creation. Sapiential imagination sets forth Woman Wisdom in Proverbs 8–9 as a goddess who was the patron of the sages and possibly even worshiped by them until the official religion of the Jerusalem cultus in the Second Temple relegates her to the lower status of the hypothesis of a divine attribute and finally to a literary metaphor. This loss of divine rank was probably due to the increasing patriarchy of the priests from the time of Ezra until the Roman destruction of Jerusalem in 70 C.E. Even so, in all three guises of goddess, hypothesis, and metaphor she becomes the sapiential means of revealing the transcendent God.

In the self-praise (panegyric) of 8:1–9:6, Woman Wisdom is adorned in the garments of a goddess who becomes the patron of the sages. As the one present with God at creation, his infant (*'āmôn*) who mediates between heaven and earth,[11] his consort in choosing kings, and the divine teacher and lover of those

---

7. Achim Müller (*Proverbien 1–9* [BZAW 291; Berlin: de Gruyter, 2000]) points to the mythical features in these texts, especially the hymns (221-50).

8. For a summary of *ma'at* in Egyptian religious and royal understandings, see Wolfgang Helck, "Maat," *LÄ* 3 (1980) 1110-19. He indicates that *ma'at* developed from a concept (justice, righteousness), to the cosmic order, to the guidance of royal rule. The term became an attribute of deities and kings and finally, in the New Kingdom, a goddess for whom temples were built.

9. Christa Bauer Kayatz, *Studien zu Proverbien 1–9. Eine form- und motivgeschichtliche Untersuchung unter Einbeziehung ägyptischen Vergleichsmaterials* (WMANT 22; Neukirchen-Vluyn: Neukirchener Verlag, 1966). By contrast, Fox continues the traditional dating of this collection to the Second Temple period, seeing it as Persian or early Hellenistic, since he argues that this section introduces the book (*Proverbs 1–9*, 6). I agree with Fox.

10. Jan Assmann, "Aretalogien," *LÄ* 1 (1975) 426-34.

11. Fox, *Proverbs 1–9*, 285-87.

who respond to her invitation to learn of her and then receive from her life and wealth, Woman Wisdom functions in comparable ways to her Egyptian prototypes. One important example is the Isis hymn on the *Metternichstele* (Saying VI, 49, 57-59).[12]

The Second Solomonic Collection: 10:1–22:16

The second collection consists of two earlier ones that have been redacted together: 10:1–15:33 and 16:1–22:16.[13] Except for occasional subunits that are formed on thematic grounds (kingship in 16:10-15), the collection lacks any overarching, coherent literary and thematic structure. Most of the collection contains two-line proverbs that are synonymous and antithetical.

Antithetical sayings dominate the literary proverbs in the first subsection,[14] while the contrast between the righteous/wise and the wicked/fool is emphasized in the second one.[15] Also characteristic of this collection is the substantial presence of Yahweh sayings (10:3; 12:2; 15:11, 25, 29; 16:1-4, 7, 9, 11, 20, 33; 17:3; 18:22; 19:3, 14; 20:12, 22, 24; 21:2-3, 30, 31; 22:2), which point to the sages redacting this collection as affirming the role of God in the maintenance of cosmic and social order by means of retributive justice and the importance of virtuous behavior of the wise in creating communal stability. The subject of kingship in 16:10-15 is evidence that the royal court is one of the locations in which the sages were active. These proverbs intimate that some of the students studying this collection are educated for service at court as officials and scribes. Thematically, the emphasis on proper speech is the primary one. This also fits well a school in which young students are preparing for careers in the royal administration.

"The Words of the Sages": 22:17–24:22

The third collection demonstrates a literary dependence on "The Instruction of Amenemope," a twelfth-century Egyptian text, due to similar content and structure. The repointing of *šilšôm* (שלשום, Ketib; "day before yesterday")/ *šālîšîm* (שלישים, Qere; "officers") to *šĕlōšîm* (שלשים, "thirty") in 22:20 paral-

---

12. Constintin Emil Sander-Hansen, *Die Texte der Metternichstele* (Analecta Aegyptiaca 7; Copenhagen: E. Munksgaard, 1956) 41.

13. P. W. Skehan, "A Single Editor for the Whole Book of Proverbs," in *Studies in Israelite Poetry and Wisdom* (CBQMS 1; Washington, DC: Catholic Biblical Association, 1971) 18-20.

14. Ibid., 18.

15. According to Udo Skladny, this subsection contains 52 synonymous, 47 antithetic, and 37 synthetic sayings out of 190 proverbs (*Die ältesten Spruchsammlungen in Israel* [Göttingen: Vandenhoeck & Ruprecht, 1962]).

lels the thirty chapters of Amenemope. While it is not possible to reconstruct thirty chapters in this proverbial collection, there is little doubt that Amenemope served as a substantial prototype for this collection, which may date from the period of the monarchy.[16]

The collection was a resource for the exercises practiced by students seeking to learn the scribal arts and to follow the virtues of the professional ethic of scribes in royal service. Especially important is the close connection of themes to chs. 1–9, suggesting that both had the same social setting, which likely was a school in which the young sons of the elite were educated. The collection possesses ten sections preceded by an introduction (22:17-21), yet it is organized into a single entity.[17]

"These Also Are (the Words) of the Wise": 24:23-34

The fourth collection contains two major sections: a partial instruction consisting of admonitions, prohibitions, and sayings that pertain to jurisprudence, and a first person narrative about the teacher's observations of indolence and its damaging consequences. The first part of the collection likely originated as part of a teaching issued to students, some of whom would enter into the legal profession as judges, scribes, and recorders following the conclusion of their education. The Israelite judicial system had three forms: the royal administration, priestly judgment, and the clan where village elders would adjudicate local disputes. Sages would have been involved in the legal system of the state bureaucracy. The second part belongs to common wisdom locations in which scribes and sages would find themselves. Consequently, the association of sloth with poverty fits any circumstances involving human activities that affect economic circumstances of life, although v. 27 points to labor in the familial household. Thus youth who finished their education would continue to function in their household responsibilities and eventually might even become the paterfamilias of the extended family.

"These Also Are the Proverbs of Solomon, Which the Men of Hezekiah, King of Judah, Edited": 25:1–29:27

This fifth collection contains a more developed superscription that identifies the scribes who redacted *(heʿtîqû)* it as the "men *(ʾanšê)* of Hezekiah." The

16. See Washington's dissertation, *Wealth and Poverty;* John Ruffle, "The Teaching of Amenemope and Its Connection with the Book of Proverbs," *TynBul* 28 (1977) 29-68.

17. Adolf Erman, "Eine ägyptische Quelle der Sprüche Salomos," *SBAW*. Phil.-hist. Kl. 15 (Berlin: Deutsche Akademie, 1924) 86-93.

Hiphil verb *he'tîqû* means to copy or to redact a text. The verb refers literally to the moving of sayings from one place to another and identifies the "Men of Hezekiah" as editors of collections of texts, a role played by Qoheleth (see Qoh. 12:9-12). The plural construct noun *'anšê*, "men of," refers to those who were in the administrative service of King Hezekiah, in this case court scribes who had the responsibility of assembling, archiving, and transmitting proverbs and other literary materials that were part of the ideology supporting the reign of the monarch. This superscription gives every appearance of a particular social role held by scribes who were members of the king's administration. Some among them had the duty of editing texts, in this case scribal collections, which likely were used in the education of youth who studied to enter into the royal administration as courtiers. The document provides then a manual not only for learning to read and write, but also to shape a professional ethic and worldview that would serve as the social and theoretical matrix for their loyal support of the ruler.[18]

This collection, which contains all of the comparative sayings present in the book of Proverbs, also brings together two subsections. The first occurs in 25:1–27:27 and possesses coherent literary and thematic eloquence that suggests a tightly woven, well-shaped collection.[19] The first part of this subsection, 25:2-27, incorporates two inclusios that mark its literary parameters: "glory" in vv. 2-27, and "wicked/righteousness" in vv. 5-26. The subsection also has several thematic units: 25:2-7 (royalty), 26:1-12 (the fool), and 26:13-16 (the lazy). The second subcollection, present in 28:1–29:27, consists primarily of antithetical sayings that contrast the behavior of the righteous and the fool.

The thematic features of the collection strongly intimate a royal school as its setting, a location in which a student would learn to embody certain moral virtues and be instructed in important religious convictions, including God as the creator and sustainer of the cosmos and the king as the sustainer of social justice. These virtues include operating as righteous officials whose activities uphold the social order, who are loyal to the king, and who serve the kingdom. The persona of the ideal ruler is determined by astute knowledge even of what is concealed from and mysterious to many sages, an intelligent and knowledgeable mind that enables him to rule wisely and successfully and to establish a rule that discriminates between righteousness and wickedness. Through judgment issued from his throne, justice supports the cosmic and societal order for which he has significant responsibility. For the sages, the king who is oppressive

18. In general see Raymond Van Leeuwen, *Context and Meaning in Proverbs 25–27* (SBLDS 96; Atlanta: Scholars Press, 1988).
19. Ibid.

brings ruin to the kingdom. Officials who are servants to kings are just, given the fact that the ruler they serve is to exhibit a sapiential and righteous character and behavior in directing the kingdom. Equally true is that oppressive kings have corrupt courtiers. The population has no power to affect this behavior, but rather it emulates the character of the ruler himself (29:2). Other themes include several sayings that deal with God, which emphasize in particular his justice and judgment, and his creation of humanity, both the rich and the poor. The emphasis placed on divine justice corresponds well with the unusually important place given to law and principled jurisprudence. Other themes cut a wide swath in the area of appropriate behavior and virtuous living, including using correct and appropriate language, avoiding boasting, and rejecting the folly of unrestrained behavior.

"The Words of Agur": 30:1-4 (+ vv. 5-33)

"The Words of Agur," originally limited to the first four verses of ch. 30, is a notoriously complex teaching to translate. However, it appears to point to an Arabian mantic sage of the tribe of Massa, who appears familiar with the *apkallu* tradition in Mesopotamia. He parodies wisdom's claim to possess knowledge of God and creation and prophetic speech that asserts divine revelation (2 Kgs. 9:25; Isa. 14:28). Instead, he offers a human "saying" *(nĕʾūm)* that is his own insight. The redaction found in vv. 5-6, 7-9, and 10 is that of a traditional scribal redactor who responds critically to this cynic. The remainder of the collection is added by traditional sages who attach sayings about the wicked, numerical sayings (vv. 15-16, 18-19, 21-23, 24-28, 29-31), a synonymous saying that speaks of the punishment of those who do not honor their parents (v. 17), another synonymous saying about the adulteress (v. 20), and an admonition warning against folly and evil (vv. 32-33).

Mantic wisdom points to an alternative sapiential tradition in Second Temple Judah, and has as one of its major themes the sage's "journey to the heavens" to obtain esoteric knowledge. In Jewish apocalyptic, Enoch returns with divine revelations that are esoteric, while Adapa and Utuabzu (another name for Adapa?) descend from heaven with wisdom. The small collection of Agur in its early form of the first four verses is the one mantic collection in Proverbs. However, the words of Eliphaz in Job 4:12-21 are suggestive of this tradition. Dating is difficult, but Jewish apocalyptic into which mantic wisdom merged began to develop significantly in the fourth century B.C.E. and is reflected in both the Joseph story and Daniel. The mantic tradition appears as a competing one with that of traditional wisdom of the First and Second Temple periods. Conservative scribes, who add their responses in Prov. 30:5-33, offer sharp criticism of this Arabian wise man.

His question appears to be catechetical, not an impossible or skeptical one: "Who has ascended to heaven and come down?" In mantic wisdom the answer would be in Mesopotamia Etana or Adapa, and then in early Judaism Enoch, all of whom made heavenly journeys to obtain as a divine gift secret knowledge of the gods, divine wisdom, or even immortality. In some of these stories, these *apkallu*s and their Jewish approximation sought to transmit their special knowledge freely to human beings. Yet the gods denied humans the comprehensiveness of divine wisdom and immortality, attributes they limited to themselves.

Since the "Sayings of Agur" as a divinatory wisdom tradition emerged from a group of seers whose descendants would morph into the sages of apocalyptic, we may imagine that a social group of mantic sages and their followers existed in a community in which this and similar teachings would have flourished. That this group was well known is demonstrated in Qoheleth's direct challenge to their claim to possess esoteric knowledge that was authoritative and certain (Qoh. 3:16-22).

"The Words of King Lemuel": 31:1-9

"The Words of King Lemuel" is the seventh and final collection in Proverbs and consists entirely of a superscription and a subsequent instruction. The instruction originates in the same Arabian tribe with which Agur is identified, Massa, and is issued by the mother, likely married to the tribe's former sheik, to her son, who appears to have recently assumed the role of his dead or indisposed father. She instructs him on behavior expected of him in ruling his people: avoid the pitfall of liaisons with unchaste women, abstain from overindulgence in strong drink, rule justly, and champion the cause of the poor. If given a ritual location, the instruction would have been issued during the son's installation that served as a rite of passage from prince to ruler. This theme of instructing a young man in the requirements of leadership would have fit best during the First Temple period.

"The Poem on the Woman of Worth": 31:10-31

This acrostic poem is added to conclude the book, providing the inclusio in which the "Woman of Virtue" is the incarnation of Woman Wisdom in chs. 1, 8, and 9. She too "opens her mouth with wisdom *(ḥokmâ)*" and her "tongue is the teaching *(tôrâ)* of kindness" (v. 26). Whom she teaches is not clearly specified, but on the basis of the social world of the household her students would have been her children and other members of her domicile.[20] This is not to say that there were no women who were considered sages, as the two unnamed women in the Succession Narrative demonstrate (2 Sam. 14, 20). Thus she is a wealthy sage whose duties and activities in the household are commensurate with her activities in the commercial world of buying and selling.

General Observations Concerning the Formal Character of the Book

In reviewing the collections, one may make the following observations concerning Proverbs:

1. The didactic poem is a major literary characteristic of chs. 1–9 and is also present in the conclusion in 31:10-31.
2. Antithetical proverbs govern the formal character of chs. 10–15.
3. Numerical sayings are primarily found in the redaction of ch. 30 (the sixth collection).
4. Instructions are especially present in the first, third, and fourth collections.
5. Comparative sayings are limited to the fifth collection.

Summary of the Collections

A number of further observations may be made about the literary character of these collections. Three of the seven collections are associated in some way with Solomon, at least in his being identified in the superscriptions (1:1; 10:1; 25:1). The superscription in each reads: "the Wisdom Sayings of Solomon" (mišlê šĕlōmōh; see 1 Kgs. 5:12 [Solomon's 3,000 wisdom sayings]; Ezek. 12:22-23; Hab. 2:6; Prov. 1:6; Pss. 49:5[4]; 78:2). The first superscription refers to him as the "son of David, king of Israel," while the third notes that the "men of Hezekiah, king of Judah, edited" them. These three collections compare to the tradition of Solomon as the "wise king" in the Deuteronomistic History and in later books: 1 Kgs. 5:9-14, 21 [4:29-34; 5:7]; 10:4, 23; Qoheleth; Sir. 47:12-17; and Wisdom of Solomon, especially chs. 7–9. Rather than noting authorship, these superscriptions are dedicatory formulae in praise of Solomon, the patron saint of wisdom (cf. the dedication of some of the psalms to David).

Three of the superscriptions contain the term "words" (dibrê, 22:17; 30:1; 31:1) of the sages. The general term "word" may refer to "proverb/saying" (1 Kgs. 10:6; Prov. 13:13; it means "history" in 1 Kgs. 11:41; Jer. 1:1; 1 Chron. 4:22 in the sense of the listing of events) or perhaps to individual lines within the collec-

20. See the essays found in Leo G. Perdue, et al., *Families in Ancient Israel.*

tions. The word "these" in the superscription in 24:23 that introduces the collection likely echoes the "words" of the embedded superscription found in 22:17. The plural noun "sages" *(hăkāmîm)* occurs in the superscriptions of 22:17 and 24:23 and is combined with the plural "words" *(dibrê)*. The "sages" are those who have become teachers in the wisdom schools of court and temple in Jerusalem and in the governors' schools in the later colonial period. In addition, the plural "words" *(dibrê)* is placed in construct with two personal names: Agur and Lemuel in 30:1 and 31:1, respectively.

Two of the collections are attributed to non-Israelite sources (30:1-2, Agur; 31:1-2, Lemuel), while a third (22:17–24:34, esp. 22:17–23:10) has appropriated and used "The Instruction of Amenemope" dating from the end of the Late Bronze Age. The geographical and historical identity of the first two collections remains uncertain, although they may have originated in Arabia (cf. Job's three friends), since both refer to "Massa" (Heb. *maśśā'*), which may be related to an Akkadian word (*maš'* postulated on the basis of Assyrian *maš'ayya,* the "Masa'aean") that may refer to an Arabian tribe.

Conclusions on the Redaction of the Book

Second Temple scribes, likely during the Ptolemaic period, shaped these seven collections and concluding poem into a scroll that served as a manual for youth studying in the sapiential schools of court (First Temple period) and later the temple and synagogue (Second Temple period and early Judaism). The content of this manual indicates that it incorporated the professional ethics required of scribes and sages in the society of Israel and Judah during the First and Second Temple periods. Its literary expression, in addition to the overarching structure of the book, is shaped by the typical wisdom genres of collection, instruction, sayings of various types, questions, and didactic poems. Themes prominently displayed include the quest for and gaining of wisdom, the importance of the proper use of wealth (indicating the sages were among the elite or at least served the aristocracy), the behavior and etiquette expected of scribes and sages as contrasted to those of fools, the acquisition of knowledge, the judicious assessment of when to speak or act and what to say and do, the metaphorical role of women enshrined in the role of goddess Wisdom or deprecated as the wicked "strange" woman to be avoided, and the religious orientation to the God of creation, order, and justice. The notion that wisdom may be divided into an earlier secular understanding of eudaemonistic success in life and a later religious activity carried out within the confines of personal piety is not supportable. Even the less ideological view that worldly wisdom became theological in the Second Temple period appears specious.

Social Features: Sages and Social Setting

Accessing the social character of wisdom in Proverbs may be done directly through the language and themes that fit the worldview of a specific social group, the institutions of importance mentioned in the literature, and the roles of sages implicit in the wisdom texts. The distinct literary forms and themes of Proverbs differ from those in other preexilic texts, with the exception of those that experienced sapiential redactions. Thus one discovers wisdom elements of language and themes in proto-Deuteronomy and hymns like Ps. 104. The following social features provide an overview of the themes of this book in both their unique and sapientially nuanced form. As I shall argue, the sophistication of their expression and insight point to an aristocratic worldview and ethos that places these texts within two milieus: royal (later gubernatorial) and temple schools for the education of youth who were to enter administrative positions in the kingdom, ranging from the scribal ranks of copyists and archivists to courtiers, judges, teachers, and officials; and a provincial school for educating youth to enter into similar roles of colonial administration. These texts were eventually used by teachers in synagogues for instructing youth in Judah to learn moral discernment and to engage in wise and pious behavior.

The Wise as a Social Group: Introduction

One of the important questions in wisdom research concerns the social identity of the sages and especially whether they were an identifiable social group. It is clear that the wise were educated people, usually wealthy, whose character was shaped by "wisdom" as knowledge, insight, and moral discernment and behavior. The literature of the ancient Near East, including the wisdom texts of ancient Israel and early Judaism, supports this view: the sages were a social group with identifiable features that point to its character and activity.

Sage (ḥākām)

The frequent occurrences of the term "sage" (or "wise person") in wisdom literature and elsewhere in the Hebrew Bible offer important evidence for regarding the wise as a social group, professional in nature, and their duties and behavior. It points to the sages as a professional social group functioning in the royal court, the temple, the office of the governors during the colonial period, and eventually the house of study often attached to the synagogue. From the introduction in Prov. 1:2-7 one discovers that two groups are addressed: the simple (young and uneducated) and the sage (one who already has gained wisdom and seeks to develop personal knowledge and skills). The sage and the youth in pursuit of wisdom are those guided by the teachings of the wise who seek to pursue and develop knowledge and skills for the effective performance of their professional duties and their variety of social roles, including those of the family and its activities.

Among the three important social groups who composed the traditions that shaped the Hebrew Bible were prophets, priests, and sages. The sages constituted a social group (Jer. 8:8; 18:18; Prov. 1:5; 22:17; 24:23; Job 15:18) serving in the administrations of the court and temple and educated in their respective schools.[21] It is wrongheaded simply to regard them as a group of aristocratic intelligentsia who discussed moral and theological issues at leisure.[22] Rather, they operated as scribes and sages in these administrations,[23] as advisors to rulers,[24] and as teachers in wisdom schools that primarily prepared young men for scribal and official positions in the government (royal or colonial) and temple.[25] Their numbers increased during the Second Temple due to the expansion of literacy, the colonial status of Judah within a succession of empires, the need to shape Jewish society based on the Torah, and the writing down and archiving of important literature.[26] By the Hellenistic period sayings and texts were called in Greek-speaking

21. First Temple sages, who were supporters of the monarchy, were criticized by the prophets. See William McKane, *Prophets and Wise Men* (SBT 1/44; London: SCM, 1965).

22. Cf. R. N. Whybray, *The Intellectual Tradition in the Old Testament* (BZAW 135; Berlin: de Gruyter, 1974). This position is opposed by Heaton, *School Tradition*, 4.

23. Ronald N. Whybray, "The Social World of the Wisdom Writers," in *The World of Ancient Israel,* ed. R. E. Clements (Cambridge: Cambridge University Press, 1989) 227-50; Joseph Blenkinsopp, *Sage, Priest, Prophet: Religious and Intellectual Leadership in Ancient Israel* (Library of Ancient Israel; Louisville: Westminster John Knox, 1995) 28-32; McNutt, *Reconstructing the Society of Ancient Israel,* 167-68; Michael V. Fox, "The Social Location of the Book of Proverbs," in *Texts, Temples, and Traditions: A Tribute to Menahem Haran,* ed. Michael V. Fox, et al. (Winona Lake, IN: Eisenbrauns, 1996) 227-39. For sages in David's and Solomon's cabinets, see 2 Sam. 8:15-18; 20:23-26; 1 Kgs. 4:2-6. See T. N. D. Mettinger, *Solomonic State Officials: A Study of the Civil Government Officials of the Israelite Monarchy* (ConBOT 5; Lund: Gleerup, 1971); E. W. Heaton, *Solomon's New Men: The Emergence of Ancient Israel as a Nation State* (New York: Pica, 1974); Ahlström, *Royal Administration.*

24. P. A. H. de Boer, "The Counselor," in *Wisdom in Israel and in the Ancient Near East,* ed. Noth and Winton Thomas, 42-71.

25. For the views and roles of women in sapiential discourse, see Athalya Brenner, "On Female Figurations in Biblical Wisdom Literature," in *Of Prophets' Visions and the Wisdom of Sages: Essays in Honour of R. Norman Whybray on His Seventieth Birthday,* ed. Heather A. McKay and David J. A. Clines (JSOTSup 162; Sheffield: JSOT Press, 1993) 192-208; Carol Newsom, "Woman and the Discourse of Patriarchal Wisdom: A Study of Proverbs 1–9," in *Gender and Difference in Ancient Israel,* ed. Peggy L. Day (Minneapolis: Fortress, 1989) 142-60.

26. The compilers of these law codes would have been scribes who were closely related to

circles the "sayings of the sages" *(logoi sophōn),* and it seems clear that the earlier sages who were teachers later became the rabbis of early Judaism and the teachers in early Christianity.[27] The mantic sages, who represented another social group of wise men and women, morphed into apocalyptic seers.

The sages developed a tradition that contains the components of their worldviews, understandings of God and religion, insights into human nature, comprehension of society and social institutions, and formative values. This common tradition that developed over the centuries gave shape to their self-understanding, virtuous behavior, and social roles pursued in a variety of communal spheres. This tradition was not only taught in a variety of different school settings by means of a curriculum *(mûsār),* but also by study and reflection pursued by accomplished scribes and sages. Through the enactment of these teachings, the sages learned to exist in harmony with the cosmos and society and to accomplish their goals of living a life in consonance with the righteous order of reality. Indeed, on a social level, their virtuous behavior that enacted wise instructions augmented the well-being of their social community and its larger relationship to the cosmos.

Grounding their worldview in a theological understanding of creation and providence, the sages viewed "righteousness" as the cohesive power permeating reality since creation and integrating its features into a congruous whole. Divine righteousness became the responsibility of the kings and their royal retinue for ruling society to integrate into human corporate life. Even after the demise of the monarchy, the sages were active in both the colonial governor's and the temple's administration in order to structure wisely just social institutions that were embodied in both instruction and civil and religious law codes. This understanding of reality is embedded in one of the key terms for the wise: they are the "righteous" *(ṣaddîq),* who follow the teachings of justice conveyed by the wisdom tradition and who behave and speak in ways that establish justice in the social world in which they live (Prov. 12:18).[28] Through the incorporation of this divine order into their teachings that continued in the wisdom tradition, the sages by their instruction and living transmitted the means by which righteousness would be observed, transmitted, and actualized.

---

sages. See Blenkinsopp, *Sage, Priest, Prophet,* 39; Moshe Weinfeld, *Deuteronomy and the Deuteronomic School* (Oxford: Clarendon, 1972).

27. James M. Robinson, "Jesus as Sophos and Sophia," in *Aspects of Wisdom in Judaism and Early Christianity,* ed. Robert L. Wilken (University of Notre Dame Center for the Study of Judaism and Christianity in Antiquity 1; Notre Dame: University of Notre Dame Press, 1975) 1-16.

28. See Leo G. Perdue, "Cosmology and the Social Order in the Wisdom Tradition," in *Sage in Israel,* 457-78, on "righteousness" *(ṣĕdāqâ),* "righteous/orderly" *(ṣedeq),* and the "righteous/orderly" *(ṣaddîq).*

In the larger social world of the kingdom and the colonial periods, the sages were members of the royal cabinet, counselors, scribes, rhetors, judges in the judicial systems of court and temple, and lower-ranked accountants, lawyers, and scribes who served in a multiplicity of business, legal, and civil activities. At the same time, the sages were also members of households with familial responsibilities that included the teaching of social values and traditions, obligations to parents, faithfulness in marriage, the attributes of a good parent and spouse, and performing the duties of the household, including its agricultural and commercial interests. Thus the teachings of Proverbs often refer to behavior and values relating to these areas.

These virtues, gleaned from Proverbs, make up the professional ethic of scribes and sages who were among the elite or at least served those who were in the political and social upper echelons of power and wealth in ancient Israel and Judah (Prov. 19:14; 31:10-31). This is seen in their value of prosperity and sociopolitical dominion properly and justly used and in their virtues of charity and legal support of the poor (14:31; 17:5; 30:9; 31:20). This set of moral values was not intended for commoners, although, through the democratization of wisdom in the Second Temple, many of these moral teachings were transferred to lay instruction by scribes and sages who were the forerunners of the rabbis. Of course, as the sages and scribes adapted their teachings to changing situations, their ethic was altered. Thus, for example, Ben Sira adds especially the emphasis on Torah piety, while Job and Qoheleth dismissed the teaching concerning retribution as the reward for righteous behavior. Proverbs and, later, Ben Sira take the form of a manual designed to guide young men and women in behavior that will enable them to know and incorporate the values and other teachings of the ancestral sages and to avoid foolish actions and language that lead to failure and even destruction.

Social Roles in the Household

The social locations for proverbial teachings, moral in content, are the extended household and the administration of court and temple. At times, these two intermingle, since household terminology is sometimes used to point to the setting of the school in which youth were educated for wise behavior and speech in both the family and the administrations of these two major institutions.

The "father" (*'ab*) is the paterfamilias of the household and assumes the responsibility for its important decisions concerning duties and responsibilities associated with different gender and familial roles. As a wise man, the father disciplines his son and requires from him obedience (Prov. 23:22). He instructs the son in the social and religious traditions of the clan and teaches him his responsibilities as a son and then as future husband and head of the household. From the familial titles given to teachers and sons in the wisdom traditions of the ancient Near East, however, it is clear that one may correctly understand these terms refer to teachers and students.[29] At times fathers who were educated, and especially those who were sages and scribes, did teach their sons to take up their social and professional roles when old age and death required it.[30]

Since there were women sages in ancient Israel (2 Sam. 14:1-24; 20:14-22), it is possible that they also were teachers of youth in the wisdom schools. We should not forget that the primary teacher in Proverbs in Woman Wisdom. However, of the fourteen times that "mother" occurs in Proverbs, most appear unquestionably to refer to biological mothers. With two exceptions, the "mother" *('ēm)* is a subject of the sayings, not the one who utters them. In the households, however, mothers would have taught their daughters the various duties and skills in performing their tasks as women, including their social roles and duties as wives and mothers. Mothers also likely taught young boys until the father assumed this responsibility as puberty approached. Proverbs 1:8 and 6:20 include mothers as the teachers of the "son," who is told not to reject his "mother's teaching" *(tōrat 'ēm)*. On occasion, however, women did hold powerful positions, including that of the "queen mother" *(gĕbûrâ)*. In 31:1-2 the mother (queen mother?)[31] of Lemuel instructs her son in the social responsibilities associated with rule,[32] while the "woman of virtue" in 31:10-31 is one who operates a large estate and teaches wisdom. Among her duties is serving as teacher, presumably of women and children who make up her family, workers, and slaves of her household. Like Woman Wisdom in Prov. 8:32-36, she "opens her mouth with teaching, and offers the instruction of kindness with her tongue" (31:26).[33]

---

29. "Big brother" is found in Sumerian wisdom texts (see the "School Dialogues," *COS* 1:588-93). Among others, consult Helmer Ringgren, *Sprüche* (2nd ed.; ATD 16; Göttingen: Vandenhoeck & Ruprecht, 1981) 25; Berend Gemser, *Sprüche Salomos* (2nd ed.; HAT 16; Tübingen: Mohr [Siebeck], 1963) 33.

30. See Kenneth A. Kitchen, "The Basic Literary Forms and Formulations of Ancient Instructional Writings in Egypt and Western Asia," in *Studien zu altägyptischen Lebenslehren*, 235-82.

31. See Herbert Donner, "Art und Herkunft des Amtes der Königsmutter im AT," *FS Johannes Friedrich zum 65. Geburtstag am 27. August gewidmet*, ed. R. von Kienle et al. (Heidelberg: Carl Winter, 1959), 105-45.

32. Claudia Camp, "The Female Sage in Ancient Israel and in the Biblical Wisdom Literature," in *Sage in Israel*, 185-203.

33. Christine Roy Yoder, *Wisdom as a Woman of Substance: A Socioeconomic Reading of Proverbs 1–9 and 31:10-31* (BZAW 304; Berlin: de Gruyter, 2001).

Sages and Scribes in the Royal, Temple, and
Gubernatorial Administrations and Schools

Most scribes and sages were more than simply intelligent people in social circles; rather they were professional officials, administrators, counselors, and teachers in the principal sociopolitical institutions of ancient Israel and early Judaism. These roles ranged from minor scribes, for example, archivists and copyists, to powerful sages who were preeminent officials in the cabinet of the monarch or in overseeing and administering the temple and its ledger of gifts, maintenance, and personnel (see the roles attributed to Shaphan in 2 Kgs. 22).

Several sages served in the royal cabinet of the king (2 Sam. 8:15-18; 20:23-26; 1 Kgs. 4:1-6; cf. Prov. 11:14 = 24:6; 12:20; 15:22). The "counselor" (*yôʿēs*) was an important officer responsible for advice that was to assure success to its recipient.[34] Among those seeking counsel and advice from sages were kings, princes, and a variety of people (see the counselors of Job) in different situations (Prov. 11:14; 12:20; 15:22; 24:6). The two best known counselors are Ahithophel and Hushai ("David's friend," *rēʿeh hammelek*, also a title for a prominent royal advisor) in the Succession Narrative (2 Sam. 15:12, 31, 34, 37; 16:15–17:23). The person in charge of administering the palace was the one "over the house" (*ʿal-habbāyit*, Gen. 41:40; 1 Kgs. 4:6). Finally the "recorder" (*mazkîr*) was apparently the cabinet official responsible for the accuracy and preservation of the minutes, annals, transcripts, archives, and all official records of the kingdom (2 Sam. 8:16; 20:24; 1 Kgs. 4:3).

A lower-placed royal official was the *měšārēt*, mentioned in Prov. 29:12. There were likely a substantial number of royal ministers who oversaw a wide variety of departments in the administration (Esth. 1:10; 1 Chron. 27:1; 28:1; 2 Chron. 17:19; 22:8). These "sages" would have included leaders in the military, administrative chiefs of royal districts, the royal treasurer, stewards of the king, and principals who directed schools.

The wise also served in the roles of officers (*śar*, Prov. 8:16; 19:10) who carried out administrative tasks assigned them by the king and cabinet officials in the administrative hierarchy and were thus responsible for assisting them in governing the kingdom (Gen. 12:15; Isa. 30:4; 1 Kgs. 4:2; 2 Kgs. 24:12, 14; Jer. 34:21; 1 Chron. 22:17; 2 Chron. 36:18). They also held the position of magistrate of a city or royal province (1 Kgs. 20:14-19; 2 Kgs. 10:1; 2 Chron. 29:20). Some were military commanders (Gen. 21:22, 32; 26:26; 1 Sam. 12:9; 2 Sam. 24:2; 1 Kgs. 1:25; 2:5; 15:20; 2 Kgs. 25:23, 26; 1 Chron. 12:22[21]; 27:3).

The content of wisdom literature indicates that the common role of sages

---

34. De Boer, "Counselor."

was that of "teacher" (môreh),[35] as the forms and content of Proverbs demonstrate. The verb yārâ means "to teach, instruct" someone in an area of knowledge (Prov. 4:4, 11; 5:13),[36] while the participial noun indicates one who "instructs or teaches with his fingers" (6:13; see 5:13; Job 6:24; 8:8, 10; 12:7-25; 27:11; 36:22). The substantive participle môreh ("one who teaches") is found in the plural in Prov. 5:13 and once in the singular in Job 36:22 to refer to Yahweh as the divine teacher. In the Second Temple period, wisdom is called the law and identified eventually with the Torah (lit. "teaching"; see Ps. 119:26, 64, 66, 108, 124, 135, 171). In Ps. 119, a wisdom psalm, Yahweh is the one who teaches, through the Torah, the one uttering the prayer of lament (cf. Pss. 25:4-5; 34:12[11]).

Another term for teacher is mĕlammēd. In the Qal lāmad means "to learn," while the Piel signifies "to teach" knowledge or skills to another or to a group. In Prov. 5:13 the term occurs in parallel to "teacher": "I did not listen to the voice of my teachers (môrāy, plural of môreh) or incline my ear to my instructors (mĕlammĕdî)" (cf. Qoh. 12:9; Job 21:22). In Ps. 119:99 the one who utters this sapiential lament to Yahweh also claims to have more understanding than all of his "teachers."

Sayings that reflect the knowledge and practice of some Israelite laws that regulated criminal and civil actions and behavior are present in the wisdom texts, including Proverbs (see the landmarks or "boundary stones" that are not to be moved, Deut. 19:14; 27:17; Job 24:2; Prov. 22:28; 23:10). Further, Deut. 4:5-8 and Jer. 8:8 remark that the sages were judges in charge of jurisprudence and the law (cf. Prov. 19:28-29), while the king in particular is to establish justice by extending it to the poor in his judgments (Prov. 31:9; cf. 16:10; 24:23; 29:14). It is also apparent that the sages were quite familiar with the filing of a legal suit or complaint (rîb, Prov. 25:9) to be adjudicated in the courtroom (Job 31; cf. Prov. 18:17). Legal matters were often handled by the complainant and the accused themselves (Prov. 25:7b-10). However, this assumes a knowledge of civil law that few outside those educated in the schools would have possessed. "Justice" (mišpāṭ) is understood as law or legal judgment in various texts in Proverbs (8:20; 17:23; 19:28; 28:4-5; also see Job 9:19; 13:16-19; 23:2-7; 31:13). In addition, Job is apparently well familiar with the legal process of the courtroom in presenting his case, demanding an indictment from his adversary (i.e., Yahweh), and requiring his day in court with his accuser (Job 31). The wisdom texts do make use of terms that refer to attorneys in the legal sphere: the adversary/prosecutor, śāṭān (Job 1–2; cf. Ps. 109 and Zech. 3:1), and the defense attorney, môkîaḥ (Job 9:33), or one who seeks to substantiate charges, yākaḥ, against another (e.g.,

---

35. Wanke, "Lehrer im alten Israel," 51-59.
36. S. Wagner, TDOT, 6:339-47.

Prov. 24:23-26). Finally, the references to witnesses and bearing witness, *'ēd* (Job 16:19; Prov. 6:19; 12:17; 14:5, 25; 19:5, 9, 28; 21:28; 24:28; 25:8), also indicate sapiential knowledge of and perhaps participation in legal proceedings. The emphasis was placed on condemning false testimony and lying witnesses. Finally, some sages also functioned as judges, or at least wisdom was a characteristic of a just and impartial judge *(šōpēṭ)*, while others were lawyers. It would seem, then, that the sages in the wisdom schools educated youth in the law and that some of them would become judges and lawyers.

It should be noted that "scribe" *(sōpēr)* and its related verb, "to write" *(sāpar)* are absent from Proverbs. The only literary activity is that of the "editing" *(he'tîqû)* of collections by the "men of Hezekiah" in 25:1. However, it is interesting to note that the cultivation of the skill of public speaking was mentioned often, pointing to the sages as rhetors who gave speeches in a variety of contexts.

While there is not a term for "rhetor" in Biblical Hebrew, the occurrence of *dābar* in the Qal (Prov. 18:13; 24:2; 25:11; 29:12) and in the Piel participle (2:12; 21:19), coupled with the numerous contrasts between proper and upright speech and foolish and lying talk, indicates that the sages were especially concerned with oral rhetoric (e.g., 10:11, 13, 18-21, 31, 32; 12:6; 25:11). Collections like Proverbs would have taught proper speech, sapiential genres, consummate oration, rhetorical enhancements like assonance, alliteration, parallelism, metaphor, and simile, knowledge of the times to speak and to keep silent, restraint in speaking (10:19), and persuasion (16:13).

Major Theological Themes

The themes of wisdom prominently displayed in the collections and poems of the book of Proverbs include several that form the conceptual and religious foundation of the ongoing worldview of the sages, while others become the subject of critical disputation. At the same time, these salient topics experienced change and reformulation in view of two factors. First, there were competing groups of sages with different emphases; second, the conceptual understandings changed in response to social and historical transformations and alterations occurring in Israel's and Judah's world.

There is no convincing argument that the collections of Proverbs, or even individual sayings, may be divided into secular/humanistic ones that contrast with pious/religious ones. This view ignores the larger contexts of the collections and the book, the fact that piety ("the fear of God/Yahweh") is the basis for wisdom, and the historical setting of ancient Israel in the context of the ancient Near East. Efforts to reshape the collections according to preconceived, modern notions of profane and religious that may be traced to the Enlightenment distort the book. Even Agur, the skeptic, does not deny the existence of God, but rather levels his criticism against the traditional sages' epistemology, that is, both its content and the means of acquiring knowledge. The theological foundation for wisdom thinking is the creation of the world and divine providence. Kingship, administration, the process of law, and the scribal profession became the instruments of the establishment and maintenance of order or justice throughout society. The theme of religious piety is found in each of the collections of the book.

Efforts made by Claus Westermann and several of his students to bifurcate the two creation traditions into older (anthropological) and later (cosmological) ones ignore numerous examples of the two occurring together in the same context in extrasapiential literature as well as in the wisdom texts themselves.[37] I find their arguments unsupportable, for they are based on the debatable assumption that wisdom moves from an anthropological orientation to a cosmological and theological formulation. Westermann's thesis, if true, would require the separation of these two traditions in dozens of texts, a necessity I find highly questionable. Furthermore, while the differences in divine names may have some theological purpose in other texts, this is not evident in the book of Proverbs. There does not appear to be any noticeable distinction between the divine names Elohim and Yahweh. The two appear to be interchangeable. Thus theological or editorial efforts inspired by this distinction lead one in directions that reach no substantiated destination.

The God(s) of the Sages

Until the rise of the Deuteronomic school in the eighth century, polytheism appears to have been practiced in some circles of Israel and Judah. Even though this largely priestly party and its later rival, the Zadokites, appear to have largely continued the emphasis on the worship of one deity, Yahweh, material culture demonstrates that the worship of numerous gods continued. The references to goddess Wisdom, Hokmah, in Prov. 1:20-33 and chs. 8–9 would best be explained as originally indicating that at least the sages worshiped her as the con-

---

37. Claus Westermann, *Elements of Old Testament Theology* (Atlanta: John Knox Press, 1978); *Creation* (Philadelphia: Fortress, 1974); Rainer Albertz, *Weltschöpfung und Menschenschöpfung* (Calwer Monographien. Reihe A: Bibelwissenschaft 3; Stuttgart: Calwer, 1974); and Peter Doll, *Menschenschöpfung und Weltschöpfung in der alttestamentlichen Weisheit* (Stuttgarter Bibelstudien 117; Stuttgart: Verlag Katholisches Bibelwerk, 1985).

sort of Yahweh. The transformation to the idea of her being viewed as a literary personification (consort, offspring) of a characteristic of Yahweh, and possibly even a hypostatization in which a divine trait takes on a type of existence apart from the deity, would perhaps have occurred in the Second Temple period (e.g., Sir. 24). At least in her early formulation during the First Temple period, however, wisdom is conceived in the images of a goddess much in the fashion of the Egyptian deities of wisdom, Sheshat, Ma'at, Isis, and Thoth. This would compare to Yahweh's fertility goddess, Asherah, found as small figurines in First Temple houses, mentioned as a goddess in Kuntillet Ajrud, and symbolized by one of the two *maṣṣēbôt* in the tenth-century *děbîr* of Arad. In Prov. 8–9 Woman Wisdom is the offspring of Yahweh who gave issue to her in procreation and also bore her as his daughter. She became the instrument of divine creation (3:19-20). She was the first of his creation, and she built her shrine, which, like Baal, she dedicated with a great festival (9:1-6). At the same time, she is, like Yahweh, the teacher par excellence whose instruction gives life and prosperity to her disciples. She has life in one hand and wealth and honor in the other, much like divine Ma'at, and she offers these gifts freely to the ones who desire her (3:16-18). She is also compared to the mythological tree of life in 3:18.

In Judahite religion God is the giver of wisdom in the divine council (Job 15:7-8) or the one who speaks the "secrets of wisdom" (Job 11:5-6). Wisdom is the gift of God to persons enabling them to become wise (Prov. 2:6-15; Job 4:12-21; Sir. 1:1; Wis. 7:7; cf. Isa. 11:2, where the spirit of wisdom granted to the future ruler comes from the spirit of Yahweh), while the organs of wisdom (hearing and seeing) are made by Yahweh (Prov. 20:12). Yahweh creates wisdom as the "first" and perhaps "best" of the divine works (Prov. 8:22; Sir. 24:3, 9).

Divine Creation and Providence

The sages in Proverbs used their imagination to give rise to a variety of metaphors to portray the cosmos as the creation of a God who established and now oversees the structures of life. Through their rhetoric, the sages developed metaphors of creation that became the major vehicles for conveying their teachings, while the literary structure of sayings, didactic poems, and instructions shaped an aesthesis of order and beauty that engaged the imagination of the audience to enter and take up residence in the imaginary world they have constructed. God is not specifically named warrior, king, judge, parent, teacher, or architect, but the sages' depiction of divine activity opens up a metaphorical description of reality in which God carries out these roles and functions. The allusion to the chaos myth is found in 3:19-20, where he splits open the deep, while the fertility myths of the origins of the gods are used to speak of God creating the world and giving birth to his daughter, Woman Wisdom (8:22-31). Furthermore, he is also the architect who constructs the cosmos like a builder laying a foundation (3:19). The cosmos is an object of art, a city, a kingdom, and even a household in which Yahweh, Wisdom, and humans dwell in harmony and joy (8:1-11; 9:1-6) under the management and oversight of God.

As the creator and sustainer of humanity, God is the divine judge who often renders his verdicts in rescuing the poor, blessing the righteous, and punishing the wicked (17:5; 22:22-23). Further, he provides both the poor and the oppressor light (a metaphor for both insight and life), and he is the creator of organs of understanding that allow humans to know the world and to grasp wisdom to understand it (20:13[12]). His role as king is implied in the metaphor of his daughter, Wisdom, who rules over the earth (ch. 8). As father he is the progenitor of his daughter, Wisdom, and as mother he gives her birth (8:22-25).

Creation and Anthropology

In their imagination, the sages categorized humans in a dualistic structure of wise/righteous and foolish/wicked. Traits of both are observed, delineated, and incorporated in the sapiential traditions. It is through the divine gift of wisdom, enhanced by study, reflection, and action, that humans learn to actualize justice in social life. God has given humans the organs of perception that enable them to gain understanding and knowledge and to become wise. And God is the one who requires justice for the poor and oppressed. Further, all people, both rich and poor, have the same origins — all are human creatures of God who deserve both respect and sustenance. According to the instructions of the sages, the poor enjoy the special protection of God. He will rise up in judgment against their oppressors and bring to destitution the wealthy who ignore their pleas. Finally, humans who respond to her invitation are Wisdom's students, lovers, and children who may receive the blessings she offers. Through obedience to wisdom, humans shape their character and make incarnate the wisdom tradition. And through their actions and speech, they shape a reality of history and language that undergirds and actualizes cosmic justice.

Creation and Goddess Wisdom

Permeated by justice, the cosmos is a world of both beauty and life. Wisdom is the first of God's creation who rejoices over the wonders of the inhabited world and its human inhabitants. Woman Wisdom, depicted in images of an ancient Near Eastern fertility goddess (e.g., Isis), is incarnate in the instruction of the wisdom tradition, assumes the role of the teacher of humanity, and offers her moral instruction to those who would accept her invitation to learn from her. She is the incarnate voice of God who provides insight into both the creator and the reality he has made and rules. Woman Wisdom is also the Queen of Heaven who dispenses wisdom and life to her devotees and chooses kings to rule in justice. The king is selected by Woman Wisdom to rule over the nation. Through the righteous rule of the divinely chosen king, justice that permeates the cosmos is actualized in the kingdom and its population that results in social order, harmony, and well-being. The wise, including especially kings, are the lovers of Woman Wisdom, who, in their passion for knowledge, gain the insight to life filled with goodness and blessing. Finally, while creation and the voice of Wisdom tell of the divine nature of God, he continues to remain largely hidden from human insight.

The figure of Woman Wisdom is especially important in understanding the sages. Woman Wisdom in 1:20-33 is portrayed as a teacher in the guise of a sage who issues her paraenetic exhortation to come and learn from her. The warning of avoiding her life-giving teaching is enfolded in the indictment that those who reject her instruction are doomed for destruction. While there are elements of the prophetic diatribe in this poem, Wisdom is a teacher, not a prophet. This same role of teacher recurs in 8:1-3 and 9:7-12, where she once again offers instructions to her followers. Most importantly, this teacher takes on the attribution of divinity in the offering of life to the wise and the warning of destruction to the fool. In a way she is the embodiment of the sapiential tradition, personified in a teacher's guise. But she is more than that. She is the goddess wisdom, Hokmah, worshiped by the sages even as Ma'at, Isis, Thoth, and Seshat were in Egypt. The worship of goddesses in Israel, especially Asherah, likely continued undisturbed through much of the monarchic period, until the reform of Josiah, especially if one views Hezekiah's "religious reform" as the creation of a Deuteronomistic, revisionist history.

In 8:4-11 and especially in vv. 12-21 and 22-31, Wisdom is no longer merely a teacher, but now is boldly portrayed as a goddess engaged in self-praise. The sophisticated argument that this is a personification, say in the manner of Jerusalem as a prostitute crying out for Yahweh's deliverance, is possible. But it is also possible that the sages viewed Woman Wisdom as the goddess they adored and followed in coming to a knowledge of Yahweh as the high god. There is no clear evidence for monotheism prior to the writing of Jeremiah and the formulation of the proto-Deuteronomic tradition that may have provided the basis for a religious reform. Monotheism was strongly advocated by Second Isaiah in the sixth century B.C.E. Following the return, official religion in Judah was mono-theistic, although other cults and their deities continued to thrive. Wisdom was the protective goddess of the sages, and the one who provided them with the scribal arts and the varieties of knowledge necessary for civilization, at least un-til the period of Josiah when she becomes personified as an attribute of God. As the goddess involved in or at least present at creation, she is the revealer of the mysterious creator who is largely concealed from human knowledge, and the friend of humanity who intercedes on their behalf to Yahweh.

In 9:1-6, now in a third person eulogy, she is portrayed as a goddess who has built her temple, slaughtered (sacrificed) the beasts for a great festival, and extends in a second person admonition the invitation to the wise to come and participate in her banquet of life, to worship her, and to follow her instruction. This is contrasted with "Woman Folly," the name given by the sages to Asherah, the goddess of fertility in Canaanite religion, who offers a similar but deceptive invitation. In the worship of her, there is not the gaining of life, as she prom-ised, but rather the fate of death. Thus two goddesses contend for the "heart/ mind" (lēb) of humanity: one is Hokmah, who bestows life upon those who worship and obey her teachings; and the other is Goddess Folly, a symbolic name for Asherah, who seduces her followers with the smooth words and hon-eyed lips of the harlot and leads them not to life but to death. This conflict be-tween the two religions was a long and contested struggle throughout the cen-turies and continued, even after the emergence of monotheism, in the expressions of popular piety.

It is only with the development of an exclusive monotheism that the figure of Wisdom becomes transformed into a metaphor representing a divine attrib-ute and ultimately, in a step back toward a divine status not fully obtained, a di-vine hypostasis giving embodiment to God's chief characteristics (Wis. 7–9). The reluctance to attribute to wisdom a divine status and instead to relegate her to the role of a personification of a divine characteristic may be based in part on the concern to project Israelite religion as distinctive and thus superior to the "paganism" of its neighbors. But with the personification and even hypostatization of wisdom, Judaism and some forms of later Christianity lost something very significant in order to preserve monotheism. Their patriarchal representation of God led to the denial of the feminine, at least among those men who were at the head of religious institutions. Males denied women a sub-stantial role in religion and society that transcended subservience. The male God led to a cheapening and a diminishment of the understanding of deity and of the role and dignity of women.

Wisdom and Mythic Metaphors

Throughout the history of the development of the collections of the book of Proverbs, from the monarchy until the Hellenistic period in the late Second Temple, the sages in Proverbs, including teachers, composers, and redactors, made substantial use of metaphors in their teachings about the two related creation traditions often presented together in the Hebrew Bible: cosmology and anthropology. They speak of the world as the creation of God brought into existence by his offspring, Wisdom, and her rule over the earth in maintaining cosmic order. And they indicate that providence continues to sustain the cosmic and social order through obedience of the sages to the wisdom tradition, which includes in particular accepting the social responsibility of the poor; social classes were believed to reflect the order of the cosmos and to result from divine initiative. This language of creation makes frequent use of metaphors that the sages appropriate from the mythic traditions of the ancient Near East, in particular the creation mythology of ancient Egypt: Wisdom is the child of the divine parent who rejoices over the inhabited world and its human population (3:13-18, 19-20; 8:22-31); Yahweh engages in a primordial struggle with chaos that continues; Wisdom is the tree of life; and Yahweh is the creator who makes both rich and poor and requires the wealthy to respect and support those in poverty. He is the one who shapes creation to bring destruction to the wicked and bestows upon humans the gifts of the organs of perception that allow them to make their way in the world. In the conservative tradition of these sages, the cosmic and social orders are intrinsically connected. In this theological construction, creation mythology and its mythic images, many of which hailed from ancient Egypt, were used by those sages who were quite familiar with this literature and the culture that produced it.

Conclusion: The Book of Proverbs and Its Sages among the Empires

In conclusion, Israel's and Judah's sages played a significant role in the administrations of the court, colonial government, and temple. This is obvious from the scribes and sages mentioned in the narratives, particularly the Deuteronomistic History. The sages saw themselves as servants to the king and his representatives, and some of them even achieved high office. Lesser scribes served various roles in the administrations, ranging from correspondence, to archiving, to taxation, to diplomacy. To achieve these positions, children of the elite attended wisdom schools that prepared them to acquire the knowledge produced by the culture, to interact with texts and persons from other cultures, and to carry on important social roles. Buttressing these social roles was the shaping of a theology in which the institution they served (i.e., the monarchy and later the colony and the temple) was viewed as the instrument through which social order was effectuated. The theology of creation, in which a divine order regulated both nature and society under the watchful eye of the creator acting through the principle of creation, was socially and politically conservative. God (or Wisdom) chooses kings, rules nations, and determines the events that affect their existence. By integrating themselves into the harmony of cosmic and social order, the sages were destined to achieve well-being and success, measured in terms of honor and respect, accumulation of resources, the familial household, and longevity. Their embodiment of sapientially prized virtues assisted in maintaining the stability of the social order based on the rule of a wise king, both indigenous and foreign, who ruled according to the dictates of justice. The sages of Proverbs had little place for radicals who demanded a more just society (e.g., the classical prophets). Of course, Agur, not incidentally an Arabian rather than an Israelite or Judahite, did lampoon the obvious limits of knowledge that constrained the epistemology of the sages. Nevertheless, his skeptical questions in Prov. 30:1-4 became a foil for the traditional sages to repudiate.

The sages derived their understandings of God, reality, and human existence from four sources: imagination, natural reason and the power of astute observation, the gift of divine wisdom that provided the ability to reason and to know, and the sapiential tradition they inherited from their wise ancestors that continued to be tested in the arena of human experience. This contrasts to prophetic revelation, which occurs in the state of ecstasy, and to priestly revelation, which occurs through the casting of Urim and Thummim (Num. 27:21). Thus the sages did not make their teachings absolute truths that were unresponsive to the times, circumstances, and human experience. They were aware that their knowledge had limits, leading to contingencies that obscured the certainty of their understanding and prescribed behavior.

It is also important to note that the sages of Israel and Judah did not limit wisdom to themselves, but rather admitted its existence outside Israel. In addition, the God of the sages in Israel is a universal deity, even when named Yahweh, not a tribal one. Israelite sages may be compared to the wise of ancient Egypt who were devoted to the "god." This deity of wisdom, both in Egypt and in Israel/Judah, is a universal being, a deity of creation and all peoples, and not an ethnic deity of a particular people interested in or limited to the guiding of their national destinies.[38]

---

38. Roland Murphy argues that even the First Temple sages of Israel affirmed the tenets of Israelite faith and religion ("Wisdom and Yahwism," in *No Famine in the Land: Studies in Honor of*

The concept of "justice" (*ṣĕdāqâ* and its synonym *mišpāṭ*) is fundamental to wisdom in Israel and ancient Egypt *(maʿat)*. It has a cosmological meaning in the sense of being the just order of the world that organizes and structures the cosmos and continues through the power of the creator to sustain its vitalization of life that enables the creation and its creatures to continue. At the same time, the state is based on cosmic order, especially symbolized in the image of the king's throne secured upon justice. "Justice" is also present in the ordering of sapiential teaching that may be embodied by its hearers in order to give them direction to life. The Egyptian sages deified justice *(maʿat)* to be a goddess, and made her the daughter of Re. Whether portrayed mythically or articulated more as a divine characteristic, Maʿat was an important virtue of the pharaoh, who was also the incarnation of Horus while ruling Egypt and then Osiris when becoming at death the ruler of the underworld. He was the offspring of Maʿat and the worshiper of Isis, who became a popular goddess of knowledge and life in Egypt. Further, *maʿat* as justice was also incorporated into law and the legal process designed to protect the well-being of both rich and poor.

In Proverbs the sages taught that the creator oversees a system of reward and punishment for human behavior, an ethical position that emerges from the aristocracy in order to justify wealth, status, and power.[39] The theory of retribution does not dismiss the freedom of God, nor does it eliminate the teaching of divine forgiveness and mercy. Retribution, in a juridical sense, appears to be assumed in the collections and sayings of Proverbs, except for Agur in 30:1-4. Morality is especially at issue in human relationships, whether in showing charity to the poor (a duty of the well-to-do), or in knowing when to speak and what to say. It has to do with avoiding vices that include many things, ranging from imbibing too much strong drink, to hubris, and even to laziness. Virtues particularly emphasized are proper speech, dispassionate yet cogent articulation of

---

John L. McKenzie, ed. James W. Flanagan and Anita Weisbrod Robinson [Missoula, MT: Scholars Press, 1975] 117-26). James Crenshaw, by contrast, points to significant differences ("Murphy's Axiom: Every Gnomic Saying Needs a Balancing Corrective," in *Urgent Advice and Probing Questions: Collected Writings on Old Testament Wisdom* [Macon, GA: Mercer University Press, 1995] 344-54). It is not clear that the sages who compiled the wisdom literature were traditional believers of the major traditions of the faith of Israel in the categories of salvation history until Ben Sira, who combined wisdom and the tenets of Second Temple Judaism. However, beginning with the earliest texts we have, the sages did avow faith in God as creator and sustainer (cf. Leo G. Perdue, *Wisdom and Creation: The Theology of Wisdom Literature* [Nashville: Abingdon, 1994]).

39. Retributive justice is hotly contested in later wisdom texts. See J. Clinton McCann, "Wisdom's Dilemma: The Book of Job, the Final Form of the Book of Psalms, and the Entire Bible," in *Wisdom, You Are My Sister,* ed. Michael L. Barré (CBQMS 20; Washington, DC: Catholic Biblical Association of America, 1997) 19-30.

views, avoiding the temptations of sexual appetites seeking satisfaction through improper carnal liaisons with either the adulteress or the married woman, and human industry to sustain life. There are, of course, troublesome exceptions that offer no real explanation. Thus one of the numerical sayings of Prov. 30 (vv. 21-23) describes a world upside-down in which the social order is so distorted that it causes disorder in the cosmos. These disturbances eventually led to the protests of Job and the skepticism of Qoheleth.

On the basis of the content of the book, Proverbs is dominated by sayings and collections that deal primarily with wise behavior and speech, topics especially appropriate for learning morality, proper speech, and etiquette for a professional life. Unlike many of the other biblical books, Proverbs omits any reference to salvation history in its two major complexes: election (exodus and covenant) and David-Zion.[40] Nevertheless, the book's content presents itself as authoritative speech on the basis of several claims: wisdom derives from astute human perception of reality and experience, the tradition based on the insights of learned ancestors, and the understanding that God, as the giver of life and insight, speaks through the teacher and the order of creation.

---

40. See Gerhard von Rad, *Old Testament Theology*, trans. D. M. G. Stalker (2 vols.; New York: Harper & Row, 1962-1965).

3. Wisdom during the Neo-Babylonian Empire: The Book of Job

General Introduction

The book of Job consists of a growing tradition that began, most likely, with the narrative in chs. 1–2 and 42:7-17. The Joban poet then composed the dialogues in chs. 3–31 and 38:1–42:6 as a response to the earlier story. The "Speeches of Elihu" (chs. 32–37) and the poem on Woman Wisdom (ch. 28) were then offered as challenges to the dialogues. The book addresses not simply the problem of evil, but more importantly the issue of the justice of God. This searing theological issue became acute during the years following the Babylonian destruction of Jerusalem, the collapse of Judah and its major social and religious institutions, the ensuing devastation and impoverishment of the land and its inhabitants, and the loss of freedom and homeland by the exiles. The extreme, negative consequences of the Babylonian conquest and exile led many in Judah and in captivity to question the related affirmations of divine justice and the theology of retribution taught in the earlier sapiential tradition as well as in Deuteronomy. Some of the destitute in Judah engaged in lamentation over the destruction of Jerusalem and its temple (see the book of Lamentations), while others wondered how the wicked Babylonians could serve as Yahweh's instrument to punish his people (Habakkuk). Some of the exiles sought solace in the preservation of the traditions of the past (especially the Priestly texts), and still others looked to the future in hope for a coming restoration of the nation in the liberation of the captives and the rebuilding of the nation (Second Isaiah and the eventual emergence of proto-apocalyptic). However, looming ever large was the critical question of divine justice. It is likely that the dialogues were written during this period of intense questioning and theological reflection.

Date and Historical Context

Finding a likely time and place for the composition of the dialogues of the book of Job is difficult, due to the lack of specific references to historical events.[1] Save for a few scholars who read the poetic book as a literary unit, most view it as developing in stages over two centuries, beginning with the Babylonian exile[2] and concluding in the late Persian period 3 (586-350 B.C.E.). The narrative may have served as a didactic tale composed in the First Temple period. The evidence for the exilic date for the poetry includes the parallels with the Babylonian texts previously mentioned; Ezekiel's reference to Job (14:14-20) in the early sixth century B.C.E., shortly before the Babylonian conquest; and the presence of many Aramaisms that may suggest that the book was composed and redacted at the time Aramaic was the lingua franca of the ancient Near East, beginning with the period of the Assyrian Empire in the eighth century B.C.E. Further, records from the Neo-Babylonian period point to the presence of Aramaic scribes at court. We have several other considerations to ponder. "The Satan" in Job 1–2 is an office (*haśāṭān*, lit. "the accuser"; cf. Zech. 3:1-2), not a personal name as it became later in the postexilic period (1 Chron. 21:1). Job 3 is likely dependent on the lament of Jeremiah in 20:14-18 (one of the prophet's confessions composed in the Second Temple period). The dialogues possess a style and vocabulary that are rather similar to those of Second Isaiah.[4] And the crisis of the exile may have instigated the questioning of divine justice in several books, including not only Job but also Habakkuk and the Confessions of Jeremiah.[5] The final redaction would have occurred during the late Persian period, sometime after the addition of the poem in ch. 28 and the speeches of Elihu in chs. 32–37.

1. Rainer Albertz dates the dialogues in the early Persian period, viewing them as a response to both the Babylonian conquest and exile and the challenges of rebuilding the colony of Judah ("The Sage and Pious Wisdom in the Book of Job," in *Sage in Israel*, 231-61).

2. Samuel Terrien, "Job," *IB* 3 (1954) 884-92.

3. Ernst Sellin, *Introduction to the Old Testament*, rev. Georg Fohrer (Nashville: Abingdon, 1968) 330; A. de Wilde, *Das Buch Hiob* (OTS 22; Leiden: Brill, 1981) 52.

4. See esp. Samuel Terrien, "Quelques remarques sur les affinités de Job avec le Deutéro-Esaïe," in *Volume du Congrès: Genève, 1965* (VTSup 15; Leiden: Brill, 1966) 295-310.

5. See esp. Karl-Friedrich Pohlmann, "Religion in der Krise — Krise der Religion. Die Zerstörung des Jerusalemer Tempels 587 v. Chr.," in *Zerstörungen des Jerusalemer Tempels. Geschehen — Wahrnehmung — Bewältigung*, ed. Johannes Hahn (Tübingen: Mohr-Siebeck, 2002) 40-60.

A question related to date is the geographical location of the poetic book. Did it originate in Babylon, Judah, or elsewhere? While we have no specific indication, other than the references to the characters in the prose story, who are apparently identified as Edomites, the issue may turn on parallels to texts more easily dated. Habakkuk also raises the question of divine justice in Yahweh's using the "wicked man" (presumably the Babylonians) to punish his admittedly sinful people, while Lamentations contains a series of city laments and those of its people concerning the destruction of the capital and its temple. These two texts, likely originating in Judah, indicate some literary activity occurring close to the time of the exile, although Habakkuk seems to have appeared as a consequence of the first exile in 597 B.C.E., some years prior to the second, more devastating exile following the sacking of Jerusalem. Lamentations could just as easily come from the community following the return home in the latter years of the sixth century B.C.E., prior to the rebuilding of the city and its temple. More important is the book of Job's close literary and linguistic parallels to Second Isaiah, written in Babylon in the mid-sixth century, when Cyrus was on the road to conquest of an area that would eventually engulf the former Babylonian Empire. This in itself would support, then, an exilic location for the poetic book of Job. In addition, a learned poet like the author of Job may have gained access to or at least heard the recitations of Akkadian texts that formed important parallels to the poetic book.[6]

Nabopolassar (626-605 B.C.E.) founded the Neo-Babylonian Empire (626-539 B.C.E.) that was to dominate Mesopotamia and the Levant for close to a century.[7] The Babylonian victory in 609 at Harran marked the defeat of the armies of the Egyptians and Assyrians, while the death blow to the remnants of the Assyrians, unsuccessfully supported by their Egyptian allies, occurred four years later in the battle at Carchemish in 605. The Egyptian forces and their administrative officials in the northern provinces were forced to evacuate Syria-Israel and withdraw to their own borders. Judah moved from the status of an Egyptian vassal in 609 when Neco II defeated the army of Josiah, the popular king who lost his life in battle, to a colony in the powerful Neo-Babylonian Empire that was soon ruled by Nebuchadnezzar II (604-562 B.C.E.), the son of Nabopolassar and the general responsible for the victories over Assyria and

---

6. See Jean Lévêque, *Job et son Dieu: Essai d'exégèse et de théologie biblique* (2 vols.; Paris: Gabalda, 1970). He reviews similar Akkadian, Ugaritic, and Egyptian texts in the first three chapters, 1:13-80.

7. See Hans-Peter Müller, ed., *Babylonien und Israel: Historische, religiöse und sprachliche Beziehungen* (Darmstadt: Wissenschaftliche Buchgesellschaft, 1991); Rainer Albertz, *Israel in Exile: The History and Literature of the Sixth Century B.C.E.*, trans. David Green (SBLStBL 3; Atlanta: Society of Biblical Literature, 2003).

Egypt. By 601 all of Syria-Israel came under the control of Babylonia. The new king in 601 even attempted to take Egypt, but was rebuffed by the forces of Neco II. In a few years the small vassal nations in Syria-Palestine, encouraged by the Egyptians and their beating back the forces of Nebuchadnezzar in 601, plotted and attempted to carry out a revolution. Jehoiakim, king of Judah (609-598 B.C.E.), joined the other rebels and withheld tribute in 601. The rebels were defeated, and Nebuchadnezzar invaded Judah and captured Jerusalem. He took Jehoiachin, the son of Jehoiakim, who apparently had been assassinated shortly before the surrender of the city in 597, and forced many leaders of the country into Babylonian captivity. The ember of rebellion flamed again within a decade when the hapless Zedekiah (598-586 B.C.E.) also withheld tribute in 589, having prepared for the eventuality of this act of war by entering in an alliance with Psammetichus II in 593. However, this Egyptian king died in 589, Egyptian support did not materialize, and the city of Jerusalem was sacked in 586. While the royal sons along with numerous other high ranking officials, priests, administrators, and royal family members were executed, a blinded Zedekiah, other leaders of the nation, and national treasures, including the temple vessels of the destroyed temple, were sent to Babylonia.

The Neo-Babylonian Empire began to weaken after the death of Nebuchadnezzar II with a quick succession of three rulers, followed by the last ruler, a former official in the court of Nebuchadnezzar II. Nabonidus (555-539 B.C.E.), whose actions bordered on the bizarre, led a religious revival in Babylonia by restoring ancient cults and their temples, worshiping as his primary deity the moon god Sin, while ignoring Marduk and alienating his powerful priesthood. He also withdrew to the desert to live in Tema for a decade. His efforts to defeat the Persians, under Cyrus the Great, led to the invasion of Babylonia and the taking, unopposed, of the city of Babylon in 539. The exiles from Judah along with Babylonia now found themselves part of an expanding Persian Empire.[8]

The destruction of Judah was extensive as is demonstrated by the evidence of both archaeology and texts. The misinformed view that there was no destruction occasioned by Babylonian conquest has been proven false due to the

---

8. See esp. Oded Lipschits and Joseph Blenkinsopp, eds., *Judah and the Judeans in the Neo-Babylonian Period* (Winona Lake, IN: Eisenbrauns, 2003). Also see Daniel L. Smith-Christopher, *The Religion of the Landless: The Social Context of the Babylonian Exile* (Bloomington, IN: Meyer-Stone Books, 1990); Bustenay Oded, "Observations on the Israelite/Judaean Exiles in Mesopotamia during the Eighth-Sixth Centuries B.C.E.," in *Immigration and Emigration within the Ancient Near East*, ed. Karel van Lerberghe and Antoon Schoors (OLA 65; Leuven: Peeters, 1995) 205-12; H. M. Barstad, *The Myth of the Empty Land: A Study in the History and Archaeology of Judah During the "Exilic" Period* (Symbolae Osloenses Fascicle Sup 28; Oslo: Scandinavian University Press, 1996).

weight of extensive archaeological evidence.[9] Excavations point to a major decline in the local economy of Judah and the near disappearance of Greek ceramics, demonstrating the radical decline of trade made possible by a strong economy, coupled with the reduction in the variety of pottery types.[10] The major cities in Judah that were destroyed included Jerusalem, Ramat Rahel, Lachish, Gezer, Beth-shemesh, En-gedi, Arad, Kadesh-barnea, Meṣad Hashavyahu, Tell Keisan, Megiddo, Dor, Acco, Tell ʿErani, Tell el-Hesi, Tell Jemmeh, Tell Malhata, and Tell er-Ruqeish, along with most of the Philistine coastal cities. They were not reconstructed during the period of the Neo-Babylonian Empire. Only a few cities escaped destruction: Tell en-Naṣbeh, Tell el-Fûl, and Bethel, and the towns in the tribal area of Benjamin and the far southern Negeb. There is no material or epigraphic evidence that the Babylonians developed the country into an organized administrative district, at least following the early assassination of Gedaliah. After his death, Eretz Israel may have been loosely divided into two regions: in the north was the province of Samaria, first established by the Assyrians, while the southern area appears eventually to have been inhabited in part by the Edomites who controlled it. Samaritan governors appear simply to have transferred their loyalty from the Assyrians to the Babylonians. However, Judah was not inserted into a heavily organized administrative system, since the new rulers focused mainly on Babylonia and regions nearby.[11] The devastation of Judah offered the Babylonians little to exploit. The survivors faced a bleak future, burdened with the requirement of annual tribute (see Lam. 2:2; 5:2-5, 9-11).[12]

The situation of the exiles is largely unknown due to the lack of concrete evidence.[13] Two opposing views have been proposed for their conditions. Peter Ackroyd, noting that the conditions were "uncongenial," still thinks the exiles lived together in their own communities, served the Babylonians, and yet also

---

9. Stern points to the archaeological evidence from this period, and concludes that the nation experienced "a state of total destruction and near abandonment" (*Archaeology*, 2:321-26).

10. Gunnar Lehmann, *Untersuchungen zur späten Eisenzeit in Syrien und Libanon; Stratigraphie und Keramikformen zwischen ca. 720 bis 300 v. Chr.* (Altertumskunde des vorderen Orients 5; Münster: Ugarit-Verlag, 1996).

11. See Stern, *Archaeology*, 2:308-9.

12. See Daniel L. Smith-Christopher, "Reassessing the Historical and Sociological Impact of the Babylonian Exile (597/587-539 B.C.E.)," in *Exile: Old Testament, Jewish, and Christian Conceptions*, ed. James M. Scott (JSJSup 56; Leiden: Brill, 1997) 7-36.

13. See Ran Zadok, *The Jews in Babylonia during the Chaldean and Achaemenian Periods according to the Babylonian Sources* (Haifa: University of Haifa, 1979); E. J. Bickerman, "The Babylonian Captivity," in *The Cambridge History of Judaism*, vol. 1: *Introduction: The Persian Period*, ed. W. D. Davies and Louis Finkelstein (Cambridge: Cambridge University Press, 1984) 342-58; Albertz, *Israel in Exile*.

were allowed to carry out a normal life of agricultural existence and to experience a good deal of localized freedom.[14] On the other hand, Oded opts for the more probable view that the exiles, while not imperial slaves or subjected to permanent physical labor, were still forced to work on projects when required to do so by their captors.[15] Since the Babylonians expressed no desire to engage in religious persecution or to force those conquered to worship their deities, the exiles would have had the option of continuing a local expression of their own religion dedicated to Yahweh without the presence of a sacred temple, now in ruins back in Jerusalem.

The elite of Jewish society, who escaped death in the defense of the city and execution, were forced into exile and included some members of the royal family, royal courtiers, highly placed administrators, chiefs of clans, the aristocracy, highly positioned priests, and skilled artisans. They were known, along with the other groups of exiles, as the ʿam haggôlâ, "the people of the exile," and were regarded by the Chronicler, Jer. 24:1-10, and Ezek. 33:23-29 as the true people of God in contrast to the ʿam hāʾāreṣ, "the people of the land," who remained behind. According to this theology, the exiles were to be the chosen vessel who would return to inherit the land, rebuild the temple, and reinstitute the institutions of the Davidic monarchy (Jer. 30–31). It is likely this ideology arose within the community of the exiles, since the royal family, headed by the captive ruler, Jehoiachin, and his surviving courtiers were imprisoned in Babylon.

The exiles of Judah lived in their own villages and urban quarters in Babylonia, were allowed to form their own communal associations, and to worship Yahweh without interference. The Murashu documents, a collection of texts from Nippur dating from the end of the fifth century B.C.E., contain many Hebrew names, thus indicating the continued existence of a Jewish community following the Persian conquest.[16] It is likely that the captives, lacking the rights of citizens, were forced to join other ethnic groups of exiles to work on their captor's construction activities.[17] It is not coincidental that the language of imprisonment and metaphors of slavery are numerous in biblical texts dating from the period of the exile (Isa. 43:6; 45:14; 52:2; Jer. 34:13; Mic. 6:4; Pss. 105:18;

---

14. Peter R. Ackroyd, *Exile and Restoration* (OTL; Philadelphia: Westminster, 1968) 32.

15. Oded, "Observations," 205-12. The Murashu documents indicate some, although not all, exiles were slaves. See M. A. Dandamayev, *Slavery in Babylonia* (Dekalb, IL: Northern Illinois University Press, 1984).

16. See Zadok, *Jews in Babylonia*.

17. Smith-Christopher *(Religion of the Landless)* refers to the building inscription of Nebuchadnezzar that points to the king's requiring the "lands of the Hattim" to engage in forced labor in building the Etemenanki (cf. Hansjörg Schmid, *Der Tempelturm Etemenanki in Babylon* [Baghdader Forschungen 17; Mainz: Philipp von Zabbern, 1995]).

107:14; and frequently in Job). Some members of the Jewish captives became corvée laborers and others perhaps royal workers who served as imperial land tenants as well as craftsmen and construction laborers for royal projects.[18] This situation would have continued throughout the entire period of their captivity under Babylonian hegemony.[19]

Rhetoric (Literary Structure and Form)

The poetic dialogues of Job represent a collage of literary features, including forms, motifs, and themes that indicate clearly it is an elegant composition of a gifted sapiential poet very familiar not only with the language of the sages but also with other literatures, Jewish and ancient Near Eastern, in particular Babylonian. The religious and sapiential literatures of Israel and Judah and Babylonia were well read and assimilated by this sage.

The large number of hapax legomena, the substantial use of disputation, and the length of the conflictive speeches between Job and his opponents characterize the distinctive features of the language of these debates. Other literary characteristics include the presence of hymns (theophanic in 5:9-16; 9:4-10; panegyric in 40:15-24; 40:25–41:26 [41:1-34]), a lengthy poem on Woman Wisdom (ch. 28), lament-like speeches of Job (chs. 6–7; 9–10; 13:20–14:22; etc.), legal language of the courtroom (9:23-35; 31:1-40), and sapiential forms that include rhetorical questions and a variety of sayings. Taken together, these forms support the sapiential identification of the entire book.

Literary Structure

The canonical book of Job breaks down into the following units:

> The Prologue (chs. 1–2)
> The Dialogues (chs. 3–27)
> The Poem on the Inaccessibility of Wisdom (ch. 28)
> The Oath of Innocence (chs. 29–31)

18. Bustenay Oded, "Judah and the Exile," in *Israelite and Judaean History*, ed. John Hayes and Maxwell Miller (OTL; Philadelphia: Westminster, 1977) 483. See, e.g., the Etemenanki cylinder, which lists the lands within the Babylonian Empire that contributed workers and lumber for the building of the ziggurat of Marduk in Babylon (E. A. Unger, *Babylon: Die Heilige Stadt nach der Beschreibung der Babylonier* [2nd ed.; Berlin: de Gruyter, 1970]).

19. Oded, "Observations," 204-12.

The Elihu Speeches (chs. 32–37)
The Speeches from the Whirlwind (38:1–42:6)
The Epilogue (42:7-17)

The prologue consists of six scenes alternating between earth and heaven in which the omniscient narrator describes the disaster that befalls Job due to the wager in heaven between Yahweh and the Satan. The one ultimately responsible for Job's descent into personal tragedy is Yahweh, whose only proscription to the Satan is not to take his servant's life. These two chapters along with 42:7-17 contain the opening and conclusion of a didactic narrative written in the First Temple period to teach youth in the wisdom schools about the issues of suffering, its causes, and the proper response that will lead to a good end. The middle of the book consists of three cycles of disputations between Job and his three opponents, Eliphaz, Bildad, and Zophar, that deal with the reasons for human suffering, seek to identify the one responsible, and determine the response to be made. These dialogues, along with the oath of innocence and the two divine speeches from the whirlwind, including two brief responses by Job, perhaps originated during the period of Babylonian captivity. Two additions were made during the Second Temple period to dull the edge of the sharp attack on the justice of God. One is the poem on the "inaccessibility of wisdom" (ch. 28), which denies that humans know true wisdom and asserts they are instead to "fear God and depart from evil." These two virtues are defined as wisdom and understanding. The other is made up of the six speeches of Elihu (chs. 32–37), the young upstart, who receives not so much as an acknowledgment from Job. The purpose is to chastise the friends for their failure to defeat Job and their cowardice in finding God to be in the wrong, to point to the reaffirmation of retribution, to anticipate the coming theophany of revelation, to know divine wisdom contrasted to Job's limited understanding, to anticipate the ascendancy of the oppressed to the position of ruling over the wicked, to condemn the hubris represented by Job, and to admonish people to praise God.

A particularly knotty problem in examining the developing composition of Job is the arrangement of the speeches and the identification of the different spokesmen in the third cycle of disputations (esp. chs. 24–27).[20] A careful reading of the third cycle indicates that there is substantial disarray in this final collection of speeches.[21] The typical pattern of alternating speeches is broken

---

20. Franz Hesse, *Hiob* (ZBK; Zurich: Theologische Verlag Zürich, 1978) 7-12; Victor Maag, *Hiob. Wandlung und Verarbeitung des Problems in Novelle, Dialogdichtung und Spätfassungen* (FRLANT 128; Göttingen: Vandenhoeck & Ruprecht, 1982) 13.

21. Markus Witte, *Vom Leiden zur Lehre: Der dritte Redegang (Hiob 21-27) und die Redaktionsgeschichte des Hiobbuches* (BZAW 230; Berlin: de Gruyter, 1994).

when Zophar does not offer a final speech and Bildad has only a truncated statement in 25:1-6. In addition, some of the comments attributed to Job represent arguments that, prior to the third cycle, have been made by his opponents (esp. 27:13-23, and probably 26:5-14). The same is true of some of the words of the opponents who came to use the arguments of Job. While there are numerous suggestions as to how to deal with these problems, I agree with Habel, who proposes the following restructuring of the third cycle that makes it consistent in argumentation with the first two and thus prepares the way for the next movement, the "oath of innocence."

> 21 — Job
> 22 — Eliphaz
> 23 — Job
> 24 — Zophar (?)
> 25:1-6; 26:5-14 — Bildad
> 26:1-4; 27:1-12 — Job
> 27:13-23 — Zophar.[22]

The poem on wisdom in ch. 28 is similar to other poems on personified Wisdom (Prov. 1:20-33; 8:1-36; 9:1-6, 13-18; Sir. 24). The theme on wisdom's inaccessibility to human beings and the affirmations that the "fear of Yahweh is the beginning of wisdom" and "to depart from evil is understanding" do not make sense in this context, if spoken either by Job or by his three friends in the dialogues. The affirmations of "fearing God/the Almighty" *(yěrē'/yir'at 'ĕlōhîm/ šadday)* and "turning away from evil" *(sûr mēra')* in the prose narrative (1:1) are repeated in the poem, which suggests an author who is associated with traditional sapiential piety that links up with the prose tale. These affirmations are neither in line with Job's early or subsequent arguments in the poetry, nor the positions of the friends in chs. 4–27. Yahweh's speeches to Job and his two responses in 38:1–42:6 are not even close to the affirmations of ch. 28, although Yahweh's questions imply his knowledge of the cosmos and Job's own limitations. Job's responses to Yahweh's two speeches could be understood as an affirmation of religious piety, although this is questionable. If these points had already been made in ch. 28, however, they would have preempted the speeches of Yahweh and the responses of Job.

This didactic poem should be seen as an addition by a pious sage who objects to all human efforts to discover wisdom. A redacted insertion, the text is similar to the attachment of the epilogue to Qoheleth by a later traditional sage

---

22. See Norman Habel, *The Book of Job* (OTL; Philadelphia: Westminster, 1985) 37.

(12:9-14). The traditional sage who adds the poem concludes that the quest of Job to obtain divine wisdom is foolhardy, for it is doomed to failure. He also is implicitly critical of Job's rather brazen assault on divine justice. The unexpected appearance of Elihu in chs. 32–37 and the lack of any response or recognition by Job suggest that this collection of four speeches is also a later addition.[23] One should additionally note that Yahweh opens his initial speech in ch. 38 with a rebuke of the one who has just finished speaking, that some of the language and content of Elihu's speeches parallel those of Yahweh (e.g., 37:14-20), thus preempting some of Yahweh's arguments, and that the content of these four speeches essentially replicates that of Job's three opponents, Eliphaz, Bildad, and Zophar. I do not find the efforts to include these speeches within the literary flow of the book convincing.[24]

Other scholars have attempted to combine the two speeches of Yahweh and the two responses of Job into a single speech and one response.[25] However, this argument is not particularly compelling. While the issues remain complex, I am inclined to accept the present arrangement and content of the two speeches and two responses.

Finally, there are several different views of the relationship between the prose narrative and the poetic dialogues. These include: an early prose tale was taken by the poet who used it to draw attention to his own radical rejection of the justice of God; the poet sought to reject the teaching that suffering was divine discipline and the proper human response is piety in spite of adversity;[26] and the poetic dialogues and the prose narrative were both written by the same author and intended to be read together.[27]

The differences between the narrative and the poetic dialogues are rather striking, ranging from literary style to content. For example, "the Satan" plays a prominent role in chs. 1–2, but then disappears altogether in the poetry, never to reemerge, even in the epilogue. Job suffers patiently and with unquestioning piety in the narrative legend, while he is the angry blasphemer in the poetic dialogues, beginning with the opening soliloquy in ch. 3. The theme of retribution, nuanced by divine discipline, is articulated in the narrative, but subverted by

23. Maag, *Hiob*, 18-19.

24. Cf. Habel, *Job*, 36-37; J. Gerald Janzen, *Job* (Interpretation; Atlanta: John Knox, 1985) 22-24. See my response to their arguments in *Wisdom in Revolt* (JSOTSup 112; Sheffield: Almond, 1991) 80-82.

25. Fohrer, *Introduction*, 327-29.

26. Georg Fohrer, "Überlieferung und Wandlung der Hioblegende," in *Studien zum Buche Hiob* (2nd ed.; Gütersloh: Gerd Mohn, 1982); Nahum Sarna, "Epic Substratum in the Prose of Job," *JBL* 76 (1957) 13-25.

27. Janzen, *Job*, 22-24; and Habel, *Job*, 35-39.

the poetic dialogues and the speeches of Yahweh. The poet seems to have taken a well-known didactic narrative and replaced part of its content with the poetic dialogues and Yahweh speeches. The connection of the narrative with the poetry results in a new and startling reading of the narrative story. Retribution, suffering as divine discipline, and a capricious God who kills in response to unwarranted suspicion are not congruous. I suggest that the first position is the most likely one, since the author of the poetic dialogues, and presumably others who have endured the Babylonian holocaust, can no longer justify the traditional teachings affirmed by the narrative.[28]

The variety of literary forms in Job has led scholars to reach numerous understandings of the overall genre of the book.[29] These include a dramatized lament,[30] a paradigm of the answered lament,[31] speeches of litigation,[32] and a sapiential disputation.[33] Considering a number of these possibilities, Pope argues that the book, largely due to the variety and combination of forms, is *sui generis*.[34] Yet his position does not consider that the preponderance of the disputations are in the rhetorical structure of the book's major sections: the speeches of controversy between Job and his three opponents in chs. 3–27, and the effort to continue the debate by Yahweh in the speeches of the whirlwind when he comes to render judgment (38:1–42:6).

From the 1970s on, several readings of Job have attempted, unconvincingly in my opinion, to view the book either as a whole, the parts of which fit together in one continuous narrative;[35] or, by looking through a postmodern lens, to see it as a steady succession of constructions and deconstructions resulting in the impossibility of achieving any single answer.[36] Thus the argument runs that the book of Job is a literary unit, or episodic groupings of ultimately

---

28. Carol Newsom prefers to read the book as a whole, with the exception of the Elihu speeches, which she considers to be a later addition ("The Book of Job," *NIB* 4 [1996] 321-23). Cf. Habel, who reads the book as a literary whole (*Job*, esp. 35-39).

29. See Roland Murphy, *Wisdom Literature* (FOTL 13; Grand Rapids: Eerdmans, 1981) 15-45, for the overarching genre of Job and the literary forms found in the book.

30. Claus Westermann, *The Structure of the Book of Job and Form-Critical Analysis*, trans. Charles A. Muenchow (Philadelphia: Fortress, 1981).

31. Hartmut Gese, *Lehre und Wirklichkeit in der alten Weisheit: Studien zu den Spruchen Salomos und zu dem Buche Hiob* (Tübingen: Mohr [Siebeck], 1958).

32. Heinz Richter, *Studien zu Hiob* (Theologische Arbeiten 11; Berlin: Evangelische Verlaganstalt, 1955) 131; "The Rîb- or Controversy-Pattern in Hebrew Mentality," in *Wisdom in Israel and in the Ancient Near East*, ed. Noth and Winton Thomas, 120-37.

33. Georg Fohrer, *Das Buch Hiob* (KAT 16; Gütersloh: Gerd Mohn, 1963).

34. Marvin H. Pope, *Job* (3rd ed.; AB; Garden City, NY: Doubleday, 1973) xxxi.

35. Habel, *The Book of Job*.

36. David Clines, *Job 1–20* (Word Biblical Commentary 17; Waco, TX: Word Books, 1989).

incoherent and unconvincing views, and not a well-constructed text that grows in stages over several centuries.[37] The variety of literary forms and the different internal responses to the book's major questions offered by the poet of the dialogues, the poem on inaccessible Wisdom, the Elihu speeches, and the narrative militate against the argument that one is to view it as a literary unit. Further, carried to a logical or nonsensical conclusion if viewed through postmodernism, the author of Job is transformed into a poet of a contemporary school of thought that had abandoned the search for truth and the discovery of any supportable philosophical orientation to life's meaning, rather than one of the religious thinkers of the ancient past who sought to address and resolve, if at all possible, the greatest of human dilemmas: the contrast between the suffering of the righteous and the justice of God.

Form-critical analyses reveal that the book contains numerous small, individual literary forms. However, three genres loom large in the text's entirety: the didactic narrative, lament, and disputation. In my view, these genres have been shaped into an overarching unit that nevertheless contains some thematic inconsistencies. It appears most likely that the one who forged the primary structure of the book is the poet who composed the dialogues (chs. 3–27; 29–31; 38:1–42:6), perhaps living as a sage in the exile or shortly after the return. This is the sage who would have attached his new dialogues to the older prose tale in chs. 1–2 and 42:7-17 and used it as the entrée into the reformulated book that reaches radically opposite theological conclusions. Following the exile and living in the Persian period when tradition is recast into a formal expression of a divine Torah, two conservative sages added the poem on wisdom in ch. 28 and the Elihu speeches in chs. 32–37 in order to lessen the extreme conclusions reached by a sage whose theology bordered on blasphemy.

Ezekiel's early-sixth-century reference (14:14-20) to Job's righteousness is likely an indication of the existence of the narrative in the First Temple period.[38] Literary analysis reveals that the book begins (chs. 1–2) and concludes (42:7-17) with a didactic story, the theology and themes of which are profoundly different from those of the poetry in the dialogues and the Yahweh speeches. The earliest form of the Joban theme is compressed into a didactic narrative composed for youth in wisdom schools in order to teach them the traditional, pious response to suffering, even by the just. Similar wisdom narratives include the Joseph Story (Gen. 37, 39–50), the Aramaic "Tale of Ahiqar,"[39]

37. J. W. Whedbee, "The Comedy of Job," *Semeia* 7 (1970) 182-200.
38. See Maag, *Hiob*, 20-90.
39. See, e.g., J. M. Lindenberger, "Ahiqar," *OTP* 2:479-508.

the Egyptian "Protests of the Eloquent Peasant,"[40] the Akkadian "Poor Man of Nippur,"[41] and the Hittite "Tale of Appu."[42] Müller analyzes the genre as composed of the following features. A third person, omniscient narrator tells the story of a sage who embodies sapiential virtues. The plot typically speaks of the misfortune of the hero or protagonist, often occasioned by his deceitful nemesis or antagonist. Maintaining his piety, the sage is finally restored to his position of divine favor and social status, while his opponent is undone. This prose narrative continues to experience a well-developed tradition that includes expansions in the Septuagint, the Targums, and the Testament of Job.

Another important genre found frequently in the book of Job is the individual lament, although its structure and themes differ from those found in the Psalter. Laments in the context of religious settings were an important part of the liturgy of Sabbath worship and also the festival of Yom Kippur. The structure of these liturgical, individual laments, which mimics that of the corporate laments, includes the invocation, the complaint, the pleas for help, the affirmation of trust in God, and on occasion a concluding vow to praise God following the rescue from distress. The "Laments of Protest" are more similar to the questioning present in the laments of Job (see Pss. 10, 13). In addition Job's disputations at times demonstrate an intensity of a radical assault on the justice and mercy of God. Subsequently, while asking God directly why he does not save his servant, he becomes distraught to the point that he expects nothing in the way of divine rescue or finally even the cessation of suffering. Indeed, he only hopes that he may die and expire quickly to end his misery. Thus there is neither an affirmation of trust in divine justice and compassion nor a concluding promise to offer a public vow following his salvation.

Regarding both the rhetorical structure and the appropriate format for the content of the book, the disputation serves as its most important genre.[43] This form is paralleled especially by "The Babylonian Theodicy."[44] Although there

---

40. The Egyptian "Protests of the Eloquent Peasant" is translated by John A. Wilson in *ANET,* 407-10.

41. "The Poor Man of Nippur" is translated in Benjamin R. Foster, *From Distant Days: Myths, Tales, and Poetry of Ancient Mesopotamia* (Bethesda, MD: CDL, 1995) 357-62; and in *TUAT* vol. 3: *Weisheitstexte,* 1:174-80.

42. See Müller, "Weisheitliche Lehrerzählung," 77-98.

43. G. J. Reinink and H. L. J. Vanstiphout, eds., *Dispute Poems and Dialogues in the Ancient and Mediaeval Near East: Forms and Types of Literary Debates in Semitic and Related Literatures* (OLA 42; Leuven: University of Leuven Press, 1991).

44. *ANET,* 601-4; see Perdue, *Wisdom and Cult: A Critical Analysis of the Views of Cult in the Wisdom Literatures of Israel and the Ancient Near East* (SBLDS 30; Missoula, MT: Scholars Press, 1977) 105-6. Sapiential debates sought to prove that one thing was superior to something else. See Jean-Jacques Glassner, "The Use of Knowledge in Ancient Mesopotamia," *CANE* 3:1816.

are some similarities to the Egyptian "Dialogue Between a Man and His *Ba*,"[45] the text is much closer in form and content to sapiential dialogues in Mesopotamia. Here disputations, whether those of fables involving the value of an animal or tree over others or of two sages debating the problem of suffering and the questioning of the personal god of the one afflicted, on occasion conclude with a divine judgment that renders the verdict as to which position is the correct one.[46] This, of course, fits the concluding narrative of Job in which Yahweh condemns the position taken by Job's opponents and finds instead Job's argument to be "correct." The literary structure of the disputation in ancient Mesopotamia contains formally four major components: the address of the opponent, accusation, argument, and concluding summary or counsel given to the opponent. In the various speeches of the opponents, the book of Job contains these features. The prominent role of the sapiential disputation in Job points to the fact that sages engaged in debates over truth thought discoverable in the intense quest for meaning, and the best way to obtain insights into issues of substance was the disputation between prominent sages.

The poetic book of Job, prior to the additions of the Elihu speeches and the hymn on wisdom, consists of chs. 3-27, 29-31, and 38:1–42:6 and is organized into two interweaving mythic patterns: one is cosmological (see the Akkadian *Enūma eliš*) and the other is anthropological (cf. the Akkadian *Atra-ḫasīs*), reflecting two of the mythic narratives of Babylonian religion. In my view, the internal structure of the poetic book of Job is a dramatic enactment of a major anthropological mythic tradition in ancient Babylon that centers on the creation of humanity by focusing on the metaphor of slaves serving the gods and relieving them from labor. Thus the thematic substructure of this myth borrowed by the poetic book of Job moves from origins, to predestination, to slavery, to revolt against the gods, to the fall and impending destruction, to final judgment and redemption, for it relates a tragic tale of a human like Adapa or Gilgamesh (at least partly human) who fails in gaining divine immortality and joining the assembly of the gods.[47]

The poet shapes the external structure of the book of Job by use of the cosmological mythic theme of conflict between the creator, who is the divine warrior, and his nemesis, the monster of chaos who threatens creation. The two best examples of this tradition are the *Enūma eliš*, a Mesopotamian myth of origins, and the Ugaritic Baal Cycle, a maintenance myth. The literary pattern

---

45. *ANET*, 405-7; see Perdue, *Wisdom and Cult*, 31-32.

46. See John B. Gray, "The Book of Job in the Context of Ancient Near Eastern Literature," *ZAW* 82 (1970) 251-69; Perdue, *Wisdom and Cult*, 95-133.

47. See Perdue, *Wisdom in Revolt*.

common to this mythic tradition moves from battle, to victory over chaos, to the proclaiming of the victor who becomes king, to judgment of the opposing force of chaos and its army of gods, to creation of the cosmos, to the building of a temple for the new conquering god. This is "the myth of the divine warrior." These two myths that were instrumental in shaping the culture and ideology of Babylonia would have been known by the sapiential poet, especially if he had been present in Babylon during the exile when he wrote the poetic book.

The poetic book of Job points to a tension between these two mythic traditions in order to depict Job's struggle with the creator. Where they intersect is noteworthy, for they do so at the point of conflict: the battle between the divine warrior and chaos monster and the struggle of the human hero with the deity of creation. Job's revolt derives from his perception that God has misruled creation and history and should be dethroned, whereas the deity understands Job's revolt as identified with the forces of chaos that must be defeated, if creation is to continue.

Babylonian Parallels

The important encounter of sages of Judah with Akkadian wisdom literature likely would have occurred during the period of captivity in Babylon. This may explain the dominant role of the disputation, which was prominent in Sumero-Assyriological wisdom. Akkadian literature appears to have been an important source of Joban literary images, including chaos, the magic of pagan priests, the first man, the battle with different figures of chaos, the restriction of the waters of chaos by divine decree, death as the final human destination, slavery to the gods, the questioning of divine justice, divine caprice, Marduk as the god of creation and providence, the divine council, the righteous sufferer, redemption by the personal deity, and the decision of the judge between the two lines of argument, that of the opponents and that of Job.[48]

Four deities and seven prediluvian semidivine humans are singled out for their great wisdom in Mesopotamian literary tradition. The gods assign to humans their roles in the social order and teach them the arts of civilization and knowledge of the world. One of them, Marduk, is even depicted as the creator of the cosmos and the lord of providence. The others are Ea, Nisaba, and Nabu. The seven humans are primordial sages of ancient lore, the *apkallus*, known for their wisdom and heroic feats. One postdiluvian *apkallu* who was the most popular among the postdiluvian sages was Adapa, who ascended to the heavens

---

48. Horst Goeseke, "Motive babylonischer Weisheitsliteratur," *Altertum* 13 (1967) 7-19.

and came close to achieving immortality as a god. Three postdiluvian *apkallus* appeared who, instructed by the gods, taught civilization to humanity.

Three deities possessing a patrilineal consanguinity (grandfather, father, and son) are associated with wisdom: Ea ("lord of wisdom," the lord of incantations, and "the sage among the gods, the one who knows all that is"); Marduk his son, the god of wisdom and exorcism, who killed Tiamat in battle, became king of the pantheon, and created the world; and Nabu, the god of the scribal profession and the son of Marduk. This theological association of wisdom is especially helpful in understanding Akkadian wisdom and the relationship to creation and providence. Nabu's cuneiform sign was a wedge, likely a writing stylus, occasionally resting upon a clay tablet.[49]

The classic creation story in Babylonian mythology is the "Epic of Creation" (*Enūma eliš*, "When on High"),[50] which tells the story of Marduk's election to the position of king over the gods, his defeat of Tiamat, his receiving fifty divine names that describe his attributes, his creation of the cosmos and humanity (from the blood of the rebel god and general of Tiamat's forces, Kingu), the establishment of the social order, and the building of Babylon, which served as the center of creation, and of Esagila, the temple for his dwelling place.[51] I have pointed to the numerous instances in Job with mythological allusions to creation in general and combat in particular in an earlier monograph.[52]

"The Babylonian Story of the Flood" in the myth of Atra-ḫasīs also resonates with the poetic Job, for both possess the important feature of human revolt, occasioned by the harshness of their forced labor and divine mistreatment.[53] The first line of the initial section of the Akkadian myth reads: "When the gods like men bore the work and suffered the toil." In primordial times the lower gods (Igigi) were slaves of the exalted deities of the divine pantheon ruled by Anu (heaven) and then followed in rank by Enlil (earth) and Enki = Ea = Apsu, the water below the earth (the sea). Following forty years of slavish drudgery, the Igigi rebelled, burning their tools and laying siege to Enlil's palace. Con-

---

49. See Francesco Pomponio and Ursala Seidl, "Nabû," *Reallexikon der Assyriologie*, 9, ed. E. Ebeling, et al. (Berlin: de Gruyter, 1998) 16-29.

50. Foster, *From Distant Days*, 9-51. Also see Thorkild Jacobsen, *The Treasures of Darkness: A History of Mesopotamian Religion* (New Haven: Yale University Press, 1976) 165-66.

51. Foster, *From Distant Days*, 9.

52. Perdue, *Wisdom in Revolt*.

53. W. G. Lambert and Alan R. Millard, *Atra-ḫasīs: The Babylonian Story of the Flood* (Oxford: Clarendon, 1969). Cf. W. L. Moran, "Some Considerations of Form and Interpretation in Atra-ḫasis," in *Language, Literature, and History: Philological and Historical Studies Presented to Erica Reiner*, ed. Francesca Rochberg-Halton (New Haven: American Oriental Society, 1987) 245-55.

vened to handle this crisis, the divine assembly issued the decree that humanity was to be created for the purpose of relieving the Igigi of this onerous labor.

The second section describes the dramatic increase in human population, which then produces a "noise" disturbing Enlil's sleep. Following the issuance of edicts to eliminate humans, which were rebuffed by humanity's friend, Enki, Enlil sends a cosmic flood and binds Enki to an oath not to interfere. However, Enki does warn Atra-ḫasīs (the one "exceeding wise") by instructing him to construct a vessel that will enable his family and him to escape death. Enlil is angry that some escaped his wrath, but the other gods realize that without humans they would have to work. Enlil then orders the society with classes and institutions (especially kingship) to reduce the "noise" that would lead to their destruction. Thus, in retrospect, the unruly humans are brought into a system of social order by Enlil, allowing them to survive. This myth serves to legitimate the autocratic society of the Assyro-Babylonian culture. Elements of this mythic tradition are found in the book of Job in the references to revolt against Yahweh, the drudgery of human slavery, and the references to the chaos monsters Yamm and Leviathan in Job 3:8; 7:12; 9:13; 38:8-11; and 40:25–41:26 (41:1-34). However, the book of Job lacks any depiction of a cosmic flood that inundates the earth, since Yahweh issues a decree to Yamm (the sea) that limits its "proud waves" (Job 38:11).

Interpretation

The poet begins the story of Job with the prologue (chs. 1–2), which consists of six scenes alternating between heaven and earth (four occurring on earth and two in heaven). Drawing on the legendary presentation of the pious and moral sage, wealthy beyond measure and blessed with a household of a wife and off-spring, Job's loyalty to God and family is underscored by his offering of burnt offerings to assuage the possible guilt of his children. Even when faced with the devastating loss of all that he has, Job continues to bless the name of Yahweh. When afflicted by the Satan (Accuser) with loathsome sores, he repudiates his wife's counsel to curse God. The omniscient narrator also describes the wager between Yahweh and the Satan, making clear that the loss of Job's children and property were due to divine caprice, unbeknownst to Job, who maintains his integrity, which disallows him from cursing God or charging him with wrongdoing. The narrative presents Yahweh as the ruler of the divine council who meets with the other gods annually, probably during the New Year Festival when he determines the fates for the coming year. Lacking any knowledge of the actions of humans, Yahweh depends on the Satan to inform him about the behavior of his servant Job. When beguiled by the Satan to doubt the integrity of Job's piety, Yahweh turns his servant over to the Satan, with the only reservation being that he could not take Job's life. Yahweh assumes responsibility for these vile actions that result in the killing of Job's children and the immense suffering of a faithful servant.

The disputations (chs. 3–27) consist of three cycles of speeches between Job and his three opponents. In Job's speeches, the sage, having been changed by the suffering he has endured in the prologue, begins to launch an attack on the justice of God and to subvert the arguments of the defenders of theodicy. Job likens Yahweh to an oppressive despot who seeks to destroy the work of his own hand. Psalm 8, a creation hymn that describes the divine exaltation of humans who are made only a little less than the gods and crowned with glory and honor, is satirically repudiated in Job 7:17-21. Later, in ch. 10, Job accuses God of having formed him in the womb for the sole purpose of doing him harm. By contrast, the friends are resolute in continuing to uphold the righteousness of God and to defend him from Job's blasphemous onslaught, concluding that he must be an outrageous sinner to merit such vile punishment. Job responds to these imputations by placing blame on God, while describing himself in images of the chaos monster that the divine warrior now torments and will ultimately destroy. Yet even his desire to die is denied him. He finally begins to give voice to his desire to prove his innocence in a courtroom and to demonstrate the guilt of his divine opponent (esp. chs. 9–10). His one fear is that Yahweh would overpower him with threats and intimidate him with fear to the point that he would condemn himself.

Following the conclusion of the disputation with the three opponents, Job then enters into the uttering of a lament followed by an "oath of innocence" in chs. 29–31. This lengthy soliloquy consists of two parts: an accusatory lament addressed to God (chs. 29–30), and a series of oaths (ch. 31) that represent Job's legal defense against the accusations of wrongdoing made by the friends.[54] He first describes his prior life when he experienced the friendship of God, his divine patron, and when he was held in honor by those he encountered in the city. He speaks of his own righteous judgment and distribution of justice like a father, counselor, and ruler to those in need (ch. 29). However, this period of honor has now been replaced by the present contempt in which he is held by those who are his social inferiors. The one responsible for his mockery is the violent God who rejects his pleas for help. It is ultimately God who will bring him to the death that is appointed for all, refusing to issue to him any respite from his unbearable torture.

54. See Georg Fohrer, "The Righteous Man in Job 31," in *Essays in Old Testament Ethics*, ed. James L. Crenshaw and John T. Willis (New York: Ktav, 1974) 1-22.

Job has no recourse other than to engage in the legal process of uttering his oaths designed to prove his innocence by stating the crimes and sins he has not committed, followed by the just punishment that would be his were he lying. Thus Job denies that he has lusted after a virgin; that he has engaged in acts of deceit; that he has committed adultery with another man's wife; that he has turned aside the just cause of his slaves who issue their complaints against him; that he has failed to offer charity to the poor, the widow, and the orphan; that he has taken comfort in gold; that he has engaged in the worship of false gods taking the shape of the moon and the sun; that he has exulted in the ruin of his enemy; that he has cursed his opponent; that he has turned aside the stranger; and that he has exploited the land by its overuse. Signing his oath in a legal procedure that attests to the truth of his negative confession, Job finally demands from God, his accuser, an indictment, which, if received, he would flaunt by carrying it publicly on his shoulder and wearing it like a crown.

The declaration of innocence consists of twelve sins or crimes positioned within the formal structure of a list of oaths consisting of one or more protases (conditions), introduced by 'im ("if") or 'im lō' ("if not"), and an apodosis (result).[55] The protasis is a conditional clause that declares the crime or sin, while the apodosis contains the punishment to be administered, if guilty.[56] Four topics follow this pattern (vv. 7-8, 9-12, 16-23, 38-40), while the others contain the protasis, but either leave out the apodosis (vv. 24-25, 33-34, common in OT oaths, since it was implied),[57] or transform it either into a declaration (vv. 26-28, 29-30, 31-32), an imperative (vv. 5-6), or a rhetorical question (vv. 1-2, 13-15).

Occasionally combined with an ordeal,[58] this type of conditional self-imprecation (normally called the 'ālâ) was used in sanctuary courts to determine by divine judgment a person's guilt or innocence (Exod. 22:6-12; Num. 5:5-28). This process occurred when there were no eyewitnesses (1 Kgs. 8:31-32).[59] The integrity of the process depended on the belief in the power inherent in the curse and ordeal and in the justice of God to find one innocent or guilty.

Also included in this chapter is Job's legal signature appended to the oaths,

---

55. Lists of ten and twelve were common for laws and curses (Exod. 23:10-19; 34:10-26; Lev. 18:6-18; Deut. 27:15-26).

56. See Sheldon H. Blank, "The Curse, Blasphemy, the Spell, and the Oath," *HUCA* 23 (1950/51) 73-95; Delbert Hillers, *Treaty-Curses and the Old Testament Prophets* (BibOr 10; Rome: Pontifical Biblical Institute, 1964).

57. The apodosis was normally omitted, since the self-imprecation was destructive.

58. See Richard Press, "Das Ordal im alten Israel," *ZAW* 51 (1933) 121-40; G. R. Driver, "Ordeal by Oath at Nuzi," *Iraq* 7 (1940) 132-38.

59. Another example comes from Elephantine. See Paul Volz, "Ein Beitrag aus den Papyri von Elephantine zu Hiob Kap. 31," *ZAW* 32, 126-27.

a wish that someone would "hear" the case,[60] and a direct appeal to his "legal adversary" (*'îš rîb;* cf. Judg. 12:2) to present a written "indictment" *(sēper)*[61] specifying the crimes of which he has been accused (vv. 35-37). The appeal becomes a direct challenge to God to appear in court to bring his charges. Job demands that the creator respond to this challenge. Were that to happen, Job boasts he would carry such a document on his shoulder and wear it as a crown for public display. The action may simply indicate Job's confidence that he could easily refute evidence arrayed against him and therefore be vindicated. Indeed, given the chance, he would approach God like a king or a prince who demands an accounting from his divine accuser.

The two Yahweh speeches (38:1–42:6) and Job's two responses provide the conclusion of the poetic book of Job, although the content and meaning are not altogether clear. Scholars have made numerous efforts to reshape the concluding speeches and Job's responses into a single speech and response. In doing so, however, they often excised praises of Leviathan and Behemoth, an editorial decision that in my judgment destroys much of the meaning of the book. Indeed, mythical images of chaos are frequently found in the poetic book, including the references to Yamm (the Sea) and Leviathan in 3:8. In these speeches Yahweh is the creator and sustainer of the cosmos who restrains Yamm with the power of his edict, while he continues to battle the two monsters of chaos for supremacy of creation: Behemoth and Leviathan (40:15–41:34). Furthermore, Yahweh declares that neither Job nor he possesses the ability to defeat and then vanquish these monsters and to remove the proud wicked from the face of the earth. Thus the presence of the mythical monsters is important in understanding the poetic book. Their elimination would subvert the poetic book's meaning and would fail to make clear that Yahweh is limited in his rule over creation. Consequently, God is not all-powerful, but rather he must continue to battle evil in the forms of chaos and wickedness.

It is also significant to underscore that Yahweh, in his lengthy speeches composed primarily of a series of impossible questions, ignores the critical charges Job has made against him in his disputation with his human opponents, and ignores the challenge to present a list of charges of crimes. Yahweh fails to explain why the righteous suffer, refuses to defend his justice denied by Job, and forsakes the responsibility to clarify why retribution is a false teaching. Instead, Yahweh rests content with asserting the superiority of his wisdom and

60. Michael B. Dick argues that the appeal for one to "hear" *(šmʿ)* the case is for an unspecified yet impartial arbiter who would preside over the civil process ("The Legal Metaphor in Job," *CBQ* 41 [1979] 37-50).

61. Habel suggests *spr* may have been a "deed of renunciation" that would have formally exonerated Job (*Job,* 439).

power to those of his human rival. Noteworthy is that Job had already conceded these two points in his earlier speeches (9:3-4, 19).

The initial speech (38:1–40:2) has two major sections: one on cosmology (chaos, heaven, earth, and underworld, 38:1-38) and the other on animals beyond human control (38:39–39:30). Following a direct challenge from Job, Yahweh issues the first section of his disputation that, like the second that follows, consists largely of impossible questions that assume that he, not Job, possesses the knowledge to answer.

Important to the first part of this initial speech is the restraining by fiat of the newborn Yamm (38:8-11), whom Yahweh, acting like a midwife, receives from the womb. This contrasts with the image of Yahweh as mother and midwife to humans (Ps. 139:13-16) and Woman Wisdom (Prov. 8:22-31). The second section of the first part of this initial speech consists of six strophes that direct questions to Job concerning the heavenly region: light and darkness, weather, precipitation, the constellations, and the clouds (Job 38:12-38). The speech concludes with a reference to the wisdom and insight of the ibis and the cock (v. 36).[62] Yahweh providentially cares for animals, especially the wild beasts untamed by human beings (38:39–39:30; see Ps. 104). It is striking that no mention is made of his nurturing of humans.

The second part of this initial speech (39:1-30) contains depictions of six pairs of animals who share similar features and are nurtured by Yahweh and the two chaos monsters (Behemoth and Leviathan, 40:6–41:26). Except for the horse, the wild creatures are beasts dwelling in regions uninhabited by human beings and uncontrolled by human efforts. Even human mastery of the horse is difficult. In the Priestly document of Gen. 9:1-17, when God establishes a covenant with Noah and the cosmos, creatures tremble in fear before human beings. In P humans are ordained to reign as God's surrogate in the world (cf. Ps. 8). This is not the case in this speech, for these are wild animals, most of which are inimical to human life and reside outside of humanity's control. If Job answers these rhetorical questions by admitting his own weakness and ignorance and the superiority of the creator, it is assumed he would abandon his questions assaulting the integrity and justice of God. However, he chooses silence instead, for he recognizes that Yahweh "holds him in contempt" (cf. Gen. 16:4, 5; 2 Sam. 1:23; Jer. 4:13; Hab. 1:8; Nah. 1:4).[63] His questions have been ignored. Now he waits for a proper response.

62. For a discussion see Robert Gordis, *The Book of Job* (New York: Jewish Theological Seminary of America, 1978) 452-53.

63. Job learns how little he (and the rest of humanity) is valued by Yahweh. The Hebrew particle *hēn* usually means "since," or "seeing that this is so," while *qallōtî* (a Qal verb) clearly means "to be held in contempt" by another.

The second divine speech (40:6–41:26[34]) offers Job the throne under one condition: he must rid the world of the proud and the wicked and then defeat the dreaded monsters of chaos, Behemoth ("mighty creature") and Leviathan (monster of the seas). The following strophes describe the fearsome power of these two chaos monsters. Yahweh describes Behemoth (40:15-24) as a creature that he "made like you" (i.e., Job). Neither humanity nor Woman Wisdom is the first and the best of those creatures made by God. Rather it is Behemoth who is the "first of El's works" *(rē'šît darkê 'ēl).*

The following section of Yahweh's second speech praises the ruler of the seas, Leviathan (40:25–41:26 [41:1-34]). Leviathan (= Ugaritic Lotan)[64] is far more fearsome than Behemoth. This praise of Leviathan concludes with the statement, "no one upon earth can rule over him." He "is king over all the proud beasts," most probably those fierce animals in the first speech who are untamed by human creatures (cf. 28:8). Leviathan knows no fear. Yahweh alone is able to subdue these ferocious mythical beasts, but even he cannot eliminate them and the threats they present.

Job's second response (42:1-6) contains at least features of the doxology in which he acknowledges that Yahweh has the power and wisdom to create and sustain the world. Whether this is praise or parody depends on the translation and meaning of 42:6. Job now recognizes that he cannot replace Yahweh as ruler, and thus ceases this element of his attack on the creator. In 42:2 ("I know you are capable of all things, and that no plan you propose will be impossible for you"), Job's words quote almost exactly Yahweh's language of judgment in Gen. 11:6, the story of the tower of Babel that points to the futility of human arrogance (Gen. 11:1-9). In Job 42:3 he uses with only slight changes Yahweh's opening words in 38:2, thus implying that Yahweh is the one "who conceals counsel," that is, hides any explanation that would lead to understanding of what is at issue: the justice of God.

Job admits he does not possess the knowledge to understand divine acts in creation and history, "wondrous things" *(niplā'ôt)* that redeem and bring life. Yet is this not a forced confession that fulfills Job's earlier fear that, face-to-face with the divine opponent, he would be intimidated into silence and incapable of responding due to his lack of knowledge? He says to Yahweh, "I have said that I do not have perception." The verb *'em'as* is either active or intransitive and does not mean, "I despise myself." As an intransitive verb, it means "to protest" (Job 7:16; 34:33; 36:5). With a direct object ("dust and ashes"), the transitive means to "feel sorry" (Ps. 90:13). The Niphal *niham,* followed by *'al,* means "comforted over" (2 Sam. 13:39; Jer. 16:7; Ezek. 14:22) and "have compassion for/

---

64. CTA 5 (Eng. trans. COS I:265).

feel sorry for" (Ps. 90:13). This construction means "repent of" only when followed by the word "evil" (Jer. 8:6; 18:8; Joel 2:13). Job is not "repenting in" dust and ashes, but rather he feels compassion/sorrow for human beings who are forced to endure divine misrule and imposed suffering.[65]

The poet has allowed the conclusion of the old didactic narrative, now appearing again in the form of the conclusion of 42:7-17, to be endowed with new meaning: Job has his integrity upheld by the ruler of the divine assembly, who now renders judgment. The friends, who had unflaggingly held to the inviolable righteousness of God, are condemned by the judge they had defended without daring to question for having spoken "incorrectly" about God, while Job's portrayal of an opprobrious and destructive deity who has vitiated the standards of justice is said to be "correct." Retribution and the refusal to question divine justice are rebuffed as false.

In the final judgment, Yahweh issues the decision that Eliphaz and his two friends have not spoken "correctly" about him and that Job must intercede for them to divert their punishment. The opponent of God, Job, is restored and receives again all he has lost along with ten new children. Thus the friends of Job are required to offer burnt offerings while Job intercedes on their behalf to assuage the anger of Yahweh and to obtain for them forgiveness. Yahweh reclaims at least some of his own integrity in the final judgment, but undoubtedly the question about the murder of Job's children and the undeserved suffering Yahweh inflicted upon him has unsettled the traditional sapiential theology based on the justice of God.

Traditional sages, unhappy with this rereading, sought to undo its effects with two additions: the hymn on the inaccessibility of wisdom (ch. 28), and the speeches of Elihu (chs. 32–37). The poem on Wisdom gives expression to Second Temple piety in which wisdom is identified with the fear of God (see 28:28 = 1:1). Not humans but rather God is both the sage and the judge who alone knows the dwelling of Wisdom and issues decrees that shape and regulate the cosmic order. Thus he oversees providentially all that exists in earth and heaven and creates both wind and rain that produces the richness of the soil. Humans are admonished to cease their search for wisdom and instead to turn to the study of the Torah and to fear God.

The speeches of Elihu (chs. 32–37) derive from a marginalized community on the periphery of political and religious power. He becomes their voice protesting the leadership of Second Temple society, that is, the politically co-opted aristocracy and the priestly hierarchy of the Zadokites. The sage who composed these four speeches (32:6–33:33; 34:1-37; 35:1-16; 36:1–37:24) was dissatisfied with

---

65. See John B. Curtis, "On Job's Response to Yahweh," *JBL* 98 (1979) 497-511.

the earlier poetic dialogues. Indeed, young Elihu was "angry at Job because he justified himself rather than God" (an accurate reading of Job's speeches) and "at the three friends of Job because they had found no answer, though they declared God guilty" (a correction of the scribes, one of the *tiqqûnê sōpĕrîm*, had changed "God" [*hā'ĕlōhîm*] to "Job" [*'iyôb*], 32:3). The sage who composes these speeches is critical of both traditional and radical wisdom to discover answers to major theological questions. Thus he claims inspiration for himself (32:8) in order to combat the typical view that wisdom came with age and experience. The "spirit" *(rûaḥ)* of the Almighty dwelling within humans and nocturnal visions are the forces of life and of inspiration.

Due to the tragedy of the exile, the righteous Job becomes the angry opponent who seeks to expose the injustice of God. Yahweh, the suspicious head of the divine pantheon, no longer is the nurturing creator and patron who protects and sustains his worshipers. The question that remains from reading the dialogues is whether this deity merits human worship. Even with the restoration of Job, there remains the question of divine justice. What God would allow or initiate the outrages done to Job, a faithful and pious man to occur, including the killing of his original ten children? Instead of answering the questions of the catastrophes of the Babylonian destruction and captivity, the transformed book serves only to intensify them. Even later attempts by traditional sages in their additions fail to rescue Job and to respond adequately to the despair of a destroyed community languishing in captivity in a land whose people mock them and their God (Ps. 137).

Social Features: Sages and Their Social Setting

From the activities and terminology of Job's opponents, Elihu, and Job himself, the participants in the disputations are obviously sages who are deeply rooted in the wisdom tradition. In addition, there are references to other sages who are engaged in a variety of roles. Albertz offers a list of terms that are important in identifying the major activities of the sages, who he contends are among the aristocracy.[66] From this list, he concludes that the sages had two primary roles: educational and pastoral.

One of the two principal social roles of the sage is the "counselor" (*yô'ēṣ*, 3:14) who "gives advice" (*yā'aṣ*, 26:3; 29:21). Thus the sage is "to console" (*niḥam*, 16:2; 21:34), "to strengthen" (*ḥizzēq*, *'immēṣ*), "to raise up" (*qûm*, 4:3-4; 21:34), "to help" *('āzar),* "to assist" (*yāśā'*, 26:2), and "to heal" (*rāpā'*, 13:4). The

66. See Albertz, "Sage and Pious Wisdom," 249-50.

instructional function of the sage becomes pastoral in giving comfort to the one who is experiencing difficulty, in this case Job. Not only the friends, but also Job is engaged in this type of counseling (4:3-5). These sages also "issue counsel" *(yāʿaṣ)* to provide guidance *(ʿēṣâ)* to others to make proper decisions and set forth a plan of action that will lead to success (Job 5:13; 18:7). As counselors, Job and his opponents are pastors, offering advice on what to do in particular situations in order to gain relief from their distress and to set a course of action that will lead to well-being, and lawyers, engaged in judicial action to charge the guilty with crimes and to defend the innocent from false accusations. Job is originally advised to confess his sins and to plead for forgiveness and mercy from the divine judge. The opponents also become the defenders of divine justice against the accusations of Job. Job speaks of having served in this dual role in advising and defending the oppressed (29:21).

The second major social role of the sage in Job is that of the instructor who "teaches" *(yārâ,* 6:24; 8:10), "transmits knowledge/perceives" *(yādaʿ, bîn,* 6:24; 26:3; 28:11), and "provides guidance and instruction" *(yāsar, yākaḥ* Hiphil; *mûsār, tôkaḥat;* 4:3; 15:2; 19:5; 20:3; 32:12).

Job is portrayed as wealthy (1:2-5; 19:13-16, 29; 30:1, 28; 42:12), virtuous ("perfect," and "turns from evil," 1:1; ch. 31), and wise (15:2, 8, one who listens in the divine council). In the poetic dialogues, he follows the ideal of the sage portrayed by his friends: 4:3-5; 15:2; 16:4-5; 30:25. He is a sheik or chief *(rōʾš)* of a clan, a pastoral nomad, with a household who, when he enters the city that is close to his tent where he resides with his family and is surrounded by his herds, is held in high esteem. He takes his place of honor in rendering righteous judgment to members of his community, both rural and urban (29:1-25). Finally, in the "oath of innocence," he articulates a list of immoral actions that he has not committed, several of which reflect the ethical code of the sages (cf. ch. 31). Among the wicked actions he has not committed are adultery and ignoring the needs of the poor.

Eliphaz, Bildad, and Zophar are traditional sages, as is the youthful Elihu.[67] Indeed, Elihu calls the three opponents of Job the three "sages" (34:2). Eliphaz

---

67. It is possible that Job and his friends are professional sages (Maag, *Hiob,* 125). R. N. Whybray changed his earlier position on the sages as a professional class of scribes and teachers in his study of the Succession Narrative (*The Succession Narrative: A Study of II Samuel 9–20, I Kings 1 and 2* [SBT 2/8; Naperville, IL: Allenson, 1968]) and came to argue that the wise were intelligent people who discussed important issues. In this later view, he understood the characters in Job not as "learned men" who belonged to a professional class, but rather as wealthy aristocrats who owned lands and substantial property. Thus the characters are in actuality "learned farmers" (*Intellectual Tradition,* 65). See also Gerhard von Rad, who denied that the contestants in the dispute were professional sages (*Wisdom in Israel,* trans. James D. Martin [Nashville: Abingdon, 1972] 20-21). Albertz ("Sage and Pious Wisdom," 243-61) largely agrees with Whybray's later decision.

has a grasp of the wisdom tradition taught by the ancestors (15:17-19), which gives authority to his instruction. He also affirms that God is the one who subverts the plans of the wise, keeping them from reaching a successful outcome (5:12-13): *'ărûmîm* (sensible ones), *ḥăkāmîm* (sages), and *niptālîm* (crafty ones). In 5:13 Eliphaz begins to insinuate that Job is among the sages who are not the pious and righteous followers of the wisdom tradition but rather, filled with craftiness, act to subvert counsel and moral behavior (see 2 Sam. 13:3). They are among the "mighty" *(ḥāzāq)* in Job 5:15 who oppress the poor and comprise the community of the wicked (20:19; 22:5-9; 24:3, 9; 29:16-17).[68] These powerful sages may have constituted a particular social class, even a group of courtiers or officials, who opposed the pious sages. The social group to which Job's opponents belonged comprised traditional sages, teachers, and counselors who instructed others, including those who sought the proper response to suffering. Yet there is one particular feature that sets them apart from the typical traditional sages: their additional role as mantic seers who receive esoteric knowledge by means of dreams (4:12-21; cf. 15:14-16; 25:2-6; 26:4). This same motif is restated by Elihu in 32:8, 18; 33:14-18; and 36:7-12. Further, Job receives esoteric insight from the theophany in the "speeches from the whirlwind."

One of the more important texts for understanding the roles and offices of sages is 12:13-25. In addition to the titles is the reference to the language of exile, indicating strongly that the captivity in Babylon is the setting for the poetic book of Job. The "counselors" *(yôʿăṣîm)* are often found in political contexts and refer to officials whose role it is to provide counsel that will prove successful for the king and his decisions (e.g., 2 Sam. 15:12; 1 Chron. 27:33). "Judges" *(šōpĕṭîm)* are those in the royal administration, who, in addition to rulers, are appointed by the kings to officiate and make rulings based on justice and law in the courts (e.g., Isa. 40:23; Prov. 8:16). If this text refers to the end of the nation due to the Babylonians, "kings" *(mĕlākîm)* were exiled (Jehoiachin, who was replaced on the throne by Nebuchadnezzar and sent into Babylonian captivity in 597 B.C.E.; and Zedekiah, blinded and taken into captivity to Babylon in 586) and one was assassinated (Jehoiakim, who died during the siege resulting in the exile in 597). "Established ones" *('ētānîm)* are those who either hold hereditary offices or have the status of wealth.[69] These may be the ones to whom 2 Kgs. 24:15 refers as the "elite of the land." "Trusted ones" *(neʾĕmānîm)* are those who are reliable (Isa. 8:2; Prov. 25:13). They may be those in government whose words and behavior may be trusted by the king, thus making them advisors or counselors. "Elders" *(zĕqēnîm)* on occasion were part of the upper stratum in the government and are often listed among

68. Albertz, "Sage and Pious Wisdom," 247.
69. BDB, 450-51.

other officials, especially royal ones (2 Kgs. 10:1, 5; Lam. 1:19). The *nādîb* ("noble," esp. in character) belongs to a social category of highly respected and powerful people due to office or status. At times, nobles or noble ones are paralleled to the *śārîm* (princes or officials) (Job 34:18-19; Prov. 8:16). Collectively, they represent the highest human power in the state (Pss. 118:9; 146:3). In Job 34:18; Prov. 8:15-16; 25:6-7; and Ps. 47:10(9) they are paralleled to the king *(melek)*, thus indicating their stature and power in the royal government. They may be a more general category to refer to the officials mentioned in 2 Kgs. 24–25: servants of the king *('ăbādîm)*, officers *(śārîm)*, and palace officials *(sārîsîm)*. They also were aristocrats due to their wealth (Prov. 18:16), and in wisdom texts often refer to the blameless, upright, and righteous sages (Prov. 8:16; 17:7, 26).[70]

In Job 12:13-25 the language of the exile includes: "lead away" *(môlîk*, v. 17; see 2 Kgs. 24:15; Hos. 2:16[14]; Ps. 125:5), "wasteland without roads" *(tōhû lō'-dārek*, v. 24; see Deut. 32:10; Job 6:18; Ps. 107:40), and "despoil" *(šôllāl*, v. 19; see Isa. 10:6; Ezek. 26:12; 29:19; Hab. 2:8; Zech. 2:12[8]). Thus among the leaders sent into exile are sages who are officials responsible for the foolish mistakes that led to the devastation of the city of Jerusalem (see 2 Kgs. 24–25). They are all the more the ones challenged, along with the rulers, to explain their and God's failure in saving the nation from this collapse.

Finally, it is important to note the divine roles and titles in this passage. God possesses "wisdom *(ḥŏkmâ)*, strength, counsel *('ēṣâ)*, and understanding *(tĕbûnâ)*" (12:13; he is "wise in heart," 9:4). In traditional theology these are the divine characteristics used in creating both the cosmos and humanity, judging human behavior, and defeating both Behemoth and Leviathan, who threaten the cosmos and all of life. Yet the passage here appears to mock this theology in view of the devastation of the nation and its people.

The book of Job points to two possible social locations: the royal administration, especially the upper echelons of officials, and the school. The officials, courtiers, and royal house sent into captivity in 12:13-25 demonstrate that one of the social locations found in the poetic book of Job is the royal court. It is possible that the sage who composed this section of the book was one of the exiles or a descendant who spent his life in Babylonian captivity functioning as a sage in the Jewish community, engaging the crisis of faith that engulfed the former leaders of Judah whose nation, capital, monarchy, temple, and religious traditions had disintegrated in the face of a cataclysmic holocaust. This sage would have found himself in the midst of former leaders whose status, power, prestige, and honor had vanished in the desolation of conquest.

The legendary narrative does mention Job's household *(mišpāḥâ)*, and this is

---

70. J. Conrad, *TDOT*, 9:224-25.

picked up once by the poet in ch. 31. In both contexts he is presented as a wealthy pastoral nomad. In the narrative he owns a large number of herds of sheep, camels, oxen, and donkeys, and has numerous servants. In addition to animals and servants, he is married and has seven sons and three daughters. Three catastrophes exterminate his entire household and herds, leaving only his wife who survives, although all is restored to him and more. Chapters 29–31 mention his tent and his male and female slaves, whom he treats with justice. In both literal and figurative applications, the term "father," 'āb, occurs throughout the book (8:8; 15:10; 15:18; 17:14; 29:16; 30:1; 31:18; 38:28; 42:15). The word "mother," 'ēm, is used literally (1:21; 3:10; 17:14; 31:18). In two places, however, the term "father" is treated to refer to sages: Bildad's reference to the fathers to refer to the wise men of the past who formed the sapiential tradition (8:8), and the reference by Eliphaz to ancient sages whose wisdom refutes the teaching of Job (15:15). But any reference to the household as the context for the teaching of wisdom is lacking.

The existence of schools suggested by the book of Job is based on several factors: the references to the instruction of the sages, the traditions of the wise ancestors, common sapiential themes and vocabulary, titles given to the disputants, and the disputations themselves. It is the disputation, a common sapiential form, that is the most important clue to a school setting for the book. Furthermore, the resemblance of Job to Babylonian wisdom texts, the author's frequent use of Aramaic terms, the existence of Akkadian schools *(bīt ṭuppi)*, and the presence of scribes who know Aramaic in the Babylonian administration are intimations of a school setting for the book. Aramaic had become the lingua franca of the Babylonian empire. The exile marked the slow transition from Hebrew to Aramaic as the dominant language of the people of Judah.

The presence of scribes and teachers among the Jewish population in Babylon may be inferred from the fact that upper-class residents of Jerusalem included administrative officials and a well-educated aristocracy who were taken into exile. Due to the lack of archaeological and written evidence, it is impossible to know with certainty if any schools were established among the exilic communities, but the large number of texts likely written and redacted during this period in order to preserve Jewish culture points to the necessity of some schools where this activity of composition, writing, and, due to the lengthy period of exile (more than two generations), education must have occurred. At least one may imagine fathers and mothers teaching their children, with some receiving scribal instruction from their fathers. Whether any of the Jewish exiles would have had access to any Neo-Babylonian literature is impossible to say, but the themes of this culture seem to be well known to Jewish exiles, as the books of Second Isaiah and Job demonstrate. This knowledge of Neo-Babylonian royal ideology and mythology would intimate that some of the educated captives had access to scribal knowledge that produced and preserved Babylonian culture. Some of these captives may have been pressed into service as scribes in the vast Babylonian Empire.

Cuneiform was known by some scribes in Eretz Israel over a lengthy period of time, from the early Assyrian period into the early Hellenistic age.[71] In addition, Isa. 28:11 possibly refers to Akkadian. The exiles' knowledge of Akkadian would likely have been necessary, although the uneducated might have relied only on Aramaic, leaving it up to Jewish scribes to master the difficult cuneiform language. This was especially possible due to the fact that the alphabetic Aramaic language was becoming the lingua franca of the empire. That Jewish scribes knew Aramaic well is recognized in the extensive influence of this language on later Hebrew texts. While most of the Jewish literature of the exile was written in Babylonia, some literary activity did occur in Judah at the same time, although there is little evidence for any extensive knowledge of cuneiform.[72]

The location in Babylonia would have provided the intelligentsia of the exiles the opportunity to have firsthand knowledge of Babylonian culture, including literature. In Babylonia past written records of Judah were reshaped by Jewish scribes and surviving leaders to take into consideration the dramatic effect the exile had on Israelite and Judahite history, theology, and religion. Thus the redaction of the past traditions was done with an eye toward their reformulation for both the Jews of the homeland and the Babylonian captives. A new sociopolitical reality had to be created to maintain some semblance of identity based on learning and the composition and redaction of texts. Thus the exiles must have had several schools that redacted the past literature and composed new texts necessary to provide continuity into an uncertain future.

Particularly significant in the prophetic literature of the period (Habakkuk, Ezekiel, and esp. Second Isaiah) are two matters: Babylonian traditions, in particular the Babylonian imperial cosmology, military adventurism, and economic policies[73] that were devastating to the victims of conquest;[74] and the literary im-

---

71. Wayne Horowitz, Takayoshi Oshia, and Seth Sanders, "A Bibliographical List of Cuneiform Inscriptions from Canaan, Palestine/Philistia, and the Land of Israel," *JAOS* 122 (2002) 753-66.

72. Horowitz, Oshia, and Sanders note that few Neo-Babylonian texts have been found (ibid.).

73. See M. A. Dandamayev, "Neo-Babylonian Society and Economy," in *CAH* 3/2: *The Assyrian and Babylonian Empires and Other States of the Near East, from the Eighth to the Sixth Centuries B.C.*, ed. John Boardman, et al. (2nd ed.; Cambridge: Cambridge University Press, 1991) 252-75.

74. See David S. Vanderhooft, *The Neo-Babylonian Empire and Babylon in the Latter Prophets* (HSM 59; Atlanta: Scholars Press, 1999) 114-202. For a contrary position that rejects Babylonian influence, see H. M. Barstad, "On the So-Called Babylonian Literary Influence in Second Isaiah," *SJOT* 2 (1987) 90-110.

pact of cuneiform on the language of Second Isaiah.[75] A strong case has been made in favor of his knowledge of the royal inscriptions.[76] In particular, his attack on cult images points to his concerted efforts to subvert the authenticity of Babylonian cosmology and imperial greatness that, among other things, pointed to Babylon as the center of the cosmos. By contrast, Second Isaiah argues against the animation and knowledge of crafted idols and asserts that Yahweh alone is creator, director of history, and determiner of human destinies.[77]

The most engaging and theologically astute texts of the Hebrew Bible were Job and Second Isaiah (Isa. 40–55). Indeed, as Terrien has argued, the two texts share a considerable number of literary images, suggesting either influence or at the least a common social world from which their contents emerged.[78] This piece of prophetic literature points to the enemy of the exiles as the Babylonians and interprets the historical movements instigated by Cyrus (c. 559-530 B.C.E.; 41:2-3, 25; 44:24–45:13; 48:14) as the new acts of God to redeem the chosen from exile. Strongly monotheistic (43:10-11; 45:21-22), as is the book of Job, this unknown prophet of the exile encouraged his fellow exiles to live in expectation of a new deliverance that took on the images of the first exodus, the one from Egyptian slavery led by Moses. Jerusalem will be restored including the temple and the returnees, although curiously no mention is made of the reconstitution of the Davidic monarchy. Now it is Judah who will enjoy God's eternal covenant, while Cyrus is the "anointed one" chosen to carry out this deliverance. This unknown prophet of the exile supported the imperial ambitions of Persia, seeing that this new power in the ancient Near East provided the best opportunity for liberation from captivity. Since the Persians discontinued the Assyro-Babylonian policy of exile and presented the view that they were tolerant of other religions, Second Isaiah placed full weight on Israel's sacred traditions of the exodus, a divinely guided and protected journey through the wilderness, the entrance in the land, and the David and Zion complex in order to shape a theology of return. The one political change designed to curry Persian favor

75. Note Shalom Paul, "Deutero-Isaiah and Cuneiform Royal Inscriptions," *JAOS* 88 (1968) 180-86.

76. J. W. Behr, *The Writings of Deutero-Isaiah and the Neo-Babylonian Inscriptions* (Publications of the University of Pretoria, Series III, Arts 3; Pretoria: University of Pretoria, 1937); Vanderhooft, *Neo-Babylonian Empire*, 170. See P.-R. Berger, *Die neubabylonischen Königsinschriften: Königsinschriften des ausgehenden babylonischen Reiches (625-539 a. Chr.)* (AOAT 4/1; Kevelaer: Butzon & Becker; Neukirchen-Vluyn: Neukirchener Verlag, 1973).

77. See esp. Angelika Berlejung, *Die Theologie der Bilder: Herstellung und Einweihung von Kultbildern in Mesopotamien und die alttestamentlichen Bilderpolemik* (OBO 162; Göttingen: Vandenhoeck & Ruprecht, 1998).

78. Terrien, "Quelques remarques."

was the transference of the messianic tradition from the house of David to the Persian conquering king, Cyrus. His response to the exile, coming near the end of the captivity in Babylonia, strongly contrasted with the laments of Job and the sapiential attack on the justice of God.

In Job the roles of the educated include the following. The term "teacher" *(môreh)* or the activity of teaching occurs several times (Job 6:24; 12:8; 27:11; 34:32; 36:22). This term in its nominal and verbal forms occurs in reference to the cosmos, whose structure and forms of life teach the observant sage (12:8), in the disputations of Job and his opponents when they seek to "teach" or instruct the other (6:24; 27:11; 34:32), and later in regard to God in the speeches of Elihu (36:22). Another term for an office held by sages is *šōpēṭ*, translated as "judge" or "lawyer/advocate" (see 12:17). It is clear that there are important legal dimensions prevalent in the book. These include the opponents' rejection of Job's accusations against the justice of God and the contention that he perverts justice in the manner of a corrupt judge (8:3; 22:4, 13; 40:8). Job asserts his own justice (29:14) and seeks to take his opponent to court (9:15, 19; 9:32; 22:3-7), though he fears that God's power would leave him speechless and overwhelmed (9:32; 27:2). His own recourse is to have speak for him an intermediary *(môkîaḥ)* to demonstrate that God is the corrupt judge who has subverted his creature's justice (14:3; 19:7; 21:22). Finally, Job demands an indictment *(sēper kātab)* from "my adversary" *('îš rîbî)* that lists the charges against him (31:35).

The references to Job's literary and reading skills indicate that he is presented as an educated graduate of a sapiential school of some type (19:23-24; 31:35). This talent and training were available only to the aristocracy, a status indicated by his enormous wealth and social status in chs. 1 and 29–31. Skilled speaking is a talent attributed to Job in 31:35-37, which refers to his legal defense. Job and his opponents boast the skills of the rhetor (4:2; 33:32; 34:3), while the sophistication of their speeches demonstrates their rhetorical skills. The term "rhetor" may be suggested by the Piel participle *mĕdabbēr*. Not only is the poet who composes the dialogues a sage, but so is his major character. Job is presented as a skilled wise man and considers his adversaries to be sages who either lack true wisdom (26:2-3) or pervert it (12:2; 13:5). He attributes wisdom to the aged (12:12) and to God (12:13). Job's speeches are also replete with typical wisdom genres: rhetorical questions (6:5, 6), sayings (12:11; 24:19), and a *māšāl* as an "example story" (27:1; 29:1).[79] Thus the book appears to be the composition of a sage, likely living in Babylonian exile, who writes a dialogue intent on addressing the horrors of the Babylonian conquest and its impact on both the under-

---

79. For the poet as a sage, see Jacques Vermeylen, *Job, ses amis et son Dieu: La légende de Job et ses relectures postexiliques* (Studia biblica 2; Leiden: Brill, 1986) 72-79.

standing of the social group of exiled sages and the other intelligentsia who made up the majority of the Jewish community in Babylonia.

Major Theological Themes

The poetic book of Job is best interpreted as a response to the devastation caused by a traumatic national experience in the life of the community of Judah. The section of Job's speech in 12:13-25, which uses the language of exile and mentions the social groups involved in the journey into captivity, suggests that the destruction of Jerusalem, followed by the forced march into captivity, is the occasion for the composition of the poetic book. It is this devastation that leads the poet to reflect on the theological implications of the Babylonian holocaust in the life of Judah. This book joins others that were written and redacted while the community of the exiles is languishing in exile: Second Isaiah, Ezekiel, the prose speeches and narratives of Jeremiah, Ps. 137, much of the Deuteronomistic History, and an early form of the Priestly document. It is noteworthy that the exile was the time for the thriving of literary activity. For this to occur, the poets and composers of the community would necessarily have had to have access to a setting where writing was possible.

The poet subverts the theological foundation of wisdom that flourished prior to the debacle of 586 B.C.E.: the righteous order that permeates creation, the justice of God the creator of the cosmos and humanity, the divine providential maintenance of the natural world and human society and events, and God's goodness and mercy. The Babylonian conquest undermined the sages' theological affirmations, leaving the wise with a faith in which Yahweh could no longer rule the world in justice. The cardinal teaching of retribution has dissolved in the face of holocaust.

Divine Creation and Providence

The poet began the story of Job with the appropriation of the older prologue (chs. 1–2), which has the mythic images of the divine council and predestination of humans. Yet the acquiescence of Job is replaced by a despairing curse in the opening soliloquy (ch. 3). This speech gives voice to curses that ironically repudiate Job's refusal to yield to the Satan's testing and to his wife's counsel in the prose tale. Now follow increasingly passionate dialogues over divine justice between Job and his three opponents, culminating in the theophany of the whirlwind speeches.

In the dialogues, Job assaults divine justice by comparing the creator to a despot who seeks to destroy the work of his own hand. The exaltation of humanity in Ps. 8 is rejected by Job in 7:17-21. The friends, who are the stalwart defenders of divine justice, reach the conclusion that Job must be a sinner to receive such punishment. Job's oath of innocence in ch. 31 indicates he has left his human opponents behind in order to challenge God to a lawsuit that would exonerate the human adversary and thereby condemn the creator.

The speeches of the "voice from the whirlwind" (38:1–42:6) speak of creation and providence, but do not address the issues at hand. God ignores the two critical questions raised by Job in the earlier dialogues with his opponents: why humans, especially the righteous, suffer, and why God is unjust. In the speeches from the whirlwind, Yahweh does not defend his justice or explain why retribution is a false teaching. Instead, he merely demonstrates his profound wisdom and asserts his superior power. However, Job had already acceded to these points, which he considered to be unquestionably the case, and simply reiterates them in his second response (42:1-6). Yahweh's ignoring of the critical questions of Job resounds with deafening silence.

While God is the heavenly creator and sustainer who has great power, he can only restrain Yamm with his edict and continue to do battle with the two monsters of chaos, Behemoth and Leviathan (40:15–41:34), for the rule of the cosmos and the sea. He admits indirectly that he cannot defeat the proud and wicked and cast them into the underworld. Consequently, God is not omnipotent. As for his own nature, God is a destructive deity who brings unbearable suffering even to his own righteous servants.

With the new poetic dialogues, the epilogue's meaning is reconstructed by the poet to indicate that Job has spoken "correctly" about God (ironically supporting his accusations against divine justice), while the friends have not (also ironic since they had adamantly defended God's righteousness). Job has his integrity upheld by the ruler of the divine assembly, who now renders judgment against his defenders. The friends are condemned by the judge they had staunchly justified and delivered only because of the intercession of the blasphemous opponent they had charged with wrongdoing. Retribution and the refusal to question divine justice are proven false. In a community of exiles whose nation had been destroyed, questioning divine justice is the proper recourse.

Creation and Anthropology

In the dialogues, Job is positioned as the "slave" of Yahweh, similar to the role of humanity in Babylonian mythology (see Atra-ḫasīs and Job 7). Afflicted with excruciating pain and subjected to social humiliation, Job unleashed his verbal assault on the divine tyrant who brings destruction against even the righteous slave who serves him loyally. No longer the passive and obedient servant of the prologue, Job engages in a titanic contest with God for supremacy over the earth. While not the perfect man of the prologue, Job now asserts his own righteousness in the poetry. He recognizes that he has committed insignificant sins and rejects the contention that unknown sins have led to his present torment. Nothing he has done, knowingly or unknowingly, should have led to this divine attack by God. By contrast, the friends set forth the innate wickedness of humans, whom Bildad even compares to maggots. For the friends, humans deserve chastisement and suffering for their evil, since wickedness permeates human nature. Furthermore, the extreme suffering of Job may be explained only as retribution for his evil. Yahweh's speeches from the whirlwind remove humans from the central role on earth. Indeed, it is Behemoth, not humanity, who is the first of God's creation. God even sends the precious rain where no humans dwell and cares for the ferocious animals that are not controlled by humans. Nowhere does God assert his care for humans or offer them mercy.

Creation and Goddess Wisdom

Traditional sages made two additions in order to attempt to lessen the radical conclusion of the addition of the poetic disputations: the hymn on the inaccessibility of wisdom (ch. 28) and the speeches of Elihu (chs. 32–37). These were likely written during the periods of Ezra and Ben Sira when Torah and retribution gained salient theological significance. The didactic poem on Wisdom indicates that she resides outside the reach of human beings. This is more than a statement about the inability to locate and understand divine wisdom. In the wisdom tradition, Wisdom is the giver of life and prosperity, but now she resides in hidden recesses and is known only by the creator. The refrain encapsulates the poem's theme in the form of an impossible question: "Where shall wisdom be found, and where is the place of insight?" (vv. 12, 20). God alone knows the dwelling place of Wisdom in the structure of and regulation of his creation. Denied the grasp of divine wisdom, humans, instead of seeking this cosmic knowledge and life-giving gift, are to "fear God and turn from evil" in the same way that the unquestioning Job of the prologue did. The later sage who added this poem expresses the view that humans should turn from the search for cosmic wisdom and instead be content with the directions for life provided in the Torah. This sage could not endure the nightmare world depicted in the speeches of Job and the voice from the whirlwind.

Metaphors of Creation and the Speeches of Elihu

The speeches of Elihu (chs. 32–37) appear to speak against the Jewish leadership of Second Temple society and the colonial power represented by the Persian rulers. Also dissatisfied with the earlier poetic dialogues, a later sage composed these speeches, since the friends had failed to give a proper answer to Job's questioning and for finding God to be in the wrong. Claiming to be inspired, Elihu asserts that he possesses the "spirit" *(rûaḥ)* of the Almighty. Like Eliphaz, he also notes that God sends visions in the night to warn people to turn from their wickedness and to gain salvation from death (4:12-21). Finally, he contends that the creator rejects the flatterer who engages in uttering wise speech.

Elihu's populism leads him to emphasize that the mighty and wealthy possess the same origins as the poor and thus are not favored by God (34:17-20). Both are shaped by God in the womb (34:19) and have the same end. God condemns those who oppress the poor (34:28), for wicked kings are not allowed to escape divine punishment and to continue to reign. In the final speech, Elihu speaks of the exaltation of the righteous, who will sit forever on royal thrones, not the wicked kings who are tyrants. Elihu knows the mythological depiction of the rebellious kings who seek to reign in the place of the God (Ezek. 28). They will be hurled to their destruction in the new world, while the righteous poor will reign supreme.

Elihu's familiarity with the Yahweh speeches that follow is particularly noted in the final strophe of the last speech (37:14-24), indicating that the composer of these speeches has borrowed from the language of the "voice from the whirlwind." Elihu also asks Job impossible questions that pertain to the "wonderful works of God." These questions are designed to humble Job, not induce within him praise of the creator. However, he adds divine justice to the content of the Yahweh speeches. Elihu's questions underline the power, justice, and mystery of the Almighty in contrast to the weakness and ignorance of Job. The design of these questions is to fill the critics of God with fear, not adoration. Yet in the context of the book in which there is a steady movement from the defiant Job demanding his right to trial to the awesome theophany of the terrible God of creation, the rantings of Elihu ring hollow. In the theophany, God demonstrates he is neither just nor concerned with the plight of the human sufferer. Job's response continues to be that of protest and a feeling of deep-seated sorrow for humans, who must suffer in the world of divine tyranny. Like the other defenders of God, Elihu fails to offer a theological response that makes sense of a world of holocaust.

4. Wisdom during the Persian Empire: The Wisdom Psalms

General Introduction

The Psalter came into existence over the centuries and contains numerous types of psalms that were sung by corporate Israel and Judah in the context of worship in the temple. This songbook includes a variety of genres used for appropriate occasions in the liturgical year: hymns, laments, and thanksgivings. However, there are other psalms not so easily classified in these three major categories. Among them are the wisdom psalms.

Wisdom Psalms in the Psalter

The debate concerning the presence of wisdom psalms in the Psalter has been ongoing for the past century. However, most scholars of the Psalter and wisdom literature have insisted that the category, if not a conventional genre similar to the other forms of psalms (laments, thanksgivings, and hymns), may be identified in terms of language and themes.[1] The exchange between James L.

---

1. See Hermann Gunkel and Joachim Begrich, *Introduction to Psalms*, trans. James D. Nogalski (Macon, GA: Mercer University Press, 1998) 293-305; Johannes Fichter, *Die altorientalische Weisheit in ihrer israelitisch-jüdischen Ausprägung* (BZAW 62; Giessen: Töpelmann, 1933) 9; Herman Ludin Janssen, *Die spätjüdische Psalmendichtung. Ihr Entstehungskreis und ihr 'Sitz im Leben'* (Oslo: Dybwab, 1937); Sigmund Mowinckel, "Psalms and Wisdom," in *Wisdom in Israel and in the Ancient Near East,* ed. M. Noth and D. Winton Thomas (VTSup 3; Leiden: Brill, 1955)

Crenshaw and J. Kenneth Kuntz has sharpened the issues at stake. Crenshaw has categorically rejected the existence of wisdom psalms, calling the designation "vague," "misleading," and "useless."[2] Crenshaw's criticism is based on the view that vocabulary and themes uniquely sapiential must determine whether a text is a work of wisdom. In my judgment, however, the issue is not the uniqueness of a word, but its frequency and particular meaning in a specific literary context (prophetic, sapiential, priestly, royal, etc.). If "uniqueness" is the sine qua non of defining the nature of a text, nothing could be designated as issuing from a social and literary milieu. This is due to the fact that a culture may understand a text only if there are a shared vocabulary and set of themes. It is not uniqueness one should identify, but rather a preponderance of terms and concepts that identify the literary origins and contexts of literature. Another semantic factor is that of the grammar and syntax of sentences, clauses, and phrases.

Wisdom psalms are an expression of didactic poems designed to teach the important themes of sapiential literature to youth seeking an education in some form of school. From these one may derive sapiential theology, morality, and piety. On occasion, some of the features of other forms of the Psalter are used in the composition of these poems, but even more frequent is the presence of the other forms of wisdom literature. Didactic poems in the Psalter make use of a sapiential lexicography (a specialized vocabulary of a group or genre), shared semantics (terms, grammar, syntax, and common forms, phrases, clauses, and brief sentences), and themes that may be compiled from the Hebrew wisdom texts in the canonical and deuterocanonical literature.

205-24; idem, "Traditionalism and Personality in Psalms," *HUCA* 23 (1950/51) 2-3; Roland Murphy, "A Consideration of the Classification 'Wisdom Psalms,'" in *Congress Volume: Bonn, 1962* (VTSup 9; Leiden: Brill, 1963) 156-67; J. Kenneth Kuntz, "The Canonical Wisdom Psalms of Ancient Israel — Their Rhetorical, Thematic, and Formal Elements," in *Rhetorical Criticism: Essays in Honor of James Muilenburg*, ed. Jared J. Jackson and Martin Kessler (PTMS 1; Pittsburgh: Pickwick, 1974) 186-222; Walter Beyerlin, *Studien zum 15. Psalm* (Biblische Studien 9; Neukirchen-Vluyn: Neukirchener Verlag, 1985); idem, *Weisheitliche Vergewisserung mit Bezug auf den Zionskult. Studien zum 125. Psalm* (OBO 68; Göttingen: Vandenhoeck & Ruprecht, 1985); Avi Hurwitz, "Wisdom Vocabulary in the Hebrew Psalter," *VT* 38 (1988) 41-52; Samuel Terrien, "Wisdom in the Psalter" in *In Search of Wisdom*, 51-72; Anthony Ceresko, "The Sage in the Psalms," in *Sage in Israel*, 217-30; R. N. Whybray, "The Wisdom Psalms," in *Wisdom in Ancient Israel*, 152-60; Oswald Loretz, *Psalmenstudien: Kolometrie, Strophik und Theologie* (BZAW 309; Berlin: de Gruyter, 2002), who examines Ps. 127 as a wisdom psalm.

2. James L. Crenshaw, "Wisdom Psalms?" *CR:BS* 8 (2000) 9-17. Jacques Trublet emphasizes semantics. Thus a term that is generally associated with wisdom may not be a wisdom expression or necessarily influenced by wisdom (Jacques Trublet and Jean-Noël, *Approche poétique et théologique des psaumes: Analyses et méthodes* [Paris: Cerf, 1983]; Jacques Trublet, "Le corpus sapiential et le Psautier," in *La sagesse biblique: De L'Ancien au Nouveau Testaments* [LD 160; Paris: Cerf, 1995] 139-74).

Wisdom Psalms outside the Psalter

There are numerous examples of wisdom psalms and didactic poems in Hebrew canonical and deuterocanonical texts in addition to those that are found
in the Psalms. Proverbs 3:19-20, the aretologies in Prov. 8, and the numerous
hymns of praise in Ben Sira are important parallels.

Proverbs 3:19-20 is a hymnic strophe that is added to the instruction in 3:13-
18. Part of a creation hymn, this strophe praises Yahweh for his founding *(kônēn)*
the heavens by means of "understanding" *(tĕbûnâ)*, demonstrating that "understanding" (a synonym for wisdom) is the instrument of creation. This hymnic
strophe in 3:19-20 (see Jer. 10:12; Ps. 104:24) indicates through means of praise that
Yahweh used his wisdom in both the origins of the earth and in supplying the life-
giving rain.[3] This imagery echoes that of God's use of divine wisdom in creating,
ordering, and sustaining the world (cf. Pss. 104:24; 136:5; Jer. 10:12; 51:15).[4] Three
verbs of creation are used to speak of God's originating the cosmos. One is *yāsad*
("established"; Amos 9:6; Isa. 24:18; 48:13; 51:13; Zech. 12:1; cf. Prov. 8:29), while a
second is *kûn* ("secured"; Prov. 24:3; Pss. 93:1; 119:90; Job 28:25, 27; cf. Prov. 8:27).
These verbs present God as the divine builder who lays down a strong foundation
and strengthens the walls and columns (cf. Prov. 9:1; 24:3-4; Job 38:4-7; Ps. 104:5).
The third verb for God's creation of the cosmos is *bāqaʿ* ("divide"), a term used in
the tradition of the combat between Yahweh and the chaos monster. Yahweh
makes use of his knowledge (= wisdom) to "divide" the primeval sea, Yamm (see
Isa. 51:9-11, echoing the parting of the Reed Sea in Exod. 15).[5]

Proverbs 8 contains three aretologies (hymns of self-praise) of Woman
Wisdom (8:2-11, 12-21, 22-31), which are then concluded by her dissemination of
a paraenetic instruction inviting her "children" to follow her teachings in order
to discover life and avoid death (8:32-36).[6] Woman Wisdom is portrayed as a
peripatetic teacher who searches out and invites human beings to learn of her
instruction, a goddess of life, the first of God's creation present at the origins of

---

3. See Norman Habel, "The Symbolism of Wisdom in Proverbs 1–9," *Interp* 26 (1972) 131-57.

4. Prov. 3:19 closely compares to Jer. 10:12 (= 51:15). A scribal redaction of Jeremiah is responsible for the occasional occurrences of wisdom forms and vocabulary.

5. See Mary K. Wakemann, *God's Battle with the Monster* (Leiden: Brill, 1973); Foster
McCurley, *Ancient Myths and Biblical Faith: Scriptural Transformation* (Philadelphia: Fortress,
1983) 11-71; Jon Levenson, *Creation and the Persistence of Evil: The Jewish Drama of Divine Omnipotence* (San Francisco: Harper & Row, 1988).

6. See Maurice Gilbert, "Le discours de la sagesse en Proverbes 8," in *La Sagesse de l'Ancien
Testament,* ed. Maurice Gilbert (new ed.; BETL 51; Leuven: Leuven University Press, 1990) 202-18;
Patrick Skehan, "Structures in Poems on Wisdom: Proverbs 8 and Sirach 24," *CBQ* 41 (1979) 365-79.
For 1:20-33 see Phyllis Trible, "Wisdom Builds a Poem: The Architecture of Proverbs 1:20-33," *JBL*
94 (1975) 509-18; Roland Murphy, "Wisdom's Song: Proverbs 1:20-33," *CBQ* 48 (1986) 456-60.

the cosmos, and the mediator between the creator and the "inhabited earth."[7] Seeking to find students in the paths and city streets (8:1-3), Wisdom utters her call to the simple to learn of her (8:4-11). In 8:12-21 Wisdom is transformed into the Queen of Heaven (cf. Asherah, Maʿat, and Isis) who possesses both the beauty and the insight of a fertility goddess to rule earthly kingdoms. Now she becomes the goddess who, similar to ancient Near Eastern goddesses, enters into the embrace of kings and chooses those who love her to rule. Her gifts are riches and honor, which she gives to those who follow her and give her their devotion. Wise and righteous rulers establish order in their societies, which reflect the harmony of the cosmos (Job 12:18; 36:7). Proverbs 8:22-31 recounts the origins of Woman Wisdom as the divine offspring fathered *(qānâ)*[8] and given birth *(ḥûl)* by Yahweh to be the first or perhaps best *(rēʾšît)* of creation, the goddess who witnesses creation, and the mediator between Yahweh and the human world.[9] While not the means of divine creation, she is Yahweh's firstborn child *(ʾāmôn)*,[10] present when he formed the spheres of the cosmos.[11] These two texts from Proverbs demonstrate that the faith of the sages is centered in a theology of creation and maintenance of the cosmos.[12]

7. Raymond Van Leeuwen also argues that the teaching of Proverbs is based on cosmic wisdom ("Proverbs," *NIB* 5 [1997] 89).

8. The verb *qānâ* means "to acquire or obtain" (Prov. 1:5; 4:5, 7), "to purchase" (Exod. 21:2), and "to create/procreate," e.g., heaven and earth (Gen. 14:19, 22) or human beings (Gen. 4:1; Deut. 32:6; Ps. 139:13). "Create/procreate" is the meaning in this occurrence, since the verb *ḥûl* is used in vv. 24 and 25 ("to writhe in birth pains"; cf. Deut. 32:18; Job 39:1; Pss. 29:9; 51:7[5]; 90:2). See Paul Humbert, "'*Qânâ*' en hébreu biblique," in *Festschrift Alfred Bertholet,* ed. W. Baumgartner, et al. (Tübingen: Mohr [Siebeck], 1950) 259-66.

9. For the poem in 8:22-31, see Othmar Keel, *Die Weisheit spielt vor Gott* (Göttingen: Vandenhoeck & Ruprecht, 1974). Also see Herbert Donner, "Die religionsgeschichtlichen Ursprünge von Prov. Sal. 8,22-31," *ZÄS* 82 (1957) 8-18; J. N. Aletti, "Proverbes 8:22-31: Étude et structure," *Bib* 57 (1976) 25-37; Bruce Vawter, "Prov. 8:22: Wisdom and Creation," *JBL* 99 (1980) 205-16; R. N. Whybray, "Proverbs VIII,22-31 and Its Supposed Prototypes," *VT* 15 (1965) 504-14; Gale A. Yee, "An Analysis of Prov. 8:22-31 according to Style and Structure," *ZAW* 94 (1982) 58-66. For Wisdom as a goddess, see Bernhard Lang, *Wisdom and the Book of Proverbs: A Hebrew Goddess Redefined* (New York: Pilgrim, 1986) 55-58.

10. For a summary of the different possible meanings of *ʾāmôn* see R. B. Y. Scott, "Wisdom in Creation: The *ʾāmôn* of Proverbs VIII 30," *VT* 10 (1960) 213-23.

11. See Jan Assmann, *Ägypten — Theologie und Frömmigkeit einer frühen Hochkultur* (Stuttgart: Kohlhammer, 1991), esp. 211, Coffin Text 80; Kayatz, *Studien zu Proverbien 1–9.*

12. Rainer Albertz, *Weltschöpfung und Menschenschöpfung: untersucht bei Deutero-Isaiah, Hiob und in die Psalmen* (Calwer theologische Monographien Reihe A, Bibelwissenschaft 3; Stuttgart: Calwer, 1974); Peter Doll, *Menschenschöpfung und Weltschöpfung in der alttestamentlichen Weisheit* (SBS 117; Stuttgart: Katholisches Bibelwerk, 1985); H.-J. Hermisson, "Observations on the Creation Theology in Wisdom," in *Israelite Wisdom: Theological and Literary Essays in Honor of Samuel Terrien,* ed. John G. Gammie, et al. (Missoula, MT: Scholars Press, 1978) 43-57;

Ben Sira composes numerous hymns that are not only to be read but also to be used in corporate worship.[13] These are didactic poems (wisdom psalms) that are present throughout the collection: 1:1-10; 17:1-24; 18:1-14; 24:1-34; 36:1-33; 39:12-35; 42:13–43:33. Ben Sira indicates that his students engaged in the singing of wisdom psalms and that he composed them. Thus in 39:15 he admonishes his students: "Ascribe majesty to his name and give thanks to him with praise, with songs on your lips, and with harps; this is what you shall say in thanksgiving." What follows this exhortation is a thanksgiving hymn to God concerning the goodness of creation and theodicy (39:16-34). He concludes this poem with the synonymous imperative: "So now sing praise with all your heart and voice, and bless the name of the Lord." In 39:12-14 he speaks of his "inspiration," demonstrating that he is the author of this psalm. Once again he admonishes his audience: "Scatter the fragrance, and sing a hymn of praise; bless the Lord for all his works" (v. 14).

The wisdom hymn of Baruch, a deuterocanonical book consisting of three different sections (a prose prayer, 1:1–3:8; a wisdom poem, 3:9–4:4; and a lament, 4:5–5:9), dates from a period between the early second century to the mid-first century B.C.E. Wisdom is known only by Yahweh, who gave her to Israel, whom he loved. Afterward, she took up habitation on the earth and dwelt among humankind. This Wisdom is identified with the Torah, which is God's gift to Israel, and now lives among only them, bringing joy to its people. The poem concludes with a "happy saying" that indicates Israel rejoices because of the knowledge of what is pleasing to God (4:4). This didactic poem is similar to Job 28 and Sir. 24. Whether it was sung by a community cannot be determined.

Other wisdom psalms and didactic poems exist outside the canon and apocryphal Jewish literature. The wisdom literature composed by the scribes of Qumran contains several writings that are best classified as wisdom psalms (or didactic poems).[14] These include 4Q411, a fragmentary sapiential hymn that praises Yahweh's act of creation;[15] 4Q426, 4Q528, and 4Q498, a fragment of

---

Walther Zimmerli, "The Place and Limit of the Wisdom in the Framework of the Old Testament Theology," *SJT* 17 (1964) 146-58.

13. See Michael Reitemeyer, *Weisheitslehre als Gotteslob. Psalmentheologie im Buch Jesus Sirach* (BBB 127; Berlin: Philo, 2000).

14. See the study of Goff on wisdom at Qumran *(Discerning Wisdom)*. Also see idem, "Reading Wisdom at Qumran: 4QInstruction and the Hodayot," *DSD* 11 (2004) 263-88; J. A. Sanders, *The Psalms Scroll of Cave 11* (DJD 4; Oxford: Clarendon, 1965), esp. p. 11. Sanders indicates that several of the *Hodayot* compare to the wisdom texts of the Hebrew Bible.

15. Annette Steudel, "Sapiential Texts," in *Qumran Cave 4: Sapiential Texts*, Part 1, ed. Torlief Elgin, et al. (DJD 20; Oxford: Clarendon, 1997) 159-67, pl. XIV; Florentino García Martínez and Eibert J. C. Tigchelaar, eds., *The Dead Sea Scrolls: Study Edition* (2 vols.; Grand Rapids: Eerdmans, 1997-98) 2:840-41.

which appears to be a wisdom hymn.[16] Another creation hymn is 11Q5 XXVI[17] (cf. 11Q6, 11Q7, 11Q8, 11Q9).

Wisdom psalms are also present in the sapiential literature of ancient Egypt in the forms of hymns, aretologies, and panegyrics. Some of the better known ones are "In Praise of Learned Scribes," "The Lament of Khakheperre-sonbe," "The Hymn to Re" found in "The Instruction of Ptah-hotep," and "The Hymn to Imhotep."[18] Lichtheim also includes in her translation five texts from the Ramesside period, which she categorizes as "Prayers Used as School Texts."[19] These include hymns and intercessory prayers.

Sumero-Akkadian wisdom literature also contains wisdom psalms, including what Lambert calls "preceptive hymns."[20] These include the "Hymn to Shamash,"[21] "The Blessing of Nisaba by Enki,"[22] and "A Bilingual Hymn to Ninurta."[23] The Shamash Hymn contains praise to the god of justice.[24] "The Blessing of Nisaba by Enki" includes, in a section of the hymn in honor of Enki, a hymnic blessing of the goddess of wisdom, "the all-knowing sage of the gods." In "The Hymn to Ninurta," the worshiper sings praise to the deity and lists the evil actions of the wicked.[25]

From the sapiential texts in Egypt and Mesopotamia, as well as Jewish texts outside the Hebrew Bible, it is clear that noncanonical wisdom texts exist in the literatures comparable to those in the Hebrew Bible that are used in worship and the schools.

---

16. See Maurice Baillet, *Qumrân grotte 4: III (4Q482-4Q520)* (DJD 7; Oxford: Clarendon, 1982) 69-72, pl. XXVI.

17. 11Q5 26.13-14 provides a close parallel to Prov. 3:19-20 and 8:22-31: "Blessed be he who made the earth with his strength, who established the world with his wisdom. With his knowledge he spread out the heavens" (ברוך עושה ארץ בכוחו מכין תבל בחוכמתו בתבונתו נטה שמים). See Martínez and Tigchelaar, *Dead Sea Scrolls*, 2:1178-83.

18. See the collection and translation of hymns by Jan Assmann, *Ägyptische Hymnen und Gebeten* (2nd improved and exp. ed.; OBO; Göttingen: Vandenhoeck & Ruprecht, 1999).

19. Lichtheim, *AEL* 3:110-14.

20. See *BWL*, 118ff.

21. See *COS* 1:419-20 (cf. *BWL*, 121-38, for the complete text).

22. *COS* 1:531-32.

23. *BWL*, 118-20.

24. *COS* 1:419.

25. Hymns that contain ethical instructions also occur in Sumerian psalms (see Adam Falkenstein and Wolfram von Soden, *Sumerische und akkadische Hymnen und Gebete* [Zurich: Artemis, 1953]). See Wolfram von Soden, "Der grosse Hymnus an Nabû," *ZA* 61 (1971) 44-71. Nabu was a god of wisdom.

The Themes and Socioreligious Context of Wisdom Psalms

Wisdom hymns deal with a variety of themes. The sages who composed them speak theologically of creation, identify wisdom with the divine Torah, admonish the audience to engage in moral actions, and address the question of theodicy. In addition, they express the piety of sages who engaged in worship of the God of wisdom, participated in praise, and meditated on the Torah that provided the guidance to human life. Most were likely written to be sung in the liturgical settings of Israelite and Jewish worship (temple and schools), although Pss. 1 and 119 may be exceptions.[26]

Date and Historical Context

The dates and historical settings of many of the wisdom psalms are impossible to establish. However, the three Torah psalms would likely have been composed and redacted during the Second Temple period when the Law became one of the major foundations for postexilic Judaism. It would make sense to place their origins during this period when the five books of Moses were edited to become the initial section of the Tanakh. Socially, the Torah became the constitution for Judaism in the Second Temple period, likely during the late Persian period of the early fourth century B.C.E. At a similar or slightly later time, in the early Hellenistic period, Chronicles and Ezra-Nehemiah would have been composed and redacted in their final form. The book of Ben Sira, in the early second century B.C.E., not only demonstrates that wisdom became identified with the Torah, but also deals with the prominence of the temple, the importance of Jerusalem, and devotion to the hierarchy of priests. The high priesthood, likely the Zadokites, served by their Levitical and administrative scribes, were given religious oversight and judicial supervision of Judaism in and near Jerusalem, while the Persians maintained political control over the province.

One also notes that Ezra 7 focuses on wisdom and the Torah in the context of the legendary Ezra, whose mission was essentially to establish Second Temple Judaism,[27] following the demise of the monarchy and the royal administration. King Artaxerxes commands this "scribe of Torah" to institute an administrative structure in Judah in order to manage and to put into practice the "laws

26. In general see Hermann Spieckermann, *Lebenskunst und Gotteslob in Israel. Studien zu Weisheit, Psalter und Theologie* (FAT, forthcoming).

27. For a discussion of the history of the traditions that make up Ezra and Nehemiah, see Reinhard G. Kratz, *Die Komposition der erzählenden Bücher des Alten Testaments* (UTB; Göttingen: Vandenhoeck & Ruprecht, 2000) 53-92.

of God" by using his "God-given wisdom." Ezra and Nehemiah have the agenda of supporting the capital and temple of Jerusalem, the high priesthood, the Torah, and scribalism as the distinctive religious and social attributes of this period. Reconstructing the dates of the activity of Ezra is especially difficult, and his actual sociopolitical and religious roles are unclear. This is due in part to the ambiguity surrounding the Persian ruler mentioned in Ezra 7. We are unclear as to whether he is the first or second king bearing this name. If the first, then the date of the seventh year of his reign would be 458 B.C.E., while the second's seventh year would have been 398 B.C.E. In addition, our knowledge of the Persian period is extremely limited due to the lack of datable texts and the insignificant amount of material culture and epigraphical data in Judah.[28] Furthermore, most of the historical records of the Persian Empire did not survive Islamic invasion and rule.

From what little we know it was apparently a matter of policy for the Achaemenid government to support native temples and hierarchies in provinces that were loyal to the empire and faithfully paid their taxes and tribute to its treasury.[29] This assistance is not based on religious tolerance or recognition of the diverse religions and gods of the peoples they conquered, but rather on the principle of expediency of ruling peacefully over the colonial kingdoms and nations that made up the empire.

The proclamation attributed in Ezra to the new emperor of the expanding Persian Empire, Cyrus, allowed exiles who chose to do so to return to Judah from Babylonia.[30] This proclamation is present in Ezra in two versions: one in Hebrew and the other in Aramaic. The Hebrew proclamation (Ezra 1:1-4) differs in several ways from the Aramaic version (6:2-5), leading to the possible conclusion that the one in Hebrew was intended for local consumption, while the second assumed the more official form.[31] The other possible explanation is that the two forms may simply belong to two separate textual traditions written by Jewish scribes on different occasions. The Hebrew version is more theological from a Jewish point of view in that Cyrus acknowledges Yahweh as the God of heaven who directs the affairs of kings. This "Lord God of heaven" is said to

---

28. See James W. Watts, ed., *Persia and Torah: The Theory of Imperial Authorization of the Pentateuch* (SBLSymS 17; Atlanta: SBL, 2001).

29. Schwartz, *Imperialism and Jewish Society,* 20-21.

30. The only sources that note that Cyrus II, during his first year of incorporating Babylon within his empire, allowed Jews in exile to return to Judah are biblical (Isa. 44:28; Ezra 1:2-4; 5:13; 6:3-5; cf. 2 Chron. 36:22).

31. For example, Lee I. Levine, *Jerusalem: Portrait of the City in the Second Temple Period (538 B.C.E.–70 C.E.)* (Philadelphia: Jewish Publication Society, 2002) 10-11; A. A. Dandamaev, *A Political History of the Achaemenid Empire* (Leiden: Brill, 1997) 63-64.

have commissioned Cyrus to build his temple in Jerusalem. This religious confession of Cyrus parallels his confession concerning Marduk and approximates the Persian king's role as the divine pharaoh of Egypt. While this rationale supports Jewish religious convictions, the Aramaic version is more practical and official in content. This form of the edict articulates the specifications for the building of the foundation and dictates that the stolen temple treasures be returned. In addition, the expenses for the rebuilding of the "house of God" (mentioned twice) are to be paid by the palace.[32]

The Reforms of Ezra and Nehemiah

Following the rebuilding of part of the city of Jerusalem and laying the foundations of the temple, Jerusalem, and thus the new Judaism that was emerging, was threatened by the Samaritans, the Egyptians, and the Transjordan provinces. Some of these difficulties were addressed by Artaxerxes' (I?) commissioning the priest Ezra to travel to Jerusalem to instigate a social and religious reform. With this partially in place, Nehemiah was later appointed governor to rebuild the city walls and to provide strong civil leadership.[33] This foreign policy of the Achaemenid court, like that of allowing a Jewish nation to be constituted, was politically expedient, since a loyal Judah would stabilize the southern part of the empire and strengthen Jerusalem's role as a fortified city to defend against the Egyptian threat to Persian rule.

Rhetoric (Literary Structure and Form)

The redaction of the wisdom psalms likely occurred in the Second Temple period when they were inserted into the developing Psalter. The Psalter, however, probably did not achieve its final form until the Hellenistic period.[34]

---

32. Cf. the Cyrus Cylinder in *ANET,* 315-16. For a discussion see Elias J. Bickermann, "The Edict of Cyrus in Ezra 1," *JBL* 65 (1946) 249-75.

33. The dating of the activity of these two leaders continues to be debated. See, e.g., H. G. W. Williamson, *Israel in the Books of Chronicles* (Cambridge: Cambridge University Press, 1977); Joseph Blenkinsopp, *Ezra-Nehemiah: A Commentary* (OTL; Philadelphia: Westminster John Knox, 1988); Sara Japhet, *1 & 2 Chronicles* (OTL; Louisville: Westminster John Knox, 1993); Lester Grabbe, *Ezra-Nehemiah* (London: Routledge, 1998).

34. See G. H. Wilson, "Shaping the Psalter: A Consideration of Editorial Linkage in the Book of Psalms," in *The Shape and Shaping of the Psalter,* ed. J. C. McCann Jr. (JSOTSup 159; Sheffield: JSOT Press, 1993) 78-82.

Scribal Redaction

The final form of the Hebrew Bible was shaped by temple scribes of Jerusalem under the direction of the Zadokite priesthood (cf., e.g., the wisdom insertion in Jer. 17:5-8) and concluded by Tannaitic Rabbis following the Great War that, for all intents and purposes, ended with the devastation of Jerusalem in 70 C.E. The scribal redaction of the Psalms by temple scribes may be determined by the following:

1. The division of the Psalter into five books reflects the five books of the Torah.
2. The correspondence of the Torah with the wisdom tradition is present in three Torah psalms: 1, 19B, and 119.
3. The initial psalm, which contrasts the righteous and the wicked and speaks of meditation on the Torah, provides the lens for reading the entire Psalter (cf. Prov. 1:2-7).
4. The scribes composed and inserted eleven wisdom psalms (Pss. 1, 19B, 32, 34, 37, 49, 73, 111, 112, 119, 127), which may be identified by lexicography, semantics, and themes common to wisdom texts.

The following sapiential terms occur in the wisdom psalms:

1. *'āwâ* ("to desire, long for"), Ps. 112:10; cf. Job 23:13; 33:20; Prov. 10:24; 11:23; 13:4, 12, 19; 18:1; 19:22; 21:10, 25-26; 23:3, 6; 24:1; Qoh. 6:2.
2. *'ôr* ("be light, shine"), Pss. 19:19; 37:6; 49:20; 112:4; 119:105, 135; cf. Job 3:9; 3:16, 20; 12:22; 18:5-6, 18; 22:28; 24:13-14, 16; 25:3; 26:10; 28:11; 29:3, 24; 31:26; 33:28, 30; 36:30, 32; 37:3, 11, 21; 38:15, 19, 24; 41:10, 24; Prov. 4:18; 6:23; 12:25; 13:9; 16:15; 17:12; 29:13; Qoh. 2:13; 8:1.
3. *bîn* ("perceive"), Pss. 19:13, 49; 32:9; 37:10; 49:4; 73:17; 119:34, 73, 95, 100, 104, 125, 130, 144, 169; cf. Job 6:24, 30; 9:11; 12:12-13; 14:21; 15:9; 18:2; 20:3; 23:5, 8; 26:12, 14; 28:12, 20, 28; 30:20; 31:1; 32:8-9, 11-12; 34:16; 37:14; 38:4, 18, 20, 36; 39:17, 26; Prov. 1:2, 5-6; 2:2-3, 6, 11; 3:5, 13, 19; 4:1, 5, 7; 5:1; 7:4, 7; 8:1, 5, 9, 14; 9:6, 10; 10:13, 23; 11:12; 12:13; 14:6, 8, 15, 29, 33; 15:14, 21; 16:16, 21; 17:10, 24, 27-28; 18:2, 15; 19:8, 25; 20:5; 21:29 (Qere), 30; 23:1, 4, 23; 24:3, 12; 28:5, 16; 29:7, 19; 30:2; Qoh. 9:11.
4. *bā'ar* ("to be brutish, stupid"), Pss. 49:11; 73:22; cf. Prov. 12:1; 30:2.
5. *gā'â* ("to be proud, be exalted, rise up"), Ps. 73:6; cf. Job 8:11; 10:16; 35:12; 38:11; 40:10-12; 41:7; Prov. 8:13; 14:13; 15:25; 16:18-19.
6. *dārak* ("to tread"), Pss. 1:1, 6; 32:8; 37:7, 14, 23, 34; 49:14; 119:1, 3, 14, 27, 29-30, 32-33, 35, 37; cf. Job 3:23; 4:6; 6:18; 8:19; 9:8; 12:24; 17:9; 19:12; 21:14, 29, 31; 22:3,

15, 28; 23:10-11; 24:4, 11, 13, 18, 23; 26:14; 28:26; 31:7; 34:27; 36:23; 38:19, 24-25; Prov. 1:15, 31; 2:8, 12, 20; 3:6, 17, 23, 31; 4:11, 14, 26; 5:8; 6:6, 23; 7:8, 19, 25; 8:2, 13, 22; 9:6, 15; 10:9, 29; 11:5, 20; 12:15, 26, 28; 13:6, 15; 14:2, 8, 12, 14; 15:9, 19; 16:9, 17, 25, 29, 32; 19:3, 16; 20:24; 21:2, 8, 16, 29; 22:5-6; 23:19; 26:13; 28:6, 10, 18; 29:27; 30:19-20; Qoh. 11:5; 12:5.

7. *hāgâ* ("to utter, speak"), Pss. 1:2; 37:30; 49:4; cf. Job 27:4; Prov. 8:7; 24:2.

8. *hîdâ* ("riddle"), Ps. 49:5; cf. 78:2; Prov. 1:6.

9. *hākam* ("be wise"), Pss. 19:8; 49:4, 11; 111:10; 119:98; cf. Job 4:21; 9:4; 11:6; 12:2, 12-13; 13:5; 15:2, 8; 17:10; 26:3; 28:12, 18, 20, 23, 28; 32:13; 33:33; 34:2, 7, 34; 37:24; 38:36-37; 39:17; Prov. 1:2, 5-6, 7, 20; 2:2, 6, 10; 3:7, 13, 19, 35; 4:5, 7, 11; 5:1; 7:4; 8:1, 11-12; 9:1, 8-10; 10:1, 8, 13-14, 23, 31; 11:2, 29, 30; 12:15, 18; 13:1, 5, 10, 14, 20; 14:1, 3, 6, 16, 24, 33; 15:2, 7, 12, 20, 31, 33, 48; 15:33, 16; 16:14, 16, 21, 23; 17:16, 24, 28; 18:4, 15; 20:26; 21:11, 20, 22, 30; 22:17; 23:23-24; 24:3, 5, 7, 14, 23; 25:12; 26:5, 12, 16; 28:11, 26; 29:3, 8, 9, 11, 15; 30:3, 24, 31; Qoh. 1:16-18; 2:3, 6, 9, 12-14, 19, 21, 26; 4:13; 6:8; 7:4-5, 7, 10-12, 16, 19, 23, 25; 8:1, 5, 16-17; 9:1, 10-11, 13, 15-16, 18; 10:1-2, 10, 12; 12:9, 11.

10. *hāpēṣ* ("to take delight"), Pss. 1:2; 37:23; 73:25; 111:2; 119:35; cf. Job 9:3; 13:3; 21:14; 22:3; 31:16; 33:32; 34:13; 40:17; Prov. 3:15; 8:11; 18:2; 21:1; 31:13; Qoh. 3:1, 17; 5:3; 8:6; 12:1, 10.

11. *hāraš* ("to be silent, dumb"), Ps. 32:3; cf. Job 13:5, 13; 33:31, 33; Prov. 11:3, 12; 17:28.

12. *hāšab* ("to think"), Ps. 119:59; cf. Job 5:12; 13:24; 18:3; 19:11; 21:27; 32:2; 33:10; 35:2; 41:19, 21, 24; Prov. 6:18; 12:5; 15:22, 26; 16:3, 9, 30; 17:28; 19:21; 20:18; 21:5; 24:8; 27:14; Qoh. 7:25, 27; 9:10.

13. *yāda'* ("to know"), Pss. 1:6; 19:3; 32:5; 37:18; 73:11, 16, 22; 119:16, 75, 79, 152; cf. Job 1:23; 5:24-25; 8:9; 9:2, 5, 21, 28, 29; 10:7, 13, 32; 11:6, 8, 11; 12:9; 13:2, 18; 15:2, 9, 23; 18:21; 19:6, 13-14, 25; 20:4, 20; 21:14, 21-22, 27; 22:13; 23:3, 5, 10; 24:1, 16; 26:3; 28:7, 13, 23; 29:16; 30:3, 23; 31:12, 23; 32:6-7, 10, 17, 22; 33:3; 34:2, 4, 33, 35; 35:15-16; 36:3-4, 12, 26; 37:5, 7, 15-16, 19; 38:2, 4-5, 12, 18, 21, 33; 39:1-2; 42:2-3, 11; Prov. 1:2, 4, 7, 22, 29; 2:5-6, 10; 3:6; 4:1, 19; 5:2, 6, 27; 7:4, 23; 8:9-10, 12, 20; 9:10, 13, 18; 10:9, 14; 11:9; 12:1, 10, 16, 23; 13:2, 16; 14:6-7, 10, 18, 21, 33; 15:2, 7, 14; 17:27; 18:15; 19:2, 25, 27; 20:15; 21:11; 22:12, 17, 19-20; 23:12, 35; 24:4-5, 12, 14, 22; 27:1, 23; 28:2, 22; 29:7; 30:3-4, 18; Qoh. 1:16-18; 2:14, 19, 21, 26; 3:14, 21; 4:13, 17; 6:5, 8, 10, 12; 7:12, 22, 25; 8:1, 5, 7, 12, 16-17; 9:1, 5, 10-11, 12; 10:14-15, 20; 11:2, 5-6, 9; 12:9.

14. *yā'aṣ* ("to give counsel"), Pss. 1:1; 73:24; 119:24, 38; cf. Job 3:14; 5:13; 10:3; 12:13, 17; 18:7; 21:16; 22:18; 26:3; 29:21; 38:2; 42:3; Prov. 1:25, 30-31; 8:14; 11:4; 12:15, 20; 13:10; 15:22; 19:20, 23; 20:5, 18; 21:30; 22:20; 24:6; 27:9; Qoh. 2:6.

15. *yārē'* ("to fear"), Pss. 19:10; 34:10, 12; 49:6, 17; 111:5, 9-10; 112:1, 7; 119:38, 63, 74, 79, 120; cf. Job 1:1, 8-9; 2:3; 4:6; 5:21-22; 6:21; 9:35; 11:15; 15:4; 19:10; 22:4; 28:28;

31:30; 32:6; 34:12; 37:22, 24; Prov. 1:7, 29; 2:5; 3:7, 25; 8:13; 9:10; 10:27; 13:13; 14:2, 16, 26-27; 15:16, 23; 16:6; 19:23; 22:4; 23:17; 24:21; 31:21, 30; Qoh. 3:14; 5:6; 7:18; 8:12-13; 9:2; 12:5, 13. A phrase often found in wisdom texts is *yir'at 'ĕlōhîm/ YHWH* ("the fear of God/Yahweh")." See Job 6:14; 28:28; Prov. 1:29; 8:13; 9:10; 10:27; 14:26-27; 15:16, 33; 16:6; 19:23; 22:4; 23:17; 31:30.

16. *yārâ* ("to instruct"), the verbal root of "Torah," Pss. 1:2; 19:8, 18; 32:8; 37:31; 119:33-34, 44, 51, 53, 55, 61, 70, 72, 77, 85, 92, 97, 113, 126, 136, 142, 150, 153, 163, 165, 174; cf. Job 6:24; 12:7-8; 8:10; 22:22; 27:11; 30:19; 34:32; 38:6; Prov. 1:8; 3:1; 4:2; 5:13; 6:13, 20, 23; 7:2; 13:14; 26:18; 28:4, 7, 9; 29:18; 31:36.

17. *yāšar* ("to be upright"), Pss. 19:9; 32:11; 37:37; 49:15; 111:1, 8; 112:2; 119:7, 28, 137; cf. Job 1:1, 8; 2:3; 4:7; 6:25; 8:6; 17:8; 23:7; 33:3, 27; 37:3; Prov. 1:3, 6; 2:7, 9, 13, 21; 3:6, 32; 4:11, 25; 8:6, 9; 9:15; 11:3, 5-6, 11, 24; 12:6, 15; 14:2, 9, 11-12; 15:8, 19, 21; 16:13, 17, 25; 17:26; 20:11; 21:2, 8, 18, 29; 22:17; 23:31; 28:10; 29:10, 27; Qoh. 7:29; 12:10.

18. *kāsal* ("to be/become stupid"), Ps. 49:11, 14; cf. Job 4:6; 8:14; 9:9; 31:24; 33:31; Prov. 1:22, 32; 3:35; 8:5; 9:13; 10:1, 18, 23; 12:23; 13:19-20; 14:7-8, 24, 33; 15:2, 7, 14; 17:10, 12, 16, 21, 24-25; 18:2, 6-7; 19:1, 10, 13, 23; 23:9; 26:1, 3-12; 28:26; 29:11, 20; Qoh. 2:14; 4:5, 17; 5:2-3; 6:8; 7:4-5, 6, 9, 25; 9:17; 10:2, 12, 15.

19. *lēb/lēbāb* (noun, "heart"), Ps. 19:9, 15; 32:11; 34:19; 37:15; 49:4; 73:1, 7, 13, 21, 26; 112:7-8; 119:2, 10-11, 32, 34, 36, 58, 69-70, 80, 111-112, 145, 161; cf. Job 1:8; 2:3; 7:17; 8:10; 11:13; 12:24; 15:12; 17:4; 23:16; 29:13; 36:5, 13; 31:7, 9, 27; 33:3; 34:14; 37:1, 24, 31; 41:16; Prov. 2:2, 10; 3:1, 3, 5; 4:4, 23; 5:12; 6:14, 18, 21, 32; 7:3, 7, 10, 25; 8:5; 9:4, 16; 10:8, 13, 20-21; 11:12, 20, 29; 12:8, 11, 20, 23, 25; 13:12; 14:10, 13-14, 30, 33; 15:7, 11, 13-15, 21, 28, 30, 32; 16:1, 5, 9, 21, 23; 17:3, 16, 18, 20, 22; 18:2, 12, 15; 19:3, 8, 21; 20:5, 9; 21:1, 4; 21:2; 22:11, 15, 17; 23:12, 15, 17, 19, 26, 33-34; 24:2, 12, 17, 30, 32; 25:3, 20; 26:25; 27:9, 11, 19, 23; 28:14, 26; 30:19; 31:11; Qoh. 1:13, 16-17; 2:1, 3, 10, 15, 20, 22-23; 3:11, 17-18; 5:1, 19; 7:2-4, 7, 21-22, 25-26; 8:5, 9, 11, 16; 9:1, 3, 7; 10:2-3; 11:9-10.

20. *lîṣ* ("to scorn"), Pss. 1:1; 119:51; cf. Job 16:20; 33:23; Prov. 1:22; 3:34; 9:7-8; 13:1; 14:6, 9; 15:12; 19:25, 28-29; 20:1; 21:11, 24; 22:10; 24:9.

21. *lāmad* ("to learn"), Pss. 34:12; 119:7, 12, 26, 64, 66, 68, 71, 73, 99, 108, 124, 135, 171; cf. Job 21:22; Prov. 5:13; 30:3; Qoh. 12:9.

22. *lāšôn* ("tongue"), Pss. 34:4; 37:30; 73:9; 119:172; cf. Job 15:5; 20:12, 16; 27:4; 29:10; 33:2; 40:25; Prov. 6:17, 30; 10:20, 31; 12:18-19; 15:2; 17:4, 20; 21:6, 23; 25:23; 26:28; 30:10; 31:36.

23. *māšal* ("to be like"), Ps. 19:14; cf. Job 13:12; 17:6; 30:19; 41:25; Prov. 1:1, 6; 6:7; 10:1; 12:24; 16:32; 17:2; 19:10, 14; 22:7; 23:1; 25:1; 27:1; 28:15; 29:1-2, 10, 12, 26; Qoh. 9:17; 10:4; 12:9.

24. *nātîb/nĕtîbâ* ("path, course of life"), Ps. 119:35, 105; cf. Job 18:10; 19:8; 28:7; 30:13; 38:20; 41:24; Prov. 1:15; 3:17; 7:25; 8:2, 20; 12:28.

25. *ʿāwal* ("to be wicked, go astray"), Ps. 119:3; cf. Job 5:15; 6:29-30; 11:14; 13:7; 15:16; 16:11; 18:21; 22:23; 24:20; 27:4, 7; 29:17; 31:3; 36:23, (33?); Prov. 22:8.

26. *ʿāwlâ* ("wicked, evil"), Pss. 37:1; 119:3; cf. Job 5:15; 6:29-30; 11:14; 13:7; 15:16; 16:11; 18:21; 22:23; 24:20; 27:4, 7; 29:17; 31:3; 36:23, (33?); Prov. 22:8.

27. *ʿāwat* ("to be bent, crooked"), Ps. 119:61, 78; cf. Job 8:3; 19:6; 34:12; Qoh. 1:15; 7:13; 12:3.

28. *ʿāmal* ("to labor"), Pss. 73:5, 16; 127:1; cf. Job 3:10; 4:8; 5:6; 7:3; 11:16; 15:35; 16:2; 20:22; Prov. 16:26; 24:2; 31:7; Qoh. 1:3; 2:10-11, 18-21, 22, 24; 3:9, 13; 4:4, 6, 8-9; 5:7, 14-15, 17, 18; 6:7; 8:15, 17; 9:9; 10:15.

29. *petî* (noun, "simple"), Pss. 19:8; 119:130; cf. Prov. 1:4, 22, 32; 7:7; 8:5; 9:4, 6, 13, 16; 14:15, 18; 19:25; 21:11; 22:3; 27:12.

30. *ṣādaq* ("to be righteous"), Pss. 1:5-6; 19:10; 32:11; 34:16, 20, 22; 37:6, 12, 16-17, 25, 29-30, 32, 39; 111:3; 112:3, 6; 119:7, 40, 42, 62, 75, 106, 121, 123, 137-138, 140, 142, 144, 160, 164, 172; cf. Job 4:17; 6:29; 8:3, 6; 9:2, 15; 9:20; 11:2; 12:4; 13:18; 15:14; 17:9; 22:3; 25:4; 27:5-6; 29:14; 31:6; 32:1-2; 33:12, 32; 34:5, 17; 35:2, 7; 36:3, 7; 37:23; 40:3, 8; Prov. 1:1, 3; 2:9, 20; 3:33; 4:18; 8:8, 15-16, 18, 20; 9:9, 20; 10:2-3, 6, 11, 16, 20-21, 24, 28, 30-32; 11:4-6, 8-10, 18-19, 21, 23, 28, 30-31; 12:5, 7, 10, 12, 13, 17, 21, 26, 28, 29; 13:5-6, 9, 21-22, 35; 14:19, 32, 34; 15:6, 9, 28-29; 16:8, 12-13, 31; 17:15, 26; 18:5, 10, 17; 20:7; 21:3, 12, 15, 18, 21; 22:19; 23:24; 24:4, 15-16, 24; 25:5, 26; 28:1, 12, 28; 29:2, 7, 16, 27; 31:9; Qoh. 3:16-17; 5:7; 7:15-16, 20; 8:14; 9:1-2.

31. *rîb* ("to strive, contend"), Ps. 119:154; cf. Job 9:3; 10:2; 13:6, 8, 19; 23:6; 29:16; 31:13, 35; 33:13; 40:2; Prov. 3:30; 15:18; 17:1, 14; 18:6, 17; 20:3; 22:23; 23:11; 25:8-9; 26:17, 21; 30:33.

32. *rāmâ* ("to deal treacherously with"), Pss. 32:2; 34:14; 119:18; cf. Job 13:7; 15:35; 27:4; 31:5; Prov. 10:4; 11:1; 12:5, 17, 20, 24, 27; 14:8, 25; 19:15; 20:23; 26:24.

33. *rāṣâ* ("be pleased with, accept happily"), Pss. 19:10; 34:10, 12; 49:6, 17; 111:5, 9-10; 119:38, 63, 74, 79, 120; cf. Job 1:1, 8-9; 2:3; 4:6; 5:21-22; 6:21; 9:35; 11:15; 15:4; 19:10; 22:4; 28:28; 31:30; 32:6; 34:12; 37:22, 24; Prov. 1:7, 29; 2:5; 3:7, 25; 8:13; 9:10; 10:27; 13:13; 14:2, 16, 26-27; 15:16, 23; 16:6; 19:23; 22:4; 23:17; 24:21; 31:21, 30; Qoh. 3:14; 5:6; 7:18; 8:12-13; 9:2; 12:5, 13.

34. *rāšaʿ* ("to be evil"), Pss. 1:1, 5, 6; 32:10; 34:22; 37:10, 12, 14, 16, 17, 20, 21, 28, 32-35, 38, 40; 112:10; 119:53, 61, 95, 110, 155; cf. Job 3:17; 8:22; 9:20, 22, 24, 29; 10:2-3, 9, 15; 11:20; 15:6, 20; 16:11; 18:5; 20:5, 29; 21:7, 16-17, 28; 22:18; 24:6; 27:7, 13; 32:3; 34:8, 10, 12, 17, 18, 26, 29; 35:8; 36:6, 17; 38:13, 15; 40:8, 12; Prov. 2:22; 3:25, 33; 4:14, 17, 19; 5:22; 8:7; 9:7; 10:2-3, 6-7, 11, 16, 20, 24, 25, 27-28, 30, 32; 11:5, 7, 8, 10-11, 18, 23, 31; 12:2, 5-7, 10, 12, 21, 26; 13:5-6, 9, 17, 25; 14:11, 19, 32; 15:6, 8-9, 28-29; 16:4, 12; 17:15, 23; 18:3, 5; 19:28; 20:26; 21:4, 7, 10, 12, 18, 27, 29; 24:15-16, 20, 24; 25:5, 26; 28:1, 4, 12, 15, 28; 29:2, 7, 12, 16, 27; Qoh. 3:16-17; 7:15, 17, 25; 8:8, 10, 13-14; 9:2.

35. *śîaḥ* ("to muse, complain"), Ps. 119:15, 23, 27, 48, 78, 97, 99, 148; cf. Job 7:11, 13; 9:27; 10:1; 12:8; 15:4; 21:4; 23:2; 30:4, 7; Prov. 6:22; 23:29.

36. *śākal* ("be prudent"), Pss. 32:8; 111:10; 119:99; cf. Job 22:2; 34:27, 35; Prov. 1:3; 3:4; 10:5, 19; 12:8; 13:15; 14:35; 15:24; 16:20, 22-23; 17:2, 8; 19:11, 14; 21:11-12, 16; 23:9.
37. *šaw'* ("emptiness, vanity"), Pss. 119:37; 127:1-2; cf. Job 7:3; 11:11; 15:31; 35:13, 15; Prov. 30:8.
38. *šā'a'* ("feel joy, delight"), Ps. 119:16, 24, 47, 70, 92, 143, 174; cf. Prov. 8:30-31.
39. *tām* ("be complete/perfect"), Pss. 19:8; 37:18, 37; 73:19; 119:1, 80; cf. Job 1:1, 8; 2:3, 9; 4:6; 8:20; 9:20-22; 12:4; 21:23; 22:3; 26:7, 9; 27:5; 31:6, 40; 36:4; 37:16; Prov. 1:12; 2:7, 21; 10:9, 29; 11:3, 5, 20; 13:6; 19:1; 20:7; 25:21; 28:6, 10, 18; 29:10.

Categories of Wisdom Psalms

In my judgment, the eleven wisdom psalms, found in various collections of the Psalter, may be placed into five types based on either genre or theme:

1. Torah Psalms. Psalms 1, 19B, and 119 are Torah psalms that praise the teachings of the Torah as the basis for divine instruction in righteous behavior.[35]
2. Instruction Psalms. These psalms make use of the features of the wisdom instructions, that is, admonitions and prohibitions in teaching the hearers the ethics of the sages. These include Pss. 32, 34, and 37.
3. Proverb (Saying) Psalms. Two psalms (112 and 127) include proverb lists that contain ethical teachings based on observations of a just and proper social order.
4. Reflective (Joban) Psalms. Two psalms (49, 73) approach the issue of the suffering of the righteous and the well-being of the wicked.
5. A Psalm of Creation. Psalm 111, a sapiential creation hymn, accentuates the "fear of Yahweh" as the "beginning of wisdom."

Torah Psalms

During the Second Temple period, scribes educated in a wisdom school and serving under the jurisdiction of the Zadokite priests edited the Psalter. They included approximately eleven wisdom psalms. Three of these are clearly Torah songs: 1, 19B, and 119. The term *tôrâ* in wisdom literature means "teaching" or "instruction" of the sages (Prov. 7:2; 13:14), of the "father" (4:1-2), and of the

---

35. See David Noel Freedman, *Psalm 119: The Exaltation of Torah* (Biblical and Judaic Studies from the University of California, San Diego 6; Winona Lake, IN: Eisenbrauns, 1999).

"mother" (1:8; 6:20). Sapiential instruction is clearly differentiated from the part of the Priestly Torah that contains laws of purity, cultic regulations, and judicial matters, since the prior is concerned with moral teaching and etiquette, while the latter attends to cultic legislation, which according to legend may be traced to Moses at Sinai. While these Torah psalms do not mention Moses, the implied teachers offer praise to the Law and meditate on its commandments.

Psalm 1

The opening psalm to the Psalter was likely placed there by the final redactors of the Psalter in order to provide the lens through which to read the entire book of five volumes. Its lexicography, semantics, and themes identify the psalm as a composition of the sages. The verbal lexemes of this psalm (along with their derivatives) include terms frequently found in wisdom literature:

dārak ("to tread"), 1:1, 6
hāgâ ("to utter, speak"), 1:2
ḥāpēṣ ("to take delight"), 1:2
yādaʿ ("to know"), 1:6
yāʿaṣ ("to give counsel"), 1:1
yārâ ("to instruct"), the verbal root of "Torah," 1:2
lîṣ ("to scorn"), 1:1
ṣādāq ("to be righteous"), 1:5-6
rāšaʿ ("to be evil"), 1:1, 5, 6

Semantically, the contrast between the righteous and the wicked is shaped by two thematically opposed strophes. Within the poem are two wisdom forms: an *'ašrê* ("happy") saying that serves as the introduction and an antithetical proverb that provides a summary for the entire psalm. Finally, the psalm has several common wisdom themes that are found in sapiential literature: the contrast between the righteous and the wicked (cf. esp. Prov. 10–15), retribution, and the meditation on the Torah, which is Yahweh's divine instruction.

Psalm 1 consists of two strophes (vv. 1-3, 4-5) arranged in a chiastic structure and concludes with a proverb that summarizes them. The first strophe depicts the righteous person with three verbs that describe the different positions of the human body: "walking" *(hālak)*, "standing" *(ʿāmad)*, and "sitting" *(yāšab)*. These verbs refer to the righteous person, who is to keep his distance from the wicked. The ungodly are described with three different terms: "wicked" *(rěšāʿîm)*, "sinners" *(ḥaṭṭāʾîm)*, and "scoffers" *(lēṣîm)*. These are those who fail to follow sapiential teaching and through their behavior subvert the social order. The sage also uses three terms for "counsel," "way," and "assembly" of the wicked: *'ēṣâ,* *derek,* and *mōšāb* (cf. Jer. 17:5-8; Ezek. 29:1-5). In the psalm's literary structure, the one theme in the first strophe that is not contrasted in the second is the "delight" *(ḥāpēṣ)* in and "meditating" *(hāgâ,* v. 2) on the Torah (cf. Ps. 119:48, 97).

This psalm offers no indication that it was used in cultic worship, but it does serve to teach its audience, presumably composed of young students in the Second Temple, that meditation on the teachings of the Torah becomes an important act of piety for the sage.[36] If the psalm does serve as the introduction to the Psalter, then its purpose is to stress both contemplation on the teachings of the Torah, now identified with wisdom, and the avoidance of the wicked, who subvert the instruction of the sages.

Psalm 19B

Psalm 19B is the second wisdom psalm, composed and attached by a scribe to an earlier creation hymn. During the First Temple period, wisdom was the instrument of creation and in mythological language also a goddess who was the offspring of Yahweh (Prov. 3:19-20; 8:22-31). In the Second Temple period, it was only a short step to the equating of wisdom and Torah. Now, with the principal focus on the Law, wisdom becomes identified with the divine teachings of the Torah. The natural revelation of God in creation is now incorporated in written form (cf. Sir. 24).

The verbal lexemes and their derivatives of this poem draw on significant sapiential terms:

> *yārâ* ("instruct"), the verbal root of "Torah," 19:8, 18
> *bîn* ("perceive"), 19:13, 49
> *māšal* ("to be like"), 19:14
> *tām* ("be complete/perfect"), 19:8
> *rāṣâ* ("be pleased with, accept happily"), 19:10
> *ḥākam* ("be wise"), 19:8
> *petî* (noun, "simple"), 19:8
> *yāšar* ("to be upright"), 19:9
> *lēb/lēbāb* (noun, "heart"), 19:9, 15
> *'ôr* ("be light, shine"), 19:19
> *yārē'* ("to fear"), 19:10
> *ṣādaq* ("to be righteous"), 19:10

---

36. "Meditating" *(hāgâ)* is found in Pss. 63:7[6]; 77:13[12]; 143:5. The noun form, "meditation" *(hegyôn),* is found in Ps. 19:15[14].

The sage's petition (cf. Ps. 106:47; and the *Amidah*, "Eighteen Benedictions," fifteenth blessing) in the concluding verse (Ps. 19:15) resembles colophons written by scribes in the ancient Near East to serve as summaries or identifications of the scribe and his role, or both. Its literary form combines a hymn in praise of Torah with a prayer for protection from the power of sin. In the Torah Yahweh provides means for this knowledge of and protection from the power of sin. Through obedience to the Law the sage is provided the insight that keeps him from wicked behavior, transgression, and insolence. Other related themes are studying and obeying the Torah, which leads to the "rejoicing of the heart" and the "enlightening of the eyes," that is, joy and knowledge. "Rejoicing the heart" is an important dimension of sapiential piety. Finally, the psalmist emphasizes the experience of joy as a central feature of Jewish spirituality. Joy derives from the gift and instruction of the Torah, as well as from meditating on its teachings (*měśamměhê-lēb*, Ps. 19:9; see 16:11; 119:14, 16, 47, 92, 111, 143).[37]

The incomparable worth of the Torah (19:10) echoes that of wisdom in Proverbs (Prov. 3:13-17; 8:18-21). The Torah is perfect, pure, and the source of righteous teaching in enabling the pious sage to identify his sins, which include presumptuous pride (cf. Prov. 29:23) and those that are hidden. It is also noteworthy that the petition of the wise psalmist in the concluding verse (Ps. 19:15) compares to colophons written by scribes in the ancient Near East and Israel to serve either as summaries or indications of roles served by the composer of the literary text, if not both. From this concluding verse, it is clear that the psalmist utters the words of this hymn to the Torah, suggesting he is its composer. This sage is devoted to the study of the Torah, which he values for teaching him about his sins. He reads and learns from the Torah, meditates upon it, and uses it to identify and to warn him against sins. Unknown sins (Job 13:13) and pride (Prov. 29:23) are two especially important categories of sins in wisdom texts.

What is particularly significant is the resulting theology of the combined psalms that has become central to wisdom faith in Second Temple wisdom: the creator has revealed himself in both the cosmos and the Torah. The written revelation of the Torah provides the needed direction on how to live faithfully. At the same time, the sage is one who observes creation and learns from it about the nature and character of God. Thus one finds the theological synthesis of creation of the cosmos (particularly in this case the heavens, the temporal polarity of day and night, and the sun that gives light and warmth), the law of

---

37. Michael Fishbane, *The Exegetical Imagination: On Jewish Thought and Theology* (Cambridge: Harvard University Press, 1998) 151-72.

Yahweh that is perfect and contains the divine commandments that "rejoice the heart" and "enlighten the eyes," and human character shaped by the Torah that keeps one from the dominion of sin. This structure indicates that cosmology and anthropology are kept in concert by means of the divine revelation of God (El) in creation and Yahweh in the Torah. In a period when the Torah has become one of the central theological themes in early Judaism, the association of the revealed law with the divine creation in wisdom, including this psalm (cf. Sir. 24), provides an important insight into the faith of the Jewish community in Jerusalem during the late Persian period.

Psalm 119

The identifying features of lexicography, semantics, and themes of this psalm are largely sapiential and legal, indicating that it is composed by a sage of the Torah.[38] The eight synonyms for "law," which were likely found in a list of words compiled by scribes of Torah, are 'imrâ, dābār, miṣwâ, ḥōq, 'ēdût, tôrâ, mišpāṭ, and pĕqûdîm. Each of the twenty-two strophes contains from six to nine of these terms. Only three lines, 3, 90, and 122, do not contain a word for "law."

The lexicography of sapiential terms in this psalm includes

> lāmad ("to learn"), 119:7, 12, 26, 64, 66, 68, 71, 73, 99, 108, 124, 135, and 171
> ṣādaq ("to be righteous"), 119:7, 40, 42, 62, 75, 106, 121, 123, 137-138, 140, 142,
>   144, 160, 164, 172
> yāšar ("to be upright"), 119:7, 28, 137
> ḥākam ("to be wise"), 119:98
> bîn ("to perceive"), 119:34, 73, 95, 100, 104, 125, 130, 144, 169
> yā'aṣ ("to counsel"), 119:24, 38
> yārē' ("to fear"), 119:38, 63, 74, 79, 120
> śîaḥ ("to muse, complain"), 119:15, 23, 27, 48, 78, 97, 99, 148
> lîṣ ("to scorn"), 119:51
> yāda' ("to know"), 119:16, 75, 79, 152
> śākal ("be prudent"), 119:99
> petî ("simple"), 119:130
> šaw' ("emptiness, vanity"), 119:37
> rāša' ("to be evil"), 119:53, 61, 95, 110, 155

38. André Robert, "Le psaume CXIX et les Sapientiaux," *RB* 48 (1939) 5-20; Alfons Deissler, *Psalm 119 (118) und seine Theologie* (Munich: Karl Zink, 1955); Jon Levenson, "The Sources of Torah: Psalm 119 and the Modes of Revelation in Second Temple Judaism," in *Ancient Israelite Religion: Essays in Honor of Frank Moore Cross,* ed. Patrick D. Miller, et al. (Philadelphia: Fortress, 1987) 559-74.

dārak ("to tread"), 119:1, 3, 14, 27, 29-30, 32-33, 35, 37

šā'a' ("feel joy, delight"), 119:16, 24, 47, 70, 92, 143, 174

ḥāpēṣ ("to take delight"), 119:35

lēb/lēbāb ("heart/mind"), 119:2, 10-11, 32, 34, 36, 58, 69-70, 80, 111-112, 145, 161

lāšôn ("tongue"), 119:172

nātîb/nĕtîbâ ("path, course of life"), 119:35, 105

'āwal ("to be wicked, go astray"), 119:3

'āwat ("to be bent, crooked"), 119:61, 78

rāmâ ("to deal treacherously with"), 119:118

rîb ("to strive, contend"), 119:154

tām ("to be complete, perfect"), 119:1, 80

yārâ ("instruct"), the verbal root of "Torah," 119:33-34, 44, 51, 53, 55, 61, 70, 72, 77, 85, 92, 97, 113, 126, 136, 142, 150, 153, 163, 165, 174

This psalm's sapiential semantics include the alphabetic acrostic[39] (22 letters that structure the strophes and make up 176 verses, each consisting of a bicolon) and two "happy" sayings *('ašrê)*, which inaugurate the initial strophe (119:1-2; each verse is a bicolon).

Drawing on features of the hymn, thanksgiving, and lamentation, the themes include the praise of the Torah as the basis not only for moral instruction and meditation but also for a lament that expresses the pleas for escape from wickedness and obtaining forgiveness. The psalm includes a thanksgiving for the gift of the Law that would lead ultimately to redemption. This psalm is appropriate for the Second Temple period, when the Torah became central to Jewish life. The lament contains the plea that the psalmist is to follow the commandments, the attestation of contrite repentance, the request for protection from both private sins and the wicked, and the appeal to God for forgiveness.

One gains from this psalm indications of the role of its composer. In v. 18 the psalmist prays: "Open my eyes that I may observe miracles from your law *(tôrâ)*." This expression likely refers to the scribe's desire for divine inspiration, especially in view of the fact that he repeatedly asked for instruction in the Torah (vv. 12, 27, 33, 64, 66, 68, 73, 108, 124). Indeed, he even echoes the priestly benediction of Num. 6:25 in v. 135, suggesting that he knew the language of the Torah and granted its keeping to the priests whom the scribes served in shaping the ongoing tradition and in preserving the *traditio*.[40] Other sapiential features

39. The acrostic, while predominantly found in wisdom literature, is not limited to sapiential writings: Pss. 25, 34, 37, 111, 112, 119, 145; Prov 31:10-31; Lam 1–4; Nah 1:2-10; Sir. 51:13-30.

40. Michael A. Fishbane, *Biblical Interpretation in Israel* (Oxford: Clarendon, 1985) 332-34, 539-42. See M. Gertner, "Midrashim in the New Testament," *JSS* 7 (1962) 276. Fishbane compares the *p* strophe with the language of the Priestly blessing in Num. 6:23-27.

include the hidden and mysterious character of both sin and wisdom (cf. Ps. 139:6; Prov. 30:18; Job 42:3). Verse 18 also reflects the prophetic inspiration found in Ezra 7:6, a subject found also in Ben Sira (39:6).[41]

This psalm is in part to be construed as a lament. The sage, enduring great difficulties that God has yet to address, repeatedly asks him to deliver his servant from both his persecutors and his suffering, something he expects, due to his faithful adherence to the teachings of the Torah. He urges God to act on his behalf and to rescue him from distress, as v. 154 makes clear. He calls upon God to serve in the role of the redeemer to exact retribution for the shedding of his blood, if it comes to that.[42] By contrast, the wicked persecutors have flouted the Law and thus deserve to be punished. As noted, the psalm begins with two 'ašrē sayings (vv. 1-2). This adds to the sapiential character of the psalm. In addition, the psalmist asks God for patience, steadfast love, continuing instruction, enlightenment, and the provision of additional wisdom (v. 34) in order that he may even more closely follow the precepts of the Torah. It is important to note that in strophe 12 the psalmist speaks of the cosmic foundation of Torah, thus placing it within the order of creation.

One recognizes that this Torah hymn is directed to God as the giver of the commandments that lead to life. Trusting in the revelation of the Torah, the psalmist tells of the deepening of the religious experience of God that derives from the study of Torah.[43] In addition, the psalmist proclaims that he has been created by God (v. 73), leading to the giving of divine instruction to the human creature that requires obedience to the Law. The association between wisdom and Torah is found in sapiential language throughout the psalm, particularly in meditation on the Torah, the creation of humanity, the prayer for wisdom, and moral instruction.

Wisdom Psalms as Poems of Instruction

The Psalter contains several wisdom psalms that are instructions, which are much the same as those found in other sapiential texts (esp. Proverbs and Ben Sira). These psalms, which include 32, 34, and 37, also may be identified as wisdom texts in terms of lexicography, semantics, and themes. However, these texts do not provide clues as to their dates.

41. See Leo G. Perdue, "Ben Sira and the Prophets," in *Intertextual Studies in Ben Sira and Tobit: Essays in Honor of Alexander A. Di Lella, O.F.M.*, ed. Jeremy Corley and Vincent Skemp (CBQMS 38; Washington, DC: Catholic Biblical Association of America, 2005) 132-54.

42. David Daube, *Studies in Biblical Law* (Cambridge: Cambridge University Press, 1947) 47.

43. Michael Fishbane, "From Scribalism to Rabbinism," in *Sage in Israel*, 447.

Psalm 32

Psalm 32 consists of a pedagogic instruction that is based on the form and theology of a typical thanksgiving. The semantics of the psalm reflect a model thanksgiving that teaches students how to write this type of text (vv. 1-7) and to understand how its theology correlates with the teaching of the retribution of the sages (vv. 8-11). The second part of the psalm, an instruction, is initiated by the stated purpose of the sage to break down his students' resistance to teaching. The lexicography of the psalm, in particular the instruction in vv. 8-11, includes:

> *bîn* ("to perceive"), 32:9
> *dārak* ("to tread"), 32:8
> *ḥāšab* ("to think"), 32:2
> *yāda'* ("to know"), 32:5
> *lēb/lēbāb* ("heart/mind"), 32:11
> *yā'aṣ* ("to counsel"), 32:8
> *yārâ* ("to instruct"), the verbal root of "Torah," 32:8
> *śākal* ("be prudent"), 32:8
> *rāša'* ("to be evil"), 32:10
> *ṣādaq* ("to be righteous"), 32:11
> *ḥāraš* ("to be silent, dumb"), 32:3
> *rāmâ* ("to deal treacherously with"), 32:2
> *yāšar* ("to be upright"), 32:11

This psalm is also composed by a traditional sage who seeks to instruct his students on the legitimacy of the teaching of retribution that is found in both the theology of the thanksgiving psalm and the wisdom tradition. To instill this teaching within their character as the basis for their actions, the youth are instructed to remove any opposition to its validity.

Psalm 34

This psalm consists of a superscription (v. 1) and two major sections: a thanksgiving (vv. 2-11) and a wisdom instruction consisting of three strophes (vv. 12-15, 16-19, and 20-23).[44] Thus a scribe appropriated a thanksgiving psalm, added a sapiential instruction, and shaped an alphabetic acrostic, a semantic

---

44. In general see H. Wiesmann, "Ps. 34 (Vulg. 33)," *Bib* 16 (1935) 416-21. See also Hans Schmidt, *Die Psalmen* (HAT 15; Tübingen: Mohr [Siebeck], 1934) 64.

feature occasionally found in, but not limited to, the writings of sages (Pss. 37, 111, 112, 119; Sir. 51:13-30; for nonsapiential acrostics see Pss. 9, 10, 25, 145; Lam. 1–4). The form of the second part of Ps. 34 reads as an instruction. It begins in v. 12 with a typical introduction (cf. Prov. 1:8; 2:1; 3:1, 21; 4:1, 10, 20; 5:1, 7; 6:1, 20; 7:1; 22:17; 23:19, 26) in which a teacher admonishes his "sons" (students) to give heed to his teaching:

> Come, O sons, listen to me,
>   I shall teach you the fear of Yahweh.

Following this address, the teacher then issues a rhetorical question (v. 13), two admonitions (vv. 14-15), seven synonymous sayings (vv. 16, 17, 18, 19, 21, 22, 23), and one antithetical saying (v. 20). Sapiential language in this psalm comprises the following terms:

> *lāmad* ("to learn"), 34:12
> *rāmâ* ("to deal treacherously with"), 34:14
> *lēb/lēbāb* ("heart/mind"), 34:19
> *ṣādaq* ("to be righteous"), 34:16, 20, 22
> *rāšaʿ* ("to be evil"), 34:22
> *yārēʾ* ("to fear"), 34:12
> *lāšôn* (noun, "tongue"), 34:4

The sapiential themes are the "fear of Yahweh," proper speech and moral action, and retribution in which Yahweh saves the righteous from their difficulties when they call for his salvation, while evil results in the wicked's condemnation. Thus the entirety of the psalm, including both the thanksgiving and the instruction, stresses that the psalmist who called upon Yahweh was delivered from his troubles when he prayed for salvation. The one delivered gives thanks to Yahweh for his salvation.

This text includes a model of a thanksgiving psalm that may be used by students who are learning how to write different genres in Hebrew literature and to understand their theology, in this case the traditional view of conservative wisdom's teaching that Yahweh redeems the righteous. The catechetical question, which asks who among the students desires life, is answered by the two admonitions. Thus life is obtained by proper language (e.g., Prov. 13:3) and by moral action, which includes avoiding evil (2:22; 3:7; 13:19), doing good (13:21), and pursuing well-being (3:2, 17; 12:20). These constitute the inclusive areas of performance for wisdom and righteousness: speech and action. The remaining sayings serve to legitimate the admonitions. In following the ethic of retribution, the teacher stresses that proper speech and moral action produce well-being for the community, while wickedness brings destruction both to the wicked one and his/her social group.

Psalm 37

Psalm 37 is an instruction shaped into an alphabetic acrostic. The psalm makes use of typical features of the sapiential instruction. Prohibitions (vv. 1-2, 27-28a, 28b), admonitions (vv. 3-4, 5-6, 7, 8-9, 34, 37-38), autobiographical observations (vv. 10-11, 25-26, 35-36), synonymous sayings (vv. 29, 30-31, 39-40), antithetical sayings (vv. 12-13, 14-15, 18-20, 21-22), and one "better" saying (vv. 16-17). The sayings are used as result and causal clauses. The semantics of this instruction psalm also include the division of the instruction into four strophes (vv. 1-11, 12-22, 23-33, 34-40). The thematic repetitions are based on the theology of retribution and knit the psalm together: "(the children of) the wicked/those cursed by Yahweh/transgressors will be cut off" (vv. 9, 22, 28, 38), as contrasted to "the ones who wait for Yahweh/the meek/righteous will inherit the land" (vv. 9, 11, 22, 29).

The lexicography of the sages reflected in this didactic poem comprises the following:

> *bîn* ("to perceive"), 37:10
> *hāgâ* ("to utter, speak"), 37:30
> *dārak* ("to tread"), 37:7, 14, 23, 34
> *yāda'* ("to know"), 37:18
> *lēb/lēbāb* ("heart/mind"), 37:15
> *'āwlâ* ("wicked, evil"), 37:1
> *tām* ("to be complete, perfect"), 37:16
> *yāšar* ("to be upright"), 37:37
> *yārâ* ("instruct"), the verbal root of "Torah," 37:31
> *ṣādaq* ("to be righteous"), 37:6, 12, 16-17, 25, 29-30, 32, 39
> *rāša'* ("to be evil"), 37:10, 12, 14, 16, 17, 20, 21, 28, 32-35, 38, 40
> *lāšôn* (noun, "tongue"), 37:30

The instruction is grounded in the teaching of retribution, which includes the temporal quality of future time: eventually the wicked will be removed from the land, while the righteous will inherit it. This is an instruction that is stressed to the students who are studying under a teacher who belongs to the conservative sages. They believe that the wicked will be removed from the community of the righteous.

Proverb Psalms

There are two proverb psalms in the wisdom corpus.

Psalm 112

Psalm 112 is a well-crafted proverb psalm that begins with the call to the audience to "praise Yahweh," giving the appearance that what is to follow is a hymn. Yet following the brief hymnic introduction in v. 1a, the psalmist, who writes as a sage, composes a didactic poem as the reason for the praise: the well-being of those who "fear Yahweh." This didactic poem is initiated by an *ʾašrê* saying that emphasizes that the God-fearer is the one about whom the poem speaks:

> Happy is the one who fears Yahweh,
>> Who takes exceeding delight in his commandments.

The poem that follows the "happy saying" is structured in three parts (vv. 2-3, 4-6, 7-9), each of which is set off by a repetitive asseveration: "their righteousness endures forever" (v. 3b), "they will be remembered forever" (v. 6b), and "their righteousness endures forever" (v. 9b). The concluding verse contrasts with the perpetuity of the righteousness and memory of the God-fearers by indicating that the wicked, seeing the well-being, wealth, and goodness of the righteous, become consumed by their anger. Indeed, their "desire will perish" (v. 10).

The lexicography of the poem is that of Second Temple sapiential piety, similar to that of Pss. 1, 19B, and 119:

> *ʾāwâ* ("to desire, long for"), 112:10
> *yārēʾ* ("to fear"), 112:1, 7
> *yāšar* ("to be upright"), 112:2
> *ṣādaq* ("to be righteous"), 112:3, 6
> *lēb* ("heart/mind"), 112:7-8
> *rāšaʿ* ("to be evil"), 112:10

This poem praises the God-fearers for delighting in and obedience to the commandments, grace, charity, justice and righteousness, and trust in Yahweh. Because of their behavior and character, they receive as a reward wealth, mighty descendants, an honored memory, and an enduring legacy of righteousness. They have nothing to fear from their enemies. By contrast, the wicked are ruined by their jealousy and ultimately perish with nothing that endures after them.

Psalm 127

One of the psalms of ascent[45] (cf. v. 1a — *šîr hamma'ălôt lišlōmōh*) is attributed to Solomon, since the reference to "building" in v. 1 appears to suggest to the redactor that the psalm should be attributed to the preeminent builder in Israelite and Jewish tradition. However, this psalm takes the form of a brief proverb psalm, composed by a sage who is writing about the household.[46] Its literary structure consists of two strophes (vv. 1-2, 3-5). The first strophe addresses Yahweh's building of the household and guarding of a city in order for it to endure. These human institutions, often mentioned in sapiential literature, will not endure (i.e., they are "vain") without the involvement of Yahweh in their construction. The second strophe speaks of the heritage of sons provided by Yahweh. "Heritage" *(naḥălâ)* is a theologically important term, usually understood as the land given by Yahweh to his people. In this strophe, however, the true heritage is "sons" who assist in the work of the household and speak on behalf of their father at the gate, that is, during legal proceedings. In addition to the literary structure of the poem and its themes, the sapiential character of the psalm is found in its individual forms used by the sage for its composition: two conditional sayings (v. 1), a synonymous saying (v. 3), a comparative saying (v. 4), and an *'ašrê* saying (v. 5).

The lexicography of this psalm includes two terms frequent in wisdom literature:

šāw' ("emptiness, vanity," noun), 127:1-2
'āmal ("to labor"), 127:1

Wisdom Psalms and Theodicy

One of the categories of wisdom psalms is named after the theme of theodicy that dominates the content.[47]

Psalm 49

One of two wisdom psalms in the Psalter that addresses the problem of divine justice is Ps. 49, which makes use of the riddle or dark saying *(ḥîdâ)* and its an-

---

45. The "psalms of ascent" are Pss. 120–134. Pilgrims would likely sing these songs while ascending the steps to the temple (cf. 122:4).

46. Perdue, et al., *Families in Ancient Israel*.

47. On theodicy see James L. Crenshaw, *Defending God* (Oxford: Oxford University Press, 2005).

swer to become the basis for reflection.[48] Theodicy is the most perplexing problem faced by the traditional sages, who sought to affirm the theology of retribution. While riddles belonged to the rhetorical forms of the sages (Prov. 1:6), there is no other example of them in wisdom literature (however, see Judg. 14:12-13, 16; 1 Kgs. 10:1 = 2 Chron. 9:1; Ezek. 17:2; Hab. 2:6).[49] Riddles are intentionally obscure and are told to confound their hearers. Intrinsic to this form is that within the language of the riddle itself is the expression of a key that, to the one who is truly wise, will be understood to be the real answer. The riddle of the psalm may have been as follows: "How is the fool like a domesticated animal?" The wrong answer is they are both stupid or lacking in knowledge. Rather, the riddle in this psalm, which is composed for the lyre to be sung, proposes a different answer: they face the same fate, that is, death, for which there is no ransom. Indeed, all people, rich and poor and wise and foolish, will eventually enter the eternal tomb from which there is no deliverance. The consolation is that for the wise psalmist even his wealthy and powerful enemies who seek to do him harm face the same death that he will experience.

The structure of the psalm consists of the following: the introduction (vv. 2-5) that is addressed to the nations and the inhabitants of the world, both the rich and the poor; strophe 1 (vv. 6-12), which speaks of the inevitability of the death even of the wealthy; strophe 2 (vv. 13-15), in which the wise psalmist asserts that Sheol is the future home of even the rich and powerful; and strophe 3 (vv. 16-21), which asserts that the wealthy will join their ancestors in the tomb, leaving behind what they have accumulated.

The sapiential vocabulary of the psalm includes:

ḥākam ("to be wise"), 49:4, 11
bîn ("to perceive"), 49:4
dārak ("to tread"), 49:14
ḥîdâ ("riddle"), 49:5
hāgâ ("to utter, speak"), 49:4
kāsal ("to be/become stupid"), 49:11, 14
yāšar ("to be upright"), 49:15
lēb ("heart/mind"), 49:4
bāʿar ("to be brutish, stupid"), 49:11

---

48. See Leo G. Perdue, "The Riddles of Psalm 49," *JBL* 93 (1974) 533-42.
49. Hans Peter Müller, "Der Begriff 'Rätsel' im Alten Testament," *VT* 20 (1970) 465-89.

Psalm 73

A second text that deals with the issue of theodicy is Ps. 73. The poem demonstrates features of the individual lament, but its theme and vocabulary point to its sapiential disposition. The psalm finds its closest parallels in its lament-like character and reflection over the issue of theodicy in Job and comparable literature from Mesopotamia, especially the Sumerian "Man and His God" and the Akkadian "I Will Praise the Lord of Wisdom" *(Ludlul bēl nēmeqi)*. In the two Mesopotamian texts and this psalm, the answer to the question of the suffering of the righteous and the well-being of the wicked is found in the process of the ritual and uttering of the lament.

The literary structure of the poem contains three strophes: strophe 1 (vv. 1-12) begins with the affirmation of the divine goodness bestowed upon the righteous and follows with the observation of the welfare of the wicked; strophe 2 (vv. 13-20) describes the psalmist's contrasting experience of suffering and the mentioning of the revelatory experience in the sanctuary; and strophe 3 (vv. 21-28) contains the psalmist's solace from taking refuge in God in contrast to the wicked, who will experience their end.

The lexicography of the psalm points to its sapiential character:

lāšôn ("tongue"), 73:9
'āmal ("to labor"), 73:5
bā'ar ("be brutish, stupid"), 73:22
bîn ("to perceive"), 73:17
yā'aṣ ("to counsel"), 73:24
yākaḥ ("to decide, prove"), 73:14
yāda' ("to know"), 73:11, 16, 22
lēb ("heart/mind"), 73:1, 7, 13, 21, 26
rāša' ("to be evil"), 73:3
gā'â ("to be proud, be exalted, rise up"), 73:6
'āmal ("to labor"), 73:5, 16

Finally, the themes of the psalm are frequently found among the literature of the sages. The theme that is the basis for the reflection of the entire psalm occurs in the initial verse that takes the form of the synonymous saying:

Surely, El is good to the upright,[50]
    Elohim to the pure in heart.

50. Reading *yāšār 'ēl* (ישר אל) for *liśrā'ēl* (לישראל).

This is the fundamental affirmation of the sages' view of divine justice and the teaching of retribution. In the initial strophe, the authenticity of the saying is at first questioned by the sage, based on his observation of the well-being of the wicked. He sees them as healthy, free from affliction, filled with violence, full of conceit, wealthy, and proud mockers of the justice of God. They express their arrogance by doubting that God is even aware of their actions. In the second strophe, however, the sage moves from a third person description of the good fortune of the wicked to a first person admission that he almost lost his faith in divine justice. What kept him from questioning God and issuing a complaint against divine justice was his experience in the sanctuary, where, based perhaps on a priestly revelation, he came to realize that God will bring the wicked to destruction. He, by contrast, finds himself led by divine counsel in which God lays hold of his right hand, a ritual action expressing victory. He regains his faith in divine justice, knowing ultimately that he will be received into the "glory" of God, that is, he will be recognized as one who continues to trust in God as his rock and portion forever. Those who distance themselves from God will ultimately perish, while the righteous will continue to enter into divine presence. This intimation of God's attestation of the psalmist's loyalty and faith will lead to his deliverance, an experience that he will recount before others, presumably in the thanksgiving he expresses before the gathered community in the sanctuary.

Psalm 111: A Wisdom Psalm of Thanksgiving and Creation

The final wisdom psalm in this list of sapiential writings is the hymn of creation and expression of thanksgiving that occurs in Ps. 111. Creation theology provided the foundation for the worldview of the sages, for God created the cosmos and continues to maintain it. In addition, God is the creator of humanity and supporter of the righteous.[51]

It should not be surprising to discover a creation hymn in the Psalter that gives evidence of redaction by a scribe, and this is certainly the case with Ps. 111. Unless the psalm is written late in the Hellenistic period, it is doubtful that a sage wrote the entire psalm, since the redemption of the people of Israel is emphasized. The psalm does appear, on the basis of language and themes, to have been edited by a wisdom scribe. The semantics of the psalm include the alphabetic acrostic, a frequent literary pattern for wisdom psalms (cf. Ps. 112 that follows). In the introductory verses in Ps. 111 (vv. 1-3), the psalmist states that his intention is to give thanks to Yahweh in the assembly of the upright. This "congregation of the upright" likely refers to those who are admitted by the priests

---

51. Perdue, *Wisdom and Creation*.

into the sacred sphere of the outer court (cf. the entrance Torah psalms, 15 and 24). Following the statement of intent, the psalm continues in the following two verses of the introduction to state the reason for the thanksgiving: the greatness, honor, and majesty of the works (creation and salvation) of God, whose "righteousness" endures forever. These works are witnessed by those who reflect on the mighty acts of God in creation and history. These who reflect on divine actions are the sages. This combination of creation, redemptive history, and wisdom points to a likely date in the late Second Temple period.

The structure of the psalm then develops into two brief strophes: strophe 1 (vv. 4-6), which addresses the gifts of Yahweh bestowed upon the God-fearers with whom he keeps his covenant obligation (obviously Israel); and strophe 2 (vv. 7-9), which speaks of the divine commandments that result in the salvation of those who are obedient to them. Finally, the sage adds a conclusion in v. 10 in which he/she combines both the "fear of God" (a major theme in wisdom literature, Prov. 1:7; 15:33; 31:30) and the theme of the praise of God that "endures forever."

The lexicography of the psalm supports its inclusion as a sapiential text.

lēb ("heart/mind"), 111:1
yāšar ("to be upright"), 111:1, 8
ṣādaq ("to be righteous"), 111:3
yārēʾ ("to fear"), 111:5, 9-10
ḥākam ("to be wise"), 111:10
śākal ("be prudent"), 111:10

Social Features: Sages and Social Setting

With the appearance of wisdom psalms, the question that emerges has to do with the identity of the sages who composed the wisdom psalms and later redacted the Psalter in its final or close to its final form.

The Province of Judah and Jewish Governors

In the Persian period, when many of the wisdom psalms were probably composed, Jerusalem became the provincial capital of the fifth satrapy, which included Syria, Phoenicia, Cyprus, and Judah.[52] This satrapy of five districts in-

---

52. Herodotus 3.89-94. For a brief overview see Levine, *Jerusalem*, 31-42.

cluded Beth-haccherem, Mizpah, Beth-zur, Keilah, and Jerusalem; the borders of the province of Judah extended westward from Mizpah to the Shephelah, to Tell el-Full in the north, to Jericho in the east, and to Ramat Rahal and Beth-zur in the south. The organization of the province included a Persian appointed Jewish governor, several of whom are mentioned in the Elephantine papyri and the Bible: Sheshbazzar (Ezra 5:14), Zerubbabel (Hag. 1:1), Nehemiah (Neh. 2:5-9; 5:14), and later on Bagohi, Urio, Hananiah, Elnathan, Yehoazar, Ahzai, and Yehizqiah.[53] While the date of the Jewish governor, Nehemiah, is disputed, the biblical chronology has him come to Judah some thirteen years after the beginning of the mission of Ezra (this would mean he served as governor 445-433 B.C.E., if the Persian king was Artaxerxes I). Judah had been separated from the political leadership of Samaria and given its own independent status as a province (*yĕhûd mĕdîntā'*, Ezra 5:8) within the empire.

The Development of Scribalism in the Persian Period

With the rebuilding of the temple and the political organization of the province under a Jewish governor, two types of scribes were required: those who served in the temple complex under the Zadokite hierarchy, and others who were scribes in the governor's administration.[54] The titles for both were *sōpēr* (Aram. *siprā'*) and *liblār*, and later in the Greco-Hellenistic period Greek *grammateus* and *liblarios*. The roles of the scribes included civil administrators and their assistants, teachers of students in scribal schools in the temple, the court, and private homes, and recorders in charge of correspondence and records. A small number held significant rank in the administration, while a few even composed literature for sages, priests, and civil administrators (e.g., historical records and the Torah's civil legislation).[55]

With the "end" of prophecy (according to the rabbis) in the Persian period, a new type of scribalism emerged in which the sage's compositions and inter-

---

53. See Bezalel Porten, *Archives from Elephantine: The Life of an Ancient Jewish Military Colony* (Berkeley: University of California Press, 1968) 289-90; Lester L. Grabbe, *Judaism from Cyrus to Hadrian* (2 vols.; Minneapolis: Fortress, 1992) 1:68-73.

54. See Fishbane, "From Scribalism to Rabbinism," 440-43.

55. See Emil Schürer, *The History of the Jewish People in the Age of Jesus Christ (175 B.C.–135 A.D.)*, ed. Geza Vermes, et al., trans. T. A. Burkill, et al. (3 vols. in 4; Edinburgh: T&T Clark, 1973-1987). Also see Martin Hengel, "'Schriftauslegung' und 'Schriftwerdung' in der Zeit des Zweiten Tempels," in *Kleine Schriften*, vol. 2: *Judaica, Hellenistica et Christiana*, ed. Jörg Frey and Dorothea Betz with contributions by Hanswulf Bloedhorn and Max Küchler (WUNT 109; Tübingen: Mohr-Siebeck, 1999) 20-35.

pretations came to be viewed as inspired and revealed.[56] The new understanding of the scribe as the authoritative and inspired interpreter of the Torah may be traced in the books of Chronicles and Ezra-Nehemiah. Ezra, the scribe and priest of God Most High, is depicted as the second Moses and later in early noncanonical Jewish writings as an apocalyptic seer.[57] He is said to have received his legitimacy as "a priest and a scribe of the God of heaven" *(kāhănâ sāpar dātā' dî-'ĕlāh šĕmayyā')*, appointed by the Achaemenid ruler Artaxerxes (I?) (Ezra 7:21). These roles are those of priest, guardian, teacher, and interpreter of the Torah. His activity as the "scribe of the God of heaven" included his inspired interpretation ("to inquire," *lidrôš*) of the meaning of the "Torah of Yahweh" (7:10). This formula refers to the earlier prophetic obtaining of a divine oracle (1 Kgs. 22:8). He is the one who teaches the Torah to the people. The composer of the narrative uses another prophetic expression, "the hand of Yahweh" coming upon him, to speak of inspiration and revelation (Ezra 7:6, 9; cf. Ezek. 1:3). Thus "Ezra is a priestly scribe who teaches the received, written revelation through his inspired study of it."[58]

Josephus (*C. Ap.* 1.40-41) indicates that the succession of the prophets stretched from Moses to Artaxerxes, strongly suggesting that he included Ezra in this list (*Ant.* 11.120-58 places Ezra earlier, during the time of Xerxes I). Later regarded as the last of the prophets, he is also among the first members of the "Great Synagogue" *(kĕneset haggĕdōlâ)*, thus connecting the Jewish scribes of Torah to those continuing into the Tannaitic period (*m. 'Abot* 1.1). Of course, this tradition of an assembly of Jewish sages who enacted and interpreted legislation and composed literature that entered the canonical sections of many of the prophets and several of the writings (Ezekiel, Daniel, Esther, and the Twelve) cannot be demonstrated conclusively to be historical. But at least the literature of Chronicles, Nehemiah, and Ezra and later traditions point to Ezra as the legendary prototype of the sages of the Persian period.[59] This evidence provides some support for the scribal positions held by Ezra, Zadok, and

---

56. See esp. Joseph Blenkinsopp, "The Sage, the Scribe, and Scribalism in the Chronicler's Work," in *Sage in Israel*, 307-15; Moshe Weinfeld, *Deuteronomy and the Deuteronomic School* (Oxford: Clarendon, 1972).

57. Louis Ginzberg, *The Legends of the Jews*, vol. 4: *From Joshua to Esther* (repr. Baltimore: Johns Hopkins University Press, 1998) 359. According to Ginzberg, Ezra was not only a member of the Great Assembly but also directed it.

58. Fishbane, "From Scribalism to Rabbinism," 441. This compares to Ps. 119:18 in which the psalmist prays for divine light in order to interpret the Torah.

59. Seals and bullae of scribes testify to their activity during the Persian period. See Nahman Avigad, *Bullae and Seals from a Post-Exilic Judaean Archive* (Qedem 4; Jerusalem: Hebrew University of Jerusalem, Institute of Archaeology, 1976).

Shimshai in the books of Ezra and Nehemiah. It is quite probable that the Jewish scribes were employed by Persians and Jews for writing documents, served as officials in the Achaemenid Empire in both the royal court and in the province, and had legal responsibilities in codifying and rendering local verdicts on the basis of Jewish law. In later Jewish literature, for example, *b. Qidd.* 30a, the scribes were called *sôpĕrîm* because they counted all of the letters of the Torah, a scribal procedure to ensure accuracy. Thus there is a line of scribes that includes copyists, supported by the temple, who were likely priests (see *m. Šeqal.* 4.2; *b. Ketub.* 106a; also see *m. Šeqal.* 6.6) and also exegetes and teachers of Scripture and the Mishnah (*m. ʿOr.* 3.9; *Ned.* 9.2; *Qidd.* 4.13).[60]

The Development of the Scribe as Interpreter of Scripture in Chronicles and Ezra-Nehemiah

The roles of the scribes and the development of Torah and wisdom are conspicuous in the literature of Chronicles, Ezra, and Nehemiah. The Torah is now identified with wisdom, giving an even more significant role to the sages as a consequence. The Persian period witnessed the growth of scribal professions throughout the empire. Aramaic had replaced Akkadian as the lingua franca of the Achaemenid Empire. In Judah the steady transition from Hebrew to Aramaic as both the spoken and the official language of the colony required scribes who knew intimately well both languages for civil responsibilities and for the translation of Hebrew into what was becoming the spoken language of Jews in Judah (see Neh. 8:1-8, which lists scribes and the Levites as the interpreters of the Hebrew Torah read by Ezra). It is conceivable that some scribes may even have known Old Persian to communicate with the empire, although the official language was Aramaic. In addition, the final formation of the Priestly document (P) became the major religious text for the temple cultus.

As noted earlier, scribes worked in two locales: the temple complex in recording sacrifices, collecting temple taxes, creating compositions of various types, and archiving these documents; and the local provincial government, which was a part of the larger Persian satrapy of Abar-Nahara ruled by a Persian governor. The local internal administration of the province of Judah was headed by Jewish governors. The commitment of the *sôpĕrîm* to the Torah was both personal, as expressed in scribal piety found in the Torah psalms, and offi-

---

60. See Isa. 28:7, an exilic text, and Jer. 18:18, belonging to the Deuteronomic redaction that dates circa the exilic to the early Second Temple period.

cial, in that some were civil servants, officials, judges, and translators involved in instituting and interpreting the Torah as the constitution for Judah.

The Scribe of Torah and the Torah Psalms

The emphasis on the priestly Torah corresponds to one of the important roles of Second Temple scribes who reflect on, interpret, and teach the law that was codified by Ezra in the early fourth century B.C.E. (perhaps an early form of P). The three Torah psalms are appropriate compositions for the scribes in this period, including Ezra and those under him, who translated and explained the law read to the assembly of Jews during the Festival of Tabernacles. One may surmise that with Ezra there emerged one type of scribe serving as the interpreter of Torah whose theology was centered on creation, the revelation of the Torah (equated with wisdom), a universal deity ("God Most High"), the temple, and the sacred city of Jerusalem. During the Persian period, the codification of the priestly law continued in part as a direct response to the Achaemenid proclamation that the nations within their empire shape their own laws for local social life. It is especially the revealed Torah that is the divine gift that enables its observers to live righteous and wise lives.[61] Each of these features is stressed also in Ben Sira. This new theology of the sages grounds the Torah in creation and providence and views the temple and its rituals as significant for the renewal of life, especially during the New Year Festival (see Job 33:26; Qoh. 4:17 [5:1]; 8:10; Sir. 24:10-11; 36:13-14; 45:9, 24; 47:10, 13; 49:6, 12; 50:1-2, 7, 11; 51:13; Wis. 9:8-9). The Torah and the temple assume both cosmological and moral characteristics and actualize divine creation, providence, and the well-being of the moral life.[62]

Ezra, the Scribe and Priest of God Most High

How much of the portrait of Ezra in the books of Ezra and Nehemiah is historical and how much is fictional is difficult to say. However, Ezra is the legendary, ideal sage of the Second Temple period and is presented as involved in a series of actions that develop the foundation for early Judaism in the later Persian pe-

---

61. Ceresko, "Sage in the Psalms," 218-30.

62. See Frank Gorman, *The Ideology of Ritual: Space, Time, and Status in the Priestly Theology* (JSOTSup 91; Sheffield: Sheffield Academic Press, 1990); Levenson, *Creation and the Persistence of Evil.*

riod. Josephus (*Ant.* 11.120-83) follows the narrative in 1 Esdras, but also attaches an account of Ezra's death in his old age. In the Bible Ezra is the sage and interpreter of the Torah.

However, there is a parallel to his role in the life and activity of the Egyptian scribe and priest Udjahorresnet, commissioned by Darius I to reinstitute the local cult and provide a unified form of local law.[63] The reverse side of the Demotic Chronicle presents the Persian king as ordering that "the wise men be assembled . . . from among the warriors, the priests and the scribes of Egypt so that they may set down in writing the ancient Laws of Egypt."[64]

Artaxerxes (I?), in his decree in Ezra 7:12-26, written in Aramaic,[65] addresses Ezra as "the priest" who is a descendant of the chief priest Zadok[66] and as "the scribe of the law of the God of heaven" ("a priest, and a scribe of the law of the God of heaven," *kāhănā' sāpar dātā' dî-'ĕlāh šĕmayyā'*).[67] In 7:6 he is called a "scribe skilled in the law of Moses" *(sōpēr māhîr bĕtôrat mōšeh)*. To be "skilled" means to have the ability to read, write, and interpret, in this case, the "Torah of Moses."[68] Ezra's title as a *sōpēr māhîr* is found in the royal marriage hymn of Ps. 45:2(1), indicating that this title may have been used in the First Temple period. In the Aramaic version of Ahiqar from Elephantine, this scribe is called a *sāpar ḥakkîm māhîr* ("a wise and skillful scribe"), who gave *'ăṭâ* ("ad-

63. Joseph Blenkinsopp, "The Mission of Udjahorresnet and Those of Ezra and Nehemiah," *JBL* 106 (1987) 409-21. For a translation of the inscription, see *TUAT* 1/6 (1985) 525-613. Also see John Baines, "On the Composition and Inscriptions of the Vatican Statue of Udjahorresnet," in *Studies in Honor of William Kelly Simpson,* ed. Peter Der Manuelian (2 vols.; Boston: Dept. of Ancient Egyptian, Nubian and Near Eastern Art, Museum of Fine Arts, 1996) 1:83-92; Günter Burkard, "Literarische Tradition und historische Realität: Die persische Eroberung Ägyptens am Beispiel Elephantine," *ZÄS* 121 (1994) 93-106; idem, "Literarische Tradition und historische Realität: Die persische Eroberung Ägyptens am Beispiel Elephantine (II)," *ZÄS* 122 (1995) 31-37; Christophe Thiers, "Civils et militaires dans les temples: Occupation illicite et expulsion," *Bulletin de l'Institut Français d'Archéologie Orientale* 95 (1995) 493-516; Bernadette Menu, "Les carrières des Egyptiens à l'étranger sous les dominations perses: Les critères de justification, leur évolution et leurs limites," *Transeuphratène* 9 (1995) 81-90.

64. See W. Spielgelberg, *Die sogenannte demotische Chronik des Pap. 215 der Bibliothèque Nationale zu Paris* (Leipzig: Hinrichs, 1914) 30-32; A. Tulli, "Il Naoforo Vaticano," in *Miscellanea Gregoriana* (Rome: Tipografia Poliglotta Vaticano, 1941) 211-80.

65. See Hans Heinrich Schaeder, *Ezra der Schreiber* (Tübingen: Mohr, 1940). However, the decree has undergone Jewish scribal editing (Blenkinsopp, "Sage, Scribe, and Scribalism," 312-14).

66. He also is called a "priest" (Aram. *kāhănā'*, Ezra 7:12) in the letter of Artaxerxes, who commissions him to go to Jerusalem, to enquire about following the Torah, and to reestablish worship at the temple by means of financial support the Persian government provided. The "official" decree of Artaxerxes also refers to Ezra as a "priest" (7:21).

67. Cf. Wisdom proceeding out of the mouth of the "Most High" (Sir. 24:3).

68. For *māhîr* see H. Ringgren, *TDOT,* 8:141-42.

vice/counsel"). In 7:11 Ezra is called "the priest, the scribe of the book of the words of the commandments of Yahweh and his statutes for Israel" *(hakkōhēn hassōpēr sōpēr dibrê miṣwōt-YHWH wĕḥuqqāyw ʿal-yiśrāʾēl)*. In the Hebrew narrative, the law is the "law of Moses" given to Ezra by Yahweh. The Aramaic proclamation refers to the law more generally as "the law of the God of heaven," a reference more in line with Zoroastrian religious expression. In the letter of commission from Artaxerxes I (?), Ezra is given a specific administrative title from the royal court: "the scribe of the law of the God of heaven." The narratives of Ezra and Nehemiah present Ezra as one who dedicated himself to study the Torah and observed (or perhaps "composed," *laʿăśōt*) and taught Israel its ordinances (Ezra 7:10). The Persian king gives him the power to appoint judges and magistrates "according to the God-given wisdom *(ḥokmâ)*" that he possesses, and to dictate punishments for violations of the law (7:25-26).

1 and 2 Chronicles, Ezra, and Nehemiah are four (or 2) volumes with tradition histories that range from the late Persian period to the time of the early Hellenistic period. In chs. 7–8, developing from the fundamental document of 7:21-22, which may date from the fourth century, before the conquest of Alexandria, Ezra is presented as a "scribe skilled in the law of Moses that Yahweh, the God of Israel, had given" (7:6). Therefore, Ezra is both a priest[69] and a scribe of the Torah. In the development of the Ezra legend, he becomes the "father" of scribal interpreters of the Torah. In the tradition, Ezra is not the composer of the law in one of its editions, but rather the one who took some form of it, studied and reflected on it, and sought to enact it in communal existence in Jerusalem as the basis for Jewish life.[70] According to the narrative in Neh. 7:73b–9:37, Ezra reads the Torah (at least an early version of it) during the first day of the seventh month, the day of the new moon that introduces the most important month of festival ("This day" refers to Tishri 1, which was later called New Year's Day, i.e., Rosh Hashanah). Following the conclusion of the reading, the scribes and the Levites went among the assembled crowd reading from the law of God, "with interpretation" *(mĕpōrāš)*. "And they read in the book in the Torah of God, providing its interpretation and meaning, and they [the people] understood" *(wayyiqrĕʾû bassēper bĕtôrat hāʾĕlōhîm mĕpōrāš wĕśôm śekel wayyābînû bammiqrāʾ*, 8:8). The ability to read, speak, and clarify the meaning of the Torah likely followed a tradition of interpretation these scribal Levites must have developed and learned in a temple school. The ones who "inter-

69. This descent of Ezra from the first high priest, Zadok, is presented in 1 Esdras 1:1 (LXX) while in latter rabbinic legend he is both priest, teacher, and, like Moses, a lawgiver (t. Sanh. 21b, b. Sanh. 21b, and b. Meg. 16b). The teaching role of the priests is seen in other biblical writings, including Mal. 2:7.

70. Hengel, "'Schriftauslegung' und 'Schriftwerdung,'" 24.

preted" *(mĕbînîm)* the Torah comprise a group of individuals listed by name who were likely scribes and Levites. The "scribes" (so we assume) are Jeshua, Bani, Sherebiah, Jamin, Akkub, Shabbethai, Hodiah, Maaseiah, Kelita, Azariah, Jozabad, Hanan, and Pelaiah. The Levites are educated in the priestly school, although they are not named in this passage. This process of reading, translation, and interpretation signifies a new development in the understanding of revelation in the Second Temple. Priestly mantic wisdom, that is, revelation through means of Urim and Thummim, had come to an end (Neh. 7:65), and cultic prophecy is now replaced with the sages' reading, translation, inspired interpretation, and instruction in Torah (8:1-8).

Scribes read from the book of the law of God, translated it into Aramaic for the populace, and made clear its meaning (8:7-9; cf. Ezra 7:25). This is the first time that the word *miqrā'* is used to refer to the reading of the Torah (Neh. 8:8). This public reading, translation, and interpretation for people assembled in Jerusalem for Rosh Hashanah (the "New Year's Festival") is presented as the precedent for reading and interpreting the Torah at common gatherings during pilgrimage festivals and eventually in the synagogues for Sabbath meetings and special sacred occasions.

Sages and Officials in the Second Temple Period

The professional roles of scribes in Chronicles, Ezra, and Nehemiah are indicated by the titles they bore during the late Persian or early Hellenistic period. The word *'āb* in this literature normally refers to the father in the household. In the genealogy of the children of Israel and Judah (1 Chron. 2), however, there is the reference to the families *(mišpāḥâ)* of Kenite scribes *(sōpĕrîm)*, who lived at Jabez, a town in Judah, probably located near Bethlehem (1 Chron. 2:55). These Kenites descended from Hammath, father *('āb)* of the house of Rechab. This refers to a family guild that indicates one way scribes were educated, that is, by their fathers, so that they would inherit their status and professional roles. This text also indicates that there may have been clusters of scribal families who lived near Jerusalem.

In this literature, some of the Levites served the temple priests and governors as counselors *(yō'ēṣ)*. Among the Levitical gatekeepers (1 Chron. 26:1-19), the keeper of the northern gate was Zechariah, a "counselor," known for his insight (26:14). Listed as one of the seven officials who were in the royal cabinet (27:32-34) and advised the king was David's uncle, Jonathan, who has three sapiential titles and likely roles: "counselor, a man of understanding, and a scribe" *(yôēṣ 'îš-mēbîn wĕsōpēr)*. As noted in the Succession Narrative,

Ahithophel is the king's counselor (2 Sam. 16:23; 17:23), a designation of the one who held the highest rank, while Hushai the Archite is the "king's friend" (2 Sam. 15:32-37), thus a close personal advisor. In addition, the officials in the cabinet include one who was "with the king's sons" (*'im bĕnê-hammelek*), likely their official tutor.[71] He is listed among the high-ranking cabinet officials as Jehiel, son of Hachmoni (1 Chron. 27:32). The "counselor" in the cabinet was an advisor to the monarch in the area of political policy and military matters, while the "man of understanding" (*'îš-mēbîn*), is a temple servant, a Levitical teacher, one who led the choir and musicians in the temple service, and an instructor of Levitical students in these musical roles (1 Chron. 15:22; 25:7-8; 27:32; Ezra 8:16). While the Davidic monarchy had ceased, the role of counselor would have been assumed by advisors to governors appointed by administrative officials of the Achaemenid rulers.

The "one over the house" (*'ăšer 'al-habbayît*) was the administrator responsible for the operations of the palace, if not the entire administration (Gen. 43:19; 1 Kgs. 16:9; 18:3; 2 Kgs. 10:5; 18:18, 37; 19:2; Isa. 22:15; 36:3, 22; 37:2). He may also have been educated in the wisdom tradition. In 2 Kgs. 18:18, 37, and Isa. 36:3, 22, the palace administrator is listed with the secretary (*sōpēr*) and the recorder (*mazkîr*). While evidence is lacking that this office continued in the Second Temple period, an official in charge of the governor's palace is likely.

One of the royal advisors was called the "friend of the king" (*rēʿeh hammelek*, 1 Kgs. 4:5 = 1 Chron. 27:33; cf. 2 Sam. 15:37; 16:16). In the Succession Narrative, David's "friend" is Hushai, the Archite, whose wise counsel overturns that of the traitor Ahithophel, David's counselor. In 1 Kgs. 4:5 the list of highly placed officials in the administration includes a reference to Zabud, who was a priest and the "king's friend." This office referred to the personal "counselor" in the administrative hierarchy. While the title would have changed in the Second Temple period, there was likely a similar advisor to the Persian appointed governor of the colony.

The recorder (*mazkîr*) was an important official in the court who wrote down the royal decrees and proclamations. His skill in language indicates that he would have had a scribal education and was included in the king's (later the governor's) cabinet (2 Sam. 8:16; 20:24; 1 Kgs. 4:3; 2 Kgs. 18:18, 37 = Isa. 36:3, 22; 1 Chron. 18:15; 2 Chron. 34:8).

A wise teacher (*'îš-mēbîn*) was the title used of the Levite who was a teacher in Chronicles and Ezra-Nehemiah. Additionally, he was in charge of the music in the temple services and thus taught students music, which was part of the curriculum (1 Chron. 15:22; 25:7-8; 27:32; Ezra 8:16). Levites appeared to have

---

71. Leslie A. Allen, "First and Second Chronicles," *NIB* 3 (1999) 457.

served in the role of the official *(miśraṭ)* who assisted the priests and carried out many of the duties in the temple, except for sacrifice (Ezra 8:17).

Chronicles also refers to teachers *(môreh)* who were priests and Levites responsible for teaching the Torah to the people (2 Chron. 15:3). God is the divine teacher in Job 36:22 in the Elihu speeches, which were likely written in the Persian period (cf. Isa. 30:20). This indicates that the God of wisdom had now become Yahweh, while Hokmah became a metaphor or divine attribute and no longer held the rank of goddess or consort/daughter of God.

In Ps. 119:99 (a Torah psalm), the sage who utters the lament to Yahweh asserts that he has more understanding *(hiśkaltî)* than all of his teachers *(mĕlammĕday)*. In 1 Chron. 25:7 the Pual form of the verb *lāmad* refers to the Levites who were "instructed" in singing to Yahweh. Those who taught in the Second Temple schools held the office of instructor *(mĕlammēd)*.

The judge *(šōpēṭ)*, who would have received a scribal education, is mentioned often in Chronicles, Ezra, and Nehemiah. During the late Persian and early Hellenistic periods, the judges knew the legal commandments and precedents of the Torah and used them in making legal decisions. The term is found in 1 Chron. 17:6 (the judges who shepherd the people); 23:4 (judges among the four groups of Levites); 26:29 (the reference to judges from the Levitical Izharites); 2 Chron. 1:2 (judges listed along with heads of families, leaders, and commanders of a hundred and of a thousand); and Ezra 10:14 (judges presiding over the assembly in order to annul marriages to foreign wives).

During the reform of Jehoshaphat based on the law, the king appointed judges in the different cities and established a central court in Jerusalem to deal with cases that are referred from the lower courts (2 Chron. 19:5-6). Amaziah, the high priest, was in charge of this legal process, indicating that the high priest assumed control over internal, legal matters in the colony of Judah. It is likely these texts reflected the legal system established during the Persian period in order to implement the Torah as the basis for religious and civil legislation in the colonial state.

The secretary in the royal cabinet was simply known as the *sōpēr* or the king's *sōpēr*. This post, something like a prime minister, was likely the office second to the king in regard to authority and power (2 Sam. 8:17; 20:25; 1 Kgs. 4:3 [Solomon had two]; 2 Kgs. 18:18, 37 = Isa. 36:3, 22; 2 Kgs. 19:2 = Isa. 37:2; Jer. 36:10-20; 1 Chron. 18:16). In colonial Judah the chief secretary would have served the Jewish governor in the administration (Esth. 3:12; 8:9), financial record keeping, the collection and use of taxes, and legal administration. There were other chief secretaries who are mentioned. Shimshai produced the letter from the provincial center in Samaria (Ezra 4:8-24), while Ezra 7:14-15 refers to counselors of the king (called sages in Esth. 1:13-14). Scribes were also active in the governmental centers of Judah (Esth. 3:12; 8:9) and in the provinces and satrapies of the Persian administrative structures (Herodotus 3.128; Elephantine papyri 17.1, 6). Other scribes included the treasurer and paymaster (2 Kgs. 12:11 = 2 Chron. 24:11; Neh. 13:13; 2 Kgs. 22:3, 8, 9, 10, 12 = 2 Chron. 34:15, 18, 20) in charge of the temple treasury (2 Kgs. 12:11 = 2 Chron. 24:11; cf. Neh. 13:13) and a recorder (1 Chron. 24:6 speaks of a Levite who recorded the divisions of the priests of the temple). The military secretary who served the commander of the army may have continued into the Second Temple period in mustering, organizing, and paying Jewish troops who served as auxiliaries in the Persian military forces (2 Kgs. 25:19 = Jer. 52:25).

The "official" *(šōṭēr)* refers to one who organizes various associations and goods and appears to refer to a lower placed scribe (2 Chron. 26:11; 34:13). This official likely served in a number of functions, including judicial recording, judging in lower courts, assistance in the mustering of troops and in forming divisions (1 Chron. 27:1), and overseeing groups of laborers. Levites held this position according to 2 Chron. 19:11 (serving the governor and the high priest) and 34:13.

The officer *(śar)* in the later narrative history refers to a number of different scribes who had important governing functions. These comprised officers under rulers, including foreign kings (2 Chron. 36:18; Neh. 9:32, 34), a district magistrate in the Persian Empire's organization of Judah (Esth. 1:3; 8:9; 9:3; Neh. 3:8-19), a citadel's magistrate (Neh. 7:2), city officials (2 Chron. 29:20), military officials (1 Chron. 13:1; 26:26; 27:1, 3; 29:6; 2 Chron. 1:2; 32:6; 33:14; Neh. 2:9), officials among the orders of the priests (2 Chron. 36:14; Ezra 8:24, 29; 10:5), Levites (1 Chron. 15:5-10, 16, 22; 2 Chron. 35:9), leaders and elders of the tribes (1 Chron. 27:22; 28:1; 29:6; 2 Chron. 24:23; Ezra 9:1-2; 10:8; Neh. 4:10; 11:1), and magistrates of Judah (Neh. 12:31-32) and of the people (Neh. 11:1). Heads of families were also called "officers," perhaps to adapt them to the administrative organization of the provincial government established by Darius I (1 Chron. 24:31; 27:1; 29:6; Ezra 8:29; Neh. 7:70). The recording of these family heads would have provided a convenient census for the collection of taxes to the local and imperial governments.

"Rulers" or "officials" *(sāgān/segen)* of Judah appear to have been part of the Persian administrative organization. This term is used to refer to the "officials" of Judah and is found only in Ezra and Nehemiah (Ezra 9:2; Neh. 2:16; 4:8, 13; 5:7, 17; 7:5; 12:40; 13:11). Their precise function is not clear, although they appeared to have held an administrative office in the Persian government of the colony.

The Sages and Scribal Schools

The scribes of Judah more than likely would have been involved in carrying out correspondence, raising taxes, accounting for produce, regulating trade, providing subscriptions for the army, and formulating lists of laborers for royal projects. These skills would have required an education in schools in Jerusalem or possibly in urban areas of the colony. Dating the didactic tales of Dan. 1–6 in the Persian period intimates that the three friends of the protagonist passed through a three-year curriculum (Dan. 1:5) and learned Akkadian literature and language (1:4) in a school likely in Jerusalem. Furthermore, 1 Chron. 2:55 refers to "families *(mišpāḥâ)* of scribes dwelling at Jabez," perhaps scribal families and guilds who lived and studied there (cf. 4:14, 21, 23). Blenkinsopp surmises that these scribes belonged to the lower ranks and served, for example, as notaries.[72]

Major Theological Themes

The theological themes of the Second Temple period reflected the new status given the Torah.

Wisdom, Torah, and Creation

Creation resided at the heart of sapiential theology, something especially noticeable in the scribal redaction of Ps. 111 and in the combination of Ps. 19B with 19A. During the Persian period, the Second Temple literature, including the three Torah psalms (1, 19B, 119), clearly indicates that the Torah, which was largely shaped in what would be its canonical form, became the theological center of traditional Judaism, including Jewish wisdom. The Torah is now identified with the order of creation that sustains the cosmos and with wisdom that instructs its followers in the proper ways to live in harmony with God and society and to achieve well-being by meditation and obedience. Since the sages in the Second Temple period begin to equate wisdom and the Torah, both are seen as the order of righteousness that integrates creation and a just society (e.g., Ps. 19; Sir. 24). Both the Torah and wisdom permeate creation, sustaining and revitalizing its forces of life and order that oppose the power of evil and chaos. To live in harmony with the

---

72. Blenkinsopp, "Sage, Scribe, and Scribalism," 310. He compares these to the *sāprayyā'* of Elephantine's Jewish community (Porten, *Archives from Elephantine*, 55-57, 192-97).

cosmos now means to follow carefully not only the teachings of the wise, but also the divine ordinances incorporated in the Torah.[73]

Wisdom and Torah: The Torah as the Basis for Social and Religious Life

The meaning of Torah in the Ezra narrative provides some insight into its understanding in the three Torah psalms.[74] The Torah involves two interweaving connections, one cosmic and the other societal. In Ezra 7:26 the royal "law" (Aram. *dātā'*) may suggest the influence of the Achaemenid royal inscriptions (also in Aramaic) in which law in the Persian understanding is identified with the cosmic order.[75] The Persian king was *dātā'*, that is, the one who represents, incarnates, and actualizes this universal order in his reign (cf. Heb. *dāt* in Esth. 1:8; 2:12; 4:8; Ezra 8:36). This cosmic dimension is central to the understanding of Torah in Ezra and the Torah psalms. Further, the Torah in Ezra and the Torah psalms is also a legal code of civil and religious commandments that provides the basis for social and individual existence.[76]

Torah as the Response to Religious Diversity in Judaism

The reason for the emphasis on Torah in the Second Temple period was that the Torah was used to provide a more unified formation of early Judaism. The significant differences of religious understanding found in the varieties of early Judaism in the Second Temple period, which included developing sects of Jews in Jerusalem and Judah, the Samaritans, and the Elephantine colony, proved to be an obstacle to religious conformity. This concern for homogeneity emerged not only internally from the Jewish religious authorities in Jerusalem, in particular the Zadokite priestly hierarchy, but also externally as part of the Persian political policy for ruling the vast empire they conquered. The codification of socioreligious law among the vassal nations and colonies was one means for achieving stability among the multiple ethnicities and cultures of the empire. Thus the efforts of Ezra and the ethos that is reflected in the Torah psalms point

73. See Reinhard G. Kratz, "Die Torah Davids. Psalm 1 und die doxologische Fünfteilung des Psalters," *ZThK* 90 (1993) 1-34.

74. Sebastian Grätz, *Das Edikt des Artaxerxes: Eine Untersuchung zum religionspolitischen und historischen Umfeld von Esra 7,12-26* (BZAW 337; Berlin: de Gruyter, 2004).

75. Pierre Lecoq, *Les inscriptions de la Perse achéménide* (Paris: Gallimard, 1997).

76. Rolf Rendtorff, "Noch einmal: Esra und das 'Gesetz,'" *ZAW* 111 (1999) 228-35.

to the desire of the Persian rulers and the Jewish authorities in Jerusalem who were loyal to the Achaemenid court to create a common expression of Judaism and brand as illegitimate other forms. This in turn led to the enhancement of the theological role of the sages who were given the primary responsibility in producing the codification of Yahweh's Torah and to the scribal administration in carrying out its dictates for Jewish social and religious life. The sages and scribes of the wisdom tradition joined with the leaders of the hierarchically differentiated priesthood to create a holistic Judaism that was held to be the authentic form of expression that was especially centered in the sacred city and temple of Jerusalem. Monotheism, the temple at Jerusalem, the Torah, and the authority of the Zadokite priesthood became the unified articulation of state and provincial legitimated Judaism. Competing shrines, religious understandings of deity, and law codes at Elephantine, Dan, Lachish (cf. the solar shrine from the Persian period), and Samaria (Mt. Gerizim) were deemed illicit.[77] Of course, this effort to unify Judaism was not successful prior to the Roman destruction of Jerusalem in 70 c.e.

Wisdom and Torah

The ethical and social features of Torah and wisdom are identified. Psalm 19 unites together a song in praise of the creator and sustainer (originally El and Shamash, respectively) with a lament in which the Torah is also extolled, and God is petitioned to keep the psalmist from transgression. Together these two texts become a meditation that the editor offers to God in praise of his creation and his gift of the Torah. The value of the Torah (19:10) reminds the audience of the incomparable worth of wisdom in Prov. 3:13-17 and 8:18-21. Psalm 119 has features of both thanksgiving and lamentation. Using eight different terms for "law," the psalmist argues that the Torah provides religious instruction. In addition, the lament into which the Torah and its synonyms are inserted expresses the psalmist's request of God to escape the wicked and to gain forgiveness for

77. See the solar shrine at Lachish and the *YHD* coins minted in the late Persian period. One is a silver Jewish drachma likely originating from Judah, which is imitative of an Athenian coin. On the obverse side is the portrait of a bearded male head in a Corinthian helmet. This figure is identical to the Syrian god Hadranos found on the coins of the Mamertines (see J. P. Six, "Observations sur les monnaies Pheniciennes," *Numismatic Chronicle* 17 [1877] 221-63). On the reverse side is a deity with a satyr's mask in a Greek *chitōn* seated on a winged wheel and holding an Egyptian falcon on his left arm. Is this Yahweh in his winged chariot (Ezek. 1) portrayed as the Egyptian sun god? The Aramaic word *YHD* ("Judea") is inscribed above the figure; see Yaʿakov Meshorer, *Jewish Coins of the Second Temple Period* (Chicago: Argonaut, 1967) 35-38, 116-17, pl. 1.

personal sins. Likewise, the thanksgiving provides the scribe's joy at the gift of the Torah to guide the wise in their efforts to be obedient to divine teaching encompassed in both the Law and the sapiential instructions.

The three Torah psalms indicate that the theological emphases of the temple sages expand the focus on creation and providence to include the temple and the Torah. Now the Torah, grounded in creation and providence, and the Temple, with its rituals, are key to the renewal of life, especially during the temple New Year Festival in which the creation is renewed by means of the temple liturgy and the reading and teaching of the Torah. The Torah and the temple take on significant cosmological and moral characteristics that actualize divine creation, providence, and human life through the obedience of the wise to the Law's prescripts.

Creation and Anthropology

The psalms of Torah also speak to the topic of creation and anthropology. This element is especially important in Ps. 119, and the sage affirms in the initial line of the tenth strophe (vv. 73-80) that God has created and enlightened him/her in order to become resolute in faithful obedience to the Law (v. 73; cf. Ps. 8 and Job 10):

> Your hands made *('āśâ)* me and fashioned *(kûn)* me,[78]
>   enlighten me so that I may learn your commandments *(miṣwōt).*

This writer points to the divine purpose of the creation of human beings. Through the life lived in commitment to the Torah, others will observe his/her example and rejoice over committed faithfulness. Even when the one engaged in the lament suffers, God's steadfast love embraces his/her life, while the wicked and the proud who have persecuted him/her will be shamed.

The psalmist expresses the belief that the Law is given by God to obedient followers to direct their lives in accordance with divine instruction. This connection between wisdom and Torah is present throughout the psalm. The emphasis on the tradition of the creation of humanity derives from the features of the lament that are strongly present in this psalm, since the lament is the seedbed for the tradition of the creation of humanity. Indeed, the tradition of the creation of the individual is appropriated to speak not only of God's creation of the psalmist, but also of enlightening her/him with the knowledge necessary to

---

78. The verb *kûn* refers to the erection of the pillars of the earth.

live a righteous existence (Ps. 19:8). Through this life of obedience to wisdom, identified with the Torah, the sage participates in the sustaining of creation and in serving as an example to others, both the wicked and those who would take up the path to wisdom. By the time Ben Sira's text is composed, the Torah's assimilation into creation's cosmological and anthropological spheres is at the heart of sapiential understanding.

The Piety of Second Temple Sages

During the Persian period the Torah obtained its esteemed position in Jewish wisdom, where it would remain central to the theology, moral philosophy, and worldview of the sages. In addition to learning, religious piety was cultivated in the wisdom schools of the Persian period. This cultivation of piety marked a major development in the character formation of the sages. Psalm 1 emphasizes meditation on the Torah as the demarcation between the wicked and the righteous. This is underscored structurally by the psalm's bifurcation into two strophes: the differentiation between the righteous, who meditate continually on the Torah and who experience life and vitality (strophe 1), and the wicked, whose end is destruction (strophe 2). In Ps. 119 the sage describes the deepening of his religious experience of God that derives from the study of Torah.[79]

The piety of the sages may be broken down into several major elements, especially as revealed by the didactic poems present in the Psalter (wisdom psalms). First, the didactic poems (wisdom psalms) witness to the character and devotional elements of piety that occur in the context of worship. Particularly in the act of confession expressed in laments and thanksgivings, the worshiper gave testimony to God's actions. It was during these public occasions that sages found their opportunity to speak of their own experiences and to offer instruction to the assembly. This is especially evident in Pss. 32:6-7; 34:6-7; and 73. Thus the divine acts of salvation on behalf of the sage to which testimony was given became instruction to the community in the faith of the righteous deity who delivers the faithful and just and punishes the wicked. This deliverance provides then the basis for the participation in praise.[80]

In addition to confession and thanksgiving, prayer was an intrinsic feature of sapiential piety (see Prov. 15:8, 29; 28:9; Job 31:26-28; 33:24-26; 42:8-10; Qoh. 5:1-2; Sir. 3:5; 4:6; 7:10, 14; 17:25; 28:2; 34:24, 26; 36:17; 37:15; 38:14, 34; 39:5-6; 46:4-

---

79. Fishbane, "From Scribalism to Rabbinism," 447.

80. Sigmund Mowinckel notes that the testimony assumes the form of an admonition ("Psalms and Wisdom," in *Wisdom in Israel and in the Ancient Near East,* 213-14).

5, 16-17; 47:5-6; 50:19; Wis. 7:7-8; 8:21; 11:3-4; 18:21). The composition and expression of prayers in the wisdom psalms may be found in Pss. 19:15(14); 32:5; 73:17, 23-25, 28; and, of course, Ps. 119. These are not limited to private prayers, since the wise psalmists admonish their audience to pray to and praise Yahweh, presumably in corporate worship (32:11; 37:3-5). Outside the Psalter, the prayers of sages for guidance, instruction, and/or wisdom include Sir. 22:27–23:6; 39:5-6; 51:13; and Wis. 9:1-18.

Two other acts of sapiential piety in the wisdom psalms consist of meditating on (*śîḥâ*, Ps. 119:15, 78, 97, 99) and delighting (*ḥēpeṣ*, 1:2; 119:48, 97; cf. 32:11) in the Torah. Meditation is more than private contemplation, but moves beyond reflection on a commandment to include the continuity of the progression from reading, interpreting, studying, to actualizing in life the teachings of the Torah. Meditation culminates in the praise of Yahweh for the gift of the life-giving Torah to his people (119:4-7, 24). To delight in the Torah is the response of the joyful sage who not only understands the meaning of a teaching, but also incorporates it in life. "Delighting" refers to the depth of religious experience when teaching and character become one.

Moral Instruction in Wisdom and Torah

Outside the traditional wisdom corpus, the clearest association of sages with the Torah is in Deuteronomy and the Deuteronomistic History. This association is attested first in Jeremiah, Deuteronomy, and the Deuteronomic redaction of various books, including Jeremiah. In Jer. 8:8 the prophet, in a poetic judgment speech from "Source A," launches his diatribe against the "wise" (*ḥăkāmîm*) for arguing the "the law of Yahweh" is with them, when, instead, their "false pen has made it into a lie (*šeqer*)." This suggests that sages and scribes were involved in the writing of the Torah in the late First Temple period. The didactic poems in the Psalter (wisdom psalms) as a whole present a number of important teachings of the sages to their students and to worshipers in the temple during the Sabbath and pilgrimage festivals. This is particularly noted in the instructions found in Pss. 32, 34, and 37. The sages teach their audience not only to avoid associations with the ungodly, but also to seek to find the righteous for fellowship (1:1), to avoid evil and to engage in good deeds (34:15; 37:3, 27), to speak with caution (34:14[13]), to control anger (37:8), to experience the well-being that comes to the faithful (34:15; 37:7), to practice charity (112:5, 9), to incorporate the virtue of integrity (112:5), to trust in Yahweh (32:10; 37:3, 5, 7, 34), to search out the will of God in all endeavors (127:1-2), and to receive the blessings of God (1:1-2; 128:1-4).

Wisdom and Retribution

Almost all the sages who composed the wisdom psalms and scribes who redacted them into the final form of the Psalter were traditional in their theology and moral teachings. The single exception was the composer of Ps. 49, who, similar to Qoheleth, dwells on the theme of death that comes to all, both the rich and the poor, the wise and the foolish. The conventional teachings of conservative sages are noted elsewhere in these psalms and especially in the repetition of the validity of the theme of retribution. In similar fashion to Prov. 10–15, people are divided into wise and foolish, righteous and wicked, based on both their response to the teachings of wisdom and the Torah (see Ps. 1). The teachings of the sages are to be incorporated in their behavior and speech (Pss. 32, 34, 37). Yahweh is the one who oversees human beings, bringing life to those who follow the sages' teachings and destruction to those who do not. While this divine judgment may reside in the future, it is inevitable (Ps. 37).

Wisdom and Theodicy

The sages address the pressing issue of theodicy in two wisdom psalms, 49 and 73. In Ps. 49 the sage, whose literary composition is similar to Qoheleth, demonstrates that all people, rich and poor, wise and foolish, face the same fate: death. The sage finds some comfort in knowing that even those rich and powerful people who persecute him will face the same death that all people and creatures will experience. The sage does not adhere to the teaching of a just God who maintains the righteous order of human society through the administration of justice in punishing the wicked and delivering the righteous. Rather, death is the common denominator that ultimately breaks down present social differentiations.

Finally, theodicy in a more traditional understanding is reviewed in Ps. 73. The affirmation of the conservative believer who trusts in the goodness of the justice of God in favoring the upright is sorely tested in the psalmist's witness of the well-being of the wicked who oppress and mock Yahweh. Yet, due to his theophanic experience in the temple, he receives the assurance that those who are evil will indeed come to an ignoble end. By contrast, he is led by divine instruction, assured of his reception into the glory of God who will deliver him, a salvation to which he will testify before the audience assembled in the sanctuary.

5. Wisdom during the Ptolemaic Empire: The Book of Qoheleth

General Introduction

The book of Qoheleth emerges from a wisdom tradition that engages critically and often opposes the conventional wisdom of the Jewish theocracy in either the late Persian,[1] or, more likely, the Ptolemaic period.[2] One encounters in the cultural areas of wisdom circles in the ancient Near East and larger eastern Mediterranean world skeptical literature that brings into question conventional religion and wisdom. Not only have the book of Job and Psalm 49 pointed to the existence of the early stages of this skepticism, but so have the literatures of Classical Greece and of Middle and New Kingdom Egypt. Alexander the Great's conquest brought more than the loss of indigenous rule to the kingdoms of the East, including Egypt and those that had been a part of a vast ancient Near Eastern empire of the Persians, whose rulers, including Xerxes I and Darius I, had attempted unsuccessfully to conquer Greece. Alexander's wars of conquest also brought the conventions of Hellenism into an eastern world with an emphasis on the superiority of Greek language and culture. While hellenization,

---

1. C. L. Seow, *Ecclesiastes* (AB; New York: Doubleday, 1997). See now his detailed essay, "The Social World of Ecclesiastes," in *Scribes, Sages, and Seers*, forthcoming.

2. James L. Crenshaw, *Ecclesiastes* (OTL; Louisville: Westminster John Knox, 1988); Norbert Lohfink, *Qoheleth*, trans. Sean McEvenue (Continental Commentary; Minneapolis: Fortress, 2003); Michael Fox, *Ecclesiastes: The Traditional Hebrew Text with the New JPS Translation/Commentary* (JPS Bible Commentary; Philadelphia: Jewish Publication Society, 2004); Thomas Krüger, *Ecclesiastes: A Commentary*, trans. O. C. Dean Jr. (Hermeneia; Minneapolis: Fortress, 2004).

that is, the processes of cultural infusion, led to the merging of local indigenous cultures with those of the Greek west, it did not have as its design the elimination of the non-Greek world's culture and languages. Rather, there was a type of supra-Hellenistic world of intellectual and artistic awareness that, deemed superior to others, became in the minds of the aristocratic and intellectual leaders of the western empire the ideal model for non-Greek regions and cities to emulate. Under the weight of assumed cultural superiority, due to military conquests, Western Asiatic artistic and intellectual attainments were viewed often with a xenophobic disdain by the Greek émigrés in the east who were seeking wealth and status through commercial, agricultural, and governmental activities in this new world of opportunity. Many Hellenes, whether soldiers rewarded for their valor with land in the new world or Greeks seeking to exploit the new treasures that awaited them in the East, had certainly lacked the wealth and status they were seeking in the lands of the east. Even some intellectual leaders of the local indigenous populations also saw the superiority of the achievements of the western empire builder and his successors in the Greek kingdoms that emerged. Thus Alexander's conquest also brought not only the rule of a new empire, but also a new cultural mood of despair and doubt cast on the assumptions of conformist conservatism of intellectuals and indigenous aristocracies of this larger world.

To rightly interpret the book of Qoheleth requires an inquiry into the intellectual and cultural world of the early Hellenistic kingdoms and especially the reactions and development of the tiny province of Judah within the larger Ptolemaic kingdom centered in Alexandria. To understand Qoheleth is to enter into the cultural world that included skeptical literature produced by thinkers who came to be known not only in the Hellenistic Jewish colonies of the eastern Mediterranean regions but also in Judah itself. The intellectual tradition of Skepticism coming from the writings of scholars and thinkers who belonged to or at least came under the influence of the New Academy begins in a substantial way with Pyrrho of Elis, who lived approximately at the same time as Epicurus (c. 365-272 B.C.E.). Egyptian sages, from the end of the Persian Empire and the early generations of Ptolemaic rule that blended Egyptian religion and tradition with Greek culture, also betray at times a high degree of doubt about traditional affirmations that were constituent of a conventional and earlier worldview. Some of these skeptical writings were preserved in tomb inscriptions of the same era.

The book of Qoheleth and the case that was made for its inclusion in the Jewish canon in the first and second centuries C.E. present the most developed form of an internal skepticism that gripped the Jewish worldview in Israel and early Judaism. Scholars like Qoheleth seriously contested traditional affirmations in Jewish religious and sapiential circles. In his skeptical views of God, wisdom, and human existence, Qoheleth appears to have drawn on similar Greek and Egyptian traditions of wisdom, religious teachings, and philosophy vibrant during his time as a teacher.[3] At least his book takes its place in a world in which skepticism was regnant in the cultural climate.

Qoheleth in the Hellenistic World

Jerusalem and the late third century B.C.E. are the likely physical location and period of activity of the sage known as Qoheleth.[4] Jerusalem was a former religious capital and intellectual center that had undergone a succession of foreign rulers located in distant imperial centers (Assyrian, Egyptian, Babylonian, Persian, and now Greek) and yet had witnessed the reinvigoration and even reinterpretation of the Jewish worldviews as evidenced by the writings of narrators, priests, historians, and sages during the late Second Temple period. The new threat the world offered, introduced to Judah by the imperial expansion under Alexander, challenged the very core of traditional Judaism (represented by Ezra and Ben Sira) as a religious and cultural entity. From the literature and material culture of the world of Hellenism in Judah, Egypt, and Syria, we are made only too aware of the spread of Greek philosophical thought (Pythagoreanism, Stoicism, Epicureanism, and Middle Platonism)[5] and the rich and varied amalgam of religions that became popular in the larger Greek world due to the decreasing attraction of earlier Greek state religion and the Olympiad deities and the growing attraction of the religions and mystery cults from the East. A city of tradition and intellectual vitality like Jerusalem points to the significant impact of Hellenism and the new challenges to its world. Thus the temple, the development of the Torah as the religious and social constitution of the population, and the theocracy of the priesthood and its advocacy of loyalty to the Greek rulers in exchange for religious control flourished at a time when encroach-

3. See the essays in *Sagesse et religion*. They point to the influence of Greece on ancient Israel and Judah, which may be traced to the ninth century B.C.E.

4. The long-standing debate over Hellenistic influence on Qoheleth continues. See Harry Ranston, *Ecclesiastes and the Early Greek Wisdom Literature* (London: Epworth, 1925); Martin Hengel, "The Political and Social History of Palestine from Alexander to Antiochus III (333-187 B.C.E.)," *The Cambridge History of Judaism*, vol. 2: *The Hellenistic Age* (Cambridge: Cambridge University Press, 1989) 35-78; idem, "The Interpenetration of Judaism and Hellenism in the Pre-Maccabean Period," *Cambridge History of Judaism*, 2:167-228.

5. See Keimpe Algra, Jonathan Barnes, Jaap Mansfeld, and Malcolm Schofield, eds., *The Cambridge History of Hellenistic Philosophy* (Cambridge: Cambridge University Press, 1999).

ments from a strange and extremely different set of worldviews were emerging to challenge their indigenous understandings of life. Resistance to these challenges of a new world dawning in the ancient city of Jerusalem came in the form of a variety of groups that opposed hellenization in favor of traditional values and beliefs. These would include the Hasidim (see Sir. 46–51) or pious traditionalists, embodied in the character and actions of past heroes; revolutionaries, later known as the Maccabees and then the Zealots; and sectarians, some of whom even withdrew from settlements in Judea and Jerusalem to the desert to develop an apocalyptic worldview that awaited the destruction of the Greek and then Roman worlds to be replaced by a new Jerusalem, cleansed of its foreign impurities. Yet other groups, classified simply as Hellenistic Jews, stood ready to embrace much of what was new and alluring and to incorporate its features into a more traditional Judaism.

While it is difficult to prove conclusively that Qoheleth was educated in Greek philosophical and cultural traditions or, for that matter, even knew well the Greek language, he would likely have encountered Egyptian and Hellenistic skepticism, which existed in the commercial and intellectual climate of third-century Jerusalem in its commercial, political, and intellectual exchanges.[6] Due to the expansion of well-maintained and guarded roads and sea lanes by the Greeks, travel to other cultural regions was becoming commonplace, especially for government officials and the well-to-do. Certainly Ben Sira points to the travel that is a part of the repertoire of activities and the location of sources of knowledge available to the ideal sage (39:4), while Clearchus of Soli, a disciple of Aristotle, referred to the Jews who, as a people, he considered to be philosophers. He mentions a Jew from Coele-Syria, who was "Hellenic not in speech only, but also in mind," representing him as having come in his travels to Asia Minor and Greece where he had conversed with Aristotle (Josephus, *C. Ap.* 1.76-183). In addition to travel abroad, a sage like the one who composed Qoheleth had frequent contact with other cultures, including that of the Hellenes, through merchants, government officials, aristocrats, and their children. If he taught in a school, as the editor of the book indicates in the epilogue in 12:9-10, he would likely have had under his tutelage Jewish youth who were preparing to enter the lives of the nobility and their scribal servants. In the larger Hellenistic world, they would have required instruction in Hellenic culture and thought as

6. For studies of Hellenistic Judea, see Tcherikover, *Hellenistic Civilization;* Martin Hengel, *Judaism and Hellenism,* trans. John Bowden (2 vols.; Philadelphia: Fortress, 1974); idem, *Jews, Greeks, and Barbarians,* trans. John Bowden (Philadelphia: Fortress, 1980); Louis H. Feldman, *Jew and Gentile in the Ancient World* (Princeton: Princeton University Press, 1993); John J. Collins, *Between Athens and Jerusalem* (2nd ed.; Biblical Resource Series; Grand Rapids: Eerdmans, 2000); Collins and Sterling, eds., *Hellenism in the Land of Israel.*

well as that of their own native traditions. Certainly, the forging of Hellenism and Egyptian tradition, which was endemic to the Ptolemaic dynasty, centered in Alexandria, would have presented a most pressing intellectual and artistic achievement that may have encountered the Judaisms present in Judah, which was much more isolated culturally and commercially in the earlier Persian Empire. The schools (Hellenistic and Jewish) in Judah would have been the center for the shaping of Hellenistic Judaism among those still residing in Jerusalem and its environs.[7] The Zenon papyri demonstrate beyond any doubt that Greek was well known among the aristocracy and military of the Jews of Judah as early as 250 B.C.E. and in many locales in the Near East had become the language of culture, political institutions, and commerce.[8] Thus in the world of Qoheleth, Hellenism and indigenous cultures shaped new intellectual and religious conventions among not only the elite but even the local classes of farmers, shopkeepers, artisans, laborers and commercial traders of Judah. This evidence of the infiltration of Hellenistic culture is present in the languages used even on grave inscriptions of Jewish burials from the Hellenistic period.[9]

Qoheleth and Skepticism

Despair is the prevailing mood that colors the content and the conclusions of Qoheleth's investigation of "the good in human living."[10] Unlike the poet who composed disputations in the book of Job, this sage confronts not a crisis like the one that engulfed the nation in the form of the Babylonian conquest and exile, but rather the confluence of severe doubts about several of traditional

7. See Josephus, *Ant.* 12.154-236, for his treatment of the Tobiads.

8. On Eupolemus see Harold W. Attridge, "Historiography," in *Jewish Writings of the Second Temple Period*, ed. Michael E. Stone (CRINT II/2; Philadelphia: Fortress, 1984) 162-66. For the Greek papyri and inscriptions, see Victor A. Tcherikover, ed., *Corpus Papyrorum Judaicorum* (3 vols.; Cambridge: Harvard University Press, 1957-1964) = *CPJ* 1-3. See the survey of Greek papyri, parchments, inscriptions, numismatics, names, and literature by Gerard Mussies, "Greek in Palestine and the Diaspora," in *The Jewish People in the First Century*, ed. Shmuel Safrai and Menahem Stern, in cooperation with David Flusser and W. C. van Unnik (2 vols.; CRINT I/1-2; Philadelphia: Fortress, 1974-1976) 2:1040-64. Greek grave inscriptions have been partially collected, translated, and studied by Imre Peres, *Griechische Grabinschriften und neutestamentliche Eschatologie* (WUNT 157; Tübingen: Mohr Siebeck, 2003).

9. Peres, *Griechische Grabinschriften*.

10. Whybray dismisses the influence of other cultures and attempts instead to discover the major themes of Qoheleth within earlier OT texts ("Conservatisme et radicalisme dans Qohelet," in *Sagesse et Religion*, 65-81). However, he does admit that Qoheleth's radical expression of faith that embraces resignation is the product of its zeitgeist (p. 81).

wisdom's affirmations, its view of retributive justice, and its understanding of revelation through the Torah and apocalyptic visions. Unable to claim a revealed knowledge of "the God" who is hidden in the dark recesses of the heavens and is far removed from the land of human dwelling, Qoheleth sets out on a quest to determine "what is good to humanity in living" (*mah-ṭôb lā'ādām běḥayyîm,* 6:12). Thus his quest is one of ethics grounded not in a list of virtues but rather in human behavior and accomplishments.

As he pursues the experiences that life yields him in his activities, he proceeds stripped of any theological attribution or preconceived conviction. Even retribution, the age-old teaching so central to the understanding of the earlier sages, is put aside in his quest. He even determines that it is a false teaching, for there is no causal nexus between deed and consequence. Indeed, he begins without any affirmation of theological conviction, and he soon discovers there is no observable and knowable relationship between God, cosmology, human society, and the individual moral life. Order, understood as righteousness and justice, does not permeate reality. Indeed, there is no effect that human behavior has on the external world or the internal reality of private experience.[11] His views of the hidden God soon dismiss the sapiential teaching of providence and election.[12] While despair encompasses his teachings, his commitment is to the empirical method of analysis and result, followed by the general conclusion of an undeterred, exacting, rational mind. The metaphor that emerges from his varied experiences of human behavior is that of *hebel* ("breath"), not so much vanity but rather "evanescence" — all things do not endure.[13]

Rhetoric (Literary Structure and Form)

The book of Qoheleth has long vexed scholars seeking to recover the rhetorical structure and the literary form of its text.[14] I suggest that the two are related in

11. See Hartmut Gese, "Die Krisis der Weisheit bei Koheleth," in *Sagesses du Proche-Orient Ancien,* 139-51.

12. See Aare Lauha, "Die Krise des Religiösen Glaubens bei Kohelet," in *Wisdom in Israel and in the Ancient Near East,* 183-91; Hans-Peter Müller, "Neige der althebräischen 'Weisheit.' Zum Denken Qohäläts," *ZAW* 90 (1978) 238-64; Frank Crüsemann, "The Unchangeable World: The 'Crisis of Wisdom' in Koheleth," in *God of the Lowly: Socio-historical Interpretations of the Bible,* ed. Willy Schottroff and Wolfgang Stegemann, trans. Matthew J. O'Connell (Maryknoll, NY: Orbis, 1984) 57-77; Roland Murphy, "The Faith of Qoheleth," *Word & World* 7 (1987) 253-60.

13. *Eudaimonia* is the common concern of every Hellenistic philosophy; see Michael Erler and Malcolm Schofield, "Epicurean Ethics," in *Cambridge History of Hellenistic Philosophy,* 642.

14. See Diethelm Michel, *Untersuchungen zur Eigenart des Buches Qohelet. Mit einem Anhang:*

that the rhetorical structure is based on its literary form. Previous investigations have seen one of two possibilities for the form of the book: sayings collections and first person narratives.[15] Sayings collections, such as those that make up most of the sections of the book of Proverbs, consist of a variety of brief sapiential forms, ranging from two-line proverbs of various types to instructions to didactic poems. Thematically, there are occasionally smaller units that cohere (e.g., 16:1-15, kingship), but none of the larger proverbial collections is thematically related to another. In the case of Qoheleth, it is clear that there are a variety of sapiential forms.[16] Yet does this mean that the book is nothing more than a collection of diverse materials devoid of both an integrating central theme and an overarching structure? Is there possibly a larger genre that encompasses these various types of smaller sapiential forms that provides a key to understanding the thematic and literary organization of the entire text? The repetitions of key words and phrases in Qoheleth do suggest that the text is structured thematically. The question is what does this larger rhetorical form resemble in the repertoire of sapiential genres from the ancient Near East. Once we identify the form, then we may examine the structure and its components parts.

A second approach to the literary form of Qoheleth is to move beyond the observation that the text is a sayings collection and to consider the book as an "autobiographical" testament (see 1:12–2:26; 3:10–4:16; 5:12–6:6; 7:15–10:7). We have this type of literary form in a number of instances in the wisdom literatures of the ancient Near East, particularly in Egypt.[17] In the testament, a first person narrator, often identified as the implied author, reveals his/her experiences in life and uses them as the basis for sapiential instruction. Two subcategories of Egyptian wisdom testaments are similar to Qoheleth as an autobiographical narrative: the testament of a royal (deceased) king to his successor,[18] and tomb inscriptions placed on graves to instruct the living who come to visit the deceased. These two types of texts both devise a literary fiction of a person

---

Reinhard Lehmann, Bibliographie zu Qohelet (BZAW 183; Berlin: de Gruyter, 1989); Michael V. Fox, *Qohelet and His Contradictions* (JSOTSup 71; Sheffield: Almond Press, 1989); W. Sibley Towner, "The Book of Ecclesiastes," *NIB* 5 (1997) 269-70.

15. Walther Zimmerli, "Das Buch Kohelet — Traktat oder Sentenzensammlung?" *VT* 24 (1974) 221-30. Zimmerli thinks that, while the book does not have a recognizable structure, it is more than simply a loose collection of different sayings, as is the case with Proverbs.

16. E.g., Aare Lauha, *Kohelet* (BKAT 19; Neukirchen-Vluyn: Neukirchener Verlag, 1978) 5.

17. There are several examples of first person narratives in Israelite and Jewish wisdom texts: Ps. 73; Prov. 4:3-9; 24:30-34; Sir. 33:16-18.

18. See the two royal testaments, "The Instruction of Amenemhet" and "The Instruction for Merikare," discussed above.

who is dead offering instruction that is based on his wisdom and life experiences to the living.[19] There are other canonical and pseudepigraphal Jewish texts that provide evidence of a similar literary form in Israelite and Jewish literature. Two examples from the Hebrew Bible include the narrative reformulation of what originally appears to have been the testament of David (1 Kgs. 2:1-12) and the "Last Words of Jacob" (Gen. 49:1-27). In the Pseudepigrapha there are numerous examples, including two that are especially well known in their sociohistorical context: the Testaments of the Twelve Patriarchs,[20] perhaps dating from the second century B.C.E., making it only approximately a century later than Qoheleth, and the Testament of Job, from the end of the first century B.C.E.[21] The fictional setting is the approaching death of the patriarch who wishes to instruct his descendants on how to live the moral life as they gather around him for the last time. The major formal difference between Jewish testamental literature and the Egyptian royal testamental instructions and autobiographical testaments found on graves is that, in the case of the first, the instruction is issued by an old and dying figure of prominence to his children, while the two Egyptian parallels are utterances of the deceased to the living.

I would suggest that the literary form of Qoheleth belongs to this corpus of testamentary literature and is similar to the autobiography of the deceased found on some Egyptian tombs that tell of the virtuous life of the occupant of the grave, who issues an instruction to the living,[22] and to Jewish testament literature that sets forth the last words of an ancient patriarch nearing death. Au-

---

19. The setting of death for instructions is a common one. See Leo G. Perdue, "The Death of the Sage and Moral Exhortation: From Ancient Near Eastern Instructions to Graeco-Roman Paraenesis," in *Paraenesis: Act and Form*, ed. Leo G. Perdue and John G. Gammie (Semeia 50; Atlanta: Scholars Press, 1990) 81-109.

20. See the introduction and brief commentary by Howard Clark Kee, "Testaments of the Twelve Patriarchs," *OTP* 1:775-828. These are represented as the last words of the twelve patriarchs, each of whom instructs his children on evils to avoid and virtues to incorporate. Predictions of the future and the closure of the narrative account of the burial of the deceased are also common elements of the literary form.

21. R. P. Spittler, "Testament of Job," *OTP* 1:829-68. This testament is formally similar to the Testaments of the Twelve Patriarchs. For a survey of Jewish testament literature, see Max Küchler, *Frühjüdische Weisheitstraditionen. Zum Fortgang weisheitlichen Denkens im Bereich des frühjüdischen Jahweglaubens* (OBO 26; Göttingen: Vandenhoeck & Ruprecht, 1979) 319-547; Eckhard von Nordheim, *Die Lehre der Alten* (Arbeiten zum Literatur und Geschichte des Hellenistischen Judentum 13; 2 vols.; Leiden: Brill, 1980). For the other testaments' translations, notes, and commentaries, see *OTP* 1:869-995.

22. I compared this correspondence of Qoheleth to Egyptian grave autobiographies in *Wisdom and Creation*, 193-242. Now see the more extensive study by Shannon Burkes, *Death in Qoheleth and Egyptian Biographies of the Late Period* (SBLDS 170; Atlanta: Society of Biblical Literature, 1999).

tobiographical tomb instructions, Jewish testaments, and the book of Qoheleth hold in common several important features.[23] These are the first person voice of the teacher (a king or a patriarch), the listing of achievements or important events during the teacher's lifetime (2:1-11), and the offering of counsel to the successors or descendants on a variety of matters, often united by a single theme (loyalty, patience, etc.). The implied narrator of the book is identified as Qoheleth, a king over Israel in Jerusalem (1:12) and a son of David (1:1), although a second voice, presumably that of a later redactor, is infrequently heard (see esp. 11:9d and 12:9-14).[24] While not explicitly named Solomon, the implication is that the primary voice belongs to this king, who in tradition was the royal patron of wisdom (cf. 1 Kgs. 3–10). The secondary voice of a later redactor was a conservative sage adding his warnings of judgment and offering his counsel to "fear God and keep his commandments." Indeed, the achievements listed in 2:1-11 suggest some accomplishments for which Solomon was renowned in Jewish tradition.

Literary Forms in Qoheleth

In addition to the larger genre that assists in the classification of Qoheleth as a wisdom testament, smaller sapiential forms are present.[25] These include the superscription in 1:1 (cf. those that introduce the wisdom collections in Prov. 22:17; 30:1; 31:1) that attributes the testament to the Teacher (Qoheleth), the son of David, king in Jerusalem (thus Solomon); sayings that make up the smaller collections in Qoh. 7:1-13 and 9:7–11:6; the instruction concerning worship (4:17–5:6); the autobiographical observation that leads to the unique feature of internal dialogue (e.g., 1:12-18); and several didactic poems (1:4-11; 3:1-8; 12:1-8).

Literary Structure

It is not evident that this wisdom text presents a disjointed collection of various forms and themes. Rather, it is highly stylized and organized into an artistic structure that revolves around the central theme of the book: the experience of

---

23. Gerhard von Rad (*Wisdom in Israel*, trans. James D. Martin [Nashville: Abingdon, 1972] 226) and Oswald Loretz (*Qoheleth und der Alte Orient* [Freiburg: Universitätsverlag, 1964] 148, 161, 212-13) have argued that the royal testament was the literary form for the entire book of Qoheleth.

24. Gerald T. Sheppard views the epilogist as a commentator who seeks to relate wisdom to Torah ("The Epilogue to Qoheleth as Theological Commentary," *CBQ* 39 [1977] 182-89).

25. See esp. Murphy, *Wisdom Literature* (FOTL), 126-49.

present joy or *carpe diem* ("seize the day"). This theme is repeated seven times in strategic places, as the following outline demonstrates.[26]

Frame 1:1-11 and 11:9–12:14

Introduction		*Conclusion*	
1:1	Title	12:9-14	Epilogue
1:2	Theme: "Breath of breaths," says Q. "Breath of breaths." "All is breath."	12:8	Theme: "Breath of breaths," says Q. "All is breath."
1:3	Central Question: "What remains to a person from all the labor at which he/she toils under the sun?"		
1:4-11	Two-Stanza Poem	11:7–12:7	Two-Stanza Poem
	Cosmology (1:4-7)		Anthropology: Carpe diem (11:7-10)
	Anthropology (toil; 1:8-11)		Cosmology and death (12:1-8)

Internal Structure: 1:12–11:6

I. 1:12-5:19. Cosmology, Anthropology, and the Moral Order: Human Activity
   Key refrain: "Breath (and a striving after life's breath)."
   1:12-18   Twofold introduction to sections I and II
   A. 1:12–2:26   Solomon's accomplishments
                   Carpe diem: Conclusion (2:24-26)
   B. 3:1-15   Time (human toil and divine action)
                Carpe diem: Interlude (3:12-13)
   C. 3:16-22   Judgment and human nature
                 Carpe diem: Conclusion (3:22)
   D. 4:1–5:19   Royal rule and the cult
                  Carpe diem: Conclusion (5:17-19)
   6:1-9   Interlude: Section on joy and its absence
II. 6:10–11:6. Cosmology, Anthropology, and the Moral Order: Human Knowing

---

26. Addison Wright, "The Riddle of the Sphinx: The Structure of the Book of Qoheleth," *CBQ* 30 (1968) 313-34.

Key refrain: "Cannot find out/who can find out?" (chs. 7–8)
"Do not know/no knowledge" (chs. 9–11)
E. 6:10–8:15   Divine sovereignty and Wisdom, Part 1
Carpe diem: Conclusion (8:14-15)
F. 8:16–9:10   Divine sovereignty and Wisdom, Part 2
Carpe diem: Conclusion (9:7-10)
G. 9:11–11:6   Risk and caution

The two poems on cosmology and anthropology/anthropology and cosmology (plus death; 1:4-11 and 11:7–12:8) and the repetition of the major metaphor ("'breath of breath,'" says Qoheleth, "'all is breath'") at the opening and conclusion of the testament proper (1:2; 12:8) present the telling inclusios for the testament. Discovering the "good" in human life, the quest that drives Qoheleth's empirical examination, has two aspects, reflected in the two parts of the literary structure: "doing" and "knowing." These are based on two pivotal expressions: "breath (and a desire for life's breath)" in the first part and "cannot find out (who can find out)" and "do not know (no knowledge)" in the second. Recurring throughout the testament is the repetition of "carpe diem" that reflects the seven major units of the book (see 2:24-26; 3:12-13, 22; 5:17-19; 8:14-15; 9:7-10; 11:7-10).[27] These repetitions point to the thematic organizing principle of the volume that contains the teacher's conclusion to each of the stages of his quest: joy that is quickly fleeting is the good in human life. An interlude (6:1-9) divides the two major parts and describes the misery of a life devoid of joy that ultimately ends in death and eternal darkness.

In my view, Qoheleth is a piece of sapiential testamental literature. It sets forth the fiction of Israel's most honored sage and patron of the wisdom tradition, Solomon, engaging in the quest to determine the "good" in human living. The discovery of this greatest good will allow one to negotiate an ethical response to a life of virtue, because its experience is to provide the impetus for human behavior. Solomon, through the imagination of a literary fiction, instructs his audience as an old king facing his own mortality. And, having lived centuries before the time of the fashioning of this testament, he also, like his Egyptian royal counterparts (Merikare and Amenemhet), instructs his audience from the grave.

---

27. Those who argue that joy and the enjoyment of life are at the heart of Qoheleth's teaching include Robert Gordis, *Koheleth — The Man and His World* (3rd ed.; New York: Schocken, 1968) 129-31; Robert K. Johnston, "'Confessions of a Workaholic': A Reappraisal of Qoheleth," *CBQ* 38 (1976) 14-28; R. N. Whybray, "Qoheleth, Preacher of Joy," *JSOT* 23 (1982) 87-98.

Grave Autobiographies

The closest parallels to the literary genre and content of Qoheleth are found in Egyptian grave autobiographies and Greek inscriptions written on tombs, including Jewish ones.[28] These stereotypical tomb autobiographies allow the visitors to the grave to honor the virtuous life and accomplishments of the deceased, who is actualized in this type of experience. These autobiographies may be divided into two types: one is a sequence of epithets and expressions that portray the deceased's character and view of life, while the second is a narrative that presents in chronological order the major events of the dead person's life.[29] Important in these autobiographies is the exhortation to visitors to provide them with the offerings of food and other gifts, actual or contained in grave formulae, that are necessary for survival in the future life. At the same time, visitors are warned against tomb desecration, since most Egyptians found it difficult to imagine eternal life in the West without a tomb. What is important to observe is that the narrator of the text is the deceased himself/herself. Thus the words are her/his continued utterances long after passing into the land of the dead to cross the river to the West.

In terms of their formal characteristics, Egyptian tomb autobiographies have three elements: an autobiographical narrative, sayings concerning morality, and instructions and exhortations. The audience consisted of visitors to the tomb, who would have included family members and others who knew the deceased, as well as strangers. The narrative usually contained the titles and accomplishments of the grave occupant, while the sayings were presented as those that guided the dead speaker through life and thus are commended to the visitors. The character of the deceased included intelligence, wisdom, piety and faithful fulfillment of cultic obligations to the patron deity, and the avoidance of evil. Additional themes were loyalty to rulers, carrying out of responsibilities to the family and other members of Egyptian society, especially the poor, and divine blessings showered on the faithful that included health, possessions, lon-

---

28. In addition to Peres, see the earlier studies of Nikolaus Müller, *Die Inschriften der jüdischen Katakombe am Monteverde zu Rom* (Gesellschaft zur Förderung des Wissenschaft des Judentums; Schriften; Leipzig: Gustav Fock, 1919); Jean-Baptiste Frey, *Corpus Inscriptionum Judaicarum* (hereafter *CIJ*) (2 vols.; Rome: Pontificio istituto di archeologia cristiana, 1936-1952); Pieter W. van der Horst, *Ancient Jewish Epitaphs: An Introductory Survey of a Millennium of Jewish Funerary Epigraphy (300 BCE–700 CE)* (Kampen: Kok Pharos, 1991); idem, "Das Neue Testament und die jüdische Grabschriften aus hellenistisch-römischer Zeit," *BZ* 35 (1992) 161-78; William Horbury and David Noy, *Jewish Inscriptions of Graeco-Roman Egypt with an Index of the Jewish Inscriptions of Egypt and Cyrenaica* (Cambridge: Cambridge University Press, 1992).

29. Olivier Perdu, "Ancient Egyptian Autobiographies," *CANE* 4:2243.

gevity, children, a proper burial, and the promise of a future life. Important to note for comparison to Qoheleth is the emphasis placed on joy. Thus the audience is to "follow the heart" *(sms ib)* in achieving what one desires, while "happiness" *(ndm ib)*[30] suggests satisfaction with life, a feeling of joy, and the comfort of contentment. On occasion those in the audience were urged to reflect on their own death. Finally, they are exhorted to offer grave offerings and sacrifices, both actual and magical through mortuary pronouncements, in memory of the occupant of the tomb. The intent of these autobiographies is to show that the deceased have lived in accordance with the principles of *ma'at,* to make a strong case for admission into the afterlife, and to receive continued offerings that would sustain them in the next world. Egyptian grave autobiographies have much in common with traditional wisdom literature, especially the instructions, likely due to their authors attending wisdom schools in order to become scribes.[31] One should observe that "The Instruction of Ptahhotep" has elements of a grave biography in its conclusion.[32]

While pessimism is the mood evoked by the autobiographical grave inscriptions as early as the Late Bronze Age, it was especially common in the later Hellenistic and Roman periods. The tyranny of the gods was viewed as damaging to the teaching of retributive justice, since divine caprice and unjust control of reality were not carried out in concert with *ma'at.*[33] This mood intensified during periods in which political stability was undermined by external or internal events. Pessimism resulted not only from political instability attributed to capricious gods, but also from a more somber view of the afterlife, which was occasionally seen to be a time of great sorrow and loss and an entrance into the void of eternal darkness. The achievement of virtue and honor, the remembrance of the living, and the experiences of joy while living were stressed in place of eternal life.[34]

The emphasis on the celebration of life in these later grave inscriptions also finds an important location in Qoheleth.[35] Included in both are eating, drinking,

---

30. On *sms ib* see Otto, *Biographischen Inschriften,* 70-71. See inscriptions 46, 58b, 58c, 127, etc. On *ndm ib* see ibid., 10c, 10h, 3e, 19, 46, 58, etc.

31. Jan Bergman, "Gedanken zum Thema 'Lehre-Testament-Grab-Name,'" in *Studien zu Altägyptischen Lebenslehren,* 73-104.

32. *ANET,* 412-14.

33. Otto, *Biographischen Inschriften.*

34. Ibid., 61.

35. The inscription on the statue of Neb-neteru reads: "The exit from life is sorrow, signifying want from what was yours formerly and emptiness of possessions. It means sitting in the hall of unconsciousness awaiting the announcement of a morning that never comes. It offers as compensation an eye that weeps — take care, for it comes! It means knowing nothing and sleep, when the sun is in the East. It means thirst for beer! Therefore, the West itself answers: 'Give . . . to the one

lovemaking, a faithful companion, and children. Indeed, the celebration of life and the mood of despair in later Egyptian grave texts find their parallels in the Jewish teacher who, assuming the voice of the speaker in an autobiographical testament, issues to his students counsel on engaging in activities that bring satisfaction and pleasure, if only for a brief and passing moment (2:24-26; 5:18-20; etc.).[36]

Perdu translates and discusses one of the latest examples of autobiographical grave inscriptions, that of Somtutefnakht, who was chief of the *wab* priests of Sakmet, the goddess of plague and pestilence. This priest (who lived during the Thirtieth Dynasty, 380-343 B.C.E.) recalls the events at the end of the Persian period shortly prior to the conquest of Alexander. In these occurrences of uncertainty and catastrophe, he sees the protection of his deity at work to preserve him from difficulties and harm: "You inspired affection for me in the heart of the Ruler of Asia [Persian king], so that his courtiers thanked god for me, when he appointed me to the office of Overseer of *wab* priests of Sakhmet. . . . You protected me through the offensive of the Greeks as soon as you repelled Asia (Persia); they killed a multitude around me; but there was none who raised a hand against me."[37] These texts provide important insight into the virtues, culture, morality, and history of ancient Egypt.[38]

One tomb autobiography from the Hellenistic period that possesses features of the wisdom instruction is found on the walls of the family tomb of Petosiris.[39] He was high priest of Thoth at Hermopolis during the late fourth century B.C.E. In this autobiography this priest assumes the role of a sage in order to instruct the visitors to the tomb to make funerary offerings on his behalf and to learn from his teachings.

---

who follows his heart! The heart is a god. Desire is its shrine. It rejoices when the body's members are in a festive mood'" (Otto, *Biographischen Inschriften*, inscription 5; cf. inscription 57).

36. Taimhotep admonishes her husband: "O (my) brother, husband, friend, high priest: do not weary of drink, food, deep drinking, and loving. Make a holiday! Follow your heart day and night! Do not set sorrow in your heart. What are the years which are not on earth? As for the West, it is a land in sleep, heavy darkness, the dwelling-place of those who are there. Sleep is in their (mummy) forms. They do not awake to see their brothers, they do not see their fathers or their mothers, their hearts lack their wives and their children. The water of life which is food for all, it is thirst for me. It comes (only) to the one who is on earth; I am thirsty (though) water is beside me" (see the translation in Burkes, *Death in Qoheleth and Egyptian Biographies*, 192-193).

37. Perdu, "Ancient Egyptian Autobiographies," 2253.

38. The three from the Late Period that are examined by Burkes (*Death*, 188-204) include Isenkhebe (a woman of the Saite period, 650-630 B.C.E.), Taimhotep (d. 42 B.C.E.), and Petosiris (a Hellenistic family tomb).

39. André Barucq, "Une veine de spiritualité sacerdotale et sapientielle dans l'Égypte ancienne," in *À la rencontre de Dieu. Mémorial Albert Gélin*, ed. Andre Barucq (Bibliothèque de la faculté catholique de théologie de Lyon 8; Le Puy: X. Mappus, 1961) 193-202.

Greek grave inscriptions, which included those on Jewish tombs in Judah and Egypt, are another rich resource for comparison to Qoheleth, although the parallels are less striking than those of Egypt. Unlike the Egyptian autobiographies, these epitaphs are largely commemorations of the deceased by a close relative, although some, including several from Egypt, do contain the voice of the deceased, thus paralleling Qoheleth and the Egyptian autobiographies on tombs. By the time of the imperial Roman period, the dominant language of Jews in Judah and other regions was Greek. Van der Horst estimates that during this time Greek was the primary language for more than two-thirds of the Jews.[40] Thus their epitaphs are largely in Greek. Even in Roman Judea, more than half of the epitaphs are in Greek. He estimates that in Jerusalem the number of Greek epitaphs equaled those in Hebrew or Aramaic. This was true not only of ordinary people but also of rabbis and their families.[41] This demonstrates unquestionably that Greek was a common, shared language of Jews, especially in the urban areas, as Aramaic was in the villages.

While the epitaphs of Hellenistic graves are written in a very poor Greek, they demonstrate a number of common features.[42] One is their great reserve in quoting the Bible. Indeed, the ancient ones will occasionally quote Prov. 10:7 — "the memory of the righteous one be [for] a blessing." Both the LXX and Aquila's more literal reading are quoted in the epitaphs. The dedications and memory in many of the inscriptions have "here lies" or "this is the tomb of." Another type mentions the names of the deceased in the dative followed by the name or names of the dedicator(s) in the nominative. These are usually the deceased's close relatives, who indicate they have prepared or dedicated the tombstone for the sake of the memory of the dead relation. In addition, a large number of expressions of grief are placed on the tombstone, especially the statement that the death of the deceased was untimely and thus the basis for lamentation. At times, these inscriptions contain an explicit or implicit protest of parents about the premature deaths of their young children, something also often contrasted with marriage and the producing of offspring. Judaism, in most instances, did not hold out hope for a resurrection. Curses are sometimes found on epitaphs, especially in Asia Minor, that are directed to those who violate the tomb, indicating the belief that there is some continued, even if dark and shadowy, existence in the tomb for the deceased.

Some epithets, titles, and virtues recur in tomb inscriptions, the last of which even invoke the themes of sapiential teachings. These, like their Egyptian

40. Van der Horst, *Ancient Jewish Epitaphs,* 23.
41. Ibid., 24.
42. Ibid., 44ff.

counterparts, may simply have been a stock collection purchased by masons from scribes. From these collections, the survivors seeing to the erection of the epitaph could choose what they considered to have been appropriate for the departed.[43] The inclusion of these was not only to honor the deceased, but also to indicate that they lived lives that exuded virtuous behavior and by implication taught the visitors and passersby that they should do the same in order to live in human memory and to become a witness to the moral life, even from the tomb. The list of virtues, found on pagan, Jewish, and Christian tombstones, included "good," "worthy," "beautiful," "everlasting remembrance," "one who caused no pain or grief," "incomparable," "asleep," "pleasantness," "wise," "pious," "gentleness," "one husband," "doer of honor," "friend of all," "noble," "chaste," "joyful," "a friendly neighbor," "one exuding brotherly love," "lover of people," "lover of humanity," "lover of God," "lover of one's mother," "lover of one's father," "lover of children," and "lover of friends."[44] Greek and Jewish epitaphs include a number of additional epithets, titles, virtues, and comments of melancholy. These are especially frequent in the Greek epitaphs of Jewish tombs: "righteous," "blessed," "holy," "lived honorably," "innocent," "chastity," "beloved," "having come to a dreadful end," "blameless," "undefiled," "unfortunate," "ill-fated," "worthiness," "faithfulness," "pleasant," "illustrious," "gentleness," "worthiness," "self-control," "pure," "causing no one harm," "blessed memory," "lover of the poor," "well taught/erudite," "lover of the law/Torah," "lover of the synagogue/community," and "having lived as a good human being." The Roman virtues stress more the duties of children to parents and wives to husbands. One who dies a virgin is especially lamented.[45]

Finally, the professional roles are frequently mentioned in Jewish epitaphs.[46] These included *archon* (an elected leader of the synagogue, who along with others served as the executive committee of the *gerousia* [elders of the synagogue]), the *grammateus* (scribe of the community), *archisynagogos* (the elected head of the synagogue who presided over the meetings, regulated services, and designated the men who were to read, recite prayers, and deliver the sermon),[47] *prostatēs* (patron of the community), the *mathētēs sophōn* (likely referring to teachers in Jewish schools; cf. *didaskalos*, "teacher"; and the teacher of

---

43. Ibid., 61-72.

44. In Latin epitaphs in Rome, the most frequently mentioned virtue is *benemerens*, which emphasizes the performance and reward of duty. Greek epitaphs in Rome refer to *glykytatos*, which points to the joy of human interaction; see Iiro Kajanto, *A Study of the Greek Epitaphs of Rome* (Acta Instituti Romani Finlandiae 2/3; Helsinki: Tilgman, 1963) 30-39.

45. Van der Horst, *Ancient Jewish Epitaphs*, 64.

46. Ibid., 84-101.

47. Ibid., 92.

the law, *nomos*), and "rabbi" (in Greek and Hebrew). Most of these come from ancient Judah.[48]

Those that do contain the voice of the deceased are more directly related to Qoheleth. From Leontopolis (no. 1512), the inscription in metrical Greek reads:

> Look on my tombstone, passer-by, weep as you gaze;
> > beat five times with your hands for a five-year-old.
> For early and without marriage I lie in the tomb.
> > My parents suffer likewise for the son that pleased them.
> My friends miss their companion and playfellow.
> > But my body lies in the place of the pious.
> Weeping say: untimely gone, much lamented, best of all,
> > who were always known for all kinds of virtue.[49]

Another autobiographical, metrical inscription on an epitaph at Leontopolis (no. 1508) speaks of death as a marriage to Hades or as a type of marriage replacing the joyous one experienced in life:

> Weep for me, stranger, a maiden ripe for marriage,
> > who formerly shone in a great house.
> For, decked in fair bridal garments, I untimely have received
> > this hateful tomb as my bridal chamber.
> For when a noise of revellers already at my doors
> > told that I was leaving my father's house, like a rose
> > in a garden nurtured by fresh rain,
> suddenly Hades came and snatched me away.
> > And I, stranger, had accomplished twenty revolving years.[50]

Noteworthy is that in many of the Greek epitaphs, including Christian and Jewish ones, the tomb occupant invites or commands the passerby to stop, read the tomb inscription, and share in the grief of the one who is dead. Van der Horst explains that in antiquity the deceased were customarily buried outside the cities and placed in tombs along the roadways that entered and left the gates. Thus from this context travelers are urged at least to pronounce the name of the deceased, proving a small degree of existence in their consciousness, if only for a

---

48. See Shaye J. D. Cohen, "Epigraphical Rabbis," *JQR* 72 (1981/82) 1-17.

49. See *CPJ* 3:158. Van der Horst also reproduces the Greek text (*Ancient Jewish Epitaphs*, 46, n. 267).

50. See *CPJ* 3:156. Van der Horst (*Ancient Jewish Epitaphs*, 48-49) notes that of the fifteen Greek metrical epitaphs found on Jewish tombstones, twelve are from Leontopolis in Egypt (see 1451, 1489, 1490, 1508-1513, 1522, 1530, and 1530A).

fleeting moment. By contrast, some of the epitaphs, pagan as well as Jewish, contain the passerby's greeting of the deceased. Again, from Leontopolis (no. 1514): "O Marion, of priestly descent, excellent one, friend of all, you who caused pain to no-one and were a friend to your neighbours, farewell." Van der Horst also points to examples of those that address the deceased with statements, including "farewell," "be of courage, for no-one is immortal," "be well," "have a good death," and "be of good cheer."[51] Another extremely interesting, metrical Jewish epitaph, in Doric, also comes from Leontopolis, a conversation between the deceased and the passerby, a common form in pagan tomb inscriptions:

> The speaking tombstone: "Who are you who lie in the dark tomb?
>   Tell me your country and birth."
> "Arsinoe, daughter of Aline and Theodosius.
>   The famous land of Onias reared me."
> "How old were you when you slipped down the dark slope of Lethe?"
>   "At twenty I went to the sad place of the dead."
> "Were you married?"
>   "I was."
> "Did you leave him a child?"
>   "Childless I went to the house of Hades."
> "May earth, the guardian of the dead, be light on you."
>   "And for you, stranger, may she bear fruitful crops."[52]

A final example from Leontopolis may date from the early Imperial period (first to the fourth century C.E.).[53] Especially interesting is that this Jewish epitaph, told in the third person concerning the deceased buried in the tomb, contains no indication of a belief in life after death.

> When he had already achieved the span of 53 years,
>   he who tames all himself snatched him off to Hades.
> O sandy earth, what a body you hide
>   of the soul of the most blessed Abramos.
> For he was not without honor in the city, but wore the wreath
>   of majesty for the whole people in his wisdom.
> For you were honored with the leadership of two places,
>   generously performing the double duty.

51. Van der Horst, *Ancient Jewish Epigraphs,* 52-53.
52. *CPJ* 3, inscription 1530.
53. *CPJ* 3, inscription 1530A.

And everything that was fitting to you, soul, before you hid yourself,
   we, your family of good children, are increasing.
But you, passerby, seeing the grave of a good man,
   say these words to him and depart:
"May the earth be light on you forever."

Finally, pagan grave inscriptions in Greece and the Hellenistic Greek world often express a deep-seated pessimism about death and the grave.[54] There is a mixed view about this topic in later Jewish epitaphs of the Hellenistic and early Roman period. The Greek and Hellenistic communities prior to the writings of the New Testament produced numerous grave inscriptions that dealt with death and the afterlife. Approximately 50,000 Greek tomb inscriptions and 2,000 Jewish ones existed in addition to perhaps 400,000 Christian Latin ones. Peres, who has worked through about 26,000 Greek inscriptions, has identified some 400 that deal positively with a place of blessing beyond the grave, including those that mentioned the Isles of the Blessed, Elysium, the netherworld, Olympus, and heaven. About 300 express a general hope in a life after death in some fashion. These date between 300 B.C.E. and 200 C.E. They encompass the Hellenistic period, the time of the early emperors, the period prior to the emergence of early Christianity, and then the time of the primitive church. These hail from Greece, Asia Minor, Syria, Egypt, Italy, and also the cities bordering the Bosporus Strait. In addition, some are found in Hungary and Libya where there were Greek colonies and cities.

In Greece and its colonies and cultures influenced by Hellenism the view was common that the original source of human existence was that to which a human returned at death (not unlike Job's remark of coming forth naked from the mother's womb [including the earth] and returning there at death, Job 1:21). Life was for a brief period and could not be retained, but rather when its final course was completed, it returned back to its origins. These words were reflected in Greek epitaphs. Sometimes this return to the source was reflected in the notion of the netherworld where one returned at death. Thus the ancient Greeks believed in the reality of death, which is to be accepted as inevitable. Whether one was pained at the lost of life or sought to hold on to it, it was fated to come to its end, and there was no possibility of escape. Life at times, according to these inscriptions, was an end, a *telos,* that could convey not only the finality of life but also a final rest from pain and suffering experienced by the body. Death is something that always follows one and finally will overtake one. Thus one inscription reads:

54. Peres, *Griechische Grabinschriften,* 1-4. See N. Walter, "'Hellenistiche Eschatologie' im Neuen Testament," in *Glaube und Eschatologie,* FS W. G. Kümmel, ed. Erich Grässer and Otto Merk (Tübingen: Mohr-Siebeck, 1985) 335-56.

For all joy and hope he had covered in the earth,
    while at home the grieving mother wails,
    and brings even the nightingale to silence with her laments.[55]

Even so, there is also the yearning for immortality. The reality of death pressed hard upon the Greek human spirit, and while humans yearned to escape its icy grip, there was little hope in Classical Greece for any escape. Thus there was an intense pessimism that is reflected in most of the literature and the early epitaphs. The great majority of the tomb inscriptions saw death in explicit terms as the negation of any future hope for life, for the tomb was the final destination of life's journey. In the tomb there is no continuing memory of what had transpired or would occur on the earth. In some of the inscriptions, there is an even more fearful dimension of death as the reaching out of the gods of the underworld to pull one within its dank region. The same image is found in regard to fate that grasps the unwilling mortals and brings them into the underworld. Thus many of the inscriptions read simply: "no one is immortal." A variant is "no one upon the earth is immortal" *(oudeis epi gēs athanatos)*.[56] An inscription attributed to a Hermes of Rome (second-third century C.E.) reads:

ouk ēmēn, genomēn, ēmēn, ouk eimi tosauta
    ei de tis allo ereei, pseusetai ouk esomai.

I was not, then I became; I was, and now am not. That is it.
    If another asserts something different, he is lying.
        I shall not exist again.[57]

Peres suggests this and similar epitaphs represent the views of life especially among the elite who resided in the great cities. These were inspired by the cultural life in the theater and the desire to enjoy life.[58]

    The emphasis on the enjoyment of life and pessimism deriving from the finality of the tomb are common themes in the Greek grave inscriptions. For example:

Chrō ton erōta pheron pasi chronōn agathois.

Enjoy all the good things in this time so long as you experience desire.[59]

55. Peres, *Griechische Grabinschriften*, 25.
56. Ibid., 26.
57. Ibid., 27.
58. Ibid., 28.
59. Peres quotes another inscription from Rome in the second-third century C.E. that speaks

One notes that many of the epitaphs even reject the view that there is any existence in the underworld following death. Denying that there is in Hades a ferryman, Charon, Aiachos (a judge of the underworld), and Kerberos (gatekeeper of Hades), one inscription (from the fourth-third century B.C.E.) goes on to read:

hēmeis de pantes hoi katō tethnēkotes
ostea tephra gegonamen, allo d' oude hen.

we all, who are dead beneath in the grave are
only ashes and bones and nothing more.

Occasionally one finds only skepticism concerning the possibility of life after death, a view expressed by Euripides, *Frag.* 638:

Tis d'oiden ei to zēn men esti katthanein,
to katthanein de zēn kato noumizetai?

who knows whether life is only death,
or what we name death, below is known as life?[60]

Finally, fate or fortune, at times personified as a deity, plays an important role in Greek grave inscriptions. The term *moira* means in essence "portion," "part," or "allotment," an expression whose Hebrew equivalent is often found in Qoheleth. There existed in the predominant Greek understanding the idea that the "lot" of humans was to participate in life, the fortunes of existence, and its end in death. These constitute the destiny of human beings. Thus one grave inscription from Samos (end of the second century B.C.E.) reads:

Moira Philoni biou pikron ethēke telos.

Fate has determined for Philo a bitter end.

Jewish epitaphs most often regard death as "sleep." The formula "May his/her/their/your sleep be in peace" occurs especially frequently. While it is possible to understand this formula as implicitly eschatological in the hope of an afterlife, I take it as simply a way of expressing the hope of the survivors that the

---

of the material aspects of life: "Take care as long as you live . . . and live as you desire. For there is no igniting of fire and no alluring repast. . . . No one who is dead awakens from the tomb to a new life" (ibid., 28-29). Another inscription (p. 29) notes that from all that the deceased has accumulated the only possession that has followed him into death is the tomb.

60. Ibid., 33.

beloved's rest in death may be undisturbed. This is certainly the case in the Hebrew Bible, which speaks of death as sleep, for example, "sleeping with or being gathered to the ancestors" (cf. the many occurrences in Genesis, Kings, and Chronicles). This undisturbed rest is no more than the hope that the tomb would not be violated. There are in later Judaism (after the time of Qoheleth, however) a number of epitaphs, found especially in Beth-Shearim and Leontopolis, that suggest that in death there is rest with the righteous and faithful ancestors who have gone before so that the idea of eternal life or resurrection from the dead of some sort may be envisioned. This is found in the literature in 1 En. 22–27; 92–105; Dan. 12; Wis. 2:22-24; 3:1-9; 4:7-11; 2 Macc. 6–7; 4 Macc. 7:3; 9:22; 13:17; 14:5-6; 15:3; 16:13, 25; 17:12, 18-19. There are even a few references to a final judgment, a teaching that the redactor of Qoheleth underscores (11:9b; 12:14).

Thus it is clear that Qoheleth's skeptical view of death is a common one in grave autobiographies of Ptolemaic Egypt and Greek epitaphs from throughout the ancient Greek and early Roman worlds. While it is impossible to know if Qoheleth had read these mournful inscriptions, it is clear that many in the cultures with which Judah came into contact shared his understanding. By contrast, the notion that there is either resurrection from the dead or even immortality is an infrequent expression in the epigraphy and literature of his period. Qoheleth himself remains skeptical about any future existence of life's breath.

Date and Historical Context

Most scholars of the wisdom corpus have placed Qoheleth in the late Second Temple period, either the end of the Persian or the early Ptolemaic Hellenistic period. My preference is the end of the Ptolemaic period, perhaps during the last quarter of the third century. The reasons for this date are linguistic and cultural. The language of Qoheleth betrays traces of Late Biblical Hebrew: *še* for *'ăšer,* the exclusive use of the abbreviated *'ănî,* the placement of *'ēt/'ēt* with an indefinite noun, the feminine demonstrative *zōh* rather than *zō't,* the use of the masculine plural pronominal suffix for a feminine plural antecedent, and the negation of the infinitive with *'ēn.*[61] Second, there are two Persian words, *pardēs* (2:5) and *pitgām* (8:11), as well as numerous Aramaisms.[62] Third, Greek and

---

61. See Antoon Schoors, *The Preacher Sought to Find Pleasing Words: A Study of the Language of Qoheleth* (OLA 41; Leuven: Peeters, 1992); Seow, *Ecclesiastes,* 12-21. Schoors finds thirty-four features of Late Biblical Hebrew in Qoheleth.

62. See Seow, *Ecclesiastes,* 12-15; W. C. Delsman, "Sprache des Buches Koheleth," in *Von Kanaan bis Kerala, FS J. P. M. van der Ploeg,* ed. W. C. Delsman, et al. (AOAT 211; Neukirchen-

Egyptian skepticism may have contributed to the cultural and philosophical world in which Qoheleth wrote his testament.[63] Other features that fit the Hellenistic period are his first person style and the description of his house, with the accoutrements of gardens, pools, and slaves (see Varro, *Rust.* 1.2.1–12.4; 3.2.1–2.18; Pliny, *Ep.* 2.17).

The Historical Setting: From Alexander to Antiochus III

Alexander's conquest led to the permission to allow the Samaritans to build a temple on Mount Gerizim, a temple that would eventually rival the one in Jerusalem for several centuries (Josephus, *Ant.* 11.306-12, 321-24; 12.254-58).[64] In Egypt Ptolemy I Soter I (305-285 B.C.E.) began the creation of a significant political state that transformed native Egyptian religion and culture into a Greco-Egyptian form of expression that, until 200 B.C.E., significantly impacted Judah and would continue to do so under the Seleucids and eventually the Romans. Hellenization became the tool for forming cultural unity within the diverse regions and states, although indigenous cultures and languages were not eradicated. Among the Jews, different responses to Hellenism developed, including both a reactionary repudiation of Greek culture and a more accommodating acceptance of many new things from the traditions of Classical and Hellenistic Greece.[65] With the exception of the persecution unleashed by Antiochus IV Epiphanes and the later pogrom under the Roman prefect Flaccus, tolerance of Judaism was the official policy of the two empires that directly affected the Jews. There was, however, a deep-seated xenophobia coupled with an expressed arrogance of superiority that was found among the Greek intellectuals and aristocracy, who tended to disparage and hold up to ridicule the assumed barbarism of the cultures of the peoples they and their Roman successors conquered. This elitism was likely a major reason for resistance from some of the local in-

---

Vluyn: Neukirchener Verlag, 1982) 341-65; D. C. Fredericks, *Qoheleth's Language: Re-evaluating Its Nature and Date* (ANETS 3; Lewiston, NY: Mellen, 1988).

63. Rainer Braun, *Kohelet und die frühhellenistische Popularphilosophie* (BZAW 130; Berlin: de Gruyter, 1973). Michael Fox has argued that the book does incorporate the basic Greek ideal of "the autonomy of individual reason, which is to say, the belief that individuals can and should proceed with their own observations and reasoning powers on a quest for knowledge and that this may lead to discovery of truths previously unknown" ("Wisdom in Qoheleth," in *In Search of Wisdom*, 123).

64. On the period in general see Günther Hölbl, *A History of the Ptolemaic Empire* (London: Routledge, 2001); Werner Huss, *Ägypten in hellenistischer Zeit. 332-30 v. Chr.* (Munich: Beck, 2001); Ernst Haag, *Das hellenistische Zeitalter. Israel und die Bibel im 4. bis 1. Jahrhundert v. Chr.* (Biblische Enzyklopädie 9; Stuttgart: W. Kohlhammer, 2003).

65. Schwartz, *Imperialism and Jewish Society*, 1-2.

habitants, who were often denied Greek citizenship in cities and positions of high social standing in the countries in which they resided, perhaps even if they were indigenous. At the same time, it is clear that hellenization streamlined commerce, communication, the rule of law formulated in Greek royal policies, administration of diverse groups, and legal decisions.[66]

The decline of the Ptolemaic Empire began in the final years of the rule of Ptolemy III Euergetes I (246-221 B.C.E.) and continued during the reign of his successor, Ptolemy IV Philopator (221-205). This weakness reached its low point under Ptolemy V Epiphanes (194-181), with the result that Egyptian control over much of the eastern Mediterranean world outside Egypt came to an end.

Dating Qoheleth to the final quarter of the third century B.C.E. corresponds to the teacher's criticism of an unjust, hierarchical government (5:7[8]) and the period of diminishing influence of the Ptolemaic presence in the eastern Mediterranean world. The decline of the Egyptian empire ruled by the Ptolemies would have occasioned a prevailing sense of pessimism in an area that included Judah.[67] This date for Qoheleth suggests that he issued his testament during the reign of Ptolemy IV Philopator (221-205) during the period of the eclipse of Ptolemaic rule, now stretching for four generations, and the imminent ascension of Seleucid dominion over Judah under the militarily strong ruler Antiochus III. With the decline of Ptolemaic power, the Jewish community of Judah, centered in Jerusalem, experienced the imminent trauma of transition to a new political power. Qoheleth, during the Ptolemaic rule of Judah and Egypt, would have been aware of larger Egyptian history and culture as they continued through the third century B.C.E. and was possibly affected by the events of this tumultuous time.

The reign of Ptolemy IV experienced a succession of internal revolts and significant military defeats abroad.[68] He ascended to the throne in 221 B.C.E. at the age of twenty,[69] having murdered Magas, his brother, in a struggle for king-

---

66. Two examples of this cultural arrogance are found in Plato and Plutarch: "Such was the natural nobility of this city, sound and healthy was the spirit of freedom among us, and the instinctive dislike of the barbarian, because we are pure Hellenes, having no admixture of barbarism in us. For we are not like many others . . . who are by nature barbarians, and by custom Hellenes, but we are pure Hellenes, uncontaminated by any foreign element, and therefore the hatred of the foreign has passed unadulterated into the lifeblood of the city" (Plato, *Menexenus* 245d); and, "The difference between Greeks and barbarians was not a matter of cloak or shield, or of scimitar or Median dress. What distinguished Greekness was excellence, while wickedness was the mark of the barbarian" (Plutarch, *Alex. fort.* 1.329d).

67. See Hengel, *Jews, Greeks, and Barbarians*, 33-41.

68. Hölbl remarks that the reign of Ptolemy IV marked the end of the "century of the Ptolemies" (*History of the Ptolemaic Empire*, 134).

69. Antiochus III had just become the Seleucid king in 223 B.C.E.

ship. Bernice, the mother, had favored the younger son Magas as successor, so that she and an uncle, Lysimachus, were also murdered. Ptolemy IV married Arsinoe III, his sister, assumed the cultic name "lover of the father" (Philopator) in order to legitimate his rule, and soon found himself threatened by the Seleucid ruler Antiochus III (223-187),[70] who became king in Antioch also at the age of twenty. The Fourth Syrian War (219-217), initiated by Antiochus III, led to the loss of some Ptolemaic possessions in Asia, and the threatened conquest of Coele-Syria by the ambitious Seleucid ruler posed difficulties for the Egyptian king. Ptolemy IV finally succeeded in defeating the army of Antiochus III at Raphia in 217 (Polybius 5.5-87; Plutarch, *Cleom.* 33; Dan. 11:11-12; cf. 3 Macc. 1–2). In a counterattack, Ptolemy IV led his troops into Syria for three weeks, resulting in a peace treaty between the two Greek states. Coele-Syria remained in the control of the Ptolemies, until its loss to Antiochus III during the early part of the reign of Ptolemy V (204-180) in the Fifth Syrian War (202-200). The earlier victory at Raphia in 217 had revived Egyptian prestige, but only for a brief period. Major building projects during the early reign of Ptolemy IV were extensive in the decade following the victory at Raphia. These included the building of a powerful navy and the erection, expansion, and renovation of temples in the north.[71] The latter was done to curry favor with the important and powerful priesthoods who legitimated his reign, yet the temple cults' massive expense was in part responsible for the increase of local taxes that overburdened the local population.

Internally, Ptolemaic sociopolitical stability was on the decline, beginning with the onerous taxation due to the high costs of the Fourth Syrian War. Southern Egypt was threatened by the secession of the Nubian kings in Upper Egypt who ruled 207-187 and by a Theban royal state over which native kings ruled as pharaohs (206-186). Major internal Egyptian revolts developed during the rule of Ptolemy IV beginning soon after the victory at Raphia in 217, because of increasing taxes, exploitation of the local Egyptian population, the lavish self-indulgence of the court, and the forcing of a continual stream of young men into the army to pursue increased military control in Asia. Out of feelings of desperation and exploitation in the populace, a serious downward spiral soon developed. Polybius (5.107.1-3) even drew a direct connection between the battle and the increase in military activity and the internal revolt that erupted soon after. From the Rosetta Stone we learn that the Delta was engaged in a full-blown civil war between the Greek court and the lower classes of Egyptians

---

70. See Hengel, *Jews, Greeks, and Barbarians*, 33-41.

71. Dieter Arnold, *Temples of the Last Pharaohs* (Oxford: Oxford University Press, 1999) 173-78.

over social injustice at the end of the reign of Philometor.[72] The hostility of the local Egyptian population against the Ptolemies is demonstrated by an edited version of the Demotic Chronicle that tells of a native king from Herakleopolis who would drive the Greek rulers off the throne, for their reign did not embody the principle of justice, the primary duty of the Egyptian pharaoh throughout Egyptian history, prior to outside conquest and rule by the Persians and then the hated Greeks.[73] The author of 3 Maccabees appears to be speaking of Ptolemy IV's return home from military success at Raphia when he stopped in Jerusalem and attempted to enter the temple. Divine intervention prohibited this sacrilege, for the ruler was thrown paralyzed to the ground. 3 Maccabees 3–7 narrates this ruler's return home, followed by his vengeful assault against the Jews, likely leading to the curtailment of their rights. The aftermath would have been compatible with the skepticism and elements of despair one finds in Qoheleth.

One other factor may have provided an appropriate background during the reign of this king for the composition of Qoheleth. Although earlier Greek rulers were addressed as divine, Ptolemy IV established a royal cult to the dead rulers and to himself while he was still alive. He identified himself with the Egyptian deity Horus in military endeavors and in cultic ritual. In addition, he named himself beloved of Isis and loved by Ptah. His wife, Arsinoe III, wore the headdress of an Egyptian goddess. Cult statues of the couple, following the model of Egyptian representations of royal pairs, were erected in Egyptian temples. Ptolemy IV also became associated with the Greek cults. Ptolemy IV became Theos Philopator, while the royal couple was called the "father-loving" gods.[74] This Ptolemaic dynastic cult in Alexandria honored deceased rulers as Theoi Philopatores. Ptolemy IV built in Alexandria a burial pyramid with a mausoleum for the dead Ptolemaic rulers, beginning with Alexander. After the victory at Raphia, he even established a cult for himself at Jaffa, a port city in Eretz Israel. In addition, inscriptions have been found in Coele-Syria in honor of the king, which attribute to him the title Theos Philopator and to his wife that of Thea Philopator. At court and in an annual festival there was the celebration of the Greek god Dionysius. After Ptolemy IV's death, however, the close relationship between the Ptolemaic dynasty and the native cults of Egypt deteriorated. This religio-historical development may provide the context for understanding Qoheleth's contrasting emphasis on the "eternal home" of the

---

72. E. A. Wallis Budge, *The Rosetta Stone* (1913; repr. New York: Dover, 1989).

73. Peter Kaplony, "Demotische Chronik," *LÄ* 1 (1975) 1056-60. See the essay by J. H. Johnson, "Is the Demotic Chronicle an Anti-Greek Tract?" in *Grammata Demotica, FS Erich Lüddeckens*, ed. Heinz-J. Thissen and Karl-Th. Zauzich (Würzburg: Zauzich, 1984) 107-24.

74. Hölbl, *History of the Ptolemaic Empire*, 168.

grave where all people, great and small, wise and foolish, and righteous and evil, reside in darkness and forgetfulness.

Judah in the Seleucid Empire

Following the Battle of Issus in 332 B.C.E., Alexander's victory paved the way for Greek control of Syria and Eretz Israel.[75] After the death of Alexander and then his son, the empire was divided among his former generals, who established their own empires. The Ptolemaic Kingdom's control over Judah (301-200) lasted until the defeat of Ptolemy V at Paneion by Antiochus III, circa 200; by 198 Judah became part of the Seleucid Empire.[76] The Jews in Jerusalem supported Antiochus III, which in turn led to his issuance of favorable edicts on their behalf. The first edict designated the Jews as an *ethnos,* called for the rebuilding of the temple and the support of its cultus, and exempted from personal taxation (poll tax, tax on produce, and salt tax) the *gerousia,* the priests, the temple scribes, and the temple singers. The Jews who had been enslaved were freed, while the entire Jewish population was permitted to "live in accordance with the laws of their fathers." The second edict prohibited non-Jews from entering the temple, while at the same time it restricted the sale of animals in Jerusalem to those that could be offered as sacrifices. Correspondence between Antiochus III and Ptolemy, son of Thrasea, discovered in Ḥefzibah near Scythopolis, refers to protecting the village populations from occupying soldiers. The life of the Jews had improved with the new regime, thus suggesting further the view that Qoheleth lived and taught prior to the Seleucid takeover when life, especially under Ptolemy IV, became more harsh.

Hellenistic Judah

Alexander's eastern empire comprised for the most part previously existing cities, although due to hellenization they underwent varying degrees of transformation into Hellenistic cities that included dimensions of both Greek and indigenous religious and cultural elements.[77] Jewish communities negotiated in

75. Evidence of engagement with Greek culture and the presence of Greeks in Eretz Israel may be found as early as the ninth century B.C.E. See, e.g., John Pairman Brown, *Israel and Hellas* (BZAW 231; Berlin: de Gruyter, 1995); idem, *Israel and Hellas* (BZAW 276; Berlin: de Gruyter, 2000). He investigates the language of social institutions and of sacred institutions.

76. A large Jewish community developed in Syria, esp. in the city of Antioch (Josephus, *J.W.* 7.43-53).

77. See Aryeh Kasher, "Jerusalem Cathedra," in *Jerusalem* 1-2, ed. Lee I. Levine (Yad Izhak Ben-Zvi Institute 1982; Detroit: Wayne State University Press, 1982) 2:63-78; idem, *Jews and Helle-*

many different ways their relationship to the ruling government. Of course, these eastern cities had had contact with previously existing Greek states through commerce since the ninth century B.C.E. Greek contact with and occasional settlement in Eretz Israel began in the region of the coastal plain that extended from Syria to the north to Egypt to the south. Indeed, this even began as early as the invasion of the Sea Peoples at the end of the Late Bronze Age and the first century of the Iron I Age. Phoenician and Philistine cities along the coast engaged in trade with the regions to the west in the Mediterranean world so that by the time of Alexander this culture had become commonly known in Syria and Israel. Indeed, examples of this may be recognized in Greek ware of various types found in inland cities. To this point, Tel Dor provides the best example of earlier Greek influence even prior to Alexander. The city has yielded materials that include a favissa of a nearby Greek temple and the existence of Attic sherds from the latter half of the fifth century B.C.E. After the conquest of Alexander, Syrian and Israelite cities were eventually assimilated into the various Greek administrative systems, and there is evidence that some even assumed Greek names. Following the establishment of the Greek empires subsequent to the conquest of Alexander, Greeks, normally soldiers and others from the lower classes, were induced to settle in Eretz Israel through land grants and the status of a ruling population. Most cities even welcomed the coming of Alexander, save for a few, including Samaria and Gaza.

In the deuterocanonical literature the terms "Judaism" (*Ioudaismos*, 2 Macc. 1:1; see 2:21; 8:1; 14:38) and "Hellenism" (*Hellenismos*, 4:13-14) were used textually as early as the end of the second century B.C.E. First Maccabees also refers to Hellenism as Greek culture (e.g. 1:13-15). By the end of the third century, Palestinian Judaism became as thoroughly hellenized as Diaspora Judaism.[78] Of course, there were differences in each expression of Judaism in the important regions of the Greek East.[79]

---

nistic Cities in Eretz-Israel: Relations of the Jews in Eretz-Israel with the Hellenistic Cities during the Second Temple Period (332 BCE–70 CE) (Tübingen: Mohr [Siebeck] 1990); T. F. R. G. Braun, "The Greeks in the Near East," in *CAH* 3/3: *The Expansion of the Greek World, Eighth to Sixth Centuries B.C.*, ed. J. A. Boardman and N. G. L. Hammond (2nd ed.; Cambridge: Cambridge University Press, 1982) 1-31; idem, "The Greeks in Egypt," *CAH* 3/3:32-56; Ephraim Stern, "The Beginning of the Greek Settlement in Palestine in the Light of the Excavations at Tel Dor," in *Recent Excavations in Israel: Studies in Iron Age Archaeology,* ed. Seymour Gitin and William G. Dever (AASOR 49; Winona Lake, IN: Eisenbrauns, 1982) 107-12; Gideon Fuks, "A Mediterranean Pantheon: Cults and Deities in Hellenistic and Roman Askelon," *Mediterranean Historical Review* 15 (1999) 27-48.

78. Hengel, *Judaism and Hellenism,* 1:104-5. Also see idem, *Jews, Greeks, and Barbarians,* 49-82; idem, "Jerusalem als jüdische und hellenistische Stadt," in *Kleine Schriften,* 2:114-56.

79. Gregory E. Sterling, "Judaism between Jerusalem and Alexandria," in *Hellenism in the Land of Israel,* 263-301. Sterling's study focuses on Jerusalem from 175 to 135 B.C.E.

Hellenistic Influence in Jewish Cities

Some thirty cities in Eretz Israel possessed Greek architecture, coinage, cultural materials, and domestic artifacts.[80] Strong evidence of Hellenistic influence on cities of Israel may be documented from the third century B.C.E.[81] The administration of the city market of Jerusalem *(agoranomos)* may be traced to the period of the Maccabean revolt (2 Macc. 3:4).[82] In addition, Qoheleth's reference to economic wealth in 2:4-9 suggests the expansion of economic resources, agricultural estates, and population, based on a system of slavery, during the third century. It may well be that the teacher himself is reflecting his own substantial wealth in his description of Solomon or that of the Greek ruler in Alexandria. The teacher's substance, if not simply a fictional account dealing with Solomon, would have come from his association (likely trade) with the "provinces" *(mědînôt,* 2:8; 5:7) and especially the coastal cities located in the western provinces of Israel *(mědînôt hayyām).*[83] Qoheleth, the son of David, may well be portraying himself as more prosperous than anyone who lived before him in Jerusalem. While the description rings with hyperbole, it represents "the growth of a new class of landlords who derive their wealth from agricultural production combined with commerce, but who reside principally in Jerusalem."[84] The development of a new aristocracy, whose wealth was centered in the ownership and cultivation of estates, commerce, slavery, and new technology, may be traced to the Persian period (Neh. 4–5).[85] One may compare the teacher's pros-

---

80. Shimon Applebaum, "Jewish Urban Communities and Greek Influences," in *Judaea in Hellenistic and Roman Times: Historical and Archaeological Essays* (SJLA 40; Leiden: Brill, 1989) 30-46. At present there is no comprehensive survey of Greek inscriptions from the Hellenistic period until the seventh century C.E. The current, most extensive collection we have is *CIJ* which covers Asia and Africa. Jonathan Price of Tel Aviv University is leading a team to produce an exhaustive collection. This will include an editing of 6,000 to 7,000 texts, each with a drawing or photograph, textual translation, and commentary. In addition to *CIJ* see Kasher, *Jews and Hellenistic Cities;* van der Horst, *Ancient Jewish Epitaphs;* J. W. van Henten and P. W. van der Horst, eds., *Studies in Early Jewish Epigraphy* (Leiden: Brill, 1994); Pieter W. van der Horst, "Greek in Jewish Palestine in the Light of Jewish Epigraphy," in *Japheth in the Tents of Shem: Studies on Jewish Hellenism in Antiquity* (Contributions to Biblical Exegesis and Theology 32; Leuven: Peeters, 2002) 9-26.

81. Shimon Applebaum, "Hellenistic Cities of Judaea and Its Vicinity — Some New Aspects," in *The Ancient Historian and His Materials: Essays in Honour of C. E. Stevens,* ed. Barbara Levick (Franborough, Hants: Gregg, 1975) 59-73.

82. The *agoranomos* referred to both the administration of the market of a city and its overseer in a Greek city (*Athenaion politeia* 51.1). This official was responsible for the supply of food. See *OCD,* 43.

83. Applebaum, "Jewish Urban Communities," 31.

84. Ibid., 32.

85. For technological developments that included the treadmill, irrigation machinery, and the

perity and status to that of the family of the Tobiads (see Josephus, *Ant.* 11.4; 12.160; cf. *CPJ* 1:115-30) who lived mainly in the region of Ammon (1 Macc. 5:9-13).[86] Josephus notes especially that one member of this family, Joseph, was the son of Tobias. Joseph was the nephew of the high priest Onias II and received the contract for the collection of taxes from the farms of Judah from his uncle. While the farmland around new Greek cities was normally either owned or controlled by the king, it should be noted that the aristocracy, Greek citizens of the city, and indigenous landowners were often allowed to maintain ownership of their estates. Even so, the taxation was high. The existence of these estates is attested both in archaeological studies and in textual witnesses. For example, in 1 Macc. 6:24 the Hellenistic Jews in Judah complain to Antiochus V that the rebels had seized their estates ("patrimonies") and divided them *(diarpazō)* among themselves. Smaller farms were owned by families who lived in villages and cultivated their own fields.[87]

Jerusalem as a Hellenistic City

Jerusalem's Greek name is listed among the cities visited by Zenon during his journey in Eretz Israel during the mid-third century B.C.E.[88] A student of Plato, Clearchus, calls the city *Hierousolēmēn*.[89] The latter Greek name is used by Jewish writers who composed in Greek (1 Esdras, Tobit, the books of Maccabees, and the Letter of Aristeas). Some Greek writers provided a fanciful etymology in which *Hiero* was an abbreviation for *to hieron* ("the temple") and *solēm* was a reference to the "famous people of Solymer" in Homer (*Il.* 6.184, 204). A second

---

introduction of new agricultural products, see Hengel, *Judaism and Hellenism*, 1:46-47; Mikhail Ivanovich Rostovtzeff, *The Social and Economic History of the Hellenistic World* (3 vols.; Oxford: Clarendon, 1941) 2:1186-97.

86. For the study of this story of the Tobiads recorded by Josephus, see Dov Gera, *Judaea and Mediterranean Politics, 219 to 161 BCE* (Brill's Series in Jewish Studies 3; Leiden: Brill, 1998) 6-58; as well as idem, "On the Credibility of the History of the Tobiads," in *Greece and Rome in Eretz Israel*, ed. Aryeh Kasher, et al. (Center for Eretz Israel Research of Yah Izhak Ben-Zvi and the University of Haifa and of Tel Aviv University; Jerusalem: Israel Exploration Society, 1990) 21-38. He concludes that the story in Josephus originates from a source that is propaganda written by a Jew of Ptolemaic Egypt to encourage both confidence among the Jewish community in Egypt of this period and their loyalty to the Ptolemies.

87. Applebaum, "Jewish Urban Communities," 37.

88. In general see esp. Levine, *Jerusalem*, 45-90; Frederick E. Brenk, "Jerusalem — Hierapolis: The Revolt under Antiochus IV Epiphanes in the Light of Evidence for Hierapolis of Phrygia, Babylon, and Other Cities," in *Relighting the Souls: Studies in Plutarch, in Greek Literature, Religion, and Philosophy, and in the New Testament Background* (Stuttgart: Franz Steiner, 1998) 354-93. On the Greek name see Hengel, "Jerusalem," 118-21. For Zenon see *CPJ* 1:121-22, no. 2a, col. I.3; cf. 2b.2.7.

89. Josephus, *C. Ap.* 1.179. Cf. Eusebius, *Praep. ev.* 9.5.7.

name for Jerusalem, or at least the more hellenized and affluent section of the city, may have been Antiocheia.[90]

The city of Jerusalem was held in great esteem among Greeks and Jews during the Hellenistic period. Although ranked as a sacred or temple city (hierapolis) due to its status as the religious center of Judaism and the location of its foremost sanctuary, it did not appear to have achieved the status of a Greek polis with a significant cultural and political position in the empire. These Greek interpretations of the name of Jerusalem raised its prestige among the Hellenists, as did speculative imaginings of the antiquity of the city that are traced back to the beginnings of history.[91]

While politically the city was administered by a Greek governor as the major temple city of a colony within the Ptolemaic Empire, it did not achieve the status of a polis. It was allowed to function on a local level as a theocracy in which the high priests and the *gerousia* of aristocratic leaders held power. However, those who sought to achieve the status of polis for their temple city probably did not view the changes necessary to become a polis radically different from those traditional features that were already integrated in its culture, architecture, religion, social structure, and governance. Thus language, paideia, and even features of Hellenistic and mystery religions, in particular the ruler cult, were new formulations that became entrenched in the colony. Judaism and Hellenism included highly diverse configurations and a variety of social, religious, political, and cultural formations, a recognition that resists the oversimplification of opposing Greek culture to Jewish religion.

From both the Jewish literature of the age and the limited material culture of Jerusalem, which has been only partially excavated, it is clear that the city blended Greek and indigenous features.[92] The land of Judah experienced some five Syrian Wars (274-271, 260-253, 246-241, 221-217, and 202-198 B.C.E.), during which there was a division of the Jewish house concerning the support of one or the other of the two Greek empires, either Ptolemaic or Seleucid. In addition there was a resistance movement, the Maccabean revolt, that finally gained the upper hand by rejecting Greek rule, presence, and influence beginning with Antiochus IV Epiphanes from 167 to 164. Most of the battles during the Syrian

90. See Brenk, "Jerusalem — Hierapolis," 379.

91. Reflecting a Greco-Roman understanding of cities as the "mothers" of cultures and nations, Plutarch and Tacitus refer to Jerusalem as the tribal ancestor of Judea (Plutarch, *Isis and Osiris* 31.363 C/D; Tacitus, *History* 5.2.2).

92. See Eric Gruen, *Heritage and Hellenism: The Reinvention of Jewish Tradition* (Berkeley: University of California Press, 1998) xv; John J. Collins, "The Hellenization of Jerusalem in the Pre-Maccabean Era," *International Renneart Guest Lecture Series* 6 (Jerusalem: Ingeborg Renneart Center for Jerusalem Studies, 1999); Brenk, "Jerusalem-Hierapolis," 364-65.

Wars preceding the Maccabean uprising occurred in the area of the coastal plain, with the result that Jerusalem was not directly affected by the military confrontations. Nevertheless, the city was occupied by garrisons of the rival Greek empires, since control of this strategically important city was critically important in the struggle for dominance in the regions of Syria and Egypt.

During the late Persian and then the Hellenistic period, Jewish texts continued to stress the importance of the temple, the Torah, monotheism, the rejection of idolatry, and the sacredness of Jerusalem. One of the common features of Greek paideia reflected in Jewish literature of the Hellenistic and even the early Roman period was the special distinction of the antiquity of a people and its early achievements that continued to influence later cultures (Theodotus, Eupolemos, Ben Sira, Pseudo-Hecataeus, and later Josephus).[93] Jerusalem was viewed by some pagan and almost all Jewish writers as the sacred site of Delphi, the navel of the earth, where divine revelation occurred and Apollo dwelt in his temple (see Jub. 8:19; 1 En. 26:1-2; 2 En. 71:35-36; cf. *b. Qidd.* 10). The author of 2 Maccabees declared that Jerusalem was the most famous city in the entire world.

Our major source for understanding the political and social operation of the city is Pseudo-Hecataeus, who wrote at the beginning of the third century B.C.E.[94] According to him, the city itself was dominated internally by a hierocracy of Sadducean priests who controlled the temple that provided them not only with enormous prestige and social status through the teaching of the Torah and the operations of the cultic sacrifices, festivals, and Sabbath worship, but also with access to vast wealth. It is not surprising that the upper echelons of the priests became quite rich as well as politically powerful. The high priest was the indigenous political and religious leader in Jerusalem and was recognized as being the primary holder of religious office in both Judah and the Diaspora. Ben Sira's praise of Simon II demonstrates that the high priest had both religious and political power in Jerusalem and among all the Jews in Palestine and the Diaspora. Hecataeus also notes that the priests constituted much of the leadership of the city, especially in overseeing and administering the laws through the courts. Qoheleth's strong criticism of the rulers (presumably Greek) and his lack of interest in the temple cult make it unlikely he would have occupied a similar position as a teacher under the auspices of the priests. It is much more likely that he operated a school for aristocratic youth in Jerusalem that would have been rather critical of the temple priests and their scribes. In

---

93. For Josephus see *C. Ap.* 2.193; cf. 1.21, 221; 2.130-31.

94. See his *Aegyptiaca*, partially preserved in Diodorus Siculus, *Bibliotheca historica* 40.3.4-7. Also see the work of the Jewish historian Pseudo-Hecataeus, *On the Jews*.

addition to the hierocracy, the lay aristocracy also wielded significant power, both economically and politically. They were represented by a council (*gerousia*, 2 Macc. 11:27; 3 Macc. 1:8; Josephus, *Ant.* 12.138, 142). However, the precise authority and duties of this group are not known.

Material Culture in Hellenistic Jerusalem

The influence of Hellenism on Judaism is mentioned by Pseudo-Hecataeus: "as a result of their mingling with men of other nations [both under Persian rule and under that of the Macedonians who overthrew the Persians], many of their traditional practices were disturbed."[95] The evidence for Greek influence is in the form of material culture, philosophical ideas, literary themes and features, and rhetoric. Greek names were used among the aristocracy at the end of the third century B.C.E., while the Tobiads had a Greek secretary and Greek teachers. It may well have been the case that there were Greek teachers in the house of Simon II.[96] It is probable, then, that there would have been multilingual (Greek, Aramaic, and Hebrew) sages in Jerusalem and its wider environs. Jerusalem coins of the early third century have been found with the images of Ptolemy I and Bernice I as well as of Ptolemy II and Arsinoe II. In addition, they also often have the eagle, which is the symbol of Ptolemaic rule.[97] Over one thousand stamped jar handles of amphorae, probably containing wine from Rhodes, have been excavated in Jerusalem. These jar handles are engraved with official Rhodian stamps and are dated by the names of local priests. The majority date between the mid-third to the mid-second century B.C.E.[98] They dem-

---

95. Diodorus Siculus, *Bibliotheca historica* 40.3.8. In general see Th. A. Busink, *Der Tempel in Jerusalem von Salomo bis Herodes* (2nd ed.; 2 vols.; Leiden: Brill, 1980); Hengel, *Judaism and Hellenism*; idem, "Jerusalem," 128-52; H.-P. Kuhnen, *Palästina in griechisch-römischer Zeit* (*Handbuch der Archäologie, Vorderasien* 2/2; Munich: Beck, 1990); Tal Ilan, "New Ossuary Inscriptions from Jerusalem," *Scripta Classica Israelica* 9 (1991/1992) 149-59; Jan Willem van Henten and Pieter van der Horst, eds., *Ancient Jewish Epitaphs* (Leiden: Brill, 1994); Levine, *Jerusalem*; Nahman Avigad, *Jewish Quarter Excavations in the Old City of Jerusalem, Conducted by Nahman Avigad, 1969-1982*, ed. Hillel Geva (3 vols.; Jerusalem: Israel Exploration Society, 2000-2006).

96. See Hengel, *Judaism and Hellenism*, 1:76. Greek tutors may have been present in the house of the high priest as early as the third century. This would help explain why Jason, the son of the high priest Simon II, was a leading hellenizer. The building of the gymnasium near the temple would have allowed the priests convenient access.

97. See Arie Kindler, "Silver Coins Bearing the Name of Judea from the Early Hellenistic Period," *IEJ* 24 (1974) 73-76; D. T. Ariel, "A Survey of Coin Finds in Jerusalem," *LÄ* 32 (1982) 273-326; Dan Barag, "The Coinage of Yehud and the Ptolemies," in *Studies in Honor of Arie Kindler*, ed. Dan Barag (Jerusalem: Israel Numismatic Society, 1999) 27-38.

98. D. T. Ariel, *Excavations at the City of David*, vol. 2: *1978-1985* (Qedem 30; Jerusalem: Institute of Archaeology, Hebrew University Press, 1990); idem, "Locally Stamped Handles and Associ-

onstrate the involvement of Jerusalem's commercial activities in the Greek world. Other evidence for commercial activities includes those mentioned in the Zenon papyri. Zenon was a Ptolemaic official who was commissioned to go to Palestine in 259 B.C.E. Some forty or so documents have been discovered that also point to the Ptolemaic involvement in commercial activities in Judah, including Jerusalem, which is specifically mentioned several times.[99] 1 Maccabees 12:20-23 (see Josephus, *Ant.* 12.225-27) reproduces in part a letter that indicates correspondence took place between the high priest Onias II and Areus, king of Sparta. More than a century later, Jonathan the Hasmonean sent a letter to Sparta that renewed the association between the two countries (1 Macc. 12:1-18). Jason, defrocked from his position as high priest, fled to Sparta, which is said to have consisted of a "kindred people" (2 Macc. 5:9).

As I will discuss in more detail later in chapter 7 on the Wisdom of Solomon, the translation of the LXX in Alexandria, beginning in the first half of the third century B.C.E. (see the Letter of Aristeas), became a major vehicle for the hellenization of many Jews, not only in the Diaspora but also in Judah. The largely legendary account of the Letter of Aristeas, nevertheless, assumes without explanation or question that there were Jewish scribes in Jerusalem who knew both Hebrew and Greek and therefore could produce a Greek translation of the Hebrew Bible.

The social composition of Jerusalem during the period of the Ptolemies is difficult to reconstruct from the limited written sources we have. However, the high priest and other Zadokite priests clearly had substantial power and wealth due to their regulatory power over the Torah and the gifts, offerings, and taxes to the temple. There was considerable involvement of the city and the colony in the commercial activity in the Greek world so that Aramaic, Hebrew, and Greek had to be known and spoken by most residents, including even laborers, and there would have to have been multilingual scribes who were able to read and write these three dominant languages. Finally, there were also apocalyptic scribes in Judah and likely in Jerusalem, as is demonstrated by the existence of the earliest sections of 1 Enoch from the third century (chs. 1–36, 72–82, 106–107).[100] The training of sages would likely have been in different schools, ranging from one attached to the temple to private ones open to aristocratic youths,

---

ated Body Fragments of the Persian and Hellenistic Periods," in Ariel, et al., *Excavations at the City of David,* vol. 6: *1978-1985: Inscriptions* (Qedem 41; Jerusalem: Institute of Archaeology, Hebrew University Press, 2000) 137-94.

99. *CPJ* 1:115-30.

100. Michael E. Stone, *Scriptures, Sects and Visions: A Profile of Judaism from Ezra to the Jewish Revolts* (Cleveland: Collins, 1980) 27-35; James C. VanderKam, *Enoch and the Growth of an Apocalyptic Tradition* (Washington, DC: Catholic Biblical Association of America, 1984) 79-88, 111-14.

to family guilds, and to tutors. My estimation is that Qoheleth, from the tenor and tone of his writing, would have been cosmopolitan in outlook, critical of traditional religion, wealthy, and quite probably a teacher of aristocratic youth in a private school that he operated, perhaps in his own house or villa. The worldly Zadokite priests, the cosmopolitan Hasidim, and the sectarian apocalyptic seers would have been his opponents, for he countered their teachings with a skepticism that reflected some of the Greek and Egyptian thought of the period.

Greek Epigraphy in Hellenistic Palestine

In addition to the epitaphs already mentioned, Greek papyri, coins, and inscriptions also demonstrate the substantial presence of Greek culture during the Hellenistic period.[101] Communication in Eretz Israel was predominantly trilingual during the rule of the Greek empire. Greek served as the official and international commercial language, Hebrew was the religious language of Torah and worship, and Aramaic was the popular, vernacular dialect among indigenous people, particularly in the villages and rural areas. It is not surprising in this setting to find the existence of hundreds of texts and inscriptions predominantly written in Greek, even in Eretz Israel.[102] If we place Qoheleth in the last quarter of the third century B.C.E., he would have lived and taught in this multilingual world that would have required scribes, sages, administrators, and those engaged in commerce to be fluent in Greek. Greek names are well attested for Jews in Judah, including even several of the later Hasmonean rulers (Hyrcanus, Aristobulus, Alexander, and Antigonus) and are also noted on a large number of epitaphs.[103] Furthermore, numismatics in Judah include coins with both Hebrew and Greek inscriptions, beginning with Alexander Jannaeus (103-76 B.C.E.) who ruled more than a century after Qoheleth. The later synagogues in Israel even had Greek inscriptions, indicating that the worshipers could read and speak Greek, which was used along with Aramaic in the assembly and worship.[104]

Since Greek became the dominant commercial language for international

101. For a convenient list of Greco-Jewish literature in Jerusalem, inscriptions in Jerusalem, ossuaries in Jerusalem, Greek manuscripts in the Judean Desert, Greco-Jewish literature in Alexandria, and nonliterary Jewish texts from or dealing with Alexandria, see Sterling, "Judaism between Jerusalem and Alexandria," in *Hellenism in the Land of Israel,* appendix, 279-90.

102. See van der Horst, *Japheth,* 12.

103. See the appendix, "Jews with Greek or Roman Names," in Harris, *Greek Athletics and the Jews,* 102-6.

104. Saul Lieberman, *Greek in Jewish Palestine* (New York: Feldheim, 1965) 16.

trade, its use was not limited to the aristocracy, but even people of more ordinary means spoke a colloquial Greek.[105] This is demonstrated by epitaphs, inscriptions in synagogues, coins, papyri, and literary sources. The scrolls of Masada and Qumran also have yielded Greek documents. Not to be ignored is that later rabbinic literature contains thousands of Greek loanwords.[106] From the Hellenistic and early Roman periods the quality of the Greek and of the material inscribed ranged from epitaphs composed of Homeric hexameters on an expensive sarcophagus to words that are scratched on an ostracon or on wall plaster.

Examples of Jewish scholars from Judah who composed in Greek include Eupolemus, who supported Judas Maccabeus,[107] and Theodotus, who wrote an epic poem, *On the Jews,* from the late third or early second century B.C.E. These works and 2 Maccabees point strongly to the intellectual tradition of Hellenistic Jewish religion, written in Greek, that existed in Eretz Israel as early as the third century B.C.E. Thus Greek was the major language for administration, trade, and a significant amount of literature in Eretz Israel during the third and second centuries B.C.E.[108]

Hellenism and Hellenization

Hellenization is "a complex phenomenon which cannot be limited to purely political, socio-economic, cultural or religious aspects, but embraces them all."[109] Thus it includes paideia, philosophy, rhetoric, traditional religion, the newly emerging mystery religions, the Greek language, and a variety of political and social features. Prior to Alexander, Israel's and Judah's contact with the Hellenic world developed as early as the ninth century B.C.E.[110]

---

105. Lieberman, *Greek in Jewish Palestine;* Rachel Hachlili, *Ancient Jewish Art and Archaeology in the Land of Israel* (HdO 35; Leiden: Brill, 1988) 103. Lea Roth-Gerson indicates that more than a third of the synagogue inscriptions in Palestine are in Greek (*The Greek Inscriptions from the Synagogue in Eretz-Israel* [Jerusalem: Yad Izhak Ben Zvi, 1987]). This is also true of Samaritan synagogues (van der Horst, *Japheth,* 17).

106. See Martin Hengel, "Zum Problem der 'Hellenisierung' Judäas im 1. Jahrhundert nach Christus," *Kleine Schriften,* vol. 1: *Judaica et Hellenistica* (WUNT 90; Tübingen: Mohr, 1996) 1-90.

107. Collins, *Between Athens and Jerusalem,* 17.

108. Van der Horst, *Japheth,* 26.

109. Hengel, *Judaism and Hellenism,* 1:3. Important discussions include Gerhard Delling, "Die Begegnung zwischen Hellenismus und Judentum," *ANRW* 2.20/1:3-39; Schwartz, *Imperialism and Jewish Society,* 22-25; Gruen, *Heritage and Hellenism;* Lee I. Levine, *Judaism and Hellenism in Antiquity: Conflict or Confluence?* (Seattle: University of Washington Press, 1998).

110. Clearchus of Soli, a former student of Aristotle, tells of a meeting, sometime between 347 and 345 B.C.E., in Western Asia Minor between his teacher and a Jew who "not only spoke Greek, but

The influence of Greek culture on Judah was significant in the Hellenistic period. Greek quickly became the lingua franca of the former eastern empire, and soon commerce and political policies required facility in the language. Even many Jewish grave inscriptions were written in Greek.[111] It may be that Jewish schools were influenced by Greek paideia (see Sir. 51:23), although there was no Greek gymnasium or *ephebeion* until the time of Jason the high priest (174-171 B.C.E.) during the reign of Antiochus IV Epiphanes (175-164). Indeed, the revolt against this Seleucid ruler was due both to the increasing influence of Jewish "hellenizers" among the upper classes in Jerusalem and to the imposed Hellenism of Greek authorities.[112] The hellenization of Jerusalem during the Ptolemaic and Seleucid dynasties is clear.[113]

Several features of Greek Hellenistic thought are found in Qoheleth, as are some terms and phrases that may have Greek derivations.[114] While there are no Graecisms, there are several Greek expressions in Qoheleth's Hebrew: the frequent use of the terms *miqreh* and *ḥēleq* are similar to the Greek terms *tychē* and *moira*, that is, "fate" and "fortune" or "portion," respectively. "Under the sun" (*taḥat haššāmeš* = *hyp' hēlio*) appears often in Greek literature to speak of human existence and the activities pursued while alive.[115] The word *hebel* ("evanescence, vanity, nonsense") suggests the Greek term *typhos*, both of which may mean "wind," "smoke," "vanity," and "darkness." In addition, *laʿăśôt ṭôb* (3:12) is the Hebrew expression of *eu prattein* or *eu dran*, while *ṭôb 'ăšer yāpeh* (5:17) compares to the common Greek expression *kalos agathos* or *kalon philon*.[116]

On the basis of these and other linguistic similarities and similar views, Antoon Schoors also thinks that Qoheleth came under the influence of Greek thought.[117] Among the possible Greek expressions he adds to the above is "to

had the soul of a Greek." See Menahem Stern, *Greek and Latin Authors on Jews and Judaism* (3 vols.; Jerusalem: Israel Academy of Sciences and Humanities, 1984) 1:47-52; Josephus, *C. Ap.* 1.179-83.

111. For a comprehensive list of Jewish names in the Hellenistic period, see Tal Ilan, *A Lexicon of Jewish Names in Late Antiquity*, Part 1: *Palestine 330 BCE–200 CE* (Texte und Studien zum antiken Judentum 91; Tübingen: Mohr-Siebeck, 2002).

112. See Fergus Millar, "The Background to the Maccabean Revolution: Reflections on Martin Hengel's 'Judaism and Hellenism,'" *JJS* 29 (1978) 1-21; idem, *The Roman Near East, 31 B.C. to A.D. 337* (Cambridge: Harvard University Press, 1993); Hannah M. Cotton and Guy M. Rogers, eds., *Rome, the Greek World, and the East* (Chapel Hill, NC: University of North Carolina, 2004).

113. See the papyrological evidence for hellenization in *CPJ* 1:18, 26, and section 1, 115-28.

114. "Influence from the Greek world of ideas is seen in Koheleth more than in any other Old Testament work" (Hengel, *Judaism and Hellenism*, 1:115).

115. Braun, *Kohelet*, 50.

116. Hengel, *Jews, Greeks, and Barbarians*, 120-21.

117. Personal correspondence, October 13, 2003.

see the sun" (Heb. *lir'ôt 'et-haššāmeš,* 6:5; 7:11; 11:7), which takes on the meaning of "live" (e.g., cf. Gk. *oude ny moi kēr ēthel' eti zōein kai horan phaos ēelioio,* "nor had my heart any longer desire to live and to behold the light of the sun"; Homer, *Od.* 4.539-40). The Hebrew expression *'āśâ yāmmîm* ("spend the days," 6:12) parallels Greek *poiein chronon.* The Hebrew word *'ôlām* assumes the meaning of Greek *aiōn* in 1:10, Hebrew *mālē'* (8:11; 9:3) means "to make full, satiate, impregnate" in the sense of Greek *plēroō,* and Hebrew *tûr* is influenced by the Greek term *skeptomai* in 1:13; 2:3; and 7:25, where the word means "mental exploration." Hebrew *yitrôn,* "what remains," is comparable to Greek *ophelos,* both of which point to excess. Another important term in Qoheleth, *'āmāl* ("toil"), brings to mind Greek *ponos,* which the LXX uses to translate the Hebrew term. Furthermore, labor or work *(ponos)* in the Greek social world is often seen in socioeconomic terms and status. Many of the educated who belong to the aristocracy and the intellectual classes (teachers, philosophers, and rhetors) hold labor in disdain, especially manual toil, that is undertaken to earn a living, and regard it as having no intrinsic worth (e.g., Cicero, *Off.* 1.150-51). Qoheleth's frequent metaphorical understanding of life as tiresome toil and dispiriting labor is shaped by a similar understanding. This is coupled with his pessimistic view of the tomb as the place of darkness when all accomplishments cease and do not continue beyond death. Qoheleth regards life as an endless succession of activities that have no value beyond the grave. This is the view of the aristocracy in the Hellenistic world and would be expected in Jewish society influenced by Hellenism. The last important parallel is *'ăšer yāpeh* (5:17), which resonates with *kalon philon* in Greek literature. The expression refers to the divine gift of the good and beauty in many texts, including those of Theognis and Euripides.[118]

John Pairman Brown notes several other close parallels with Qoheleth coming from Greek literature. Two of these include the important statements: "everything comes from the dust, and everything returns to the dust" (3:20; Gen. 3:19; Xenophanes, *Frag.* 27; Lucretius 2.999-1000; Euripides, *Frag.* 195), and "eat, drink, and rejoice" (Qoh. 9:7; Tob. 7:10; Luke 12:19; Aristobulus of Alexandria, *Athenaeus* 12.530AB: *esthie, pine, paize,* written on a monument of Sardanapallus [= Ashurbanipal?] in Cilicia).

From the composite of evidence we have, the testament of Qoheleth may be a collection of reflections of a Hellenistic Jewish sage who, likely wealthy, engaged in the education of children of some of the Jewish aristocracy within the city and outlying areas of Jerusalem. While well versed in the traditions of wis-

---

118. Braun, *Kohelet,* 55. He notes that the majority of similarities derive from Greek literary and philosophical texts that deal with tragedy and pessimism.

dom in ancient Israel and Judah, Qoheleth appears to have been knowledgeable of Greek culture and philosophy, at least in a very general way.[119] Hellenistic teachings find their expression in his book, including the important place given to fate and determinism and the conclusion that death in the tomb is the final end of the human journey. His cautious view of cultic religion and the absence of important Jewish views of divine creation and revelation, the Torah, and redemptive history permit the teacher to enter and dwell within a Hellenistic world that is not incompatible with his culture's own expressions of value and religious understanding. He became familiar with the features of Greek paideia and Hellenistic Greek through the impact of the Hellenic world on Israel and Judah. He would have had numerous opportunities to inculcate Greek paideia into his thinking, including the school of Greek Skepticism that dominated the New Academy in Athens. In addition, traveling sophists would have likely made their way into the eastern colonies and kingdoms and presented their teachings to people receptive to Hellenistic culture and thought. This pervasive influence of Hellenism in the Jewish world of Judah and the Diaspora is also reflected in the writings of numerous Hellenistic Jews, including Aristobulus, who lived several generations after Qoheleth, wrote the first Greek commentary on the Torah, argued that the great Greek philosophers (including Pythagoras, Socrates, and Plato) learned of the one universal God from Moses, and concluded that "all philosophers agree that it is necessary to hold devout convictions about God, something our (Jewish) school prescribes particularly well."[120]

The Struggle with Hellenism in Jerusalem

The Jewish encounter with Hellenism in Jerusalem produced varied reactions, ranging from wholesale adoption to complete rejection.[121] Zenon's visit of Jerusalem circa 259 B.C.E. led him to depict it as a provincial temple city with a rather politically and commercially small area making up its domain. We know from elsewhere that the most influential and wealthiest Jew from the period was the brother-in-law of the high priest Onias II, Tobias, who resided in a military colony in Jordan and not, as did his son Joseph, in Jerusalem. Joseph was the first financial banker from outside Palestine who took up residence in the

119. Braun, *Kohelet.*

120. Carl R. Holladay, *Fragments from Hellenistic Jewish Authors*, vol. 3: *Aristobulus* (SBLTT 39; Pseudepigrapha 13; Atlanta: Scholars Press, 1995) 70-75. Hengel refers to another Jewish scholar who, several decades later, tells King Ptolemy that the God of the Jews "is the overseer and creator of all, whom all men worship including ourselves . . . except that we have a different name." See Hengel, "Judaism and Hellenism Revisited," in *Hellenism in the Land of Israel*, 21.

121. In general see Hengel, "Jerusalem," 128-32.

temple city, thus underscoring its increasing cosmopolitan and influential status in the Greek world. The knowledge of Greek culture among most Jews would have been limited until the early second century, since most local Jewish citizens did not enjoy a Greek education in a gymnasium. However, the aristocracy, including people like Qoheleth and the Tobiads, were not hostile to the new civilization, but rather were inquisitive, worldly, and open-minded regarding its culture and ideas.[122] Furthermore, the radical rejection of images was not enforced when it came to the minting and use of Greek coins that had images of rulers (especially Ptolemy I and his wife Bernice with the topographic reference of Yehud), while the zeal for the Torah is not present in the family of Tobias, the writings of Josephus, and the testament of Qoheleth. These suggest a Jerusalem with a rather religiously, socially, and culturally diverse Jewish and non-Jewish population.

Eventually, this situation became more openly conflictual. An important segment of the lower class priestly and lay social stratum engaged in religiosocial strife over hellenization's influence, eventuating in the revolution against Antiochus IV Epiphanes. The Jewish communities of the Diaspora and the party of the Hellenists in Jerusalem were not the primary initiators of this revolt, but rather the less cosmopolitan Jews in the smaller cities, towns, and villages in the countryside. In the prelude to Seleucid rule and the Jewish revolt, Qoheleth's criticisms of traditional Jewish beliefs and practices are well understood. His teachings would have been directed not simply against the wisdom of the past, represented by the book of Proverbs, but also toward sapiential, priestly, and apocalyptic contemporaries who wrote and taught during the same cultural and political climate in which he lived. Indeed, what he teaches echoes many of the issues discussed in the Hellenistic Jewish writings of the time.

A Jewish poet who wrote in Judah close to the period of Qoheleth (third to second century B.C.E.), Theodotus, composed an epic poem, *On the Jews*.[123] Eight fragments have survived with 47 hexameter lines. Each of these partial sections includes a prose introduction serving as a summary. The first-century B.C.E. Greek historian Alexander Polyhistor preserved these fragments, which were included in Eusebius, *Praep. ev.* 9.22.1-11, under the heading of "Jacob." These stories cover a variety of themes, including the rape of Dinah at Shechem

---

122. See ibid., 129.

123. In general see John J. Collins, "The Epic of Theodotus and the Hellenism of the Hasmoneans," *HTR* 73 (1980) 91-104; Francis T. Fallon, "Theodotus," *OTP* 2:785-793; Carl F. Holladay, *Fragments from Hellenistic Jewish Authors 2. Poets: The Epic Poets Theodotus and Philo and Ezekiel the Tragedian* (SBLTT 30; Pseudepigrapha Series 12; Atlanta: Scholars Press, 1989) 151-204. It is possible that Theodotus was a Samaritan Jew.

(Gen. 33:18–34:31),[124] the divine revelation of the unchangeable Torah, moral behavior, and circumcision. God is also the one who reveals his will and activity in prophetic oracles and oversees retributive justice.[125] Qoheleth's testament stands in contrast to this epic poem, especially in the rejection of retribution and the silence concerning both the Torah (except by the second voice) and circumcision.

A second Jewish poet of the late third or early second century B.C.E. who wrote in Greek was Philo the Poet.[126] His probable residence in Jerusalem is based on his detailed description of the water system in the city. He appears to have been the Philo mentioned in Josephus (*C. Ap.* 1.218) and Clement of Alexandria (*Strom.* 1.14.3). Six fragments of his epic poem *On Jerusalem*, consisting of twenty-four hexameter verses, survive in Eusebius (*Praep. ev.* 9.17.1–19.3), who copied them from Alexander Polyhistor. The stories include two that refer to Abraham, one that speaks of God's blessing of the patriarchs and Joseph in particular, and three more that describe Jerusalem and its water supply. The reference to Abraham is in the form of a panegyric (cf. Sir. 44:19-21; cf. Wis. 10:5). The themes include Israel as the chosen people and the "blessed dwelling place" (likely Jerusalem). This epic poem tells the story of the Jews and Jerusalem and praises them. These emphases find no place in Qoheleth, but the work of this Philo does testify to the existence of Greek literature in Eretz Israel in a period close to that of Qoheleth.

Writing during the second century B.C.E., the Greek historian Eupolemus appears to have been Jewish (see Eusebius, *Hist. eccl.* 6.13.7; Jerome, *Vir. ill.* 38), in spite of Josephus's denial (*C. Ap.* 1.218). He wrote during the period of the early Maccabees.[127] According to 1 Macc. 8:17, Eupolemus, the son of John, the son of Accos, served as an envoy along with Jason, the son of Eleazar, to Rome during or just before 160 B.C.E. in order to negotiate a treaty of friendship between the two countries. Holladay suggests that his major writing was probably called *Concerning the Kings in Judea.* The first four fragments were likely preserved by Alexander Polyhistor in *On the Jews* (c. mid-first century B.C.E.),[128]

---

124. This topic is found also in the books of Judith, Jubilees, and the Testament of Levi, all three of which derive from Eretz Israel in the third-first centuries B.C.E.

125. See Fallon, "Theodotus," 788.

126. Harold W. Attridge, "Philo the Epic Poet," *OTP* 2:781-84; Yehoshua Gutman, "Philo the Epic Poet," *Scripta Hierosolymitana* 1 (Jerusalem: Magnes, 1954) 36-63.

127. For an overview see Attridge, "Historiography," 162-66; Robert Doran, "Jewish Hellenistic Historians before Josephus," *ANRW* 2.20/1:263-70. See the detailed study by B. Z. Wacholder, *Eupolemus: A Study of Judaeo-Greek Literature* (Cincinnati: Hebrew Union College–Jewish Institute of Religion, 1974).

128. Alexander Polyhistor wrote a treatise concerning the Jews that was cited by Jewish, Samaritan, and Gentile writers (esp. Eusebius, *Praep. ev.* 9.17-39; see Stern, *Greek and Latin Authors,* 157-66).

which were then incorporated by Eusebius into his *Praep. ev.* 9. Although in an altered form, these four fragments are also preserved by Clement of Alexandria. There are parallels to the panegyric to the Hasidim in Sir. 44–50. The first fragment is dedicated to Moses, the second to the prophets from Moses through Samuel and the reigns of David and Solomon and the building of the temple, the third to Solomon's decoration of the temple with golden shields and his death, and the fourth to the apocryphal prophecy of Jeremiah about the Babylonian captivity. A fifth fragment, found only in Clement, presents a chronology from Adam to the fifth year of Demetrius and the twelfth year of Ptolemy (c. 40 B.C.E.).[129] These fragments suggest that he was a Jewish scholar associated with the leaders of the Maccabean revolt and knowledgeable of the larger Hellenistic world. While his text was composed in a rather poor Greek, his encomium and apology extol the glories of the Jewish people, heroes, and institutions.[130] His recounting of Jewish history and institutions, including especially the temple and the kingships of David and Solomon, called to mind the glories of the Jewish past and presented its features to pagan readers. While remarking that the Jews were opposed to idolatry, Eupolemus does not criticize the Greeks. His writing points to the influence of Hellenistic culture on the Jews of Eretz Israel during and following the Maccabean revolt.[131] The emphasis on Solomon points to his continuing importance in Jewish tradition, and parallels Qoheleth's fictional authorship. However, the content and form of Eupolemus are quite different from Qoheleth.

Social Features: Sages and Social Setting

While information is sketchy, there is little doubt that schools of several kinds existed in Eretz Israel, beginning in the First Temple period and lasting well into the period of the Roman Empire.[132]

---

129. Eupolemus joins other writers who wrote in Greek and glorified their national traditions. Among them are Manetho of Egypt, Berossus of Babylon, Philo of Byblos (or his source, Sanchuniathon), and Hecataeus of Greece.

130. Holladay, *Fragments*, 1:95. Also see Sir. 44–50.

131. Attridge, "Historiography," 163.

132. See esp. H. L. Strack and Günter Stemberger, *Introduction to the Talmud and Midrash*, trans. Markus Bockmuehl (2nd ed.; Minneapolis: Fortress, 1996) 8-14. Also see Eliezer Ebner, *Elementary Education in Ancient Israel during the Tannaitic Period* (New York: Bloch, 1956); Haim Z. Dimitrovsky, ed., *Exploring the Talmud*, vol. 1: *Education* (New York: Ktav, 1976).

Hellenistic and Jewish Schools

Of course, familial education was one form that continued,[133] but tutors and institutional schools also existed. Some fathers, who were responsible for the education of sons, would seek on occasion to hire teachers to enable the youth to memorize and even read the Torah.

In the first century B.C.E. we have schools established in Eretz Israel (cf. *p. Ket.* 8.11, 32c) during the reign of Salome Alexandra (76-67), the wife of Alexander Janneus who became queen following her husband's death. Other references to schools for young boys in the first century C.E. (*b. B. Bat.* 21a) and in the second (*b. Sanh.* 17b) are mentioned in the comment that sages were forbidden to dwell in towns and cities that did not have a teacher for the instruction of youth.

The rabbinic literature mentions primary and more advanced schools, beginning with the *bêt sēper,* often connected to the synagogue, when young boys, beginning at six or seven and continuing until twelve or thirteen (*Gen. Rab.* 63.9), were taught to read and write in order to engage in the study of the Torah (*'Abot R. Nat.* A6 [Schechter ed. 29]; *Meg.* 3.1, 74a; *Lev. Rab.* 7.3). Among the methods for learning were reading aloud (*b. 'Erub.* 53b-54a) and repetition (*b. Ḥag.* 9b).[134] The more advanced school was the *bêt midrāš,* normally attached to the synagogue (Sir. 51:23; cf. 33:16-19), where older students studied tradition and halakah, learned to interpret the Torah, and were taught to compose and present synagogue homilies. Since the academy *(bêt midrāš)* was in existence during the lifetime of Ben Sira, who taught and wrote perhaps two generations after Qoheleth, it is likely that the latter taught in some type of school (Qoh. 12:9). Whether it was a Torah school or one more open to Hellenistic paideia is difficult to know. However, it is likely that the latter is the case.

On the basis of the epilogue, Qoheleth likely studied and later taught in a school that was influenced by Hellenistic paideia.[135] While gymnasia were usually limited to access by citizens of Greek cities where they were located, schools of rhetoric were more common and did not require citizenship of their students. The first mention of a Jewish gymnasium is 2 Macc. 4:7-22, when the

---

133. According to *Sipre Deut.* 46, the father teaches his son in sacred language. Girls did not receive instruction (see *m. Soṭ.* 3.4).

134. Strack and Stemberger, *Introduction to Talmud and Midrash,* 9.

135. See Hock, "Paul and Graeco-Roman Education," 198-227. In addition, see Cribiore, *Writing, Teachers, and Students;* idem, *Gymnastics of the Mind;* Morgan, *Literate Education;* Kah and Scholz, *Hellenistische Gymnasion.* Our best source for Greco-Roman education is Plutarch (c. 46-119 C.E.), who has four tractates on education. See Giuliano Pisani, *Plutarco, L'educazione* (Pordenone: Edizioni Biblioteca dell'Imagine, 1994).

high priest Jason sought to transform Jerusalem into a Greek polis. Jason's plan was to make it possible for Jerusalem to receive the coveted status of a Greek polis, meaning that the gymnasium he constructed would have provided its students a Greek education. He also paid a large sum to Antiochus IV for the citizens of Jerusalem (or perhaps a more limited Hellenistic Jewish group) to receive the title of citizens of Antioch. Prior to the reign of Antiochus IV Epiphanes (175-163 B.C.E.), however, there is no reference to a gymnasium in the Jewish literature. In addition, none of the material culture in Eretz Israel points to one. But some type of education in Greek language and culture must have existed. This is indicated by the number of Greek forms used by Ben Sira and the presence of Greek epigraphic materials and texts from Eretz Israel from the Hellenistic period.[136] Some Greek paideia could have been taught by wandering sophists, but they would have needed a receptive audience composed of people in Israel who sought this type of learning and knew Greek.

The major instrument for the hellenization of the eastern colonies and states of the Greek empires was paideia. Thus the medium for paideia and the hellenization of the East was the school. While entrance to these gymnasia was normally limited to Greeks and Hellenes whose parents were born in the polis, it is likely that Jewish schools in these Hellenistic cities adopted some of the Greek curriculum and structure of education that issued from the Greek schools. These Greek schools were divided into primary, secondary, and tertiary levels. The curriculum consisted of a variety of subjects, ranging from the linguistic skills of reading, writing, and grammar to rhetoric (including the composition and delivery of speeches), to the study of literature, philosophy, the sciences, medicine, music, math, and athletics. At the highest level and the postgraduate education of the *ephebeion,* specializations in a variety of professions were offered.

But what of Jewish schools influenced by Hellenism in both Eretz Israel and the Diaspora?[137] As noted, in 2 Macc. 4:7-22 Jason established a gymnasium and an *ephebeion* in Jerusalem, following his purchase of the office of the high priest from Antiochus IV Epiphanes, thus removing his brother, Onias III, who was the legitimate holder of the position. The school, based on a Greek model, was constructed near the citadel at the northwest corner of the temple. Since education was closely connected to the religious and political life of the polis, this meant for Jerusalem that Jason, as high priest, would have had enormous

---

136. A. A. Fischer understands Qoheleth to be a school book (*Skepsis oder Furcht Gottes* [BZAW 247; Berlin: de Gruyter, 1997]).

137. Doran, "High Cost," 94-115. Other important studies are those by Nilsson, *Hellenistiche Schule;* Marrou, *History of Education;* Kah and Scholz, *Hellenistische Gymnasion.* Also see Delorme, *Gymnasion,* 253-315; Pélékidis, *Histoire de l'Éphebie.*

power over the city and would have exerted significant influence in shaping the religious, political, and cultural life of both the urban population and those living elsewhere in Judah. He only had to transform Jerusalem into a polis by making it into a Greek center for Jewish life to succeed in his ambitions. However, there was substantial resistance to his efforts at hellenization, as evidenced in particular by the Maccabean revolt (167-164 B.C.E.), which opposed a forced acceptance of Hellenism and the forbidding of significant Jewish religious practices and customs.

In the Diaspora, some Jews attended Jewish schools that were influenced by Hellenistic paideia. Some wealthy Jews, who were granted citizenship in some of the eastern cities, also appear to have attended gymnasia. This may have been the case with Philo Judaeus, who belonged to one of the most prominent families in Alexandria. Philo speaks of education ("encyclical training") of wealthy families in several places in his writings (*Spec.* 2.230; *Prov.* 2.44-46; *Congr.* 74-76).[138] According to Philo, *enkyklios paideia* refers to education in the liberal arts and the sciences. His writings give evidence both to his study of Greek philosophy, language, grammar, rhetoric, literature, mathematics, astronomy, and music, and engagement in physical activity. Thus it is likely that he received an education in a gymnasium. His Jewish family would have instructed him at an early age, and later they employed "divinely gifted men" (*Spec.* 1.314) to teach him. Thus as his writings indicate, he knew the Tanakh and traditions passed down by the "elders of the nation" (*Mos.* 1.4).[139] His exegetical method was allegory, a hermeneutic that flourished in some writings of the Greeks of his period.

He also speaks of "Sabbath schools" in *Mos.* 2.216: "The Jews every seventh day occupy themselves with the philosophy of their fathers, dedicating that time to the acquiring of knowledge and the study of the truths of nature. For what are our places of prayer throughout the cities but schools of prudence and courage and temperance and justice and also of piety, holiness and every virtue by which duties to God and men are discerned and rightly performed?" In *Opif.* 128 he notes the divine requirement to dedicate the Sabbaths to philosophy "with a view to the improvement of character and submission to the scrutiny of conscience." In this setting the faithful focus on "theoretical" issues on the Sabbath: duty to God and duty to others. These lead to the "knowledge and perfection of the mind" (*Spec.* 2.63-64).[140]

---

138. See esp. Harris, *Greek Athletics;* Mendelson, *Secular Education.*

139. Barclay, *Jews in Mediterranean Diaspora,* 161.

140. A list of *ephēboi* from the early Roman period includes Jewish names (Robert, "Corpus des Inscriptions Juives," 73-86).

In *Vita* 7-12 Josephus speaks of his education and describes his intellectual development in the conventions of Greco-Roman society. Thus he extols his intellectual prowess even as a youth, who at the age of fourteen was approached by the wise men of his city to seek his counsel. He indicates that at sixteen he entered into an extensive philosophical study in the major Jewish schools of the day: Pharisees, Sadducees, and Essenes. This was followed, so he says, by becoming the disciple of an ascetic teacher, Bannus, in the Wilderness of Judea.[141]

It is clear from existing literary sources that Jewish assimilation into the surrounding Hellenistic and later Roman world was a decision made by many Jews in both the Diaspora and Judea.[142] While there is no explicit evidence that Qoheleth attended a gymnasium, he became familiar with popular Greek philosophy, most likely knew Greek, and appears to describe the structure and architecture of the Hellenistic villa (2:4-8). Many of his themes and literary sayings have strong parallels with Greek literature. Taken together, a reasonably plausible case may be made that Qoheleth came to know the Greek world through some sort of scholastic or tutorial environment.

The Symposium

Another Greek social setting, in addition to schools (gymnasia and schools of rhetoric), may be reflected in Qoheleth's frequently stated emphasis on "eating and drinking" as one of the sources in human living. Indeed, the teacher's emphasis on "carpe diem" fits well the social institution of the symposium, which was central to Greek life.[143] The symposium, which appeared in pre-Classical Greece and as early as the Sumerian period in the third millennium in southern Mesopotamia and continued well into the history of the Roman Empire, even had parallels with, if not origins in, similar festive meals from the East. Bonhomie and the establishment of close bonds between the participants were the

---

141. Steve Mason, *Josephus and the New Testament* (2nd ed.; Peabody, MA: Hendrickson, 2003).

142. Tcherikover, *Hellenistic Civilization,* 352.

143. The best description is Xenophon's *Symposium,* a dialogue occurring in the context of an Athenian supper party. The key elements in this case included drinking, flute playing, a dancing girl from Syracuse, and most importantly the "table talk" of Socrates. For a brief overview see Oswyn Murray, "Symposium," *OCD* 1461. Also see William J. Slater, ed., *Dining in a Classical Context* (Ann Arbor: University of Michigan Press, 1991); Oswyn Murray, "The Greek Symposium in History," in *Tria Corda. Scritti in onore di Arnaldo Momigliano,* ed. Emilio Gabba (Como: Edizioni Nuova, 1983); idem, "The Symposium as Social Organisation," in *The Greek Renaissance of the Eighth Century B.C.: Tradition and Innovation,* ed. Robin Hägg and N. Marinatos (Stockholm: Svenska institutet i Athen, 1983) 195-99.

central features and purposes of these meals. The symposium (*symposion*, lit. "drinking together"), a "drinking party," was a scripted social gathering where men drank together, conversed, and enjoyed themselves in a setting that enhanced conviviality. Many topics were discussed and debated in this social setting, including those of philosophy. Greek poetry at times was written for reading at the symposia, while philosophers recruited their disciples, discussed the formation and curricula of schools, and set forth their teachings within this context. Dining became the means by which conversation and behavior occurred that conformed to the highest cultural traditions of a society. The terms for this decorum included *euphrosynē* ("merriment"), *charis* ("elegance"), and, for the poets, *eunomia* ("good order"), while the philosophers stress *koinōnia* ("community/fellowship") and *philanthrōpia* ("benevolence, courtesy").[144] Entertainment, in addition to festive eating and drinking, could be presented by performers, dancers, and magicians. Indeed, the Greeks and later the Romans celebrated their own formulation of carpe diem, or "eat, drink, and be merry, for tomorrow you die." In the celebration of life, there is the defiance of death.[145]

Normally, participants wore garlands and reclined (one or two) on a couch in a room designed to hold seven to fifteen couches with cushions and low tables. Many such rooms have been identified archaeologically in domestic households. The best representation is found on the richly decorated walls of the Tomb of the Diver at Paestum.[146]

The Sage (Sophos) *in the Hellenistic World*

The sophists became important educators in Greece as early as the mid-fifth century B.C.E. They were usually itinerant teachers traveling throughout Greece and the later Hellenistic empire, offering lectures on a number of wide-ranging subjects, teaching the main features of the important philosophies, and even becoming tutors of wealthy patrons who hired them to teach their young.[147] In Athens the sophists became the primary educators by the beginning of the Classical Age. This resulted in three developments. First, they became teachers in the circles of higher education (the Academy, the Lyceum, and the schools of

144. Slater, "Introduction," in *Dining*, 3.

145. Ibid., 4.

146. R. Ross Holloway, "The Tomb of the Diver," *American Journal of Archaeology* 110 (2006) 365-88.

147. See *OCD*, 1422. None of their original writings has survived, leaving us with only references to them in Greek literature. For an overview of the sophists, see Kerferd, *Sophistic Movement*.

the rhetoricians). Second, they eventually became associated with a particular type of philosophy (Stoic, Epicurean, Skeptical, and Pythagorean). Third, they became the models of virtue for emulation by their students.[148]

Egypt is another region important for understanding the sage in the cultural world of Qoheleth. "The Sayings Collection of Ankhsheshonqy" is a collection of proverbs written in demotic script that may date from the third century b.c.e.[149] It bears similarities in themes and forms to "The Instruction of Ahiqar,"[150] Ben Sira, and Greek *gnomologia*. Like Ahiqar, the sayings of this teacher to his son are positioned within a narrative that tells of Ankhsheshonqy's imprisonment for having plotted the death of the king.

Two other sayings collections are "The Teaching of Papyrus Insinger" and "The Teaching of Pordjel," which is given by a scribe to his "beloved son."[151] A conservative text, the latter instruction contains significant themes, including controlling the passions, avoiding intercourse with a married woman, keeping good company, and honoring the god and the master and giving them their due. The Papyrus Insinger contains twenty-five numbered teachings arranged according to subject matter.[152] Central to this last text is the idea of balance that is important for understanding cosmic and social order. Like Qoheleth, this sage teaches that the deity is inscrutable. However, it differs from Qoheleth in that in this Egyptian text divine justice is not brought into question. Other themes comparable to Qoheleth include moderation, the contrast between the wise person and the fool, and personified Fate and Fortune.[153] This teaching reflects a popular form of Greek philosophy, in particular Stoicism and Epicureanism.

---

148. George B. Kerferd, "The Sage in Hellenistic Philosophical Literature," in *Sage in Israel*, 319-28. See esp. F. L. Vatai, *Intellectuals in Politics in the Greek World from Early Times to the Hellenistic Age* (London: Croom Helm, 1984); Long and Sedley, *Hellenistic Philosophers*.

149. In general see Lichtheim, *AEL* 3:159-84; idem, *Late Egyptian Wisdom Literature*, 13-92; Burkard, *TUAT* 3: *Weisheitstexte*, 2:222-50; Brunner, *Die Weisheitsbücher der Ägypter*, 257-91. Also see Heinz-Josef Thissen, *Die Lehre des Anchscheschonqi (P.BM 10508)* (Papyrologische Texte und Abhandlungen 32; Bonn: Habelt 1984). On the script see Williams, "Egyptian Wisdom Literature," 397.

150. The sayings are placed within a narrative that tells of Ankhsheshonqy's imprisonment for having plotted the death of the king.

151. See Lichtheim, *Late Egyptian Wisdom Literature*, 93-106. Also see *TUAT* 3: *Weisheitstexte*, 2:277-80.

152. Lichtheim, *AEL* 3:184-217; idem, *Late Egyptian Wisdom Literature*, 107-234; Burkhard, *TUAT* 3: *Weisheitstexte*, 2:280-319; Brunner, *Weisheitsbücher der Ägypter*, 295-349.

153. See Williams, "Egyptian Wisdom Literature," 397.

Jewish Scribes in the Hellenistic World

The Hellenistic period witnessed a substantial increase in the scribes who served in administrative and public positions. This led to the composition of numerous texts and categories of inscriptions. Greek was well known in Judah and became the lingua franca for official, literary, and commercial writings, while Aramaic was the local dialect. Hebrew continued to be the religious language for worship and the composition of some literature. Qoheleth would have read and studied Jewish literature written in Hebrew and Greek, and he appears to have read earlier Greek texts. He likely taught aristocratic youth in a private Jewish school he would have operated, possibly in his house.[154] These youth, once they received their education, became government officials and administrators, accountants, scribes, lawyers, and clerks. He addressed his students with the term of familiarity, "youth" (bāḥûr, 11:9). The activities of Qoheleth as a teacher and scribe are listed in 12:9-10. These include "weighing" (i.e., "evaluating," 'izzēn), "seeking out" (ḥiqqēr), and "ordering" (tiqqēn) "many sayings" (mĕšālîm harbēh). Thus he assayed the wisdom he collected in order to determine its authenticity and truth.

The Editor as a Scribe

Finally, one hears a second voice in the book, especially in the epilogue (12:9-14) and 11:9b.[155] This suggests a piety issuing from traditional wisdom that taught obedience to the Torah, the "fear of God" (yir'at hā'ĕlōhîm), moral obedience, and retribution.[156] Qoheleth's skepticism and excessive reading and writing that are wearisome toil become the basis for the editors' countermeasures and warnings issued to the students who read Qoheleth. Instead, they should study the Torah and the sayings of the sages, while being aware of divine judgment.

---

154. See Christine Schams, *Jewish Scribes in the Second-Temple Period* (JSOTSup 291; Sheffield: Sheffield Academic Press, 1998) 73-83.

155. See, e.g., Walther Zimmerli, "Das Buch des Predigers Salomo," in Helmer Ringgren and Zimmerli, *Sprüche/Prediger* (ATD 16/1; Göttingen: Vandenhoeck & Ruprecht, 1962) 123-251. The editor was a traditional scribe whose theology was similar to Ben Sira's. In general see Roland E. Murphy, "The Sage in Ecclesiastes and Qoheleth the Sage," in *Sage in Israel*, 263-71.

156. Gerald Sheppard, *Wisdom as a Hermeneutical Construct* (BZAW 126; Berlin: de Gruyter, 1980) 126.

Major Theological Themes

The age in which the teacher writes is one of growing skepticism, taking form in both Hellenistic Skepticism and in some of the Egyptian wisdom literature written in the formal conventions of grave autobiographies. Hellenistic Skepticism, both from Greece and Egypt, was to have a significant impact on the culture in which Qoheleth wrote; and numerous ideas, unknown to Jewish thinking in earlier times, were cultivated by these foreign texts. These ideas included the denial of the Olympian gods, practical atheism that denied the gods were active in human affairs or that they truly mattered in human life, the inability to find a plausible epistemology that would identify truth and empirical data, the emphasis on equilibrium deriving from the recognition of the principle of constancy and the rejection of overemphasis on any particular passion or pursuit, and the view that tranquility derives from human activities that were in essence the simplicities of life. The joyful celebration of life, before the eternal night descended upon human life, was encouraged. These ideas found a ready recipient in Qoheleth.

Skepticism

The skeptical tradition, which is particularly strong in Egypt in the Hellenistic period, is paralleled by Greek Skepticism in literature and philosophy that became especially important during the same period.[157] While the rule of the Ptolemies over Eretz Israel (301-198 B.C.E.) was not only peaceful but also apparently popular among contemporary Jews until the later period of its hegemony over Judah,[158] some skepticism penetrated the Jewish worldview at the same time. This is particularly true of Qoheleth. While apocalyptic was emerging in the late Persian and then Hellenistic periods and offering a hopeful view of resurrection and an afterlife, it was given birth by the view that the current world was corrupt and in the control of demonic forces incarnated in the rule of Judah by foreign empires.

With one possible exception, the "Instruction of Agur" (Prov. 30:1-4), the skepticism present in Qoheleth is unparalleled in the Jewish Bible. But the strong presence of skepticism in Qoheleth may be paralleled by Greek and Egyptian literature, philosophy, and epitaphs. Skepticism became strong in Greek philosophical thought, poetry, and tragedy, which also finds its kinship

---

157. In general see Long, *Hellenistic Philosophy.*
158. Tcherikover, *Hellenistic Civilization*, 59-75. See Polybius 5.86.10.

with this Jewish testament. Greek literary compositions, in particular tragedies, contain a strain of skepticism that is analogous to the thought of Qoheleth. Similarities to Qoheleth from Greek sources include the following views: (1) justice avails nothing; (2) truth (or authentic wisdom) cannot be obtained; (3) both sides of a contention may be equally argued; (4) the outcome of an action cannot be previously known; (5) the gods are capricious, far removed from human perception and experience, and cannot be known; (6) the human quest to determine the good is doomed, epistemologically speaking; (7) the brevity of life ends in eternal death; and (8) human life is subject to fate.[159]

The term in Greek, *skeptikos,* means an "inquirer" who, doubting the veracity of current knowledge that led to truth, continued to search for the verifiable and authentic. Skepticism is found in Greek literature as early as Homer's heroic characters (c. 750 B.C.E.) who lived lives that were of short duration in contrast to the eternity of the cosmos.[160] Their "fortune" was determined by a capricious Zeus.[161] The poet Hesiod (c. 700 B.C.E.) composed literature that also was filled with skepticism, for he pointed to social oppression and penury due to the capricious gods' support of evil over good.[162] The one pursuit that humans could follow that provided meaning was investment in human celebration and moral living and creations of art and philosophy. Sophocles and Euripides (contemporaries in the fifth century B.C.E.) also depicted the skepticism that increased during the Classical Age. Sophocles depicted the gods as unknowable, while tragedy enabled people to become truly human. Euripides held the classical myths in disdain, for they depicted the gods as unjust and capricious. While the gods ignored human efforts, humans were irrational creatures subject to chance and disorder whose tragic ends resulted from their disorder and lack of reason.

While at times Skepticism entered schools of Greek philosophy, including the Cynics, the Stoics, the Epicureans, it developed its own distinct school of thought eventually in the Academy of Plato.[163] Empirical in its approach to

---

159. See Braun, *Kohelet,* 56-66; Hans Peter Müller, "Plausibilitätsverlust herkömmlicher Religion bei Kohelet und den Vorsokratikern," in *Gemeinde ohne Tempel Community,* ed. Beate Ego, Armin Lange, and Peter Pilhofer (WUNT 118; Tübingen: Mohr Siebeck, 1999) 99-113; Reinhold Bohlen, "Kohelet im Kontext hellenistischer Kultur," in *Das Buch Kohelet. Studien zur Struktur, Geschichte, Rezeption und Theologie,* ed. Ludger Schwienhorst-Schönberger (BZAW 254; Berlin: de Gruyter, 1997) 327-62.

160. Wilhelm Nestle, "Der Pessimismus und sein Überwindung bei den Griechen," *Neues Jahrbuch für die klassische Altertumswissenschaft* 24 (1921) 81-97.

161. Braun, *Kohelet,* 15.

162. See Hesiod, *Opera et dies.*

163. Braun, *Kohelet,* 27-31.

knowledge and critical of any epistemology based on reason that could not be verified by experience, Skepticism found adherents who doubted that anything could be regarded as unquestionably true in most areas of knowledge: metaphysics, ethics, the sciences, and religion. Sextus Empiricus, a physician and Pyrrhonist Skeptic (end of the second century C.E.), regarded the goal of skepticism to be "the hope of attaining freedom from disturbance" (*Pyr.* 1.8, 12). What then was the criterion by which to establish and then differentiate between "truth" and "falsity"? This criterion could ultimately not be found. Thus in all matters, save practical reason, it was necessary to suspend judgment (*Pyr.* 1.29).

The Skeptics taught that philosophers are to suspend judgment on the reliability of data derived from the senses and live in reality as it appears, not necessarily as it is. The world (i.e., things as they are) cannot be known by either reason or the senses. The New Academy (269 B.C.E. to the mid-first century C.E.) flourished in Athens by interpreting Plato through the lens of Skepticism. Thus the New Academy would have been one of the leading schools of Greek thought during the period in which Qoheleth likely lived and taught.[164] It largely contended with the Stoics, due to their strong emphasis on reason that permeated the world and human nature and the affirmation that truth could be known. New Academy philosophers set forth the teaching of *akatalēpsia,* the idea that absolute knowledge or truth was impossible to obtain. Two of the early, important heads of the New Academy were Arcesilaus, scholarch from about 268 to 242/41, and Carneades (214/213-129/128).[165]

Skepticism in Qoheleth

With the flourishing of Skepticism in the third century B.C.E., Qoheleth likely would have encountered this philosophy through literature and wandering sophists in Judah. This, coupled with the evidence of epitaphs written in Greek that point to a popular appropriation of themes of Skepticism, including especially the brevity of life, suggests a pervasive influence that would have been available to the sage who portrays himself as Solomon who speaks from the grave.

164. John Glucker, *Antiochus and the Late Academy* (Hypomnemata 56; Göttingen: Vandenhoeck & Ruprecht, 1978); M. Ostwald and John P. Lynch, "The Growth of Schools and the Advance of Knowledge," *CAH* 6:592-633.

165. On Arcesilaus see Schofield, "Academic Epistemology," 32. On Carneades see David N. Sedley, "Academy," *The Oxford Companion to Classical Civilization,* ed. Simon Hornblower and Antony Spawforth (Oxford: Oxford University Press, 1998) 1.

Viewing "the God" as beyond human understanding and realizing that the cosmos was simply the constant, circular movement of wind, rivers, and the rising and setting of the sun (1:4-7), while human generations followed one after another throughout time (1:8-11), the teacher Qoheleth turned to a consideration of human nature in order to discover the "good" that humans could determine and actualize. While they were destined to a brief life that ended in the eternal tomb, Qoheleth still sought a limited good that could be grasped and affirmed as the basis for human existence. The teacher's quest for the "good" in human living (*mah-ṭôb lāʾādām baḥayyîm,* 6:12) was based on his own experience. He sought to find something during the brief life span of human existence ("under the sun") that would provide the basis for knowing and doing. Thus empiricism was the one epistemology, not the teachings of former sages or rational thought, which prompted and sustained Qoheleth's undertaking. This was an ethical search, for morality necessitated a virtue or a criterion for the determination of and differentiation between good and evil as well as an absolute ground for knowledge and behavior. This discovery would also provide the one essential truth that was open to human knowing and living. The "good" was sought in the accomplishment of something that would endure in human memory, including honor, teaching, wisdom, or possessions. However, Qoheleth failed in this pursuit of the unquestionable good. Thus there was no absolute truth based on the good in human life that could provide it a moral center for a course of virtuous living.

Instead, what Qoheleth discovered was that all things open to human acquiring and doing were nothing but *hebel.* The testament begins (1:2) and ends (12:8) with this key expression:

> *hăbēl hăbālîm,* says Qoheleth,
> *hăbēl hăbālîm,* all is *hābel.*

This motif is found 38 times in the testament.[166] The definitions scholars give to the term include:

---

166. Klaus Seybold, *TDOT,* 3:313-20. Seybold gives *hebel* a rather wide semantic range, while Michael Fox has argued that *hebel* in Qoheleth has one overriding meaning: "absurd/absurdity" ("The Meaning of *Hebel* for Qohelet," *JBL* 105 [1986] 409-27). Graham Ogden thinks that *hebel* means "enigmatic" (*Qoheleth* [Sheffield: Almond, 1987] 22). Murphy prefers the meaning "incomprehensible" ("On Translating Ecclesiastes," *CBQ* 53 [1991] 573). Also see Douglas B. Miller, *Symbol and Rhetoric in Ecclesiastes: The Place of Hebel in Qohelet's Work* (Academia Biblica 2; Atlanta: Society of Biblical Literature, 2002), who notes that the word is indeed polyvalent, but in some sense always relates to the key meaning of "vapor."

1. "Vanity," a metaphor for "meaninglessness," or "emptiness."[167]
2. "Absurdity," the difference between what is expected and what occurs.[168]
3. The "irrational" that negates "human actions of significance and undermines morality."[169]
4. That which is inconsistent, unpredictable, and mysterious.[170]
5. "Ephemerality/evanescence," that is, everything quickly passes.[171]

Associated with this key word is the metaphorical phrase, "pasturing the wind" or perhaps better translated, "desiring the spirit" *(rĕʿût/raʿyôn rûaḥ),* which occurs seven times (1:14; 2:11, 17, 26; 4:4, 16; 6:9) and is used to extend the meaning of *hebel.* Thus life and all of its possessions and accomplishments are *hebel* and the "pasturing of the wind/desiring the spirit." The literal meaning of *hebel* is "breath" (Job 7:16; 9:29; Pss. 39:6-7, 12; 62:10; 94:11; 144:4). The metaphor evokes ephemerality or evanescence and is used especially to refer to the brevity of human existence (Qoh. 6:12). The entire expression *hakkōl hebel ûrĕʿût rûaḥ* is to be translated "all is ephemeral and a desire for (life's) vital spirit." While existence and its accomplishments are ephemeral, humans still desire[172] to retain the life-giving breath given them by the creator (Qoh. 12:7; Ps. 104:30). Thus the internal consternation of humans is that they are ephemeral creatures desiring the impossible: to retain the divine spirit that animates human life. Thus a more elegant paraphrase would be: "all is breath quickly passing and a desire to retain life's animating spirit." Even the remembrance of the dead quickly vanishes.

The leitmotif *hebel* ("ephemerality") is followed by the central question of the first section.

What is the *yitrôn* to a person in all his labor,
at which he labors under the sun (1:3)?

---

167. Crenshaw, *Ecclesiastes,* 23; Rudi Kroeber, *Der Prediger* (Schriften und Quellen der Alten Welt 13; Berlin: Akademie, 1963) 122; Lauha, *Kohelet,* 18.

168. Fox, "Meaning of *Hebel,*" 410.

169. Ibid.

170. W. E. Staples, "Vanity of Vanities," *CJT* 1 (1955) 141-56.

171. Seow, *Ecclesiastes,* 112; Kurt Galling, *Prediger Salomon* (HAT 18; Tübingen: Mohr [Siebeck], 1940) 79; Gordis, *Koheleth,* 20; Scott, *Proverbs, Ecclesiastes,* 202; Oswald Loretz, *Qohelet und der alte Orient. Untersuchungen zu Stil und theologischer Thematik des Buches Qohelet* (Freiburg: Herder, 1964) 223. Loretz suggests other meanings as well, including "Gewichtlos-Leichten, Wertlos, Leer, Macht- und Hilflos."

172. In Late Hebrew and Aramaic *rĕāʾ* also means "to take pleasure in, to desire" (Marcus Jastrow, *A Dictionary of the Targumim, the Talmud Babli and Yerushalmi, and the Midrashic Literature* [repr. New York: Judaica, 1985] 1486).

The term *yitrôn* occurs only in Qoheleth and is usually translated "profit" or "advantage." These translations are not correct. The verb *yātar* means "to remain" (1 Sam. 15:15) and also occurs often in the Niphal, "to be left behind, remain," and the Hiphil, "to leave over, leave." Qoheleth desires to find not something that "profits from" or is an "advantage to" living, but rather something that endures beyond death, if only in human memory. Thus *yitrôn* in Qoheleth suggests "continuation" or "endurance."[173] However, when Qoheleth concludes his quest, he finds nothing that continues beyond death. The other important word in this programmatic question (1:3) is *ʿāmāl,* meaning "toil," "labor," and "activity," which for Qoheleth is onerous (2:20). This term occurs thirty-five times in the testament. Seow submits that the word "refers to the routine struggle of humanity to achieve some end or other. Toil is the tiresome effort expended over an enterprise of dubious result."[174]

The Hidden God

Qoheleth assumes the existence of "the God" *(hāʾĕlōhîm),* and portrays him as a tyrant who rules the world in secrecy. While this mysterious deity determines the fate of every person, even the sage cannot find out what his fate will be. The only thing of which the wise person may be certain is that all people, himself included, are destined for the tomb (2:14-16; 9:3). At death everyone returns to the dust *(ʿāpār),* while his spirit *(rûaḥ)* returns to God (3:16-22; 12:7). Humans are weak, intrinsically corrupt, and mortal creatures whose one certainty resides in the recognition that they are destined for the grave. Not the present or coming world, but rather the tomb is humanity's final abode. Death for Qoheleth is oblivion, the complete cessation of every element of life, when there is no memory of the past or awareness of the present. From this fate there is no escape and no return. Death, like coming forth from the womb, naked and without any possession or accomplishment, is the reversal of human birth. Similar to Job in the prologue (Job 1:21), one returns, in death, naked to the place from which one originated (Qoh. 5:14[15]). The grave is the "eternal or enduring home" into which one ultimately enters, never to depart.

Divine decisions are capricious so that every action one undertakes has no relationship to retributive justice. Most importantly, the deity alone decides to whom to give the gift of "joy" *(śimḥâ,* 2:24-26), the one feature of human expe-

173. The word *yitrôn* occurs ten times in Qoheleth (1:3; 2:11, 13, 13; 3:9; 5:8, 15; 7:12; 10:10, 11), *yōtēr* seven times (2:15; 6:8, 11; 7:11, 16; 12:9, 12), and *môtar* once (3:19).

174. Seow, *Ecclesiastes,* 113.

rience that provides its recipient some alleviation from laborious toil or a diversion from meaningless existence. While Qoheleth does not abandon wisdom or advise his students to do so in order to pursue the experience of joy, he does note that "much sagacity adds to vexation, and the increase of knowledge leads to pain" (1:18). What adds to this vexation is that "the God" has placed *hā'ōlām* ("the age") in their hearts, that is, the awareness of the comprehensive structure of time, yet without the ability to understand it or to know when to act successfully (3:1-15). Indeed, the acts and purposes of "the God" occurring within the context of time are beyond human grasp. Hence the ethical life that traditional sages sought, based on the comprehension of the times to know when to act and what to say, was denied them. Also beyond their ability to know were the actions of the God who resided in "heaven" in deep mystery, while humans dwelt on the earth (5:1[2]), or "under the sun" (*taḥat haššāmeš*, 1:14; 2:17-22). This creator is not revealed in nature, human history, priestly Torah, or sapiential teaching.

While humans could engage in foolish actions (especially failing to fulfill their vows, 5:1[2]) that would incite a destructive response from "the God" and thus die before the time that had been determined for them, they could never predict divine action. This mystery of the remote and hidden God, the *deus otiosus*, including both divine nature and activity, led to Qoheleth's loss of confidence in beneficent providence. "The God" is absent from the world of human dwelling, but he still issues unalterable decrees.[175] This deity takes on some of the character of El in Ugaritic mythology, who is removed from human understanding but often still issues decrees that determine what happens among the gods and on earth. Order is not an all-embracing righteousness that permeates the cosmos, but rather is equated with the autocracy of divine rule. For Qoheleth, "the God" is not the just creator and providential guide of cosmos and history, but rather a hidden and capricious deity whose power cannot be challenged. In the sphere of human dwelling wickedness prevails in the place of righteousness (3:16-17). Even those leaders charged with maintaining justice are corrupt and tyrannical.

Qoheleth does not counsel his students to ignore the worship of this unknown God. He submits that humans are to "fear God" (5:6[7]), emphasizing that they should submit to the reality of divine sovereignty. Humanity is not the center of reality, nor are humans the measure of all things.[176] "The God," not

---

175. Qoheleth's reference to God as "the God" *(hā'ĕlōhîm)* may emphasize both the distance of the *deus otiosus* and universal monotheism.

176. Scott, *Proverbs, Ecclesiastes,* 205; Walther Zimmerli, "'Unveränderbare Welt' oder 'Gott ist Gott'?" in *"Wenn nicht jetzt wann dann?" Aufsätze für Hans-Joachim Kraus zum 65. Geburtstag,* ed. Hans-Georg Geyer, et al. (Neukirchen-Vluyn: Neukirchener Verlag, 1983) 103-14.

humanity, rules over creation and directs history, although without any revelation of action or purpose. Unlike "the God," humans are incapable of achieving something lasting, whether accomplishments or fame, that enables them to transcend the limits of human mortality. Finitude weighs heavily upon the human breast, since nothing associated with human being and doing endures. All is breath, quickly passing. Thus is there anything that humans should pursue in directing their existence in a world that is hidden in the dark recesses of apparent futility? To this question Qoheleth responds with the capacity of humans to experience joy obtainable from the conviviality of eating and drinking, the warmth and embrace expressed and experienced in moments of intimacy, and the labor or activity that one pursues.[177] However, even this experience is ultimately contingent on the caprice of "the God." Joy may come only to those who please "the God," but there is no way of existing that Qoheleth can find that is sure to warrant divine favor. Joy is a divine gift that may or may not come. Of course, like the swift passing of life and the abrupt end of human accomplishments, even joy quickly passes.

Death and Carpe Diem

The teaching that derives from his quest for the feature of existence that provides the basis for the good that the teacher discovers within the human capacity to experience is assimilated into the literary design of the testament. This rhetorical structure of Qoheleth envelops the sevenfold occurrence of the carpe diem (lit. "seize the day"): 2:24-26; 3:12-13, 22; 5:17-19; 8:15; 9:7-10; and 11:7-10.[178] The teacher issues the first five occurrences on the basis of his personal experience that comes from his quest for the good in human living. In the last two, however, he exhorts his students in second and third person admonitions. What should be noticed in the rhetorical organization of the testament is the interlude in 6:1-9, which speaks of the worthless character of human living, if it is not accompanied by moments of joy. Wealth, possessions, honor, numerous offspring, and longevity have no intrinsic value or worth if one does not experience joy.

Thus for Qoheleth the one important thing in human experience is the capacity for joy. Four things provide the potential of joy in human living: labor, eating and drinking, the lover, and youth. Labor appears in Qoheleth to be the

---

177. Robert Gordis, "The Wisdom of Qoheleth," in *Poets, Prophets, and Sages* (Bloomington: Indiana University Press, 1971) 337-38.

178. See Fischer, *Skepsis oder Furcht Gottes?* 137-46.

human activity that gives one some sense of involvement in human productivity, even though nothing that is done can endure. If Qoheleth is an aristocrat speaking to the offspring of the upper echelon of society, then he is addressing the pursuit of tasks that are available only to the wealthy and the life of leisure. Thus one would expect him to specify his affirmation with references to reading, writing, directing an estate, and so forth, although these may only be surmised. Youth is the temporal apogee of the capacity to experience joy, for the senses are not yet dulled by repetition and the decline in their potency. Eating and drinking echo the experience of conviviality, bonding, and the ambience of the male symposium in which feasting and drinking were the central activities, coupled with stimulating conversation, the reading of poetry, entertainment in the form of the performances of dancers and singers, and the warmth of embrace.[179] Finally, taking delight in the lover of one's youth is another occasion for joy.

Even if "the God" does grant one the experience of joy, there are still inherent limitations that point to the limits of this one boon to human existence: no one is able to know what happens on earth after death (3:22), joy serves only as an anesthetic that allows one to escape the despair of a meaningless existence for a brief moment and that makes one temporarily forget the past (5:19[20]), excess may lead to the loss of exuberance in human living, and the sobering realization to which one comes is that the days of darkness are many in contrast to the brief time one is alive.[180] Even so, if joy does come, it should be savored, for it is the one experience that anesthetizes the pain of meaninglessness and the irresistible beckoning of eternal darkness. If it is not fully experienced, then life is indeed without meaning and value. While joy is a rather limited good, it is the one and only good in human living.[181]

179. See Oswyn Murray, ed., *Sympotica: A Symposium on the Symposion* (Oxford: Clarendon, 1994).

180. See Denis Buzy, "La notion du bonheur dans l'Ecclésiaste," *RB* 43 (1943) 494-516.

181. See Whybray, "Qoheleth, Preacher of Joy," 87-98. He notes: "These seven texts are clearly more than mere marginal comments or asides. They punctuate the whole book, forming a kind of leitmotiv; they increase steadily in emphasis as the book proceeds" (p. 88). See also Norbert Lohfink, "Qoheleth 5:17-19 — Revelation by Joy," *CBQ* 52 (1990) 625-35.

6. Apocryphal Wisdom Literature in the Seleucid Empire: The Book of Ben Sira

General Introduction

The Apocrypha or deuterocanonical texts contain two books that in their entirety are sapiential in form and content: Ben Sira (Sirach) and the Wisdom of Solomon. As one might expect, other, less comprehensive wisdom texts are present in other apocryphal books, the most notable being the hymn to Wisdom in Bar. 3:9–4:4. However, my emphasis will be on the two wisdom books from this corpus, beginning in this chapter with Ben Sira.

Hellenization shaped a variety of different cultural blendings of indigenous traditions with elements of Greek civilization through sociopolitical rule, commerce, the location of Greek populations in the Near East, the variety of Hellenistic religions, and above all paideia, taught in the gymnasia and schools of rhetoric that were established in the major poleis of the Greek kingdoms. This enculturation of local and Greek social and cultural conventions led to many different forms of Hellenism in the East and not one universal expression that swept over the nations conquered by Alexander. These heterogeneous cultural, social, and religious expressions were still largely viewed by the Greeks and the elite who held positions of power and wealth as an amalgam in which Greek civilization was viewed as superior to local expressions. Thus for local peoples seeking to advance in the new world of Hellenism, the accommodation to Greek culture and its cultivation proved to be the path to success in the achievement of a highly respected status.

The book of Ben Sira, composed originally in Hebrew, is the first Jewish writing to provide the author's name, pointing to one of the influences of Greek culture on this sapiential Jewish writing. Ben Sira is a "sage" who teaches in a school and possibly a temple scribe who was among the group mentioned by the decree of Antiochus III.[1] As a scribe, Ben Sira adapts his understanding of traditional Judaism to that of Hellenism, both of which were strongly present in the city of Jerusalem by the time of Seleucid rule, which began in 200 B.C.E.

The important appropriation of Greek language and ideas by Ben Sira likely occurred through his teaching as a sage in a Jewish school in a period in which Hellenistic culture permeated the urban sites of Eretz Israel.[2] Greek language, literary forms and grammar, and philosophy enter his world through the administrative and social institutions of Hellenism, the availability of anthologies that presented summaries of philosophical teachings, and perhaps the education offered by sophists who traveled and taught in the cities of the eastern Mediterranean world.[3]

Numerous passages in Ben Sira suggest the plausibility of the sage's knowledge of Greek and important Greek philosophers and literary composers. This is suggested especially by Greek literary expressions and themes that appear to reside behind some of the language and thought expressed in this sage. Possible influence of Greek vocabulary on the Hebrew of Ben Sira includes: *syneidēsis* ("consciousness," "knowledge"), *hybris* ("pride"), *kairos* ("time"), *eukardia* ("good for the heart," "stout heart"), *kardia* ("heart"), *daimōn* or *daimonion* ("power," "divine power"), *moira* ("fate"), *tychē* ("fortune"), *anankē* ("force," "necessity"), *paideia* ("education," "teaching"), *aretē* ("virtue"), *physis* ("nature"), *sōprosynē* ("prudence," "discretion"), *didachē* ("teaching"), and *eusebeia* ("piety"). In addition, one notes several Greek themes and philosophical ideas that appear to have influenced Ben Sira.[4] These include the praise of heroes for their lives of virtue (see Suetonius, *De viris illustribus*), friendship, sexist representation of women, self-control, rhetorical skill, behavior, satisfaction, proper

---

1. Josephus, *Ant.* 12.138-44. See Hengel, *Jews, Greeks, and Barbarians,* 121.

2. Theophil Middendorp, *Die Stellung Jesu Ben Siras zwischen Judentum und Hellenismus* (Leiden: Brill, 1973) 7-34. While some of the parallels are overstated, Middendorp has outlined possible parallels between Ben Sira and Hellenistic texts and ideas.

3. Octave Guéraud and Pierre Jouguet, eds., *Un livre d'écolier du IIIe siècle avant J.-C.* (Publications de la Société Fouad I de papyrologie; Cairo: L'Institut français d'archéologie orientale textes et documents 2, 1938).

4. Middeldorp, *Stellung,* 28-31. Others include Johannes Marböck, *Weisheit im Wandel: Untersuchungen zur Weisheitstheologie bei Ben Sira* (BZAW 272; Berlin: de Gruyter, 1999) 267; Raymond Pautrel, "Ben Sira et le Stoïcisme," *RSR* 51 (1963) 535-49. Hengel sees less Greek influence than these scholars (*Judaism and Hellenism,* 1:132-57).

etiquette and decorum, guests, the interpretation of dreams, self-love, the doctor, the superiority of the scribal craft to manual labor, death as a friend, two kinds of shame, contact with slaves, and the intoxication of wine. Especially noteworthy are the parallels with Stoicism: the emphasis on reason (see Sir. 4:23-24; 5:10; 38:5; 44:3; 45:5), creation in which everything has its purpose (39:16, 21b, 33), and the theory of opposites (33:15; 42:24; also see Pythagoras and Heraclitus). Ben Sira adapts Greek cultural and ideological forms and thoughts to fit his understanding of Judaism. Middendorp concludes this section of his study of Ben Sira's relationship to Hellenism and Judaism with the following summation:

1. Ben Sira wrote a schoolbook after a Greek model.
2. He was familiar with Greek and especially schooled in the sayings of Theognis.
3. Traveling outside Judah was a desired activity that parallels the popular tale of Odysseus. Ben Sira himself was well traveled.
4. He was especially familiar with Stoic literature and thought, as well as the Old Testament.
5. Behind a Hebrew idea often stands a concept from Hellenistic literature.
6. The Greek school system must have been a pattern for the school in which Ben Sira taught and offered in the curriculum his compendium of sayings.
7. The nationalism of Ben Sira occurs by going beyond the Stoic concept of world citizenship.
8. The fact of Greek influence points to a time prior to rebellion against Antiochus IV.
9. His knowledge of Greek must have been influential in the composition of the book and its literary text.[5]

The literary forms that he appropriates from Greek literary expression include the panegyric in ch. 24 and the brief narrative list of famous ancestors and their character and activities in chs. 44–50 that parallels the form and function of the encomium. Thus Ben Sira, both conceptually and compositionally, combined Judaism in a traditional form with features of Greek culture, language, and thought to shape his book of teachings directed to young men who were educated in his school in Jerusalem. Thus he chose the middle path that maneuvered between a strong commitment to Hellenism and a conservative reaction against what were considered to be foreign intrusions.

5. Middendorp, *Stellung,* 33-34.

Date and Historical Context

The Identity and Time Period of Ben Sira

This collection of wisdom teachings is known as "The Book (or Instruction) of Ben Sira" (in Hebrew and in rabbinic tradition), "The Wisdom of Jesus, Son of Sira" (Greek), or "Ecclesiasticus" (Latin). The prologue, written by the grandson of Ben Sira, attributes the text to a scholar of the Law, Prophets, and other ancestral books who bore the name of Yeshua. He is also called Simon, ben Yeshua, ben Eleazar, ben Sira in 50:27 (Ms. B). Because of the numerous manuscript differences, 50:27 is problematic. In Ms. B "Simon" is presented as the author, although the more likely place for this name occurs at the end of v. 24, which brings to conclusion the elegy to Simon II. In v. 27 the LXX adds "the one of Jerusalem" in order to clarify the specific author by his location, while the Syriac does not contain this bicolon. When one takes into consideration the name Yeshua in the prologue, the most likely conclusion to be reached would be to identify Eleazar as Ben Sira's father and his grandfather as Sira. The grandson in the prologue indicates that his grandfather combined *paideia* ("education, teaching," "the state of being educated," and a "cultured mind") with *sophia* ("wisdom").

The grandson states in the prologue that in the thirty-eighth year of the reign of Euergetes (i.e., Ptolemy VIII Euergetes II, coregent 170-164, solo reign 145-117 B.C.E., nicknamed Physcon, "basket" or "potbellied") he came to Egypt to study. The thirty-eighth year of Ptolemy VIII's reign is 132, thus allowing one to infer that Ben Sira composed his text sometime between 200 and 175 (prior to the pogrom initiated against practicing Jews by Antiochus IV Epiphanes). Ptolemy VIII had his nephew, Neos Philopator, assassinated in order to claim the throne, since the latter was in line to replace his father. Physcon had ruled as coregent with Ptolemy VI and Cleopatra II (170-164) and as sole ruler in 164-163. Due to the decision of Rome, Physcon was made king of Cyrene in 163. Finally, in 145 he returned to Egypt and claimed the Alexandrian throne. He ruled as king or possibly shared the throne with Cleopatra II and Cleopatra III, his two rival wives, until his death in 117. This reference to Euergetes (Ptolemy VIII Euergetes II) provides the historical basis for dating Ben Sira. It is likely that shortly before 175 Ben Sira, who would presumably have been about 60 at the time, published his lengthy text during the reign of Seleucus IV Philopator (187-175). This would have allowed his grandson, possibly a child when this occurred, to travel to Egypt when he was in his forties (c. 132) and then to translate into Greek and to publish the volume in his sixties (c. 117).[6]

---

6. See the argument by D. S. Williams, "The Date of Ecclesiasticus," *VT* 44 (1994) 563-66.

During his sojourn in what was likely Alexandria, the grandson wrote the prologue in Greek and proceeded to translate his grandfather's book from Hebrew into Greek, resulting in its inclusion in the Alexandrian canon. It is possible that his translation was finished soon after the death of Ptolemy VIII.[7]

The reign of Seleucus IV Philopator, the son of the powerful Antiochus III, began in 187 B.C.E. after the defeat of the father at Magnesia by the Romans in 190 B.C.E. The treaty of Apamea (188) led to the young king, who had ruled briefly as coregent with his aged father, having to renounce any aspirations of conquest west of Taurus in order to proceed further into Asia Minor. The war reparations forced upon him by the terms of the treaty led to his having to obtain funds from his conquered nations, including raiding the temple treasury in Jerusalem. He sent his emissary Heliodorus to the temple, although 2 Macc. 3:7-39 notes he was not allowed into the sanctuary due to an apparition of a rider on a horse. While the reign of Seleucus, restrained financially and politically by the *Pax Romana,* was one of tranquility, the same Heliodorus later assassinated him in a failed attempt to gain the throne. Instead, the younger brother of Seleucus IV, Antiochus IV Epiphanes, became the new king. Thus Ben Sira's teachings would likely have been produced during the reign of Seleucus IV when hostilities due to earlier Seleucid adventurism were at an end. Even so, the sage lived and wrote in a period in Jewish history that had recently witnessed the transition from an increasingly difficult rule of the Ptolemies to another Greek dynasty to the east (200 B.C.E.) in the form of the Seleucid kings, hailed by many Jews as a much desired development.[8] Ben Sira's strong support of the temple and priesthood may have been shaped by the Seleucid raiding of the sanctuary's treasury in order to meet the large indemnity imposed by Rome.

The Seleucid practice of rule was the stationing of garrisons of troops in the various satrapies of the empire. The governance of the satraps was given to the ruling dynast's friends and relatives, who received large land grants for loyal service.[9] The Seleucid rulers also made important military alliances in the form of royal charters. One of these was the one mentioned by Josephus, when Antiochus III came into control of Judah following the victory over the army of

7. This date is suggested by John J. Collins, *Jewish Wisdom in the Hellenistic Age* (OTL; Louisville: Westminster John Knox, 1997) 18; Rudolf Smend, *Die Weisheit des Jesus Sirach erklärt* (Berlin: Reimer, 1906) 3-4; Patrick W. Skehan and Alexander A. Di Lella, *The Wisdom of Ben Sira* (AB; Garden City, NY: Doubleday, 1987) 134.

8. See Gera, *Judaea and Mediterranean Politics;* Susan Sherwin-White and Amélie Kuhrt, *From Samarkhand to Sardis* (Berkeley: University of California Press, 1993); Amélie Kuhrt and Susan Sherwin-White, eds., *Hellenism in the East: The Interaction of Greek and Non-Greek Civilizations from Syria to Central Asia after Alexander* (Berkeley: University of California Press, 1987).

9. Sherwin-White and Kuhrt, *From Samarkhand to Sardis,* 47-48.

Ptolemy V at Paneion in 200 B.C.E. (*Ant.* 12.138-46). Antiochus III in his letter to Ptolemy, son of Thraseas, who was governor of Coele-Syria and Phoenicia, writes that the Jews of Judah warmly received his troops and gave them provisions. In addition, some had supported the Seleucid army in expelling the Egyptian garrison from Jerusalem. As rewards, the Seleucid king restored the sections of the city destroyed in the war and repopulated it with those Jews who had been dispersed to other areas. He supplied their temple with sacrificial animals, wine, oil, and frankincense, which were valued at 20,000 pieces of silver, and fine flour that met the ritual requirements of the Jewish law. In addition, Antiochus decreed that work on the completion of the temple should resume and that the importation of timber for this task should be provided without any toll tax. This was also allowed for other materials needed to make the temple resplendent. In addition, he allowed the Jews to have their own internal form of government in accordance with their own laws. Further, the senate, the priests, the temple scribes, and the temple singers were granted freedom from various taxes imposed on others (poll, crown, and salt). The returnees who came before October of that year were allowed to be exempt from taxes for three years, and they were compensated for their losses. In addition, they would not have to pay a third of their tribute. Finally, those who were taken from the city as slaves were set free, along with their children, and their property was returned. While some cities such as Hierapolis and Jerusalem had to pay royal taxation imposed by the king, they also benefited from royal bequests of money and land.[10] The local priesthoods and their hierarchies were allowed to be hereditary, and the high priest's position was normally not to be questioned. This resulted in the priestly hierarchy's wealth and growth in power and influence. They also were allowed to receive on behalf of the temple significant tithes from Jews in the homeland and in the Diaspora. Cities with prominent temples had high priests with whom the Seleucid administration would correspond. Thus the latter part of Ben Sira's life occurred when Jerusalem was a royal city, received support from the Seleucid dynasty in the form of money and land, and witnessed the enhanced position of the high priesthood. These developments would explain Ben Sira's emphasis on Torah, the temple, and the high priesthood of Simon II. Ben Sira's panegyric to Simon II occurs in ch. 50.

The office of high priest was contested during the period immediately following the death of Simon II in 196 B.C.E. Onias III (c. 190-175) succeeded to the position, although his brother Jason, intent on carrying out a program of hellenization of Judaism especially in Jerusalem, eventually bribed Antiochus IV with 360 talents of silver to give the post to him (2 Macc. 4:7-16), in 175. After

---

10. Ibid., 60-61.

holding the office three years, however, Jason was removed in 172 when Menelaus purchased it with an even larger bribe (2 Macc. 4:23-26). While nothing in Ben Sira suggests that the selling of the office had yet occurred, his growing concern with the disputes developing over the high priestly office are evident (7:4-7; 45:26-27; 50:23-24). The description in 1 and 2 Maccabees of the efforts of Antiochus IV Epiphanes to bring Judaism to its dissolution, including the prohibition of the observance of the Mosaic laws and the setting up of an idol of the Olympian Zeus in the temple, appears to have occurred after the conclusion of Ben Sira's writing and possibly at the end of his life were he still alive.

The Seleucid Empire was divided into a group of hyparchies so that Judah may have had its own native governor *(dioiketēs)*, as did Syria and Egypt, although we cannot be certain.[11] Judah was also likely a royal land, and perhaps was ruled internally by a native governor. Each hyparchy had its own local *oikonomos* that functioned as the local authority within the larger empire. The external Seleucid administration of the hyparchy was headed by a governor, who also held the rank of *stratēgos* and had supreme military control of Judah. He was assisted by a Greek finance minister. The Jewish *gerousia* or council of elders (Heb. *'ēdat šĕbā'îm*) was empowered to deal with legal matters on a local scale according to its own traditions. The high priest may have presided over the *gerousia*, which was likely drawn from the elite of the country. The local priesthood had a great deal of internal power and was responsible to the ruling house of the Seleucids and their administration. With this system, the Seleucids offered to the Jews significant internal authority to handle local matters and allowed them to practice their own laws and traditions. This time of relative tranquility helps to explain why Ben Sira does not offer any criticism of the dynasty or of Hellenistic culture.

Jerusalem during the early period of Seleucid rule was a small temple city, a classification that the Seleucids gave to poleis that had important temples. Jerusalem continued to be the center of all Judaism, although the prominence of the Jewish community in Alexandria was increasing. Joseph and his sons, who were members of the prominent Tobiad family in Ammon (Josephus, *Ant.* 12.160ff.), moved to Jerusalem, perhaps one indication of the increasing hellenization of the city. Increasing hellenization is also indicated by the archaeological excavations in western Jerusalem by Nahman Avigad and of the Temple Mount by Benjamin Mazar.[12] Some of the wealth came from the economic engine of the temple that

11. Tcherikover, *Hellenistic Civilization,* 61-62.

12. Nahman Avigad, *Archaeological Discoveries in the Jewish Quarter of Jerusalem: The Second Temple Period* (Jerusalem: Israel Museum, 1976); Eilat Mazar, et al., *Excavations in the South of the Temple Mount: The Ophel of Biblical Jerusalem* (Qedem 29; Jerusalem: Hebrew University, 1989). Also see Hillel Geva and Nahman Avigad, "Jerusalem" in *The New Encyclopedia of Archaeological*

required faithful Jews to give an annual tax and to travel to the city for pilgrimage festivals. The excavations and multilingual inscriptions point to a culturally diverse city that was increasingly open to Greek culture.

A teacher, Ben Sira ran a boarding school to which the youth of the aristocracy came to study.[13] He mentions his *bêt midrāš* in 51:23, which provided room, board, and instruction for students, presumably for a fee.[14] We do not know the school's location, although the sage's strong support of the priesthood and temple could be taken to suggest it was located near the sanctuary. Ben Sira, as an interpreter of Scripture, would have been involved in deriving the meaning of the Torah.

Judaism in Eretz Israel and Hellenization

Hellenization was the major cultural force in shaping some semblance of unity among the polyglot of nations and cultures brought under Hellenistic hegemony through Alexander's wars of conquest.[15] This unification enhanced the spheres of commerce and political administration, but did not allow indigenous populations, save in very infrequent cases of individuals, to obtain Greek citizenship. The process of hellenizing local cultures still allowed the continuation of indigenous traditions at the same time local peoples were introduced to all things Greek and learned to function socially, politically, and economically with the Greek language and culture. In addition, hellenization was varied, for it took different shapes and forms in the variety of regions where it took root. This process fused Hellenistic culture with non-Greek cultures through the institutions of education and the composition of various genres, including the literary products of Jewish teachers who were familiar with its major writings and philosophies.[16]

Hellenistic culture has been described as a "civilization of *paideia*,"[17] since

---

Excavations in the Holy Land, ed. Ephraim Stern (2nd ed.; 4 vols.; Jerusalem: Simon & Schuster, 1993) 2:698-767; Levine, *Jerusalem*.

13. Robert Gordis, "The Social Background of Wisdom Literature," *HUCA* 18 (1944) 85-86. See Smend, *Weisheit des Jesus Sirach*, xxi.

14. See H. Stadelmann, *Ben Sira als Schriftgelehrter* (WUNT 2/6; Tübingen: Mohr, 1980). He argues that this education was free, basing his interpretation on 51:25, where he understands the teacher to tell his potential students that they may acquire wisdom without gold.

15. For a discussion of the historical and social background, see Hengel, *Judaism and Hellenism*; Tcherikover, *Hellenistic Civilization*.

16. For Ben Sira in the Hellenistic context, see Hengel, *Judaism and Hellenism*, 1:131-53.

17. Marrou, *History of Education*, 95. There is little information about Jewish education in Eretz Israel during Ben Sira's period. The first evidence comes from two legends that are found in

Greek schools were established throughout Alexander's empire. Florilegia, which summarized the major philosophies and literatures of the Greeks, were written for schools in order to teach Hellenism to youth, regardless of their national origins.[18] Yet it is also true that the local traditions shaped the Greek ones that infiltrated their culture, a fact that explains the variety of mixed and integrated cultures throughout the Greek empire. This mixture is noted in the variety of gods worshiped throughout the empire, ranging from the old Olympian deities to those of the new mystery cults. Education was a primary source for hellenization, but only Greeks and those who could prove Greek descent were allowed to enter gymnasia and the *ephebia*. Presumably, the first gymnasium was built in Jerusalem after the time of Ben Sira's publication. However, his grandson, responsible for the prologue, would not only have known of the existence of this gymnasium but also would have seen it and possibly studied in it. As for the sage himself, there appears to be Greek influence on Ben Sira, for his writings suggest a basic knowledge of Hellenistic philosophical thought, although there is no evidence that he could read Greek.[19] However, one cannot imagine that a teacher in Jerusalem during the first quarter of the second century B.C.E. did not know and use Greek, not only in daily discourse but also in formulating a worldview. Indeed, to conduct commerce the knowledge of Greek was an absolute necessity. Further, it would be unreasonable to think that Greek culture, including philosophy, literature, art, and religion, available at least in summary form through the florilegia, would not have been known by Ben Sira.

The persecution of Antiochus IV, followed by the Maccabean revolt, is not mentioned in the literary traditions of Ben Sira, although the sage does point to tensions with political powers (4:26-27; 8:1). In addition, Ben Sira's teachings, whether his own or those of the larger sapiential community to which he belonged, reflect some minor degree of tension between openness to Hellenism and a conservative affirmation of more traditional Judaism.[20] But until Antiochus IV, there was no major accommodation to Greek culture required by the new rulers, the house of Seleucus, and there were no hostilities that threatened the life or religion of Jews in Jerusalem and Judea. Rather, the Jews were allowed

---

the Jerusalem Talmud that place schools after the beginning of the first century B.C.E. (see, e.g., *b. B. Bat.* 21a; Shemuel Safrai, "Education and the Study of the Torah," in *Jewish People*, I/2:947-48.

18. Wilhelm Schubart, *Einführung in die Papyruskunde* (Berlin: Weidmann, 1918) 71 and 131; Tcherikover, *Hellenistic Civilization*, 114.

19. Alexander Di Lella, "Conservative and Progressive Theology: Sirach and Wisdom," *CBQ* 28 (1966) 139-54.

20. Smend, *Weisheit des Jesus Sirach*, xxxiii-xxxiv; Hengel, *Judaism and Hellenism*, 1:134-53. These scholars stress more the antagonism between Ben Sira and Hellenism than I do, although they recognize the Jewish teacher was influenced in a limited way by Greek philosophy and culture.

to live according to their own laws and traditions. As one would expect of a traditional Jewish sage, the text contains emphases on the Torah as the authoritative basis for Jewish life, Israel's sacred history, the theocratic character of postexilic Judaism most clearly expressed in the temple and its worship, and loyalty to the office of the high priest.

The text of the sage also provides some evidence of limited acquaintance with Hellenistic culture, including the ideals of paideia, important Greek values, and the social organization of the Hellenistic city. However, the book does not present so much a contrast between a conservative Ben Sira and a liberal Hellenistic Jewish aristocracy; rather it reflects a developing sapiential tradition that Ben Sira assisted in forging that had deep roots in the Jewish past and still made use of current Greek and Jewish culture. Standing between Judaism and Jewish wisdom and a basic understanding of Hellenistic paideia,[21] Ben Sira was content primarily to articulate a teaching that was traditional in its Judaism and yet open to encountering elements of Greek culture. Hellenization had not yet become the threat it posed during the tyrannical rule of Antiochus IV in the generation following the completion of his book of wisdom. Thus Ben Sira represented many of the tenets of traditional Jewish wisdom and yet remained open to many features of Hellenistic culture.[22] He did not engage in a concerted effort to oppose directly an encroaching Hellenism, nor did he seek to idealize and then force many of its features into Jewish tradition for the Jewish community and their youth whom he taught. For Ben Sira, however, it was the Torah, not Greek philosophy, that provided the path of truth for the sage.[23]

---

21. Mack, *Wisdom and Hebrew Epic.* Also see Pautrel, "Ben Sira et le Stoïcisme," 535-49; Middendorp, *Stellung;* Lee, *Studies in Sirach 44–50.* They recognize a far more positive adaptation of Jewish thought and culture to Hellenism than do Smend and Hengel.

22. Several studies have appeared since the late 1990s that relate different features of Ben Sira's thought to Stoicism, especially the doctrine of providence. See Otto Kaiser, "Die Rezeption der stoischen Providenz bei Ben Sira," *JSNL* 24 (1998) 41-54; and the dissertation of his student, Ursel Wicke-Reuter, *Göttliche Providenz und menschliche Verantwortung bei Ben Sira und in der Frühen Stoa* (BZAW 298; Berlin: de Gruyter, 2000). See idem, "Ben Sira und die Frühe Stoa. Zum Zusammenhang von Ethik und dem Glauben an eine göttliche Providenz," in *Ben Sira's God: Proceedings of the International Ben Sira Conference Durham-Upshaw College 2001,* ed. Renate Egger-Wenzel (BZAW 321; Berlin: de Gruyter, 2002) 268-281. For a judicious assessment of the relationship of Ben Sira to Hellenistic philosophy, in particular Stoicism, see David Winston, "Theodicy in Ben Sira and Stoic Philosophy," in *Of Scholars, Savants, and Their Texts,* ed. Ruth Link-Salinger (New York: Peter Lang, 1989) 239-249. Also see S. L. Mattila, "Ben Sira and the Stoics: A Reexamination of the Evidence," *JBL* 119 (2000) 473-501.

23. Blenkinsopp, *Sage, Priest, Prophet,* 19.

The Judaism of Eretz Israel in the Seleucid Empire

Thanks to Ben Sira's grandson, who wrote the prologue, we are on much firmer ground in dating this text than other pieces of wisdom literature. Written during a period when the Seleucids had recently gained control of Judah (due to the victory of Antiochus III at the battle of Paneion, 200 B.C.E.) and when hellenization continued to transform Jewish culture, society, and religion in important Jewish communities in the Diaspora and in Judah, the book of Ben Sira represents a conservative, although not reactionary, position of those Jews of Eretz Israel who did not wish to participate too dramatically in the new social and cultural metamorphosis of Judaism in the province, including Jerusalem, and yet were still open to engaging new insights and challenges. This sage lived during a period when the shift from the Ptolemies to the Seleucids occurred and when Judaism was beginning to change significantly, even in Judah, at least in regard to its increasing diversification of culture and religion. His life preceded the vigorous struggles over the priesthood and temple when Hellenists began to seize this venerable office leading to the abdication and murder of Onias III, the withdrawal of Onias IV to Leontopolis in Egypt, the erection of a rival temple, and the establishment of the Dead Sea community in Qumran that was opposed to the Zadokite priesthood and its ritual pollution.[24] Qumran and Leontopolis became reactionary centers against the hellenization of Jerusalem and Jewish religion. Finally, in 167 B.C.E., rebellion in the countryside broke out due to the desecrations of the temple by Antiochus IV Epiphanes and to the hellenization of Jerusalem and its religious blending of Hellenism and traditional Judaism.

The law continued to serve as a type of "constitution" for religious and social life, as long as there was no encroachment on fundamental Seleucid policies (24:23; 32:17; 41:8; 42:2; 45:5, 17; 46:14; 49:4). While Antiochus IV Epiphanes later declared a number of ancient cities (*poleis*) to be Greek cities that enjoyed the benefits of this privileged status, he did not include Jerusalem. However, the Seleucid policy of noninterference dramatically changed during his reign in order to generate the capital necessary to support his military efforts against the threat of the Ptolemies from the south. Thus he allowed Jason to purchase the high priesthood and to remove the contemporary ruling high priest, Onias III, from his position. Jason began then a major effort to hellenize Jerusalem in order to transform it into a Greek polis in order to achieve the sociopolitical status and prestige in the Hellenistic world that the city lacked. He renamed Jeru-

---

24. See C. T. R. Hayward, "The Jewish Temple at Leontopolis: A Reconsideration," *JJS* 33 (1982) 432-33.

salem as Antioch-at-Jerusalem (2 Macc. 4:9, 19) and built a gymnasium with an attached *ephebeion*. This would have occurred about 174 B.C.E., shortly after the completion of Ben Sira's book of wisdom. We cannot ascertain what the curriculum of Hellenistic Jewish schools was, although, as we have seen in chapter 5 above on Qoheleth, it is likely that in Jerusalem there would have been Jewish schools and teachers who taught ancestral traditions, including especially the wisdom literature and the Torah, and some of the key elements of Greek culture (language, literature, and philosophy). This would have been necessary for anyone to operate within a social world and market economy that was largely dominated by Greek kingdoms in the eastern Mediterranean world.

The International Setting of Wisdom in the Hellenistic Period

The sapiential texts from the Hellenistic period in Egypt, Eretz Israel, and Mesopotamia point to an international tradition that had developed throughout the Near East and the Aegean world. Texts like the book of Ahiqar were known in both Egypt (the Elephantine library) and Mesopotamia (Warka in the Seleucid period). This internationalization of wisdom, which had been indigenous to the ancient Near Eastern traditions throughout the period of the Israelite monarchy, continued to expand throughout the region. The Egyptian wisdom tradition was prolonged well into the Hellenistic period and was likely known by Jewish sages who taught in schools in Egypt (at least Alexandria) and somewhat in Eretz Israel. As noted earlier, the "Satire on the Trades" ("The Instruction of Duauf") was extremely popular, with citations from this Twelfth Dynasty Egyptian text continuing as late as a text dating from 264 B.C.E.[25] A variety of later texts, including Sir. 38:24–39:11, take up the same theme. It seems quite possible that Ben Sira was familiar with this Egyptian text, since it was cited well into the Hellenistic period. The proverbial collections, instructions, and the hymn to the creator (present in the Papyrus Insinger) found in Egyptian wisdom of the Hellenistic period certainly parallel the literary forms and content found in Ben Sira.

The Wisdom of Hellenistic Egyptian Sages

Demotic wisdom literature is found as late as the Roman Empire of the second century C.E., with the earliest wisdom text being in the form of a tomb biogra-

---

25. Williams, "Egyptian Wisdom Literature," 398.

phy of the family of Pesostris appearing in the fourth century B.C.E.[26] In addition to this particular tomb biography, one also finds wisdom texts, including "The Instruction of Ankhsheshonqy," "The Teaching of Pordjel," and "The Papyrus Insinger."[27] Furthermore, Lichtheim has also noted the impact of other cultures, especially the languages of Aramaic and Greek, on Egyptian wisdom.[28] This points to the importance of cultural exchange during the Hellenistic period, allowing for the Jewish sages cross-cultural knowledge of literature in Egypt written by native Egyptian sages.

It is clear from these Egyptian collections and Ahiqar that the sages of the eastern Mediterranean world, ranging from Greece into western Asia and northern Africa, carried out their activities as teachers and scribes in an international setting in which they were familiar not only with their own cultural literature but also with that of other civilizations of this part of the world. This is underscored by Lichtheim, who notes that these teachers and scribes "worked in a medium which they recognized as being an international one. And they were all the more ready to spread and trade their wares as their subject matter was designed for teaching, persuasion, and the widest possible consumption."[29] Perhaps the most important example of this cultural exchange is provided by ostraca from Deir al-Bahri, where temples to the healing gods Imhotep and Amenhotep, son of Hapu, two deified sages, were located. These ostraca included votive inscriptions and graffiti in demotic script and in Greek. One is a Greek ostracon in which a certain Polyaratos tells of his healing by Amenotes (the Greek name of Amenhotep). The text indicates the date as the twenty-fifth year of Ptolemy II (285-246 B.C.E., thus c. 260). Another is "The Counsels of Amenotes," which is written in Greek and attributed to the deified Egyptian sage and savior, Amenhotep, son of Hapu. This text contains eighteen fragmentary lines and teaches virtue through the sayings of a variety of Greek sources, including the "Sayings of the Seven Sages." This text was likely written by a hellenized Egyptian sage who incorporated Greek wisdom into his native traditions.[30]

---

26. See Lichtheim, *Late Egyptian Wisdom Literature,* 1-12. She hesitates to call these Egyptian sayings "proverbs." In my view, like the sayings in Proverbs and Ben Sira, these Egyptian sayings are primarily sayings, admonitions, and prohibitions. In addition to the instructions examined below, there is the Tefnut Legend, a late demotic text that has a frame narrative into which are inserted gnomic speeches, fables, and songs.

27. See Williams, "Egyptian Wisdom Literature," 397.

28. Lichtheim, *Late Egyptian Wisdom Literature,* 22-28, and passim.

29. Ibid., 106.

30. See ibid., 104-6.

Rhetoric (Literary Structure and Form)

Literary Structure

The book has three sections: 1–24, 25–43, and 44–51, each concluding with a poem or psalm.[31] These are ch. 24, a panegyric hymn of wisdom's self-praise; 42:15–43:33, a hymn on creation; and 51:13-30, a poem describing Ben Sira's search for wisdom — three themes that shape the content of their respective sections and indeed the entire book. Typical for other collections (cf. Proverbs, after which Ben Sira is modeled), the text contains largely sayings, instructions, and poems.[32] There are also features of Greek literature, in particular the "Praise of the Pious" in chs. 44–50 that compares to a Greek encomium.[33] Due to the fact that Ben Sira is a teacher of Scripture, other literary forms from the prophets and psalms are also used.[34] The opening poem that sets forth the twin features of wisdom and creation (1:1-10), preserved in Greek but not in Hebrew, provides the dominant theme of the entire book (cf. the poems on personified Wisdom: 4:11-19; 6:18-37; 14:20–15:10; 24:1-34).[35]

Jewish and Greek Literary Forms

Greek forms either present in or similar to some of those in Ben Sira include florilegia, gnomologia = paroimia, apostrophe, aretology, paraenesis, protrepsis, panegyric, and encomium.[36] The florilegium served as a useful summation of the major schools and teachings of Greek philosophy. The gnomologia = paroimia were lists of sayings quite similar to the lists of sayings one discovers in the book of Proverbs. Since works were read out loud, the apostrophe in-

---

31. In general see Johann Marböck, "Structure and Redaction History of the Book of Ben Sira: Review and Prospects," in *The Book of Ben Sira in Modern Research*, ed. P. C. Beentjes (BZAW 255; Berlin: de Gruyter, 1997) 62-79; W.-W. Jungling, "Der Bauplan des Buches Jesus Sirach," in *"Den Armen eine frohe Botschaft." FS Franz Franphaus*, ed. Josef Hainz (Frankfurt am Main: Peter Lang, 1997) 89-105; Georg Sauer, "Gedanken über den thematischen Aufbau des Buches Ben Sira," in *Treasures of Wisdom: Studies in Ben Sira and the Book of Wisdom. FS Maurice Gilbert*, ed. N. Calduch-Benages and J. Vermeylen (BETL 143; Leuven: Leuven University Press, 1999) 51-61.

32. See J. T. Sanders, *Ben Sira and Demotic Wisdom* (SBLMS 28; Chico, CA: Scholars Press, 1983); Crenshaw, "Book of Sirach," 613-20.

33. For a discussion of the encomium, see Lee, *Studies in Sirach 44–50;* Mack, *Wisdom and the Hebrew Epic.*

34. Walter Baumgartner, "Die literarischen Gattungen in der Weisheit des Jesus Sirach," *ZAW* 34 (1914) 161-98.

35. The book does not possess a detailed literary structure (Collins, *Jewish Wisdom*, 45-46).

36. In general see Skehan and Di Lella, *Wisdom of Ben Sira*, 21-30.

volves a reference to imaginary opponents and was indicated by voice modulation in which the speaker imitated the speech of the adversaries (cf. Sir. 2:15-17; 16:17-23; 31:1-11). Ben Sira uses this form in challenging his Hellenistic Jewish opponents who had abandoned much of Jewish religious tradition (2:15-17; 16:17-23; 31:1-11).[37] The aretology, or speaking of the virtues of gods and humans, at times in hymnic form, is used in the praise of Simon II in ch. 50.[38] Protrepsis is exhortation, designed to persuade youth to enter a teacher's course of instruction (e.g., 51:23-30). Paraenesis is instruction in moral behavior.[39] The panegyric originated in the funeral eulogy and came to be used in the praise of gods and humans. Finally, the encomium was especially important in Greek rhetoric (see Aristotle, *Rhet.* 2.20, 1393a23-1394a18).[40]

Some sapiential forms in Ben Sira are also present elsewhere in the wisdom literatures of the eastern Mediterranean world. The typical forms from Jewish literature present in his writing include sayings or proverbs, the instruction, the hymns (1:1-10; 18:1-7; 39:12-35;[41] 42:15–43:33; 50:22-24; 51:1-12), the *Lehrgedicht* or didactic poem (ch. 24, Woman Wisdom), the prayer of petition (22:7–23:6; 36:1-22), the autobiographical narrative (33:16-18; 51:13-15), onomastica (43:32-33), and the didactic narrative (7:22-23, 24-27; 41:1-15). Sayings ("commonly held opinions") were to be used in argumentation and in determining the limits of their application.[42]

Language and Text (Text Criticism)

The Hebrew and Greek Texts of Ben Sira

Approximately two-thirds of the text of Ben Sira has survived in the original Hebrew language.[43] These include several fragmentary or incomplete texts.[44]

---

37. See Stanley K. Stowers, "Apostrophe, προσωποπία, and Paul's Rhetorical Education," in *Early Christianity and Classical Culture,* ed. John T. Fitzgerald, Thomas H. Olbricht, and L. Michael White (NovTSup 110; Leiden: Brill, 2003) 351-69.

38. See Hans Conzelmann, "The Mother of Wisdom," in *The Future of Our Religious Past: Essays in Honour of Rudolf Bultmann,* ed. J. M. Robinson, trans. Charles E. Carlston and Robert P. Scharlemann (New York: Harper & Row, 1971) 230-43; Marböck, *Weisheit im Wandel,* 48-54; Mack, *Logos und Sophia.*

39. See Gammie and Perdue, eds., *Paraenesis: Act and Form.*

40. See Lee, *Studies in Sirach 44–50;* Mack, *Wisdom and the Hebrew Epic.*

41. Jan Liesen, *Full of Praise: An Exegetical Study of Sir 39,12-35* (JSJSup 64; Leiden: Brill, 2000).

42. Doran, "High Cost," 101.

43. For a brief overview of the Hebrew, Greek, and other translations, see Skehan and Di Lella, *Wisdom of Ben Sira,* 55-62.

44. Important discussions of the textual history of Ben Sira include those of Hans-Peter

The Greek translation (LXX) is better preserved, since it contains the entire book, although there are two major recensions: a short text (GI) and a longer expanded one (GII).[45] However, the differences between the LXX and the surviving Hebrew manuscripts are often substantial, indicating the likelihood that the translators did not consider themselves to be restrained by a desire to present a literal rendering in their rendering, paraphrasing, and interpreting of the Hebrew copies they used. The appropriate procedure with the matters of textual history is to use the major Hebrew recension that has survived (Ms. B), and then to use variants from other Hebrew manuscripts in the case of difficulties arising due to the occasionally poor state of preservation of Ms. B. The LXX is to be consulted only when there are lacunae in the Hebrew manuscripts, and then it is necessary to keep in mind the particular linguistic and thematic considerations of this Hellenistic tradition.

The Hebrew text is partially preserved in six medieval manuscripts (from the Cairo Genizah:[46] A, B, C, D, E, and possibly F), several fragments from Qumran (2Q18; 11QPsa), and twenty-six fragments plus a lengthy section (39:27–44:71) found at Masada (M). The acrostic poem (51:13-20b, 30b) is found in the first Psalms Scroll of Qumran, indicating that this poem was used in a variety of other texts and may not have been originally part of Ben Sira. The Ben Sira fragments found in Qumran and Masada may be dated on paleographic grounds to the first century B.C.E., although the Genizah manuscripts also represent an ancient literary tradition. Di Lella and Skehan find in these Genizah manuscripts two different recensions: a short text (HTI), representing the closest text we have to the original of Ben Sira, and a longer, expanded text (HTII) that is lengthened briefly by a later redaction. The short Greek text (GI) is likely closer to the translation of the grandson, while the longer one (GII) is an edited

---

Rüger, *Text und Textform im hebräischen Sirach* (BZAW 112; Berlin: de Gruyter, 1970); Skehan and Di Lella, *Wisdom of Ben Sira*, 51-82; Maurice Gilbert, "L'Ecclésiastique: Quel texte? Quelle autorité?" *RB* (1987) 233-50; B. G. Wright, *No Small Difference: Sirach's Relationship to Its Hebrew Parent Text* (SBLSCS 26; Atlanta: Scholars Press, 1989). For the extant Hebrew mss., see Pancratius Cornelis Beentjes, *The Book of Ben Sira in Hebrew: A Text Edition of All Extant Hebrew Manuscripts and a Synopsis* (VTSup 68; Leiden: Brill, 1997). A comprehensive review of the texts of Ben Sira and the listing of comparative columns are found in Friedrich V. Reiterer, *Zählsynopse zum Buch Ben Sira* (Fontes et Subsidia ad Bibliam pertinentes 1; Berlin: de Gruyter, 2003) 1-86. Reiterer presents his own versification in order to provide a convenient way of correlating Ben Sira's Greek and Hebrew manuscript traditions (pp. 87-247).

45. Joseph Ziegler, *Sapientia Iesu filii Sirach* (Septuaginta 12/2; Göttingen: Vandenhoeck & Ruprecht, 1965). For a succinct study of the Greek translations of the Bible, including esp. the LXX, see Emanuel Tov, "Die griechischen Bibelübersetzungen," *ANRW* 2.20/1:121-89.

46. *Genizah* means "storeroom," where worn manuscripts were stored that no longer were read.

text that is created later.[47] The Hebrew manuscripts have been placed into columns by Beentjes.[48]

Social Features: Sages and Social Setting

The Social Status of Ben Sira and the Roles of the Scribes

Ben Sira was the first known scribal interpreter of Scripture since Ezra, who had been commissioned to codify Jewish law and to organize Jewish society on its basis.[49] It is interesting to observe that Ben Sira's understanding of the sage and of his own role is very similar to that of the Deuteronomic scribe: fear, love, serve God, and keep his commandments (Deut. 6:1-2; 10:12-13; 30:16).[50] Ben Sira's canon has expanded from the Torah to include the Prophets and the "rest of the Books," although this third section was as of yet undefined. His grandson indicates that Ben Sira devoted his life to the study of Scripture and the writing of instruction and wisdom so that those who "love learning" should be better able to follow the Torah. The colophon at the end (50:27-29) describes the book as one that contains the sayings and wisdom teachings of Ben Sira, whose stated purpose in writing was to become a source of teaching for all of those who wished to become wise. The prologue, epilogue, and contents of the book indicate that Ben Sira was a wise teacher who operated a boarding school for students (51:23-25).[51] His strong interest in and support of the temple and the high priesthood suggest he had an important connection with this institution and its hierarchical personnel. He seems to have worked under the auspices of the Zadokite high priesthood. From the information we have, then, Ben Sira is a scribal interpreter of Scripture who taught in an academy (51:23; cf. 33:16-19), perhaps a Torah school of the temple in Jerusalem or a synagogue school, and a "sage" who compiled a list of his teachings, poems, and hymns into a book that

---

47. See *Sapientia Iesu Filii Sirach.*

48. Beentjes, *Ben Sira in Hebrew.*

49. In general see Hengel, "'Schriftauslegung' und 'Schriftwerdung,'" 20-35. Cf. Hengel, *Judaism and Hellenism,* 1:132-57; Johann Marböck, *Weisheit im Wandel;* Küchler, *Frühjüdische Weisheitstraditionen;* E. J. Schnabel, *Law and Wisdom from Ben Sira to Paul* (WUNT 2/16; Tübingen: Mohr Siebeck, 1985); John G. Gammie, "The Sage in Sirach," in *Sage in Israel,* 355-72; Schams, *Jewish Scribes,* 98-106.

50. Alexander A. Di Lella, "God and Wisdom in the Theology of Ben Sira: An Overview," in *Ben Sira's God,* 15.

51. Michael E. Stone, "Ideal Figures and Social Context: Priest and Sage in the Early Second Temple Age," in *Selected Studies in Pseudepigrapha and Apocrypha: With Special Reference to the Armenian Tradition,* ed. Michael E. Stone (SVTP 9; Leiden: Brill, 1991) 259-70.

has undergone later redaction. He is the first person in the canon (that includes the deuterocanonical texts) to be identified as the author (the end of the work, as well as the identification by his grandson) whose own character and personal attributes are set forth, thus mimicking the Greeks' emphasis on the individuality of an author. In speaking of the scribe, in a poem that may be autobiographical, Ben Sira compares this profession favorably to many others (38:24–39:11).[52] He appears to have been wealthy, and, unlike common scribes, he likely would have been a member of Jewish society's elite (see 23:14; 39:4) whose audience consisted of aristocratic youth who came to him for an education.[53] Ben Sira was clearly an elitist due to his personal wealth, education, literary prowess, and profession of teaching male students of aristocratic Jewish families.[54] In addition to the excellent education he obviously received in the teachings of the biblical texts and Greek rhetoric, he owned land (7:3, 15, 22) and slaves (7:20-21; 33:25-33; 42:5). Even though he was himself apparently quite well-to-do, he recognized the deceit of wealth and its many pitfalls and warned his students of its dangers. While he recognized the social advantages of the wealthy in contrast to the poor (12:9; 13:21-24), he spoke of God's special protection of the poor (21:5), cautioned students against trusting in or exulting in riches (5:1, 8; 9:13; 13:3-7), advised them against miserliness (14:3-10) and the love of wealth (31:1-7), and spoke of the responsibility to provide for the poor, who along with the wealthy are predestined for their roles by God (11:14; 31:23-24). This notation of predestination is found in a number of Hellenistic writers in terms of the concept of "fate." Finally, he taught that those who profit from ill-gotten gain will perish (40:13-14). Ben Sira implied that he traveled extensively, although this may only be a reference to the diplomatic service in which some scribes were active (31:9ff.; 39:4), and he pointed to the necessity of leisure time in order to carry out the activities of the sage, who read and wrote (38:24ff.). This status and reputation would have added to the personal prestige necessary for the wide distribution of his texts and enhanced the chances of his text's entrance into the canon. Ben Sira fully expected to gain entrance to the Hebrew canon, a concept that was developing at the time he wrote, for he considered his teachings to be inspired (24:30-34). While his book did enter the Alexandrian canon (LXX) and

---

52. Cf. the Egyptian "Satire of the Trades" (*ANET*, 432-34).

53. Smend, *Weisheit des Jesus Sirach*, 345-46; Gordis, "Social Background," 77-118. For Ben Sira's positive view of wealth, see 3:17-18; 10:27; 13:24; 14:11-16; 25:3; 34:3; 40:18; 44:6; 47:18. Opposite to my view is that of Stadelmann, who regards him as a priestly, scribal interpreter of law who is of ordinary means and instructs the "middle class" (*Ben Sira als Schriftgelehrter*, 12, 36-39).

54. Benjamin G. Wright, "The Discourse of Riches and Poverty in the Book of Ben Sira," *SBLSP 1998* (2 vols.; Atlanta: Scholars Press, 1998) 2:559-78; Oda Wischmeyer, *Die Kultur des Buches Ben Sira* (BZNW 77; Berlin: de Gruyter, 1995) 181.

thus is regarded as deuterocanonical, it failed to be included in the later Jewish Hebrew canon probably due to the fact that the legend developing after his time held that inspiration began with Moses and ended with Ezra. Consequently, a book that acknowledges that it is later by identifying its author and providing concrete information about its time of origin precludes its inclusion into the Hebrew canon. But it appears he made every effort at inclusion. Perhaps this is why he followed the literary structure of Proverbs in beginning his book with a poem of personified Wisdom (1:1-27) and concluded it with an acrostic poem in 51:13-30 (cf. Prov. 31:10-31). Indeed, the language and literary style of Scripture inform the writings of Ben Sira in a notable way.[55]

Hengel surmises that Ben Sira may have held an important position as a judge or political counselor and perhaps was even a member of the *gerousia* or council of elders.[56] Because of his devotion to the temple and loyalty to the high priesthood, Ben Sira could have been one of the temple scribes mentioned in one of the royal decrees of Antiochus III (Josephus, *Ant.* 12.138-39).[57] His outlook is certainly Sadducean in noticeable areas, including the importance placed on the temple, the identification of wisdom with the Torah, the panegyric to Simon II, the omission of any reference to oral tradition or to resurrection from the dead, and the lack of apocalyptic themes and literary features. It is interesting to note that the term "scribe" occurs only once in the surviving Hebrew manuscripts (38:24) and once more in the Greek of 10:5. In 38:24ff. wisdom and the scribe are connected and then explained in the following praise of the scribes in Jewish society. The introduction to the poem notes that if one does not need to spend time in business activities, one has the opportunity of leisure time to pursue study to become wise (38:24).[58] The elite sage has the ability to significantly increase in wisdom; that is, study exponentially expands knowledge. Ben Sira also betrays his elitist position in Jewish society by his deprecation of common laborers and their tasks (38:24-34).

55. Hilaire Duesberg and Irene Fransen, *Ecclesiastico* (La Sacra Bibbia; Turin: Marietti, 1966) 69; J. G. Snaith, "Biblical Quotations in the Hebrew of Ecclesiasticus," *JTS* 18 (1967) 1-12; J. L. Koole, "Die Bibel des Ben-Sira," *OTS* 14 (1965) 374-96.

56. *Judaism and Hellenism*, 1:131-62. See Josephus, *Ant.* 12.138-44.

57. *Judaism and Hellenism*, 1:247. See Marböck, *Weisheit im Wandel*, 83.

58. This downplaying of the work of common laborers belonged to the elitist class attitude of the aristocracy in the Greco-Roman world. For many of those in the upper class, work had no intrinsic value, and the type of work one did reflected social status. Manual labor, in particular, was disparaged by most of the aristocracy. Aristocrats usually held in highest regard the life of the patrician who owned land, lived on an estate, and pursued the life of culture and learning. Ben Sira's disdain for common labor is evidence of his aristocratic status.

The Sage, Torah, and Wisdom

It is important to recognize that Ben Sira equates wisdom and the Torah (see ch. 24). This is noticeable in a number of texts that point to the law and the commandments. Especially noteworthy is the brief panegyric to Moses in the larger "Praise of the Pious," in which Moses is both the giver of the Law and the patron of the sages (44:23–45:6). God gives to him "the law of life and understanding," and he "taught his [God's] precepts to Jacob, his covenant decrees to Israel." This description of Moses as the one who taught the Law adds to the eminence of the sage who is the interpreter of Scripture in general and the Torah in particular. The equating of wisdom and Torah and the sage as the teacher and interpreter of the Law are strong indications that the sages are professionals under the oversight of the priestly ranks who operated the temple. Thus the sages emphasize the importance of the support of the priests, especially the high priest (see Simon II in ch. 50), as well as the performing of temple rituals.[59] Indeed, Ben Sira claims he composed hymns under the impress of inspiration, which may well have been used in the temple worship.

The Sage as Prophet

The sage in Ben Sira appropriates some of the characteristics of prophecy.[60] In some circles of Judaism the prophet had been discredited (Zech. 13:2-6), leading to transformation into the seer, who combined elements of esoteric wisdom, divine inspiration, and revelatory visions. For Ben Sira, the sage who was chosen by God to receive the spirit of understanding is inspired (39:6-8), but other elements of the prophetic institution are not assumed, particularly the social criticism directed against the injustice of foreign nations (except for the possibly spurious condemnation of foreign rulers and peoples in 36:1-10), rulers, the priesthood, and the temple cult. Rather, important for Ben Sira is the prophetic inspiration that comes to the sage, who then writes sapiential writings under divine guidance.

---

59. See James L. Crenshaw, "The Book of Sirach," *NIB* 5 (1997) 628.

60. See Perdue, "Ben Sira and the Prophets." For a detailed list of references to the Hebrew prophets in Ben Sira, see Stadelmann, *Ben Sira als Schriftgelehrter*, 177-270. Also see Middendorp, *Stellung*, 6-71; Koole, "Bibel des Ben-Sira."

The Sage and the Temple

No archive in Jerusalem has yet been discovered. Nevertheless, on the basis of parallels from the ancient Near East, it is likely there would have been one in close proximity to the temple and palace, possibly within the walls of the sacred precinct on Mount Moriah. These would have included state documents and religious literature produced by scribes active in the temple and the ruler's (later, governor's) palace. If Ben Sira was part of the scribal ranks of the temple or a teacher who was legitimated by the Zadokite priesthood, then he would have had access to various texts, including religious literature, from within Judah and possibly even texts from other regions of the eastern Mediterranean world. The archive and library would explain his many references to what became canonical literature and other types of texts, including some composed in Greece. Thus sapiential, ritual, legal, and administrative documents would have been the types of material found in a library and archive during the Seleucid period.

The temple became the economic center for Jerusalem and Judah and received sacrifices, gifts, and the temple tax. Indeed, it may have been at the center of a banking system for the colonial economy. The temple and its priestly overseers would have earned profits from the number of pilgrims and sacrifices necessary to keep the cultic operation functioning. Agricultural produce and farm animals were sold to dealers and possibly directly to worshipers for sacrifices and meat, while byproducts that included the hides for the production of leather would have been a means of income.

The Sage and the Synagogue

Ben Sira also likely attended and later taught in a Jewish school in Jerusalem connected to the temple or perhaps to a synagogue.[61] The synagogue became a place of assembly for the local community, a house of worship (reading of Scripture, prayer, singing of psalms, and issuing homilies), and often, if a *bêt midrāš* was attached, a location for study, including a formal school. Along with the temple and the Torah, the synagogue became one of the major pillars of Second Temple Judaism. The origins of the synagogue (*bêt hakkĕnesset,* "place

---

61. See the study by Louis H. Feldman, "Diaspora Synagogues: New Light from Inscriptions and Papyri," in *Studies in Hellenistic Judaism,* ed. Louis H. Feldman (AGAJU 30; Leiden: Brill, 1996) 577-602. Feldman notes that by the time of the writing of his book the papyri and inscriptions had pointed to sixty-six synagogues in antiquity, dating from the third century B.C.E. to 500 C.E. Of the various activities taking place in these assembly places, education was an important one. They were "houses of study," or at least had such a facility attached to them.

of the congregation" = Gk. *synagōgē*), based on excavations and epigraphical references, may be traced to the third century B.C.E. in Egypt. For example, two synagogue dedications have been found in this century in Hellenistic Egypt,[62] and a papyrus letter dating from 218 B.C.E. in the town of Alexandrou-Nesos refers to a third synagogue. Other inscriptions point to Egyptian synagogues in Alexandria, Xenephyris, and Nitriai.[63] Archaeological evidence for synagogues in the Diaspora prior to 70 C.E. also includes Delos (second–first century B.C.E.), Ostia (reign of Claudius in 41-54 C.E.), and Rome.

The material data in Eretz Israel derive from the second century B.C.E. and later. Synagogues have been discovered in Qumran, Gamla, Masada, Herodium, Capernaum, and Hasmonean Jericho.[64] Philo speaks to the education ("encyclical training") of youth of wealthy families in *Spec.* 2.230, *Prov.* 2.44-46, and *Congr.* 74-76.[65] The rabbinic tradition (*y. Meg.* 3, I, 73d; *y. Ketub.* 13, 35c; *b. Ketub.* 105a) mentions a highly exaggerated number of 480 synagogues in pre–70 C.E. Jerusalem, each with a primary school *(bêt sēper)* and a more advanced school *(bêt talmûd)*. Nonetheless, it is likely that future scribes and teachers studied in this type of educational setting (see Josephus, *C. Ap.* 2.204). A synagogue was located on the Temple Mount (*m. Yoma* 7.1; *m. Soṭ.* 7.7-8), as was a *bêt midrāš* (*t. Sanh.* 7.1; *t. Ḥag.* 2.9). Possibly the two were related. An assembly in part composed of sages met in the *bêt midrāš* on the Temple Mount to hold judicial proceedings during the week and to debate the meaning of the commandments on the Sabbath and festivals. This meeting place was called the "Chamber of Hewn Stone" in the temple. Subsequent to 70 C.E., a *baraita* in *b. Sanh.* 32b mentions the scholars of the *yěšîbâ (yeshiva)* in a variety of cities.

The Sage and the School

The sage is primarily a teacher in a *bêt midrāš*, most likely a school that is associated with either the temple or a synagogue. Ben Sira would have worked under the auspices of the high priest and the priestly hierarchy in Jerusalem as a teacher

---

62. The inscriptions were found in Schedia near Alexandria and Crocodilopolis. For the list of synagogues see *CPJ* 1:8; 3:9, 13, 22, 24-25, 27-28, 117, 125-27.

63. See Donald Binder, *Into the Temple Courts: The Place of the Synagogues in the Second Temple Period* (SBLDS 169; Atlanta: Society of Biblical Literature, 1999).

64. Ehud Netzer's discovery of a Hasmonean synagogue near the Hasmonean winter palace in Jericho is the oldest synagogue yet discovered in Eretz Israel ("A Synagogue from the Hasmonean Period Recently Exposed in the Western Plain of Jericho," *IEJ* 49 [1999] 203-21). There were likely other synagogues in Judah predating the Roman sacking of Jerusalem. These would have included possibly those at Chorazin, Kiriath-sepher, Magdala, and Shuafat.

65. See Harris, *Greek Athletics;* Mendelson, *Secular Education.*

of Scripture and interpreter of Torah. Subsequently, Ben Sira's praise of the high priest, Simon II, support of the priesthood, adoption of a Zadokite theology, and instruction to support the temple and its priests through worship and sacrifices were not only religiously motivated but also grounded in the economic structure of Hellenistic Jerusalem. Through teaching aristocratic youth and educating scribes to serve in the administration of the government and of the temple, the sage contributed to sustaining the social and economic reality in which Zadokite priests and their assistants, the scribes and sages, played an important role. By educating temple scribes, these individuals would clearly have entered into the various roles that attended to archives of religious texts and documents, the legal corpora and the interpretation of laws, and financial records for sacrifices and gifts to the temple. Likewise, the education of scribes for the secular administration of the city would have provided a necessary learned profession for the political and economic direction of the colony within the Seleucid Empire. From the content of the book, one may surmise he taught a curriculum that included Greek and Hebrew rhetoric, medicine, cosmology, anthropology, and moral philosophy.

The sage in Ben Sira has the responsibility of teaching his students. One of his titles is "father" (*'āb*), and his student is "son" (*ben*; see 4:1, 20; 10:28; 11:8, 10, 20; 14:11; 37:27; 38:9; 40:28; 42:11). What is taught is rhetoric, the law, the importance of study, discipline, moral behavior, obedience to parents, etiquette, following the commandments, piety and worship (prayer, sacrifice, support of priests), proper burial and burial ceremonies for the deceased that motivate one to remember one's own mortality, rejection of the life of the beggar, and care for biological children. Three texts are important in presenting the teaching of students: 6:32-33; 30:1-13; and 51:23-30. Especially in the third text, a poem of instruction, Ben Sira, like a youth seeking instruction, searches for Wisdom, finds and learns from her, and then offers her charms to students who would study in his house of inquiry.

In many respects the ideal sage, who we assume is incarnated in the life and work of Ben Sira during the early Seleucid period, is presented in this book in the traditional guise of the sage of Proverbs with features of the Deuteronomic scribe. Part of this continuity may be explained by the duration of the sapiential tradition through the centuries, in spite of the disruption of the Babylonian destruction of Jerusalem and the exile. It also is possible that he is an opponent of disciples of Qoheleth,[66] further suggesting a continuity of sapi-

---

66. See the seminal essay by Johannes Marböck, "Kohelet und Sirach," in *Das Buch Kohelet*, ed. Ludger Schwienhorst-Schönberger (BZAW 254: Berlin: de Gruyter, 1995) 275-301. He argues that Ben Sira may have sought to correct some of Qoheleth's radical teachings that would have been known and preserved in the Jewish schools.

ential tradition. The existence of the book of Ben Sira points to the durative quality of the wisdom tradition in Babylonia, Persia, and the Hellenistic empires. In addition, part of this continuation of the traditional sage is indirect evidence that scribes were active in Jerusalem during the Persian period and edited much of the canon, including especially the Torah.

Ben Sira's virtuous sage, who is described in an aretology in 38:24–39:11, also may be reconstructed from the various teachings of the book. This description may even be a self-portrait. Among the important characteristics of the sage's morality and behavior are the following. He is pious and prayerful (14:20a; 15:1; 18:27; cf. Prov. 14:2; 15:29, 33), engaged in the study of rhetoric (including not only the Hebrew language and its classics, but also the great compositions of Greek and possibly Egyptian literature, Sir. 39:1-2), knows the teachings of past sages (6:35), composes wisdom (18:27-29; 24:31-34), is able to conceal both his thoughts and the secrets of others (8:19; 9:18; cf. Prov. 10:19; 12:23), avoids improper relations with women (Sir. 42:12-14; cf. Prov. 23:26-28), controls his appetites (Sir. 31:12-21; cf. Prov. 20:25-26), is generous to the needy (Sir. 4:1-10; cf. Prov. 11:17, 24-25), and reflects on and implements the Torah and other wisdom traditions in his behavior (Sir. 38:34). Ben Sira holds in common numerous teachings with the earlier traditional sages with whom he shared a similar worldview in which a knowing God created and oversees the world, sustaining life and operating in the world and society largely through the principle of retribution (7:1-3; 29:11-13; 40:12-27; cf. Prov. 10:25, 30). In addition, the sage's primary virtue is the "fear of Yahweh," which is expressed in piety, faith in the creator and sustainer of the cosmos, trust in the providential guide of human history, and obedience to the revealed commandments (Sir. 1:10-20; 19:20; 32:24–33:1; 34:13-14).

The Counselor (Yôʿēṣ)

The sage in Ben Sira is also a counselor. Ben Sira in 37:7-15 instructs students about seeking counsel from one who has the insight to offer wise advice. Yet he warns them to scrutinize critically what a counselor may advise them to do. There are good counselors who offer proper advice and imposters who are deceptive. It is the latter group that Ben Sira warns his students against. There are imposters who offer counsel on the basis on their own self-interest: a woman concerning her rival, a captive concerning war, a merchant regarding the price for his goods, the wicked concerning compassion, the masochist about doing good to the body, and the hired laborer regarding his work. Ben Sira instructs his students to seek out those who are like themselves, that is, God-fearers who are obedient to the commandments. Finally, he notes that it is God alone who is able to direct one's steps.

The Teacher (Mĕlammēd)

The term for "teacher" is missing from Ben Sira's text, but the verb "to teach" (*lāmad*) does occur.[67] In 4:11-16 Woman Wisdom (*ḥokmôt*) teaches her "sons" (*bānîm*) and counsels those who "seek to understand her." Her "sons" are those who love life and serve her ministers (*mĕšārĕtîm*, that is, her priests, judges, rulers, and kings). These demonstrate that Ben Sira is a loyal sage within the Seleucid colony and a supporter of the priests active in the temple.

The grandson states that his grandfather was among those who "were eager for knowledge"; he occupied himself with both *paideia* and *sophia*, and devoted himself to read the Law and the Prophets and the other books of the ancestors. This he did in order that those who "were eager for knowledge" might "make progress" in living according to the Law by becoming familiar with these texts. Ben Sira indicates that the wise man "will manifest the learning of his teaching," indicating that he incorporates wisdom in his character and acts according to its teachings (39:8). In 51:28 he exhorts students to hear his instruction and tells of many who listened to his instruction.

Professional teachers were sought out for instruction at their private homes or in their schools by young men (3:29; 6:34, 35; 8:8, 9). These teachers served as tutors of those youth who were seeking instruction (9:14), while the "righteous" were their hosts (9:16).[68] Even so, Ben Sira's students were both young men as well as leaders in the community (33:19; 37:19-26). Indeed, he even engaged in the teaching of the people (*hā'ām*), suggesting that he taught them in their religious assemblies.[69] Students were taught to become wise, which was both a type of behavior and a profession. By contrast, the "fool" (*sākāl*) was the one who was uneducated and incapable of learning (cf. 19:23). Choosing not to "fear God" or to obey the Torah, the fool rejected self-control, did not speak properly, and lacked intelligence. Teaching and learning for Ben Sira appear in part to be oral, and in part to be reading written texts.[70]

---

67. In general see Wischmeyer, *Kultur*, 174-200.

68. Ibid., 177.

69. See Stadelmann, *Ben Sira als Schriftgelehrter*, 296ff.

70. See Martin S. Jaffee, *Torah in the Mouth: Writing and Oral Tradition in Palestinian Judaism, 200 BCE–400 CE* (Oxford: Oxford University Press, 2001).

The Physician (Rōpē')

Medicine was a subject in the curriculum of the gymnasium, and it appears to have been so in the school of Ben Sira as well. In 38:1-23 he describes physicians as well as Yahweh, the divine healer. Imhotep, who was the vizier of Pharaoh Djoser (2686-2687 B.C.E.) of the Third Dynasty and a renowned sage, architect, astrologer, and administrator, was also a physician who became enshrined in Egyptian mythology as the god of medicine. Later, in the Greco-Roman world, he became identified with Asclepius, the god of healing.[71]

In Greece the treatment and curing of the sick and physically infirm was associated with both the healing powers of the physician and religious rituals, in particular those practiced in the cult of Asclepius. Priests of Asclepius and physicians were considered to possess the ability to cure.[72] In Israel Yahweh was the God of healing (Gen. 20:17; Num. 12:13; 2 Kgs. 20:5, 8; Ps. 107:20) whose redemption of the pious and faithful from illness and death was celebrated in psalms of thanksgiving. Ben Sira regarded the physician as a sage who had learned his medical knowledge in a school.

Ben Sira's presentation of the sage as a physician is found in an instruction (38:1-23) that consists of three parts: the divine knowledge of the wise physician, the wise physician and the God of healing, and mourning rites for the dead.[73] The last section is likely in opposition to the Hellenistic view that Asclepius and magicians were said to possess the powers of resuscitation of the dead.[74] The king appoints physicians in order to license them and thus distinguish between authentic doctors and quacks. Further, the physicians are found at court and stand above even the nobles in order to demonstrate their significant official status.

---

71. See Hans-Josef Klauck, *The Religious Context of Early Christianity: A Guide to Graeco-Roman Religions,* trans. Brian McNeil (Minneapolis: Fortress, 2003) 154-68.

72. Some physicians were thought to have miraculous healing powers, including the ability to raise the dead. For example, see Asclepiades in Pliny the Elder, *Nat. Hist.* 7.37.

73. For physicians in the ancient world, see Walter Muri, *Der Arzt im Altertum: Griechische und lateinische Quellenstücke von Hippokrates bis Galen* (Tusculum Bücherie; Munich: Heimeran, 1979); Antje Krug, *Heilkunst und Heilkult: Medizin in der Antike* (2nd ed.; Munich: Beck, 1993); Louise Wells, *The Greek Language of Healing from Homer to New Testament Times* (BZNW 83; Berlin: de Gruyter, 1998).

74. Klauck, *Religious Context,* 154-68.

The Scribal Interpreter of Scripture

The scribes were interpreters of Scripture and tradition as early as the eighth century B.C.E. (see, e.g., Jer. 18:18; Ezek. 7:26; 22:26; 44:23-24; Hos. 4:6; Mic. 3:11; Zeph. 3:4; Hag. 2:10-13; 2 Chron. 15:3; 17:7-9; 19:5-10; 35:3). It is also important to note that the Levites taught the law according to Deut. 33:9b-10, while Mal. 2:7-9 mentions that priests had the responsibility of offering instruction to the people (see Let. Aris. 130-170; Jub. 32:1, 3, 9; 45:16; T. Levi 4:8).

From the prologue and elsewhere, we learn that Ben Sira and the scribes are interpreters of Scripture, sayings, and parables (Sir. 39:1-11). The interpreter of Scripture and the scribe of Torah is now the office in which its holders become divinely inspired (see 24:30-34), especially those privileged by divine selection (39:6). Those honored in the "Praise of the Pious" are great heroes, the important leaders, the "righteous," and the authors of biblical books, scribal interpreters, and poetic writers (44:5). Ben Sira and presumably other learned scribes do not simply quote texts, but rather adapt and expand the words they read. Thus the learned scribe is a scholar steeped in Scripture and skilled in the interpretation of the Law, the Prophets, and the Prologue, "rest of the Books" (24:30-31; 33:16; 38:34–39:8).[75]

Summary: The Scribe in the Seleucid Period

The incorporation of Judah into the Ptolemaic and then the Seleucid Empire led to a number of changes in the office of the scribe. The increase in literary records points to the expansion of the ranks of the scribes and their activities at all levels of governmental, temple, and private arenas.[76] In addition, the archaeological and literary evidence for the origins of the synagogue from Egypt would imply the role of scribes included teachers in the local assembly houses and houses of study throughout the Hellenistic world. This points to an increased democratization of learning that would have included both sages who interpreted the Torah and other traditions of Jewish tradition, and laypeople offering instruction during the Sabbath and festival periods. Some Jewish scribes served as officials in Greek governments, while others, like Ben Sira, were teachers who educated leaders and scribes for various roles in Judah as a Seleucid colony. In addition to Ben Sira, others would have worked under the auspices of the priestly hierarchy of Jerusalem.

75. See the detailed study of Stadelmann, *Ben Sira als Schriftgelehrter*.
76. Schams, *Jewish Scribes*, 312-21.

The Family Household (Mišpāḥâ)

Those who were held in prominence in Ben Sira's social world were the aristocratic males, and this included the family household. The family was a traditional and conservative institution; the roles of the father and mother included teaching the household the commandments and the traditions of Israel (30:1-13). Children were to respect their parents by obeying their instruction.

The major text that focuses on the family is 3:1-16, an instruction of three strophes that interprets in detail the commandment to honor the parents (Exod. 20:12 = Deut. 5:16). Functioning as an interpreter of the Torah, Ben Sira emphasizes first obedience to the father in particular, and then honoring both parents. The act of honoring refers both to respect and to obeying their directives. The first strophe occurs in Sir. 3:1-6. The commandment, "honor your father and mother," includes the imperative, coupled with one motive clause taken from Exod. 20:12: "that your days may be long upon the earth" (see Deut. 5:16). Thus wealth, long life, and atoning for sin accrue to the students who follow Ben Sira's instruction.

The second strophe (Sir. 3:7-11) relates the honoring of the parents with blessing, while failing to do so brings about cursing. Furthermore, when the parents are disgraced, the offspring share in that abasement. The father's blessing results in the strengthening of the houses of the children, while dishonoring the mother leads to the uprooting of their foundations.

In the third and final strophe (3:12-16), honoring the father is to continue, even when he becomes old and feeble. This act of kindness will serve as a sin offering and in times of difficulty it will bring an advantage. Indeed, honoring the father will result in the removal of sin. However, the one who demeans the father is a blasphemer who provokes God, and the one who is angry with the mother receives the curse of God.

Ben Sira's views of the family may be representative of the Jewish aristocracy of Jerusalem and Judah in his period.[77] The restrictions placed on women are not unusual in the Bible, for the Torah includes similar views. Women were usually not engaged in social roles outside the household, and also were subject to the head of the family as well as to her husband.[78] While Ben Sira indicates

77. Silvia Schroer, *Die Weisheit hat ihr Haus gebaut. Studien zur Gestalt der Sophia in den biblischen Schriften* (Mainz: Matthias-Grünewald Verlag, 1996) 99.

78. See, among other studies, Léonie J. Archer, *Her Price Is beyond Rubies: The Jewish Woman in Graeco-Roman Palestine* (JSOTSup 60; Sheffield: JSOT Press, 1990); P. J. Botha, "Through the Figure of a Woman Many Have Perished: Ecclesiasticus 41:14–42:8," *OTE* 9 (1996) 20-34; Claudia V. Camp, "Understanding a Patriarchy: Women in Second Century Jerusalem through the Eyes of Ben Sira," in *"Women Like This": New Perspectives on Jewish Women in the Greco-

that wives and mothers possessed important roles within the domestic household and were respected, those outside these roles who were disobedient and flagrantly immoral were severely chastised and subject even to execution.

Ben Sira is often criticized for his sexism, although this view, grounded in the patriarchy of the social elite of his day, would not be unique among Jewish writers of the Hellenistic period. His sexism is expressed especially in 25:13–26:27 ("The Wife"), where he blames a woman, unnamed but obviously Eve, for the sin that resulted in the sentence of death that all people consequently must bear. The Hebrew text (in this case Ms. C) is only partly preserved and rather corrupt. Thus the best procedure is to follow the LXX's rendition. The section on the wife includes the following parts.

25:13-26   The Wicked Wife
26:1-4   The Good Wife
26:5-12   The Wicked Wife and Her Various Vices
26:13-18   The Beauty of a Wife
26:22-27   The Contrast between Good and Evil Wives[79]

Ben Sira's teaching stresses his fear of the wicked wife who renders her husband powerless. The husband who is not obeyed and honored by his wife (25:22) experiences anger, recklessness, and, above all, shame. Indeed, the evil wife is blamed for numerous difficulties experienced by her husband, ranging from his despair to disturbance of his silent surroundings. The attractive woman may cause a man to intensify his desire, thus "ensnaring" him if he is not careful. The wife who is disobedient to her husband should be divorced. Especially shameful is the wife who participates in illicit sexual liaisons. But if she is one who pleases her husband, he should not divorce her. If he despises her, however, he should deny her his trust (see 7:26). By contrast, the good wife is a source of her husband's joy; she is silent, obedient, trustworthy, and charming. Her beauty brings him great delight.

The father has the special responsibility to guard his daughter's fidelity (42:9-14), since she is potentially a seducer and adulteress (26:10-12). Her headstrong behavior leads to sexual iniquity and brings great shame to her father.

Roman World, ed. Amy-Jill Levine (SBLEJL 1; Atlanta: Scholars Press, 1991) 1-39; Alexander A. Di Lella, "Women in the Wisdom of Ben Sira and the Book of Judith: A Study in Contrasts and Reversals," in *Congress Volume: Paris, 1991*, ed. J. A. Emerton (VTSup 61; Leiden: Brill, 1995) 39-52; Jack Levison, "Is Eve to Blame? A Contextual Analysis of Sirach 25:24," *CBQ* 47 (1985) 617-23.

79. See Renate Egger-Wenzel, "'Denn harte Knechtschaft und Schande ist es, wenn seine Frau ihrer Mann ernährt' (Sir 25,22)," in *Der Einzelne und seine Gemeinschaft bei Ben Sira*, ed. Renate Egger-Wenzel and Ingrid Krammer (BZAW 270; Berlin: de Gruyter, 1998) 23-49.

The father's maintenance of his daughter's chastity is important, and in arranging her marriage, he should see that she marries one who is wise (7:24-25). Ben Sira shared the primal anxiety about the male's inability to control women's sexuality,[80] for a lack of sexual dominance subverts male patriarchy at the heart of his view of society and marriage. He also greatly fears his sexual attraction to women other than his wife, including especially the "strange woman" (the prostitute, the virgin, another's wife, and one whose sexual dalliances are frequent; cf. 9:1-9). Failure to control this desire can destroy the man's life, for, if found out, he is executed or murdered by the woman's offended family.

Ben Sira, himself a man of means, followed the traditional Jewish and sapiential teaching to care for the poor. This responsibility is especially tempered by the duty incumbent upon the aristocracy to see to it that the needs of the impoverished in Jewish society were met with charity. The instruction in 4:1-10 contains care for the usual categories of the poor in Jewish society, the orphans and widows.[81] Yet these two groups are extended to include the destitute (the providing of clothing, shelter, food, and provisions for health), the beggar, and those exploited by the oppressor. The theological basis for this charity is the teaching that Yahweh gives an attentive ear to the cries of the poor and will deliver them, while bringing punishment to those who oppress them. For Ben Sira, charity was no longer a royal responsibility, but now rested on the shoulders of the aristocracy.

Major Theological Themes

Ben Sira was the first known sage to combine creation theology with salvation history. He is similar in this regard to the prophet Second Isaiah. As a sage, however, he integrated a national theology of election and divine redemption into a universal one that pertained to all nations. His was the first sapiential text that integrated a particularistic theology into a ubiquitous one. He was thus a transitional figure in blending together these two theological traditions and paved the way for future sages.

---

80. Lewis J. Eron, "'The Women Have Mastery over Both King and Beggar' (TJud. 15.5) — The Relationship of the Fear of Sexuality to the Status of Women in Apocrypha and Pseudepigrapha: 1 Esdras (3 Ezra) 3–4, Ben Sira and the Testament of Judah," *JSP* 9 (1991) 43-66.

81. See Pancratius C. Beentjes, "'Sei den Waisen wie ein Vater und den Witwen wie ein Gatte': Ein kleiner Kommentar zu Ben Sira 4,1-10," in *Einzelne und seine Gemeinschaft*, 51-64.

The Creation of the Cosmos

The centrality of creation in the book is recognized in key locations in its literary structure. The book opens with a hymn to Wisdom (1:1-10). The first act of creation is the forming of Wisdom (1:4), thus echoing Prov. 8:22-31. This universal wisdom, known in its entirety only by God, informs reality and is given by him to those who worship and love him (Sir. 1:9-10). Ben Sira's view of the universal presence of Wisdom and its dwelling in human beings is comparable to the Stoic view of the Logos. At the conclusion of the first major section (24:1-34), the sage returns to cosmic Wisdom, while Yahweh is proclaimed to be the "creator of all things" (24:8). Wisdom utters her hymn of self-praise before the assembly of the Most High and in the midst of her people, that is, the people of Israel (24:1-2), speaking once more of her origins ("came forth from the mouth of the Most High"). She then describes her search for a dwelling place on the earth; and, at God's command, she takes up residence among the people of Israel, to dwell in the temple in Jerusalem, and to become present in its cultic worship. Now Wisdom is with the chosen people and is identified with the Mosaic law. Thus Wisdom and Torah take on both a universal meaning in creation theology and a particular one in describing Wisdom's election of Israel. Finally, she is identified with the cultic service in the temple in Jerusalem, giving this sacred space and its rituals a universal meaning.

The conclusion of the second section of the book once more highlights creation, this time in a hymn sung by the sage in praise of the wonders of creation (42:22–43:33). Finally, the third section (chs. 44–51) contains the theme of divine providence through the leadership of "pious men" whose deeds and character led the ancestors to the present day. "The assembly declares their wisdom, and the congregation proclaims their praise" (44:15). This encomium of famous heroes is followed by a concluding thanksgiving hymn to the Lord in which Ben Sira describes his search for Wisdom and, having found her, he indicates he gained from her understanding. He declares his undying devotion for her, and affirms he will never leave her. He then issues to potential students the invitation to come and learn from him and to take up the yoke of Wisdom, resting assured that God will provide them their reward (51:1-30).

The Creation of Humanity

Ben Sira also significantly emphasizes the creation of humanity and, in so doing, draws from a variety of biblical texts. Similar to the book of Proverbs, Ben Sira affirms that the poor enjoy the protection of the one who "formed" them

(21:5; cf. Prov. 14:31; 17:5). As the divine potter who creates humanity from the earth (Gen. 2:7), God fashions both the nature and destiny of humans. Ben Sira also speaks of conception as an act of God that shapes humans in their mother's womb and then provides them with the gifts of piety and wisdom (cf. Ps. 139:13-18; Job 10:1-17). Making use of Gen. 1:26-28, Ben Sira tells of humans as created in the divine image who rule over the other creatures who fear them (Sir. 17:4; see Gen. 9:2). They receive from God the gift of wisdom in order to rule justly (see 1 Kgs. 3:3-14). Created to have freedom of the will (Sir. 15:11-20), humans acquire their knowledge of the creator through their "fear of God," which they receive in the womb (1:14) and which is equated with reflection on and living according to the commandments (1:26-27).

Creation and Wisdom

Wisdom is the dominant theme in Ben Sira.[82] Wisdom is the first of God's acts of creation, made to permeate reality. She also is given to the sages in order to understand both God and the world. With this knowledge, the sage is able to interpret correctly the Torah and thus to live a moral life. This cosmic wisdom also becomes the divine inspiration that fills the heart and mind of the sage who writes hymns in praise of God and teaches youth how to behave in order to experience well-being. As the means of divine immanence, Woman Wisdom is the agent of God in revitalizing creation.

Ben Sira begins his text with his initial poem (1:1-10 LXX), declaring that Wisdom originates with God as the first of his divine works (1:4). He alone is wise and to be feared (1:8). In this hymn she is said to be preexistent, originating before all else (1:4). God gives her to those who love him, but he alone knows her intimately, for he created *(ektisen)* her. God also pours her out over all of creation so that it becomes intelligible to the wise (1:9). The following poem (1:11-30), an acrostic psalm, identifies wisdom *(sophia, synesis)* with the fear of God *(phobos kyriou,* 1:14), which serves as the theme of this sapiential psalm. Thus the piety and worship of humans serve as the basis for their receiving the gift of Wisdom. For Ben Sira humans who possess wisdom do so from the womb and enhance it by means of their "fear of God."

Chapter 24 is a most significant text about Woman Wisdom in the book,[83] although it is preserved only in the LXX. The first three strophes are a hymn of self-praise by Wisdom (vv. 3-6, 7-12, 13-17) who dwells in the divine assembly.

---

82. Marböck, *Weisheit im Wandel.*
83. See esp. Maurice Gilbert, "L'Éloge de la Sagesse (Siracide 24)," *RTL* 5 (1974) 326-48.

This hymn is comparable to the Isis hymns of self-praise (vv. 1-17).[84] She then issues her protrepsis by which she invites those who desire her to eat of her fruits and to drink to quench their thirst in order to escape shame and avoid sin (vv. 19-22). The concluding strophes (vv. 23-29, 30-34) are written in the voice of Ben Sira, who first identifies her with the Torah and then speaks of his own offering of instruction to leave to future generations. Cosmic Wisdom, created by God in the beginning, before the ages, came forth from his mouth and sought her resting place in creation. As the universal spirit of knowledge of creation, she goes in quest of a resting place among a people. Obedient to the creator's command, she takes her place in Israel. She then dwells on the Temple Mount (= Zion) where she is identified with both the temple service and the law of Moses. What is particularly striking in this hymn is the closely drawn connection between wisdom, election, the temple, and creation.

Ben Sira tells of cosmic Wisdom taking up her abode in the "holy tabernacle" of the wilderness, now in Zion in the form of the temple, and in Jerusalem the "beloved city" and serving as a priest ("one who ministers before him") in the tent (v. 10). This hymn incorporates the cosmic myth of Wisdom in which she is described as a goddess. The sage makes use of important mythical images that include the "vault of heaven" (cf. Prov. 8:27-28), the "deep abyss" (cf. Prov. 8:24), the sacred grove of trees, the cosmic waters that originate in the center of the earth and stream in different directions throughout the world from Zion, the cosmic mountain. Wisdom is like the tributaries of the cosmic rivers that flow from the sacred garden surrounding the holy temple where the deity dwells. The water source for the temple was the Siloam spring, and its sacred waters were used especially during the Festival of Tabernacles.

For Ben Sira, Wisdom, Israel as her dwelling place, the temple services, and the Torah are merged theologically in order to describe the order of creation and to speak of the means by which it receives its stability and vitality.[85] This text marks the most important theological synthesis in the corpora of wisdom texts.

The Praise of Pious Men (Chs. 44–50)

Included among the literary genres of Jewish historiography in the Hellenistic period (chronicles, romances, and epic poetry) is a fourth category: the enco-

---

84. Conzelmann, "Mother of Wisdom," 230-43; Burton L. Mack, *Logos und Sophia: Untersuchungen zur Weisheitstheologie im hellenistischen Judentum* (SUNT 10; Göttingen: Vandenhoeck & Ruprecht, 1973) 40-42.

85. Robert Hayward, *The Jewish Temple: A Non-Biblical Sourcebook* (London: Routledge, 1996) 6-17.

mium.[86] In Sir. 44–50 there is an encomium that surveys Jewish history known as the praise of "pious men" (Heb. 'anšê ḥăsādîm). This Greek form originated in the eulogy delivered at funerals and consisted of the praise of the deceased.[87] As the form developed in its extensive use in a variety of religious and social settings, it became a panegyric of human saints and heroes as well as of cities that was delivered during festivals.

Historiography was a highly valued literary form in Greece. Greek historians of note included Herodotus in the fifth century B.C.E., Hecataeus of Miletus at the end of the fourth century B.C.E., and Diodorus of Sicily in the first century B.C.E.[88] Especially valued among the Greeks was the antiquity of a people. Nations that came under Greek control during the Hellenistic period often composed their own histories in order to establish the prestige of their cultures.[89] Thus Ben Sira makes this effort in his encomium that traces Jewish history from the origins of humanity to his present time by focusing on the noble heroes of Judaism.

The encomium belongs to epideictic literature (Gk. *epideixis*), which, according to Aristotle, is one of the major types of rhetorical presentations: deliberative, forensic, persuasive, and epideictic (*Rhet.* 1.3.3). The first three have different social settings: the assembly, the courtroom, and the ordinary audience, respectively. Epideictic oratory referred to speeches in which the rhetor sought to impress, rather than persuade, his audience. In Ben Sira's example, the audience is a Jewish one, presumably an assembly during a festival celebrated in a synagogue. He extols the heroes of Jewish history whose great deeds and deepseated piety led to the shaping and continuation of the chosen people.[90] Thus he combines Jewish history with the elegance of language by lauding the great

---

86. On these chapters see Theodore C. Burgess, *Epideictic Literature* (New York: Garland, 1987); Mack, *Wisdom and the Hebrew Epic*; Lee, *Studies in Sirach 44–50*; R. N. Whybray, "Ben Sira and History," in *Treasures of Wisdom*, 137-45; J. L. Ska, "L'éloge des Pères dans le Siracide (Sir. 44-50) et le canon de l'Ancien Testament," in *Treasures of Wisdom*, 181-93; Teresa R. Brown, "God and Men in Israel's History: God and Idol Worship in Praise of the Fathers (Sir. 44–50)," in *Ben Sira's God*, 214-20; Alon Goshen-Gottstein, "Ben Sira's Praise of the Fathers: A Canon-Conscious Reading," in *Ben Sira's God*, 235-67. For a comprehensive overview of the encomium, see Robert Doran, "Jewish Hellenistic Historians before Josephus," *ANRW* 2.20/1:246-97.

87. Arnaldo Momigliano, *Alien Wisdom: The Limits of Hellenization* (Cambridge: Cambridge University Press, 1975) 98; Wacholder, *Eupolemus,* 12.

88. Diodorus Siculus, *Bibliotheca Historica* 40.3.

89. See Berossus for Babylonian history and Manetho for Egyptian history (G. P. Verbrugghe and J. M. Wickersham, *Berossos and Manetho, Introduced and Translated: Native Traditions in Ancient Mesopotamia and Egypt* [Ann Arbor: University of Michigan Press, 1996]). The style of the chronicle used by Demetrius is identical to that found in Berossus and in Manetho.

90. Lee, *Studies in Sirach 44–50,* 84.

accomplishments and esteemed virtues of the pious and notable ancestors. These ancestors include: Enoch, Noah, Abraham, Isaac and Jacob, Moses, Aaron, Phinehas, Joshua, Caleb, the judges, Samuel, Nathan, David, Solomon, Rehoboam, Jeroboam, Elijah, Elisha, Hezekiah, Isaiah, Josiah, Jeremiah, Ezekiel, Job, the Twelve Prophets, Zerubbabel, Jeshua, Nehemiah, Joseph, Shem, Seth, Enosh, Adam, and Simon. By tracing Israel's history back to the beginning of time, Ben Sira thus seeks to extol the glories of his people within a Hellenistic world that highly values the antiquity of an ethos.

Ben Sira's encomium excludes for the most part, but not completely, disgraced sinners. He focuses on noble heroes whose qualities enhance their character, deeds, and prestige.[91] He at times engages in a revisionist, romanticized history in order to praise the great heroes of the past who were pious, righteous, faithful, honored, and thus to be remembered. In his view, it is because of their deeds and virtues that their descendants will continue for all times. His approach is selective; he does not refer to Saul or Ezra, while the great priests, Aaron, Phinehas, and Simon II, receive significant praise. Indeed, there is more about Aaron than Moses. While his omitting of Saul is understandable, it is striking that he makes no mention of Ezra. One can only guess why. However, the emphasis placed on the great high priests, culminating with Simon II, underscores the close relationship of this sage to the priesthood and the value he places on this important office. As one would expect from the other sections of the book, Ben Sira does not refer to any women in his encomium. In addition, he speaks of only five southern kings (David, Solomon, Rehoboam, Hezekiah, and Josiah). Rehoboam is belittled as the fool whose policies led to the northern revolution, while Solomon, extolled for his wisdom, still brought shame to himself and wrath upon his descendants due to his defiling his bed with women. In the summation about the kings, he exempts from the cast of royal sinners who abandoned the law only David, Hezekiah, and Josiah (49:4). As for northern kings, Ben Sira mentions by name Jeroboam (I), who is portrayed as leading Israel into sin and initiating a process of wickedness that eventuated in the Assyrian exile. Among the prophets, he gives only passing notice to Jeremiah and Ezekiel, while extolling Isaiah in a lengthy section. The Twelve Minor Prophets are briefly mentioned, and then only as a group. In eliminating any stain from the character of those saints who were truly heroes, he does not refer to their sins, save in a very general way (thus David's sins are taken away by the Lord). In speaking of the perfect and righteous Noah, he makes no mention of either his drunkenness or the sin of Ham.

The sage's encomium follows a hymn on the works of creation (42:14–

---

91. Ibid., 206.

43:33). The encomium then opens with the call to worship by the sage (v. 1), followed by a proem (vv. 2-14). The heroes who performed righteous and noble deeds in Israel's history then follow. Theologically speaking, this structure reveals a movement from creation, to history, to the temple service and the grandeur of the figure of the high priest Simon II.[92] The grand finale is the description of the high priest during the Festival of Tabernacles. This festival brings to culmination the order of creation and history for Judah and the nations. To participate in the Festival of Tabernacles is to participate in the final actualization of the salvific order of creation and history, not just of Israel but also of all peoples. Thus the preceding creation hymn and this recounting of the praise of the pious ancestors are integrally connected into one grand mythic scheme of creation, history, and fulfillment in the celebration of Tabernacles in the temple. The glory of creation now is shared by the great heroes of Israel who lead to the fulfillment of the salvific order of creation and history.[93]

Wisdom, creation, the pious heroes of Jewish history, the temple, and the priesthood provide the major theological emphases in the book of Ben Sira. The forming of Woman Wisdom, the first act of creation, enables God to shape the order of creation and history and to guide providentially reality to its culmination in the glorious high priesthood of Simon II and the celebration of the Feast of Tabernacles. Wisdom becomes identified with the Torah, which guides the behavior of the faithful. The celebration of the temple ritual and the obedience to the Torah enable the righteous to participate in the ongoing order of cosmos and history.

92. See Mack, *Wisdom and the Hebrew Epic,* Appendix A, 189-93. He argues that the hymn on creation and the "Praise of the Pious" belong together: "Now I will remember God's works/praise pious men." Both literary pieces are held together by the theme of the revelation of "glory." In addition, each of the introductory proems refers to important wisdom themes: the limits of wisdom and death without memory.

93. Mack, *Wisdom and Hebrew Epic,* 65; Maurice Gilbert, "L'action de grâce de Ben Sira (Sir 51,1-12)," in *Ce Dieu qui vient. Études sur l'Ancien et le Nouveau Testament offerts au Professeur Bernard Renaud,* ed. Raymond Kuntzmann (LD 159; Paris: Cerf, 1995) 231-242; Johannes Marböck, "Der Hohepriester Simon in Sir 50," in *Treasures of Wisdom,* 215-29.

7. Wisdom during the Roman Empire: The Wisdom of Solomon

General Introduction

The author, date, and context for the Wisdom of Solomon are not precisely known. Most scholars who have worked extensively in the analysis of this book have argued, however, that a Jewish sage,[1] living in Alexandria of Egypt,[2] wrote this text in an accomplished, if not very elegant, Greek[3] between the first century B.C.E. and 40 C.E., that is, at the end of the Ptolemaic period to the early pe-

---

1. The author was well educated and may have attended both a Jewish Torah school and a school of rhetoric where he would have been introduced to Greek literature and philosophy (see Collins, *Jewish Wisdom*, 150-57). Otherwise, he would at least have listened to lectures in the agora or studied under a sophist who was employed by his parents to teach him a variety of subjects, including popular renditions of current philosophies. The author probably taught either in a Jewish school, or as a private tutor employed in Alexandrian families of privilege to teach their children (see Philo, *Spec.* 2.62; *Mos.* 2.16). While he appears to be familiar with Hellenistic philosophy, he fits better the social model of a sophist especially trained in rhetoric in setting forth a speech of artful persuasion than as a philosopher who, like Philo, sought to transform Judaism by means of the important features of Middle Platonism or Stoicism.

2. While there is little evidence to identify the provenance of the book, the origins in Alexandria are implicitly supportable. The way he shapes his presentations of the exodus and the polemic against idolatry and animal worship strongly suggest an Egyptian origin, as we shall see below.

3. The best critical Greek text is that of Joseph Ziegler, *Sapientia Salomonis* (Göttingen Septuagint 12/1; Göttingen: Vandenhoeck & Ruprecht, 1962). Also see Peter Arzt, et al., eds., *Sprachlicher Schlüssel zur Sapientia Salomonis (Weisheit)* (2nd ed.; Institut für Neutestamentliche Bibelwissenschaft Salzburg 1. Sapientia Salomonis; Salzburg: Verlag Institut für Ntl. Bibelwissenschaft, 1997).

riod of the Roman rule of Egypt.[4] The author gives evidence of being a well-educated wisdom teacher, or rhetor, who either had studied under a sophist or was a graduate of a school of rhetoric. The author composed an exhortatory speech that had the purpose of encouraging faithful Jews to maintain their loyalty to their ancestral faith in the face of persecution, persuading apostate Jews to return to their religious tradition, and convincing Hellenes of the superiority of Jewish religion and the moral life. The Jews in his community were apparently experiencing persecution, which led him to write this book as an apologia to defend his community against the outrages of xenophobia and to encourage loyalty to the traditional faith.

This teacher, or perhaps better said, rhetor, merged redemption history and creation with familiar Hellenistic literary forms and thought in order to provide a theology that would appeal to Jews who lived in the Egyptian Diaspora.[5] While he was knowledgeable of both his own Jewish history and religion and Hellenistic philosophy, he did not shape a philosophical treatise. Rather, he wrote a sermon of exhortation *(logos protreptikos)* that united Greek literary forms and thought with the religious traditions of the ancestors of Israel.

Date and Historical Context

Following the defeat of Marc Anthony and Cleopatra in 31 B.C.E. and their subsequent deaths, Octavian brought the wealthy nation of Egypt into the Roman Empire.[6] Cleopatra's dream, shared by Anthony, was to build an expansive empire that would unite the east and west. Yet this ambitious vision failed to reach

---

4. The earliest references to the Wisdom of Solomon are those of Irenaeus (140-202 C.E.; *Haer.* 3.4; 7.5), Clement of Alexandria (175-230 C.E.), and the Muratorian Fragment (180-190 C.E.), which includes it within the NT canon. In addition, the similarities of Wisdom to Philo (20-50 C.E.) also are suggestive of the date. For discussions of possible dates of composition and the probable location of Alexandria, see Peter Dalbert, *Die Theologie der hellenistisch-jüdischen Missionsliteratur unter Ausschluss von Philo und Josephus* (Hamburg-Volksdorf: Herbert Reich, 1954) 71-72. Also see David Winston, *The Wisdom of Solomon* (AB; Garden City, NY: Doubleday, 1979) 12-25; Hans Hübner, *Die Weisheit Salomos* (ATD Apocryphen 4; Göttingen: Vandenhoeck & Ruprecht, 1999). Winston points to the early first century C.E. as the period of composition on the basis of the occurrence of numerous Greek words and phrases that do not appear before this period. In my judgment he has the better of the argument.

5. Walter Vogels, "The God Who Creates Is the God Who Saves: The Book of Wisdom's Reversal of the Biblical Pattern," *Église et théologie* 22 (1991) 315-35.

6. In general see Barclay, *Jews in the Mediterranean Diaspora*, 48-81; Allan K. Bowman, et al., eds., *CAH* 10: *The Augustan Empire, 44 B.C.–A.D. 69* (2nd ed.; Cambridge: Cambridge University Press, 1996).

its culmination due to the pivotal sea battle at Actium in which the Roman navy destroyed its Egyptian opposition. The suicides of Anthony and Cleopatra a year later led to the end of the Ptolemaic dynasty. Even so, Alexandria remained a city of advanced culture and wealth, made possible by its successful commercial enterprises and rich harvests of grain from the Nile Valley.[7] After the fall of the Ptolemies, Rome ascended to the rank of the most prominent city in the empire, followed then by Alexandria. The Ptolemaic rulers were replaced by Roman-appointed prefects accountable directly to Rome. Roman prefects did not ingratiate themselves to the Egyptian vassals, who held considerable resentment against their overlords, as they did of the Greek kings who preceded them. After the death of Augustus, the Egyptians lost their status of privilege in their own country.[8]

The Jews of Alexandria initially cultivated good relations with Rome. This began when they supported Gabinius's effort to reestablish the rule of Ptolemy XII Auletes in 55 B.C.E. and then Julius Caesar's support of Cleopatra in 47 B.C.E. Thus early in the period of Roman influence and ultimately domination of Egypt, Jews enjoyed overseeing and enacting their own internal civil regulation and were permitted to live according to their ancestral laws. The Letter of Aristeas 310 even indicated that the Jewish community was allowed to organize itself in Alexandria as a *politeuma* (an ethnic religious community), although they did not possess the status of a political organization essentially involved in self-rule. This term had three differently nuanced uses: the political composition of a polis, the inhabitants of an area, including a city, and a community of aliens living in a Greek polis. For the Jews, this term would be valid only in the third sense.[9] The legal powers of the Jews of a city were limited to administering internal affairs, although they were prohibited from executing the death penalty. Each Greek city in Egypt was under the control of the hierarchical bureaucracy of the dynasty. A charter was required for any city and any ethnic group within it to exist. One would assume that the Jews of Alexandria possessed this charter. Their privileges granted by this supposed charter would have included the right to build and attend synagogues, to follow their own laws and customs, to establish their own courts and thus make legal decisions, to teach the Torah, and to elect their own officials for administering their community.

The Jewish *politeuma* consisted of the following structure. Originally, dur-

7. See P. M. Fraser, *Ptolemaic Alexandria* (2 vols.; Oxford: Clarendon, 1972); Jean-Yves Empereur, ed., *Alexandria* (2 vols.; Cairo: Institut Français d'Archéologie Orientale, 1998, 2002); idem, *Alexandria Rediscovered* (New York: George Braziller, 1996).

8. See E. M. Smallwood, *Philonis Alexandrini Legatio ad Gaium* (2nd ed.; Leiden: Brill, 1970) 11-12.

9. Tcherikover, *Hellenistic Civilization*, 299.

ing the Ptolemaic period, the ethnarch "ruled the people, judged its cases and supervised the implementation of contract and orders, like the ruler of an independent state" (Strabo, as quoted by Josephus, *Ant.* 14.117). In the period of Imperial Rome, Augustus replaced the ethnarch with a *gerousia* (Philo, *Flacc.* 74) composed of seventy-one members (*b. Sukkah* 51b). Philo calls them "archons," although this term may have been limited to the most powerful and prominent among the *gerousia* (cf. Josephus, *J.W.* 7.47). Josephus calls these leading members "the heads of the *gerousia*" (*J.W.* 7.412). The archons and the larger *gerousia* made the most important decisions. Other important positions in the Jewish community included the head of the *gerousia* (the *gerousiarchēs*), the head of the synagogue *(archisynagōgos),* the overseer *(phōnētēs),* and the secretary *(grammateus);* there were also less important positions. While there were Jewish courts (Josephus, *Ant.* 14.235), Jews could also appeal their cases to the secular city court.

Among the privileges of the Jews, granted to them by charter by Augustus[10] and later reaffirmed by Claudius, was religious freedom, which could be exercised by refusing to participate in state and city pagan cults and to offer sacrifices to other deities. Jews were also granted the right to observe the Sabbath and other religious holidays without having to work or to schedule events like legal decisions by Greek courts, to be exempt from military service largely because of Sabbath observance, and to collect the temple tithes and gifts that were permitted to be sent to Jerusalem. Conditions for the Jewish community in Alexandria deteriorated, beginning with Germanicus, a position that became more pronounced during the reigns of Tiberius and Gaius Caligula (37-41 C.E.). The pogrom under Flaccus was later followed by the slaughter of thousands of Jews during the disturbances incited by the Great Revolt and by Trajan's extermination of the Alexandrian community due to their revolt in 115-117 C.E.

Hellenism and the Jews of the Diaspora

Among the sociopolitical concerns voiced in the Wisdom of Solomon, three stand out as especially important: the attraction of Hellenistic culture, the

---

10. Augustus issued this charter in the form of a proclamation, engraved on a stele. This proclamation thanked the Jews for support and granted them their specified privileges (see Josephus, *C. Ap.* 2.37, who wrongly attributes this stele to Julius Caesar and also incorrectly assumed that this guaranteed their full citizenship in the polis). While Augustus had allowed the Jews of Alexandria to be led internally by their own ethnarch and council, he withdrew this advantage c. 11 C.E. These privileges created strong tensions between Jews and their ethnic neighbors, the Greeks and especially the Egyptians.

question of Greek citizenship in a polis, and xenophobia, which was occasionally behind the outbreak of persecution.

The struggle between religious heritage and ethnic identity on one hand and Hellenism and its advantages on the other led some Jews to abandon Judaism. During this period, several prominent Jews either renounced their Jewish heritage or sought to reshape Judaism into a largely Hellenistic religion and culture. These include Jason, the high priest; Tiberius Julius Alexander, who was the nephew of Philo; Dositheus, son of Drimylus (3 Macc. 1:3; *CPJ* 1:230-36); and Antiochus, a son of the archon of the Jews of Antioch at the end of the Great Revolt (Josephus, *J.W.* 7.44-56).

Tiberius Julius Alexander, the son of Alexander Lysimachus, who belonged to one of the most prominent Jewish families in Jerusalem, was an Egyptian Jew who rose to prominence in Roman circles.[11] He served as the Roman governor first of Judea (46-48 C.E.) and then of Egypt (68-69), and was one of the commanders during the Roman siege of Jerusalem (70). The father served as chief customs officer and had offered financial help to Antonia, the mother of the emperor Claudius. The father's brother was the philosopher Philo (c. 15 B.C.E.–c. 50 C.E.), and his younger son was Marcus, the husband of princess Bernice, the daughter of the Jewish king Herod Agrippa. Thus Tiberius Julius Alexander belonged to one of the most influential families in the Roman east, a family that stood in three cultural traditions: Jewish, Greek, and Roman. His first known office was that of commander of the Theban district in southern Egypt. Later he was appointed prefect of Judea (46-48), during which time he executed the two Zealot sons of Judas the Galilean, who earlier had instigated a revolt. He assisted the Roman general Corbulo in the war against the Parthians in 63. In 68 Alexander was made prefect of Egypt by the emperor Nero. He now commanded two legions, III Cyrenaica and XXII Deiotariana, which he used against the Jews of Alexandria during the early years of the Great Revolt in Judah. Josephus states that no less than fifty thousand Jews were killed when Alexander sent the legions to the Jewish quarter. Finally, he was one of the Roman commanders in the siege of Jerusalem, which fell in 70.

According to 3 Macc. 1:3, "Dositheus, known as the son of Drimylus, a Jew by birth but who renounced the law and abandoned his ancestral beliefs," learned of the plot of a certain Theodotus and some of Ptolemy's (Ptolemy IV Philopator) best soldiers to assassinate the king at night in order to end the war with Antiochus III. He convinced the king to hide in another tent and placed someone else in the royal tent to suffer the intended fate. With Ptolemy saved

---

11. See Viktor Burr, *Tiberius Iulius Alexander* (Antiquitas. Reihe 1: Abhandlungen zur alten Geschichte 1; Bonn: R. Habelt, 1955).

from this assassination attempt, his forces were then victorious at Raphia over those of Antiochus.

When Vespasian landed in Syria at the beginning of the Great Revolt, Antiochus, the son of the archon of Antioch, instigated a persecution of his fellow Jews in the city (Josephus, *J.W.* 7.44-56). According to Josephus, prior to this time the Jews were well treated by the Seleucid kings and allowed to settle in Syria, with a significant community formed by those choosing to live in Antioch. He argued that the Seleucid rulers gave them citizenship rights equal to those held by Greeks and that the Jews incorporated themselves amicably into the population of the city. Josephus also stated that Antiochus, at the height of anti-Judaism in the city, was the chief magistrate of the Jews, and during an assembly in a theater gave a speech in which he denounced his father and other Jews, including some non-Syrian Jews, accusing them of planning to incinerate the city. The people's response was one of great fury. To inflame them even further, Antiochus, who sought to prove he detested his Jewish tradition by offering sacrifices to the pagan Greek gods, suggested that other Jews be forced to do the same. This would allow the conspirators to be exposed by their refusal to follow suit. While a few did submit to this outrage, the ones who would not were massacred. With the support of a Roman general, Antiochus then humiliated the Jews by disallowing them to observe the Sabbath, a prohibition that resulted in eliminating this day from observance not only in Antioch but in other Syrian cities as well.

The enticement of Greek culture was especially strong in eastern provinces, where hellenization blended with ancient traditions.[12] Greek intellectuals, of course, held to the view that their culture was infinitely superior, although their rulers generally did not force hellenization on their subjects, save for the futile efforts of Antiochus IV Epiphanes. However, that the lingua franca of the Greek empires, states, and colonies was Greek, that the cultural values were steeped in Hellenism, and that commerce and diplomacy required fluency in the language meant that a mastering of Greek and an accommodation by other ethnicities to Greek civilization held major advantages for those in pursuit of wealth and social acceptance. Thus the attraction of Hellenistic culture proved appealing to many Diaspora Jews, especially those who resided in Alexandria.

This enticement of Hellenistic culture for Jewish literati is seen in a variety

---

12. Hellenistic elements included the original composition in Greek, several central Stoic teachings (the four cardinal virtues of Stoicism, 8:7; the harmony of the elements in ch. 19; the argument from design, 13:1-5; and the Stoic ideal of a world soul). Also important in Wisdom is the Platonic conception of the immortality of the soul. See esp. Chrysostome Larcher, *Études sur le Livre de la Sagesse* (Études bibliques; Paris: Gabalda, 1969) 201-2; J. M. Reese, *Hellenistic Influence on the Book of Wisdom and Its Consequences* (AnBib 41; Rome: Pontifical Biblical Institute, 1970).

of writings, including historians, philosophers, and sages. Among the better known are Pseudo-Hecataeus, Artapanus, Ezekiel the Tragedian, the unknown author of the so-called Letter of Aristeas, Aristobulus, Philo Judaeus, Pseudo-Phocylides, 3 Maccabees, and the Third Sibylline Oracle. Some of these Jewish scholars sought to explain and defend Judaism from pagan criticism, while others attempted to present their ethnicity and religion in ways that would appeal to a contemporary Greek and then Greco-Roman audience. They also indicated how a Jew should respond to Hellenistic culture in ways that, in their view, would be acceptable. Some were sympathetic and adaptable to Hellenism, while others were sharply critical. Among these Jewish intellectuals is the rhetor who composed the Wisdom of Solomon.

A Jewish historian and writer of romance, Artapanus wrote *Judaica* and *Concerning the Jews,* three fragments of two manuscripts that have survived in Eusebius (*Praep. ev.* 9.18.1; 9.23.1-4; 9.27.1-37), who quoted them from Alexander Polyhistor.[13] Drawing from the LXX, his romantic history, *Concerning the Jews,* is also characterized by the presence of the encomium and apologia, which one also finds in Ben Sira and the Wisdom of Solomon.[14] His encomium, functioning as an apology, praises three heroes of Jewish history: Abraham, Joseph, and Moses. Similar to Ben Sira and to the Wisdom of Solomon, he lived and wrote between 250 and 100 B.C.E. in Egypt.[15] His time period is difficult to pinpoint, but perhaps the most feasible, general date of his writing activity is the reign of Ptolemy VI Philometor (180-145 B.C.E.).[16] Due to its scholarly

13. Holladay, *Fragments from Hellenistic Jewish Authors,* 1:189-243; Attridge, "Historiography," 166-68; John J. Collins, "Artapanus," *OTP* 2:889-903; Doran, "Jewish Hellenistic Historians before Josephus," 257-63.

14. The *apologia* is a form of Greek rhetoric used by several Jewish writers during the Hellenistic period in order to defend Judaism and make it acceptable to Gentiles. See Mark Edwards, Martin Goodman, and Simon Price, in association with Christopher Rowland, eds., *Apologetics in the Roman Empire: Pagans, Jews, and Christians* (Oxford: Oxford University Press, 1999); Elisabeth Schüssler Fiorenza, ed., *Aspects of Religious Propaganda in Judaism and Early Christianity* (University of Notre Dame Center for the Study of Judaism and Christianity in Antiquity 2; Notre Dame, IN: University of Notre Dame Press, 1976). In his essay in the preceding collection ("In Defense of the Spirit: Paul's Letter to the Galatians as a Document of Early Christian Apologetics," 99-114), Hans Dieter Betz describes Christian and Jewish apologetics as follows: literature that sought to add new members, to compete with other religions for people's allegiance, and to prevent persecution. In addition, apologetics seeks to explain or correct its "misunderstandings," "errors," "relativity," or "embarrassments."

15. Collins, *Between Athens and Jerusalem,* 39. He dates Artapanus at the end of the third century B.C.E., thus shortly before Ben Sira's composition. He argues for an Egyptian origin for this work, although not necessarily Alexandria.

16. Holladay, *Fragments,* 1:190.

activity and large Jewish population, Alexandria is the best location for the origin of both this writer and his compositions.

Abraham is credited with teaching astrology to the Egyptians, while Joseph is portrayed not only as the "lord of Egypt" but also as the one who provided significant cultural developments to the Egyptians. Moses was also the teacher of important cultural advances to the Egyptians as well as their military strategist who allowed them to defeat the Ethiopians. He is credited with having invented for the Egyptians ships, architectural devices, military equipment, and waterworks, and for writing philosophy for them. He also was supposed to have founded the Egyptian cults, and to have taught hieroglyphics to the various Egyptian priesthoods. Hermopolis was said to be built to recognize his achievements for Egypt. He himself was worshiped by the Egyptians as a god, Hermes (= Thoth).[17] Artapanus even claimed that Moses' envious stepfather, Pharaoh Chenephres, ordered a failed assassination plot to remove him, died later for uttering blasphemy against the Jewish God, but was revived by a forgiving Moses. In the plague narrative, Artapanus omits the Passover, although he does summarize the exodus and replaces the miraculous character of the Red Sea crossing with a rational explanation. For Artapanus, these three Jewish ancestors are the founders of culture. Portraying the Jews as benefactors of the ancient Egyptians, Artapanus sought to establish favorable relations with their Hellenistic descendants.[18] A liberal Hellenistic Jew, he sought to merge features of Egyptian Hellenism with Hellenistic Judaism.[19] In ascribing to Moses the founding of a number of Egyptian cults, he may have been attempting to repudiate the charge that Jews were atheists, that is, denied the existence of other gods. Yet he still held the view that the Jewish God was the "master of the universe," while the Egyptian gods and animals they worshiped were explained euhemeristically as useful inventions.[20] However, he did not attack them. Artapanus stressed not Jewish faithfulness to the requirements of the Torah, but rather the virtuous character and heroic deeds of the noble Jewish ancestors. This lack of criticism of Egyptians and their gods stands in sharp contrast to the author of the Wisdom of Solomon.

Ezekiel the Tragedian, a Hellenistic Jew of the second century B.C.E. who

17. The Ethiopians are said to have been so impressed by Moses that they began to practice circumcision.

18. Carl H. Holladay, *Theios Anēr in Hellenistic Judaism* (SBLDS 40; Missoula, MT: Scholars Press, 1977) 199-232.

19. Holladay, *Fragments,* 1:193. This liberal view contrasts with the legalistic and narrow one of Theodotus, writing likely in Judea during the rule of John Hyrcanus.

20. Collins, *Between Athens and Jerusalem,* 42. In Wis. 14:15 idolatry is attributed to a grieving father erecting a statue of his dead son and worshiping it in secret rites (thus, a mystery religion).

most likely lived in Alexandria, wrote a tragedy that he entitled the *Exagōgē* ("Leading Out") (seventeen fragments preserved in Eusebius, *Praep. ev.* 9.28.1, who says he uses Alexander Polyhistor; cf. Clement of Alexandria, *Strom.* 1.23; Clement also preserves several fragments).[21] Using the LXX, he combined biblical materials with legends to speak of Moses from his birth to the wilderness wandering. Writing in the literary poetry of tragedy, iambic trimeter, he also used Greek writers (cf. Homer, Aeschylus, Sophocles, Euripides, and Herodotus). This usage indicates that he was well familiar with and even educated in the Greek literary tradition. His purpose was to glorify Moses and to speak of the exodus as an event under the direction of God (cf. Wis. 11–19). Yet he also omitted features that would prove embarrassing when read by a pagan audience. This emphasis on the exodus from Egypt is a key theme in the Wisdom of Solomon, and demonstrates its special importance in the religious celebration of Jews in Alexandria.

The so-called Letter of Aristeas was written by an unknown Jewish author, likely living in Alexandria in the second half of the second century B.C.E.[22] It purports to be a letter of the Greek courtier of Ptolemy II Philadelphus who addresses his brother Philocrates. This literary fiction covers up the fact that the writing is a legendary apology,[23] which describes the translation of the Torah into Greek by seventy-two Jewish scholars chosen by the high priest Eleazar who were experts in Greek and Hebrew, for the great library of King Ptolemy.[24] The text's purpose was to encourage the Jews to adapt to Greek culture and society.[25] At the same time, the Jewish audience was to use their piety and traditions to gain respect from the Greeks and tolerance for their religious practices. Thus this text seeks to achieve a synthesis of Hellenism and Judaism, something that is intrinsic to the Wisdom of Solomon. An encomium (Let. Aris. 121-122; cf. Ben Sira

21. Carl Howard Jacobsen, *The Exagōgē of Ezekiel* (New York: Cambridge University Press, 1983); R. G. Robertson, "Ezekiel the Tragedian," *OTP* 2:803-7.

22. See Victor Tcherikover, "The Ideology of the Letter of Aristeas," *HThR* 51 (1958) 59-68; Sidney Jellicoe, "The Occasion and Purpose of the Letter of Aristeas: A Re-Examination," *NTS* 12 (1966) 144-50; George Howard, "The Letter of Aristeas and Diaspora Judaism," *JTS* 22 (1971) 337-48; R. J. H. Shutt, "Letter of Aristeas," *OTP* 2:7-34; Mary Ann L. Beavis, "Anti-Egyptian Polemic in the Letter of Aristeas 130-165 (The High Priest's Discourse)," *JSJ* 18 (1987) 145-51. The translation of the LXX began in the third century B.C.E. and was concluded by the end of the second century B.C.E.

23. Howard's view is that the "letter" was written in part to respond to conservative Jews in Jerusalem who claimed one could practice true Judaism only by studying the Torah from the Hebrew Bible preserved in Jerusalem. Aristeas wishes to show that the translation was as accurate and inspired as the original Hebrew Bible. The apology was directed not to the Greeks but rather to the Jews of Jerusalem and its environs ("Letter of Aristeas," 348).

24. Barclay, *Jews in the Mediterranean Diaspora,* 138-50.

25. Tcherikover, *Hellenistic Civilization,* 61.

and Wisdom of Solomon) praises the translators for their excellent paideia, their family ancestors, their mastery of Jewish literature, and their knowledge of Greek literature.[26] Mutual respect,[27] God as creator and provider for Jews and Greeks, and the worship of the same deity under different names (i.e., Zeus and Jove) are important moral and theological themes. Kashrut is provided both an ethical and allegorical connotation, and the great banquet at the end suggests Jews and Greeks ate together. Jewish religion is affirmed as the superior religion, especially because of the emphasis placed on monotheism, while, similar to the Wisdom of Solomon, polytheism is described in euhemeristic terms. Also similar is their common disdain for Egyptian idolatry and the worship of animals, living or dead. Jewish religion is superior to all others. This text also describes the glorious office of the high priest (cf. Sir. 50) and the wonders of the temple in Jerusalem, including its awe-inspiring liturgy.[28] Thus the text attempts to strike a happy medium between Judaism and Greek culture.

Another Alexandrian Jewish intellectual writing in the second century B.C.E. was Aristobulus.[29] Five fragments of his writings have been preserved (Eusebius, *Hist. eccl.* 7.32.16-18; *Praep. ev.* 8.10.13.12),[30] and they underscore their author's intent to relate Hellenistic culture to Judaism.[31] He also made use of elements of the encomium and the apologia (cf. Wisdom of Solomon). Dedicating his text to Ptolemy, probably Ptolemy VI Philometor (180-145 B.C.E.), he spoke of a variety of themes, including the nature of God (particularly addressing the problem of anthropomorphism); the similarity of the views of Moses with several Greek writers; the dependence of certain Greek philosophers, including Socrates, Plato, and Pythagoras, on the law of Moses; the similarities of the ideas of Orpheus and Aratus to those of Moses; and the Sabbath, which was said to parallel the Greek idea of cosmic order found in Homer and Hesiod (both of whom were said to regard the seventh day as holy). The exodus once again receives an important thematic emphasis. Aristobulus sought not only to explain certain features of Judaism that an educated Hellenistic audience might consider offensive, for example, a deity who possessed human features, but also to extol the greatness and even superiority of the teachings and figure of Moses

26. See Ben Sira's description of the sage in 38:34b–39:11.

27. Barclay, *Jews in the Mediterranean Diaspora*, 141.

28. Shutt, "Letter of Aristeas," 10.

29. Adela Yarbro Collins, "Aristobulus," *OTP* 2:831-42; Holladay, *Fragments*, vol. 3: *Aristobulus*; Nikolaus Walter, *Der Thoraausleger Aristobulos. Untersuchungen zu seinen Fragmenten und zu pseudepigraphischen Resten der jüdisch-hellenistischen Literatur* (Berlin: Akadamie Verlag, 1964).

30. Clement of Alexandria preserved fragments 2-5 that were more paraphrases than quotes (*Strom.* 1, 5, 6).

31. An Aristobulus is mentioned in 2 Macc. 1:10–2:18, possibly the same person.

and the importance of the Jewish law. Rejecting the possibility of a contradiction between the Bible and philosophy, like Philo he gave the Torah an allegorical interpretation.[32] He emphasized the unity of all truth and stressed that Judaism is the most significant "philosophical school." The deity of the Jews and the god of the Gentiles are one and the same, showing that the author sought to forge a compatible relationship with the Greek community. Likewise, he mentioned that both Greeks and Jews regarded the number seven as holy.

The presentation of Judaism by Philo Judaeus (c. 15 B.C.E.–50 C.E.),[33] who was both a philosopher and exegete of the Greek Pentateuch and a prolific writer who composed more than forty treatises, may be characterized as an example of the interpretation of Judaism through a variety of Hellenistic lenses, including, in particular, Middle Platonism. His writings included elements of Stoicism, mysticism, and Pythagorean numerology.[34] In the interpretation of Scripture, he made significant use of allegory. He also undertook, though unsuccessfully, to obtain Alexandrian citizenship for Jews living in the city in which he lived and worked. He sought to present the major features of ancestral Jewish beliefs and practices in Hellenistic dress, appropriating from his religious tradition what he deemed most important to maintain, and to explain its features to a Hellenistic audience.[35] Philo came from one of the most prominent families in Alexandria (see the roles and accomplishments of his brother, Alexander Lysimachus, whose son was the infamous apostate who slaughtered large numbers of his fellow

32. See David Dawson, *Allegorical Readers and Cultural Revision in Ancient Alexandria* (Berkeley: University of California Press, 1992).

33. E. R. Goodenough, *The Politics of Philo Judaeus* (New Haven: Yale University Press, 1938) 52-74; Harry Austyn Wolfson, *Philo: Foundations of Religious Philosophy in Judaism, Christianity, and Islam* (2nd ed.; 2 vols.; Cambridge: Harvard University Press, 1948); idem, *Introduction to Philo Judaeus* (2nd ed.; Oxford: Blackwell, 1962); David Winston, *Logos and Mystical Theology in Philo of Alexandria* (Cincinnati: Hebrew Union College Press, 1985); Peder Borgen, "Philo of Alexandria," in *Jewish Writings*, 233-82; Samuel Sandmel, "Philo Judaeus: An Introduction to the Man, His Writings, and His Significance," *ANRW* 21/1.2:3-46; Alan Mendelson, *Philo's Jewish Identity* (BJS 161; Atlanta: Scholars Press, 1988); Ellen Birnbaum, *The Place of Judaism in Philo's Thought: Israel, Jews, and Proselytes* (BJS 290; Atlanta: Scholars Press, 1996); Dorothy Sly, *Philo's Alexandria* (London: Routledge, 1996); Barclay, *Jews in the Mediterranean Diaspora*, 158-80; Collins, *Between Athens and Jerusalem*, 131-38; David Winston *The Ancestral Philosophy: Hellenistic Philosophy in Second Temple Judaism*, ed. Gregory E. Sterling (BJS 331; Providence: Brown Judaic Studies, 2001); M. R. Niehoff, *Philo on Jewish Identity and Culture* (Tübingen: Mohr Siebeck, 2001).

34. See Winston, "Was Philo a Mystic?" 151-70. Winston gives the basic understanding of mysticism as "a timeless apprehension of the transcendent through a unifying vision that gives bliss or serenity and normally accrues upon a course of self-mastery and contemplation" (p. 151). Thus Philo seeks a timeless union of humanity with the "All" of existence, serenity that derives from this union, and ecstasy (p. 170).

35. Barclay, *Jews in the Mediterranean Diaspora*, 125-80.

Jews). Philo's brother appears to have served as both the chief customs official of eastern Egypt and the protector of Antonia, the mother of Claudius.[36]

Because of the prominence of his family and his clear, elegant Greek, it is possible that he was a citizen and graduate of an Alexandrian gymnasium.[37] His writings reveal that he was a man who knew both Jewish and Greek literatures. However, his Bible was the LXX, which he considered to be an inspired translation, and we cannot be certain he knew Hebrew (see *Mos.* 2.37-41). In his essay *De congressu eruditionis gratia,* he describes Greek paideia practiced in the schools and notes that the standard curriculum consisted of philosophy, grammar, geometry, and music. Philosophy was the "lawful wife" (*Congr.* 74-76), while other subjects were "handmaidens." Philosophy, he says, consisted of logic, ethics, and physics (esp. cosmology).[38]

Philo examined a wide variety of subjects.[39] His religious beliefs are stated in a creed of five affirmations: God exists from eternity, God is one, the world had a beginning, the world is one, and God exercises divine forethought for the cosmos and its inhabitants.[40] He also created the world through means of the divine *logos* even as an architect plans and builds a city (*Spec.* 1.80-81; cf. Wis. 7:22).[41] These themes resonate well with the Wisdom of Solomon. God was also the providential director of reality and the divine judge rewarding the just and punishing the wicked. In his hierarchical cosmology, Philo sets forth the highest reality in its purest form as "the One" (= God) and then descends to lower (earth and creatures) and lower forms (inanimate). Men are higher in this ranking than women, who are more encumbered by the corporeal. Men also are superior to women, for the male has the ability to use his mind more than the female. The highest creature, below God, is the man who is rational, free, and liberated from captivity to the body and passions.

Bringing together Stoicism and the Torah, he argues that the soul of the cosmos is in harmony with the Jewish Torah, while the Torah replicates the order of nature in the world. Conversely, the person who follows the Torah exists in concert with the cosmos. Similarly the Logos is the emanation of the creator and shapes the world into a rational entity that responds favorably to the thoughts and behavior of rational humans. Yet it is only through means of a type of mystical illumination of the soul that one's reason enables him/her to

36. Abraham Schalit, "Alexander Lysimachus," *EncJud* 2 (1971) 582.

37. Sly, *Philo's Alexandria,* 7.

38. Kah and Scholz, *Hellenistische Gymnasion.*

39. See H. Graf Reventlow, *Die Epochen der Bibelauslegung* (4 vols.; Munich: Beck, 1990), vol. 1.

40. Sly, *Philo's Alexandria,* 136-37.

41. This metaphor is also found in rabbinic writings. See Ephraim Urbach, *The Sages: Their Concepts and Beliefs,* trans. Israel Abrahams (2nd ed.; 2 vols.; Jerusalem: Magnes, 1979) 2:200-201.

know God. For Philo the Logos refers to the Divine Mind, the Idea of Ideas, the firstborn Son of the Uncreated Father, the shadow of God, the pattern of creation, Scripture, Mosaic laws, human and heavenly beings, the archetype of divine order actualized through reason, and human reason. Philo's Logos has many similarities to Sophia in the Wisdom of Solomon.

For Philo reality is dualistic: the soul (the higher, immortal part of humanity) and the body (the lower, mortal element), evil originating in matter and good coming from reason, and thought and the senses in contrast to passion and feelings. His mystical views configure his affirmation that the goal of life is to reject fleshly pleasures and to obtain a beatific vision of God. The high priest is the symbol of the perfect human being and has the cosmic role of separating the clean from the unclean that exists in the world. His vestments are the symbol of the entire cosmos (cf. Sir. 50:6-22; Wis. 18:24). The Jews serve the significant role of intercessor for humanity, for they are the priests of all peoples who intercede between humanity and God.[42] Their sacrifices and prayers are for all of humanity. Indeed, they become the vehicle for universal providence.[43]

In similar language to the Wisdom of Solomon, Philo praises Judaism's piety and virtues and contrasts them with the irrational, carnal character of the Egyptians, who are yoked to the body and its passions. The plagues were God's wrath against the Egyptians (cf. Wis. 11:6–19:22). In using allegory, Philo declares that every human who wishes to obtain the beatific vision of God must flee Egypt. This strong condemnation of the Egyptians and Egyptian religion and emphasis on the exodus were among the major features of the conflict between Jews and Egyptians in Alexandria particularly, and explain part of the hostility between the two ethnic groups that fueled the fires of hatred of the Jews. He also depicts the Greeks as wicked, gluttonous, and licentious. He is harsh in his criticism of the gymnasium's discrimination against the Jews and its serving as a social center for Judeophobia.[44]

Philo remained passionately linked to his Jewish heritage. The temple, the payment of the temple tax, the high priesthood, the obedience to and interpretation of the Torah, the rejection of polytheism and the practice of idolatry, and worship in the synagogue were frequent themes in his writings and figure prominently in his religious interpretation of Judaism.[45] He also was politically active in attempting to resolve the Alexandrian crisis by obtaining from Claudius the rights of citizenship of the polis for Jews in Alexandria, a topic to

42. Other mediators between God and the world include Moses and angels.

43. Borgen, "Philo of Alexandria," 251.

44. Ibid. For explication of the term "Judeophobia" see Peter Schäfer, *Judeophobia* (Cambridge: Harvard University Press, 1997).

45. See esp. Goodenough, "Politics of Philo Judaeus," 5-7.

which he devotes two treatises. In *In Flaccum,* Philo explains the Jewish tenacity to maintain their faith at any cost, asserting they are willing to give up their lives in order to maintain certain elements central to Judaism: temple worship, worship in synagogues, the Sabbath, and observing the law of Moses.[46] He rejected all Jewish temples, save the one in Jerusalem, because of his affirmation of the oneness of God. He saw Jews as those who served an intercessory role for the rest of the world, and he castigated apostate Jews who sacrificed their religious heritage for Hellenistic paganism. In *Legatio ad Gaium* he stressed that the deliverance of the Jews from Alexandrian and Jerusalem crises was proof of God's providential care for both the Jews and all of humanity for whom they interceded. While he did not ignore the hope of a future eternal kingdom, he was more concerned with piety and virtue in the present.

Pseudo-Phocylides of Alexandria,[47] a Jewish poet whose preserved writings are dated as early as the third century B.C.E. to as late as the latter part of the first century B.C.E., wrote a poem that blended features of Jewish sapiential poetry and Greek gnomology in rough dactylic hexameters in the Ionic dialect. These monostichs are sayings dealing with ethics and the making of decisions. There is no evidence of tensions between Jews and non-Jews, thus suggesting that the piece was composed at a time in which the heightened tensions between Jews and especially Egyptians had not yet climaxed. The work is primarily a summary of the moral teachings of the Torah in order to instruct Jews in the way of the ethical life. It could well have been used in a Jewish school.[48] The blending of Greek and Jewish features served to encourage Hellenistic Jews to be loyal to their ancestral virtues while accepting features of Hellenism amenable to Judaism. An apologetic function is also present in persuading Greeks to honor Jewish virtues based on monotheism. The aim of his work is the description and cultivation of paideia, or a higher wisdom, which consists of the *theou bouleumata* ("counsels of God," line 1) and *dikaiosynēs mysteria* ("mystery of righteousness," line 231). That lines 5-79 are also present in the Sibylline Oracles (2.55-149) demonstrates its popularity in Hellenistic Judaism. Topics covered

---

46. See Pieter van der Horst, *Philo's Flaccus,* vol. 2: *The First Pogrom. Introduction, Translation and Commentary* (Philo of Alexandria Commentary Series 2; Leiden: Brill, 2003).

47. See the translation and introduction by P. W. van der Horst, "Pseudo-Phocylides," *OTP* 2:565-82. Also see idem, *The Sentences of Pseudo-Phocyclides, with Introduction and Commentary* (VTSup 4; Leiden: Brill, 1978); idem, "Pseudo-Phocylides and the New Testament," *ZNW* 69 (1978) 187-202. In addition, see Pascale Derron, *Sentences/Pseudo-Phocylide: Texte établi, traduit et commenté* (Collection de Universités de France; Paris: Société d'Édition [Les Belles Letters], 1986); and Johannes Thomas, *Der Jüdische Phokylides: Formgeschichtliche Zugänge zu Pseudo-Phokylides und Vergleich mit der neutestamentlichen Paränese* (Göttingen: Vandenhoeck & Ruprecht, 1992).

48. See Pieter van der Horst, "Pseudo-Phocylides Revisited," *JSP* 3 (1988) 19.

include marriage, chastity, the family, charity, the rejection of greed, modesty, self-control, moderation, the avoidance of envy, the cultivation of wisdom, proper speech, and the value of work, with little emphasis on worship.

The text is an eclectic combination of philosophical elements: Stoicism (vv. 63-67),[49] Neopythagoreanism (vv. 124-128), and the thought of both Theognis (vv. 143, 199-204) and Hesiod (vv. 159-160).[50] This writer positions morality within the context of ethical monotheism, which teaches that people are to live according to the will of the eternal God (v. 17).[51] God is the lawgiver, the creator (humans are created in the divine image), and characteristically wise, mighty, and bountiful. In addition, Pseudo-Phocylides offers contradictory under-standings of the future life, the bodily resurrection, and the immortality of the soul (lines 102-15; cf., e.g., Wis. 3:1-12). While mentioning most of the Ten Com-mandments, he omits the prohibition against idolatry, likely in order to appeal to a pagan audience and to counter the criticism that Jews were atheists who re-jected even the practice of placing idols at the entrance to their synagogues. Of course, in the Wisdom of Solomon idolatry is the root cause of human sinful-ness and thus is roundly condemned.

The book of 3 Maccabees[52] is presented as a Jewish history in the Greek style of historiography and was perhaps written in the mid-first century C.E. shortly after the Wisdom of Solomon.[53] The book makes use of the style of Greek "pathetic" historiography, which appeals to the emotions by means of narrating stories of great heroes, atrocities suffered by the chosen, and divine actions of providence and redemption.[54] Covering the ancient past from cre-ation to the exodus, this book seeks to persuade Jewish apostates to return to

49. Van der Horst, *Sentences of Pseudo-Phocylides*, 57-58.

50. Maurice Gilbert, "Wisdom Literature," in *Jewish Writings*, 314, n. 113.

51. Monotheism was especially appealing to many Greek and Roman intellectuals. It began to appear in Greek thought in the fifth century B.C.E. (see Antisthenes) and continued among the Stoics (see Cleanthes' "Hymn to Zeus," Heraclitus, Xenophanes, and Zenon). Also see M. P. Nilsson, *Geschichte der griechischen Religion* (3rd ed.; 2 vols.; HAW 5/2.1-2; Munich: Beck, 1977) 2:546-52.

52. See esp. André Paul, "Le troisième livre des Macchabées," *ANRW* 2.20/1:298-336. He argues that the Letter of Aristeas and 3 Maccabees have such striking similarities that it is likely they were both written in the same place, most probably Alexandria. Also see Hugh Anderson, "3 Maccabees," *OTP* 2:509-29; Aryeh Kasher, "Anti-Jewish Persecutions in Alexandria in the Reign of Ptolemy Philopator, According to III Maccabees," in *Studies in the History of the Jewish People and the Land of Israel*, vol. 4 (mod. Heb.), ed. Uriel Rappaport (Haifa: University of Haifa, 1978) 59-76; David S. Williams, "3 Maccabees: A Defense of Diaspora Judaism?" *JSP* 13 (1995) 17-29.

53. Collins, *Between Jerusalem and Athens*, 128-30; Moses Hadas, *Third and Fourth Maccabees* (New York: Harper & Row, 1953) 19-21.

54. G. W. E. Nickelsburg, "Stories of Biblical and Early Post-Biblical Times," in *Jewish Writings*, 80.

their ancestral faith and to encourage others who are wavering due to the enticement of Hellenism to stay the course, even in the face of persecution. Thus addressing a Jewish audience, this work is comparable to the Wisdom of Solomon in these areas. This book also was likely written in Alexandria.

While the original beginning did not survive, the first section (chs. 1–2) begins with the battle at Raphia in 217 B.C.E. when Ptolemy IV Philopator defeated Antiochus III to stave off, at least for almost another generation, Seleucid control of Eretz Israel. When Ptolemy returned to Egypt, he stopped over in Jerusalem and tried to enter the holy of holies of the temple (1:8–2:24). However, a miracle occurred that paralyzed him and prohibited this defilement (2:21-24). Ptolemy returned to Alexandria and sought to have his revenge by ordering all of the Jews to become devotees of Dionysus. If they acceded to this request, they would receive Alexandrian citizenship, but should they refuse, they would be reduced to slavery (2:25-30). Most resisted, and the apostates were ostracized. The second section, chs. 3–7, narrates the divine deliverance of the Jews from Ptolemy IV. Due to the refusal of most Jews to convert, Ptolemy ordered the extermination of the entire Jewish community. He forced them to gather in Alexandria and imprisoned them in a hippodrome, planning to crush them with a stampede of a herd of five hundred intoxicated elephants. After they were miraculously saved twice, the king then had the Jews released, a seven-day festival ensued, the Jews were promised protection, and they were allowed to slaughter the apostates who had turned against the faithful. Following a second seven-day festival at Ptolemais, the Jews were allowed to return home.

Unlike the Wisdom of Solomon, this reactionary text rejects anything that has to do with Greek paganism or Hellenistic culture, and instead exhorts loyalty to the Torah.[55] Even Alexandrian citizenship should not sway Jews to forsake their heritage and identity. This text speaks of the sacredness of the temple, obedience to the law, monotheism, the efficacy of priestly prayer, and the divine guidance of history.

Ecstatic women prophets (sibyls) were known in the Greco-Roman world from the sixth century B.C.E. into the seventh century C.E.[56] The Third Sibylline

---

55. Paul, "Troisième livre des Macchabées."

56. See the Sibyl's description by Heraclitus found in Plutarch, *De Pythiae Oraculis.* Modern studies include that of H. W. Parke, *Sibyls and Sibylline Prophecy in Classical Antiquity,* ed. B. C. McGing (London: Routledge, 1988). Also see John J. Collins, *The Sibylline Oracles of Egyptian Judaism* (SBLDS 13; Missoula, MT: Scholars Press, 1974); idem, "Sibylline Oracles," *OTP* 1:317-472; idem, "The Sibylline Oracles," in *Jewish Writings,* 357-81; idem, *Between Athens and Jerusalem,* 83-97; idem, "The Sibyl and the Potter: Political Propaganda in Ptolemaic Egypt," in *Religious Propaganda and Missionary Propaganda in Ptolemaic Egypt,* ed. Lukas Bormann, et al. (NovTSup 74; Leiden: Brill, 1994) 57-69; Barclay, *Jews in the Mediterranean Diaspora,* 216-28.

Oracle is the oldest such prophecy that was written by a Jewish author, being composed perhaps as early as the second century B.C.E. This writing likely originated in Egypt during the period of Ptolemy VI Philometor (180-146 B.C.E.). Its author was a Hellenistic Jew who was a member of the inner circle of Onias IV. This son of the deposed and murdered Onias III fled to Egypt, where he became a loyal supporter of Ptolemy VI and the builder of a Jewish temple at Leontopolis that rivaled the one in Jerusalem. The sibyl, identified as a pagan priestess from Erythrae, although she claims to come from Babylon (*Sibyl. Or.* 3.809-10), utters political prophecies concerning the Jews that serve as religious propaganda.[57] These prophecies predict the destruction of numerous pagan nations and the restoration of Israel. The only escape for pagans is to convert to the true God and to offer gifts to his temple. Following the time of destruction and restoration, all people will come to recognize the one God and accept his law as the basis for moral instruction.

Greek mythology was used in this prophetic history, and a euhemeristic argument was constructed to explain the origins of the gods (cf. Wis. 14:15). It is clear from the contents of the oracles that the author attempts to adapt Judaism to Hellenistic culture. Hebrew prophets and Hellenistic Greek oracles merged to shape the identity and message of this sibyl. In the sibyl's eschatology, the author speaks of a new kingdom to be inaugurated during the reign of an Egyptian king.[58] This seventh ruler of the house of Ptolemy is a messianic figure, and during his time the Gentiles will be converted to Judaism. Ultimately, they, along with the Jews, will bring their offerings to the Jerusalem temple.[59] The praise of the Ptolemies represented this author's attempt to establish good relations between the Jews in Egypt and the ruling Ptolemaic dynasty.

Summary

The rhetor who composed the Wisdom of Solomon likely lived in Alexandria in the first half of the first century B.C.E., and produced his *logos protreptikos* perhaps during the pogrom of Flaccus in 38 B.C.E. He lived in a time and an area in which Hellenistic literature was flourishing, including some texts written by Jewish historians, rhetors, and literary authors. Some Jewish writers accommodated Judaism in various ways to certain Hellenistic features, while others, especially 3 Maccabees, assumed a defiant posture against this threatened encroachment of a foreign culture and religion. There were also numerous texts

---

57. Collins, "Sibylline Oracles," *OTP* 1:320.
58. Collins, *Between Athens and Jerusalem*, 88.
59. Collins, "Sibylline Oracles," in *Jewish Writings*, 366.

by non-Jews who were especially critical of Judaism, although there was an oc-casional pagan piece that was favorable toward certain Jewish practices and be-liefs. We also know of certain former Jews who were apostates and renounced their heritage and identity, including most prominently Tiberius Julianus Alex-ander.

The author of the Wisdom of Solomon, while an apologist defending Juda-ism against pagan assaults and exhorting those wavering due to the attraction of Hellenism, used both Greek rhetorical and literary features and popular philosophical ideas from a variety of sources to compose his literature. These included the Stoic understanding of the Logos and the four cardinal virtues, the Platonic teaching of the immortality of the soul and the corruptibility of the flesh that proved to be a hindrance to the moral life, and Wisdom's guidance of the heroic leadership of unnamed ancestors whose deeds and virtues led to sal-vation. He also admired Greek philosophical religion in rejecting idols, al-though it failed to deduce from the beauty and order of the world that the cre-ator transcended that which was made. Thus while accommodation was his approach, he rejected full-scale acculturation in Hellenistic culture.[60] There does not appear to be any active desire to convert pagans to Judaism, although he clearly sought to develop a spirit of tolerance toward the Greeks. However, this was certainly not the case with regard to the despised Egyptians.[61] He likely would have been aware of the aforementioned texts and used some of them in shaping his own teaching. The book takes its proper place among the apolo-getic literature that made substantial use of arguments and themes shaped in Greek rhetorical form.

Critics of Judaism were repelled by the practice of animal sacrifice, charg-ing the Jews with atheism for rejecting idolatry and polytheism in favor of one deity. These critics interpreted Judaism's strong communal ties and laws of kashrut as misanthropic, and even accused Jews of an annual ritual murder of a Greek. Some pagan writers attributed philosophical irrationality to Jews. Finally, some concerns were raised that Jewish failure to acculturate was moti-vated by the desire to subvert the order of the empire. In Egypt, particularly, new Egyptian renditions of the story of the exodus led to the interpretation that it was the expulsion of unclean and leprous people to appease the wrath of the

60. Hengel uses acculturation to explain hellenization and the Jews, and not syncretism or as-similation (*Judaism and Hellenism*, 1:114).

61. The contention that Hellenistic Jewish literature sought to convert non-Jews to Judaism has been advocated by a number of scholars, including Feldman, *Jew and Gentile*, 293. However, this was not its primary intention. See Victor Tcherikover, "Jewish Apologetic Literature Recon-sidered," *Eos* 48 (1956) 169-93; Martin Goodman, *Mission and Conversion: Proselytizing in the Reli-gious History of the Roman Empire* (Oxford: Clarendon, 1994).

native Egyptian gods.[62] The rhetor responded to these claims by charging Greeks and Egyptians with religious devotion that honored idols, condoned cult murders, worshiped beasts, promoted immoral ecstatic rites, and created ineffectual idols and gods that sought merely to glorify deceased humans, including children and rulers.

Citizenship

There remain uncertainties about the citizenship of Jews in the Ptolemaic period, although it is doubtful that Jews, save for a few, possessed the full array of the rights of citizens as long as they maintained their Jewish ethnicity. However, the Ptolemaic rulers gave the various peoples they ruled the freedom to worship their own gods and to follow their native traditions. This included the Jews, who possessed the right to attend their synagogues and to follow the Torah. Jews in Ptolemaic Egypt were not organized into "civic communities" (politeuma),[63] but rather were a religious, ethnic community.[64] While they were not full Greek citizens, they appear to have been included in the general civic body of the "Hellenes,"[65] that is, peoples who were acculturated, while still maintaining an ethnic identity other than Greek. Full citizenship was highly desired, for it offered political and economic advantages not enjoyed by noncitizens. Greeks were automatically "citizens," regardless of their place of birth. This citizenship extended beyond the urban areas and even included the countryside.

After the conquest of Ptolemaic Egypt by the Romans, citizenship of Alexandria continued to be desirable and was sought by leaders among the Jewish population. The Romans established a social classification that varied from the Ptolemies and led to a further demotion of Jews in the new empire. The three major social classes were Romans, citizens of Greek cities, and peregrini ("foreigners"), that is, free citizens of any community other than Rome. In the Impe-

---

62. For the debate about the exodus in Jewish and anti-Jewish literature, see Claude Aziza, "L'utilisation polémique du récit de l'exode chez les écrivains alexandrins (IVème siècle ap. J.-C.)," ANRW 2.19/1 (1979) 41-65. He deals especially with Lysimachus, Chaeremon, and Apion.

63. Gert Lüderwitz, "What Is the Politeuma?" in Studies in Early Jewish Epigraphy, ed. Jan Willem van Henten and Pieter Willem van der Horst (AGAJU 21; Leiden: Brill, 1994) 183-225.

64. See Sterling, "Judaism between Jerusalem and Alexandria," 266; E. M. Smallwood, The Jews under Roman Rule: From Pompey to Diocletian: A Study in Political Relations (Boston: Brill, 2001).

65. J. M. Modrzejewski, The Jews of Egypt: From Rameses II to Emperor Hadrian (Princeton: Princeton University Press, 1995) 82.

rial period, people were permitted to be citizens both of a non-Roman community and of Rome. Both Egyptians and Jews of Alexandria were classified in the third category, the *peregrini*. In Alexandria some Jews could be both Roman citizens and Jews, but they were denied the right in most cases to be Alexandrian citizens. Jews could no longer be Hellenes as many were during the Ptolemaic dynasty. Caesar Augustus continued the policy of the Ptolemies in allowing the Jews freedom of religion and the right to follow their own traditions.[66] However, he did not allow them to be citizens of Greek cities. Jews sought full Greek citizenship as citizens of Alexandria for increased social status, access to the gymnasium, the right to establish internal self-rule through a *gerousia*, and to avoid poll taxes, but they were denied this standing. In spite of the fact that they possessed important political rights and called themselves Alexandrians during the Roman period, they still had to pay the Roman poll tax.[67]

Internal details of the text suggest that the Wisdom of Solomon may date to the final year of the Roman prefect Avilus Flaccus (32-38 C.E.) when the pogrom against the Jews was in full effect.[68] Tiberius (14-37), who succeeded Augustus, executed Sejanus, one of his advisors, in 31 for seeking to usurp his throne. Among the actions of Sejanus causing civil disturbances was his persecution of the Jews in Italy. Tiberius ordered this to stop. In 32, however, he gave Flaccus the post of prefect of Egypt. Flaccus, born in Rome, was the classmate and boyhood friend of the grandchildren of Augustus.[69] Thus Flaccus was closely associated with the emperor's court. He was also a close advisor to Tiberius. However, when Tiberius was murdered in 37 and the throne passed unexpectedly to Gaius Caligula (37-41), this development proved threatening to Flaccus. Flaccus had been involved in the banishment of Agrippina, the mother of Caligula, in 29. Further, Flaccus had supported Gemellus, the grandson of Tiberius, in his efforts to succeed his grandfather to the throne. The situation deteriorated further when Caligula forced Macro, a powerful man at court and a supporter of Flaccus, to commit suicide. Later, Herod Agrippa, who had received from Caligula the throne over Palestine, was mocked when he visited Alexandria. The great celebration of the Jews caused Flaccus and the Greek leaders of Alexandria to fear that an insurrection might occur due to the nationalism evoked by the Jewish king. Flaccus, perhaps seeking to gain Caligula's favor, yielded to the Alexandrian Greek citizens and the Egyptians who sought to remove the privileges of the Jews of the city. Launching a wholesale pogrom against the Jews in 38,

---

66. Michael Kolarcik, "The Book of Wisdom," *NIB* 5 (1997) 439-40.

67. Erich Gruen, *Diaspora: Jews amidst Greeks and Romans* (Cambridge: Harvard University Press, 2002) 77.

68. Van der Horst, *Philo's Flaccus: First Pogrom*.

69. See ibid., 34-38.

Flaccus allowed them to be attacked physically, tortured, and murdered, their homes ransacked and burned, their shops plundered, and their synagogues desecrated with images.[70] Jewish women were forced to eat pork or suffer the humiliation of physical abuse (rape? see Philo, *Flacc.* 96). Part of the animosity was due to the Jewish efforts to obtain Greek citizenship and part to special privileges Jews had continued to enjoy since the reign of the Ptolemies. Flaccus denied Jews civic privileges and declared them to be foreigners and aliens (Philo, *Flacc.* 65-72, 127-31). Flaccus sentenced the *gerousia* to flogging and even executed some Jews as a macabre way of celebrating Caligula's birthday. The uproar caused by this pogrom was finally ended by Caligula, who had Flaccus arrested, brought to Rome, tried, banished, and finally murdered. However, the Jewish difficulties were not over. When Caligula proclaimed himself a god in 40, the Jews refused to worship him, thus leading to his growing anger against them.

Philo headed the first delegation of Jews to ask Caligula to reinstate their privileges and to allow them to be citizens of Alexandria. But Caligula, miffed at the obstinacy of the Jews in refusing to worship him as a god, dismissed them without responding to their request. Indeed, he even threatened the erection of his idol in the temple of Jerusalem. His death in 41 kept this crisis from reaching its climax, and his replacement by Claudius improved the lot of the Alexandrian Jews, although he did not grant their appeal to him to be recognized as citizens of the polis, a claim based on the argument that Augustus had regarded them as such. Whether or not Claudius knew that claim was without merit, he still denied them this coveted status.[71] For a second time Philo had led a Jewish embassy, but he did not achieve his desired goal of obtaining citizenship for the Jews of Alexandria. Claudius decided that, while the Jews did not enjoy Alexandrian citizenship, their ancestral religious customs should be permitted as they had been during the reign of Augustus. He did indicate that participation in the gymnasium required Greek citizenship, thus denying Jews the ability to enter the category of the elite Hellenes in Alexandria. At the same time, the emperor warned the Jews against any efforts to destabilize the *Pax Romana* (see the edict in Josephus, *Ant.* 19.283-85). He also instructed them not to seek anything more than what they had previously held as regards their civil and religious rights *(dikaia)*. Thus the Jews of Alexandria, even those whose families had lived there for generations, lost in their efforts to become citizens of the city. Only extraor-

70. See Gruen, *Diaspora,* 54-68. The pogrom of Antiochus IV Epiphanes in Palestine is described in 2 and 3 Maccabees.

71. See Diana Della, *Alexandrian Citizenship during the Roman Principate* (American Classics Studies 23; Atlanta: Scholars Press, 1991) 42. She notes the one known exception is the masseur of Pliny the Younger, Harpokras, who was the freedman of a peregrine patron (p. 41). See Pliny, *Ep.* 10.5-7.

dinary circumstances, significant wealth, and political influence would allow a Jewish inhabitant of Alexandria to have the coveted citizenship of the polis.[72]

The Wisdom of Solomon and Citizenship

Elements of the text of the Wisdom of Solomon indicate that serious conflict had broken out between the Egyptians, the Greeks who were citizens of the polis, and the Roman authorities on the one hand, and the Jewish community on the other. These included a number of factors. First, there are strong indications that the audience of the text, experiencing overt persecution and suffering, is the subject of a pogrom. This is suggested primarily by the description of the views, language, and actions of the wicked in 1:16–2:24 against the righteous man. Second, in the midst of the discussion of the Egyptians having afflicted those whom they had welcomed to their land with grievous sufferings, there is the reference in 19:16 to the fact that both Egyptians and Jews shared the same rights *(dikaia)*. This notation would make sense during the period when both Jews and Egyptians were classified as *peregrini* and would have been allowed the freedom to practice their customs and religions.

Xenophobia

The pogrom that rocked the Jewish community of Alexandria in 38 c.e. led to the murder of Jews, destruction of their property, and the desecration of their synagogues. When Emperor Claudius (41-54) granted the Jews their historic rights but continued to deny them Alexandrian citizenship, the Jewish community did not respond well. Later their situation deteriorated greatly due to the Jewish revolt in Judea against Rome in 66 and the slaughter of many Alexandrian Jews by the two Roman legions led by the apostate Tiberius Julianus Alexander. Their revolt in 115-117 led to Trajan's obliteration of the Jewish community in the city by means of massacre and slavery. Before this revolt, apologetic literature sought to steady those Jews harassed by the sharp diatribes of Hellenistic critics and to bring Jewish apostates back into the fold. However, it should be noted that for a period of nearly four centuries, from the time of Alexander to the Great Revolt in 66 c.e., the Jews enjoyed, with two important exceptions, largely peaceful relations with the Greeks and often even with the

---

72. Documentary evidence attests to the fact that some Jews obtained Roman citizenship (see *CPJ* 2:151; Josephus, *Ant.* 14.236).

Egyptians, even though some of the leaders and intellectuals of these two ethnicities harbored an intense dislike for their Jewish neighbors and sought to castigate and ridicule their traditions and historical understandings going back to the time of the exodus from Egypt. While there were not frequent pogroms launched against the Jews of Egypt, there were xenophobic flames fanned against them by certain Greek, Egyptian, and Roman authors.

Peter Schäfer, who uses the term "Judeophobia" to describe the intense feelings against Jews in the Greco-Roman period, traces this largely to the psychological hatred and fear of practices and traditions that were strange to that cultural environment.[73] This sentiment was heightened due to the strong sense of community amongst those Jews who sought to maintain their social and religious identity through separation from the larger milieu in which they lived and the nationalism among some who hoped for the restoration of the Jewish kingdom in Eretz Israel. Apocalyptic writers even spoke on occasion of a messianic kingdom and at times a future Messiah. Then too the granting of privileges and the strong desire for citizenship led to increased animosity and especially rankled the Egyptians. Jewish ethnocentrism led to some non-Jews fearing that Jews would succeed in forging new legal practices, religious practices, and social customs and impose them on their ethnic neighbors. Yet we should not overlook that hostile and xenophobic views of groups other than Jews were expressed in Greek and Latin literature. The charges of ritual cannibalism, for instance, were made not only against Jews but also against other groups.

This anti-Judaism had a long history, particularly in Egypt, as evidenced by the enslavement of Jewish ancestors by the pharaoh who knew not Joseph, the exodus, and the Elephantine pogrom originating due to the sacrifice of lambs in the Jewish temple. Lambs were the sacred animals of the god Khnum. Yet, in the early Roman period, the only official policy of anti-Judaism was the converting of the temple tax into a tax for the upkeep of the temple of Jupiter Capitolinus, harshly enforced by Domitian long after the time of the sage who wrote the Wisdom of Solomon. Thus the official Roman policy was to tolerate and even protect Judaism as long as there were no threats of proselytism or revolution against the empire. There was normally a positive alliance of Jews with Rome, and the few exceptions were the fears of Jews growing too large through proselytism and their possible resistance to imperial rule.

73. Schäfer, *Judeophobia*. In addition to Schäfer, among the studies of early xenophobia in Alexandria and the Roman Empire see Feldman, *Jew and Gentile*. Alexandrian anti-Jewish libel often assumed the shape of Egyptian argument, which had a xenophobic orientation from as early as the New Kingdom, and this explains the evoking of the conflict with the Egyptians in Wis. 19:13-16; see Dominique Valbelle, *Les neufs arcs — L'Egyptien et les étrangers de la préhistoire à la conquête d'Alexandre* (Paris: Colin, 1990).

Some pagan writers vilified the Jews' ancestors as lowly, leprous, and diseased slaves who ate animals that represented the gods and thus angered them. These dreadful conditions led the Egyptians' ancestors to drive the Jews out of their country. They returned several centuries later as unwelcome settlers. They were depicted as physically inferior and despised by the gods.[74] The most virulent animosity developed between the indigenous Egyptians and the Jews in Alexandria (Josephus, *C. Ap.* 2.69).[75]

The portrayals of Judaism by Gentile writers varied from intense disparagement to noteworthy praise.[76] The pagan writers (including some Egyptians) who were critical of Jews included Manetho,[77] Posidonius,[78] Apollonius Molon, Cicero,[79] Horace,[80] Chaeremon, Lysimachus, Apion, and Tacitus.[81] Yet more sympathetic views came from Strabo, Clearchus of Soli, Varro, and Pompeius Trogus, who admired some of the Jewish teachings and traditions. The anti-Jewish views of several writers are summarized in the following.

Manetho (c. 300 B.C.E.) was an Egyptian priest at Heliopolis and scholar who enjoyed the patronage of Ptolemy I Soter I (305-282 B.C.E.) and Ptolemy II Philadelphus (282-246).[82] He may have assisted in establishing a cult of Serapis during the reign of Ptolemy I. Ptolemy I brought one hundred thousand Jew-

74. Modrzejewski, *Jews of Egypt,* 136-37.

75. Gruen, *Diaspora,* 64; Feldman, *Jew and Gentile.*

76. Collins, *Between Athens and Jerusalem,* 6-13. Stern's volumes on *Greek and Latin Authors* are a detailed presentation of the Greek and Latin writers who refer to Judaism. See esp. "Strabo of Amaseia," 1:261-315.

77. Said to have composed eight books, Manetho's most significant writing was *Aegyptiaca.* A small part of the work has survived in quotations in Josephus (*C. Ap.* 1.238, 249, 264, 309), Sextus Julius Africanus (c. 160-240 C.E.), and Eusebius (c. 260-341 C.E.). See the translation and notes by W. G. Waddell, in Manetho, *Aegyptiaca* (LCL; New York: Putnam, 1940); Stern, *Greek and Latin Authors,* 1:62-85.

78. For the text, see Stern, *Greek and Latin Authors,* 1:141-47. Also see Feldman, *Jew and Gentile,* 126.

79. For overviews of Cicero, see Thomas N. Mitchell, *Cicero, the Ascending Years* (New Haven: Yale University Press, 1979); idem, *Cicero, the Senior Statesman* (New Haven: Yale University Press, 1991). For Cicero's views of the Jews, see *Pro Flacco* (59 B.C.E.), *De provinciis consularibus* (see Stern, *Greek and Latin Authors,* 1:193-206).

80. See Niall Rudd, *The Satires of Horace* (2nd ed.; Berkeley: University of California Press, 1982); idem, *Themes in Roman Satire* (Bristol: Bristol Classical, 1998). For Horace's satire of the Jews, see Feldman, *Jew and Gentile,* 171.

81. For the anti-Semitism of Tacitus, see Bilhad Wardy, "Jewish Religion in Pagan Literature," *ANRW* 2.19/1:592-644.

82. Gerald P. Verbrugghe and John M. Wickersham, *Berossos and Manetho, Introduced and Translated: Native Traditions in Ancient Mesopotamia and Egypt* (Ann Arbor: University of Michigan Press, 1996).

ish captives to Egypt, and thirty thousand were positioned in fortresses to guard the frontier. The rest were given to his soldiers to be their slaves (Let. Aris. 12-14). Ptolemy II Philadelphus purchased the Jews from their owners and set them free (Let. Aris. 22-24). Thus all of the Jews in Egypt were freedmen. The Jews viewed this release as a "new exodus," while Judeophobic Egyptians like Manetho, displeased with this action, engaged in their literary assault on Judaism. He and others after him especially sought to discredit the Jewish account of the exodus from Egypt. Seeming to identify the Hyksos with the ancient Jews, Manetho presented them as lepers who were exiled from Egypt or sent to the quarries to work. He accused the Jews of misanthropy, since Osarsiph (his name for Moses) commanded that the Jews should not associate with non-Jews. He also charged them with the destruction of the temples and altars of the gods, the slaughter and slavery of Egyptians, the consumption of animals revered by the Egyptians, forcing Egyptian priests and prophets to cook them and then to be turned out of these sanctuaries stark naked, and the ridicule of the gods and religious beliefs of other peoples. Osarsiph is identified as a priest of Heliopolis, implying that Egyptian religion was the source of Judaism. However, Osarsiph convinced the Jews to repudiate the gods of Egypt and to adopt a new religion. Eventually he led them to Jerusalem, which they subsequently conquered. During the journey from Egypt they committed many crimes.

Apollonius Molon, a rhetor who dates to the first century B.C.E., was, according to Josephus, a virulent Jew hater. His two most famous pupils were Cicero and Julius Caesar. It was at Rhodes that he encountered the anti-Jewish ideas of Posidonius (135-51 B.C.E.) and began to propagate similar charges.[83] In his *syskeuē*, a polemical treatise (Eusebius, *Praep. ev.* 9.19), Apollonius interpreted the exodus as the expulsion of Jews from Egypt due to a terrible disease. Moses was a sorcerer whose work lacked moral worth. Jews were depicted as atheists (*atheos*, Josephus, *C. Ap.* 2.148) for not honoring the gods of other people and as misanthropes (*misanthrōpoi*, Josephus, *C. Ap.* 2.258) for refusing to associate with non-Jews and for not offering them any acts of kindness. They also were charged with offering an annual sacrifice consisting of a fattened Greek (Josephus, *C. Ap.* 2.79).[84] Lacking virtues, Jews were said to be cowards, fanatics, and the least talented of all the barbarians (Josephus, *C. Ap.* 2.148).

An Alexandrian Stoic and priest of Serapis, Chaeremon lived during the first century C.E. and wrote a "History of Egypt" that presented Egyptian reli-

---

83. For the text, with introduction and notes, see Stern, *Greek and Latin Authors,* 1:148-49.

84. Diodorus Siculus made similar accusations (40.3.4). He wrote the *Bibliotheca Historica* sometime during the first century B.C.E.; see Stern, *Greek and Latin Authors,* 1:167-89.

gion as an allegorical worship of nature (Josephus, *C. Ap.* 1.289).[85] He recounts that the goddess Isis appeared to King Amenophis in a dream and blamed him for the destruction of her temple during a war. His counselor advised him to remove from Egypt those filled with pollutions in order to allay the wrath of the goddess. Moses and Joseph, who were formerly Egyptians, came to Pelusium and joined in league with 380,000 slaves who had been placed there by Amenophis. These slaves, led by Moses and Joseph, attacked Egypt, forcing the king into exile into Ethiopia where his wife gave birth to a son, Messene. Once grown, he defeated these enemies and drove them out as far as Syria, returning Egypt to his father. This narrative identifies the Hebrews as the Hyksos. Thus impurity and defeat in war led the Egyptians to expel the Jews.

Lysimachus was an Alexandrian Greek and the head of the great library during the first century B.C.E.[86] His views of the exodus are similar to those of Manetho and Chaeremon. He sought to discredit the important place of the exodus and the Passover celebration in Jewish life. According to Lysimachus, the Jews, suffering from leprosy and other terrible afflictions, took refuge in the temples, where they begged for food. This impurity led to the failure of crops. When Ammon was consulted, the king was told to expel these infected people from Egypt. With Moses as their leader, they came to Judea and founded the city that came to be called Hierosolyma. He held the Jews in disgust and even criticized the influence of Jewish military leaders in the army of Cleopatra III.

The Alexandrian Egyptian whose opposition to the Jews Josephus challenged was Apion, a prominent politician and writer of the first century C.E.[87] He was the leader of the Greco-Egyptian delegation to Rome to oppose the Jewish appeal to Caligula to obtain citizenship of Alexandria and to have their privileges restored, which were lost due to the pogrom of Flaccus (Josephus, *Ant.* 18.257-60). His history (*Aegyptiaca;* cf. Josephus, *C. Ap.* 2.147) depicted the antiquity of the Egyptian people, culture, and religion in order to impress the Romans about the accomplishments and antiquity of his people. More to the point, he also made use of the Greek rhetorical form of the reviling of nations and cities to slander Jewish character (see Clement of Alexandria, *Strom.* 1.21 [101.3-4]).[88] His

---

85. See Pieter Willem van der Horst, *Chaeremon, Egyptian Priest and Stoic Philosopher: The Fragments Collected and Translated with Explanatory Notes* (Études preliminaires aux religions orientales dans l'Empire romain 101; Leiden: Brill, 1984).

86. Josephus, *C. Ap.* 1.305-11.

87. The text is partially preserved in Josephus, *Against Apion;* Tatian, *Oratio ad Graecos* 38; Clement of Alexandria, *Strom.* 1.21 (101.3-4); Eusebius in *Praep. ev.* 10.10.16. For notes and introduction see Stern, *Greek and Latin Authors,* 1:389-416.

88. See David L. Balch, "Josephus, *Against Apion* II.145-296," *SBLSP 1975* (Missoula, MT: Scholars Press, 1975) 187-92. This rhetorical form, which was used to revile nations and cities, is

slander included the charges that the expulsion of the Jews from Egypt was due to their diseases, lameness, and blindness (*C. Ap.* 2.21), the behavior of misanthropy, especially toward the Greeks (*C. Ap.* 2.258), cannibalism (*C. Ap.* 2.95), and, most significantly, sedition against Roman rule (*C. Ap.* 2.68).[89] Apion also identified Moses as an Egyptian and native of Heliopolis (*C. Ap.* 2.11) and even contended that the Jews were originally Egyptians (*C. Ap.* 2.28).

Greek and Latin Writers Sympathetic to Judaism

Among the writers in Hellenistic and early Imperial Roman periods who were largely complimentary of Judaism were Strabo, Clearchus,[90] Varro, and Pompeius Trogus. Strabo (born c. 64 B.C.E.), who composed seventeen volumes of the *Geographica*, praised Moses for introducing an imageless deity and portraying him as universal in encompassing all that exists.[91] He interpreted this rejection of images as a view based on reason, since no image could resemble God. While viewing Moses as a great mantic prophet who founded Jerusalem, Strabo interpreted the Judaism of his day as having declined into a superstitious religion concerned with diet. Its militancy of this period was bent on destroying Hellenistic centers of culture. Varro (c. 116-27 B.C.E.) was a well-known scholar of republican Rome who was rather favorable to Judaism.[92] The appropriate references to Judaism (no. 72 a-b) are taken from *Res Divinae*, which is part of his *Antiquitates Rerum Humanarum et Divinarum*, put together between 63 and 47 B.C.E. Equating the God of Judaism with Jupiter, he also noted that Judaism did not allow idolatry. This rejection of divine images was grounded in Greco-Roman understanding.[93]

Pompeius Trogus (end of the first century B.C.E. and beginning of the first century C.E.) wrote a Latin history of the Macedonian-Hellenistic states and set forth certain views of the Jews.[94] He accepted the Egyptian argument that they

---

employed both by Apion and by his opponent, Josephus (*C. Ap.* 1.220-21). Also see the discussion by Menander of Laodicea, *How One Praises Cities*.

89. Feldman, *Jew and Gentile*, 96, 126-28, 143, 224, 229-39, 505 n. 58.

90. See Stern, *Greek and Latin Authors,* 1:47-52.

91. See François Lasserre, "Strabon devant l'Empire romain," *ANRW* 2.30/1 (1982) 867-96. For views of Moses see John Gager, *Moses in Graeco-Roman Paganism* (SBLMS 16; Nashville: Scholars Press, 1972).

92. See Stern for the translation of the text, introduction, and notes (*Greek and Latin Authors,* 1:207-12).

93. Ibid., 207.

94. Feldman, *Jew and Gentile,* 174.

were lepers forced to leave Egypt, and viewed Moses as the son of Joseph. However, Joseph was praised for his intelligence and numerous talents shared by his people.[95] While he noted that Jews had no associations with non-Jews, this was due not to misanthropy but rather to their having spread an infection. Consequently they did not wish to become odious to their neighbors.

The Wisdom of Solomon and Xenophobia

This literary anti-Judaism led to the counter-literature of Alexandrian Jews in opposing authors like Manetho and Lysimachus (see Pseudo-Hecataeus, Artapanus, the poet Ezekiel, and, of course, the Wisdom of Solomon) that defended Judaism and even proposed the superiority of Jewish history and tradition. The strong criticism of pagan religions and especially the Egyptians in the Wisdom of Solomon, particularly found in chs. 10–19, is a reaction to this assault on Jewish identity, national character, traditions, religion, and privileges granted by Greek and Roman rulers. Especially important was his lengthy description of the exodus to counteract the strong criticism of this tradition by pagan writers.

Summary

This summary of the literature of the last two centuries B.C.E. and the first century C.E. that deals with Judaism reveals the climate in which the sage who composed the Wisdom of Solomon lived.[96] This text merges themes, rhetorical forms, schools of thought, social institutions, and the religions of Judaism and Hellenism. However, anti-Judaism in Egypt continued to oppose and threaten Jews dwelling in this region, extending a long history of conflict that originated in the exodus at the end of the Late Bronze Age. Egyptian and Greek writers charged the Jews with ritual murder, atheism that involved the rejection of other gods, misanthropy, and acts of sedition against the Roman Empire. The reinterpretation of the exodus as the expulsion of diseased Jews was made in order to strike at the heart of Jewish tradition and identity. Xenophobia, the allure of Hellenism, and the opposition of Greeks and Egyptians to Jews having

95. Ibid., 205.

96. Marie-Françoise Baslez, "L'autore della Sapienza e l'ambiente colto di alessandria," in *Il Libro della Sapienza: Tradizione, Redazione, Teologia,* ed. Guiseppe Bellia and Angelo Passaro (Studia biblia Biblica 1; Rome: Citta Nuova, 2004) 47-66.

citizenship in the Greek cities were enormous pressures directed against Jews, especially those living in Alexandria.

The Jews had different responses to these charges and to acculturation. Some abandoned their identity and became hellenized in order to accommodate to these pressures and to gain the status of citizenship. Others completely rejected Hellenism and regarded any accommodation as ill-considered. Many, however, including the rhetor who composed the Wisdom of Solomon, represented a middle path between these two extremes. Thus a form of Hellenistic Judaism developed that blended the two cultures in different ways. While citizenship, attendance of a gymnasium, and skills in the Greek language were desirable elements that many upper-class Jews sought, they still affirmed monotheism (which included opposition to ruler worship), rejected the worship of images, supported the Jerusalem temple and priesthood financially and ideologically, assembled and worshiped in synagogues, studied their traditions in schools associated with these places of assembly, honored the teachings of the Torah, and observed the Sabbath. As we shall see, many of these important themes, goals, and virtues are present in the Wisdom of Solomon.

Rhetoric (Literary Structure and Form)

The art of public speaking became an increasingly important subject in both the gymnasia and especially the schools of rhetoric in spite of criticisms that it lacked a definable body of knowledge and was nothing more than a handmaiden to philosophy. This earlier Greek attitude changed dramatically with the Romans. In the early empire, rhetoricians were held in greater esteem than philosophers.[97] The art of rhetoric included clarity, brevity, forms, and a suitable relationship between form, style, and content. The *technē*, a speech or text characterized as the art of persuasion, resided at its center. The handbooks of tropes, figures, and quotations were developed for ready use by the speaker. Rhetors often wrote out their speeches in order to practice their presentations. The author of the Wisdom of Solomon was not a philosopher, although he was familiar with the rudiments of the major philosophical schools, but rather a rhetor and possibly a teacher of rhetoric. This is seen in a variety of features of

97. In his treatise *On the Ancient Orators*, Dionysius of Halicarnassus related how he came to Rome as a rhetorician, teacher, and historian sometime after Augustus's defeat of Marc Anthony at Actium (31 B.C.E.). Seeking to convince Greeks of the nobility of Rome and to reconcile them to Roman rule, he wrote that history had allowed the return of rhetoric to its place of honor. He then turned to the consideration of the eloquence of the greatest orators (Kennedy, *Art of Persuasion*, 337-40).

his writings. The text may be a written version of a longer speech he had prepared for delivery in a social or religious context.

Greek Forms in the Wisdom of Solomon

The rhetor who composed the Wisdom of Solomon merged a variety of Greek forms and ethics, Jewish teachings of creation and redemptive history, in particular the plagues and the exodus, and elements of Philonic mysticism.[98] While he affirmed the superiority of Judaism in comparison to the pagan religions of the Hellenists, he still used Greek rhetoric and morality to coalesce these two different cultures.[99]

Perhaps the most noticeable feature of the Greek literary influence on the book is its overarching form that combines protreptic (*protreptikos*, "hortatory"), epideictic (*epideiktikos*, "declamation, exhibition, display"),[100] and encomium (*enkōmion*, "praise, eulogy, panegyric").[101] Other common forms and elements of Greek rhetoric present in this book include the diptych (*diptycha*, "doubled, folding"), *synkrisis* ("comparison: a comparison of opposite or contrary things"),[102] apostrophe (*apostrophē*, "when one turns away from all others to address one"), *prosōpopoiia* ("the putting of imaginary speeches into one's own or another's mouth"),[103] eulogy (*eulogia*, "praise"),[104] synecdoche (*synekdochē*, "a figure of speech in which a more comprehensive term is used for a less comprehensive one, or vice versa"), and *diairesis* ("separation").[105] The literary form of the text is a speech of persuasion (*logos protreptikos* =

98. Winston, "The Sage as Mystic in the Wisdom of Solomon," in *Sage in Israel*, 383-97.

99. Modrzejewski, *Jews of Egypt*, 67; Collins, *Between Athens and Jerusalem*, 13.

100. Winston indicates that it is difficult to determine which of the two is dominant ("Review of 'Il libro della sapienza: Struttura e genere letterario,'" *CBQ* 48 [1986] 527).

101. Maurice Gilbert, "Wisdom Literature," in *Jewish Writings*, 307-8.

102. The *synkrisis* is a literary technique of contrasts, in Wisdom's case five, between the features of creation that brought salvation to Israel and those that effectuated disaster for the Egyptians.

103. LSJ, 1533. See the speech of the wicked in Wis. 2.

104. This use of Greek rhetorical forms does not suggest the writer was sophisticated in his use of Greek rhetoric. His work was a less elegant type of protreptic uttered by a moral teacher.

105. *Diaeresis* is the classification of the world of phenomena according to the dialectical principle of the separation of things that are similar and yet different. The author makes use of this principle in arguing that what punishes one group benefits another (thus the plagues). Allegory is expressed through diaeresis. The argument is that there exists a factual commonality between the symbol, the wording of the biblical text, and the meaning that comes from the spheres of ideas, ethics, or cosmology.

protreptic)[106] that has as its purpose to convince an audience to pursue a particular course of life (e.g., Wis. 6:12).[107] While the *panēgyrikos* ("panegyric, praise at a festival") is a major form in Wisdom (cf. 19:2), the rhetor also makes use of additional types of oratory, including the accusation (*katēgoria;* cf., e.g., 2:21-24), apology (*apologia;* cf. the apology for the conquest of Canaan in 12:3-18, and the punishment of the Egyptians in 11:15–12:2), praise (*ainesis;* cf. 7:22–8:1), and the funeral oration (*epitaphios [logos];* cf. 3:1-9).

A final form in Wisdom that draws from Greek oratory is that of "self-praise" *(periautologia)* issued by Solomon in chs. 7–9.[108] While praise is legitimate when uttered by others, self-praise is to be avoided, though it is acceptable in defense of one's good name or when pleading for justice to those who have defamed one. Further, Plutarch justifies legitimate boasting to enhance one's reputation in order to achieve a greater good.[109] This would be the case with Solomon, who presents himself in Wisdom as the paragon of royal virtue and righteous rule for pagan kings and a model of virtue for youth in Jewish schools to emulate.

The typical intention of the rhetor's use of protreptic becomes obvious from the content of the text. He exhorts Jews to remain steadfast in their loyalty to their traditions, ethnicity, and religious identity, especially when they are suffering ridicule and abuse at the hands of their opponents. The references to the explanation of the origins of death and the immortality of the righteous suggest, as noted earlier, that this persecution may have taken place in a state-sponsored pogrom, and if so, the one initiated and pursued by Flaccus in 38 C.E. would be the obvious candidate. The epideictic character of this *protreptikos logos* points to a literary and rhetorical adeptness acquired by one whose skills of combining content with elegant language are reasonably well presented. This suggests that the author was a rhetor who had studied in a rhetorical school, while his audience consisted of Jews present in an assembly in a synagogue. Since he addresses "kings of the earth" in a speech that makes use of features of

---

106. Winston, *Wisdom of Solomon,* 18-20; Reese, *Hellenistic Influence,* 117-18. Reese notes (118): "The protreptic, then, is not a formal treatise on the abstract aspects of philosophy, but an appeal to follow a meaningful philosophy as a way of life."

107. Burgess, *Epideictic Literature,* 229-30; Stanley E. Porter, ed., *Handbook of Classical Rhetoric in the Hellenistic Period, 330 B.C.–A.D. 400* (Leiden: Brill, 1997); Stanley K. Stowers, *Letter Writing in Graeco-Roman Antiquity* (LEC; Philadelphia: Westminster, 1986) 92.

108. Plutarch, "On Praising Oneself Inoffensively," *Mor.* 7; Dio Chrysostom, *Fifty-seventh Discourse;* Quintilian, *Inst.* 11.1.15-28. See Hans Dieter Betz, "De Laude ipsius (Moralia 539A-547F)," in *Plutarch's Ethical Writings and Early Christian Literature,* ed. Hans Dieter Betz (SCHNT 4; Leiden: Brill, 1978) 367-93.

109. See Duane F. Watson, "Paul and Boasting," in *Paul in the Graeco-Roman World,* ed. J. Paul Sampley (Harrisburg: Trinity International Press, 2003) 77-100.

the apology, it is not impossible that he addressed the prefect's court. But it is more likely that an assembly of Jews is the audience gathered to hear his exhortation.

The primary group to which the rhetor spoke consisted of Jews, perhaps gathered together at a synagogue or of the *gerousia* charged with leadership of the Jews in Alexandria. What intensified the occasion of the protreptic was Jewish suffering from persecution. Jews of Alexandria were in need of encouragement to continue to maintain their heritage of faith and practice. Some in the audience appear to have wavered in their commitment to Judaism. Thus this speech of exhortation provided confirmation that Jews have a rich and noble history and may expect immortality, if they remain loyal and are righteous. Some in the audience may have crossed the line into the acceptance of features of Hellenism the rhetor opposed, including, for example, the worship of other gods and the honoring of images.[110] Thus these are warned of the punishment, in particular the loss of immortality, that comes to those who forsake the key features of their religious identity and teaching. The rhetor exhorts them to return to the practice of the primary features of Judaism.[111] Apologetic features in the book suggest that the rhetor also sought to provide a justification of Jewish faith and life to Greek and Egyptian intellectuals who would have been sympathetic to Alexandrian Jews and their practices. There is no evidence that the Alexandrian Jews were actively seeking to proselytize non-Jews. There may have been in the city "God-fearers," that is, non-Jews sympathetic to Judaism, if this is the major connotation of the term. If the assembly in the synagogue is the context for the delivery of this speech, warned indirectly are the Jews who were threatened by Judeophobia and a pogrom unleashed against them due to their state-granted privileges and their continuing quest for citizenship in the polis. What was at stake was nothing less than the survival of the Jewish community in Alexandria.[112]

The Author as Rhetor

The author's knowledge of Greek and Greek philosophy, Hellenistic religion especially as practiced in Egypt, and Jewish tradition point to his role as a Jewish rhetor *(rhētorikē)*, who previously attended a Greek school of rhetoric and

---

110. See Wolfson, *Philo*, 1:73-74.

111. John G. Gammie, "Paraenetic Literature: Toward the Morphology of a Secondary Genre," in *Paraenesis: Act and Form*, 52.

112. See Johannes Pedersen, "Wisdom and Immortality," in *Wisdom in Israel*, 238-46.

studied in a Jewish school, likely attached to a large synagogue.[113] He may have studied as well under Greek sophists who were not members of any particular school of philosophy but offered lectures and tutoring to students for a price. Rhetoric developed originally within the contexts of public praise, ceremonies celebrating gods and heroes, funerals, and embassies seeking a favorable ruling. Yet these same occasions were the places in which speeches of blame were delivered. As the formulation of rhetoric took on more precise shape, different types of rhetoric were developed: epideictic that shaped the elegant character of the literary artistry, forensic speech delivered in the courtroom, political and deliberative oratory that was delivered before the assembly and occasionally even larger crowds, and protreptic or persuasive speech articulated by teachers, polemicists, and sophists seeking to prove the authenticity of their teaching, to attract students and other adherents, and to prevail in an argument. Rhetoric achieved its greatest significance in the Hellenistic period and the early centuries of the Roman Empire as it became increasingly a discipline of study for the spread and deepening of Hellenistic culture and Roman knowledge and values. Some of the Greek philosophical schools, for example, Stoicism, included rhetoric as one of their disciplines for study. In his *Controversiae* and *Suasoriae,* Seneca the Elder (c. 50 B.C.E. to c. 40 C.E.), a Roman patrician of Corduba, Spain, gives evidence that Roman youth were trained in the scholia of rhetoric in order to engage in the arts of persuasion and deliberation and that adults were keen to display their epideictic skills in public speaking in a variety of settings.[114] During the Roman period, rhetoric took on a greater emphasis and was highly valued as an art and skill.[115] In the years prior to the reigns of the emperors (Julius Caesar and following), some rhetoric began to assume an antityrannical character, since the principate's assumption of autocratic power led to the clamping down on free and open debate among the Roman elite.[116]

113. See "Rhetoric, Greek," *OCD* 1312-14. The best ancient discussion of rhetoric is that of Philodemus (c. 110-40/35 B.C.E.). See Dirk Obbink, ed., *Philodemus and Poetry: Poetic Theory and Practice in Lucretius, Philodemus and Horace* (Oxford: Oxford University Press, 1995).

114. See Stanley Frederick Bonner, *Roman Declamation in the Late Republic and Early Empire* (Berkeley: University of California Press, 1949).

115. Tacitus contended that the health of the Roman state was directly related to the wisdom and persuasive abilities of highly intelligent speakers *(Dialogue on Orators).* This is not a call to *libertas,* but rather an exhortation to reject the decisions being made by "an ignorant multitude" and to establish a hierarchy of one or more gifted orators who maintain the social structure that culminates in elitism of the wealthy and highly educated (Habinek, *Ancient Rhetoric and Oratory,* 12-13).

116. Habinek, *Ancient Rhetoric and Oratory,* 11-12. This is especially noticed in the orations of Cicero, a defender of the Republic, who attacked the despotism of some of the Roman elite, including Marc Anthony, whom he accused of being despotic and "un-Roman."

While this diminished their power, it did allow for the increased social status of plebeians and less powerful patricians. Wisdom's criticism of pagan kings who, unlike the Jewish Solomon, disregarded justice and ruled in terms of repressive power (6:1-2), fits well pro-republican criticism of despotic behavior of rulers and prefects of the empire and its kingdoms (e.g., Cicero). In addition, his tone, less than reproachful, may also be a means of attempting to encourage the leaders of the Jewish community to seek to persuade the prefect and other Roman officials in Alexandria and possibly elsewhere to allow the Jews to assume an increased social status that might even lead to the attainment of citizenship and other privileges given to the powerful in the polis and the larger empire. This theme of despotism is especially influential in the Latin literature of late republican and early Imperial Rome. The literary structure of these texts often includes the antithesis of despotism and resistance to tyranny.

The important features of rhetoric included the following.[117] First are the main features of speech: the prologue, narrative, argument, counterargument, and epilogue. These elements are basic to the structure of the Wisdom of Solomon: prologue (the general exhortation to justice, 1:1-15), narrative (the encomium in 10:1–11:1 and the history of the exodus in 11:2–19:22), argument and counterargument (found throughout the book; the debate with the wicked in 1:16–2:24 is especially illustrative), and epilogue (briefly stated in the abrupt ending in 19:22). Second, the basic classification of rhetoric mentioned above — forensic, deliberative, persuasive, and epideictic — is partially reflected in this Jewish text. Wisdom is a combination of the second and third types with features of epideictic that enhanced the literary artistry. Third, "invention" *(heuresis)* sets forth the means by which to discover things to say to respond to the issues under discussion. These include conjecture, definition, quality, and transference. These are found throughout the protreptic of Wisdom: the origin of death due to the envy of the devil involves conjecture; the rhetor defines wisdom in terms of its many characteristics and major functions; quality, which has to do with the nature of an action, is seen in the example of the argument that immortality comes to one who is righteous while the acts of the wicked intended to bring harm to the righteous lead to destruction; and transference used in the affirmation that the Egyptians suffered the devastation of the plagues due to their sinful actions and oppression of God's people. "Disposition" *(oikonomia)* deals with the various divisions of subjects within parts of speech and the ability to follow the teacher's instruction on ways to make and strengthen an argument. "Diction" (*lexis; phrasis* has to do with types of style, figures, tropes, word order, rhythm, and euphony, which also characterize the semiticized Hellenistic Greek of Wis-

---

117. "Rhetoric, Greek," *OCD* 1313.

dom. "Delivery" (*hypokrisis*, "acting a part, pretense") is an important skill, but cannot easily be recovered from literary texts, including Wisdom. The only obvious element is the rhetor's assuming the role of King Solomon addressing his royal peers about justice. Finally "memory" (*mnēmē*) was important, since orations were not to be read but delivered by the power of recall and memorization. Presumably, the Wisdom of Solomon was written out carefully and then committed to memory. Aids to memory could be used that allowed the speaker to associate the major points of the oration, including visual elements in the surroundings or perhaps a few notes. The rhetorical structure of Wisdom allows the rhetor to deliver his oration from memory.

Speaking as the long-dead Solomon (cf. chs. 7–9), the rhetor addresses the "judges of the earth" and kings (1:1; 6:1), likely only a rhetorical device, and yet it was possible for rhetors who represented constituencies to address public assemblies, gathered for open lectures, or to make a presentation in the prefect's court. In addition, the setting could have been a public forum in which a rhetor would have uttered his speech.[118] However, pretense as a possible feature of the oration would have allowed him, as Solomon, to address orally an audience in a Jewish assembly by feigning an audience of rulers.

His opponents in the oration were especially the Egyptians of Alexandria, some of whom would have gained a Hellenistic education and consequently were largely hellenized. However, they too were denied citizenship in the polis and the opportunity to attend gymnasia in the city. He especially describes his and his community's Egyptian antagonists in 1:16–2:24, where he sets forth their own thoughts about life and their opposition to the Jews for their religious beliefs, cultural practices that were deemed foreign to the environment, and claim to righteousness. This speech of the wicked is an apostrophe (*prosōpopoiia*) in which the arguments of the absent opponents of the sage are spoken.[119] Their identity has been debated, but they were likely prominent Egyptians who had a Greek education, although not in a gymnasium, and appropriated a popularized, vulgar, and not altogether correct understanding of Epicureanism.[120] A materialistic understanding of human nature is evident in 2:2ff.: breath is generated by smoke and thought by the beating of the heart. At death the body returns to ashes and the spirit evaporates into the air. Death is final, and there is no return from Hades. Therefore joy and the sweetness of life at its peak during youth

118. See John G. Gammie, "The Sage in Hellenistic Royal Courts," in *Sage in Israel*, 147-53.

119. Stowers, "Apostrophe," 351-69.

120. This pessimistic view of human existence is common in many writers of the Hellenistic and early Roman period. Winston refers to numerous citations that are similar to the pessimism of the opponents of the teacher (*Wisdom of Solomon*, 115). For Epicureanism see Elizabeth Asmis, "Epicurean Epistemology," in *Cambridge History of Hellenistic Philosophy*, 260-94.

become the objects of human pursuits. This is the lot or fate given to humans, and there is nothing more. They oppose the righteous man who calls himself a child of God and disapprove of his actions. His manner of life "is unlike that of others and his ways are strange" (the statement reflects xenophobia). Since he has become a reproach and a burden, avoiding the "wicked" for impurity and ways that are unclean, he should be removed through murder. He should be tortured in order to see if God indeed will rescue him. They fail to recognize he is a child of God and that the creator made humans to be immortal, but the devil, through his envy, brought death into the world. The righteous man is one who separates himself from not only the wicked, but also non-Jews, and he knows that righteousness leads to immortality. The torture of a pogrom is intimated in this speech as is the separation of practicing Jews from the unclean wicked. Their monotheism is based on a firm belief in the faithfulness of God, while the wicked have no view that God is involved with human beings and behavior. Indeed, they doubt God will do anything to save the righteous. This compares to the Epicurean view of divine disinterest.

Literary Structure

In the shaping of this text, the rhetor has made substantial use of Greek forms (protreptic, epideictic, and encomium) along with several features of Hebrew poetry, including in particular parallelism.[121] The literary rhetoric and the content are combined to shape and transmit the meaning of the text. Addison Wright has shown that the book is arranged into two major sections, each consisting of 251 verses of poetry: 1:1–11:1 (560 stichoi), and 11:2–19:22 (561 stichoi).[122] His rhetorical structure for the book, partially modified, appears as follows:

I. The Praises of Wisdom (1:1–11:1)
    A. Immortality is the reward of wisdom
        (1:1–6:21 — "The Book of Eschatology")
        1. Exhortation to justice (1:1-15)
        2. The wicked invite death (1:16–2:24)
        3. The hidden counsels of God (3:1–4:20)
        2'. The final judgment (5:1-23)
        1'. Exhortation to seek Wisdom (6:1-21)

---

121. Kolarcik, "Book of Wisdom," 437.

122. Addison Wright, "The Structure of the Book of Wisdom," *Bib* 48 (1967) 165-84; idem, "The Structure of Wisdom 11–19," *CBQ* 27 (1965) 28-34. Cf. James M. Reese, "Plan and Structure in the Book of Wisdom," *CBQ* 27 (1965) 391-99.

    B. The nature of Wisdom and Solomon's quest for her
    (6:22–11:1 — "The Book of Wisdom")
      1. Introduction (6:22-25)
      2. Solomon's speech (7:1–8:21)
      3. Solomon's prayer for Wisdom (9:1-18)
II. God's Fidelity to His People in the Exodus
    (11:2–19:22 — "The Book of History")
    A. Transitional section: Wisdom saves her own (10:1–11:1)
    B. Introductory narrative (11:2-4)
    C. Theme: Israel is benefited by the very things
    that punish Egypt (11:5)
    D. Illustration of the theme in five antithetical diptychs (11:6–19:22)
      1. Water from the rock contrasted to the plague
      of the Nile (11:6-14)
      2. Quail instead of the plague of little animals (11:15–16:14)
      (Digression: critique of pagan religions, 13:1–15:19)
      3. A rain of manna instead of the plague of storms (16:15-29)
      4. The plague of darkness and the pillar of fire (17:1–18:4)
      5. The tenth plague and the exodus (18:5–19:22).[123]

This structure demonstrates literarily a progressive movement from creation and cosmology ("The Book of Eschatology"), to cosmic Wisdom's encounter with and appropriation by Solomon ("The Book of Wisdom"), to cosmic Wisdom's guidance of Israel out of slavery in Egypt, to the transformation of creation ("The Book of History"). This structure provides a rhetorical depiction of the themes of the text: cosmic Wisdom's active participation in creation and cosmology, the lives of the faithful, the movement of history, and the transformation of the cosmos.

Social Features: Sages and Social Setting

Schools in Greece and the Egyptian Greek Diaspora

Schools were the major means for the dissemination of art forms, philosophies, literature, and sociopolitical structures in the Greek world.[124] This continued

---

123. "Structure of the Book of Wisdom," 168-69.

124. See Nilsson, *Hellenistische Schule*; Delorme, *Gymnasion*; W. V. Harris, *Ancient Literacy* (Cambridge: Harvard University Press, 1989); N. M. Kennell, *The Gymnasium of Virtue: Education*

in the Hellenistic period in the forms of the variety of different schools operating in Greek society. Select treatises by Greek and Hellenistic philosophers (e.g., Aristotle, Dionysius, Aristippus, Theophrastus, Cleanthes, Zeno, Chrysippus, and Clearchus) provide us some insight into the nature and practice of various forms of education. Education was offered for the payment of tuition, usually by affluent parents of youth, although some teachers in certain cases received support from especially wealthy patrons (e.g., Artistotle was the teacher of young Alexander). Students also came to the great centers of learning to be instructed by famous teachers and philosophers in their various schools. This meant that Alexandria was one of the major cities attracting intellectuals, scholars, and pupils.

Schools of Rhetoric

Rhetoric was one of the key features of education in Greece and Rome in formal gymnasia, in the public lecturing and private tutoring of sophists, and especially the schools of rhetoric. Rhetorical schools were established in the eastern Mediterranean world likely in congruence with hellenization, although the curriculum varied from one school to another. Greek citizenship was not a requirement for participation in these schools. The learning process included the following. The first level was the formal education in Greek grammar (from around age seven until twelve to fourteen). Following the successful completion of this period, the student moved to the second level, that is, he/she entered a rhetorical school to study theory, lectures, literature, the speeches of great orators, and the declamation of his/her teacher.[125] The third level involved the practice through imitation of various types of declamation and their composition for the most advanced students who sought to master rhetoric. To study in one of these schools required a lengthy stay in one of the great cultural cities, especially Rome, Athens, Antioch, Pergamum, or Alexandria.[126]

The schools of rhetoric considered declamation to be the quintessential subject of education and its mastery the much desired pinnacle reached by the cultured and learned man. The student began by learning to master the *progymnasma*, which was the preliminary rhetorical exercise that taught stu-

---

and Culture in Ancient Sparta (Chapel Hill, NC: University of North Carolina, 1995); Cribiore, *Writing, Teachers, and Students;* idem, *Gymnastics of the Mind;* Kah and Scholz, *Hellenistische Gymnasion.*

125. Kennedy, "Historical Survey of Rhetoric," 18-19.
126. Habinek, *Ancient Rhetoric and Oratory,* 60.

dents the basic techniques of writing and how to select themes to develop.[127] Learning to write began with shorter and simpler genres (for example, fables, encomia, *chreiai* [sayings], and proverbs of various types). These and other genres taught students the skills and styles needed to compose speeches. The exercise involved taking a *chreia* or another simple form and formulating a thesis concerning it. The student then sought to develop and prove the thesis in a convincing manner. This included comparison, contrast, and quotation of significant literati and orators. The student would point out the results of following or not adhering to the thesis. Metaphorically, students on occasion were viewed as athletes and teachers as trainers. Hard work and practice in writing and declamation, including the essential argumentation, were the key elements on the path to mastering the rhetorical art, in much the same way that physical exercise developed the muscles of the physique. This metaphor is used of virtue (Wis. 4:2) and of the righteous who endure to the end and even in death are rewarded with immortality, thus receiving the crown of victory (5:16).

Handbooks *(hermeneumata)* or *colloquia* were written and shaped to set forth rules and sayings *(chreiai)* for learning to speak and write, to memorize, and to enhance rhetorical oratory and composition through the addition of quotations from public wisdom and famous men (philosophers, rhetoricians, historians, and public figures). The handbooks that have survived consist of four sections: a general glossary, a glossary that was divided by topics, vignettes of common life, and short texts of stories, fables, and sayings.[128] More complicated and cultured literature that included the works of Homer, Euripides, and other great poets were read and imitated by students at more advanced levels. Historians were also read and imitated, especially the major characters and their speeches of rhetorical display that occurred within the context of the narrative. And, of course, the great orators and their speeches were read and imitated. Even so, it was the teacher's own skills of speaking and writing that were the focal point of imitation by his students. He served as a model for students in writing, oratory, and behavior. For the teachers of rhetoric, the exercises of impersonation and praise *(ēthopoiiai* and *enkōmia)* were the most common types of exercises in the school.[129] The first type of exercise involved declamations that allowed students to play the roles of mythological, heroic, or literary figures (see the fifth- and early-fourth-century B.C.E. orator Lysias, particularly orations 1, 7, 9, and 21). These impersonations gave students the opportunity to

127. Cribiore, *Gymnastics of the Mind*, 222.
128. Ibid., 15.
129. Ibid., 228.

develop the figure's arguments within the context of the speech. The student usually selected the literary pattern appropriate for the occasion, ranging from exhortation to the request for forgiveness, although the same literary type of speech in the writing was often simply imitation. The second type is a prose or poetic panegyric that praises a significant person, thing, or idea.[130] This was occasionally combined with the historical recounting of the past through the praise of ancestors, gods, and cities (encomium). These two elements of impersonation and praise were important in the Wisdom of Solomon. Thus the rhetor plays the role of the legendary king, Solomon, honored for his wisdom (chs. 7–9), and the encomium is used to praise Wisdom's guidance of the ancestors in 10:1–11:1.

While no Greek orations survive that come from the Hellenistic period, the "Second Sophistic" included epideictic models of declamation by such great orators as Dio Chrysostom (late first century B.C.E.) and Aelius Aristides (mid-second century C.E.). Plutarch's *On the Lives of the Ten Orators* preserves the classic Greek orators and some of their oratory: Antiphon, Andocides, Lysias, Isaeus, Isocrates, Demosthenes, Aeschines, Hyperides, Lycurgus, and Dinarchus (cf. the canon of Cicero, *Brut.* 32-37; the one by Dionysius of Halicarnassus; and that of Caecilius of Calacte, whom we know only by the name of the title of the work: *On the Character of the Ten Orators*). The Roman Quintilian (first century C.E.) composed an incisive essay on education that was devoted to rhetoric ("The Training of an Orator," *Institutio Oratoriae*). Cicero (first century B.C.E., *De oratore*) and he were the two leading scholars of rhetoric in the early empire.

Synagogues

The Ptolemies permitted the building of synagogues *(synagōgē)*, allowed public assemblies at these houses of prayer *(proseuchē)*, and permitted Jewish worship (engagement in prayer, delivering a homily, singing psalms, and reading Torah) to be practiced without interference.[131]

---

130. See Aristotle, *Rhet.* 2.20, 1393a23-1394a18. See also Lee, *Studies in Sirach 44–50;* Mack, *Wisdom and the Hebrew Epic.*

131. *CIJ* 2, no. 1440; Horbury and Noy, *Jewish Inscriptions*, no. 22; and *CPJ* 3, Appendix I, no. 1532A; Horbury and Noy, no. 117. See the discussion in Modrzejewski, *Jews of Egypt*, 88. In the reign of Cleopatra VII, there is evidence of another synagogue in the Alexandrian suburb of Gabbary (*CPJ* 2, no. 1432; Horbury and Noy, no. 13). The Ptolemaic monarchy granted the right of asylum to synagogues and did not require either royal statues or those of their patron deity, Dionysus, to be erected in them.

Jews were not required to place pagan idols at their entrances. The generally held view that synagogues emerged in Egypt as houses of assembly and eventually worship is based on the inscriptional evidence for *proseuchē*, which most scholars equate with synagogues.[132] Nine inscriptions on private dedicatory plaques presuppose a building used at least for the purpose of prayer.[133] The principal Egyptian inscriptions are the following:

1. Schedia: "On behalf of King Ptolemy and Queen Berenice, his sister and wife, and their children, the Jews [dedicated] this prayerhouse *(proseuchē)*."[134]

2. Lower Egypt, where an older inscription was included in a later one: "King Ptolemy Euergetes [bestowed the right of asylum] on the prayerhouse."[135]

3. Athribis: "On behalf of King Ptolemy and Queen Cleopatra, Ptolemy son of Epicydus, the commander of the guard, and the Jews in Athribis [dedicated] the prayerhouse to the Highest God."[136]

4. Athribis: "On behalf of King Ptolemy and Queen Cleopatra and their children, Hermias and his wife Philotera and their children [dedicated] this *exedra* for the prayerhouse."[137]

5. Nitriai: "On behalf of King Ptolemy and Queen Cleopatra his sister and Queen Cleopatra his wife, benefactors, the Jews in Nitriai [dedicated] the prayerhouse and appurtenances."[138]

6. Xenephris: "the Jews of Xenephris [dedicated] the gateway of the prayerhouse when Theodorus and Achillion were benefactors [*prostatai*]."[139]

7. Alexandria: "To the highest God [who hears prayer] the holy [precinct, *(peribolos)* and] the prayer[house and the app]urtenances [were dedicated]."[140]

8. Alexandria: "On behalf of the Qu[een] and K[ing], Alypus made the prayer ho[use] for the Highest God who hears prayer, in the fifteenth year in the month Mecheir."[141]

9. Arsinoe-Crocodilopolis in the Fayum: "On behalf of King Ptolemy son of

---

132. See Schürer, *History of the Jewish People*, 2:245.

133. The following translations are taken from Peter Richardson, *Building Jewish in the Roman East* (JSJSup 92; Leiden: Brill, 2004) 115-16.

134. *CIJ* 2:1440. This inscription dates sometime during the years 246-221 B.C.E. (the reign of Ptolemy III Euergetes).

135. *CIJ* 2:1449, 246-221 B.C.E.

136. *CIJ* 2:1443, 180-145(?) B.C.E.

137. *CIJ* 2:1444, 180-145 (?), B.C.E.

138. *CIJ* 2:1442, 144-116, B.C.E.

139. *CIJ* 2:1441, 144-116 B.C.E.

140. *CIJ* 2:1433, second century B.C.E.

141. *CIJ* 2:1432, 36 (?) B.C.E.

Ptolemy and Queen Berenice his wife and sister and their children, the Jews of the city of the Crocodiles [dedicated] the prayerhouse."[142]

It is likely that the *proseuchē* of Egypt was indeed a synagogue. This was the place of assembly for civic meetings and worship of a Jewish community. Synagogues were usually dedicated to rulers, and in this way approximated the "loyalty shrines" *(proseuchē)* dedicated to Hellenistic rulers,[143] with the important difference that the Jewish *proseuchē* was dedicated "on behalf of" rulers, not to recognize their divinity, to "serve their interests," or to seek their approval. Rather, the synagogues are centers of the worship of God, and not the divine rulers or other gods.[144] Philo indicates that *proseuchai* were used for both worship and education (*Vit. Mos.* 2.39),[145] and he calls them the *didaskaleion* (*Mos.* 2.216). In *Spec.* 3.171 he also refers to the synagogue as the *hieron*. Synagogue inscriptions in Egypt and elsewhere do not refer to sacrifices of any kind, although it is possible that gifts of food, wine, money, and incense were offered.

It is possible that, following Philo's remark, education of some sort was offered in the synagogue complex. It may have been the locale for teaching the Torah to laypeople and for scholars and students to study the Torah. Teachers associated with the synagogues would have instructed young students in the tradition of Judaism and its interpretation. Perhaps in this type of environment the rhetor taught young boys who were seeking an education. While the Wisdom of Solomon makes no reference to the synagogue, prayer house, or associated school building, the text may have been used in this locale for its delivery, reading, and study.

Empire/Kingdom/King

The social world of the Wisdom of Solomon included kingship, as indicated by the address of kings in 1:1 and 6:1, the instruction of rulers in 6:1-11, and the relationship of wisdom and King Solomon in chs. 7–9. While it is not impossible

142. *CPJ* 3:164, 1532A, 246-221 B.C.E. Richardson, *Building Jewish*, 116, notes two papyrus fragments that match with this inscription and provide additional information about the prayer house (whether the same building is in mind or not). *CPJ* 1:129, from the Fayum, 246-221 B.C.E., mentions a thief who stole a cloak and deposited it "in the prayerhouse of the Jews." From Arsinoe in the Fayum comes a papyrus, *CPJ* 1:134, from the late second century B.C.E., giving a list of properties with two references to "a prayerhouse of the Jews" that had a "holy garden" *(hiera paradeisos)*.

143. Rachel Hachlili, "The Origin of the Synagogue: A Re-assessment," *JSJ* 28 (1997) 34-47.

144. Joseph Gutmann, "Origin of the Synagogue: The Current State of Research," in *The Synagogue: Studies in Origins, Archaeology and Architecture* (LBS; New York: Ktav, 1975) 74.

145. Schürer, *History of the Jewish People*, 2:425.

for the rhetor to have addressed the prefect's court in Alexandria, the numerous references to Jewish tradition suggest that the audience is a Hellenistic Jewish one.[146] This group would likely have been among the elite in Jewish society, as indicated by 7:8-11. Among the things valued are beauty, nobility, knowledge, wealth, practical wisdom, justice, and virtue (8:2-6).

In the exhortation to kings who rule the earth (6:1-11), the rhetor criticizes them for failing to judge with righteousness and to rule according to law and counsel. Those who rule the earth would likely be the emperors, yet they are told that their sovereignty is due to divine providence. Kings are expected to judge righteously according to the dictates of law (Roman law) and to rule righteously. If they fail to do so, they will be judged severely.

Solomon's lengthy speech and prayer deal with a variety of matters according to kingship. In the world of Ptolemaic kings, who together form the cult of the divine rulers, a tradition appropriated by the later Caesars, Solomon becomes the paradigm of royal rule (7:7–9:18). Rejecting the divine kingship of Ptolemaic kings and Roman rulers, the rhetor, who plays the role *(prosōpopoiia)* of Solomon, presents himself as a mere mortal with the same origins as all human beings. Solomon prefers Wisdom to scepters and thrones and considers her to be more valuable than gold, silver, and jewels. Additionally, she is the source of wealth and all good things, provides friendship with and knowledge of God, enables him to speak elegantly and rightly, grants him the gift of unerring knowledge of all that exists, and teaches him the common virtues of self-control, prudence, justice, and courage, along with the knowledge of divine works and commandments. Wisdom also grants to Solomon knowledge of the past and foreknowledge of things yet to come. Finally, God has chosen Solomon to be king and to judge the people, to build a temple on the holy mountain, and to construct an altar in the city of God's habitation. This temple construction is an action similar to the temple of Isis built by Alexander and the temples of Serapis and Harpocrates built by Ptolemaic kings. Thus the ideal ruler is the one who is dedicated to the worship of the divine, constructs temples, and honors his presence and temple through gifts.

Sophists

Itinerate sophists in the Greco-Roman world, while unattached to gymnasia and schools of rhetoric, gave lectures and tutored students for a fee.[147] They

146. See Reese, *Hellenistic Influence*, 146-51.

147. See *OCD*, 1422, for a review essay. For important studies see Kerferd, *Sophistic Movement;*

spoke and taught about many areas, ranging from mathematics and metaphysics to ethics and schools of philosophy. The sophists especially stressed language, and offered to their students expertise in the features of rhetoric and helped them learn to cultivate the facility of argument. Students who desired to be rhetors and lawyers as well as those seeking a general education often learned from them. Philosophers of note tended to hold them in disdain for their lack of a fully developed system of thought and their claims to know what was not within their grasp. They were not known for rigorous thinking, but rather they set forth, albeit usually superficially, a miscellany of learning. Unlike priests who spoke mythologically about the forces of the cosmos being subject to the will and actions of the gods, they stressed a literate and logical approach to life that was philosophically informed by a variety of schools and individuals. It is true that they often did not represent an informed and accurate portrayal of writers and philosophers about whom they sought to present a précis. They tutored wealthy youth who had the luxury of time and resources to study and to advance in the skills and learning offered. Hippius of Elis, Georgias of Leontini in Sicily, Antiphon of Athens, and Protagonos of Abdera were well-known sophists.[148] Hellenistic Jews who could not attend gymnasia and schools of rhetoric would have sought out sophists to deepen their knowledge of Greek culture and thought. It is possible that the composer of Wisdom received his knowledge of Hellenism from one or more sophists.

The rhetor makes use of the term *sophos* in several places with two meanings. It may refer to those who possess wisdom due to the education they have received and to the divine wisdom that dwells within them. In 4:17 the unrighteous will see the end of the "wise," and will not understand what the Lord had in mind for them, that is, immortality. At times, however, the term may also refer to the sophists. In his exhortation to kings (6:1-25), the rhetor says: "The multitude of the wise is the salvation of the world, and a sensible king is the stability of any people. Therefore, be educated *(paideuesthe)* by my words, and you will profit" (6:24-25). Thus the vocation of the sophist or rhetor is to teach the king, and to offer the king knowledge and understanding. The rhetor also remarks that God is the one who corrects the wise *(sophon,* 7:15-16). The rhetor places himself in a public arena, likely a synagogue or other type of assembly of

Robin Waterfield, *The First Philosophers: The Presocratics and Sophists* (Oxford: Oxford University Press, 2000); Bruce W. Winter, *Philo and Paul among the Sophists: Alexandrian and Corinthian Responses to a Julio-Claudian Movement* (2nd ed.; Grand Rapids: Eerdmans, 2002); John Dillon and Tania Gergel, *The Greek Sophists* (Penguin Classics; New York: Penguin, 2003).

148. The Presocratics include Thales, Anaximanes, Anaximander of Miletus, Heraclitus, Zeno, Xenophanes of Colophon, Anaxagorus of Acragas in Sicily, Empedocles, Democritus of Abdera, Diogenes of Apollonia. They lived between 600 and 400 B.C.E.

Jews in the city, where he plays the role of the wise Solomon, who begins his prayer for wisdom with a reference to sophists who also receive their learning and ability from God.

Teachers

Teachers, who often bore the specific, functional titles of grammarians and rhetors, usually held the highest social status in the Greek world.[149] In Wisdom the key nouns *didaskalos* ("teacher") and *mathētēs* ("student") do not occur, but the participles *didachthentes* ("teaching") and *mathēte* ("learning") are found in a section on royal instruction in 6:9-11.[150] Further, *paideuthēsesthe* ("to be educated") occurs in 6:11. Another occurrence of *didaskō* ("teach") is present in Solomon's prayer for Wisdom (7:21). Wisdom, the skilled artisan of all things, taught *(edidaxen)* Solomon. Cosmic Wisdom is the teacher who instructs King Solomon on how to rule in justice. Later, the rhetor points to Wisdom as the one who instructed the ancestors whom she saved. These righteous ones from the Jewish past were "taught" *(edidaxēsan)* what was pleasing to God and thus delivered because of their righteous and faithful actions (9:18). In God's judgment of the wicked, including the Canaanites, he brings divine punishment against them. And by means of his acts of judgment and redemption, the rhetor glorifies God as the one who thus has taught *(didaskalō)* his people.

Rhetors

Rhetoric *(rhetoreia)* is the art of persuasion (Plato, *Gorg.* 453a2),[151] which was important to the public oratory practiced by lawyers and public officials.[152] It

---

149. Robert A. Kaster, *Guardians of Language: The Grammarian and Society in Late Antiquity* (Berkeley: University of California Press, 1988). See, e.g., Libanius. However, this economic status often varied due to a number of circumstances, ranging from the renunciation of wealth to the frequent travels of sophists.

150. See Cribiore, *Gymnastics of the Mind*, 45-73.

151. For example, see Dio Chrysostom, *Dic. exercit.* (= *Or.*) 18. Important works on rhetoric include D. L. Clark, *Rhetoric in Greco-Roman Education* (New York: Columbia University Press, 1957); G. A. Kennedy, *The Art of Persuasion in Greece* (Princeton: Princeton University Press, 1963); Thomas Cole, *The Origins of Rhetoric in Ancient Greece* (Ancient Society and History; Baltimore: Johns Hopkins University Press, 1991). For rhetoric in the Wisdom of Solomon, see Larcher, *Études*, 185-87.

152. George A. Kennedy, "Historical Survey of Rhetoric," in *Handbook of Classical Rhetoric*, ed. Porter, 3-41. Quintilian added the concept of morality (*Inst.* 2.15.34).

was embodied also in texts, including especially the classics, which were read and appreciated for their literary elegance and persuasive qualities by educated people who had access to them.[153] While this "art of discourse" *(technē)* was intended to be public oratory, the speeches were often written down, both for committing them to memory and for study by students. The *technē* did not consist of rules, but rather was the combination of features of rhetoric that have been discussed (see above). As a work of a Jewish rhetor, the Wisdom of Solomon was not intended for the common masses of uneducated Jews, who lacked the resources and thus the time to learn and to study, but rather for the educated, who possessed the knowledge of elegant and persuasive language as well as the traditions, which the discourses set forth.

Religion in Greco-Roman Alexandria

Fraser points to a fourfold classification of gods and their cults in Ptolemaic Alexandria: the important Greek deities (Zeus, Hera, Artemis, Apollo, Aphrodite, Adonis, Demeter, Dionysus, and the Alexandrian deity Agathos Daimon associated with the founding of the city), the dynastic cult or ruler worship centered on the royal family (Alexander and the Ptolemaic rulers), Egyptian religions (including the ancient and later gods Serapis, Isis, Harpocrates = Horus, and Anubis), and cults of non-Egyptian, oriental deities (Cybele, Atargatis, and the Jewish deity).[154] Another classification of religion is the mysteries, which became prominent in the Greek and Roman empires. These different religions, including the Dionysian mystery, which were practiced in Alexandria, were known by the author of Wisdom, who criticized some of them in chs. 11–19, especially chs. 13–15.[155]

Greco-Roman State Religion

The rhetor of Wisdom would also have known the Imperial state religion, which appropriated largely Olympian religion from the Greeks and is found in

---

153. Cole, *Origins of Rhetoric*. Perhaps the greatest of the rhetors was Isocrates (436-338 B.C.E.), who founded and taught in a school in Athens.

154. The religions of Alexandria are discussed in Fraser, *Ptolemaic Alexandria*, 1:189-301. The classic study of Greek religion is Nilsson's *Geschichte der griechischen Religion*. For Roman religions see Kurt Latte, *Römische Religionsgeschichte* (2nd ed.; HAW 5; Munich: Beck, 1992); Robert Turcan, *The Cults of Ancient Rome* (Oxford: Blackwell, 1996).

155. Sly, *Philo's Alexandria*, 103-19.

particular in the worship of gods like Zeus (= Jupiter). This was coupled with the emperor cult, in which the divine nature of the emperor was to be recognized throughout the empire. Offerings to images of the emperors demonstrated loyalty to the state. Jews were able to avoid the erection of idols to the emperors in their synagogues, and they usually satisfied the emperors by uttering prayers and making gifts on their behalf. The author of the Wisdom of Solomon is careful not to attack the worship of the emperors, but he does strongly criticize idolatry and offers a euhemeristic explanation for its origins (14:11-31).[156] Indeed, the idealized Solomon becomes an important contrast, albeit recondite, to divine emperors (chs. 7–9). Solomon's ordinary birth and mortality are stressed with the comment that "no king has had a different beginning of existence" and with the notation that all humans, including kings, have the same origins and the same end (i.e., death; 7:5-6). Instead of being the recipient of worship, Solomon is the pious devotee of the true God (7:7-8). His knowledge is not that of a god, but rather is that granted him by God and actualized through Wisdom, the divine consort (now a hypostasis). Solomon returns in ch. 9 to emphasize his humble beginnings and the weakness and short life span due to his mortality (v. 5). Like all human beings, he too has a "soul" that is weighed down by a "perishable body."

Native Egyptian Religions

Many native Egyptians continued to practice their ancient religions made up of numerous gods with temples, priests, and festivals. The antiquity of the various cults, the magnificence of their temples, and the education of the priests were held in admiration by the Greeks and Romans, but not so by our author. Certain animals and heavenly bodies that served as symbolic vehicles for deities were largely misunderstood by many Greeks, Romans, and Jews as the veneration of animals. Both Philo and the author of the Wisdom of Solomon criti-

---

156. Pierre Boyancé, *Le culte des Muses chez les philosophes grecs. Études d'histoire et de psychologie collectives* (Paris: Boccard, 1972) 330-32. Baslez ("L'autore della Sapienza," 55) notes that the Greek practice of immortalizing humans, including rulers, heroes, and children, lay behind the rhetor's argument that one form of immortality results from one's children (Wis. 4:1). However, the rhetor of Wisdom argues not only that true immortality resides in virtue and not in sons but also that the offspring of the wicked are good for nothing (Wis. 4:3-5), an opprobrious view, given the Greek religious practice of honoring and immortalizing the dead noted in the giving of food to the deceased and the transference of some to the realm of the immortals. Indeed, for the rhetor of Wisdom, an early death may come to the virtuous, whose lives of honor position them next to God and remove them from the destructive nature of sin (4:7-14).

cized the Egyptians for animal worship. Thus Egyptian religion was ridiculed by the Jewish community, as were also the Egyptians, who were foolish for worshiping the animals as divine.

Native Egyptian religion was a continuation of the religions of the pharaohs that had thrived during periods prior to hellenization. Even after the establishment of Greek rule, these religions continued to affect the lives of both prominent and lower classes of ethnic Egyptians and impacted the religion and culture of the Ptolemies. As already noted, the Egyptian historian Manetho was a priest, likely of the sun god Re, at Heliopolis and may have participated in the establishment of the cult of Serapis during the reign of Ptolemy I Soter. These cults of the numerous Egyptian gods continued to operate during the syncretistic Hellenistic period, which merged numerous gods. The gods Re, Geb (the earth), and Nut (the sky) were worshiped throughout Egypt, while others were more regional. These polytheistic religions were also characterized by an orientation to animal cults. Numerous deities had sacred animals who represented them (e.g., Horus, the falcon; Bast, the cat; and Thoth, the ibis and the baboon), leading eventually to the mummification of these creatures in large numbers. There was also a tendency to identify Egyptian gods with Greek ones during the Ptolemaic period (Amon with Zeus, Hathor with Aphrodite, Horus with Apollo, and Thoth with Hermes). Finally, the mummification of humans of all classes continued and pointed to the belief in a future life beyond earthly existence. Large numbers of mummies from the Greco-Roman period have been discovered. Later, the Roman practice of entombment in catacombs began to be emulated in Egypt in which the dead in the burial chambers would gather in a common banquet hall, together with the tomb visitors who came to mourn their passing. While the earliest of these in Alexandria date from the second century C.E., it is not implausible to think that this practice may have existed much earlier, especially since tomb reliefs from older Egyptian burial chambers depict the deceased dining with visitors to the tomb. Thus the rhetor's emphasis on immortality of the righteous soul takes on an especially important role in a world in which life beyond death was often expected by the Roman, Greek, and Egyptian populations who engaged in the mysteries. The celebration of ancient religions and the process of mummification, the dining together of the deceased and the living mourners, the mystery religions and their emphasis on life beyond death, and the Platonic concept of the immortal soul point to the common belief of a future life in the world of the rhetor of Wisdom.

The rhetor devotes considerable space to conflict with the Egyptians, due to their oppression of the Jews throughout Jewish history into the teacher's present period. Much of his criticism is centered on their worship. He condemns and ridicules animal worship in three separate texts: 11:15-26; 12:23-27;

and 15:14-19. In the first text he illustrates his thesis, "one is punished by the very things by which he sins," by noting the Egyptians' worship of "foolish reptiles and worthless animals" led to their destruction. Similar animals are at work in the second, third, and fourth plagues in bringing punishment to the Egyptian oppressors. This was a divine warning to abandon the foolishness of this worship. In 12:23-27 the rhetor again argues that the Egyptians were punished by means of the same animals they venerated. This affliction came in order that the Egyptians might eventually recognize the one true God. They worshiped these animals, the rhetor concluded, for two reasons: folly and unrighteousness. He devotes a small section to Egyptian religion (15:14-19) in his criticism of pagan religions and particularly idolatry in his digression in chs. 13–15. He especially condemns the Egyptians for idolatry and the worship of animals.[157] He begins with the statement that the enemies who oppressed God's people (i.e., the Egyptians) are the most foolish of all the people who engage in idolatry. His idol satire, long an established form in Judaism since Second Isaiah (Isa. 44:9-20), is followed by his ridicule of the Egyptian "worship of despised animals." He points to two features that make this practice even more absurd: the animals worshiped are often intellectually inferior to others, and they are lacking in beauty. As he resumes his second diptych on quails in contrast to the plague of the little creatures in 16:1, he remarks that similar animals were the instrument of divine chastisement of the Egyptians.

The Ruler Cult

The ruler cult assumed different forms in the Ptolemaic and Roman empires and involves a number of conundrums that prohibit clarity about several important issues, including the date of origin.[158] The deity's major characteristic in Greco-Roman religion was redemption from distress. The ruler's participation in this divine role led eventually to the divine metamorphosis of kings.[159] Ruler worship in the Greek world is first attested in Samos in the deification of

157. For the criticism of pagan gods in Wisdom, see Maurice Gilbert, *La critique des dieux dans le Livre de la Sagesse* (AnBib 13; Rome: Pontifical Biblical Institute, 1973).

158. In general see Lucien Cerfaux et Julien Tondriau, *Un concurrent du christianisme: Le culte des souverains dans la civilization gréco-romaine* (Bibliothèque de théologie 3/5; Tournai: Desclée, 1957); Antonie Wlosok, ed., *Römischer Kaiserkult* (WdF 372; Darmstadt: Wissenschaftliche Buchgesellschaft, 1978); S. R. F. Price, *Rituals and Power: The Roman Imperial Cult in Asia Minor* (Cambridge: Cambridge University Press, 1984); Klauck, *Religious Context*, 250-330.

159. Christian Habicht, *Gottmenschentum und griechische Städte* (2nd ed.; Zetemata 14; Munich: Beck, 1970).

Lysander (404 B.C.E.).[160] Lysander, the Spartan general, liberated Samos from the Athenians and restored its rightful oligarchy, which then established a cult to this hero in thanksgiving for his deliverance. Thus the human deliverer who redeems an oppressed people or city is one who partakes in divine power. The cult eventually develops from a civic one in honor of a ruler into the cult of a dynasty. Later, Euhemeros of Messene (c. 340-260 B.C.E.) described the ideal state in which he claims to have discovered a sacred inscription that tells of the deification of Uranos, Kronos, and Zeus originally as great kings who were given the status of gods. This account may have represented part of the effort to legitimate the ruler cult in the Hellenistic period.[161]

The Ptolemaic ruler cult partook of both the cult dedicated to the heroic deliverer, a king who rescued and sustained a city or people, and the pharaonic cult of divine kings that reaches back to the Old Kingdom in Egypt. Indeed, it is quite possible that Alexander the Great used divine kingship in ancient Egypt as a fitting explanation for his own rule and the dynasty he hoped to establish;[162] but, in any case, he became the forerunner of the dynastic ruler cult that the Ptolemies established in Alexandria and their extended empire.[163] Ptolemy I Soter established a new state cult dedicated to the worship of Alexander as a god. Ptolemy II Philadelphus then made his father a god and his wife, Bernice, a goddess. Together they were the *theoi sōtēres* ("savior gods") who had their temples and priests. He eventually gave his wife (who was his sister) and himself divine status, making them the *theoi adelphoi* ("sibling gods"). They were assimilated into the imperial cult of Alexander. Henceforth, all of the Ptolemaic rulers were divinized in this state cult in order to sanction the political rule of the Ptolemaic Empire.

The ruler cult in Rome developed out of this tradition in Ptolemaic Egypt and not from indigenous conventions.[164] Beginning with Julius Caesar, we witness both the divinization of the human ruler who bore many divine features, due to his heroic deeds, and his apotheosis that followed his death in which he joined the immortals.[165] In 42 B.C.E. Caesar was provided a temple, cult statue, priesthood, and rites of sacrifice. Even Octavian, the adopted son of Caesar, was

---

160. Ibid., 3-6.

161. Klauck, *Religious Context*, 261.

162. This is the explanation of Eduard Meyer, "Alexander der Grosse und die absolute Monarchie," in *Römischer Kaiserkult*, 203-7.

163. Klauck, *Religious Context*, 277-79; Habicht, *Gottmenschentum und griechische Städte*, 42-126.

164. Klauck, *Religious Context*, 285-307.

165. Helga Gesche, *Der Vergottung Caesars* (Frankfurter althistorische Studien 1; Kallmünz: Lassleben, 1968).

called *Divi filius* ("son of God"), beginning in 29 B.C.E. Henceforth, at their deaths Roman emperors, unless extremely unpopular, became apotheosized *(consecratio)* and were included among the civic gods. This required the resolutions of the people and the senate and a witness who testified that he saw the soul of the deceased ruler ascending into heaven. On occasion and in different places Augustus was viewed as a ruling deity, although he did not attempt to establish in Rome his veneration in the form of cultic images, a temple, and a priesthood. However, these demonstrations of divinity were included among the honors paid him in various places in the east. Apotheosis also followed his death, and in Rome he was included among the civic gods. Tiberius followed, and eleven cities in Asia Minor have been excavated that were dedicated to his cult. In Rome, however, he continued to be regarded as a human until his death. Thus balance between divinity and humanity in the ruler's earthly existence was achieved. Caligula came to the throne with great fanfare, with Philo remarking that he was greeted as one who would bring great blessings to people in Europe and Asia as benefactor and savior (*Legat.* 22). Yet he turned into a monstrous ruler and even placed himself for the first time in competition with the ancient gods (Suetonius, *Cal.* 22.2-3).[166] According to Suetonius, he commanded the statues of the great gods be brought to Greece, whereupon his head replaced the original ones. He dedicated a temple to his divine self, accompanied with priests and sacrifices, called himself "Jupiter of Latium," and had erected a golden statue of himself in his temple. Indeed, during Philo's first encounter with Caligula, the emperor chastised the Jews for not worshiping him as a god. Simply to offer sacrifices for him was not enough, he contended, since these were given to another god and not to him as a deity (*Legat.* 353). His murder in 41 C.E. kept him from carrying out his threat to have an image of himself erected in the temple in Jerusalem. Finally, for our purposes, the emperor Claudius rejected the extreme attempts at self-deification by Caligula. He too experienced apotheosis after death and joined the state cult of the deified emperors.

The ruler cult in Ptolemaic and Roman Alexandria provides the backdrop for the lengthy speech and prayer of Solomon in 7:1–9:18. He became the paragon of the ideal ruler in contrast to the Ptolemies and Roman divine kings: "I also am a mortal *(thnētos)* like other humans" (7:1a). In 9:5 he confesses he is a "man, weak and of short duration" *(anthrōpos asthenēs kai oligochronios)*, thus noting his common human nature. These texts are a clear rebuff to the Ptolemaic and Roman rulers who reigned under the pretense of divine immortality, either at birth or in their consecration at death. In a clear rebuff to the ruler cult, Solomon asserts, "No king has had a different beginning of existence, for

166. Klauck, *Religious Context*, 303.

there is one entrance into life and one way out" (7:5-6; cf. Philo, *QE* 2.673). This indication that no ruler is born divine or becomes a god at death is a rejection of divinity during life and apotheosis at death. Solomon's reign is characterized not by divinity but rather by a series of virtues necessary for righteous rule to be practiced that were taught to him by Wisdom, who was given to him by God. Virtue and divine selection became the means by which legitimation of his rule is obtained (9:7). His immortality comes in the same way as that of the righteous — through Wisdom's dwelling within him. The rhetor describes Solomon's extolling of Wisdom by indicating his preference for Wisdom to scepters and thrones and for value that exceeds gold, silver, and gems (cf. Prov. 3:14-15; 8:10-11; 16:16). At the same time, she is the source of wealth and all good things, provides friendship with and knowledge of God, enables him to speak elegantly and rightly, gives him unerring knowledge of all that exists, and teaches him the common virtues of self-control, prudence, justice, and courage, and the knowledge of divine works and commandments. Further, as his teacher and the one who dwells within him, Wisdom enables Solomon, the ideal monarch, to have knowledge of the past and foreknowledge of things yet to come. Wisdom, the "artificer" of all things and an intimate of God, dwells within Solomon's "undefiled body" (Wis. 8:20), a view that expresses the Platonic dualism of body and soul.[167] Finally, God has chosen Solomon, reflecting the theology of divine selection of Israel's rulers (cf. 2 Sam. 7 and Ps. 89), only in this case it is Solomon, the paragon of human virtue and righteous rule, not his father, David. Solomon is commanded to build a temple on the holy mountain, and to construct an altar in the city of God's habitation. However, this temple is not like those constructed to honor Ptolemaic and Roman rulers, following their deaths, but rather is the divine dwelling place for God. While the sage never expected his rhetorical composition to enter the court of the ruling emperor (Caligula?), he did make allusions to divine kingship and knew his audience was well aware of the state cult of the ruler, beginning with the Ptolemies and continuing into the reigns of the emperors.

Mystery Religions

New religions in the Greco-Roman world were adopted from the east, beginning with the Hellenistic period and continuing into Imperial Rome.[168] These

---

167. Winston, *Wisdom of Solomon*, 199.

168. For the mystery religions in general see Walter Burkert, *Ancient Mystery Cults* (Cambridge: Harvard University Press, 1987); Klauck, *Religious Context*, 81-152; Antonia Tripolitis, *Reli-*

included the religions of Dionysus, Isis, and Serapis, who were both public deities in the worship of people and households and private deities for a group of initiates whose rites were to be held in secret.[169] The boundary between public worship and sacred cult is ambiguous, since many of the rites held in open view are the same as those privately experienced. As a manifestation of a mystery religion, the public religion takes on the form of secret cults in which rites are carried out only by the initiated. According to myth, Dionysus (the "twice-born"), the son of Zeus and Semele (a mortal), was the deity with whom Alexander the Great identified. He became the patron deity of the royal religion of the Hellenistic kings. Dionysus was born twice, since Zeus took him from the womb of his dying mother and placed him in his thigh to bring him to term. Those who were initiated into his mystery, especially the Maenads (women worshipers), demonstrated his indwelling by entering into ecstasy. Other features included "enthusiasm," in which the god dwelt within his worshipers, and "mania" or madness, the result of the intoxicating revelry of the worship of the god. Alexandria was the chief center of worship for this half-god, half-man. In Alexandria he was the god adored during his public festival. In the form of his mystery, partakers participated in the drinking of wine, since he was the god of the vine and the giver of fertility. What is particularly interesting is that people from every social arena and class, including men and women, could practice this mystery.

The rhetor of Wisdom is familiar with the mysteries of Alexandria, including this one. In his explanation of the origins of the gods, similar to Euhemeros, he remarks that a father, due to his grief over the death of his son, makes an idol of him and eventually worships him, although he was a "dead human being." He then handed on to his descendants "mysteries" *(mystēria)* and "initiation rites" *(teletas)*.

By means of disguising his criticism of Dionysian religion as an ancient one from the days of the Canaanites, the rhetor engages in a major criticism of this pagan religion, avoiding the direct rebuff of the deity associated with the former Ptolemaic dynasty. He indicted the Canaanites for participating in "sorcery" and "unholy mystery rites" (12:4; cf. 14:23), along with murdering their helpless children and sacrificial feasting on flesh and blood (12:3-6). This appears to echo the myth of Bacchus in which the deity eats raw flesh *(ōmophagion)* and rips apart living animals and even human beings. In

---

gions of the Hellenistic-Roman Age (Grand Rapids: Eerdmans, 2001). For a discussion of religions in the Hellenistic period, see Luther H. Martin, *Hellenistic Religions* (2nd ed.; New York: Oxford University Press, 1987); for Roman religions, see Robert Turcan and Antonio Nevill, *The Cults of the Roman Empire* (Oxford: Blackwell, 1996).

169. See Euripides, *Bacchae.*

Bacchae, written by Euripides, the women (Maenads), who rip apart living animals, set upon Pentheus; and they, along with his mother (Agaue), tear him to pieces. His grandfather (Cadmus) gathers the pieces, while his mother brings his head to the city. Then the inhabitants engage in a festival with Pentheus serving as the meat that is consumed.

The worshipers who participate in the Dionysian mystery eat pieces of a sacrificial animal with the belief that they are partaking of the god Dionysus himself (theophagy).[170] Through this mystery, the worshiper expected to attain not only vitality and joy in this life, but more especially eternal existence following death. While the rhetor condemns the heinous actions of the ancient Canaanites, in reality they serve as a cipher for the worshipers of Dionysus ("the initiates of the mystery," 12:5). In his exaggerated description, he increases the hideousness of these rituals to include such heinous acts as the murder of children and the feasting on human flesh. These monstrous practices were due to the creation and worship of lifeless idols, for idolatry is at the basis of all human sin. This is also a criticism of Ptolemaic kings, since Dionysus was the god of the rulers.

Isis was the most popular goddess of all the deities in the Hellenistic religions.[171] Worshiped publicly and in secret rites, Isis was originally the ancient Egyptian goddess and the mother of the divine ruler, who resurrected Osiris, her consort, from the dead by finding the pieces of his body, reassembling them, and through the magic of ritual, resurrecting him. He then becomes the lord and judge of the underworld. The reigning pharaoh is identified with Horus, her child, but at death he becomes Osiris, ruling in the underworld. She continues to grow in importance, reaching her apex as a divinity during the Hellenistic and early Roman period. This feature of transformation to new life, especially the resurrection of the dead, was central to the mystery of Isis and its popularity in the Greco-Roman world. Through the performance of the correct rituals, individuals, regardless of class, may participate in the future life through resurrection.

Isis, of course, became important in influencing the depiction of Sophia in the Wisdom of Solomon. However, she also became the major rival to the Jewish God. Isis was a goddess of love and immortality, and she also was the religious reason for the high status of women in Hellenistic Egyptian society.[172]

---

170. Klauck, *Religious Context,* 110-11.

171. See Apuleius, *Metamorphoses;* Plutarch, *De Iside et Osiride.* Important studies include R. E. Witt, *Isis in the Graeco-Roman World* (Ithaca, NY: Cornell University Press, 1971); Reinhold Merkelbach, *Isis regina — Zeus Sarapis: Die griechisch-ägyptische Religion nach den Quellen dargestellt* (Stuttgart: Teubner, 1995).

172. Michael Grant, *A Social History of Greece and Rome* (New York: Scribner's, 1992) 5-26. He writes: "But religion was the women's great strength. It had always been so, but now priestesses were abundant and honored on a scale that had not been seen hitherto" (p. 26).

Egyptian women were accorded the highest position in the Greco-Roman world.[173] Isis raised their social level to that of men, at least in Egypt, requiring the respect of children and faithfulness from men in marriage.

The mystery cult of Serapis, the consort of Isis, was also practiced in Alexandria. Serapis combined the Apis bull and Osiris. Serapis was killed by his brother Seth. Resurrected by Isis, he became lord and judge of the world of the dead. He was revered as the great and powerful deity (thus like Zeus), the god of healing (like Asclepius), and the lord of fertility (like Dionysus). His cult was likely founded by Ptolemy I Soter. Ptolemy I built a temple to Serapis alone, while Euergetes built a temple to Harpocrates in Alexandria. This dynasty chose Serapis to be their Greco-Egyptian patron, whose main temple (Serapeum) was placed on the hill of Rhacotis, located on the shore at Alexandria.[174] In the third century B.C.E. private dedicatory plaques to Serapis and Isis together, which occasionally included Harpocrates, indicate that in private devotion the two belonged together, although there is no evidence that a Ptolemaic king built a single temple to both of them. However, most private shrines in Alexandria were dedicated to Serapis and to Isis. In the Roman period, he was depicted as a bearded deity sitting on a throne and bearing on his head the sacred calathus, symbolic of fertility and the fruits of nature.[175] In his mystery, he became the lord of the sacred meal in which celebrants participated by invitation only in secret meals in homes and his temple.[176]

In the Wisdom of Solomon, Wisdom as the hypothesis of God is portrayed as his female consort who permeated creation, ruled the cosmos, gave it life, chose kings to rule, and entered the pure souls of the righteous, guiding their behavior and giving them eternal life. It is clear that Isis was a model for the portrait of Wisdom in the rhetor's *protreptikos logos* (see esp. chs. 7–9). Yahweh and Sophia parallel in a number of ways the divine pair Serapis and Isis in Alexandria.

In the Greco-Roman period of Egypt, temples were often built or renovated according to Egyptian design, although Greek features were added.[177] Thus architectural syncretism is a recognizable trait. This may be seen in the Ptolemaic and Roman temples at Dendera, Edfu, and Philae. Since Alexandria was a new

---

173. Susan Pomeroy, *Women in Hellenistic Egypt* (New York: Schocken, 1984).

174. "Sarapis," *OCD* 1355-56.

175. Fraser, *Ptolemaic Alexandria*, 1:256.

176. Klauck, *Religious Context*, 139.

177. Examples of the adornment of the Serapis temple are listed by Fraser, *Ptolemaic Alexandria*, 1:265-66. For Egyptian temples see Richard H. Wilkinson, *The Complete Temples of Ancient Egypt* (London: Thames & Hudson, 2000); Byron E. Shafer, ed., *Temples of Ancient Egypt* (Ithaca, NY: Cornell University Press, 1997).

city, the temple built by Alexander to Isis and the Serapeum a century later includes elements of Greek architecture. In Greek religion each deity has its own temple *(naos)*, viewed as the "house of the deity" and located on its sacred land *(temenos)*. Most significant was the altar, which was especially associated with the divine presence. The altar stood in the open air where sacrifices to the god were offered and worshipers assembled. The core of the temple was the cella, a rectangular room. Its sides are often extended by means of the porch. More elaborate temples were surrounded by rows of columns that duplicate the cella.[178]

The teacher's reference to the Jerusalem temple, located on the mythical Mount Moriah, occurs in the context of Solomon's lengthy prayer in chs. 7–9.

> You have given (me) the command to build a temple
> > on your sacred mountain,
> an altar in the city you inhabit,
> a copy *(mimēma)* of the holy tent that you prepared from the beginning.
> > > > > > > > > > > > > > > (9:8)

The Platonic idea of the eternal form, in this case that of the holy tent, is used here to indicate that its pattern and nature existed from all eternity.[179] The feature of the archetype is common in Philo (*Mos.* 2.74-76; *Her.* 1.2; *Det.* 160-61; *Congr.* 116) and in other writers influenced by Platonism. The mention of the sacred space, in this case the "sacred mountain," and the altar are especially important elements of the Greek temple.

Hellenistic Philosophy

Not as accomplished in his knowledge of Greek and Hellenistic philosophy as Philo,[180] the rhetor of Wisdom still was aware of some of the major features of the leading schools in his day.[181] He at least would have had access to and perhaps used a florilegium that set forth in summary form the thoughts and themes of leading philosophers and writers (poets and historians).[182]

---

178. Richard Allen Tomlinson, "Temple," in *Oxford Companion to Classical Civilization*, 705-6.

179. This term is frequently used by Plato to indicate that the archetype is the ideal form possessing a far greater authenticity of what is real than mere earthly copies (e.g., *Pol.* 300E; *Tim.* 48E; *Leg.* 668B).

180. See the classic study of Wolfson, *Philo*.

181. For an overview of Hellenistic philosophy, see Long, *Hellenistic Philosophy*. A two-volume sourcebook that includes both the texts and critical translations of selected literature is Long and Sedley, *Hellenistic Philosophers*.

182. For Hellenistic philosophy and the book of Wisdom, see Larcher, *Études*, 201-23.

Middle Platonism

Middle Platonism is an expression used to refer to the eclectic philosophical thinking of many writers and thinkers in the Hellenistic period.[183] Thus important virtues, the supreme principle or the "One," the dichotomy of body and soul, immortality, and the problem of evil are features of Middle Platonism that are found in Wisdom. Albinus, Apuleius, and Chaeronea are among the best-known Middle Platonists in the second–first century B.C.E. These are themes of importance in the Wisdom of Solomon, although they are given a Jewish nuance.

Stoicism

In Wisdom, Stoic teachings are present in the rhetor's statements about the world soul, logic, ethics, and metaphysics (e.g., the change in the elements while nature continues to be stable).[184] For the Stoics and the rhetor, virtues and the desire for their realization are part of the human participation in the cosmos that is rationally founded and maintained. As is the case with the Stoics, the rhetor stresses that ethical behavior is rational. The "good" is understood as virtue and is to be actualized in human behavior. Important virtues in Wisdom are self-control, prudence, justice, and courage (8:7), found also in Stoicism. Reason, not the passions, is the highest aspect of human nature for both Stoics and the rhetor and should be realized by moral human beings to control the passions and to follow consistently the ordered world. For the Stoics the life of virtue is to conform to the natural order, which permeates the cosmos and is present in human nature. For Wisdom, Sophia assumes this role as the cosmic principle also dwelling in the souls of the righteous. The sorites in 6:17-19 recalls the mystical ascension in Plato (*Symp.* 210–12).[185] This concept of the ascension to the world of the ideal is a significant element of the religious and philosophical understandings of mystical harmony in Philo and Wisdom. In

183. Dillon, *Middle Platonists.*

184. For Stoicism in general see *Cambridge History of Hellenistic Philosophy,* in particular, Brad Inwood and Pierluigi Domini, "Stoic Ethics," 675-738; Long, *Hellenistic Philosophy,* 107-209. One of our best sources for Stoicism is Diogenes Laertius of Cilicia (third century B.C.E.), whose *Lives of the Philosophers,* consisting of ten books, provides an overview of many of the Greek and Roman philosophers and schools of thought.

185. For a discussion of mysticism in Philo and the Wisdom of Solomon, see E. R. Goodenough, *By Light, Light: The Mystic Gospel of Hellenistic Judaism* (New Haven: Yale University Press, 1935); Winston, *Logos and Mystical Theology;* idem, "Sage as Mystic."

Stoic logic, a sorites is a succession of valid arguments (thus a "chain") that results in a correct conclusion. The rhetor, working out of his Jewish faith, moves from the love of wisdom, instruction, and keeping of laws to immortality, then God, and then a kingdom. Here in Wisdom, however, the sorites is a rhetorical device, for it is not grounded in logic.

For the Stoic understanding of physics, nature is part of the cosmos, and in Wisdom nature responds to the righteous deeds with blessings, while punishment comes to those who are wicked and irrational. In Stoicism and Wisdom, the elements of the universe combine to form a unity due to the Logos (= Sophia or Spirit of God) identifying both the righteous and the foolish led astray by irrational behavior (1:7). This interpretation of the miracles of the exodus conforms to Stoic physics (11:17, i.e., the creation of the world from formless matter). According to the rhetor, in building on Stoic physics, creation is shaped in such a way as to punish the wicked by the same element or action that brings blessing to the righteous.

Epicureanism

In describing the opponents of the righteous person, the rhetor may have in mind a type of distorted Epicureanism.[186] While Epicurean philosophy taught that virtuous people were to avoid injustice, this is not true of the rhetor's depiction of the wicked. They torment the righteous and ignore the plight of widows and the aged. In condemning the righteous person, the wicked seek to condemn him for holding them and their views as contrary to law and morality. It appears that they have the power to execute the righteous. They assert that power prevails over the deeds of the righteous. Their condemnation of the righteous to death will test the truthfulness of his words and affirmations. The righteous man contends that he is patient in the face of persecution, and he knows that God will redeem him, if not in the present, then in the future life. This persecution, in which the villains are depicted as powerful and destructive, suggests a pogrom in which Jews find themselves victims. Finally, the wicked in ch. 2 reject the belief in immortality and instead present a materialistic view of existence in which people are born by chance, will die as though they had never been, view breath as nothing but smoke, and understand reason as due to the spark ignited by the beating heart. While they believe in fate, which is set for

---

186. In general see *OCD*, 532-34; Phillip Mitsis, *Epicurus' Ethical Theory: The Pleasures of Invulnerability* (Ithaca, NY: Cornell University Press, 1988); Michael Erler and Malcolm Schofield, "Epicurean Ethics," in *Cambridge History of Hellenistic Philosophy*, 644-74.

them, presumably by God, they do not engage in obedience to the law and in worship. These things being so, the goal of life is pleasure, for this is the "lot" to which humanity is destined. The wicked do not know the "mystery" of God, that is, the knowledge of the righteous that they were made to be incorruptible and to possess the image of God.[187] The rhetor rejects their teachings, for he affirms that God created humans to be incorruptible. Death entered the world through the envy (Ps. 108:6 LXX) of the devil and is shared only by those who belong to his followers. While the righteous have the hope that they possess the immortality for which humans were made (Wis. 3:1-10), the wicked are condemned to suffering and death without hope (3:11–4:6). Their only pact is with the one who brings death, the devil.

Neopythagoreanism

Major concepts in Neopythagoreanism included the transmigration of the soul, the kinship of all creatures, and harmony present in numbers and proportion. The goal of life (salvation) was to achieve unity with the cosmos. The concept of opposites was also important (good-evil, right-left, and male-female), and may have influenced the idea of opposites in creation in both Ben Sira and in Wisdom of Solomon. Thus the rhetor may have been influenced by Neopythagoreanism in speaking of the mystical harmony of the cosmos as mediated through the harmony of numbers, musical notes, and heavenly immortality.[188] Passages in the Wisdom of Solomon that resonate with this philosophy include 6:3-4, which may reflect the idea of the king as the living incarnation of the law. Other comparable ideas are the beginning and end of time (7:18), and the measure, number, and weight of things in the structure of the universe (11:20). The divine nature of Pythagoras (an incarnation of Apollo) could be a point of refutation in 7:1-6, and the divine monadism that formed a monotheistic feature of their religious understanding is found in numerous places in Wisdom. Thus, with a few exceptions, Hellenistic Judaism was an appropriate vehicle for this Alexandrian philosophy.[189]

187. The divine "mystery" about immortality is found also in 1 En. 103:2. The term *aphtharsia* ("immortality") is also an Epicurean term, but it refers only to the immortality of the physical atom or matter, which is eternal.

188. Kolarcik, "Book of Wisdom," 441. Also see Winston, "Sage as Mystic."

189. Larcher, *Études*, 218-21.

The Theology of the Wisdom of Solomon

The theology of the Wisdom of Solomon draws heavily from Jewish tradition and recasts much of it in Hellenistic terms. The dominant themes are creation and redemption, Sophia, and anthropology.

Creation and Redemption

The rhetor combines creation and redemption in a new theological casting that makes use of prevailing Hellenistic philosophical, religious, and cultural elements.[190] Central to redemption are the elements of justice and wisdom, which is the divine spirit that permeates creation (1:7), dwells within the souls of the righteous and pure (7:27), is the architect *(technitis)* of all things (7:21; cf. 8:6), and guides and delivers the righteous throughout history (10:1–11:1). The fusion of salvation history and creation theology also is strikingly present in the five antithetical diptychs in which the elements of creation that punish the Egyptians conversely bless the Israelites, giving them life and redemption.

Following earlier examples of salvation history (cf. Pss. 78, 105, 106, 135, 136; Second Isaiah; Sir. 44–50), the rhetor refers to those saved by Wisdom from creation (Adam) to the exodus and wilderness (Moses, Wis. 10:1–11:1), although he describes but does not name those who were redeemed by Sophia. In "The Book of History" (11:2–19:22), he narrates God's deliverance of the ancestors from the Egyptians in the exodus event. The cosmos is created to respond to the salvation of the righteous with the same events and means that destroy the wicked, in this case the oppressive Egyptians. This emphasis on the exodus tradition is due to its serving as the narrative for the Passover celebration. This was the Jewish festival that Egyptian opponents had attempted to discredit by undermining the Jewish telling of the story. Instead of redemption from oppression, they saw it as the casting out of a diseased people who had defiled the land. The rhetor, however, speaks of the ten plagues and the exodus to contrast the divine destruction of the Egyptians and the redemption of God's people. This part is more than a rehearsing of the past. Instead, the event became the archetypal action of the chosen people's salvation, especially during the period of the pogrom that sought to destroy them in Alexandria.

According to the rhetor, God creates the world, rules over the cosmos, providentially redeems the chosen, and guides the chosen to the final days (i.e.,

---

190. In general see Michael Kolarcik, "Universalism and Justice in the Wisdom of Solomon," in *Treasures of Wisdom*, 289-301.

eschatology). In a period of intense persecution in which many die young, the rhetor seeks to impress upon his Jewish audience that the creator who has redeemed them in the past will do so again. Those who die will serve as judges to condemn their persecutors (4:7-20). The Jews who remain loyal to their faith, in spite of persecution, are guaranteed immortality and will reign with God over the nations.

Sophia

The rhetor draws on three sources for shaping his discourse on Sophia: the Stoic Logos, the Greco-Egyptian Isis, and Woman Wisdom in earlier Jewish texts (Prov. 1:20-33; 8; 9; Job 28; Sir. 24). The nature of Sophia is described in divine categories as noted especially in Solomon's speech in Wis. 7:15-22a. She possesses twenty-one characteristics of nature and virtue, and as the divine consort she sits by the side of God. She is a "pure emanation" of divine glory and the "effulgence of eternal light," thus reflecting the light that comes from the glory of God. In addition, she is the "image of his goodness" (7:26) at work in renewing all things and in dwelling in the souls of the righteous so that they become holy souls, friends of God, and prophets. She is both transcendent, in basking in the heavenly glory of her consort, and immanent, in imbuing the cosmos as the divine spirit of order and vitality. The rhetor's understanding of Sophia may be placed under six categories: the divine spirit that permeates the cosmos, the instrument of creation, the redeemer of the chosen, the instructor of the righteous, the highly sought lover, and the medium of immortality.

Similar to the Stoic understanding of the Logos as the world soul, Sophia is the divine spirit who is the instrument of divine creation and oversees and actualizes its order, vitality, and direction (7:25). As noted above, God's providential redemption of Israel's ancestors and the present community is accomplished through the agency of Sophia.

Sophia is also the teacher of the righteous whose paragon of virtue and justice is King Solomon (chs. 7–9). She is the divine spirit that enters into the souls of the righteous and blesses them with the munificence of her gifts (cf. Prov. 3:13-18), and she is the tutor of the wise and righteous. In Solomon's prayer he lists a variety of areas of knowledge that reflect the disciplines of Greek paideia: physics, chronology, the solstices and the changes of the seasons, the different cycles of the year, astronomy, zoology, psychology, and medicine (the drugs of plants and roots). Wisdom, who is responsible for shaping and creating the cosmos and human beings as the divine artisan, becomes Solomon's learned tutor in these areas of human knowledge (Wis. 7:15-22a). Without the gift of Sophia, no human may know God's will and thus act in ways that are pleasing to him, for the rational capacity is limited by a mortal body that restricts the mind's ability to think and to learn. Wisdom's teaching is the source of divine revelation (9:13-18; cf. Prov. 30:1-4), and she becomes the instructor of the righteous who seek to know her. Making use of Solomon's request for wisdom to rule the kingdom in 1 Kgs. 3:3-15,[191] the rhetor sets forth the prayer of Solomon in Wis. 9:1-18, making it into both a royal petition for Wisdom to enable him to rule and judge a people and the commission to have dominion over the creatures (Gen. 1:26-28).

Solomon speaks of Wisdom as the object of his passion. She becomes his lover, serving not only as the consort of God but also as the sought-out object of human affection. By means of their love for Wisdom that succeeds in taking her into their embrace, humans come to possess her and through her experience the gift of immortality (Wis. 8:13). Wisdom grants to all people who are righteous and will learn of her the means to become the "friends of God and the prophets" (7:27). "Friends" are those who are loved by God, while "prophets" are inspired by Wisdom to know the divine will. The "holy souls" are likely the righteous who seek from her instruction and embody it in their character and actions. Immortality is received by the righteous and pure souls in whom Sophia dwells and who follow her laws (6:17). In the attainment of eternal life, one comes near to God (6:18).

Anthropology

The anthropology of the rhetor is based on the tradition of the creation of the individual in the Hebrew Bible[192] and merged with features from Hellenistic philosophical and religious understandings. The most important representation is that of the duality of human nature: soul and flesh, and its impact on the important matter of immortality. He mentions Platonic dualism in 9:15, "A perishable body *(sōma)* weighs down the soul *(psychē)*, and an earthly tent burdens the thoughtful mind *(nous)*." Also, the idea of the incorruptible spirit in human beings (12:1) is a Stoic conception, as is the idea of the eternal renewal of the cosmos by means of the Logos or spirit (7:27).[193] The divine spirit, at times identified with Sophia, is among other things the rational principle that exists

191. Cf. the royal prayers of David in 1 Chron. 29:10-19 and Solomon in 1 Kgs. 8:22-53 = 2 Chron. 6:12-42).

192. See Claus Westermann, *What Does the Old Testament Say about God?* (Atlanta: John Knox, 1979), esp. 41-42.

193. Larcher, *Études,* 218.

in the cosmos and in human nature. Reason is to control and to bring into subjection the passions. What affects adversely the rational intellect is the body (corruptible and the seat of emotions), while the soul is immortal.

The rhetor begins in 1:13-15, in the context of his discussion of the origins of death, to declare that "the creator made all things to exist and things that are alive to continue *(sōtērioi hai geneseis)*." There is not in them a "destructive poison, and the kingdom of Hades is not upon the earth, for righteousness is immortal." God did not intend for living things to die, but rather gave them life and created them to continue to exist. But the "ungodly summoned Death" (personified) by their words and deeds, considering him to be their "friend" and making a "covenant" with him. What is immortal is righteousness (1:15; cf. 1:5, 8; 3:1), a virtue that humans may possess with the understanding that, though they may die, they have in confidence the realistic hope that they will live forever (3:4). The second passage is 3:23-24, in which God created humanity "for incorruption" *(aphtharsia)* and in the "image *(eikōn)* of his eternity *(aidiotētos)*." The reference to "image" likely reflects the language of Gen. 1:26-28. The rhetor understands this text to refer to immortality, a divine characteristic, and not sovereignty or serving as a surrogate of God.

As noted earlier, Solomon confesses that he is a "mortal" like all other humans and a descendant of the "first-formed" (*prōtoplaston,* i.e., Adam) child of the earth (Wis. 7:5), whose gestation lasted ten months. He was conceived by the "pleasure of marriage," breathed the air common to all, and participated in both the common human entrance into life and exit (i.e., in death). In 10:1 Wisdom (lit. "she") protected the "first-formed" *(prōtoplaston),* who alone was "created" *(ktizō),* that is, only he (Adam) was created in this manner among all of humanity. The noun for "formed" recalls the metaphor of the potter, who fashions from clay an object to fire and then to use when hardened. In Greek literature the expression is found in the description of the divine act of creating.[194] The rhetor does take up the matter of human sovereignty when he describes the righteous as those who are destined in the future age of divine visitation to serve as kings over the nations in God's creation.

In contrast to the divine creation of humanity, some wicked humans foolishly engage in making gods in the form of idols (13:10–14:31). The folly of idolatry is that it is an aberration of the theology of God as the creator of humanity. The rhetor criticizes humans trying to fashion a god who is greatly inferior to themselves (Isa. 45:20–46:13).

---

194. See, e.g., Hephaestus's forming of Pandora; Hesiod, *Op.* 70-71.

Conclusion: Creation and Redemption

During a time of intense persecution, the rhetor reshapes Jewish theological traditions with contemporary Hellenistic forms, rhetoric, and thought to construct a theological synthesis that is common to numerous texts in Hellenistic Judaism.[195] While he places a strong emphasis on election, especially in the second part of the book, he is a universalist, due to his belief that righteousness is a virtue that any person, regardless of ethnicity, may possess. Because of God's love for creation and for all his creatures, he offers pagans as well as Jews the opportunity to pursue righteousness and to gain immortality for which they, the descendants of Adam, were originally created.

In the Wisdom of Solomon God is creator, sustainer, and redeemer, and he acts in these capacities largely through his consort, Woman Wisdom. With tinges of eschatology emerging in the text, the righteous, who are given and then taught by Wisdom, may wait in confident hope for immortality. Though their corruptible bodies will die, even at times prematurely, they in the form of their immortal souls may expect to reign forever. In his shaping of creation, God created a cosmos in which the same element brings blessing to the righteous and destruction to the wicked. The story of the exodus is given new emphasis, for it becomes the means of reassurance of salvation for Jews undergoing persecution by the wicked, especially their Egyptian opponents. Sophia suffuses creation, structures and orders it, and renews all life. Cosmic Wisdom also dwells in righteous souls, making them pure and holy, friends of God, and prophets, all the while punishing the wicked. Through her comes immortality that enables even those who suffer and die due to the malicious acts of their persecutors to have eternal life. Finally, Sophia, the consort of God, is also the lover of the righteous, teaching her followers to know God (9:13-18) and to follow justice. She is a lover, both as the consort of God and the object of the righteous who pursue her. She is the means of eternal life for those who are righteous. Through the teaching of God's actions actualized by his consort and mediator, a hopeful word is issued to those who are enduring persecution.

195. Vogels, "God Who Creates."

8. Continuing Streams:
Apocalypticism and Wisdom

General Introduction

One of the continuing streams of biblical and apocryphal sapiential discourse is what may best be termed mantic wisdom, and it serves as one of the important wellsprings for apocalypticism. Of course, apocalypticism represents a significantly new and different worldview from that of the biblical and apocryphal sages so that it would be wrongheaded to see a direct line of development from biblical and apocryphal wisdom literature to apocalypticism. Yet at the same time the composers of apocalyptic literature made use of traditional and mantic wisdom to give expression to their understandings of creation, eschatology, and knowledge, even as the sages who collected and wrote sapiential texts in the third century B.C.E. and later also made use of elements of apocalypticism, especially eschatology. What one sees in apocalyptic and wisdom texts is a merging of the two types of understanding into what is best seen as a new worldview that gives place to both of these types of understanding.

Significant differences between the two kinds of literature include apocalypticism's emphasis on the supernatural world in contrast to traditional wisdom's reality consisting of the observable world of nature and society; a variety of genres that vary significantly (e.g., apocalypticism's use of revelation through dreams and visions to obtain esoteric knowledge about heaven and the future and wisdom's focus on sayings, instructions, riddles, questions, and didactic poems and narratives to articulate human understanding empirically and logically obtained); modes of discourse including apocalypticism's colorful, imaginative, and mythical imagery and wisdom's contrasting concrete details about nature and human behavior; apocalypticism's primary interest in eschatology that is incongruous with wisdom's emphasis on present experience; and apocalypticism's view of the world as corrupt in opposition to what is wisdom's essentially positive estimation of the world and life as inherently good as long as its teachings are observed and followed. While wisdom and apocalypticism present at times radically different worldviews and offer divergent discourses, there are similarities, especially in the use of wisdom forms and themes in apocalyptic literature. Indeed, the merging of these two traditions shapes a number of different texts from the third century B.C.E. to the late first century C.E.

The Jewish sources of apocalyptic as a mode of thought coupled with its associated language are prophecy and wisdom,[1] while external influence, from especially Babylonian mythical and magical texts and perhaps even Persian religious literature with its strong emphasis on dualism, was also pivotal in the rise of this new religious worldview. Unveiling these sources is helpful in understanding the thought and function of apocalypticism, but this should not detract us from viewing it in its own terms as both a worldview and a genre of religious and social literature that addresses important crises confronting Judaism for approximately four centuries.

"'Apocalypse' is a genre of revelatory literature with a narrative framework, in which a revelation is mediated by an otherworldly being to a human recipient, disclosing a transcendent reality which is both temporal, insofar as it envisages eschatological salvation, and spatial, insofar as it involves another, supernatural world."[2] The major features of apocalyptic include esoteric knowledge obtained from visions and dreams, mysterious revelations often disclosed by angels, the references to a supernatural world that is dualistic (God and his angels, and the evil one or Satan and his forces), the division of world history into aeons of time, eschatology (cosmic transformation following the final battle between good and evil, resurrection and judgment of the dead, retribution that results in the reward of the righteous and punishment of the wicked), and pseudonymity in the attributing of the revelations to hoary figures honored in Jewish memory (e.g., Enoch, Daniel, Ezra, and Baruch).[3]

---

1. For the former see Paul Hanson, *The Dawn of Apocalyptic* (Philadelphia: Fortress, 1975); for the latter see Gerhard von Rad, *Old Testament Theology,* trans. D. M. G. Stalker (2 vols.; New York: Harper & Row, 1962-1965) 2:303-8.

2. John J. Collins, ed., *Apocalypse: The Morphology of a Genre* (Semeia 14; Missoula, MT: Scholars Press, 1979) 9.

3. D. S. Russell, *The Method and Message of Apocalypticism, 200 B.C. to A.D. 100* (OTL; Philadelphia: Westminster, 1964); idem, *Divine Disclosure: An Introduction to Jewish Apocalyptic* (Minneapolis: Fortress, 1992).

Apocalypses are of two types: historical and visionary. The first responds to a crisis that endangers Jewish existence and looks forward to the end of the present age of corruption and death and the beginning of a new one in which the crisis has been dispelled by the elimination of evil and demonic forces and the reward of the righteous in a life beyond the current one. The second consists of those in which an esoteric vision is obtained by a seer who either ascends to the heavenly world and obtains divine knowledge that discloses the meaning of the present and reveals the future, or receives divine insight into the approaching transformation of the world. As a worldview apocalypticism designates the phenomenon of the disclosure of heavenly secrets in the forms of dreams and visions to a seer for the benefit of a religious community experiencing suffering or perceiving itself victimized. Socially, apocalypticism is the theological undergirding of some marginalized communities who considered themselves victims of powerful colonizers and local rulers, especially Hellenists, the Maccabees, and the Sadducees. The apocalyptic communities, denied an active role in shaping the religious, social, and political character of a new expression of Judaism, anticipated a final transformation of history by God, who was expected to usher in a new life beyond the current one that was to be the reward of the faithful and religiously observant members of the apocalyptic community, while the wicked forces of the present rulers and their evil supporters were to be destroyed.[4]

Rhetoric: Apocalyptic Literature and Wisdom

Numerous Jewish apocalyptic texts appeared as both appendages to prophetic texts (e.g., Isa. 24–27; Zech. 9–14; Joel 2:1–4:1) and independent texts (Daniel, 1 Enoch, 2 Enoch, 4 Ezra, 2 Baruch, and Jubilees among others), which are edited and shaped over a period of generations and in some cases even centuries. As we shall see, the seer who obtains esoteric knowledge through divine revelation plays the central role in these texts and thus represents a modification of the social role of the sage known in biblical and apocryphal wisdom texts.

While many of the sapiential sayings (an exception is the blessed/happy saying) and their larger collections are not found in apocalyptic texts, one does discover on occasion instructions and their embedded admonitions and prohibitions that generically parallel the biblical and apocryphal wisdom texts.[5] In

---

4. John J. Collins, *The Apocalyptic Imagination* (2nd ed.; Grand Rapids: Eerdmans, 1998).

5. See John J. Collins, "Wisdom, Apocalypticism, and Generic Compatibility," in *In Search of Wisdom*, 174-79.

1 Enoch 91–104 (the Epistle of Enoch), which perhaps dates from the early second century B.C.E., there is an instruction that contains the typical address of Enoch's children (91:3), followed by the contrast between the wise and the foolish. Urging the wise to follow the path of righteousness, Enoch notes that they will avoid the destruction that will come to the wicked. Focusing on the exploitation of the poor by the rich, Enoch emphasizes that only the righteous will enter the "gate of heaven" (104:2). Thus the content of this wisdom instruction is shaped in part by apocalyptic themes. The sage's teaching is based on the order of creation, which he observes during his heavenly journeys, and the heavenly revelation that comes to him. Another instruction occurs in 2 Enoch 39–66, opening with the address to the teacher's sons. This text, from the first century C.E., also contains a sapiential instruction with apocalyptic content. Following his trip to the heavens, the seer is given thirty days to instruct his sons before he is taken from them. Included are happy sayings, also a typical form of wisdom literature (42:1-6; 52:1-15), as well as curses. These two sapiential instructions, which also include apocalyptic themes, are reminiscent of the Testaments of the Twelve Patriarchs, a text which includes the instructions that the patriarchs on their deathbeds gave to their children.[6]

Daniel and Apocalyptic Wisdom

The book of Daniel is written in Aramaic and Hebrew. Linguistic features suggest that the Aramaic texts (2:4b–7:28) in Daniel originated during the early Hellenistic period, save for ch. 7, which appears to have a Maccabean date of composition,[7] while the Hebrew sections came together during the Maccabean period. It is likely that 1:1–2:4a was translated into Hebrew from Aramaic. The Hebrew part of Daniel was added during the Maccabean rebellion against Antiochus between 167 and 164 B.C.E.[8] The completed work consists of two sections: the first is a series of narratives about a legendary figure, Daniel, a dream interpreter in Nebuchadnezzar's court in Babylon, and his three companions, who are said to have been exiled following the Babylonian sacking of Jerusalem

---

6. See Eckhard von Nordheim, *Die Lehre der Alten,* vol. 1: *Das Testament als Literaturgattung im Judentum der Hellenistisch-Römischen Zeit* (Leiden: Brill, 1980); idem, *Die Lehre der Alten,* vol. 2: *Das Testament als Literaturgattung im Alten Testament und im Alten Vorderen Orient* (Leiden: Brill, 1985); Harm W. Hollander and Marinus de Jonge, *The Testaments of the Twelve Patriarchs: A Commentary* (SVTP 8; Leiden: Brill, 1985). Collins also points to the Sibylline Oracles as embodying a wisdom instruction in an apocalyptic context ("The Sibylline Oracles," *OTP* 1:345-53).

7. John J. Collins, *Daniel* (Hermeneia; Minneapolis: Fortress, 1993) 13-18, 24.

8. Ibid., 20-23.

(chs. 1–6). These narratives do not presuppose (as do the visions) the persecution of Antiochus IV and were likely a collection of originally independent tales. The second section (chs. 7–12) is a biblical apocalypse in which Daniel the dreamer and visionary, thanks to angelic revelation, explains the aeons of past history and forecasts the future.[9]

In the legendary narratives, Daniel and his companions are introduced as "skillful in all wisdom (ḥōkmâ)" and endowed with knowledge. Unlike Enoch, who is a prediluvian patriarch and visionary, Daniel is situated in the Babylonian court of Nebuchadnezzar II, following the destruction of Jerusalem and the subsequent exile to Babylonia. This location in more recent times compares to the figures of Ezra and Baruch in their respective apocalypses. However, there appears to have existed in the First Temple period a tradition of an ancient sage and visionary in Israelite tradition named Daniel, as reflected in Ezek. 14:14 and 28:3 (cf. Dnil in the Legend of Aqhat from Ugarit).[10] Daniel and the companions understood learning, knew Akkadian and Aramaic, and gave instruction to the court. Their wisdom in all matters surpassed that of the other wise men in the court (1:17). They also assumed the social role of the sage who serves in the Babylonian court. They took their place among the magicians, sorcerers, and other sages of Babylon, three groups who had their origins in Babylonian mantic wisdom. The key role of the wise counselor in this text is that of dream interpreter, specifically the one who provides the meaning of King Nebuchadnezzar's dreams (see 1:17, which identifies wisdom with the interpretation of dreams, a gift that Daniel and his friends possess). In the stories of the revelatory meaning of the dreams that follow, Daniel alone has the ability to offer the king the revealed and correct interpretation of his dreams. Although the lives of Daniel and his companions are threatened because of their strict observance of the Torah, divine intervention enables them to survive plots to execute them. The genre of these tales approximates that of the Joseph Story in Gen. 37, 39–50. As didactic wisdom or court tales,[11] these legends were shaped to present to students of wisdom and disciples of the sages the ideal wise person who, in spite of intense persecution, remained pious and righteous and was given the gift to interpret dreams that speak of the future. These sages in turn were to inspire their extended communities to continue their loyalty to Judaism, knowing that the righteous and faithful would enjoy the same fate.

Daniel 7–12 consists of visions of Daniel the seer, which he receives from an

---

9. In general see ibid., e.g., 48-50, 69-70.

10. *ANET,* 149-55.

11. Hans-Peter Müller, "Die weisheitliche Lehrerzählung im Alten Testament und seiner Umwelt," *WO* 9 (1977) 77-98.

angel, that forecast the future in terms of the Maccabean kingdom. Daniel and his companions are named *maśkîlîm* (11:33, 35; 12:3) who are to instruct the masses *(rabbîm)*. In Qumran these two terms describe the master and the members of the sect. Daniel, as an apocalyptic sage, is the recipient of divine revelation in the form of visions and their interpretation provided him by an angel. As an apocalyptic visionary, Daniel not only sees the divine throne but also foresees the future judgment that leads to both the salvation of the Jews who, along with the resurrected righteous who have already died, are to participate in the kingdom established by God, and the destruction of the wicked. The social role of Daniel and his companions in the apocalyptic section is that of wise teachers who instruct the Jewish community in a time of persecution. Through this teaching they achieve the state of righteousness and may look forward to exaltation. Indeed, some of them also are to suffer martyrdom, but they will enjoy resurrection from the dead in the end time. Thus for the book of Daniel true wisdom comes from the hero's dreams and visions, not from the Torah.

The book in its various stages of development emerged in a sapiential community located in Egypt in the early second century and made its way to Judea, probably Jerusalem, no later than the reign of Antiochus IV. In Judea the collected narratives were taken up by an apocalyptic community in which wisdom continued to play an important role in shaping their worldview, which is expressed in a series of eschatological visions concerning the future.

First Enoch and Apocalyptic Wisdom

First Enoch points to an apocalyptic-sapiential group of sages and seers who respond to the Hellenistic crisis of Judaism in Judea.[12] One should note that the Mosaic Torah and the covenant of Sinai were not of importance to this developing text. Rather, its scribal teachers, composers, and redactors emphasized instead an esoteric wisdom, which was revealed to the primordial patriarch Enoch (see Gen. 5:18-24) by his heavenly vision, the words of the holy angels, and the tablets of heaven (1 En. 93:2). He is presented as having written down this wisdom and then transmitted it to his followers. This gift of a revealed wisdom will provide life to the chosen and enable them to live righteously (5:8). Thus what are important are the prediluvian past and the current age that an-

---

12. In general see James C. VanderKam, *Enoch and the Growth of an Apocalyptic Tradition* (CBQMS 16; Washington, DC: Catholic Biblical Association of America, 1984); Randal A. Argall, *1 Enoch and Sirach: A Comparative Literary and Conceptual Analysis of the Themes of Revelation, Creation and Judgment* (SBLEJL 8; Atlanta: Scholars Press, 1995).

ticipates an eschatological end in judgment and heavenly redemption, which await the righteous followers of Enoch.

The entire book is available only in Ethiopic, although large parts of the first and fifth sections and a piece of the fourth have been found in Greek. At Qumran, fragments of 1 Enoch in Aramaic also have been discovered. Most of the book was likely written originally in Hebrew and was then translated into different languages. The completed book is a collection of different sections, giving indications of their composite nature and multiple redactions: the Book of the Watchers (1–36), the Similitudes (37–71), the Astronomical Book (72–82), the Book of Dreams (83–90), and the Epistle of Enoch (91–108). The Apocalypse of Weeks (93:1-10; 91:11-17) is embedded in the Epistle of Enoch.

The earliest parts of this book, which include the Astronomical Book and perhaps some of the composite Book of the Watchers, appear to have been composed in the mid-third century B.C.E., while later additions are made until the book reaches its final form sometime during the first century B.C.E. This book became the central document of Enochic Judaism, an opposition party that advocated key elements of apocalypticism and shaped a theology and practice of religion that rivaled Zadokite Judaism and responded to the encroachment of Hellenism on Jewish religion, culture, and political power.[13]

The esoteric wisdom of Enoch concerns the nature and order of the cosmos, the two ways of conduct leading to an eschatological reward for the righteous and punishment for the wicked in an eschatological judgment.[14] Only by transcendent wisdom could divine redemption from the earth (which was corrupted by the Watchers or fallen angels, Gen. 6:1-8) and the proper way of righteous existence come to fruition. This revealed wisdom, which the sage wrote down to transmit to future generations, came from Enoch's journeys to the heavens and his return to the earth. Subsequently, the term "wisdom" and its parallel *māšāl* ("parable"; 1:2-3; cf. 37:5; 93:1-3) are found throughout the sections of Enoch as the major connecting theme: 2:1–5:3; 37:1-3; 82:2-3; 92:1; and 104:12. Chapter 48 especially focuses on wisdom that includes knowledge of heaven and the Son of Man and the righteousness of the followers of Enoch.

13. Gabriele Boccaccini, *Roots of Rabbinic Judaism: An Intellectual History, from Ezekiel to Daniel* (Grand Rapids: Eerdmans, 2002) 89-102.

14. George W. E. Nickelsburg, "Enochic Wisdom: An Alternative to the Mosaic Torah?" in *Hesed Ve-Emet: Studies in Honor of Ernest S. Frerichs*, ed. Jodi Magness and Seymour Gitin (BJS 320; Atlanta: Scholars Press, 1998) 123-32. Collins notes the parallels of Enoch with the seventh king in the Sumerian King List, Enmeduranki, who ruled over Sippar, founded a guild of diviners and recipients of revelations, and ascended into heaven. This city was the center of the cult of Shamash (thus the connection made with the solar calendar in Enoch), the sun god. His sage, Utuabzu, was the seventh sage who was taken into heaven (*Apocalyptic Imagination*, 45).

This true wisdom is opposed to the primordial sin, that is, false teaching, of Asael and others similar to him who practice magic and teach a bogus revelation (7:1; 8:1-3; 9:6-8; 69:1-21). The chosen are those who not only possess the wisdom of redemption revealed to them by Enoch (5:8; 93:10), but also actualize its teachings in their deeds of righteousness (99:10). Finally, in the Similitudes (chs. 37–71) there are three parables and a twofold epilogue, all of which are introduced as a "vision of wisdom." The first parable contains a poem (ch. 41) on Wisdom, who found no place on earth and returned to heaven to take her place among the assembly of the angels, leaving the earth in the throes of wickedness. This poem emphasizes the belief that wisdom is not to be found on earth, but rather may come to human beings only through supernatural revelation. While wisdom is present in the order of the cosmos, it cannot be obtained by human means due both to its concealment and to its obscuring by wickedness, which infects human beings.

The major themes of the book include the corruption of the earth by fallen angels, in particular the angelic leaders Asael, who is the teacher of false revelation, and Shemihazah, whose Watchers intermarried with the daughters of men and produced the race of giants (Gen. 6:1-4). Enoch's journeys to heaven, his seeing of the heavenly tablets that indicate this state of corruption is only transitory, and the final retributive judgment of the world hold out the hope that the righteous will one day be redeemed.

In the Book of Watchers, Enoch is comparable to the *apkallu*s in Mesopotamian mythology and is the scribe who serves as the intermediary between the angels in heaven and the fallen on the earth (1 En. 12:1-4). In the Book of Giants, he is the "scribe of distinction" who is a dream interpreter, while in the Astronomical Book he is a seer who has visions that enable him to know the mysteries of the cosmos (1 En. 72–82). Thus Enoch is a sage, but he belongs more to the mantic tradition that influenced apocalypticism than to the empirical and rational type of sage represented by Proverbs and Ben Sira that focused on obtaining insight that would allow the wise to master present existence.

Second Enoch and Wisdom

Second Enoch, a text from the first century c.e., includes a sapiential instruction embedded in an apocalyptic text. Similar to testament literature, the sage instructs his sons after his heavenly tour. Similar to earlier sapiential instructions, this text issues the call: "Give heed, my children, to the admonition of your father." The content of this instruction includes what Enoch has learned in heaven, coupled with ethical exhortation (42:6-14; 52:1-15). Enoch's journeys resulted in his seeing the order of creation, and these form the basis for his ethical teaching (44:1). Yet there is also a final judgment in which retribution will be distributed to the righteous and the wicked (44:5; 52:15).[15]

Wisdom in 4 Ezra and 2 Baruch

These two apocalypses are closely tied together by common themes, a typical seven-part structure, and a shared setting in the aftermath of the Roman destruction of Jerusalem and the temple. In 4 Ezra, preserved in Latin, the three dialogues between the seer and an angel address the problem of theodicy, but the final part of the book places this issue within the context of visions and an apocalyptic worldview. Ezra, the revered sage of the past, engages in dialogue with the angel Uriel and then receives visions from him. Ezra writes these things down into texts intended for the people and the scribes. In regard to the theological problem of theodicy, Ezra makes the transition from the skeptic who questions divine righteousness to the believer. Whether there is an answer to his probing questions is debated, but at least one may surmise that both the skeptic and the believer are given theological credibility in the difficult task of trying to negotiate the crisis posed by 70 C.E.

Second Baruch, preserved in Syriac, also takes up the sapiential form of dialogue, but finds the answer in apocalyptic vision in which human history and the salvation of the Jews are eschatologically realized in the final judgment. This apocalyptic hope is based on national restoration and the eschatological future of a new world and new life. Baruch assumes the role of the recipient and interpreter of visions and dreams concerning future redemption. These two texts view wisdom as encompassing both the Mosaic Torah and its interpretation by the sages, and are not interested in the speculation of the heavenly world found in 1 Enoch.[16]

Date and Historical Context

Jewish apocalypticism first emerges clearly in the Hellenistic age, even though some initial elements began to appear in the Persian period. Some of

---

15. Testaments are ethical instructions of a dying father to his sons. See von Nordheim, *Lehre der Alten*, vols. 1 and 2. This form in 2 Enoch makes use of apocalypticism to shape the content of what is taught (Collins, "Wisdom, Apocalypticism, and Generic Compatibility," 177).

16. Collins, *Apocalyptic Imagination*, 194-225.

the redactors of several prophetic books during the later rule of the Achaemenid dynasty in the fifth and early fourth century B.C.E. were among the scribes working in the temple precinct under the Zadokite priesthood. This is noticeable in apocalyptic additions to Zechariah (chs. 9–14), Isaiah (chs. 24–27), and Joel (2:1–4:1). However, this centrist group of scribes or a similar group of marginal ones fell out of favor with the Zadokite priesthood sometime during the early Hellenistic period due to its envisioning of an overthrow of the ruling empire. Thus these scribes, finding their heroes among the seers, especially Enoch and Daniel, no longer were accepted by the accommodationists, including particularly the priesthood in Jerusalem. During the Hellenistic rule of Judea, sectarian communities formed consisting of Jews who for the most part were marginalized and restricted from participation in the powerful circles of Jewish priests and political leaders who led the colony that was under Greek and then Roman domination. Some of these, particularly the Essenes, embraced an apocalyptic, sapiential worldview and wrote texts that addressed the crisis of foreign rule and the threat to a more conservative form of Judaism that included Zadokites and their sapiential supporters. As a social, religious, and political ideology, apocalypticism remained a vibrant phenomenon during the Greco-Roman period of Judea's existence as a dependent colony until the Roman destruction of Jerusalem in 70 C.E. Afterward it lost much of its commanding appeal and cohesive influence among Jewish communities who chose to follow the leadership of the early rabbis. This tendency gained momentum with the failure of the Bar Kokhba revolution (132-135 C.E.).

Apocalyptic and Mantic Wisdom

Gerhard von Rad's well-known thesis, articulated in the second volume of his *Old Testament Theology*, that apocalyptic grew out of the wisdom tradition is at least partially correct, since both prophecy and wisdom provided the Jewish sources for the origins of the apocalyptic tradition.[17] Indeed, wisdom in the

17. Von Rad, *Old Testament Theology*, 2:303-8. In general see Hans-Peter Müller, "Mantische Weisheit und Apokalyptik," in *Congress Volume: Uppsala, 1971* (VTSup 22; Leiden: Brill, 1972) 268-93; idem, "Magisch-mantische Weisheit und die Gestalt Daniels," *UF* 1 (1969) 79-94. For the question of divination in the Dead Sea Scrolls, see A. Lange, "The Essene Position on Magic and Divination," in *Legal Texts and Legal Issues: Proceedings of the Second Meeting of the International Organization for Qumran Studies Cambridge 1995*, ed. M. Bernstein, Florentino García Martínez, and J. Kampen (STDJ 23; Leiden: Brill, 1997) 377-435; James VanderKam: "Mantic Wisdom in the Dead Sea Scrolls," *DSD* 4 (1997) 336-53.

apocalyptic texts comes not from human experience and reflection, but rather through revelation. This means that apocalyptic wisdom is esoteric, not inductive, traditional, or open to the human insights of international sages and their disciples, as is the case in sapiential writings like Proverbs and Ben Sira. Qoheleth demonstrates there were also sages in the Hellenistic period who opposed both traditional and mantic wisdom while expressing criticism of some of the claims of temple worship. In his criticism of mantic wisdom as baseless, Qoheleth denies that anyone may know that at death the spirit of a human ascends to heaven and that of an animal descends to the underworld. Rather, both animals and humans are made from the dust and will return to dust.[18] The sages belonged to different schools in the Second Temple period, ranging from the scribes working under the Zadokite priests (Ben Sira), to the critics like Qoheleth, to the mantic sages (Enoch).

The Apkallus in Myth, Legend, and History

One of the backgrounds of Jewish apocalypticism appears in Mesopotamian and Israelite mantic wisdom.[19] While there is no evidence that the Babylonians ever developed an apocalyptic tradition, some aspects of their thought influenced Jewish wisdom in the Second Temple period, which aspects then entered into apocalyptic and sapiential thought that was current among certain sectarian communities in Judea.

The Babylonian sages traced their origins to primordial times prior to the cosmic deluge, when there were primeval heroes who received from the gods the knowledge necessary for the forging of human culture.[20] These were the *apkallus*, who had access to divine knowledge of all things. One of the most renowned human *apkallus* was Utnapishtim, who escaped the destruction of the flood due to the warning from the wise and benevolent deity, Ea. After the flood

---

18. Leo G. Perdue, "Wisdom and Apocalyptic: The Case of Qoheleth," in *Wisdom and Apocalypticism in the Dead Sea Scrolls and in the Biblical Tradition,* ed. Florentino García Martínez (BETL 168; Leuven: Leuven University Press, 2003) 231-58; idem, "The Mantic Sage in Ancient Near Eastern Wisdom," *The Contribution of the Dead Sea Scrolls towards Understanding Prophecy in the Hebrew Bible,* ed. Kristin de Troger and Armin Lange (Leuven: Peeters, 2008).

19. W. G. Lambert, *The Background of Jewish Apocalyptic* (London: Athlone, 1978); VanderKam, *Enoch and Growth;* Helge S. Kvanvig, *Roots of Apocalyptic: The Mesopotamian Background of the Enoch Figure and the Son of Man* (WMANT 61; Neukirchen-Vluyn: Neukirchener Verlag, 1987).

20. This compares to the satirical charge Eliphaz leveled against Job in 15:7-16, and to the mythological imagery used by Agur in Prov. 30:1-4.

had completed its destruction and the earth was re-created, Utnapishtim, now granted the status of a god, provided for the continuity of civilization.[21]

While the tradition of the seven prediluvian *apkallus* is sketchy, several texts indicate they were recipients of divine wisdom from Ea, their patron deity, and gave to humanity the arts of civilization. From the information we have, the seven *apkallus* were apparently semidivine sages who maintained an intermediate position between the world of the gods and that of human beings.[22] They were the ones later sages honored as types of patron saints. But only Utnapishtim was granted immortality for escaping the ravages of the deluge. Following the flood, a new group of ancient *apkallus* taught culture and the elements of social life to humanity.

The Myth of Adapa and the Apkallu Tradition

Adapa was known primarily for being one of the antediluvian *apkallus*, a king, a priest of Ea, and a man of holiness, piety, and wisdom.[23] Due to Ea, the god of fresh water and wisdom, Adapa was given great intelligence and provided humans instruction about the ordinances of the earth. While Ea gave him wisdom, he withheld immortality, thus assuring the continued separation between gods and humans. Adapa became his loyal servant. As the legend goes, however, when journeying across the sea he was thrown into the water by the blast of the South Wind, thus imperiling his life. He then uttered a curse, breaking the South Wind's wing so that she fell into the sea and drowned. Adapa was summoned to the court of an angry Anu to answer for his destructive curse.[24] Before ascending to heaven for his meeting, Adapa was instructed by his divine advisor, Ea, to refuse the food and drink offered him by Anu, the ruler of the gods and the judge, for in consuming them he would supposedly die. Adapa followed his god's advice, but then a spurned Anu rendered the judgment that humanity was denied immortality. Is this a case of Ea's deception so that humanity would not be able to obtain the status of the gods? After all, this would have provided Adapa with immortality, thus removing the separation between humans and the gods. In either case, humans, even the great and wise Adapa, cannot live forever. In the legends of their civilization, the sages of Mesopota-

21. *ANET*, 72-99, 503-7.

22. Denning-Bolle, *Wisdom in Akkadian Literature*, 48.

23. Shlomo Izre'el, *Adapa and the South Wind: Language Has the Power of Life and Death* (Mesopotamian Civilizations 10; Winona Lake, IN: Eisenbrauns, 2001); Benjamin Foster, "Wisdom and the Gods in Ancient Mesopotamia," *Or* 43 (1976) 344-54.

24. See *ANET*, 101-3.

mia were fascinated with these heroes who dared to cross these thresholds separating the worlds of gods and humans.[25]

In addition to the seven *apkallus*, other great sages who are human beings appear after the deluge. Adapa is one of these human sages, a primordial *apkallu* who ascends into heaven and learns divine knowledge and then descends to present that knowledge to humanity.[26] One of the Sumerian king lists contains seven pairs of rulers and their *apkallus* or sages. The sages are advisors to the seven ancient kings along with one sage after the flood and then nine *ummanu* or wise men.[27]

There is an interesting development in this regard. First, the gods created the *apkallus*, who were bearers of knowledge and crafts. Second, these first *apkallus* were succeeded by *apkallus* of human origin. Finally, these in turn were followed by the *ummanus*, the "scholars" (*UVB* 18:44-45).[28] Rulers also were known at times as *ummanus* in order to govern their kingdoms wisely and justly. It is interesting also to note that these seven semidivine *apkallus* were the possessors of the Tablets of Destiny.[29] While the deity of providence (Ea and Marduk) decreed the fates of humans, the seven semidivine *apkallus* were apparently responsible for carrying out these sentences of destiny.

Of interest to us is the *apkallu* Adapa, who was in Mesopotamian tradition "the sage." His name may derive from *adapu*, meaning "wise" in a number of Akkadian texts. In Sumero-Akkadian texts he is described as the "one who emerged from the sea," and is pictorially represented as a "fish-man." In one account of the primordial sages, a purification priest of Eridu ascended into heaven. Then follows the statement: "They are the seven brilliant *apkallus*, *purādu*-fish of the sea, [sev]en *apkallus* 'grown' in the river, who insure the correct functioning of the plans of heaven and earth" (K 5519:1'-9').[30] In another

25. Such heroes included Lugalbanda, Enmerkar, and Enkidu. For an application of "rites of passage" to the Adapa materials that involve both magic and ritual, see Piotr Michalowski, "Adapa and the Ritual Process," *Rocznik Orientalistyczny* 41 (1980) 77-82.

26. See Anne Kilmer, "The Mesopotamian Counterparts of the Biblical *Něpîlîm*," in *Perspectives on Language and Text: Essays and Poems in Honor of Francis I. Andersen's Sixtieth Birthday*, ed. Edgar W. Conrad and Edward G. Newing (Winona Lake, IN: Eisenbrauns, 1987) 39-43.

27. W 20 030, 7. See *Vorläufiger Bericht über die von dem Deutschen Archäologischen Institut und der Deutschen Orient-Gesellschaft aus Mitteln der Deutschen Forschungsgemeinschaft unternommenen Ausgrabungen in Uruk-Warka* (Berlin: Gebr. Mann, 1983) 18. Other important references to the seven *apkallus* include the "Poem of Erra" (see Luiggi Cagni, *The Poem of Erra* 1 [Malibu: Undena, 1977], esp. 127, 147, 162); Reginald Campbell Thompson, *Assyrian Medical Texts*, 105:22-23; Erich Ebeling, *Literarische Keilschrifttexte aus Assur* (Berlin: Akademie, 1953) 146.

28. Denning-Bolle, *Wisdom in Akkadian Literature*, 49-50.

29. Ebeling, *Literarische Keilschrifttexte aus Assur*, 146.

30. Erica Reiner, "The Etiological Myth of the 'Seven Sages,'" *Or* 30 (1961) 1-11, esp. 2, 4.

text the last of the seven sages is Utuabzu, the one who ascended to heaven and perhaps is to be identified with Adapa or Utnapishtim.[31] According to Berossus, who wrote the *Babyloniaca* in the early third century B.C.E., the "fish-man" Oannes (= Adapa) is responsible for giving humans the gifts of writing, laws, sciences, and crafts. From him humans learned how to found cities, build temples, and engage in farming, harvesting crops, and gathering fruits. In other words, he gave to them the gift of civilization. In Jewish apocalyptic, Enoch returns from his heavenly journeys with his supernaturally revealed wisdom, while Adapa and Utuabzu descend from heaven with wisdom associated with human culture and civilization.

This connection between Enoch, Utuabzu, Adapa, Utnapishtim, and the *apkallu* tradition, to which several biblical texts allude, demonstrates that mantic wisdom is not only a source for apocalyptic texts, in particular the Enoch tradition, but also speaks of a type of sage during the First and Second Temple periods whose supernatural knowledge was received by means of visions and dreams and the ability to interpret them correctly (Joseph, Gen. 40–41; Eliphaz, Job 4:12-15; Elihu, Job 33:13-18; Daniel). Traditional and mantic sages in Israel and Qumran rejected the knowledge that included magic, divination, sorcery, augury, and consultation of the dead and spirits (Deut. 18:9-14; Mic. 5:11[12]). Among the mantic sages in Israel and Judah, Isa. 3:2-3 mentions diviners *(qōsēm)*, skilled magicians *(ḥăkam ḥărāšîm)*, and expert enchanters *(nĕbôn lāḥaš)*. The composers and editors of biblical texts were familiar with this type of wisdom in Egypt and particularly Mesopotamia (Gen. 41; Dan. 1–2; Isa. 47:12-13; Esth. 1:13). There may have been mantic sages in Israel who were perhaps associated with the temple priesthood in the Second Temple period, for they served on the temple staff and edited earlier biblical texts. This best explains the origins of the apocalyptic traditions appended to several prophetic texts. But with the radicalization of the mantic tradition in apocalyptic texts that became a means by which to speak of the downfall of ruling nations, the temple priesthood who collaborated with ruling empires could no longer countenance their scribes' participation in the ritual and political center of Jewish life. Thus the break between the priesthood and the mantic sages led to the development of apocalyptic communities who considered among their opponents the Zadokites, whom they portrayed as wicked and polluters of the tem-

31. See Rykle Borger, "Die Beschwörungsserie bit mēseri und die Himmelfahrt Henochs," *JNES* 33 (1974) 193-95, esp. 193-94. Cf. Prov. 30:1-4, where Agur asks the question about the identity of the one who ascended into the heaven and then descended ("what is his name, and what is the name of his son?"). On the basis of the mythical images of the seven *apkallu*s, Utuabzu, and Enoch, Agur's question does not appear to be an impossible one, but rather a rhetorical or catechetical inquiry that has answers known from sapiential tradition.

ple. The break between apocalyptic sages and the temple became final when Antiochus IV inserted himself into the selection of high priests in order to raise money for his military adventurism and to declare the practice of Judaism illicit. Apocalyptic communities, some militarily engaged and others nonviolent, developed a worldview in which the new age would dawn and the wicked rulers and their Jewish supporters would be overthrown and punished. Those deemed loyal to Judaism shaped by an apocalyptic worldview would finally be honored and exalted.

Major Theological Themes

The merging of Jewish apocalypticism with wisdom, beginning in the early Hellenistic period and continuing into the second century c.e. during the Roman Empire, led to the shaping of a new worldview for some Jewish communities, in particular those who existed on the social and political margins and yet were persecuted for their loyalty to their religion and their opposition to some of the developments occurring in Jewish leadership. Marginalized groups longed for a hopeful future in which liberation from foreign opponents and their Jewish allies would occur. The new worldview that emerged blended features of prophetic thought with that of wisdom, both the scribal wisdom represented by Ben Sira and the mantic wisdom that emerged in the Second Temple period (e.g., Agur in Prov. 30:1-4).

Wisdom and Knowledge

Apocalyptic communities and their teachers appropriated elements of wisdom, both esoteric and traditional, in their use of mythic and prophetic imagery to speak of the obtaining of knowledge concerning the future that would guide and undergird a righteous way of life during times of oppression. While traditional sages sought knowledge from human observation and experience in order to master life, apocalyptic sages required esoteric knowledge from great sages of the past to present an eschatological reading of the future on which to base their existence in the present. Supernatural revelation, coming from dreams, visions, angelic messengers, and seers who ascended into heaven and returned in order to reveal to their followers what was to transpire, was a key feature of apocalyptic thought. Yet traditional wisdom also furnished forms and some thematic content in providing insight into living ethically. The future held out the promise that God would defeat the foreign rulers and their wicked

Jewish collaborators, while the present could be endured through righteous behavior. Thus in apocalyptic wisdom sapiential instruction was reshaped with revealed knowledge concerning the hoary past and the eschatological future to encourage Jews to remain faithful to their religious beliefs and to practice their religion in spite of persecution.

Eschatology

For persecuted communities, a principal question concerned the fate of those who remained loyal to Judaism and even suffered death. It was not enough to promise traditional wisdom's goals of mastering life, gaining a caring family, and living a long and honored life in the face of brutal treatment. Thus the apocalyptic sages spoke of a future transformation of the world in which the wicked would be defeated, the righteous who died for their faith would experience resurrection, retribution to the just and the wicked would be meted out, and the loyal Jews would be exalted to experience a heavenly reign free of corruption and the persecution of the wicked. While traditional sages spoke often of retribution, with the exception of the Wisdom of Solomon they did not give voice to any eschatological themes. This Egyptian Jewish sage does speak of immortality of the soul, borrowing from Platonic teaching, and the origins of evil through the wicked's invitation, but not eschatological themes beyond the hope in divine deliverance. Subsequently, in both the Wisdom of Solomon and apocalypticism the origins of evil are traced to demonic forces contesting God for rulership of the earth, but God and those loyal to him would prevail in the approaching future.

9. Continuing Streams:
Apocalyptic Wisdom in Qumran

General Introduction

A second stream of wisdom that continues the biblical and apocryphal tradition as well as an early apocalyptic worldview is found in the texts of the sectarians of Qumran in the region near the Dead Sea. The Qumran community, which was likely the center for the scribal copying and collecting of the writings of numerous related communities, probably consisted of the Essenes described by Josephus or perhaps one group of Essenes. The center at Qumran was founded perhaps as early as the mid-second century B.C.E., when the Hasmonean rulers assumed the high priesthood, and certainly no later than the latter half of this century.[1] This sectarian group, consisting of many diverse though similar communities, whose leaders were sages, scribes, and priests, may have broken with the temple and its high priesthood in the period during the first half of the second century B.C.E., although this is not stated by the texts themselves. They were strongly opposed to the priesthood in Jerusalem (indicated, e.g., by references to "the Wicked Priest"), considering it illegitimate and corruptive of the temple and its ritual practices. The Hasmonean high priesthood is not given as the reason in the scrolls for the founding of the sect and its

1. See Frank Moore Cross, *The Ancient Library of Qumran* (3rd ed.; Minneapolis: Fortress, 1995) 59; Florentino García Martínez and Julio Trebolle Barrera, *The People of the Dead Sea Scrolls* (Leiden: Brill, 1995) 35; Collins, *Apocalyptic Imagination*, 148-50. For the reconstructed Hebrew texts, transliteration, and English translation of the Scrolls, see Martínez and Tigchelaar, *Dead Sea Scrolls Study Edition.*

community center at Qumran, although this change in priestly lineage appears to occur close to the period when the sect was founded. The cultic points of issue mentioned explicitly are those about following the correct liturgical calendar and purity laws (see the Damascus Document, 4Q269 2; and the Halakhic Letter, 4QMMT). However, the Qumran sectarians may have become disaffected in part by the growing hellenization of Judea and even Jerusalem and in part by the illicit appointment of the high priesthood by the Seleucid rulers. Antiochus IV Epiphanes sold the office of the high priest first to Jason (175-172 B.C.E.) and then to Menelaus (172-162 B.C.E.). Demetrius I (162-150 B.C.E.) later appointed Alcinus (from 162 to 160/159 B.C.E.) to the office. He was an anti-Maccabean high priest who descended from a Babylonian priestly family that was not from the lineage of Aaron and thus not an appropriate holder of the high priesthood. Considering it a matter of royal entitlement and political expediency, Hellenistic kings appointed priests to the high priesthood who supported them and their policies. Thus the Seleucids and the Maccabees followed a privilege that was common in the period.[2]

After the persecution of Jews in Judea by Antiochus IV led to the Maccabean revolt, the Hasmonean monarchy was established by the family of Mattathias and his five sons. During the Maccabean period, the Hasmoneans eventually assumed the role of high priest, beginning either with Judas Maccabeus, a leader of the rebel forces from 167 to 160(?) who possibly became a rival high priest to Alcinus, or more likely with his brother Jonathan in 152 B.C.E. This assumption of the role of high priest by the Hasmoneans ended with their last ruler and priest, Antigonus (40-37 B.C.E.), the son of Hyrcanus II. However, political appointments to the office continued. When Rome appointed Herod to the office of king in 37 B.C.E., he chose Ananel, a priest from Babylon who supported his reign, to hold the office.

This means that the points of issue in this contest for the office of high priest were not only cultic, theological, and lineal, but also political. The high priesthood was a powerful and wealthy post so that either the rulers themselves or their appointees who owed them allegiance assumed the office. The priestly control of this central cultic site led to significant prestige, financial wealth, and internal political power for the families of the high priests.[3]

2. See the detailed study of the office of high priesthood by James C. VanderKam, *From Joshua to Caiaphas* (Minneapolis: Fortress, 2004).

3. See E. P. Sanders, "Aristocrats and Sadducees," in *Judaism: Practice & Belief* 63 BCE–66 CE (Philadelphia: Trinity Press International, 1992).

Historical Setting

The Teacher of Righteousness

By the middle to the later second century B.C.E., the sectarians (Essenes?) withdrew from Jerusalem, and many settled in the desert adjacent to the western shore of the Dead Sea. The Teacher of Righteousness, mentioned in Pesher Habakkuk, Pesher Psalms[a], Pesher Psalms[b], and Pesher Micah, was the leader of either an initial group of sectarians taking up residence in the area near the Dead Sea or a later one that followed him when he joined one of the preexisting sectarian groups.[4] An enigmatic figure, the Teacher is called by the titles *môreh haṣṣedeq* ("the Teacher of the Righteousness," 1QpHab 10; see *môreh ṣedeq*, CD 1:11; 20:32; and *môreh haṣṣĕdāqâ*, "the Teacher of Righteousness," 1QHab 2:2), the "teacher of the community," "the teacher of the law," "the interpreter of knowledge," and the "unique teacher." Viewing the temple as defiled and advocating a different interpretation of the law from that of the high priests in Jerusalem, the Teacher left Jerusalem for the wilderness in order to pursue what he considered to be the proper interpretation of the law, correct ethical behavior, and necessary rites of purification in order to await the future transformation that would rid the temple and its rituals of its pollutions and would assert the true meaning of the law.

He may be understood not as a rival high priest but rather as a sage or teacher *(maśkîl)* who not only is wise but also imparts wisdom through his teaching.[5] Indeed, he is the primary authority in wisdom; the one who understands the divine will (especially expressed in the Torah); the one who admits members to the *yaḥad* ("community"); an inspired exegete; the teacher of ethical, proper sectarian behavior; and the revealer of the approaching time of chastisement of sinners and the reward of the righteous. Those who are obedient to the Teacher and his instructions will escape the punishment of the final judgment. Not all sectarian documents refer to this teacher, including 4QInstruction and 4QBeatitudes, although he and his teachings possibly influenced these and other texts. The historical identification of this enigmatic figure cannot be established.

---

4. See John J. Collins, "Teacher, Priest, and Prophet," in *The Scepter and the Star: The Messiahs of the Dead Sea Scrolls and Other Ancient Literature* (ABRL; New York: Doubleday, 1995) 102-35; Michael A. Knibb, "Teacher of Righteousness," *Encyclopedia of the Dead Sea Scrolls*, 2:918-21.

5. Carol Newsom, "The Sage in the Literature of Qumran: The Functions of the Maśkîl," in *Sage in Israel*, 373-83; John J. Collins, "Wisdom Reconsidered in Light of the Scrolls," *DSD* 4 (1997) 280; Goff, *Discerning Wisdom*, 6.

The Man of Lies and the Wicked Priest

The Man of Lies (mentioned in Pesher Habakkuk and Pesher Psalms[a]; 1QpHab 7:1-5; 2:7-10; 4Q171 1:26–2:1) is one of the opponents of the Teacher of Righteousness and is perhaps the leader of a splinter group among the Essenes who contested the teaching and the authority of the Teacher of Righteousness.[6] While the historical identity of the Man of Lies is impossible to know, he was apparently a teacher of the Torah whose interpretation strongly differed from the Teacher of Righteousness.

The Wicked Priest *(hakkōhēn hārāšāʿ)* also was opposed to the Teacher of Righteousness and was likely one of the Maccabean rulers and high priests, possibly Jonathan (152-143 B.C.E.) or a later Hasmonean king. Indeed, it is possible that no single historical person meets all of the criteria identifying this figure, and instead he is symbolic of numerous Hasmonean rulers. This high priest, deemed illegitimate by the Qumran sect and condemned as well for his greed and arrogance, made an attempt on the life of the Teacher, because of his opposition to the temple and its high priesthood. Thus this sage, the Teacher of Righteousness, withdrew to Qumran. In any event, on the basis of the evidence from Qumran it is impossible to identify specifically either the Man of Lies or the Wicked Priest.

While the sect constituted a nonviolent group of related communities, its apocalyptic texts spoke of the coming destruction of the Kittim (Greeks and then Romans) and the removal of the Wicked Priest (probably the high priesthood in Jerusalem). The sectarian writings are permeated with apocalyptic eschatology. Apocalyptic shaped the sectarians' interpretation of Scripture that included the final battle in which the wicked would be defeated and the righteous would be exalted. To prepare for this apocalyptic upheaval, separation from the corrupt and evil opponents and the achievement of purity by ritual and ethical means were required. The community center of Qumran was destroyed when the Roman Tenth Legion moved through the desert communities along the western coast of the Salt Sea, with the ultimate goal of conquering Herod's fortifications, especially the one at Masada.

---

6. A. S. van der Woude, "'Wicked Priest' or 'Wicked Priests'? Reflections on the Identification of the Wicked Priests in the Habakkuk Commentary," *JSS* 33 (1982) 349-59. Van der Woude is among those who think that Pesher Habakkuk refers to wicked high priests in general, not a single one. This is also part of the Groningen Hypothesis (Florentino García Martínez, "Qumran Origins and Early History: A Groningen Hypothesis," *Folia orientalia* 25 [1988] 113-36).

Wisdom in the Dead Sea Scrolls

Wisdom, past and present, had a significant influence on the worldview, theology, and moral teaching of the sectarians.[7] The numerous wisdom texts in the literature of the Dead Sea Scrolls demonstrate that sages and scribes were active among the sect's intellectual leadership. As noted above, there are a variety of sapiential texts in the Bible and the Apocrypha, ranging from traditional wisdom's quest to discover a divine order in the cosmos and society and the quest to master life to questioning of divine justice to a rejection of cosmic and social order. Many of the wisdom texts found in Qumran not only examine and teach the proper course of the moral life, but also project a theological worldview based on the creation of the cosmos viewed through an apocalyptic lens.[8]

Not surprisingly, some of the same eschatological themes are present in 1 Enoch and in a less pronounced manner in the later Wisdom of Solomon, originating in Alexandria perhaps in 38 B.C.E. However, the Wisdom of Solomon is not apocalyptic literature. The worldview of the sect, by contrast, points to a pronounced evil and extreme suffering caused by external oppression and internal corruption of sacred beliefs and practices. Believing they lived in the last days, these sectarians anticipated that matters would climax in a great war that would be won by God, the good angels, and the community of the righteous. Their ethos for this approaching time was shaped by study of the ancestors, the composition of commentaries or pesharim on the prophets, the engagement in piety and ritual cleansing designed to prepare them for the final days and the restoration of the purified cosmos and temple, the knowledge of sacred things, and a proscribed moral behavior.

While there is disagreement concerning the sapiential identification of some of the scrolls, a probable list of wisdom texts includes: 4QInstruction (1Q26, 4Q415-18, 423); the Book of Mysteries (1Q27, 4Q299-301); 4QWiles of the Wicked Woman (4Q184); 4QSapiential Work (4Q185); Words of the Sage (Maśkîl) to All Sons of Dawn (4Q298); 4QWays of Righteousness (4Q420-421); the Instruction of 4Q424; 4QBeatitudes (4Q525); Cave 11 Psalms Scroll (11QPs^a), containing several wisdom psalms or psalms influenced by wisdom (11QPs^a 18; 11QPs^a 21:11-17; 22:1; 11QPs^a 26:9-15); a number of minor texts that may be sapiential, although the data are not always sufficient to made a judgment (4Q302, 4Q303-305, 4Q412, 4Q413, 4Q425); and three sapiential-hymnic texts (4Q411, 4Q426, 4Q528).[9]

---

7. In general see esp. the detailed study by Goff, *Discerning Wisdom*.

8. See esp. Torlief Elgvin, et al., *Qumran Cave 4: Sapiential Texts* (DJD 34; Oxford: Oxford University Press, 1997).

9. This list is that proposed by Goff, *Discerning Wisdom*. Armin Lange provides a convenient summary of those texts he considers to be sapiential in his essay, "Die Weisheitstexte aus Qumran:

Especially important among these writings are the fragments that point to the existence of a major sapiential text: 4QInstruction (4Q415-418, 423; cf. 1Q26).[10] The fragments, difficult to edit together into a composite text, make up the most detailed wisdom text found at Qumran, and it is similar to 1 Enoch, in particular the Book of Watchers and the Epistle of Enoch (1Q26, 4Q415-18, 423).[11] The sapiential elements of this instruction are similar to other traditional wisdom texts, including Proverbs (esp. 22:17-24) and Ben Sira. This instruction, perhaps dating from the early second century B.C.E., combines wisdom teaching with the earlier sages' understanding of the cosmological order and a later, apocalyptic interpretation of creation and history that would culminate in the destruction of the wicked and the vindication of the righteous (e.g., 4Q416 1). 4QInstruction's identification as a sapiential text with features of eschatology is based on formal and thematic arguments.[12] It is an instruction that is addressed to the "understanding one/ones" or "the one/ones who is/are the teacher/teachers" *(mēbîn)*, and deals not only with revealed wisdom and providence but also with a variety of everyday topics, including marriage, economics, farming, and learning. The recipients considered themselves to belong to the poor. The elect wise one is ordained to his place in the structure of the cosmos and its unfolding in history. He is compared to Adam in the garden of Eden in a text (Gen. 2:4b–3:24) that metaphorically describes his wisdom being

---

Eine Einleitung," in *The Wisdom Texts from Qumran and the Development of Sapiential Thought,* ed. Charlotte Hempel, Armin Lange, and Hermann Lichtenberger (BETL 159; Leuven: Leuven University Press, 2002) 3-30. Also see Daniel J. Harrington, *Wisdom Texts from Qumran: The Literature of the Dead Sea Scrolls* (London: Routledge, 1996); Torlief Elgvin, "Wisdom with and without Apocalyptic," in *Sapiential, Liturgical and Poetical Texts from Qumran (Proceedings of the Third Meeting of the International Organization for Qumran Studies, Oslo, 1998),* ed. Daniel K. Falk, Florentino García Martínez, and Eileen Schuller (Leiden: Brill, 2000) 15-38; Florentino García Martínez, ed., *Wisdom and Apocalypticism in the Dead Sea Scrolls and in the Biblical Tradition* (BETL 168; Leuven: Leuven University Press, 2003); Hempel, et al., eds., *Wisdom Texts from Qumran and Development;* John J. Collins, et al., eds., *Sapiential Perspectives: Wisdom Literature in Light of the Dead Sea Scrolls* (Leiden: Brill, 2004).

10. For the text see John Strugnell and Daniel J. Harrington, *Qumran Cave 4: 24. Sapiential Texts, Part 2. 4QInstruction (MŪSĀR LĚ MĒVÎN): 4Q415ff. With a re-edition of 1Q26* (DJD 34; Oxford: Clarendon, 1999). See also M. Goff, "The Mystery of Creation in 4QInstruction," *DSD* 10 (2003) 163-86. This article is developed in greater detail in his published dissertation, *The Worldly and Heavenly Wisdom of 4QInstruction* (STDJ 50; Leiden: Brill, 2003).

11. Torlief Elgvin, "Wisdom, Revelation, and Eschatology in an Early Essene Writing," *SBLSP* 1995, 440-63. For an overview of eschatology in the writings of Qumran, see John J. Collins, "The Expectation of the End in the Dead Sea Scrolls," in *Eschatology, Messianism, and the Dead Sea Scrolls,* ed. Craig A. Evans and Peter W. Flint (Grand Rapids: Eerdmans, 1997) 74-90.

12. See John J. Collins, "The Eschatologizing of Wisdom in the Dead Sea Scrolls," in *Sapiential Perspectives,* 49-65.

obtained from the tree of knowledge. In addition, God created the world by means of his wisdom *(hokmâ)* and by the "mystery that was, is, and is to be" *(rāz nihyeh)*.[13] The order of the cosmos is revealed to and known by only the elect, including the recipients of the instruction who are to reflect on and learn from this divine knowledge. The relationship between the one who utters the instruction and the recipient(s) is that of teacher and student(s). The recipients, who were from a variety of occupations and are male and female from ordinary circumstances, obtain wisdom through the revelation of the *rāz nihyeh*, "the time which was, is, is to come," and the appeal to a heavenly book (the vision of Hagu). Among the recipients would have been those who were training to be scribes, teachers, and officials, as well as commoners who held secular occupations. In addition to incorporating the instruction's teaching for daily existence and gaining revealed knowledge about creation, history, and the end time, the recipients are to engage in ceaseless praise of God.

As other Qumran wisdom instructions, Harrington points to 4Q413 as the initial part of a hymn praising the obtaining of wisdom, 4Q298 as introducing an instruction by the *maśkîl* of the "sons of dawn," 4Q525 as listing five beatitudes as well as other materials too fragmentary to read, and the Book of Mysteries, 1Q27 and 4Q299-301, the last text of which indicates clearly the connection between wisdom and apocalyptic.[14] 4QWays of Righteousness and 4QBeatitudes formulate a connection between wisdom and the Torah and occasionally halakah (4Q420-21; 4Q525 4; 4Q185).[15] Of course, instructions address a variety of issues pertaining to practical wisdom (e.g., 4Q424, which may not have been produced by a member of the sect, focuses on a more well-to-do person who employs others and engages in trade). The sectarians also produced several writings that are best classified as wisdom psalms (or didactic poems). These include 4Q411, a fragmentary sapiential hymn that refers to Yahweh's creation,[16] and 4Q426, 4Q528, and 4Q498, a fragment of which appears also to be a

13. A similar expression in 4QInstruction is the "vision of Hagu" *(hāzōn hāhāgûy)*, a revealed source of heavenly knowledge to be studied by the recipient of the instruction (Goff, *Discerning Wisdom*, 29-36).

14. Harrington, *Wisdom Texts from Qumran*, 60-74. Noting the Herodian script, Lange points to a late date for the composition of this text, second or first century B.C.E. ("Weisheitstexte aus Qumran," 13).

15. The connection of wisdom with the Torah is also found in the Book of Mysteries (see Lange, "Weisheitstexte aus Qumran," 15). See also Lawrence H. Schiffman, "Halakhic Elements in the Sapiential Texts from Qumran," in *Sapiential Perspectives*, 89-100. Schiffman demonstrates the relationship between wisdom at Qumran and Pharisaic-rabbinic wisdom that emerges in the Mishnah.

16. Annette Steudel, "Sapiential Texts," in *Qumran Cave 4: Sapiential Texts*, part 1, ed. Torlief Elgvin, et al. (DJD 20; Oxford: Clarendon, 1997) 159-67, pl. XIV; García Martínez and Tigchelaar, *Dead Sea Scrolls*, 2:840-41.

sapiential psalm.[17] A creation hymn similar to those in Proverbs (Prov. 3:19-20), the wisdom psalms (Ps. 19A, possibly Ps. 104), and Ben Sira occurs in 11Q5 XXVI (cf. 11Q6, 11Q7, 11Q8, 11Q9).[18] Thus the Dead Sea sect's literature reflects the activities of sages, seers, and former priests who transmitted and at times merged their compositions for the benefit of its members. The wisdom texts of 4QInstruction, the Mysteries (1Q127, 4Q299-301), and the Treatise of the Two Spirits (1QS 3:13–4:26) demonstrate that the streams of sapiential and apocalyptic tradition merged in the sect's literature, thus following the early parts of 1 Enoch. The Qumran texts may be understood as wisdom compositions with major elements of apocalyptic thought. Other sapiential texts identify wisdom with the Torah (esp. 4QBeatitudes and 4Q185), thus continuing the tradition of Ben Sira and the Torah psalms, and the association of wisdom with salvation history (4Q185; 4Q413; see Sir. 46–51; Wis. 10–19).[19] Subsequently, the scrolls demonstrate continuity with earlier sapiential and apocalyptic texts.

Some of the nonsectarian, pre-Qumran texts appear to have been written in a different social and religious context. Words of the Heavenly Luminaries (4Q504-506), the Mysteries of Creation (4Q304-305), and 4QInstruction (4Q416-18, 423 + 1Q26) have no known place of origin; they appear to have originated outside the Dead Sea community and its geographical and social location. The Qumran sectarians used these texts in the composition of some of their own writings, including 1QS 3:13–4:26. While these sectarians used sapiential language and thought in creation theology and in moral discourse, they came to interpret history apocalyptically and viewed the prophets of the past as speaking to the present social and historical context of the sect (cf. the pesharim). But in so doing, they joined other, even earlier texts and communities that had come to use apocalyptic wisdom in the shaping of their worldview and moral instruction (e.g., 1 Enoch).

Social Features of the Dead Sea Scrolls

Due to its archaeological and textual data, Qumran provides the single instance of the social organization of an apocalyptic sect that has elements of wisdom

17. See M. B. Baillet, *Qumrân Grotte 4: III* (DJD 7; Oxford: Clarendon, 1982) 69-72, pl. XXVI.

18. Note esp. the language, "Blessed be he who made the earth with his strength, who established the world with his wisdom. With his knowledge he spread out the heavens." See García Martínez and Tigchelaar, *Dead Sea Scrolls*, 2:1178-83.

19. Other possible sapiential texts include part of the Damascus Document (CD 2); the Aramaic Levi Document, which ends with a didactic poem in praise of the teaching of wisdom (4Q213 1 I 14); and several of the *Hodayot* (Goff, *Discerning Wisdom*, 7-8).

and observance and interpretation of the Torah. The community center of Qumran was the location for sectarian worship, for study and teaching of the texts of the sect, and for producing at least some of the scrolls found in the nearby caves, as demonstrated by the scriptorium.[20] It is likely that part of this literature was written elsewhere by another group of Essenes, perhaps even in Jerusalem, and was brought to Qumran, where it was preserved in the caves with locally produced manuscripts. Except for leadership roles, most Essenes appear to have been laypeople engaged in agriculture, limited crafts, and some commerce in different sites in the region of the Dead Sea.

Sages and Scribes

One of the more interesting observations is that the term for "scribe" occurs only four times in Qumran literature (4Q274 1:7; 4Q282q 1; 4Q461 2:1; 11Q5 27:2), in spite of the fact that the sect's activities included both the composition of new texts and the copying of old manuscripts. The word *spr* ("write, writing") refers to scribes, the activity of writing, books, and as a predicative adjective, "written." One of these references to "scribe" is particularly important. It occurs in the first-century C.E. Psalms Scroll (11QPs[a] 27:2-5) and mentions King David (not Solomon!) as the one who was known for his wisdom and sapiential writings as well as composition of psalms. In column 27 David is the object of praise for having written 3,600 psalms and 4,050 songs. He is called a wise man (*ḥākām*) and scribe *(sôpēr)* whose "light" was like the "light of the sun" and who received from God a "discerning and wise spirit" (*nĕbûnâ wā'ûrâ*). This is the single place in the texts of early Judaism where David is called a "scribe." His wisdom, discerning spirit, and enlightenment, coupled with his talent for writing psalms and songs, point to his description as a sage not unlike the one in Sir. 38:24–39:11. Most important in the Qumran literature is the discussion of the *maśkîl*, whose functions comprise those of the liturgical performer, the teacher, and the keeper of knowledge, including esoteric knowledge.[21]

The non-Essene literature refers to the sage by a variety of terms, which we have encountered in the earlier biblical texts and Ben Sira: *ḥākām* ("the wise

---

20. See Jodi Magness, *The Archaeology of Qumran and the Dead Sea Scrolls* (Studies in the Dead Sea Scrolls and Related Literature; Grand Rapids: Eerdmans, 2002) 60-61, 71. Magness notes the exceptional discovery of three inkwells in L30 (the "scriptorium") and discounts efforts to explain the benches as part of a triclinium of a Roman villa.

21. See the essay by Armin Lange, "Scribes and Sages in the Qumran Literature," in *Scribes, Sages, and Seers.* The following linguistic and social description of the sages and scribes in the Dead Sea Scrolls is based largely on this essay.

one/sage"), *yôdēaʿ* ("the knowing one"), *mēbîn* ("the understanding one/the one who causes understanding/teacher"), *maśkîl* ("the one who causes understanding/teacher"), *nābôn* ("the perceptive one"), and *sôpēr* ("scribe"). The Aramaic texts use the terms *ḥakkîm* ("the wise one") and *sāpar* ("scribe").

We can assume that these terms designate a social group of sages who composed texts and instructed the sectarians. They are depicted as active in a variety of activities. They are obedient to the Torah, engage in religious acts of piety, embody and live according to ethical instruction in contrast to the wicked, provide the gift of insight, memorize and recite psalms and didactic teachings, and participate in sapiential prophecy and dream interpretation. Particularly the *mēbîn* ("the understanding one/the one who causes understanding/ teacher") and the *maśkîl* ("the one who causes understanding/teacher") appear to refer to sapiential and priestly functionaries.[22] The sage as a diviner (mantic wisdom) is present in the Aramaic wisdom texts of Qumran, especially in the figures of Abraham and Enoch. These sages have visions, possess the ability to interpret dreams, engage in divination and magic, and conjure and exorcise demons.[23] In these Aramaic texts, Enoch is at times called a scribe.

The Essene literature from Qumran has most of the terms found in the non-Essene texts, with the exception that *sôpēr* ("scribe") does not occur. This may not be an especially important absence, since the same is true of Proverbs. Certainly the scriptorium and its inkwells point to the existence of scribal activity in the composition and copying of manuscripts. The Teacher of Righteousness is designated by the terms *ḥākām* ("the wise one"), *nābôn* ("the perceptive"), and *mēbîn* ("the understanding one/the one who causes understanding/teacher") and at times appears as a wise teacher who imparts special knowledge to all members of the sect (*mēbînîm*, "understanding ones"). The *maśkîl* on occasion becomes the wise official who memorizes and recites psalms and didactic texts and has some administrative and legal interpretive responsibilities.[24] In addition, there is the mantic sage, including Enoch, who engages in speaking of the future.

The Theology of Wisdom in the Dead Sea Scrolls

The texts of the Dead Sea are strongly apocalyptic, although there are important elements of wisdom that combine to form a type of apocalyptic wisdom similar to texts like 1 Enoch and Daniel.

22. Ibid.
23. For this role of the mantic sage see Müller, "Magisch-mantische Weisheit," *UF* 1 (1969) 79-94.
24. Lange, "Scribes and Sages."

Wisdom and Apocalypticism

Aside from fragments of biblical and apocryphal documents, there are no apocalypses in the Scrolls written by the community that approximate those of Enoch and Daniel.[25] Even so, many of the texts of Qumran, including some of the sapiential writings, incorporate a number of apocalyptic themes, which, while at times distinctively articulated, are still seen in other similar writings of the third–second century c.e.[26] Accordingly, the sectarian scrolls describe the current world as the scene of conflictive forces, divine/demonic and human, that ultimately will end in the destruction of the wicked. History is determined to play out this antagonism until the eschatological war issues in the defeat of evil and the forces of wickedness leading to the final judgment in which the good, including the resurrected righteous who have died, will be rewarded and the wicked will be punished. However, these fundamental teachings are set forth not by the visions and revelations of ancient sages from the past, but rather by the Teacher of Righteousness.

Redemption comes from following the teachings of the sages that would lead the righteous in the path of the moral life, culminating in their eventual participation in the world to come. Important is the role of the sage in the interpretation of the Torah and the Prophets, which are significant sources of authority and revelation in the Scrolls. The emphasis on the Torah at Qumran distinguishes the community's thought from that of Enoch and Daniel. The traditional wisdom categories of the opposing groups of the wise/righteous and the wicked/foolish of Proverbs are categories now used to identify two different classifications of people: those who are the "children of light" and those who belong to the "children of darkness."[27] In addition, 1QS 3:13–4:26 contains a list of virtues and vices. Thus the apocalyptic sages who write this text appropriate the ethical dualism of Proverbs in order to divide humans into the two groups of good/righteous and evil/sinful (cf. Prov. 10–15). This dualism is also projected to exist on a cosmic level. Apocalyptic and sapiential forms of dualism are present in the literature of Qumran.[28] This is also noted in 4Q185, which contains three instructions that speak of the brevity of human life, the obtain-

25. In general see John J. Collins, *Apocalypticism in the Dead Sea Scrolls* (London: Routledge, 1997).

26. For the judgment of the wicked and the faithful, see 4Q416 fr. 1, D.

27. Philip Davies, G. Brooke, and P. Calloway, eds., *The Complete World of the Dead Sea Scrolls* (London: Thames and Hudson, 2002).

28. Benedikt Otzen, "Old Testament Wisdom Literature and Dualistic Thinking in Late Judaism," in *Congress Volume: Edinburgh, 1974* (VTSup 28; Leiden: Brill, 1975) 146-57; Hengel, *Judaism and Hellenism*, 1:218-47.

ing of wisdom from God's historical actions, the two ways that are open to humanity, divine judgment, and the fear that results from the beholding of divine power. Here the sage warns his listeners against choosing the way of foolishness and exhorts them instead to take the path of wisdom and righteousness.[29] One Mystery text (4Q301) presents God as promising the reward of the elect and punishment of the wicked.

Finally, the literary personification of folly in the guise of the wicked woman (cf. the "strange woman" in Prov. 2:16-19; 5:1-23; 6:23-26; 7:1-27; 9:13-18) is present in 4QWiles of the Wicked Woman (4Q184); she is presented as a mythological figure who seeks to keep people from observing the Torah and leads them to their death in the underworld.[30] 4QSapiential Work (4Q185) and 4QBeatitudes (4Q525) mention Woman Wisdom, but only incidentally.[31] Unlike this figure in Prov. 1, 8–9, and Sir. 24, she is more comparable to Bar. 3:9–4:4. Nevertheless, the dualism between the Wicked Woman and Wisdom is present, though restrained, in the corpus of texts.

Wisdom and Creation

The creation of humanity and human nature portrayed in dualistic terms were important themes in the Scrolls. Within human nature reside two spirits, one of righteousness and the other of evil (1QS 3:15-19). This leads to the conflict between the wicked and the just until the end of the age when God will destroy evil and the wicked forever (1QS 4:18-19). Sectarian texts that may be sapiential and speak of creation, although their poor state of preservation makes them difficult to understand, are those that are commonly called the "Meditation on Creation" (4Q303-305).[32] Particularly important in considering these fragments as sapiential is their dependence on Gen. 1–3: the knowledge of good and evil, light and the void, Adam's obtaining a wife, the call to the "understanding ones" to "listen" (*šm'w mbyn*) in 4Q303, and the fruit-bearing trees. The tree involves

---

29. Lange indicates that copies of this text (4Q185) include six fragments in a late Hasmonean script. The original was at least as early as 150 B.C.E. ("Weisheitstexte aus Qumran," 11). Thomas H. Tobin points to the late third or early second century B.C.E. as the likely date ("4Q185 and Jewish Wisdom Literature," in *Of Scribes and Scrolls: Studies on the Hebrew Bible, Intertestamental Judaism and Christian Origins*, ed. H. W. Attridge, et al. (Lanham, MD: University Press of America, 1990) 145-52.

30. Goff, *Discerning Wisdom*, 104-21.

31. Sidnie White Crawford ("Lady Wisdom and Dame Folly at Qumran," *DSD* 5 [1998] 355-66) points to Lady Wisdom in 4Q185, but exaggerates her prominence.

32. Goff, *Discerning Wisdom*, 268-70; Lange, "Scribes and Sages."

a parable for the wise who follow the path of wisdom, while ignoring the tree leads to its failure to bear fruit, that is, to act wisely. The "Hymn to the Creator" (in 11QPs[a])[33] incorporates the language and thought of wisdom's creation theology and is quite similar to other sapiential poems on creation in the canonical and deuterocanonical texts.[34] The rule of God over creation and its cosmic order reflects divine beneficence that is bestowed upon the human creatures and his acts of creation through his wisdom (cf. Prov. 3:19; Ps. 19A; Sir. 24). The angels are those who witness and then sing praise to creation, reflecting Job 38:7. Whether this is a wisdom hymn or a hymn to divine creation is open to debate. However, its theology certainly fits that of the sages in biblical and apocryphal wisdom writings.[35]

This community's wisdom texts, listed above, seek the proleptic realization of the future through wise actions. The sectarians believe that by their ritual purity and ethical behavior they are able to live eschatological reality into existence and to participate in the transformation of the new creation. Thus for the sages of Qumran and those who "understand," wisdom includes not only knowledge of the world through study and reflection on human experience, but also esoteric understanding of the cosmos, history, and the divine world (e.g., 11QPs[a]; see Ps. 154 in col. 18, v. 3) that derives from divine revelation to the chosen who exist in the sectarian community. Salvation comes from both the possession of this knowledge and its embodiment in human life.[36]

Wisdom and Revelation

For Harrington, the two most important contributions to wisdom made by the Qumran texts are "the insistence on wisdom as a gift from God and on the need for understanding the 'mystery that is to be/come'" or "a mystery that is coming into being," that is, *rāz nihyeh* (see 4Q415-418, 423; 1Q26).[37] Esoteric wisdom in

---

33. See Goff, *Discerning Wisdom*, 257-60 ("The Hymn to the Creator" [11QPs[a] 26,9-15]). Cf. Prov. 8–9; Job 28; Sir. 24.

34. See Perdue, *Wisdom and Cult*, and the assessment of wisdom psalms.

35. Goff, "Mystery of Creation," 163-86.

36. Sarah Jean Tanzer, "The Sages at Qumran: Wisdom in the Hodayot" (Ph.D. diss., Harvard University, 1987).

37. Harrington, *Wisdom Texts from Qumran*, 40-41; see idem, "The *Raz Nihyeh* in a Qumran Wisdom Text (1Q26, 4Q415-418, 423)," *RevQ* 17 (1996) 549-53. Also see Armin Lange, *Weisheit und Prädestination: Weisheitliche Uordnung und Prädestination in den Textfunden von Qumran* (STDJ 18; Leiden: Brill, 1995) 62, 91.

the Scrolls is knowledge of a "mystery" *(rāz)*.[38] This term of Persian derivation is not limited to events and things that are only in the future, but rather includes those that are present within the entirety of the temporal order, past, present, and future. *Rāz nihyeh* therefore represents "a body of teaching that involves creation, ethical activity, and eschatology" (e.g., 4Q417 fr. 2 i 8-9).[39] This mystery, which is the revealed understanding of the creation of the cosmos, is not only eschatological[40] but also historical, for it includes the divinely determined events of human history.[41] The "Mysteries" (1Q27; 4Q299-300) belong to the wisdom texts and tell of "God's foreknowledge and predestination of all events and plans in history."[42] Humans do not know this wisdom that God used in creation and that contains the knowledge for life and salvation. It must be given as a divine

38. Alexander Rofé indicates that this divine and esoteric knowledge is given to the chosen to allow them to understand the wondrous actions of God, including what happened and will happen ("Revealed Wisdom: From the Bible to Qumran," in *Sapiential Perspectives*, 1-2). As Goff notes, *rāz* most frequently communicates the idea of revelation of secretive knowledge of divine origin in early Jewish texts (e.g., Dan. 2:18-19, 27-30, 47; 4:6; 1 En. 103:2). See "Mystery of Creation in 4QInstruction," 165. However, *rāz nihyeh* is rare, found only in the Scrolls (the Book of Mysteries, 1Q27, 4Q299-302; and the Rule of the Community, 1QS). The first text understands the idiom in the context of divine providence in guiding history and culminating in a final judgment, while the second (1QS 11:3-4) uses it as the revelation of God's truth, power, and nature. Goff concludes, then, that the expression refers to the divine determination of reality, both creation and history, that is revealed to the chosen (cf. 4Q417 1 i 18-19). Indeed, Goff notes that the idiom could just as easily be translated as the "eternal mystery" or "the mystery that exists always" (p. 169).

39. Harrington, *Wisdom Texts from Qumran*, 83. Eschatology is an important theme in the Book of Mysteries (1Q27 1; 4Q300 3); see Lange, "Weisheitstexte aus Qumran," 15.

40. Torlief Elgvin, "Wisdom and Apocalypticism in the Early Second Century BCE — the Evidence of 4QInstruction," in *The Dead Sea Scrolls Fifty Years after Their Discovery: Proceedings of the Jerusalem Congress, July 20-25, 1997*, ed. Lawrence H. Schiffman, Emanuel Tov, and James C. VanderKam (Jerusalem: Israel Exploration Society/Shrine of the Book, Israel Museum, 2000) 239.

41. Goff, "Mystery of Creation," 179. He notes that this equating of *rāz* with divine creation is also found in the *Hodayot* (e.g., 1QH 5:19).

42. Lawrence H. Schiffman, "4QMysteries: A Preliminary Translation," in *Proceedings of the Eleventh World Congress of Jewish Studies, Division A* (Jerusalem: World Union of Jewish Studies, 1994) 199-206; idem, "4QMysteries[b], a Preliminary Edition," *RevQ* 16 (1993) 203-23; idem, "4QMysteries[a]: A Preliminary Edition and Translation," in *Solving Riddles and Untying Knots: Biblical, Epigraphic, and Semitic Studies in Honor of Jonas C. Greenfield*, ed. Ziony Zivit, Seymour Gitin, and Michael Sokoloff (Winona Lake, IN: Eisenbrauns, 1995) 207-26. Taking a broader overview, Lange argues that the crisis of knowledge in wisdom was solved through the appropriation of a pre-Qumran eschatology. This eschatology included a dualistic interpretation of history that was grounded in creation in order to explain the difficulties encountered by the delay of the eschaton and the concurrent persecution of the Hasmoneans. The Essene community expounded this view and combined it with the sapiential understanding of the order of creation in order to explain the delay of the end time that, nonetheless, was still imminent. Thus Lange agrees with von Rad's view that apocalyptic grew out of failed wisdom *(Weisheit und Prädestination)*.

gift, but it comes only to those chosen by God who search it out and meditate upon it. Thus wisdom is the result of both gift and quest. Even so, wisdom's foundation is located in creation from its inception and provides practical moral counsel that has the authority of this primeval origin. Thus God is the creator of an ordered cosmos whose wisdom is open to the sage and, once followed, leads to well-being. However, the nature of knowledge, revealed and esoteric, contrasts with the more traditional view of wisdom as rational insight present in Proverbs and Ben Sira. This revelation in the form of esoteric wisdom comes directly to the Teacher of Righteousness (1QpHab 7:3-4; 1QH 9:21, assuming he is the author of some of the *Hodayot;* 1QS 11:3) and not from an ancient seer of primordial times or from a vision or dream. Thus the Teacher of Righteousness was the direct mediator of revelation from God to the community.[43] This is expanded to the view that the sages of the community who interpreted the Torah and the Prophets were inspired by the divine gift of wisdom.

Moral Instruction and the Ethical Life

Like the literature of its sapiential forebears, the wisdom of the sectarians is pedagogical, for its purpose is to teach people the commandments and virtues that, once actualized in speech and behavior, lead to well-being. The sages of Qumran urge the community's members to search for and obtain the wisdom God has reserved for them as his elect in order that they may shape their character and participate in the future exaltation of the righteous (4Q185; 4Q525).

Biblical Interpretation

The Qumran sages cited Scripture for the following functions: to inform and teach the community, to encourage its members with a hopeful eschatology, and to warn of the consequences for disobedience and false teaching.[44] Berstein writes: "nearly all of the writings of the Qumran community, whether formally linked with scripture or not, are pervaded with scriptural interpretation."[45] The

43. Collins, *Apocalyptic Imagination,* 151.

44. In general see James C. VanderKam, "To What End? Functions of Scriptural Interpretation in Qumran Texts," in *Studies in the Hebrew Bible, Qumran, and the Septuagint, Presented to Eugene Ulrich,* ed. Peter W. Flint, Emanuel Tov, and James C. VanderKam (VTSup 101; Leiden: Brill, 2006).

45. Moshe J. Berstein, "Interpretation of Scriptures," *Encyclopedia of the Dead Sea Scrolls,* 1:376.

sages based their teachings on their inspired interpretation of Scripture that provided insight into the ethical and faithful life and taught the community to incorporate proper ways of living in order to be prepared for the time to come.[46] The Jewish opponents either misinterpreted the message of Scripture or simply disobeyed it (see CD 6:14-20; cf. 4Q3 2:20-25), and thus would join the wicked who face the coming judgment.

---

46. See Michael Fishbane, "Use, Authority and Interpretation of Mikra at Qumran," in *Mikra: Text, Translation, Reading, and Interpretation of the Hebrew Bible in Ancient Judaism and Early Christianity*, ed. M. J. Mulder (CRINT 2/1; Philadelphia: Fortress, 1988) 360-67.

10. Continuing Streams:
Rabbinic Wisdom

Historical Introduction

A final stream of Jewish wisdom that continues beyond the biblical and apocryphal traditions is rabbinic wisdom.[1] As noted in the preceding chapter, halakic features of legal interpretation in the Dead Sea Scrolls indicate that halakah is not limited to the Pharisaic-rabbinic tradition. Tracing the history of Rabbinic Judaism is extremely complex due to the lacunae in sources, lack of precise dating, and unidentified sociohistorical contexts in which the teachings of the rabbis emerged. We may, however, brush some broad strokes to give a general depiction of the period of Rabbinic Judaism during the first six centuries C.E. Rabbinic Judaism is founded on the myth of the two Torahs, the written and the oral Torah revealed to Moses at Mount Sinai ("the Judaism of the dual Torah").[2] While there were important preliminary teachers and their instruction that ushered in the development of Rabbinic Judaism, the sages of Israel shaped its comprehensive articulation in the first–sixth centuries C.E., during the peri-

1. In general see Y. Gafni, "The Historical Background," in *Jewish Writings*, 1-31; Lee I. Levine, *The Rabbinic Class of Roman Palestine in Late Antiquity* (New York: Jewish Theological Seminary, 1989); Strack and Stemberger, *Introduction to Talmud and Midrash;* Lester Grabbe, *Judaism from Cyrus to Hadrian* (Minneapolis: Fortress, 1992); Schwartz, *Imperialism and Jewish Society;* Jacob Neusner, *Introduction to Rabbinic Litearture* (ABRL; New York: Doubleday, 1994); Peter Schäfer, *The History of the Jews in the Greco-Roman World* (rev. ed. with corrections; London: Routledge, 2003); Stemberger, "Sages, Scribes, and Seers in Rabbinic Wisdom," in *Scribes, Sages, and Seers.*

2. Neusner, *Introduction to Rabbinic Literature*, xix-xx.

ods of the Tannaim (first three centuries c.e.)[3] and the Amoraim (fourth–sixth centuries c.e.). The Gaonim (sixth–eleventh centuries c.e.) continued in the footsteps of their predecessors in the formation and transmission of additional traditions.

To use the language of Shaye Cohen, the transition from the end of the Second Temple period to the beginning of Rabbinic Judaism (c. 200 b.c.e.) involves a "substantive change" in the history of the Jews.[4] The rabbis and their traditions in this time period of some four to five hundred years are both unified and divergent, due to chronological, social, and religious differences in which each generation existed. Even among the same generation, opinions often varied widely on what were considered to be key issues. Thus the effort was undertaken to achieve a unified Judaism under the rabbis that reflected the majority views of these sages. Major historical developments during these centuries included the Roman rule of Judea, beginning with Pompey's conquest in 63 b.c.e. and the end of an independent Jewish state. This led to a complete political reorganization, including the various Roman administrative systems for governing Judea (a vassal state under Hyrcanus II, 63-40 b.c.e.; Herodian rule, 37 b.c.e.–6 c.e.; the brief reign of Agrippa, 41-44 c.e.; and direct Roman rule, 6-66 c.e. through procurators), ill-fated revolutions to overthrow Roman control (the Great Revolt in 66-74 c.e., the revolt in 114-117 that included Egypt, North Africa, Cyprus, and perhaps elements in Judea, and the Bar Kokhba revolution in 132-135 c.e.), the expulsion of the Jews from Jerusalem by Hadrian in 136 c.e., and the relocation of the center of Judaism to Galilee beginning in 70 c.e. with the destruction of Jerusalem and the temple.

Social and religious transformations included the loss of the temple due to the Roman devastation of Jerusalem in 70 c.e., the ending not only of political (local royal rulers) but also traditional and successive priestly leadership, the development of new social and religious institutions including the Sanhedrin, the expansion of the synagogue, the establishment of the patriarchate, the formation of schools *(bêt sĕpārîm, yĕšîbôt,* and *bêt midrāš),* and the rise of the rabbis as the new religious leaders of Judaism. The early rabbis faced the need to respond to the loss of the temple by reshaping Jewish religion and piety, the writing down

---

3. The Tanna (*tannā',* "repeater" or "memorizer") is a teacher who is devoted to the study, interpretation, transmission, and instruction of Jewish tradition, ranging from the Tanakh to oral and written sources (halakah, haggadah, Mishnah, Tosefta, Midrashim, and Palestinian Talmud). Although early Judaism may be traced to Ezra (c. 400 b.c.e.), the period of the Tannaim (*tannā'îm,* i.e., "repeated teachings or tradition") is viewed as the beginning of the Common Era (Hillel and Shammai, if not earlier) to the end of the patriarchate of Yehudah ha-Nasi in the third century c.e.

4. Shaye J. D. Cohen, *From the Maccabees to the Mishnah* (2nd ed.; Louisville: Westminster John Knox, 2006) 205-23.

of their sayings and other types of literature (the Mishnah, Tosefta, and the Midrashim), the effort to shape a unified Judaism by stating the majority views while still listing the views of the minority, and the development of the view that the three sources of equal authority for Judaism are the Torah, the Mishnah (thus the dual Torah), and the sayings and deeds of the rabbis.

Some of the earliest rabbis and their circles of disciples are known to have originated around the beginning of the Common Era: Hillel (first century B.C.E., considered the first patriarch)[5] and Shammai (50 B.C.E.–30 C.E.). With the Roman conquest of Jerusalem in 70 C.E. and the destruction of the temple as the center of Jewish religion and life, any degree of Jewish independence, even as a Roman colony, ended. The wisdom tradition continued beyond the fall of Jerusalem among important rabbis in the Pharisaic sect that survived the elimination of the other Jewish parties that had developed in the period of early Judaism in the Hellenistic and early Roman periods. While the Zealots continued their resistance to Roman rule until the crushing of the Bar Kokhba revolt (132-135 C.E.), the destruction of the temple during the sacking of Jerusalem led to the end of the Sadducean priestly sect, while the apocalyptic dreams of the Essenes began to lose their credibility. The two last substantial Jewish apocalyptic books, 2 Baruch and 4 Ezra, were written after the destruction and contained lamentations questioning why this tragedy happened and how it was possible for the Jewish people to survive without a temple.

While the sources are fragmented and provide little certainty about the major contours of Early Judaism, it does appear that there were sects, among them the practitioners of Enochic Judaism and the Pharisees, who contested the Sadducean teaching and control of the temple. The Pharisees, from whom many of the later rabbis may be traced, appeared during the Hasmonean period and sought influence in the courts of John Hyrcanus through the time of Herod the Great. The Pharisees had important sages who were the predecessors of the Tannaitic rabbis in the second and third centuries C.E.[6] Within 150 years of the fall of Jerusalem, the first rabbinic texts began to appear. Jerusalem and

---

5. The patriarch was the head of the Sanhedrin and represented the Jewish community in Israel to the Roman authorities. See L. I. Levine, "The Jewish Patriarch (Nasi) in Third-Century Palestine," *ANRW* 2.19/2:649-88.

6. Our early information concerning the Pharisees comes from Qumran, whose texts appear to call them the "Expounders of Smooth Things" and regards them as a rival group; the NT (Q, Synoptics, Paul), which regards them largely as teachers who held to an ancestral tradition that kept them from responding favorably to Jesus; and a few references in early rabbinic sources of the Mishnah, Tosefta, and Midrashim. However, while they were concerned with purity, they placed authority in the traditions of significant ancient teachers that were transmitted through their oral and written teachings to their disciples; see Jaffee, *Torah in the Mouth*, 39-61.

Judea no longer were the locations for the teachers and scribes, some of whom had been associated with the temple and served as literary scholars under the priesthood. This change took place after 70 C.E. Due to the Roman hostility to the Jews in Jerusalem, expanded especially in 136 C.E. by Hadrian, who forbade Jews to live in Jerusalem, renamed it Aelia Capitolina, and also renamed Judea as Palestina in order to limit the identification of the country with the Jews, the early rabbis located their scribal and instructional activities as well as their primary population of followers in Galilee. After the death of Hadrian in 138 C.E., the Jews remaining in Palestine reconciled with the Roman authorities. The center of Judaism moved from Yavneh, to Usha, to Beth-shearim, to Sepphoris, and finally to Tiberias. Thus it was no longer Judea that served as the geographical location of religious leadership, but rather Galilee and eventually other geographically dispersed states and regions in the Diaspora. As for Jews in Babylonia, the Parthians followed by the Sassanid Persians ruled the larger empire and by the mid-third century C.E. the Jews were allowed religious autonomy in exchange for subservience to the state. The rabbis of Babylonia established an intellectual tradition that produced eventually the Babylonian Talmud.

The rabbis, including scholars like Yohanan ben Zakkai (first century C.E.), and the scribes provided the guidance and direction of Jews who faced the challenges of existing without a priesthood, temple, and political leadership. A student of Hillel and Shammai, Yohanan was the major figure who reconstructed local Jewish religious and ethical authority following the desolation of Jerusalem and the temple. He and later sages provided the leadership for Judaism in its transition from the fragmented existence of numerous sects and the Sadducean priesthood in control of the temple to a religion of various communities scattered throughout Israel and the Diaspora. Judaism in the Second Temple was extremely diverse, and it was to remain so throughout its history, meaning it would be incorrect to speak of a normative Judaism at any period. Rather, there are numerous Judaisms, as noted in the biblical texts preceding and following Ezra, all of which have their basis in the inspired interpretation of the Torah and wisdom traditions (Ps. 119:12, 18, 27, 33-35; Sir. 39:1-6) and continue in the formation of the many different understandings of Scripture and ways of righteous living by sages and teachers.[7] The rabbis did their best to routinize behavior and belief by means of their teachings, and to negate sectarian Judaism, but of course they never succeeded. To make this effort to standardize acceptable Jewish belief and practice, they set forth majority views of important

---

7. James L. Kugel and Rowan A. Greer, *Early Biblical Interpretation* (LEC 3; Philadelphia: Westminster, 1986).

matters but also continued to note minority ones. They undertook this task in Yavneh and continued it in other communities and later periods through the codification of their teachings in the Mishnah and later writings.

According to tractate *'Abot,* the earliest generations of the rabbis were the "Five Pairs" *(zûgôt),* starting with Simon the Just (c. 200 B.C.E.; cf. *'Abot* 1.1-2) and ending with Hillel and Shammai around the beginning of the Common Era. This period lasted for approximately two centuries. The next period included the early Tannaim in first-century Pharisaism and the academy at Yavneh. Among these were the schools of Hillel and Shammai. This group of teachers was followed by other sages (90-130 C.E.) who included such important rabbis as Gamaliel II, Ishmael, and Akiba. This group of rabbis lasted from 130 C.E. to the death of Yehudah ha-Nasi (Judah the Patriarch or Prince) in approximately 220 and the continuation of his school late into the third century.

In the third century the Mishnah was redacted in the circle of Yehudah ha-Nasi (c. 135-220).[8] This unified document of oral law, which was written down as it developed, brought together many diverse traditions and rabbinic opinions and was completed perhaps by his successor, his son Gamaliel III. Largely due to Yehudah's efforts, the Mishnah became the legal tradition for Judaism that replaced the academy *(yěšîbâ),* which had substituted for the temple as the seat of Jewish learning and worship after 70 C.E., situated first in Yavneh and then in other locations in Galilee.[9] The Mishnah was destined to become the primary resource for uniting many of the diverse and scattered Jewish communities.

Rhetoric (Literary Structure and Form) and Collections

Rabbinic literature consists of the written Tanakh and the oral tradition, which began with the Mishnah (third century C.E.) and continued with the Tosefta (300 C.E.), the Midrashim (third century C.E. and following), the Palestinian Talmud (400 C.E.), and the Babylonian Talmud (600 C.E.). It should be noted that the authors and editors of the literature of these sages are anonymous. While esteemed rabbis are ostensibly quoted, not a single rabbinic text is attributed to the authorship of one composer. In the self-presentation of the teachings in the Mishnah, however, all of the documents are believed to speak with one voice the

8. He was the head of the Sanhedrin in Beth-shearim and then in Sepphoris (see Daniel Sperber, "Yehudah Ha-Nasi," *The Oxford Dictionary of the Jewish Religion,* ed. R. J. Zwi Werblowsky and Geoffrey Wigoder [Oxford: Oxford University Press, 1997] 739-40).

9. Jacob Neusner, "The Formation of Rabbinic Judaism: Yavneh (Jamnia) from A.D. 70 to 100," *ANRW* 2.19/2:3-42; Shaye J. D. Cohen, "The Significance of Yabneh: Pharisees, Rabbis, and the End of Jewish Sectarianism," *HUCA* 55 (1984) 27-53.

words that are understood as coming from God revealed at Sinai. This revelation, and not an author, is the basis for the authority of the oral Torah.

While the genres of the early rabbinic tradition are generally quite different, there are present in the text wisdom forms that were also found in previous wisdom texts. Especially common are sayings of various kinds, often attributed to particular rabbis, which may be found also in the biblical wisdom tradition.[10] These include specific forms of the *māšāl* (e.g., sayings, numerical sayings, rhetorical questions and riddles, parables, and fables). In addition, another ancient wisdom form, the list, occurs often. The following is one example of a saying:

> Whoever does a single commandment — they do well for him and lengthen his days. And he inherits the Land. And whoever does not do a single commandment — they do not well for him and do not lengthen his days. And he does not inherit the Land.
>
> Whoever has learning in Scripture, Mishnah, and right conduct will not quickly sin. . . . And whoever does not have learning in Scripture, Mishnah, and right conduct has no share in society (*m. Qidd.* 1.10).

In later rabbinic texts, especially the two Talmuds, there is information concerning not only medicine but also mantic wisdom (magic and interpretation of dreams). However, these come after the Tannaitic period, although they build on earlier biblical and apocryphal wisdom found especially in texts that speak of dreams and ascents into the heavenly world.

Halakah and Haggadah

Two primary kinds of rabbinic tradition formulated by the sages are halakah (*hălākâ*) and haggadah (*'aggādâ*). Halakah, present in the Mishnah, Tosefta, and Talmud, alludes to legal materials that interpret and expand upon laws found in the Torah. Its creators are the sages who set forth their opinions to their disciples originally in oral form and eventually written down and shaped into collections that edited together make up the Mishnah.[11] Some of the halakot (plural of halakah) are attributed to Moses, but most are not. The point is that Moses is called upon to legitimate the authority of the mentioned sages who created and taught the halakot that reflected their own times and circumstances (*m. 'Abot* 1.1–2.8). Moses is not considered the originator of the oral law

10. Stemberger, "Sages, Scribes, and Seers."
11. See the discussion by Jaffee, *Torah in the Mouth,* 79-82.

or the Mishnah, but rather serves as the first in a list of sages, the greatest of whom were active in the period following the destruction of the temple in 70 C.E. and participated in the school of Yehudah ha-Nasi. This tractate does not attribute the oral law to Moses, but speaks only of "torah," not "the Torah" (i.e., the first section of Scripture). Most of the ancestral tradition behind the halakot reflects the Hasmonean-Herodian period.[12] Their origins came from important sages during this time who passed down their teachings within the groups of their students. The purpose of halakah is to provide direction for social and individual living according to the precepts of God revealed to Moses at Sinai in the dual Torah. This process of interpreting the law is distinctive from the work of Ezra and his scribes and continued on through the rabbis of the Tannaitic period and well beyond.[13] The rabbis developed rules for the formulation of halakic interpretation.

Haggadah refers to nonlegal materials found in the Midrashim and Talmud and consists of moral instruction, prayers, praise, dream interpretation including that applied to dreams of messianic faith, folklore, sayings, legends, historical data, and theological interpretation.[14] Haggadah likely began in the late Second Temple period, although its edited collections did not begin to appear until the early Amoraic period. While haggadah gives insight into law and halakah, it does not possess their obligatory requirements. In addition, it is as concerned with the elucidation of the Prophets and Writings as of the Torah. Further, haggadah continues to be created in an ongoing fashion and is not linked necessarily to recognized teachings in the past.

Mishnah (Mišnâ)

The term *mishnah* ("repetition") first of all refers to a brief expression of a legal or ethical teaching that usually does not cite or refer to biblical support or other types of quotation.[15] It is important to note that the Mishnah cites rabbis as authorities, but rarely Moses, the Bible, or the written Torah. Consequently, it would be incorrect to conclude that the Mishnah presents itself as an oral Torah that together with the written Law forms one revelation given to Moses at Sinai.

12. Ibid., 82.

13. Daniel Sinclair, "Halakhah," *Oxford Dictionary of Jewish Religion*, 293-94.

14. Chaim Milikowsky, "Aggadah," *Oxford Dictionary of Jewish Religion*, 23-24.

15. In general see Abraham Goldberg, "The Mishnah — A Study Book of Halakha," in *The Literature of the Sages*, ed. Shmuel Safrai (CRINT II/3/1; Philadelphia: Fortress, 1987) 211-62; Jacob Neusner, *The Mishnah: An Introduction* (London: Aronson, 1989); idem, *Introduction to Rabbinic Literature*, 99-128.

Rather, this view of the dual Torah is a rabbinic formative myth that finds expression in Gaonic and later Judaism in order to give the developing oral tradition its authority. While the term "Mishnah" includes the religious law fashioned until 200 C.E., the Mishnah as a literary text refers to the collection of halakot redacted by Yehudah ha-Nasi and his successors.[16] Even so, its various halakot and tractates began to be orally formulated and written down no later than the first century C.E., and quite possibly even earlier. With the editing of the classical expression of the Mishnah by the circle of Yehudah ha-Nasi, the disciples heard it read or delivered by the master by memory, which is then not simply received and handed down but reflected upon and engaged in order to develop its meaning in the current situation. Unfortunately, however, we do not find either the audience addressed or the purpose of the collection clearly identified.

Furthermore, the Mishnah is a philosophical anthology that sets forth explanations and instructions that are theoretical and practical. The mode of thought and literary forms are those of the scribal profession, although it does not identify its own author(s).[17] Formally, the Mishnah consists of lists, one of the literary forms of wisdom literature that may be traced back to Egypt. As a collection of lists, the Mishnah sets forth highly organized information that is the work of scribes who write and redact the orders and tractates of the Mishnah. Examples in the Mishnah include lists of thirty-nine types of work forbidden on the Sabbath, ten degrees of holiness, and ten degrees of uncleanness. In addition the scribes who shaped the Mishnah set forth interpretations of key terms, bringing precision to what is listed. For example, implied by the rabbis in their understanding of work prohibited on the Sabbath is labor that is creative, meaningful, and productive of something enduring.[18]

There are also social and political features of the Mishnah, for example, the rights and duties of the king, including in particular the requirement that he must be submissive to the Torah. This is also true of the high priest, the other leader of the Jewish people. However, most important is the setting forth of the judicial system, which requires that guilt must be determined on the basis of evidence and decreed by the majority of judges hearing a case.[19] The Mishnah, which presents itself as the written code for the patriarch's (prince's) adminis-

---

16. While the Mishnah is largely legal in nature, its philosophical character should not be overlooked. See Jacob Neusner, *Judaism: The Evidence of the Mishnah* (2nd ed.; BJS 129; Atlanta: Scholars Press, 1988); idem, *Judaism as Philosophy: The Method and Message of the Mishnah* (Columbia: University of South Carolina Press, 1991); idem, *Jerusalem and Athens: The Congruity of Talmudic and Classical Philosophy* (JSJSup 52; Leiden: Brill, 1997).

17. Neusner, *Judaism: Evidence of the Mishnah*, 241.

18. Stemberger, "Sages, Scribes, and Seers."

19. Ibid.

tration of the land of Israel, sought to set forth a just and harmonious society. This ideal served as the basis for social, political, cosmic, and ethical spheres of reality, which led to the accord and well-being of social and individual life. While it was adopted as the law of Jewish communities in the Roman Empire, the land of Israel, Babylonia, and Iran, the Mishnah is essentially ahistorical, ignoring the political structure of the lands in which it governed Jewish life. Indeed, it fails to identify any political institution as authoritative, including the patriarchate.

The Mishnah faced the problem of forging its authoritative status in early Judaism. In providing no stated rationale for obedience to its teachings and lacking any theological claim, including that of Scripture or Moses and Sinai, its acceptance proved problematic. It also lacked the usual claims of pseudonymity, divine revelation, relationship to Tanakh, a sacred style that imitated the Bible, and a myth of beginnings or underpinning of a final revelation that points to the final age. Even so it eventually entered into the law courts and communities of the Jewish people. This appropriation was achieved in three different ways. First, the Mishnah pointed to the sages as those who stood within a chain of tradition that reached back to Moses and Sinai. Second, the Mishnah was regarded as torah, that is, law as a generic classification, which was dependent upon the Torah revealed at Sinai. This became especially developed in the Tosefta. Finally, the Sifra, Aramaic midrashim on Leviticus, Numbers, and Deuteronomy, redefined torah as the Torah, which required amplification in order to achieve its understanding. Thus the oral Torah was transformed into the Torah given to Moses at Sinai. These solutions to the crisis of a philosophical law, which lacked any stated or identifiable authority, underscored the importance given to the sages who carried Judaism into a future devoid of king, high priest, and temple. The Mishnah in due course received a position of privilege for most Jews along with that of Scripture. It alone came to be regarded as the oral part of Torah.[20]

The Mishnah consists of six main divisions or orders (*sědārîm* or *'ărûkîm*), each of which has seven to twelve tractates (*massekôt;* altogether sixty-two) that in turn are subdivided into chapters *(pěrāqîm)*. The arrangement is essentially thematic, with each division/order containing a large topic and its subtopics. The six divisions/orders are rhetorically fashioned to support memorization. They are:

1. *Zera'yim* ("Seeds"): agricultural laws
2. *Mo'ed* ("Festival Days"): laws of holy periods (festivals, Sabbath, temple

---

20. Neusner, *Introduction to Rabbinic Literature*, 126-28.

tax, Day of Atonement, observations on holy days, fasting, "scroll" [Esther and Purim]), "lesser holy days," and laws concerning festival celebrations

3. *Nashim* ("Women"): levirate marriage, marriage contracts, vows, Nazirite vow, the adulteress, divorce, and betrothal

4. *Neziqin* ("Damages"): theft, bodily harm, claims, division of property and its use, inheritance, wedding presents, issuance of documents, surety, law court, legal procedures, judges and witnesses, litigation (civil and criminal), testimony, the death penalty punishments, oaths, testimonies of teachers about earlier ones, idolatry, Sayings of the Fathers *('Abot)*, chain of tradition, teachings of these teachers, and instruction or decision about errors in judgment about religious law, the sin offering, and distinctions between priests

5. *Qodashim* ("Holy Things"): sacrifices, purification, the priestly portion, blood, meal offerings, profane things not suitable for sacrifice, clean and unclean animals, meat not boiled in milk, priestly portion, firstfruits of sheepshearing, law of the bird's nest, the firstborn, priestly rights to redemption money, tithing, assessments paid for a vow, inheritance, exchange of sacrificial animals, redemption of property, extirpations, embezzlement, use of consecrated things, daily burnt offering, priestly watch in the temple during the night, clearing the altar, priestly tasks, offering of the sacrificial lamb, morning prayer, smoke offering, high priest's sacrificial service, priestly blessing, Levitical songs, temple "measures" and furnishings, temple gates, the fireplace, the holocaust altar, the temple mount and its walls and courts, the temple, outer court and chambers, the Chamber of Hewn Stone, and the offering of pigeons by the poor

6. *Tohorot* ("Purities"): laws of purity and impurity concerning utensils, a corpse, leprosy and other skin diseases, the red heifer, defilements lasting until sunset, prohibitions of sacrifices of unclean animals, degrees of defilement, defilements involving liquids, including oil and wine during trading, immersion pools for purification, uncleanness due to menstrual flow, classes of women, puberty, unclean emissions, uncleanness that defiles offerings and consecrated things, purification of the hands, and the transmission of uncleanness by stalks, peels, and kernel.[21]

The arrangements of the tractates are inconsistent and thus reveal the changing interests of the rabbis. While in general the six orders are fixed, the various topics that the tractates address are not always consistent with one an-

---

21. For this list of orders and their content, see Strack and Stemberger, *Introduction to Talmud and Midrash*, 109-18.

other, indicating that their history changes repeatedly. Thus there is not a single proposition that unites the rhetorical structure and themes, but a variety that guide the composition and transmission of the orders and the tractates' themes over the years.[22] This lack of uniformity suggests the possibility of recovering the redactional stages of the Mishnah on the basis of form, language, dependence, and contradiction. It is incorrect to argue that the Mishnah was originally conceived either as a law code, a teaching manual, or even a collection of halakot. Rather it sets forth legal categories and principles, which are discussed, defined, and delimited. From these statements about the meaning of various laws, legal decisions concerning behavior could be made. Thus the Mishnah is more of an anthology or digest than a complete law code.[23]

The text was produced in a school (perhaps the first patriarchate of Yehudah ha-Nasi) that sorted through and brought together a variety of orders and tractates in as consistent a form as deemed possible. This effort had in view the establishment of a uniform Judaism, while respecting the views of many diverse rabbis over the generations, under the direction of this patriarchate. While changes were made by the school through even the grandsons of this patriarch for the next fifty years in order to correct mistakes, it was not an easy matter to effect revisions and amendments. Even when the Mishnah was "fixed," it did not preclude later changes during the Amoraic period.

Tosefta (Tôseptā')

The Tosefta bears the meaning of "addition" or "supplement" and refers either to the additional materials of halakah that were to be added to the current Mishnah or that were to be incorporated into a book of supplements.[24] In either case, it was concluded perhaps around 300 C.E. The Tosefta as a collection cannot be understood without reference to the Mishnah and possesses in essence the same structure as the Mishnah: the identical six orders (sĕdārîm) and the equivalent tractates, which vary only slightly from those of the Mishnah. Only 'Abot, Tamid, Middot, and Qinnim in the Mishnah have no equivalent in the Tosefta, while Kelim in the Tosefta is divided into three parts. The Tosefta is approximately four times the size of the Mishnah. Its writings consist of three

22. "Complete coherence and uniformity are by definition not to be expected in the system of the rabbis" (Strack and Stemberger, Introduction to Talmud and Midrash, 124).

23. Cohen, From Maccabees to Mishnah, 207.

24. In general see Jacob Neusner, The Tosefta: An Introduction (Atlanta: Scholars Press, 1992); idem, Introduction to Rabbinic Literature, 129-52; Strack and Stemberger, Introduction to Talmud and Midrash, 150-63.

types of materials: verbatim citations and glosses of the Mishnah, freestanding statements that enhance the Mishnah's meaning, and autonomous statements understandable without any reference to the Mishnah.[25] The Tosefta's origins and attribution are debated, but one prominent view is that the collection represents largely the work of rabbis Hiyya and Hoshayah and is early Amoraic. The exact relationship between the Mishnah and the Tosefta is impossible to determine, although it is likely that the Tosefta appeared after the Mishnah. The former is similar but not completely identical to the Mishnah; the numerous differences may be explained only by recognizing the different origins of the tractates of each. In addition, unlike the Mishnah, the Tosefta does understand itself as based on the Tanakh as well as on the Mishnah.

Midrashim

The Midrashim are commentaries on the Bible that began to appear in the early part of the third century c.e. They include the sayings of rabbis whose conflicting interpretations and understandings often need not only clarification but also additional commentary. These commentaries represented themselves as tracing the rabbinic teachings back to the time of Moses. Beginning with the Tosefta and even more clearly in the Midrashim, the halakic tradition is seen to have its roots in the authority of Scripture and to derive from the Mosaic revelation at Sinai. Indeed, it was ultimately the rabbis of the Amoraic period who clearly formulated the myth of the dual Torah, written and oral, both of which are traced back to Moses.

The Midrashim contain halakic interpretation that sets forth the basis for the righteous way of life and haggadic examples and explanations that illustrate and clarify the halakhic materials. The commentaries developed principles of biblical interpretation called *middôt.* The earliest Midrashim are written on four books of the Torah: Exodus, Leviticus, Numbers, and Deuteronomy. Their composers "wrote with Scripture" in identifying the proposition implicitly and in citing evidence of its truth. The style varies, from the exposition of the biblical book in a verse-by-verse approach coupled with the setting forth and verification of particular propositions, to a propositional setting forth of a variety of different verses from biblical books, along with explanation together with the frequent repetition of the same point. The sages who wrote these commentaries knew the biblical and mishnaic materials quite well and sought to discover religious and moral understandings to guide people in their daily life.

25. Neusner, *Introduction to Rabbinic Literature,* 130.

The Tannaitic Midrashim

The Tannaitic sages and their successors produced five commentaries on the Torah, in particular the legal sections (thus halakhic midrashim), a fact demonstrated by both their language (Mishnaic Hebrew) and the teachers mentioned in them.[26] While their origins go back to the Tannaitic period, their final editing occurred later. Any of the attributions of these texts to particular rabbis is useful as a principle of categorization, but they lack any confirmable historical basis. These five midrashim are a compilation of haggadic and halakhic materials that come from a variety of sources.

The two Tannaitic commentaries on the book of Exodus known as Mekilta (mĕkîltā', Aramaic for "norm," "rule") are the Mekilta of Rabbi Ishmael and the Mekilta of Rabbi Simeon ben Yohai.[27] The first commentary (Ishmael) interprets sections from Exod. 12–35, focusing primarily though not exclusively on the legal sections. It interprets these biblical texts in three ways: exegeses of some passages at irregular intervals, propositional, occasionally disputative, exegetical essays, and topical essays usually addressing important matters of the written and oral Torah. This Mekilta is accredited to Rabbi Ishmael, a contemporary of Rabbi Akiba (thus around the end of the second century C.E.), although this attribution cannot be verified. It derives halakah from biblical verses. This Mekilta perhaps was edited in its final form in the mid-third century C.E., although this date is debated. While this commentary provides authoritative materials for proving propositions, it does not represent sages who wrote with Scripture, which is inert, meaning that statements are made about biblical texts, not through them. Thus it is more of a biblical encyclopedia, compiling data for people to read in understanding the major subjects of the biblical text.[28]

The second Mekilta (Simeon ben Yohai) appears to have derived from the Mekilta of Rabbi Ishmael. It too is attributed to the school of Rabbi Akiba. This exegetical commentary, fragmentary in its current form, is largely a halakhic midrash on scattered texts from Exod. 3–35, although there are also haggadic features. The fragmentary character of the text does not allow one to know if the original Mekilta was larger. The original structure of this text also cannot be determined. While some interpreters date it to the fourth or fifth

26. Ibid., 247-351.

27. W. David Nelson, *Mekhilta de-Rabbi Shimon Bar Yohai* (Edward E. Elson Classic; New York: JPS, 2006).

28. Neusner, *Introduction to Rabbinic Literature*, 250-51. For a full discussion of this Mekilta, see Neusner's *Mekhilta Attributed to R. Ishmael: An Introduction to Judaism's First Scriptural Encyclopedia* (Atlanta: Scholars Press, 1988).

century on the basis of similarities to the Mekilta of Rabbi Ishmael, this remains at issue.[29]

The multiauthored Sifra on Leviticus was attributed to the tradition of Rabbi Akiba, although it likely contains additions from the school of Rabbi Ishmael.[30] Its content is largely a composite of midrashic exegeses on Leviticus. Its nucleus perhaps originated in the third century as an explanation and commentary on the Mishnah, and continued to receive its shaping for some time thereafter. It combined the written Torah and the Mishnah (oral Torah) into one document. The authors' criticism of the Mishnah demonstrates that it could not exist as a separate source, but rather has to be interpreted with the written Torah. Both the oral and the written Torah were read into each other in order to derive the proper meaning.

The Sifre to Numbers is a commentary that is largely halakhic, although some narratives from the biblical book are included, leading to some haggadah as well. It is not a uniform text, since it includes a lengthy haggadic section in 78-106. Its authorship is traditionally attributed to the school of Ishmael and is dated to the mid-third century C.E.[31] It operates on the basis of two unstated principles: reason without the support of the Tanakh leads to uncertain affirmations; and reason within the context of Scripture produces truth. However, while the Torah has priority in divine revelation, there is still a sanctioned role for human reason.[32]

The Sifre to Deuteronomy is an exegetical midrash on texts from Deuteronomy that includes both halakah and haggadah. It too is not a uniform text, for the legal commentary is found in 55-305 and the haggadic sections are 1-54 and 304-57. The halakhic material is likely to be attributed to the school of Akiba, while texts said to come from Rabbi Ishmael and his school, which are largely haggadic, are later additions. The halakhic sections derive from the late third century, while the central material may have been redacted around the mid-third century and continued to be edited for some time.[33] In following the view of Deuteronomy, the sages who composed this Sifre used the book to render an account of the history of Israel with the hermeneutical emphasis being to allow the Jews to recover that destiny. Written Torah once again had priority in understanding divine revelation, but logic also had its place in the analysis of the biblical text.

29. Strack and Stemberger, *Introduction to Talmud and Midrash*, 257-59.

30. Ibid., 259-65; Neusner, *Introduction to Rabbinic Literature*, 271-304.

31. Neusner, *Introduction to Rabbinic Literature*, 305-27; Strack and Stemberger, *Introduction to Talmud and Midrash*, 266-68.

32. Neusner, *Introduction to Rabbinic Literature*, 306-7.

33. Ibid., 328-51; Strack and Stemberger, *Introduction to Talmud and Midrash*, 270-75.

Teachings of the Sages

The teachings of the sages are also extant in the freestanding tractate 'Abot (originally a mishnaic tractate), which collects sayings of the sages, and the 'Abot de Rabbi Nathan, which includes stories about them. Many scholars have pointed to tractate 'Abot as the chief exemplar of rabbinic wisdom that suggests a connection with the sages of the Tanakh; its final editing is usually dated to about 250 C.E.[34] Consisting of five chapters that create a chain of tradition ("receive" and "hand on" from teacher to disciple) from Moses to the great assembly to the rabbis, many of whom are mentioned in the Mishnah, it contains a selection of the well-known sayings of these teachers (chs. 1–2), other wisdom sayings in the name of these and additional teachers (chs. 3–4), and a variety of anonymous numerical sayings (ch. 5). This tractate provides the authentication of the authority of the sages who are the quintessence of the dual Torah and thus an equal authority to both the revelation at Sinai and the oral Torah. The tractate also legitimizes the Mishnah as equal in authority to the written Torah and to the sages, for it too is part of the Torah revealed at Sinai. A sixth chapter, Qinyan Torah ("the acquisition of the Torah"), was added when this text was used in the synagogue.[35] The sayings are attributed to specific rabbis and largely deal with their wise and righteous behavior and insight. The central theme is the quest for wisdom, which is identified with Torah. Thus

> If there is no Torah, there is no worldly occupation, if there is no worldly occupation, there is no Torah. If there is no wisdom, there is no reverence; if there is no reverence, there is no wisdom. If there is no knowledge, there is no understanding, if there is no understanding, there is no knowledge. If there is no flower, there is no Torah, if there is no Torah, there is no flower. (3:17)

In this saying, Torah, wisdom, reverence, knowledge, and creation shape and organize the structure of creation, society, and life.

The 'Abot de Rabbi Nathan is an expansion of tractate 'Abot and may have

---

34. Judah Goldin, *The Living Talmud: The Wisdom of the Fathers and Its Classical Commentaries* (New York: New American Library, 1957); Max Küchler, *Frühjüdische Weisheitstradtionen. Zum Fortgang weisheitlichen Denkens im Bereich des frühjüdischen Jahweglaubens* (Göttingen: Vandenhoeck & Ruprecht, 1979) 176-98; Isaac Gottlieb, "Pirqe Abot and Biblical Wisdom," *VT* 40 (1990) 152-64; Amran Tropper, *Wisdom, Politics, and Historiography — Tractate Avot in the Context of the Graeco-Roman Near East* (Oxford Oriental Monographs; Oxford: Oxford University Press, 2004). Also see the discussions by M. Bialik Lerner, "The Tractate Avot," in *Literature of the Sages*, 263-82; Neusner, *Torah from Our Sages: Pirke Avot: A New American Translation and Explanation* (Chappaqua, NY: Rossel/Behrman House, 1983); idem, *Introduction to Rabbinic Literature*, 571-90.

35. Stemberger, "Sages, Scribes, and Seers."

been finalized around 500 C.E.[36] The rabbis of the earlier tractate are provided narratives about the sayings they uttered. The sayings of the earlier tractate are augmented by the provision of a secondary expansion, or the citing of a biblical proof text, or the writing of a parable of illustration. At times a large composition or a lengthy story of a sage's saying and/or deed is added. Materials are occasionally added that have nothing to do with the original sayings. In all of these expansions, the intent was to provide greater clarity to the meaning of individual sayings in the earlier document by the addition of narratives.

Social Features: Sages and Social Settings

While the rabbis included many Pharisees following the destruction of Jerusalem and the temple in 70 C.E., there were others also who were among these spiritual leaders. Certainly, some of these leaders included former priests, scribes who served the temple or government, copyists, and writers of documents. Their status derived from their knowledge and the attraction of disciples who studied under them. Only with the rise of the patriarchate at the end of the second century did some rabbis work in his administration or in his school. By the third century, rabbis also began to serve as teachers in Jewish communities, courts, and synagogues.[37]

The Rabbis

While originally a title of respect, the term *rabbî* ("my master") became the name of an office, which one attained following the completion of a course of study.[38] The rabbis were often called the *ḥăkāmîm*, who sought wisdom to guide their lives and those of both their disciples and the larger Jewish communities.[39] Along with the Tanakh and the oral tradition, they became the human

---

36. M. Bialik Lerner, "The External Tractates," in *Literature of the Sages*, 369-79; A. J. Saldarini, *The Fathers According to Rabbi Nathan (Abot de Rabbi Nathan) Version B: A Translation and Commentary* (Leiden: Brill, 1975); Küchler, *Frühjüdische Weisheitstradtionen*, 176-98; Neusner, *Introduction to Rabbinic Literature*, 591-608.

37. In general see Catherine Hezser, *The Social Structure of the Rabbinic Movement in Roman Palestine* (TSAJ 66; Tübingen: Mohr Siebeck, 1997).

38. Neusner, *Introduction to Rabbinic Literature*, e.g., 6ff.; Strack and Stemberger, *Introduction to Talmud and Midrash*, 56-100.

39. In general see Stemberger, "Sages, Scribes, and Seers." He examines the rabbis as sages in early rabbinic literature. Also see Neusner, *Introduction to Rabbinic Literature*, 549-70.

embodiment of the dual Torah in their teachings and actions. In addition, their identity was formed by their incarnation of the paradigm of Moses.

The Torah also is actualized in the teachings and moral behavior of the sage even as the sage's teachings and ethics are realized in the Torah. The authority of the sages is situated not in their genealogies or scribal skills, but rather in their mastery of wisdom, which they learned from earlier masters who were ultimately traced back to Moses at Sinai.[40] The rabbinic literature consequently could be understood as wisdom literature.[41] While the sages' teachings and actions were the norms for righteous existence, prior to the Middle Ages they were unpaid, and thus they had to exist by means of income gained from a variety of different occupations.

The rabbis remain essentially hidden from historical view, lacking any detailed biographies or even compilations of collections of sayings or other forms of teachings. The authors and editors of the larger compositions wished to avoid focusing on a particular sectarian view that could develop, had certain rabbis received detailed biographies. Thus the rabbinic literature itself is anonymous, with attributions of teachings and sayings to certain sages and schools and brief exemplary stories told about them, but without detailed examinations of the authors or even complete compositions of the lives of the rabbis mentioned. Even tractate 'Abot and 'Abot de Rabbi Nathan deal with the sayings ('Abot) of the sages and stories (Nathan) about them, but do not limit themselves to a few specific individuals. It is the anonymous tradition itself, going back to Sinai, that serves as the focus of rabbinic literature, not its authors, editors, and great teachers. The deeds and sayings of the rabbis present in the literature provide examples and proof texts for the teachings of the statements in the larger composition. As embodiments of Torah, their teachings and deeds provided authority for particular teachings. Certainly by the Gaonic period, the rabbis, like the Torah and the Mishnah, are authoritative, standing on an equal plane. God's revelation comes not only through words but also through the lives of the rabbis, who epitomize the divine teachings.[42]

In addition to the setting of legal jurisprudence, including the Sanhedrin and academies (yĕšîbôt), other social settings for rabbinic teaching included the delivery of sermons in the synagogue and particularly instruction in the schools.[43]

---

40. Jaffee, *Torah in the Mouth*, 67.
41. Stemberger, "Sages, Scribes, and Seers."
42. Neusner, *Introduction to Rabbinic Literature*, 566-67.
43. Haim Z. Dimitrovsky, ed., *Exploring the Talmud*, vol. 1: *Education* (New York: Ktav, 1976).

The Synagogue

The early rabbis, prior to the fall of Jerusalem and as early as the turn from B.C.E. to C.E., began to have significant influence among the Jewish laity. After 70 C.E. the Pharisees were one of the Jewish parties, along with the Zealots, to survive the Roman destruction. The rabbis were active in two institutions: the synagogue *(bêt kěnesset)* and the house of study *(bêt midrāš)*. Synagogues existed in the Diaspora in Egypt and likely elsewhere, especially Babylonia, as early as the third century B.C.E.[44] They were located in Jerusalem prior to its destruction by the Romans.[45] The synagogue, which was described in numerous, divergent ways, served as the place of communal worship (which included prayers, biblical readings, and sermons) and assembly especially, while the house of study was the location for the study and interpretation of the Bible and the developing oral tradition. It is here that the sages began to function as an important and independent group separate and apart from the Sadducees and the temple they controlled. Once the temple was razed, the synagogue continued as the sole place of assembly and worship. Control, even after 70 C.E., was not held by any rabbinic group, but rather came under the authority of the community in which a synagogue existed.

The School

The second location for rabbinic activity was the school. This supplemented a rabbi's private teaching of his disciples. The house of study was either attached to the synagogue or located in an adjacent but separate building. The inscription of Theodotus, which dates prior to the destruction of Jerusalem in 70 C.E., indicates that this synagogue in Jerusalem was built for "the reading of the law and the teaching of the commandments, and the guest-chamber and the rooms and the water installations for lodging for those needing them from abroad."[46] Prayer offered by the pilgrims who visited this synagogue and resided in its hostel would likely have occurred in the temple.

---

44. In general see Safrai, "The Synagogue," in *Jewish People in First Century,* 2:908-44; Lee I. Levine, *The Ancient Synagogue: The First Thousand Years* (New Haven: Yale University Press, 2000).

45. See the synagogue inscription of Theodotus that indicates a house of assembly existed on Mount Ophel prior to 70 C.E. Ehud Netzer's discovery of a Hasmonean synagogue near the Hasmonean winter palace in Jericho is the oldest synagogue yet discovered in Eretz Israel ("A Synagogue from the Hasmonean Period Recently Exposed in the Western Plain of Jericho," *IEJ* 49 [1999] 203-21).

46. CIJ 2.1404.

Education

Familial education began with a father who instructed his children (almost always males, not females). This was followed by instruction in elementary schools *(bêt sēper)* that were established in towns and villages following the mid-second century C.E. Rabbis could not dwell in a place that did not have a teacher of children *(b. Sanh.* 17b).[47] Elementary schools were usually located in the synagogue or an attached room where students were taught to read Hebrew and the Tanakh. The students were eventually taught to read the Mishnah and the Talmud. The learning process involved reading the text aloud and memorizing it by means of constant repetition *(b. Ḥag.* 9b). While male students studied until the age of twelve or thirteen (Gen. Rab. 63.9), secondary education beyond this time involved learning from a teacher of the Mishnah in an academy *(bêt midrāš* or *bêt talmûd).* In this setting, the principles of halakah and haggadah were studied and learned. Of course, synagogue sermons and Sabbath schools were additional contexts for learning.

Other schools were not buildings, located in or adjacent to synagogues, but rather were circles of disciples who followed sages to learn from their instruction. Students, at least by the second century, in effect lived and traveled with their teachers and learned firsthand from their teachings and their applications of halakah to particular cases. These schools (buildings or circles or both) continued to be important in Eretz Israel. There were also important academies of rabbis in Babylonia. Through the Tannaitic period, these schools were private, not public, and were not regulated by any higher authority.

The Sanhedrin

The strikingly divergent views of the Sanhedrin in Jewish sources complicate efforts to delineate its nature and functions.[48] The following summary provides a brief overview of this institution that became a setting for important sages in the articulation of their understandings of halakah. The *sanhedrîn* appeared originally during the early stages of Roman rule of Judea and consisted of a body of leaders headed by the high priest to engage in issuing rulings for the Jewish people in the areas of political and judicial matters. Later it was the court that possessed the highest authority in the areas of religion, local political mat-

---

47. Strack and Stemberger, *Introduction to Talmud and Midrash,* 8-9.

48. In general see Christine Hayes, "Sanhedrin," *Oxford Dictionary of the Jewish Religion,* 606-8; Shemuel Safrai, "Jewish Self-government," in *Jewish People in First Century,* 2:377-92.

ters, and legislation binding on the Jewish community in Palestine during the Roman period. After the destruction of Jerusalem in 70 c.e., the body consisted of an assembly of sages. The number of sages who made up this body was seventy-one, presided over no longer by a high priest but now by two rabbinic scholars, the *nāśî'* ("prince" or patriarch) and the *'ab bêt dîn* ("the father of the house of judgment") and guided by halakah in their decisions. This latter form of the assembly was established first in Yavneh and then in other locations in Galilee. The communities in the Diaspora could accept the authority of this body if they so chose.

Major Religious Themes

Actions, based on the proper understanding and interpretation of ancestral traditions, not dogmas, were decisive for Rabbinic Judaism,[49] although theological themes undergirded righteous behavior. Obviously, the God of Israel, who was the sole deity and the creator and providential guide of the universe, was the fundamental expression of belief, but faithfulness was demonstrated by living out the commandments. The Torah, written and oral, was the center of rabbinic religious thought. The rabbis debated among themselves in the effort to interpret the meaning of the dual Torah in order to conduct life according to the will of God revealed in the commandments. Their teachings eventually were arranged into themes and then into tractates. The tractates were then collected in the Mishnah, while commentaries on the Bible were then written to set forth both halakhic and haggadic teachings.

The Dual Torah

The rabbis spoke of two forms of Torah, the written (biblical) and the oral (particularly the Mishnah). Both were eventually traced back to Sinai, meaning then that Second Temple Judaism was essentially unimportant in the thought of the Tannaitic sages. This understanding of the two Torahs originating at Sinai formed the founding myth of Rabbinic Judaism. Thus Rabbinic Judaism was understood to possess the same antiquity as that of the Mosaic revelation at Sinai. Even the rabbi became an authority equal to the two Torahs when it came to understanding and exemplifying a righteous life lived according to the divine will.

49. Josephus, *Ant.* 20.38, 43-48; 20.100.

The Torah and Wisdom

The rabbis, following the Second Temple sages beginning with Ezra and continuing with Ben Sira, equated wisdom with Torah. The rabbis and the *sōpĕrîm* were the early biblical scholars who sought to apply the Law and its commandments to the evolving circumstances of life. This adaptation of the Torah to recent developments in social existence was made possible by the oral and written tradition of halakah and haggadah that provided either fresh insights into biblical texts or justified additional changes by reference to the Bible.[50] The principles they followed in biblical interpretation were shaped by rules known as *middôt*. The rabbis held to the synchronic understanding of the Bible and nowhere held to a diachronic or developmental understanding. According to the Midrashim, the oral tradition was attributed to Moses, who was believed to have received it on Mount Sinai, while the Mishnah viewed oral tradition to be the expanded meaning of the written Torah.[51] The rabbis believed that the written Torah could be fully understood only by means of oral traditions that were written down as they were formulated. However, the oral and subsequently written tradition was not handed down in a precise fashion, but rather consisted of individual sayings and groupings that were eventually redacted together at the stage of their composition. In any event, the rabbis believed that originally there were two *tôrôt,* or Laws, one written down and the other oral prior to its composition and transmission in numerous copies, which usually varied.

The Recognition of the Canon

The rabbis rejected Greek literature, the various apocalypses, and other literature that included apocryphal and pseudepigraphal writings. Although the sages did debate the legitimacy of certain books, like Esther, they formalized a canon and recognized as authoritative those books that were commonly known and studied by many of the Jewish communities of the first century C.E. Fur-

---

50. The rabbis in Tannaitic literature referred to knowledge in the Bible as that which is "recited" or "read" *(qārā'),* thus the Miqra, while what was heard *(šĕmûʿâ)* is the listening to the audible recitation of the text, whether biblical or other. The biblical interpretation of the rabbis is grounded in the principle of halakah, which involved the adaptation of the law and daily living out of the commandments to changing circumstances. Haggadah, which is not connected to changing understandings of law and tradition, provided insight into ethical behavior (see Strack and Stemberger, *Introduction to Talmud and Midrash,* 16).

51. Strack and Stemberger, *Introduction to Talmud and Midrash,* 31-44.

thermore, this recognition did not involve an anti-Christian polemic. The rabbis did compose and preserve Targums and prayers and began to write commentaries on the biblical books, beginning with the Torah. Mystical literature did preserve some of the ideas found in apocalypticism and developed a corpus simply known as *Heikhalot*. Of course, most important was the compilation and edition of the Mishnah, followed eventually by the two Talmuds (Palestinian and Babylonian).

Rules for Interpretation of the Tanakh

The rabbinic rules *(middôt)* for interpretation of the Scriptures were collected together in some catalogues, which continued to be expanded over the course of time. The oldest list of seven rules was put together and placed in the tradition under the name of Hillel, who worked in the second half of the first century B.C.E.[52] These had to do with the rules that in essence were common to the ancient period and were not written by this rabbi himself. They consisted of the following:

1. *Qal waḥomer; ḥomer weqal:* "Lighter to weightier; weightier to lighter," or *Argumentum a minori ad maius/a majori ad minus,* corresponding to the scholastic proof a fortiori.
2. *Gezerah shawah:* "Equal law/statute" or an argument from analogy. Biblical passages containing synonyms or homonyms are subject, however much they differ in other respects, to identical definitions and applications.
3. *Binyan ab mi-katub eḥad:* "A founding of a family from a single text." Application of a stipulation found in one passage to topically related passages that do not contain the stipulation in question.
4. *Binyan ab mi-shnê ketubim:* "A stipulation from two passages of Scripture." The same as the preceding, except that the stipulation is generalized from two biblical passages.
5. *Kelal uperat* and *perat ukelal:* "General and particular, particular and general." Definition of the general by the particular, and of the particular by the general.
6. *Ka-yoṣe bô mi-makom aḥer:* "Like that in another place." Similarity in content to another biblical passage.
7. *Dabar ha-lamed me-ʿinyano:* "Something proved by the context." Interpretation is deduced from the context.

---

52. See ibid., 16-20. For the thirteen *middôt* of Rabbi Ishmael see ibid., 20-22.

These seven rules were expanded into the traditional number of thirteen, mostly through a subdivision, which was ascribed traditionally to Rabbi Ishmael, who taught around 135 C.E., before Bar Kokhba.[53] He contested Akiba's position that meaning resided in individual words, but rather taught that the "Torah speaks in human language" (Sifre Num. §112; Horovitz ed., 121). However, a close reading of the sayings attributed to Akiba indicates that his method of interpretation included more than this single principle. While all of these thirteen rules certainly did not derive from Ishmael, his *middôt*, found in the beginning of Sifra, were understood in the Middle Ages as handed down on Mount Sinai and became the "canonical" form of the principles of interpretation. The completely new one in Ishmael's list is number 13: If two passages contradict each other, this contradiction must be reconciled by comparison with a third passage. This list of principles continued to develop to become the thirty-two *middôt*, perhaps from either the Amoraic or Gaonic period.[54] As the rules of interpretation developed, they were used by the rabbis in their debates concerning the proper meaning of the traditions and their implementation in daily life.

Religious Life

For the early rabbis, Torah study took precedence over all other acts of piety, including prayer. The divine will could be known only through the commandments of God, which, when properly understood, learned, and followed, became the essential foundation for the moral life lived in concert with God's will. Practice, not creedal dogmas, resided at the heart of rabbinic religion. Of course, the rabbis believed in the world to come, the advent of a future messiah who would deliver his people from their wicked oppressors, an everlasting covenant, the resurrection of the dead, the reward of the righteous and punishment of the wicked, and the one God who guided the world providentially. The rabbinic mystical literature *(hēkālôt)*, written in Babylonia between the third and seventh centuries C.E., does refer to the ascent of certain sages to the seventh heaven, where the vision of God sitting on his throne and the singing of the angels in praise of his holiness unfolds. Otherwise, most of the rabbis, especially following the revolts against Rome in 66-70 and 132-135, essentially ignored apocalyptic.

Several Jewish sects prior to the destruction of the temple in 70 C.E. had already begun to question the purpose and degree of importance of this institution, so that its razing did not appear to some laity and rabbis to be catastrophic

---

53. This is the traditional number. The actual count can identify 16.
54. Strack and Stemberger, *Introduction to Talmud and Midrash,* 16-30.

for Judaism. Rather, daily prayer, attendance at the synagogue to worship, the study of the Torah, and the observation of the commandments became the major elements of Jewish religious life in the post-temple era. Thus the end of the temple and its cult did not pose for them a great catastrophe. Rather, Judaism shifted from the temple to different institutions, including the synagogue, the schools, and the patriarchate.

Conclusions

The rabbinic tradition likely began in the late Hellenistic and early Roman periods. The beginning of this process is traditionally attributed by the rabbis to Ezra and the mysterious "Great Synagogue" (Neh. 8–10; 'Abot 1.1-2), either the forerunner to the Sanhedrin or representatives of the people during times of crisis.[55] Ezra was regarded in rabbinic tradition to be the transitional figure between the sages of the traditional (Proverbs and Ben Sira) and critical (Job) wisdom literature and the early rabbis in Judea who worked to produce their understandings of the Torah as the embodiment of the divine will that taught people how to live in concert with the commandments. This chain of teachers, prophets, and sages began with Moses and continued to the Tannaitic rabbis after the Great Synagogue (Simon the Just was one of its last members; 'Abot 1.1-2).

The rules of interpretation attributed to Hillel, the literary forms used by the rabbis, and the collections of the Mishnah, the Tosefta, and the early Midrashim point to the interpretive work on the dual Torah by the early rabbis in the Tannaitic period, including especially the houses of Hillel and Shammai, Rabban Gamliel, Eliezer ben Hyrcanus, Akiba, and Yehudah ha-Nasi. These point to a developing rabbinic tradition emerging at the same time that other texts and wisdom teachers appeared, including the scribes of Qumran, Philo, Josephus, the Wisdom of Solomon, Q in the New Testament, and the Sayings Gospel of Thomas. The variety of methods of interpretation in early Judaism and primitive Christianity reveal the many different schools of teachers and their social locations during the first three centuries c.e. These schools formulated their traditions, shaped their respective understandings of authority, set forth different ways of interpreting the Bible, and developed distinctive worldviews that varied among the different groups whose sages disputed among themselves as to the proper course of life.

55. See H. D. Mantel, "The Development of the Oral Law during the Second Temple Period," in *World History of the Jewish People*, vol. 8: *Society and Religion in the Second Temple Period*, ed. Michael Avi-Yonah and Zvi Baras (New Brunswick: Rutgers University Press, 1977) 44-52.

11.   Summary and Observations

Introduction

This introduction has placed the wisdom texts of Israel and early Judaism within the sociocultural and historical context of the eastern Mediterranean world, from the period of Iron Age I (the monarchy) to the first century C.E. Indications from these texts point to the changing social locations, roles, and functions of the scribes and sages, the literary forms and structures of their texts, and the specificity of their diverse theologies. While the precise dates and settings of these texts are open to debate, there is little question that wisdom literature responded to the changes and developments in the social history of Israel and early Judaism. The erroneous notion that wisdom literature was understood by the sages to contain unchanging themes forever true is not accurate.

The sages who compiled the wisdom texts in the Bible represent a group of intellectuals whose fundamental efforts were to determine the order present in the cosmos and to set forth the major features of righteousness that were to be incorporated in human character and to guide moral behavior that would master life. With the apocryphal texts, the divine direction of the history of the chosen people and immortality were additional elements of wisdom's worldviews. In addition, the sages did not conclude their observations of order as the basis for the moral life with the apocryphal texts. Instead, the wise continued their work in streams of traditions that flowed into apocalyptic, sapiential, and rabbinic wisdom present in apocalypticism, the Dead Sea Scrolls, and Rabbinic Judaism.

The Wisdom Literature of the Hebrew Bible

The Book of Proverbs

The seven collections and concluding poem of the book of Proverbs were edited together during a period of several centuries. These dates range from the time of the Israelite monarchy (Hezekiah) to the Second Temple period (prior to the rise of early Judaism and its emphasis on the Torah under Ezra, i.e., late fifth to early fourth century B.C.E.). These materials point to the theological view of righteousness as the order of creation, society, and the life of the individual sage. Through wise and just behavior of the sages, the stability of creation and the sustainability of society are strengthened and given new vitality. Thus both the study of the sapiential tradition, incorporated within the teachings of the ancestors, and the experience of the sage who responds to the order of the cosmos shape a just society.

The Book of Job

The book of Job also came together over a period of several centuries and continued to be changed in its retellings in the Septuagint, the Aramaic Targum, and the Testament of Job. The prologue and epilogue form an older folktale that describes the eventual restitution and restoration of a pious, wealthy, and wise patriarch whose enduring faith led to his eventual salvation. His opponents, the three sages whose narrative speeches are replaced by the later poetic ones, were perhaps condemned for counseling their peer to curse God and die. The poetic dialogues between Job and his three adversaries, and then the two speeches and responses by Yahweh and Job, responded to the Babylonian destruction of Judah, speeches crafted by a wise poet who may have lived among the exiles. Who is to blame for the horrors of holocaust: wicked rulers (Deuteronomistic History), a capricious God (Job), or someone else? The justice of God is at issue throughout the dialogues of the human characters. Job's "oath of innocence" substantiates both his integrity and the legitimacy of his indictment of the unjust God. In the theophany, Yahweh seeks to silence Job through intimidation, but fails. The guilt of Yahweh who destroys both the just and the unjust has been exposed by the wise sage. He will not cower in submission to the worship of a cruel and destructive deity. Due to discomfort with this conclusion, later, more traditional sages add to the book with the poem on the inaccessibility of wisdom (ch. 28) that admonishes obedience to the Torah and the four speeches of Elihu (chs. 32–37), who attempts to reclaim the justice of God and to prove Job guilty.

Wisdom Psalms

It appears clear that sages composed wisdom psalms, some of which were included in the Psalter. Ben Sira and the scribes of Qumran composed similar psalms. Identified by common wisdom themes and forms, the wisdom psalms in the canonical Psalter include Pss. 1, 19, 32, 34, 37, 49, 73, 111, 112, 119, and 127. Dating these psalms is extremely difficult, although the so-called Torah psalms presuppose the period of Ezra in the later Second Temple period as the general time of their composition. The role of the Torah, theodicy, righteous and wise behavior, and retributive justice are recurring themes in this collection.

Qoheleth

Writing and teaching in Jerusalem during the Ptolemaic period of the third century B.C.E., Qoheleth speaks as King Solomon in a testament that comes from the grave. Seeking to discover the good in human existence, he does not discover either a cosmological or a theological basis for his quest. Even abstract truth obtained through reason and instruction is illusive, for the only certainty of which humans may rest assured is the grave, humanity's eternal home. The cosmos is characterized, not by justice and meaning, but by endless repetition, while God is the *deus otiosus* who hides in secret, usually unaffected by human behavior. Seeing that this deity arbitrarily has determined the fates of all human beings, the only divine gift God may choose to give to selected individuals is the capacity of enjoyment. The sources for joy are human labor, the wife of one's youth, and eating and drinking, perhaps within the context of human companionship in a symposium. He does not forsake the wisdom he has learned, but he simply concludes that it provides no advantage in enhancing life, avoiding death, or experiencing joy. Life is but a fleeting moment, soon to pass.

Wisdom Literature in the Apocrypha

Ben Sira

Ben Sira was a teacher in a "house of study," which he operated either out of his home or managed as an institution among many such schools in Jerusalem during the Seleucid period immediately preceding the outbreak of a pogrom by Antiochus IV Epiphanes (175-163 B.C.E.) who sought to exterminate Judaism and any Jews loyal to its teachings. This sage, a devotee of the temple and the high priest Simon II and a scribal interpreter of Torah in the early Seleucid period, offered a variety of instructions on obtaining wisdom and living according to its dictates. Major themes included wisdom's identification with the Torah, the order of creation, sapiential piety, and the encomium that sets forth the praise of the righteous heroes of ancestral faith. While maintaining his allegiance to Judaism, he also made use of several of the literary features of Greek rhetoric and incorporated some of the major ideas of Greek philosophical teaching into his teachings.

The Wisdom of Solomon

An unnamed Jewish rhetor and teacher offers an exhortative address to Hellenistic Jews in Alexandria to continue in their faith and traditions, even if this results in death during a pogrom (Flaccus, 38 c.e.?). Schooled in Greek rhetoric, he seeks to persuade his listeners of the superiority of Jewish religion, divine deliverance, immortality for the righteous who maintain their faith, and the folly of Hellenistic religions, including the cult of the deified rulers, Egyptian animal worship, idolatry, and Dionysian religion. As Wisdom has rescued the righteous ancestors, so she will save those who are in dire straits in the present by becoming the means by which they may obtain immortality. But this will occur only if they have righteous souls entered by Wisdom and remain faithful to their ancestral religion.

Continuing Streams: Apocalypticism and Mantic Wisdom

First Enoch

Mantic wisdom is largely suppressed in the biblical and apocryphal texts, save for the element of dreams that certain sages were said to have had that revealed to them esoteric knowledge provided by this manner of divine revelation. First Enoch is a composite text that combines apocalyptic themes with elements of mantic and traditional scribal wisdom. This text traces wisdom not to the Torah or to the revelation of divine order in the cosmos, but rather to supernatural revelation. Enoch, an enigmatic figure borrowed from biblical tradition (Gen. 5:18-24), is a prediluvian sage who ascends to the heavens, where he comes to know the hidden mysteries of divine wisdom. In addition, his esoteric wisdom comes from the tablets of heaven that he is allowed to read and from the words of angels. This wisdom is then taught by the sage or seer to his disciples and their ongoing communities in order that they may live righteously and experience heavenly redemption following an eschatological judgment.

Daniel

The book of Daniel is also a mantic piece of wisdom that takes shape in the form and content of apocalypticism. This book is divided into two major parts. The first part, chs. 1–6, consists largely of court tales that describe the faithful obedience of Daniel and his companions and their role as sages in the Babylonian court. Significant is their ability to interpret dreams concerning the future, in particular those of Nebuchadnezzar. The second part, chs. 7–12, involves visions of the future and their interpretation by an angel. In his visions, Daniel not only sees both God and the Son of Man, but also foresees the future judgment that leads to the salvation of righteous Jews and the destruction of the wicked. While some of the righteous will experience death, especially those who are martyrs for their faith, they will also be resurrected from the dead. As is the case with 1 Enoch, the book of Daniel traces wisdom to supernatural revelation and not to human observations and the Torah.

Continuing Streams: Apocalyptic Literature and Wisdom in Qumran

The Wisdom Texts of Qumran

The Dead Sea Scrolls consist of a large variety of texts that are especially concerned with the life and the worldview of the sectarians living along the western shores of the Dead Sea. Apocalypticism, wisdom, commentaries on prophets, and halakhic texts are present in this corpus and had as their purpose the instruction of the sectarians in the ways of ethics and purity, the eschatological war between good and evil leading to a retributive judgment, and the understanding of their current existence as a community engaged in opposition both to political forces and other Jewish communities in religious matters. The former included Greeks and then Romans, while the latter consisted of the false teachers and likely the corrupt high priesthood in control of the temple. Sapiential texts among these writings included 4QInstruction, the Book of Mysteries, 4QWiles of the Wicked Woman, 4QSapiential Work (4Q185), Words of the Wise (Maśkîl) to All Sons of Dawn, 4QWays of Righteousness (4Q420-421), the Instruction of 4Q424, 4QBeatitudes (4Q525), several psalms from the Psalms Scroll, and several minor texts. Redemption comes from the faithful following of the instruction of the Teacher of Righteousness and later sages and from the proper interpretation of the Torah.

4QInstruction

The most significant sapiential text preserved in the corpus of the Dead Sea Scrolls is 4QInstruction. Combining apocalyptic with sapiential elements, this text sets forth an instruction for moral behavior similar to that of earlier wisdom texts, but it also speaks of an esoteric wisdom called the "mystery that was, is, and is to be" *(rāz nihyeh)*. Only the elect (i.e., the sectarian covenanters) have this hidden knowledge of the past, the present, and the future and may base their behavior and worldview on its revelation. The interpretation of creation and history indicates that there will be a final judgment in which the righteous are rewarded and the wicked destroyed.

Continuing Streams: Rabbinic Wisdom

The Mishnah

The Mishnah is a philosophical halakhic anthology that sets forth explanations and instructions that are meant to provide a well-organized expansion of the legal portions of Jewish tradition. Its purpose is to provide clear instructions about living an ethical and ritually pure life. As oral tradition that finally is codified in written form by the end of the third century C.E., the Mishnah came to find its authority primarily as part of the revelation to Moses at Sinai even though it does not make this claim for itself. While many of the literary forms and much of the content of the Mishnah are quite different from earlier wisdom texts, it does contain lists and rabbinic sayings in a variety of forms that approximate earlier sapiential rhetoric. Furthermore, it points to and cites the honored sages who stood within a chain of tradition that reaches back to Moses and Sinai.

Tosefta

The Tosefta is a significant amount of halakhic materials that either are to be added to the current Mishnah or are a book of supplements, concluded perhaps around 300 C.E. These additions consist of verbatim citations and glosses of the

Mishnah, freestanding statements that enhance the Mishnah's meaning, and autonomous statements that are understandable without any reference to the Mishnah. It continues the sapiential characteristics of the language of the Mishnah.

Midrashim

The Tannaitic sages and their successors produced commentaries on the four legal books of the Torah (Exodus through Deuteronomy), in particular the legal sections (thus halakhic Midrashim). These texts, written over many centuries including and going beyond the Tannaitic period, represented themselves as tracing the rabbinic teachings back to the time of Moses. While the Mishnah does not indicate that its interpretations and expansions find their locus in Scripture, this is not true of the Tosefta and the Midrashim. Beginning with the Tosefta and even more clearly in the Midrashim the halakhic tradition is seen to have its roots in the authority of Scripture and to derive from the Mosaic revelation at Sinai. The early commentaries were written on the Torah to explain the meanings of particularly the legal sections.

Teachings of the Sages

Finally, among the texts of rabbinic wisdom are two that stand out for providing additional information about the wisdom and the lives of the rabbis. These are tractate 'Abot, which collects sayings of the sages and the 'Abot de Rabbi Nathan, which includes stories about them. While the dating of tractate 'Abot is debated, there is the important reference to a chain of tradition that begins with Moses and continues to the elders, the prophets, the great assembly, and finally the rabbis, many of whom are mentioned in the Mishnah ('Abot 1.1ff.). Important sayings attributed to these teachers include a number that are similar to sapiential literature in the Tanakh and likewise concern wise and righteous behavior and insight. The central theme is the quest for wisdom, which especially is identified with the Torah.

The 'Abot de Rabbi Nathan expands tractate 'Abot by adding narratives about the sayings of the honored rabbis whose sayings it quotes. These sayings are augmented by expansions, the citation of a biblical text that is viewed as verifying the truthfulness of the sayings, parables, and stories about the sages and their sayings. At times, unique materials are added that do not find a point of contact with the sayings. The purpose is to provide greater clarity to the earlier tractate's sayings and to incorporate the teachings.

Conclusion

Wisdom also enters into the literature, language, and worldview of early Christianity, as witnessed by the Sayings Source, the Coptic Gospel of Thomas, the Teachings of Silvanus, and the Sayings of Sextus. With the divergent paths taken by the various groups within Judaism and Christianity, wisdom, originating in the ancient Near East, continued to influence the worldviews and ethical teachings of both of these religions for centuries to come. Early Christian sources have been explored by several scholars who have recognized the importance of Israelite and early Jewish wisdom literature for understanding the development of early Christian didactic and theological expressions.[1]

---

1. For example, see John S. Kloppenborg, *The Formation of Q: Trajectories in Ancient Wisdom Collections* (Studies in Antiquity and Christianity; Philadelphia: Trinity Press International, 2000); Ben Witherington III, *Jesus the Sage: The Pilgrimage of Wisdom* (Minneapolis: Fortress, 2000).

Afterword

This history of wisdom literature places the texts of the sages within the context of empires and colonies in the ancient Near East, with a particular focus on Israel, Judah, and Early Judaism. The biblical literature of the Tanakh is largely written from the colonial context of its writers, who take "pen in hand" to set forth their own teachings and world views within the context of the large empires that ruled the Ancient Near East and the larger Eastern Mediterranean world. While these texts, including those of the sages, vary in their understandings of their common history, most of them share the same social and cultural location, that of a largely nondescript colony dominated by powerful imperial forces that shaped Western Asia, Eastern Europe, and Northern Africa. This common setting was highly significant in shaping the religious and political ideologies found among the metropoles of empires, but also among the colonies they dominated. This volume travels a long and winding road that encompassed nearly three millennia of history and the writings of the sages of different cultures that were necessary to give meaning and provide understanding to the rise and fall of empires and nations.

No author succeeds in writing a volume without the assistance of many people and institutions along the way. In mentioning institutions, I am indebted in particular to the support I received while carrying out research, not only in my own Divinity School, but also in several academic schools that included Durham University, Heidelberg, Göttingen, Cambridge, and Chinese University Hong Kong. In each location I received financial support, an office, secretarial assistance, and access to wonderful libraries that provided me with every type of text necessary for completing my research. My colleagues who assisted me in providing for these settings and in helping to clarify my thinking included Toni Craven, H. Graf Reventlow, Erhard Gerstenberger, Manfred Oeming, Konrad Schmid, Hermann Spieckermann, James D. G. Dunn, and Katharine Dell. I am especially indebted to Nancy Ramsey, my Dean at the Divinity School, who has been more than supportive in assisting my research. In addition, several gifted Ph.d. assistants helped by completing with acumen and skill the arduous tasks of putting together indices and checking footnotes and citations: Katherine Low, Amy Justice, Dyan Dietz, and Chang-An Yeh. Indeed, Ms. Justice has labored many hours on this volume in order to produce and review the lengthy biblical and apocryphal index and the manuscript as a whole. I could not have produced this volume without her support. Finally, I am once again indebted to Suzanne, Stone, my trusty proof reader who is an excellent teacher of grammar and syntax. Ms. Stone is the Administrative Assistant to the Executive Price President and Dean of the Divinity School.

Deans often have to put aside, at least for a time, their own teaching and writing in order to contribute their skills and knowledge to the operation of their schools. For these selfless tasks, they are often given little thanks for their labors on behalf of their schools' academic programs and faculty development. Nancy J. Ramsey, Vice President and Dean of Brite Divinity School, is one of those selfless persons who has toiled with unbounded energy in the many tasks required to build a stronger and more humane institution. It is to her that I dedicate this book, knowing full well it is but a gesture to one who deserves far more.

Bibliography

Ackroyd, Peter R. *Exile and Restoration* (OTL). Philadelphia: Westminster, 1968.

Ahlström, G. W. *Royal Administration and National Religion in Ancient Palestine* Leiden: Brill, 1982.

Albertz, Rainer. *Israel in Exile: The History and Literature of the Sixth Century* B.C.E. Atlanta: Society of Biblical Literature, 2003.

Albertz, Rainer. "The Sage and Pious Wisdom in the Book of Job." *The Sage in Israel and the Ancient Near East*, ed. John G. Gammie and Leo G. Perdue. Winona Lake, IN: Eisenbrauns, 1990, 231-261.

Albertz, Rainer. *Weltschöpfung und Menschenschöpfung. Untersucht bei Deutero-Isaiah, Hiob und in die Psalmen* (Calwer Theologische Monographischen Reihe A, Bibelwissenschaft 3). Stuttgart: Calwer, 1974.

Aletti, J. N. "Proverbes 8:22-31: étude et structure." *Bib* 57 (1976) 25-37.

Algra, Keimpe, Jonathan Barnes, Jaap Mansfeld, and Malcolm Schofield, eds. *The Cambridge History of Hellenistic Philosophy.* Cambridge: Cambridge University Press, 1999.

Allen, Leslie A. "First and Second Chronicles." *NIB* 3 (1999) 267-659.

Alster, Bendt. *Instructions of Šuruppak: A Sumerian Proverb Collection* (Mesopotamia. Copenhagen Studies in Assyriology 2). Copenhagen: Akademisk Forlag, 1974.

Alster, Bendt. "Proverbs from Ancient Mesopotamia: Their History and Social Implications." *Proverbium. Yearbook of International Proverb Scholarship.* University of Vermont 10 (1993) 1-19.

Alster, Bendt. *Proverbs of Ancient Sumer: The World's Earliest Proverb Collection.* Bethesda, MD: CDL, 1997.

Alster, Bendt. *Studies in Sumerian Proverbs* (Mesopotamica 3). Copenhagen: Academisk Forlag, 1975.

Alster, Bendt. *Wisdom of Ancient Sumer.* Bethesda, MD: CDL, 2005.

Alster, Bendt, and H. L. J. Vanstiphout. "Lahar and Ashnan. Presentation and Analysis of a Sumerian Disputation." *ActSum* 9 (1987) 1-43.

Alter, Robert. *The Art of Biblical Poetry.* New York: Basic Books, 1985.

Anderson, Hugh. "3 Maccabees." *The Old Testament Pseudepigrapha* 2. *Expansions of the "Old Testament" and Legends, Wisdom and Philosophical Literature, Prayers, Psalms, and Odes, Fragments of Lost Judeo-Hellenistic Works* (ABRL), ed. James H. Charlesworth. New York: Doubleday, 1985, 509-529.

Annas, Julia. "Stoicism." *Oxford Classical Dictionary,* 3rd rev. ed., ed. Simon Hornblower and Antony Stallworth. Oxford: Oxford University Press, 2003, 1446.

Applebaum, Shimon. "Hellenistic Cities of Judaea and Its Vicinity — Some New Aspects. *The Ancient Historian and His Materials; Essays in Honour of C. E. Stevens,* ed. Barbara Levick. Franborough, Hants: Gregg, 1975, 59-73.

Applebaum, Shimon. "Jewish Urban Communities and Greek Influences." *Judaea in Hellenistic and Roman Times. Historical and Archaeological Essays.* Leiden: E. J. Brill, 1989, 30-46.

Archer, Léonie J. *Her Price Is beyond Rubies. The Jewish Woman in Graeco-Roman Palestine* (JSOTSup 60). Sheffield: Sheffield University, 1990.

Argall, Randal A. *1 Enoch and Sirach: A Comparative Literary and Conceptual Analysis of the Themes of Revelation, Creation and Judgment* (SBLEJL 8). Atlanta: Scholars Press, 1995.

Ariel, D. T. *Excavations at the City of David 1978-1985* (Qedem 30). Jerusalem: Institute of Archaeology, Hebrew University, 1990.

Ariel, D. T. "Locally Stamped Handles and Associated Body Fragments of the Persian and Hellenistic Periods." *Excavations at the City of David 1978-1985 Directed by Yigal Shiloh 6: Inscriptions* (Qedem 41). Jerusalem: Institute of Archaeology, Hebrew University, 2000, 137-194.

Ariel, D. T. "A Survey of Coin Finds in Jerusalem." *LÄ* 32 (1982) 273-326.

Arnaud, D., and D. Kennedy. "Les texts en cuneiform syllabiques découverts en 1977 à Ibn Hani." *Syria* 56 (1979) 319-324.

Arnold, Dieter. *Temples of the Last Pharaohs.* Oxford: Oxford University, 1999, 173-178.

Arzt, Peter, et al., eds. *Sprachlicher Schlüssel zur Sapientia Salomonis (Weisheit),* 2nd ed. (Institut für Neutestamentliche Bibelwissenschaft Salzburg 1. Sapientia Salomonis). Salzburg: Verlag Institut für Ntl. Bibelwissenschaft, 1997.

Asmis, Elizabeth. "Epicurean Epistemology." *The Cambridge History of Hellenistic Philosophy,* ed. Keimpe Algra, et al. Cambridge: Cambridge University Press, 1999, 260-294.

Assmann, Jan. *Ägypten — Theologie und Frömmigkeit einer frühen Hochkultur.* Stuttgart: Kohlhammer, 1991.

Assmann, Jan. *Ägyptische Hymnen und Gebeten,* 2nd improved and exp. ed. (OBO Sonderband). Göttingen: Vandenhoeck & Ruprecht, 1999.

Assmann, Jan. "Aretalogien." *LÄ* 1 (1975) 426-434.

Attridge, Harold W. "Historiography." *Jewish Writings of the Second Temple Period.*

Apocrypha, Pseudepigrapha, Qumran Sectarian Writings, Philo, Josephus (CRINT 2), ed. Michael Stone. Philadelphia: Fortress, 1984, 162-166.

Attridge, Harold W. "Philo the Epic Poet." *The Old Testament Pseudepigrapha 2. Expansions of the "Old Testament" and Legends, Wisdom and Philosophical Literature, Prayers, Psalms, and Odes, Fragments of Lost Judeo-Hellenistic Works* (ABRL), ed. James H. Charlesworth. New York: Doubleday, 1985, 781-784.

Avigad, Nahman. *Archaeological Discoveries in the Jewish Quarter of Jerusalem. The Second Temple Period.* Jerusalem: The Israel Museum, 1976.

Avigad, Nahman. *Bullae and Seals from a Post-Exilic Judaean Archive* (Qedem 4). Jerusalem: Hebrew University of Jerusalem, Institute of Archaeology, 1976.

Avigad, Nahman. *Jewish City Excavations in the Old City of Jerusalem. Conducted by Nahman Avigad, 1969-1982*, ed. Hillel Geva. Jerusalem: Israel Exploration Society, 2000.

Aziza, Claude. "L'utilisation polémique du récit de l'exode chez les écrivains alexandrins (IVème siècle ap. J.-C.)." *ANRW* 2.19/1. Berlin: Walter de Gruyter, 1979, 41-65.

Baillet, Maurice. *Qumrân grotte 4 — III (4Q482-4Q520)* (DJD 7). Oxford: Clarendon Press, 1982, 69-72.

Baines, John. "On the Composition and Inscriptions of the Vatican Statue of Udjahorresnet." *Studies in Honor of William Kelly Simpson* 1, ed. Peter Der Manuelian. Boston: Dept. of Ancient Egyptian, Nubian and Near Eastern Art, Museum of Fine Arts, 1996, 83-92.

Balch, David L. "Josephus, AGAINST APION II.145-206." *SBLSP.* Missoula, MT: Scholars Press, 1975, 187-192.

Barag, Dan. "The Coinage of Yehud and the Ptolemies." *Studies in Honor of Arie Kindler,* ed. Dan Barag. Jerusalem: Israel Numismatic Society, 1999, 27-38.

Barclay, J. M. G. *Jews in the Mediterranean Diaspora from Alexander to Trajan (323 BCE–117 CE).* Edinburgh: T&T Clark, 1996.

Barstad, H. M. *The Myth of the Empty Land: A Study in the History and Archaeology of Judah During the "Exilic" Period* (Symbolae Osloenses Fascicle Supplement 28). Oslo: Scandinavian University, 1996.

Barstad, H. M. "On the So-Called Babylonian Literary Influence in Second Isaiah." *SJOT* 2 (1987) 90-110.

Barta, Winfried. "Das Gespräch des Ipuwer mit dem Schöpfer Gott." *Studien zur altägyptischen Kultur* 1. Hamburg: H. Buske, 1974, 19-33.

Barta, Winfried. "Das Schulbuch Kemit." *ZÄS* 105 (1978) 6f.

Barta, Winfried. "Der anonyme Gott der Lebenslehren." *ZÄS* 103 (1976) 78-79.

Barta, Winfried. "Die Erste Zwischenzeit im Spiegel der pessimistischen Literatur." *JEOL* 24 (1975-76) 50-61.

Baruq, André. "Une veine de spiritualité sacerdotale et sapientielle dans l'Égypte ancienne." *La rencontre de Dieu. Mémorial Albert Gélin,* ed. André Barucq (Bibliothèque de la faculté catholique de théologie de Lyon 8). Le Puy, France: X. Mappus, 1961.

Baslez, Marie-Françoise. "L'autore della Sapienza e l'ambiente colto di alessandria." *Il*

Libro della Sapienza: Tradizione, Redazione, Teologia, ed. Giuseppe Bellia and Angelo Passaro (Studia biblia Biblica 1). Rome: Citta Nuova, 2004, 47-66.

Bauer, Walter, and Frederick William Danker, *A Greek-English Lexicon of the New Testament and Other Early Christian Literature,* 3rd ed. Chicago: The University of Chicago, 2001.

Beavis, Mary Ann L. "Anti-Egyptian Polemic in the Letter of Aristeas 130-165 (the high priest's discourse)." *Journal for the Study of Judaism in the Persian, Hellenistic and Roman Period* 18 (1987) 145-151.

Beentjes, Pancratius C. "'Sei den Waisen wie ein Vater und den Witwen wie ein Gatte': Ein kleiner Kommentar zu Ben Sira 4,1-10." *Der Einzelne und seine Gemeinschaft bei Ben Sira,* ed. Renate Egger-Wenzel and Ingrid Krammer (BZAW 270). Berlin: Walter de Gruyter, 1998, 51-64.

Beentjes, Pancratius Cornelis. *The Book of Ben Sira in Hebrew: a text edition of all extant Hebrew manuscripts and a synopsis* (VTSup 68). Leiden: Brill, 1997.

Behr, J. W. *The Writings of Deutero-Isaiah and the Neo-Babylonian Inscriptions* (Publications of the University of Pretoria, Series III, Arts, n. 3). Pretoria: University of Pretoria, 1937.

Berger, P.-R. *Die neubabylonischen Königsinschriften: Königsinschriften des ausgehenden babylonischen Reiches* (625-539 a. Chr.) (AOAT 4/1). Kevelaer: Butzon & Becker; Neukirchen-Vluyn: Neukirchener, 1973.

Bergman, Jan. "Discours d'adieu. Testament, Discours posthume. Testaments juifs et enseignements égyptiens." *Sagesse et religion: [actes du] colloque de Strasbourg, octobre 1976* (Bibliothèque des centres d'études supérieures specialisé d'histoire des religions de Strasbourg). Paris: Les Universitaires de France, 1979, 21-50.

Bergman, Jan. "Gedanken zum Thema 'Lehre-Testament-Grab-Name.'" *Studien zu Altägyptischen Lebenslehren,* ed. Erik Hornung and Othmar Keel (OBO 28). Göttingen: Vandenhoeck & Ruprecht, 1979, 73-104.

Berlejung, Angelika. *Die Theologie der Bilder: Herstellung und Einweihung von Kultbildern in Mesopotamien und die alttestamentlichen Bilderpolemik* (OBO 162). Göttingen: Vandenhoeck & Ruprecht, 1998.

Berstein, Moshe J. "Interpretation of Scriptures." *Encyclopedia of the Dead Sea Scrolls* 1. Oxford: Oxford University Press, 2000, 376-383.

Betz, Hans Dieter. "De Laude ipsius (Moralia 539A-547F)." *Plutarch's Ethical Writings and Early Christian Literature,* ed. Hans Dieter Betz (SCHNT 4). Leiden: E. J. Brill, 1978, 367-393.

Beyerlin, Walter. *Studien zum 15. Psalm* (Biblische Studien 9). Neukirchen-Vluyn: Neukirchener Verlag, 1985.

Beyerlin, Walter. *Weisheitliche Vergewisserung mit Bezug auf den Zionskult. Studien zum 125. Psalm* (OBO 68). Göttingen: Vandenhoeck & Ruprecht, 1985.

Bickel, Susanne, and Bernard Mathieu. "L'écrivain Amennakht et son Enseignement." *BIFAO* 93 (1993) 31-51.

Bickerman, E. J. "The Babylonian Captivity." *The Cambridge History of Judaism* 1. Intro-

duction: The Persian Period, ed. W. D. Davies and Louis Finkelstein. Cambridge: Cambridge University, 1984, 342-358.

Bickermann, Elias J. "The Edict of Cyrus in Ezra 1." *JBL* 65 (1946) 249-275.

Binder, Donald. *Into the Temple Courts: The Place of the Synagogues in the Second Temple Period* (SBLDS 169). Atlanta: SBL, 1999.

Birnbaum, Ellen. *The Place of Judaism in Philo's Thought: Israel, Jews, and Proselytes* (BJS 290). Atlanta: Scholars, 1996.

Blank, Sheldon H. "The Curse, Blasphemy, the Spell, and the Oath." *HUCA* 23 (1950/51) 73-95.

Blenkinsopp, Joseph. *Ezra-Nehemiah. A Commentary.* London: SCM, 1989.

Blenkinsopp, Joseph. "The Mission of Udjahorresnet and Those of Ezra and Nehemiah." *JBL* 106 (1987) 409-421.

Blenkinsopp, Joseph. *Sage, Priest, Prophet. Religious and Intellectual Leadership in Ancient Israel* (Library of Ancient Israel). Louisville: Westminster John Knox, 1995.

Blenkinsopp, Joseph. "The Sage, the Scribe, and Scribalism in the Chronicler's Work." *The Sage in Israel and the Ancient Near East,* ed. John G. Gammie and Leo G. Perdue. Winona Lake, IN: Eisenbrauns, 1990, 307-315.

Bloch, Renee. "Midrash." *Ancient Judaism,* ed. William S. Green. Missoula, MT: Scholars Press, 1978, 29-50.

Blumenthal, Elke. "Die literarische Verarbeitung der Übergangszeit zwischen Altem und Mittlerem Reich." *Ancient Egyptian Literature. History and Forms,* ed. Antonio Loprieno. Leiden: E. J. Brill, 1996, 105-135.

Boccaccini, Gabriele. *Roots of Rabbinic Judaism. An Intellectual History, from Ezekiel to Daniel.* Grand Rapids: Eerdmans, 2002.

Boer, P. A. H. de. "The Counselor." *Wisdom in Israel and in the Ancient Near East,* ed. Martin Noth and D. Winton Thomas (VTSup 3). Leiden: Brill, 1955, 42-71.

Bohlen, Reinhold. "Kohelet im Kontext hellenistischer Kultur." *Das Buch Kohelet. Studien zur Struktur, Geschichte, Rezeption und Theologie,* ed. Ludger Schwienhorst-Schönberger (BZAW 254). Berlin: Walter de Gruyter, 1997, 327-362.

Bonner, Stanley Frederick. *Roman Declamation in the Late Republic and Early Empire.* Berkeley: University of California, 1949.

Borgen, Peder. "Philo of Alexandria." *Jewish Writings of the Second Temple Period. Apocrypha, Pseudepigrapha, Qumran Sectarian Writings, Philo, Josephus* (CRINT 2), ed. Michael Stone. Philadelphia: Fortress Press, 1984, 233-282.

Borger, Rykle. "Die Beschwörungsserie bit meseri und die Himmelfahrt Henochs." *JNES* 33 (1974) 193-195.

Botha, P. J. "Through the Figure of a Woman Many Have Perished: Ecclesiasticus 41:14–42:8." *OTE* 9 (1996) 20-34.

Bottéro, Jean, Clarisse Herrenschmidt, and Jean-Pierre Veernant. *L'Orient ancien et nous: l'écriture, la raison, les dieux* (Bibliothèque Albin Michel). Paris: Albin Michel, 1996.

Bowman, Allan K., and et al., eds. *The Augustan Empire, 44 B.C. to 69 A.D.,* 2nd ed. (*The Cambridge Ancient History* 10). Cambridge: Cambridge University Press, 1996.

Boyancé, Pierre. *Le culte des Muses chez les philosophes grecs. Études d'histoire et de psychologie collectives.* Paris: Éditions E. de Boccard, 1972.

Braun, Rainer. *Kohelet und die frühhellenistische Popularphilosophie* (BZAW 130). Berlin: Walter de Gruyter, 1973.

Braun, T. F. R. G. "The Greeks in the Near East." *The Expansion of the Greek World, 3/3. Eighth to Sixth Centuries B.C.,* 2nd ed., ed. J. A. Boardman, et al. Cambridge: Cambridge University Press, 1982, 32-56.

Brenk, Frederick E. "Jerusalem — Hierapolis. The Revolt under Antiochus IV Epiphanes in the Light of Evidence for Hierapolis of Phrygia, Babylon, and Other Cities." *Relighting the Souls. Studies in Plutarch, in Greek Literature, Religion, and Philosophy, and in the New Testament Background.* Stuttgart: Franz Steiner, 1998, 364-393.

Brenner, Athalya. "On Female Figurations in Biblical Wisdom Literature." *Of Prophets' Visions and the Wisdom of Sages: Essays in Honour of R. Norman Whybray on His Seventieth Birthday,* ed. Heather A. McKay and David J. A. Clines (JSOT 162). Sheffield: JSOT, 1993, 192-208.

Brown, John Pairman. *Israel and Hellas* (BZAW 231). Berlin: Walter de Gruyter, 1995.

Brown, John Pairman. *Israel and Hellas* (BZAW 276). Berlin: Walter de Gruyter, 2000.

Brown, Teresa R. "God and Men in Israel's History. God and Idol Worship in Praise of the Fathers (Sir. 44-50)." *Ben Sira's God. Proceedings of the International Ben Sira Conference Durham-Upshaw College 2001,* ed. Renate Egger-Wenzel (BZAW 321). Berlin: Walter de Gruyter, 2002, 214-220.

Brug, J. F. "Biblical Acrostics and Their Relationship to Other Ancient Near Eastern Acrostics." *The Bible in the Light of Cuneiform Literature,* ed. William W. Hallo, et al. (Scripture in Context 3; Ancient Near Eastern Texts and Studies 8). Lewiston: E. Mellen, 1990, 283-304.

Brunner, Hellmut. *Altägyptische Erziehung.* Wiesbaden: Otto Harrassowitz, 1957.

Brunner, Hellmut. *Die Weisheitsbücher der Ägypter: Lehren fur das Leben.* Zurich: Artimus & Winkler, 1998.

Brunner, Hellmut. "Die Weisheitsliteratur." *Ägyptologie* (HdO 1). Leiden: Brill, 1952, 90-110.

Brunner-Traut, Emma. "Der Lebensmüde und sein Ba." *ZÄS* 77 (1944) 18-29.

Buccellati, Georgio. "Tre saggi sulla sapienza mesopotamica." *OrAnt* 11 (1972): "III. La teodicea: condanna dell'abulia politica," 161-178.

Buccellati, Georgio. "Wisdom and Not: The Case of Mesopotamia." *JAOS* 101 (1981) 35-47.

Budge, E. A. Wallis. *The Rosetta Stone.* New York: Dover Publications, 1989 reprint.

Burgess, Theodore C. *Epideictic Literature.* New York: Garland Publishers, 1987.

Burkard, Günter. "Literarische Tradition und historische Realität: Die persische Eroberung Ägyptens am Beispiel Elephantine." *ZÄS* 121 (1994) 93-106.

Burkard, Günter. "Literarische Tradition und historische Realität: Die persische Eroberung Ägyptens am Beispiel Elephantine (II)." *ZÄS* 122 (1995) 31-37.

Burkard, Günther, et al., eds. *Texte aus der Umwelt des Alten Testaments 3. Weisheitstexte 2.* Gütersloh: Gerd Mohn, 1991.

Burkert, Walter. *Ancient Mystery Cults*. Cambridge, MA: Harvard University, 1987.

Burkes, Shannon. *Death in Qoheleth and Egyptian Biographies of the Late Period* (SBLDS 170). Atlanta, GA: SBL, 1999.

Burstein, S. M. *The Babyloniaca of Berossus*. Malibu, CA: Undena, 1978.

Busink, Th. A. *Der Tempel in Jerusalem von Salomo bis Herodes* 1 & 2, 2nd ed. Leiden: Brill, 1980.

Buzy, Denis. "La notion du bonheur dans l'Ecclesiaste." *RB* 43 (1943) 494-516.

Cagni, Luiggi. *The Poem of Erra* 1. Malibu, CA: Undena, 1977.

Caminos, Ricardo Augusto. *Late-Egyptian Miscellanies*. London: Oxford University, 1954.

Camp, Claudia. "The Female Sage in Ancient Israel and in the Biblical Wisdom Literature." *The Sage in Israel and the Ancient Near East,* ed. John G. Gammie and Leo G. Perdue. Winona Lake, IN: Eisenbrauns, 1990, 185-203.

Camp, Claudia V. "Understanding a Patriarchy: Women in Second Century Jerusalem through the Eyes of Ben Sira," *"Women like This": New Perspectives on Jewish Women in the Graeco-Roman World,* ed. Amy-Jill Levine (Early Judaism and Its Literature 1). Atlanta, GA: Scholars Press, 1991, 1-39.

Camp, Claudia. *Wise, Strange and Holy: The Strange Woman and the Making of the Bible* (JSOT 320). Sheffield, England: Sheffield Academic, 2000.

Carl, Edward H. *What Is History?* with a new introduction by Richard J. Evans. Basingstoke, England: Palgrave, 2001.

Carr, David M. *Writing on the Tablet of the Heart: Origins of Scripture and Literature.* New York: Oxford University, 2004.

Ceresko, Anthony. "The Sage in the Psalms." *The Sage in Israel and the Ancient Near East,* ed. John G. Gammie and Leo G. Perdue. Winona Lake, IN: Eisenbrauns, 1990, 217-230.

Cerfaux, Lucien and Julien Tondriau. *Un concurrent du christianisme: le culte des souverains dans la civilization gréco-romaine* (Bibliothèque de théologie, 3/5). Tournai: Desclée and Cie, 1957.

Chaney, Marvin L. "Systemic Study of the Israelite Monarchy." *Semeia* 37 (1986) 53-76.

Civil, Miguel. "Sur les 'livres d'écolier' à l'époque paléo-babylonienne." *Miscellanea Babylonica,* ed. J.-M. Durand. Paris: Éditions Recherche sur les Civilisations, 1985.

Clark, D. L. *Rhetoric in Graeco-Roman Education*. New York: Columbia University Press, 1957.

Clifford, Richard J. *Proverbs: A Commentary* (OTL). Louisville: Westminster/John Knox, 1999.

Cohen, Shaye J. D. "Epigraphical Rabbis." *JQR* 72 (1981/82) 1-17.

Cohen, Shaye J. D. *From the Maccabees to the Mishnah,* 2nd ed. Louisville: Westminster/John Knox, 2006.

Cohen, Shaye J. D. "The Significance of Yabneh: Pharisees, Rabbis, and the End of Jewish Sectarianism." *HUCA* 55 (1984) 27-53.

Cole, Thomas. *The Origins of Rhetoric in Ancient Greece* (Ancient Society and History). Baltimore, MD: Johns Hopkins University, 1991.

Collingwood, R. G. *History as Imagination,* rev. ed. Oxford: Oxford University, 1994.

Collins, Adela Yarbro. "Aristobulus." *The Old Testament Pseudepigrapha* 2. *Expansions of the "Old Testament" and Legends, Wisdom and Philosophical Literature, Prayers, Psalms, and Odes, Fragments of Lost Judeo-Hellenistic Works* (ABRL), ed. James H. Charlesworth. New York: Doubleday, 1985, 831-842.

Collins, John J. *The Apocalyptic Imagination,* 2nd ed. Grand Rapids: Eerdmans, 1998.

Collins, John J. *Apocalypticism in the Dead Sea Scrolls.* London: Routledge, 1997.

Collins, John J. "Artapanus." *The Old Testament Pseudepigrapha* 2. *Expansions of the "Old Testament" and Legends, Wisdom and Philosophical Literature, Prayers, Psalms, and Odes, Fragments of Lost Judeo-Hellenistic Works* (ABRL), ed. James H. Charlesworth. New York: Doubleday, 1985, 889-903.

Collins, John J. *Between Athens and Jerusalem,* 2nd ed. (The Biblical Resource Series). Grand Rapids: Eerdmans, 2000.

Collins, John J. *Daniel* (Hermeneia). Minneapolis: Fortress, 1993.

Collins, John J. "The Epic of Theodotus and the Hellenism of the Hasmoneans." *HThR* 73 (1980) 91-104.

Collins, John J. "The Expectation of the End in the Dead Sea Scrolls." *Eschatology, Messianism, and the Dead Sea Scrolls,* ed. Craig A. Evans and Peter W. Flint. Grand Rapids: Eerdmans, 1997, 74-90.

Collins, John J. "The Hellenization of Jerusalem in the Pre-Maccabean Era." *International Renneart Guest Lecture Series* 6. Jerusalem: Ingeborg Renneart Center for Jerusalem Studies, 1999.

Collins, John J. *Jewish Wisdom in the Hellenistic Age* (Old Testament Library). Louisville: Westminster/John Knox, 1997.

Collins, John J. "The Sibyl and the Potter: Political Propaganda in Ptolemaic Egypt." *Religious Propaganda and Missionary Propaganda in Ptolemaic Egypt,* ed. Lukas Bormann, et al. Leiden: Brill, 1994, 57-69.

Collins, John J. "The Sibylline Oracles." *Jewish Writings of the Second Temple Period. Apocrypha, Pseudepigrapha, Qumran Sectarian Writings, Philo, Josephus* (CRINT 2), ed. Michael E. Stone. Philadelphia: Fortress, 1984, 357-381.

Collins, John J. "Sibylline Oracles." *The Old Testament Pseudepigrapha* 1. *Apocalyptic Literature and Testaments* (ABRL), ed. James H. Charlesworth. New York: Doubleday, 1983, 317-472.

Collins, John J. *The Sibylline Oracles of Egyptian Judaism* (SBLDS 13). Missoula, MT: Scholars Press, 1974.

Collins, John J. "Teacher, Priest, and Prophet." *The Scepter and the Star: The Messiahs of the Dead Sea Scrolls and Other Ancient Literature,* ed. John J. Collins (ABRL). New York: Doubleday, 1995, 102-135.

Collins, John J. "Wisdom Reconsidered in Light of the Scrolls." *DSD* 4 (1997) 280.

Collins, John J., ed. *Apocalypse: The Morphology of a Genre* (Semeia 14). Missoula, MT: Scholars Press, 1979.

Collins, John J., et al., eds. *Sapiential Perspectives: Wisdom Literature in Light of the Dead Sea Scrolls* (STDJ 51), Leiden: Brill, 2004.

Conzelmann, Hans. "The Mother of Wisdom." *The Future of Our Religious Past*, ed. J. M. Robinson. New York: Harper, 1971, 230-243.

Corbett, Edward P. J. *Classical Rhetoric for the Modern Student*, 4th ed. Oxford: Oxford University, 1999.

Cotton, Hannah M., and Guy M. Rogers, eds. *Rome, the Greek World, and the East*. Chapel Hill, NC: University of North Carolina, 2004.

Crawford, Sidnie White. "Lady Wisdom and Dame Folly at Qumran." *DSD* 5 (1998) 355-366.

Crenshaw, James L. "The Book of Sirach." NIB 5 (1997) 601-867.

Crenshaw, James L. *Defending God*. Oxford: Oxford University, 2005.

Crenshaw, James L. *Ecclesiastes: A Commentary* (OTL). Louisville, KY: Westminster/John Knox, 1988.

Crenshaw, James L. *Education in Ancient Israel* (ABRL). New York: Doubleday, 1998.

Crenshaw, James L. "Murphy's Axiom: Every Gnomic Saying Needs a Balancing Corrective." *Urgent Advice and Probing Questions: Collected Writings on Old Testament Wisdom*. Macon, GA: Mercer University, 1995, 344-354.

Crenshaw, James L. "Wisdom and Authority: Sapiential Rhetoric and Its Warrants." *Congress Volume: Vienna, 1980*, ed. J. A. Emerton (VTSup 32). Leiden: Brill, 1981, 10-29.

Crenshaw, James L. "Wisdom Psalms?" *CR:BS* 8 (2000) 9-17.

Cribiore, Rafaella. *Gymnastics of the Mind*. Princeton, NJ: Princeton University, 2001.

Cribiore, Rafaella. *Writing, Teachers, and Students in Graeco-Roman Egypt* (American Studies in Papyrology 36). Atlanta, GA: Scholars, 1996.

Crites, Stephen. "Unfinished Figure: On Theology and Imagination." *Unfinished . . . : Essays in Honor of Ray Hart*, ed. Mark C. Taylor (JAAR Thematic Studies). Chico, CA: Scholars, 1981, 155-184.

Cross, Frank Moore. *The Ancient Library of Qumran*, 2nd ed. Minneapolis: Fortress, 1995.

Crüsemann, Frank. "The Unchangeable World: The 'Crisis of Wisdom' in Koheleth." *God of the Lowly*, ed. Willy Schottroff and Wolfgang Stegemann. Maryknoll, NY: Orbis, 1984, 57-77.

Curtis, John B. "On Job's Response to Yahweh." *JBL* 98 (1979) 497-511.

Dalbert, Peter. *Die Theologie der hellenistisch-jüdischen Missionsliteratur unter Ausschluss von Philo und Josephus*. Hamburg-Volksdorf: Herbert Reich, 1954.

Dandamayev, M. A. "Neo-Babylonian Society and Economy." *Cambridge Ancient History 3/2. The Assyrian and Babylonian Empires and Other States of the Near East, from the Eighth to the Sixth Centuries B.C.*, 2nd ed., ed. J. A. Boardman, et al. Cambridge: Cambridge University Press, 1991, 252-275.

Dandamaev, A. A. *A Political History of the Achaemenid Empire*. Leiden: Brill, 1997.

Dandamaev, M. A. *Slavery in Babylonia*. Dekalb, IL: Northern Illinois University, 1984.

Daube, David. *Studies in Biblical Law*. Cambridge: Cambridge University Press, 1947.

Davies, G. I. "Were There Schools in Ancient Israel?" *Wisdom in Ancient Israel*, ed. John Day, et al. Cambridge: Cambridge University Press, 1995, 199-211.

Davies, Philip, G. Brooke, and P. Calloway, eds. *The Complete World of the Dead Sea Scrolls*. London: Thames and Hudson, 2002.

Dawson, David. *Allegorical Readers and Cultural Revision in Ancient Alexandria*. Berkeley: University of California, 1992.

Deissler, Alfons. *Psalm 119 (118) und seine Theologie*. Munich: Karl Zink, 1955.

Della, Diana. *Alexandrian Citizenship during the Roman Principate* (American Classics Studies 23). Atlanta, GA: Scholars Press, 1991.

Delling, Gerhard. "Die Begegnung zwischen Hellenismus und Judentum." *ANRW* 2.20.1. Berlin: Walter de Gruyter, 1987, 3-39.

Delorme, Jean. *Gymnasion. Étude sur les monuments consacrés à l'éducation en Grèce (dès origines à l'empire romain)*. Paris: Boccard, 1960.

Delpha, Annette. "Women in Ancient Egyptian Wisdom Literature." *Women in Ancient Societies*, ed. Léonie J. Archer, Susan Fischler, and Maria Wyke. London: Macmillan, 1994, 24-52.

Delsman, W. C. "Sprache des Buches Koheleth." *Von Kanaan bis Kerala*, ed. W. C. Delsman, et al. (AOAT 211). Neukirchen-Vluyn: Neukirchener Verlag, 1982, 341-365.

Denning-Bolle, Sara. "The Notion of Wisdom in Ancient Mesopotamia." *Epoche* 8 (1980) 80-90.

Denning-Bolle, Sara. "Wisdom and Dialogue in the Ancient Near East. *Numen* 34 (1987) 214-234.

Denning-Bolle, Sara. *Wisdom in Akkadian Literature. Expression, Instruction, Dialogue* (Mededelingen en Verhandelingen van het Vooraziatisch-Egyptisch Genootschap "Ex Oriente Lux" 28). Leiden: Ex Orient Lux, 1992

Derron, Pascale. *Sentences/Pseudo-Phocylide: texte établi, traduit et commenté* (Collection de Universités de France). Paris: Société d'Édition (Les Belles Letters), 1986.

Deutsches Archäologisches Institut. Abteilung Baghdad, *Vorläufiger Bericht über die von dem Deutschen Archäologischen Institut und der Deutschen Orient-Gesellschaft aus Mitteln der Deutschen Forschungsgemeinschaft unternommenen Ausgrabungen in Uruk-Warka* (Abhandlungen der Deutschen Orient-Gesellschaft). Berlin: Gebr. Mann, 1983.

Dever, William. "Social Structure in Palestine in the Iron II Period on the Eve of Destruction." *The Archaeology of Society in the Holy Land*, ed. Thomas E. Levy. Leicester: Leicester University, 1998, 416-431.

Diakonoff, I. M. "A Babylonian Political Pamphlet from about 700 B.C.E." *AS* 16 (1965) 343-349.

Dick, Michael B. "The Legal Metaphor in Job." *CBQ* 41 (1979) 37-50.

Dietrich, Manfried. "Babylonian Literary Texts from Western Libraries." *Verse in Ancient Near Eastern Prose*, ed. J. C. de Moor, et al. Neukirchen: Neukirchener Verlag, 1993, 41-67.

Dietrich, Manfried. "Der Dialog zwischen Supe-ameli und seinem 'Vater'. Die Tradition babylonischer Weisheitssprüche im Westen." *UF* 23 (1991), 33-68.

Dietrich, Manfried. "'Ein Leben ohne Freude . . .': Studie über eine Weisheitskomposition aus den Gelehrtenbibliotheken von Emar und Ugarit." *UF* 24 (1993) 9-29.

Dietrich, Manfried and J. Klein. 'The Ballad About Early Rulers' in Eastern and Western Traditions," in K. van Lerberghe and G. Voet, eds., *Languages and Cultures in Contact at the Crossroads of Civilizations in the Syro-Mesopotamian Realm* (OLA 96). Leuven: Leuven University, 1999, 203-16.

Dietrich, Manfried, and Oswald Loretz. "Die Weisheit des ugaritischen Gottes El im Kontext der altorientalischen Weisheit." *UF* 24 (1993) 31-38.

Dietrich, Manfried, Oswald Loretz, and Joaquin Sanmartin, eds. *Die keilalphabetischen Texte aus Ugarit* (Alter Orient und Altes Testament 24). Neukirchen-Vluyn: Neukirchener Verlag, 1976.

Dijkstra, M. "The Akkado-Hurrian Bilingual Wisdom-Text RS 15.010 Reconsidered, *UF* 25 (1993), 163-71.

Di Lella, Alexander. "Conservative and Progressive Theology: Sirach and Wisdom." *CBQ* 28 (1966) 139-154.

Di Lella, Alexander A. "God and Wisdom in the Theology of Ben Sira: An Overview." *Ben Sira's God: Proceedings of the International Ben Sira Conference, Durham, Ushaw College, 2001*, ed. Renate Egger-Wenzel (BZAW 321). Berlin: de Gruyter, 2002, 3-17.

Di Lella, Alexander A. "Women in the Wisdom of Ben Sira and the Book of Judith: A Study in Contrasts and Reversals." *Congress Volume: Paris, 1991*, ed. J. A. Emerson (VTSup 61). Leiden: Brill, 1995, 39-52.

Dillon, John M. *The Middle Platonists. 80 B.C. to A.D. 220*, rev. ed. Ithaca, NY: Cornell University, 1996.

Dillon, John and Tania Gergel. *The Greek Sophists* (Penguin Classics). London: New York: Penguin, 2003.

Dimitrovsky, Hayim Zalman, ed. *Exploring the Talmud* 1: *Education*. New York: Ktav, 1976.

Doll, Peter. *Menschenschöpfung und Weltschöpfung in der alttestamentlichen Weisheit* (SBS 117). Stuttgart: Katholischer Bibelwerk, 1985.

Donner, Herbert. "Art und Herkunft des Amtes der Königinmutter im alten Testament." *Aufsätze zum Alten Testament, aus vier Jahrzehnten* (BZAW 224), ed. Herbert Donner. Berlin, New York: W. de Gruyter, 1994, 105-145.

Donner, Herbert. "Der 'Freund des Königs.'" *ZAW* 73 (1961) 269-277.

Donner, Herbert. "Die religionsgeschichtlichen Ursprünge von Prov. Sal. 8, 22-31." *ZÄS* 82 (1957) 8-18.

Doran, Robert. "The High Cost of a Good Education." *Hellenism in the Land of Israel*, ed. John J. Collins and Gregory E. Sterling (Christianity and Judaism in Antiquity 13). Notre Dame, IN: University of Notre Dame, 2001, 94-115.

Doran, Robert. "Jewish Hellenistic Historians before Josephus." *ANRW* 2 20/1. Berlin: Walter de Gruyter, 1987, 246-297.

Dover, Kenneth James. "Chreia." *Oxford Classical Dictionary*, 3rd rev. ed., ed. Simon Hornblower and Antony Stallworth. Oxford: Oxford University Press, 324-325, 2003.

Driver, G. R. "Ordeal by Oath at Nuzi." *Iraq* 7 (1940) 132-138.

Duesberg, Hilaire, and Irene Fransen, *Ecclesiastico* (La Sacra Bibbia). Turin: Marietti, 1966.

Ebeling, Erich. *Literarische Keilschrifttexte aus Assur.* Berlin: Akademie-Verlag, 1953.

Ebner, Eliezer. *Elementary Education in Ancient Israel during the Tannaitic Period.* New York: Bloch, 1956.

Edwards, Mark, Martin Goodman, and Simon Price in association with Christopher Rowland, eds. *Apologetics in the Roman Empire: Pagans, Jews, and Christians.* Oxford: Oxford University, 1999.

Egger-Wenzel, Renate. "'Denn harte Knechtschaft und Schande ist es, wenn seine Frau ihrer Mann ernährt' (Sir 25,22)." *Der Einzelne und seine Gemeinschaft bei Ben Sira,* ed. Renate Egger-Wenzel and Ingrid Krammer (BZAW 270). Berlin: Walter de Gruyter, 1998) 23-49.

Elgvin, Torlief. "Wisdom and Apocalypticism in the Early Second Century BCE — The Evidence of 4QInstruction." *The Dead Sea Scrolls Fifty Years after Their Discovery: Proceedings of the Jerusalem Congress, July 20-25,* ed. Lawrence H. Schiffman, Emanuel Tov, and James C. VanderKam. Jerusalem: Israel Exploration Society/ Shrine of the Book, Israel Museum, 2000.

Elgvin, Torlief. "Wisdom, Revelation, and Eschatology in an Early Essene Writing." *SBL Seminar Papers.* Atlanta: Scholars Press, 1995, 440-463.

Elgvin, Torlief. "Wisdom with and without Apocalyptic." *Sapiential, Liturgical and Poetical Texts from Qumran (Proceedings of the Third Meeting of the International Organization for Qumran Studies Oslo 1998),* ed. Daniel Falk, Florentino García Martínez, and Eileen Schuller. Leiden: Brill, 2000, 15-38.

Elgvin, Torlief, et al. *Qumran Cave 4: Sapiential Texts* (DJD 34). Oxford: Oxford University, 1997.

Empereur, Jean-Yves. *Alexandria Rediscovered.* New York: George Braziller, 1996.

Empereur, Jean-Yves, ed. *Alexandrina* 1 & 2 *(Institut français d'archéologie orientale).* Cairo: Institut Français d'Archéologie Orientale, 1998, 2002.

Erler, Michael, and Malcolm Schofield. "Epicurean Ethics." *The Cambridge History of Hellenistic Philosophy.* Cambridge: Cambridge University Press, 1999, 642.

Erman, Adolf. "Eine ägyptische Quelle der Sprüche Salomos." *Sitzungsberichte der Bayerischen Akademie der Wissenschaften. Philosophisch-Philologische und Historische Klasse.* Berlin: Deutsche Akademie, 1924, 86-93.

Erman, Adolf. *The Literature of the Ancient Egyptians.* London: Methuen, 1927.

Eron, John Lewis. "The Women Have Mastery over Both King and Beggar" (Tjud. 15.5) — The Relationship of the Fear of Sexuality to the Status of Women in Apocrypha and Pseudepigrapha: I Esdras (3 Ezra) 3-4, Ben Sira and the Testament of Judah." *JSP* 9 (1991) 43-66.

Falkenstein, Adam, and Wolfram von Soden. *Sumerische und akkadische Hymnen und Gebete.* Zurich: Artemis-Verlag, 1953.

Fallon, Francis T. "Theodotus." *The Old Testament Pseudepigrapha 2. Expansions of the "Old Testament" and Legends, Wisdom and Philosophical Literature, Prayers, Psalms, and Odes, Fragments of Lost Judeo-Hellenistic Works* (ABRL), ed. James H. Charlesworth. New York: Doubleday, 1985, 785-793.

Faulkner, R. O. "The Admonitions of an Egyptian Sage." *JEA* 51 (1965) 53-62.

Faulkner, R. O. "The Man Who Was Tired of Life." *JEA* 42 (1956) 21-40.

Fecht, Gerhard. *Der Habgierige und die Maat in der Lehre des Ptahhotep* (Mitteilungen des Deutschen archäologischen Instituts 10). Glückstadt: J. J. Augustin, 1958.

Fecht, Gerhard. *Der Vorwurf an Gott in den 'Mahnworten des Ipu-wer* (Abhandlungen der Heidelberger Akademie der Wissenschaften, Philosophisch-Historische Klasse 1). Heidelberg: C. Winter, 1972.

Feldman, Louis H. "Diaspora Synagogues: New Light from Inscriptions and Papyri." *Studies in Hellenistic Judaism*, ed. by Louis H. Feldman (Arbeiten zur Geschichte des Antiken Judentums und des Urchristentums 30). Leiden: Brill, 1996), 577-602.

Feldman, Louis H. *Jew and Gentile in the Ancient World.* Princeton, NJ: Princeton University, 1993.

Fichter, Johannes. *Die altorientalische Weisheit in ihrer israelitisch-jüdischen Ausprägung* (BZAW 62). Giessen: Alfred Töpelmann, 1933.

Finkelstein, Israel. *The Archaeology of the Israelite Settlement.* Jerusalem: Israel Exploration Society, 1988.

Finkelstein, Israel. "The Emergence of the Monarchy in Israel: The Environmental and Socioeconomic Aspects." *JSOT* 44 (1989) 43-74.

Finkelstein, Israel, and Nadav Na'aman, eds. *From Nomadism to Monarchy: Archaeological and Historical Aspects of Early Israel.* Jerusalem: Israel Exploration Society, 1994.

Fiorenza, Elisabeth Schüssler, ed. *Aspects of Religious Propaganda in Judaism and Early Christianity* (University of Notre Dame Center for the Study of Judaism and Christianity in Antiquity 2). Notre Dame, IN: University of Notre Dame, 1976.

Fischer, A. A. *Skepsis oder Furcht Gottes* (BZAW 247). Berlin: Walter de Gruyter, 1997.

Fischer-Elpert, Hans-Werner. *Die Lehre eines Mannes für seinen Sohn. Eine Etappe auf dem 'Gottesweg' des loyalen und solidarischen Beamten des Mittelerens Reiches* (Ägyptologische Abhandlungen 60). Wiesbaden: Harrassowitz, 1999.

Fishbane, Michael A. *Biblical Interpretation in Israel.* Oxford: Clarendon, 1985.

Fishbane, Michael A. *The Exegetical Imagination: On Jewish Thought and Theology.* Cambridge, MA: Harvard University, 1998.

Fishbane, Michael. "From Scribalism to Rabbinism." *The Sage in Israel and the Ancient Near East*, ed. John G. Gammie and Leo G. Perdue. Winona Lake, IN: Eisenbrauns, 1990, 439-456.

Fishbane, Michael. "Use, Authority and Interpretation of Mikra at Qumran." *Mikra: Text, Translation, Reading, and Interpretation of the Hebrew Bible in Ancient Judaism and Early Christianity*, ed. M. J. Mulder (CRINT 2). Philadelphia: Fortress, 1988, 360-367.

Fohrer, Georg. *Das Buch Hiob* (KAT 16). Gütersloh: Gerd Mohn, 1963.

Fohrer, Georg. *Introduction to the Old Testament,* by Ernst Sellin (revised and rewritten). Nashville: Abingdon, 1968.

Fohrer, Georg. "The Righteous Man in Job 31." *Old Testament Ethics*, ed. James L. Crenshaw and John Willis. New York: Ktav, 1974, 1-22.

Fohrer, Georg. "σοφία." *TDNT* 7. Grand Rapids, MI: Eerdmans, 1971, 465-526.

Fohrer, Georg. "Überlieferung und Wandlung der Hioblegende." *Studien zum Buche Hiob,* 2nd ed. Gütersloh: Gerd Mohn, 1982.

Foster, Benjamin R. *From Distant Days: Myths, Tales, and Poems of Ancient Mesopotamia.* Bethesda, MD: CDL Press, 1995.

Foster, Benjamin. "Wisdom and the Gods in Ancient Mesopotamia." *Or* 43 (1976) 344-354.

Fox, Michael V. *Ecclesiastes: The Traditional Hebrew Text with a New JPS Translation/ Commentary* (JPS Bible Commentary). Philadelphia: Jewish Publication Society, 2004.

Fox, Michael V. "The Meaning of *Hebel* for Qohelet." *JBL* 105 (1986) 409-27.

Fox, Michael V. *Proverbs: A New Translation with Commenatary* (AB 18A & B). New York: Doubleday, 2000.

Fox, Michael V. *Qohelet and His Contradictions.* Sheffield: JSOT, 1989.

Fox, Michael V. "The Social Location of the Book of Proverbs." *Texts, Temples, and Traditions,* ed. Michael V. Fox, et al. Winona Lake, IN: Eisenbrauns, 1996, 227-239.

Fox, Michael V. "Wisdom in Qoheleth." *In Search of Wisdom,* ed. Leo G. Perdue, et al. Louisville: Westminster/John Knox, 1993, 115-131.

Fraser, P. M. *Ptolemaic Alexandria* 1 & 2. Oxford: Clarendon, 1972.

Fredericks, D. C. *Qoheleth's Language: Re-evaluating Its Nature and Date* (ANETS 3). Lewiston, NY: Mellen, 1988.

Freedman, David Noel. *Psalm 119: The Exaltation of Torah* (Biblical and Judaic Studies from the University of California, San Diego 6). Winona Lake, IN: Eisenbrauns, 1999.

Frey, Jean-Baptiste. *Corpus Inscriptionum Judaicarum* 1-2. Rome: Pontificio istituto di archeologia cristiana, 1936-1952.

Fritz, Volkmar, and Philips R. Davies, eds. *The Origins of the Ancient Israelite States* (JSOTSup 228). Sheffield: Sheffield Academic, 1996.

Fuks, Gideon. "A Mediterranean Pantheon: Cults and Deities in Hellenistic and Roman Askelon." *Mediterranean Historical Review* 15 (1999) 27-48.

Gadd, C. J. *Teachers and Students in the Oldest Schools.* London: School of Oriental and African Studies, 1956.

Gafni, Isaiah M. "The Historical Background." *Jewish Writings of the Second Temple Period. Apocrypha, Pseudepigrapha, Qumran Sectarian Writings, Philo, Josephus* (CRINT 2), ed. Michael Stone. Philadelphia: Fortress Press, 1984, 1-31.

Gager, John. *Moses in Graeco-Roman Paganism* (SBLMS 16). Nashville: Scholars Press, 1972.

Galling, Kurt. *Prediger Salomon* (HAT 18). Tübingen: J. C. B. Mohr (Paul Siebeck), 1940.

Galter, Hannes D. "Die Wörter für 'Weisheit' im Akkadischen." *Megor Hajjim. Festschrift für Georg Molin.* Graz, Austria: University of Graz, 1983, 89-105.

Gammie, John G. "Paraenetic Literature: Toward the Morphology of a Secondary

Genre." *Paraenesis: Act and Form,* ed. John G. Gammie and Leo G. Perdue. *Semeia* 50 (1990) 52.

Gammie, John G. "The Sage in Hellenistic Royal Courts." *The Sage in Israel and the Ancient Near East,* ed. John G. Gammie and Leo G. Perdue. Winona Lake, IN: Eisenbrauns, 1990, 147-153.

Gammie, John G. "The Sage in Sirach." *The Sage in Israel and the Ancient Near East,* ed. John G. Gammie and Leo G. Perdue. Winona Lake, IN: Eisenbrauns, 1990, 355-372.

Gammie, John G., and Leo G. Perdue. *The Sage in Israel and the Ancient Near East.* Winona Lake, IN: Eisenbrauns, 1990.

Gardiner, A. H. *The Admonitions of an Egyptian Sage.* Leipzig: J. C. Hinrichs, 1909.

Gardiner, A. H. *Hieratic Papyri in the British Museum* 1, 3rd series. London: The British Museum, 1935.

Gemser, Berend. "The Instructions of 'Onhsheshonqy and Biblical Wisdom Literature." *Congress Volume: Oxford, 1959* (VTSup 7). Leiden: Brill, 1960.

Gemser, Berend. "The Rîb — or Controversy Pattern — in Hebrew Mentality." *Wisdom in Israel and in the Ancient Near East,* ed. Martin Noth and D. Winton Thomas (VTSup 3). Leiden: Brill, 1955, 120-137.

Gemser, Berend. *Sprüche Salomos,* 2nd ed. (HAT 16). Tübingen: J. C. B. Mohr (Paul Siebeck, 1963.

Gera, Dov. *Judaea and Mediterranean Politics, 219 to 161 BCE* (Brill's Series in Jewish Studies 3). Leiden: Brill, 1998.

Gera, Dov. "On the Credibility of the History of the Tobiads." *Greece and Rome in Eretz Israel,* ed. Aryeh Kasher, et al. (The Center for Eretz Israel Research of Yah Izhak Ben-Zvi and the University of Haifa and of Tel Aviv University). Jerusalem: The Israel Exploration Society, 1990, 21-38.

Gertner, M. "Midrashim in the New Testament." *JSS* 7 (1962) 267-292.

Gesche, Helga. *Der Vergottung Caesars* (Frankfurter Althistorische Studien 1). Kallmünz/Opf.: Lassleben, 1968.

Gesche, Petra. *Schulunterricht in Babylonien im ersten Jahrtausend v. Chr.* (AOAT). Münster: Ugarit-Verlag, 2001.

Gese, Hartmut. "Die Krisis der Weisheit bei Koheleth." *Les Sagesses du Proche-Orient Ancien* (Bibliothèque des Centres d'Études supérieures spécialisés). Paris: Les Universitaires de France, 1963, 139-151.

Gese, Hartmut. *Lehre und Wirklichkeit in der alten Weisheit.* Tübingen: J. C. B. Mohr (Paul Siebeck), 1958.

Gilbert, Maurice. *La critique des dieux dans le Livre de la Sagesse* (AnBib 13). Rome: Pontifical Biblical Institute, 1973.

Gilbert, Maurice. "L'action de grâce de Ben Sira (Sir 51, 1-12)." *Ce Dieu qui vient. Mélanges offerts à Bernard Renaud* (Lectio Divino 159). Paris: Editions du Cerf, 1995, 231-242.

Gilbert, Maurice. "L'Ecclésiastique: Quel texte? Quelle autorité?" *RB* (1987) 233-250.

Gilbert, Maurice. "Le discours de la sagesse en Proverbes 8." *La Sagesse de l'Ancien Testament,* new ed., ed. Maurice Gilbert. Leuven: Leuven University, 1990, 202-218.

Gilbert, Maurice. "L'Éloge de la Sagesse (Siracide 24)." *RTL* 5 (1974) 326-348.

Gilbert, Maurice. "Wisdom Literature." *Jewish Writings of the Second Temple Period. Apocrypha, Pseudepigrapha, Qumran Sectarian Writings, Philo, Josephus* (CRINT 2), ed. Michael Stone. Philadelphia: Fortress Press, 1984, 283-324.

Gilderhus, Mark T. *History and Historians: A Historiographical Introduction,* 5th ed. Englewood Cliffs, NJ: Prentice-Hall, 2002.

Ginzberg, Louis. *The Legends of the Jews. From Joshua to Esther* 4. Baltimore: The Johns Hopkins University Press, 1998.

Glanville, S. R. K. "The Instruction of 'Onchsheshonqy.'" *Catalogue of Demotic Papyri in the British Museum* 2. London: Printed by order of the Trustees, 1939.

Glassner, Jean-Jacques. "The Use of Knowledge in Ancient Mesopotamia." *CANE* 3 (1995) 1815-1823.

Glucker, John. *Antiochus and the Late Academy* (Hypomnemata, Untersuchungen zur Antike und zu ihrem Nachleben 56). Göttingen: Vandenhoeck & Ruprecht, 1978.

Goedicke, Hans. "Die Lehre eines Mannes für seinen Sohn." *ZÄS* 94 (1967) 62-71.

Goedicke, Hans. *The Report about the Dispute of a Man with His Ba.* Baltimore: The Johns Hopkins University, 1970.

Goeseke, Horst. "Motive babylonischer Weisheitsliteratur." *Altertum* 13 (1967) 7-19.

Goff, Matthew. *Discerning Wisdom: The Sapiential Literature of the Dead Sea Scrolls* (VTSup 116). Leiden: Brill, 2007

Goff, Matthew. "The Mystery of Creation in 4QInstruction." *DSD* 10 (2003) 163-186.

Goff, Matthew. "Reading Wisdom at Qumran: 4QInstruction and the Hodayot." *DSD* 11 (2004) 263-288.

Goff, Matthew. *The Worldly and Heavenly Wisdom of 4QInstruction* (STDJ 50). Leiden: Brill, 2003.

Goldin, Judah. *The Living Talmud: The Wisdom of the Fathers and Its Classical Commentaries.* New York: New American Library, 1957.

Golka, Friedemann. *The Leopard's Spots: Biblical and African Wisdom in Proverbs.* Edinburgh: T&T Clark, 1994.

Goodenough, E. R. *By Light, Light. The Mystic Gospel of Hellenistic Judaism.* New Haven, CT: Yale University, 1935.

Goodenough, E. R. *The Politics of Philo Judaeus.* New Haven: Yale University, 1938.

Goodman, Martin. *Mission and Conversion: Proselytizing in the Religious History of the Roman Empire.* Oxford: Clarendon, 1994.

Gordis, Robert. *Koheleth — The Man and His World,* 3rd aug. ed. New York: Schocken, 1968.

Gordis, Robert. "The Social Background of Wisdom Literature. *HUCA* 18 (1944) 85f.

Gordis, Robert. "The Wisdom of Qoheleth." *Poets, Prophets, and Sages.* Bloomington, IN: Indiana University, 1971, 337-338.

Gordon, E. I. "A New Look at the Wisdom of Sumer and Akkad." *BO* 17 (1960) 122-152.

Gordon, E. I. *Sumerian Proverbs.* Philadelphia: The University of Pennsylvania, 1959.

Gordon, Richard L. "Sarapis." *The Oxford Companion to Classical Civilization,* ed. Simon Hornblower and Anthony Spawforth. Oxford: Oxford University, 1355-1356.

Gorman, Frank. *The Ideology of Ritual: Space, Time, and Status in the Priestly Theology* (JSOTSup 91). Sheffield: Sheffield University, 1990.

Goshen-Gottstein, Alon. "Ben Sira's Praise of the Fathers: A Canon-Conscious Reading." *Ben Sira's God, Proceedings of the International Ben Sira Conference Durham-Upshaw College 2001*, ed. Renate Egger-Wenzel (BZAW 321). Berlin: Walter de Gruyter, 2002, 235-267.

Goshen-Gottstein, M. H. *The Wisdom of Ahiqar: Syriac and Aramaic.* Jerusalem: Hebrew University of Jerusalem, 1965.

Gottlieb, Isaac. "Pirqe Abot and Biblical Wisdom." *VT* 40 (1990) 152-164.

Grabbe, Lester. *Ezra-Nehemiah.* London: Routledge, 1998.

Grabbe, Lester L. *Judaism from Cyrus to Hadrian* 1 & 2. Minneapolis-St. Paul: Fortress, 1992.

Grant, Michael. *A Social History of Greece and Rome.* New York: Charles Scribner's Sons, 1992.

Grätz, Sebastian. *Das Edikt des Artaxerxes: Eine Untersuchung zum religionspolitischen und historischen Umfeld von Esra 7,12-26* (BZAW 337). Berlin: Walter de Gruyter, 2004.

Gray, John B. "The Book of Job in the Context of Ancient Near Eastern Literature." *ZAW* 82 (1970) 251-269.

Grintz, Jehoshua M. "'The Proverbs of Solomon': Clarifications on the Question of the Relation between the Three Collections in the Book of Proverbs Attributed to Solomon," in Daniel C. Snell, *Twice-Told Proverbs and the Composition of the Book of Proverbs.* Winona Lake, IN: Eisenbrauns, 1993, 87-114.

Gruen, Erich. *Diaspora. Jews amidst Greeks and Romans.* Cambridge, MA: Harvard University, 2002.

Gruen, Eric. *Heritage and Hellenism. The Re-invention of Jewish Tradition.* Berkeley, CA: University of California, 1998.

Grumach, Irene Shirun. "Die Lehre des Amenemope." *TUAT* 3. *Weisheitstexte* 2. Gütersloh: Gütersloher Haus, 1991, 222-250.

Guéraud, Octave, and Pierre Jouguet, eds. *Un livre d'écolier du IIIe siècle avant J.-C.* (Publications de la Société Fouad I de papyrologie). Textes et documents 2. Cairo: L'Institut français d'archéologie orientale, 1938.

Gunkel, Hermann, and Joachim Begrich. *Einleitung in die Psalmen.* Göttingen: Vandenhoeck & Ruprecht, 1933.

Gutman, Yehoshua. "Philo the Epic Poet." *Scripta Hierosolymitana* 1. Jerusalem: Magnes, 1954, 36-63.

Gutmann, Joseph. "Origin of the Synagogue: The Current State of Research." *The Synagogue: Studies in Origins, Archaeology and Architecture* (LBS). New York: Ktav, 1975.

Haag, Ernst. *Das hellenistische Zeitalter. Israel und die Bibel im 4. bis 1. Jahrhundert v. Chr.* (Biblische Enzykopädie 9). Stuttgart: Kohlhammer, 2003.

Habel, Norman. *The Book of Job* (OTL). Philadelphia: Westminster, 1985.

Habel, Norman. "The Symbolism of Wisdom in Proverbs 1–9." *Interp* 26 (1972) 131-157.

Habicht, Christian. *Gottmenschentum und griechische Städte*, 2nd rev. ed. (Zetemata 14). Munich: Beck, 1970.

Habinek, Thomas. *Ancient Rhetoric and Oratory* (Blackwell Introductions to the Classical World). Oxford: Blackwell, 2005.

Hachlili, Rachel. *Ancient Jewish Art and Archaeology in the Land of Israel* (HdO 35). Leiden: Brill, 1988.

Hachlili, Rachel. "The Origin of the Synagogue: A Re-assessment." *JSJ* 28 (1997) 34-47.

Hadas, Moses. *Third and Fourth Maccabees.* New York: Published for the Dropsie College for Hebrew and Cognate Learning by Harper, 1953.

Hallo, William W. "Lamentations and Prayers in Sumer and Akkad." *CANE* 3 (1995) 1876-1881.

Hallo, William W. "The Limits of Skepticism." *JAOS* 110 (1990) 187-199.

Hallo, William H., and K. Lawson Younger. *The Context of Scripture* 1-3. Leiden: Brill, 2003.

Hanson, Paul. *The Dawn of Apocalyptic.* Philadelphia: Fortress, 1975.

Haran, Manahem. "On the Diffusion of Literacy and Schools in Ancient Israel." *Congress Volume: Jerusalem 1986*, ed. J. A. Emerton (VTSup 40). Leiden: Brill, 1988, 81-95.

Harrington, Daniel. "The *Raz Nihyeh* in a Qumran Wisdom Text (1Q26, 4Q415-418, 423)." *RevQ* 17 (1996) 549-553.

Harrington, Daniel J. *Wisdom Texts from Qumran. The Literature of the Dead Sea Scrolls.* London: Routledge, 1996.

Harris, H. A. *Greek Athletics and the Jews.* Cardiff: University of Wales, 1976.

Harris, Rivkah. "The Female 'Sage' in Mesopotamian Literature." *The Sage in Israel and the Ancient Near East*, ed. John G. Gammie and Leo G. Perdue. Winona Lake, IN: Eisenbrauns, 1990, 3-17.

Harris, W. V. *Ancient Literacy.* Cambridge, MA: Harvard University, 1989.

Hayes, Christine. "Sanhedrin." *The Oxford Dictionary of the Jewish Religion*, ed. R. J. Zwi Werblowsky and Geoffrey Wigoder. New York: Oxford University Press, 606-608.

Hayward, C. T. R. "The Jewish Temple at Leontopolis: A Reconsideration." *JJS* 33 (1982) 432-433.

Hayward, Robert. *The Jewish Temple. A Non-Biblical Sourcebook.* London: Routledge, 1996.

Heaton, E. W. *The School Tradition of the Old Testament.* Oxford: Oxford University, 1994.

Heaton, E. W. *Solomon's New Men: The Emergence of Ancient Israel as a Nation State.* New York: Pica Press, 1974.

Helck, Wolfgang. *Der Text der Lehre Amenemhets I. für seinen Sohn*, 2nd. ed. (Kleine Ägyptische Texte 1). Wiesbaden: Harrassowitz, 1988.

Helck, Wolfgang. *Die Prophezeiung des Nfr.tj* (Kleine ägyptische Texte). Wiesbaden: Harrassowitz, 1970.

Helck, Wolfgang. "Ma'at." *LÄ* 3 (1980) 1110-1119.

Hempel, Charlotte, Armin Lange, and Hermann Lichtenberger, eds. *The Wisdom Texts from Qumran and the Development of Sapiential Thought* (BETL 159). Leuven: Leuven University Press.

Hengel, Martin. "The Interpenetration of Judaism and Hellenism in the Pre-Maccabean Period." *The Cambridge History of Judaism* 1, ed. W. D. Davies and Louis Finkelstein. Cambridge: Cambridge University Press, 1984, 167-228.

Hengel, Martin. "Jerusalem als jüdische und hellenistische Stadt." *Judaica, Hellenistica et Christiana. Kleine Schriften* 2, ed. Martin Hengel (WUNT 109). Tübingen: J. C. B. Mohr, 1999, 114-156.

Hengel, Martin. *Jews, Greeks, and Barbarians. Aspects of the Hellenization of Judaism in the Pre-Christian Period.* Philadelphia: Fortress, 1980.

Hengel, Martin. *Judaica et Hellenistica: Kleine Schriften* 1. Tübingen: J. C. B. Mohr, 1996.

Hengel, Martin. *Judaism and Hellenism* 1-2. London: SCM, 1974.

Hengel, Martin. "The Political and Social History of Palestine from Alexander to Antiochus III (333-187 B.C.E.)." *The Cambridge History of Judaism* 1, ed. W. D. Davies and Louis Finkelstein. Cambridge: Cambridge University, 1984, 35-78.

Hengel, Martin. "'Schriftauslegung' und 'Schriftwerdung' in der Zeit des Zweiten Tempels." *Judaica, Hellenistica et Christiana. Kleine Schriften* 2, ed. Jörg Frey and Dorothea Betz with contributions by Hanswulf Bloedhorn and Max Küchler (WMANT 109). Tübingen: Mohr-Siebeck, 1999, 20-35.

Henten, Jan Willem van, and Pieter van der Horst, eds. *Ancient Jewish Epitaphs.* Leiden: Brill, 1994.

Henten, J. W. van, and P. W. van der Horst, eds. *Studies in Early Jewish Epigraphy.* Leiden: Brill, 1994.

Hermann, Alfred. "Das Gespräch eines Lebensmüden mit seiner Seele." *OLZ* 34 (1939) 345-351.

Hermisson, H.-J. "Observations on the Creation Theology in Wisdom." *Israelite Wisdom,* ed. John G. Gammie, et al. Missoula: Scholars Press, 1978, 43-57.

Hermisson, H. J. *Studien zur israelitischen Spruchweisheit* (WMANT 28). Neukirchen-Vluyn: Neukirchener Verlag, 1968, 97-136.

Herrmann, Siegfried. "Die Naturlehre des Schöpfungsberichtes." *TLZ* 86 (1961) 413-423.

Herrmann, Siegfried. *Untersuchungen zur Überlieferungsgestalt Mittelägyptischer Literaturwerke* (Deutsche Akademie der Wissenschaften zu Berlin Institut für Orientforschung 33). Berlin: Akademieverlag, 1957.

Hesse, Franz. *Hiob* (Zürcher Bibelkommentar). Zurich: Theologische Verlag Zürich, 1978.

Hezser, Catherine. *The Social Structure of the Rabbinic Movement in Roman Palestine.* TSAJ 66. Tübingen: Mohr-Siebeck, 1997.

Hillers, Delbert. *Treaty-Curses and the Old Testament Prophets* (BibOr 10). Rome: Pontifical Biblical Institute, 1964.

Hock, Ronald F. "Paul and Graeco-Roman Education." *Paul in the Graeco-Roman World: A Handbook,* ed. J. Paul Sampley. Harrisburg, PA: Trinity International, 2003.

Hock, Ronald F., and Edward O'Neil. *The Chreia and Ancient Rhetoric: Classroom Exercises.* Atlanta, GA: Society of Biblical Literature, 2002.

Hock, Ronald F., and Edward O'Neil. *The Chreia in Ancient Rhetoric* 1: *The Progymnasmata*. Atlanta: Scholars, 1986.

Hölbl, Günther. *A History of the Ptolemaic Empire*. London: Routledge, 2001.

Holladay, Carl F. *Fragments from Hellenistic Jewish Authors* 2. *Poets: The Epic Poets Theodotus and Philo and Ezekiel the Tragedian* (SBLTT). Atlanta: Scholars Press, 1989.

Holladay, Carl H. *Theios Aner in Hellenistic Judaism* (SBLDS 40). Missoula, MT: Scholars, 1977.

Holladay, Carl R. *Fragments from Hellenistic Jewish Authors* 3. *Aristobulus* (SBLTT: Pseudepigrapha Series). Atlanta: Scholars, 1995.

Hollander, Harm W., and Marinus de Jonge. *The Testaments of the Twelve Patriarchs: A Commentary* (SVTP 8). Leiden: E. J. Brill, 1985.

Horbury, William, and David Noy. *Jewish Inscriptions of Graeco-Roman Egypt with an Index of the Jewish Inscriptions of Egypt and Cyrenaica*. Cambridge: Cambridge University, 1992.

Hornung, Erik. *Meisterwerke altägyptischer Dichtung*. Zurich: Artemis Verlag, 1978.

Horowitz, Wayne, Takayoshi Oshia, and Seth Sanders. "A Bibliographical List of Cuneiform Inscriptions from Canaan, Palestine/Philistia, and the Land of Israel." *JAOS* 122 (2002) 753-766.

Horst, Pieter W. van der. *Ancient Jewish Epitaphs. An Introductory Survey of a Millennium of Jewish Funerary Epigraphy (300 BCE–700 CE)*. Kampen: Kok Pharos, 1991.

Horst, Pieter Willem van der. *Chaeremon, Egyptian Priest and Stoic Philosopher: the Fragments Collected and Translated with Explanatory Notes* (Études préliminaires aux religions orientales dans l'Empire romain 101). Leiden: E. J. Brill, 1984.

Horst, Pieter W. van der. "Das Neue Testament und die jüdische Grabinschriften aus hellenistisch-römischer Zeit." *BZ* 35 (1992) 161-178.

Horst, Pieter W. van der. "Greek in Jewish Palestine in the Light of Jewish Epigraphy." *Japheth in the Tents of Shem. Studies on Jewish Hellenism in Antiquity* (Contributions to Biblical Exegesis and Theology 32). Leuven: Peeters, 2002, 9-26.

Horst, Pieter W. van der. *Philo's Flaccus 2. The First Pogrom. Introduction, Translation and Commentary* (Philo of Alexandria Commentary Series). Leiden: Brill, 2003.

Horst, Pieter W. van der. "Pseudo-Phocylides." *The Old Testament Pseudepigrapha 2. Expansions of the "Old Testament" and Legends, Wisdom and Philosophical Literature, Prayers, Psalms, and Odes, Fragments of Lost Judeo-Hellenistic Works* (ABRL), ed. James H. Charlesworth. New York: Doubleday, 1985, 565-582.

Horst, Pieter W. van der. "Pseudo-Phocylides and the New Testament." *ZNW* 69 (1978) 187-202.

Horst, Pieter W. van der. "Pseudo-Phocylides Revisited." *JSP* 3 (1988) 3-30.

Horst, Pieter W. van der. *The Sentences of Pseudo-Phocylides, with Introduction and Commentary* (VTSup 4). Leiden: E. J. Brill, 1978.

Horwitz, W. J. "The Ugaritic Scribe." *UF* 11 (1979) 389-394.

Howard, George. "The Letter of Aristeas and Diaspora Judaism." *JTS* 22 (1971) 337-348.

Hübner, Hans. *Die Weisheit Salomos* (ATD Apocryphen Band 4). Göttingen: Vandenhoeck & Ruprecht, 1999.

Huizanga, John. "A Definition of the Concept of History." *Philosophy and History: Essays Presented to Ernst Cassirer,* ed. Raymond Kiblansky and H. J. Paton. New York: Harper Torchbooks, 1963.

Humbert, Paul. "'*Qana*' en hébreu biblique." *Festschrift Alfred Bertholet,* ed. W. Baumgartner, et al. Tübingen: J. C. B. Mohr (Paul Siebeck), 1950, 259-266.

Hurwitz, Avi. "Wisdom Vocabulary in the Hebrew Psalter." *VT* 38 (1988) 41-52.

Hus, Werner. *Ägypten in hellenistischer Zeit. 332-30 v. Chr.* Munich: C. H. Beck, 2001.

Ilan, Tal. *A Lexicon of Jewish Names in Late Antiquity,* Part 1: *Palestine 330 BCE–200 CE* (Texte und Studien zum antiken Judentum 91). Tübingen: Mohr-Siebeck, 2002.

Ilan, Tal. "New Ossuary Inscriptions from Jerusalem." *Scripta Classica Israelica* 9 (1991/ 1992): 149-159.

Inwood, Brad. *Cambridge Companion to the Stoics.* Cambridge: Cambridge University, 2003.

Inwood, Brad. *Ethics and Human Action in Early Stoicism.* Oxford: Clarendon, 1985.

Izre'el, Shlomo. *Adapa and the South Wind. Language Has the Power of Life and Death* (Mesopotamian Civilizations 10). Winona Lake, IN: Eisenbrauns, 2001.

Jacobsen, Carl Howard. *The Exagoge of Ezekiel.* New York: Cambridge University, 1983.

Jacobsen, Thorkild. *The Treasures of Darkness. A History of Mesopotamian Religion.* New Haven, CT: Yale University, 1976.

Jaffee, Martin S. *Torah in the Mouth. Writing and Oral Tradition in Palestinian Judaism, 200 BCE–400 CE.* Oxford: Oxford University, 2001.

Janssen, Herman Ludin. *Die spätjüdische Psalmendichtung. Ihr Entstehungskreis und ihr 'Sitz im Leben.'* Oslo: I. Kommisjon Hos Jacob Dybwab, 1937.

Janzen, J. Gerald. *Job* (Interpretation). Richmond: John Knox Press, 1985.

Japhet, Sara. *1 & 2 Chronicles* (OTL). Louisville, KY: Westminster/John Knox, 1993.

Jastrow, Marcus (compiler). *A Dictionary of the Targumim, The Talmud Babli and Yerushalmi, and the Midrashic Literature.* London: Luzac & Co./New York: G. P. Putnam's Sons, 1903.

Jellicoe, Sidney. "The Occasion and Purpose of the Letter of Aristeas: A Re-Examination." *NTS* 12 (1966) 144-150.

Johnson, J. H. "Is the Demotic Chronicle an Anti-Greek Tract?" *Grammata Demotica, FS Erich Lüddeckens,* ed. Heinz-J. Thissen and Karl-Th. Zauzich. Würzburg: Zauzich, 1984, 107-124.

Johnston, Robert K. "'Confessions of a Workaholic.' A Reappraisal of Qoheleth." *CBQ* 38 (1976) 14-28.

Junge, Friedrich. *Die Lehre Ptahhoteps und die Tugenden der ägyptischen Welt* (OBO 193). Göttingen: Vandenhoeck & Ruprecht, 2003.

Junge, Friedrich. "Die Welt der Klagen." *Fragen an die altägyptische Literatur,* ed. Jan Assmann, Erika Feucht, and Reinhard Grieshammer. Wiesbaden: Reichert, 1977.

Jungling, W.-W. "Der Bauplan des Buches Jesus Sirach." *"Den Armen eine frohe*

Botschaft." *FS Franz Franphaus,* ed. Josef Hainz. Frankfurt am Main: Peter Lang, 1997, 89-105.

Kah, Daniel, and Peter Scholz. *Das hellenistische Gymnasion* (Wissenskultur und gesellschaftlicher Wandel 8). Oldenbourg: Akademie Verlag, 2004.

Kaiser, Otto. "Die Rezeption der stoischen Providenz bei Ben Sira." *JSNL* 24 (1998) 41-54.

Kajanto, Iiro. *A Study of the Greek Epitaphs of Rome* (Acta Instituti Romani Finlandiae, v. 2:3). Helsinki: Tilgman, 1963.

Kaplony, Peter. "Demotische Chronik." *LÄ* 1 (1975) 1056-1060.

Kaplony-Heckel, Ursula. "Schüler und Schulwesen in der ägyptischen Spätzeit." *Studien zur altägyptischen Kultur* 1. Hamburg: H. Buske, 1974, 227-246.

Kasher, Aryeh. "Anti-Jewish Persecutions in Alexandria in the Reign of Ptolemy Philopator, According to III Maccabees." *Studies in the History of the Jewish People and the Land of Israel* 4, ed. Uriel Rappaport. Haifa: University of Haifa, 1978, 59-76.

Kasher, Aryeh. "Jerusalem Cathedra." *Jerusalem* (Yad Izhak Ben-Zvi Institute 1982). Detroit: Wayne State University, 1982, 63-78.

Kasher, Aryeh. *Jews and Hellenistic Cities in Eretz-Israel. Relations of the Jews in Eretz-Israel with the Hellenistic Cities during the Second Temple Period (332 BCE–70 CE).* Tübingen: J. C. B. Mohr (Paul Siebeck), 1990.

Kaster, Robert A. *Guardians of Language: The Grammarian and Society in Late Antiquity.* Berkeley, CA: University of California, 1988.

Kayatz, Christa Bauer. *Studien zu Proverbien 1–9. Eine form- und motivgeschichtliche Untersuchung unter Einbeziehung ägyptischen Vergleichsmaterials* (WMANT 22). Neukirchen-Vluyn: Neukirchen Verlag, 1966.

Kee, Howard Clark. "Testaments of the Twelve Patriarchs." *The Old Testament Pseudepigrapha* 1. *Apocalyptic Literature and Testaments* (ABRL), ed. James H. Charlesworth. New York: Doubleday, 1983, 775-828.

Keel, Othmar. *Die Weisheit spielt vor Gott.* Göttingen: Vandenhoeck & Ruprecht, 1974.

Kennedy, G. A. *The Art of Persuasion in Greece.* Princeton, NJ: Princeton University, 1963.

Kennedy, G. A. *Greek Rhetoric under Christian Emperors.* Princeton: Princeton University, 1983.

Kennedy, George A. "Historical Survey of Rhetoric." *Handbook of Classical Rhetoric in the Hellenistic Period, 330 B.C.–A.D. 400,* ed. Stanley E. Porter. Leiden: Brill, 2001, 3-43.

Kennedy, George A. *A New History of Classical Rhetoric.* Princeton: Princeton University, 1994.

Kennel, N. M. *The Gymnasium of Virtue.* Chapel Hill, NC: University of North Carolina, 1995.

Kerferd, G. B. *The Sophistic Movement.* Cambridge: Cambridge University, 1981.

Kerferd, George B. "The Sage in Hellenistic Philosophical Literature." *The Sage in Israel and the Ancient Near East,* ed. John G. Gammie and Leo G. Perdue. Winona Lake, IN: Eisenbrauns, 1990, 319-328.

Khanjian, John. "Wisdom." *Ras Shamra Parallels,* ed. L. R. Fisher (AnOr 50). Rome: Pontifical Biblical Institute, 1975, 371-400.

Kilmer, Anne. "The Mesopotamian Counterparts of the Biblical Nepilim." *Perspectives on Language and Text. Essays and Poems in Honor of Francis I. Andersen's Sixtieth Birthday,* ed. E. W. Conrad and E. G. Newing. Winona Lake, IN: Eisenbrauns, 1987, 39-43.

Kindler, Arie. "Silver Coins Bearing the Name of Judea from the Early Hellenistic Period." *IEJ* 24 (1974) 73-76.

Kitchen, Kenneth A. "The Basic Literary Forms and Formulations of Ancient Instructional Writings in Egypt and Western Asia." *Studien zu altägyptischen Lebenslehren,* ed. Erik Hornung and Othmar Keel (OBO 28). Göttingen: Vandenhoeck & Ruprecht, 1979, 235-282.

Kitchen, Kenneth A. "Studies in Egyptian Wisdom Literature — I: The Instruction by a Man for His Son." *OrAnt* 8 (1969) 189-208.

Klauck, Hans-Josef. *The Religious Context of Early Christianity: A Guide to Graeco-Roman Religions.* Minneapolis: Fortress, 2003.

Klein, Jacob. "'Personal God' and Individualized Prayer in Sumerian Religion." *AfO Beiheft* 19 (1982) 295-306.

Kloppenborg, John S. *The Formation of Q: Trajectories in Ancient Wisdom Collections* (Studies in Antiquity and Christianity). Philadelphia: Trinity Press International, 2000.

Knibb, Michael A. "Teacher of Righteousness." *Encyclopedia of the Dead Sea Scrolls* 2, 918-921.

Kolarcik, Michael. "The Book of Wisdom." *NIB* 5. Nashville, TN: Abingdon Press, 1997, 435-600.

Kolarcik, Michael. "Universalism and Justice in the Wisdom of Solomon." *Treasures of Wisdom, Studies in Ben Sira and the Book of Wisdom. FS Maurice Gilbert,* ed. Núria Calduch-Benages and Jacques Vermeylen (BETL 143). Leuven: Leuven University, 1999, 289-301.

Koole, J. L. "Die Bibel des Ben-Sirah." *OTS* 14 (1965) 374-396.

Kottseiper, Ingo. "The Aramaic Tradition: Ahikar." *Scribes, Sages, and Seers* (FRLANT 210). Göttingen: Vandenhoeck and Ruprecht, forthcoming.

Kottsieper, Ingo. "Die Geschichte und die Sprüche des weisen Achiqar." *TUAT* 3. *Weisheitstexte* 1. Gütersloh: Gütersloher Haus, 320-347

Kottsieper, Ingo. *Die Sprache der Ahiqarsprüche* (BZAW 194). Berlin: Walter de Gruyter, 1990.

Kramer, S. N. "'Man and His God.' A Sumerian Variation on the 'Job' Motif." *VTSup* 3 (1955) 170-182.

Kramer, Samuel N. "The Sage in Sumerian Literature." *The Sage in Israel and the Ancient Near East,* ed. John G. Gammie and Leo G. Perdue. Winona Lake, IN: Eisenbrauns, 1990, 32-37.

Kramer, S. N. "Sumerian Wisdom Literature: A Preliminary Survey." *BASOR* 122 (1951) 30-31.

Kratz, Reinhard G. *Die Komposition der erzählenden Bücher des Alten Testaments* (UTB). Göttingen: Vandenhoeck & Ruprecht, 2000.

Kratz, Reinhard. "Die Torah Davids. Psalm 1 und die doxologische Fünfteilung des Psalters." *ZThK* 90 (1993) 1-34.

Krentz, Edgar. *The Historical Critical Method* (Guides to Biblical Scholarship: Old Testament). Philadelphia: Fortress, 1975.

Kroeber, Rudi. *Der Prediger* (Schriften und Quellen der Alten Welt 13). Berlin: Akademie, 1963.

Krug, Antje. *Heilkunst und Heilkult: Medizin in der Antike*, 2nd ed. Munich: C. H. Beck, 1993.

Krüger, Thomas. *Ecclesiastes: A Commentary* (Hermeneia). Minneapolis: Fortress, 2004.

Küchler, Max. *Frühjüdische Weisheitstraditionen. Zum Fortgang weisheitlichen Denkens im Bereich des frühjüdischen Jahweglaubens* (OBO 26). Göttingen: Vandenhoeck & Ruprecht, 1979, 319-547.

Kugel, James L., and Rowan A. Greer. *Early Biblical Interpretation* (Library of Early Christianity 3). Philadelphia: Westminister, 1986.

Kuhnen, H.-P. *Palästina in griechisch-römischer Zeit* (*Handbuch der Archäologie, Vorderasien* 2/2). Munich: C. H. Beck, 1990.

Kuhrt, Amélie, and Susan Sherwin-White, eds. *Hellenism in the East. The Interaction of Greek and Non-Greek Civilizations from Syria to Central Asia after Alexander.* Berkeley: University of California, 1987.

Kuntz, J. Kenneth. "The Canonical Wisdom Psalms of Ancient Israel — Their Rhetorical, Thematic, and Formal Elements." *Rhetorical Criticism: Essays in Honor of James Muilenburg* (PTMS 1). Pittsburgh: Pickwick, 1974, 186-222.

Kurth, Dieter. *Maximen für Manager. Die Lehre des Ptahhotep.* Darmstadt: Primus Verlag, 1999.

Kvanvig, Helge S. *Roots of Apocalyptic. The Mesopotamian Background of the Enoch Figure and the Son of Man* (WMANT 61). Neukirchen-Vluyn: Neukirchener Verlag, 1987.

Lambert, W. G. "Ancestors, Authors, and Canonicity." *JCS* 11 (1957) 1-14.

Lambert, W. G. *The Background of Jewish Apocalyptic.* London: The Athlone Press, The University of London, 1978.

Lambert, W. G. "The Development of Thought and Literature in Ancient Mesopotamia," *Babylonian Wisdom Literature.* Winona Lake, IN: Eisenbrauns, 1996.

Lambert, W. G., and Alan R. Millard. *Atra-ḫasīs: The Babylonian Story of the Flood.* Oxford: Clarendon, 1969.

Landsberger, Benno. "Babylonian Scribal Craft and Its Terminology." *Abstract in the Proceedings of the 23rd Congress of Orientalists.* Cambridge: Cambridge University, 1954, 123-126.

Landsberger, Benno. "Scribal Concepts of Education." *City Invincible: A Symposium on Urbanization and Cultural Development in the Ancient Near East Held at the Oriental Institute of the University of Chicago, December 4-7, 1958*, ed. Carl H. Kraeling and Robert M. Adams. Chicago: University of Chicago, 1958, 94-123.

Lang, Bernhard. "Schule und Unterricht im alten Israel." *La Sagesse l'Ancien Testament*, new ed., ed. Maurice Gilbert (BETL 51). Leuven: Peeters, 1990, 186-201.

Lang, Bernhard. *Wisdom and the Book of Proverbs. A Hebrew Goddess Redefined.* New York: Pilgrim, 1986.

Lange, Armin. "The Essene Position on Magic and Divination." *Legal Texts and Legal Issues: Proceedings of the Second Meeting of the International Organization for Qumran Studies Cambridge 1995,* ed. M. Bernstein, Florentino García Martínez, and J. Kampen (STDJ 23). Leiden Brill, 1997, 377-435.

Lange, Armin. "Scribes and Sages in the Qumran Literature." *Scribes, Sages, and Seers* (FRLANT 210). Göttingen: Vandenhoeck & Ruprecht, forthcoming.

Lange, Armin. "Weisheitstexte aus Qumran: Eine Einleitung." *The Wisdom Texts from Qumran and the Development of Sapiential Thought,* ed. Charlotte Hempel, Armin Lange, and Hermann Lichtenberger (BETL 159). Leuven: Leuven University Press, 2002, 3-30.

Lange, Armin. *Weisheit und Prädestination: Weisheitliche Urordnung und Prädestination in den Textfunden von Qumran* (STDJ 18). Leiden: Brill, 1995.

Lanham, Richard A. *A Handlist of Rhetorical Terms,* 2nd ed. Berkeley: University of California, 1991.

Larcher, Chrysostome. *Études sur le Livre de la Sagesse* (Études Bibliques). Paris: J. Gabalda et Cie, 1969.

Lasserre, François. "Strabon devant l'Empire romain." *ANRW* 2 30/1. Berlin: Walter de Gruyter, 1982, 867-896.

Latte, Kurt. *Römische Religionsgeschichte,* 2nd ed. (HAW 5). Munich: Beck, 1992.

Lauha, Aarre. "Die Krise des Religiösen Glaubens bei Kohelet." *Wisdom in Israel and in the Ancient Near East,* ed. Martin Noth and D. Winton Thomas (VTSup 3). Leiden: Brill, 1955, 183-191.

Lauha, Aarre. *Kohelet* (BKAT 19). Neukirchen-Vluyn: Neukirchener, 1978.

Lausberg, Heinrich. *Handbook of Literary Rhetoric. Foundation for Literary Study.* Leiden: Brill, 1998.

Lecoq, Pierre. *Les inscriptions de la Perse achéménide.* Paris: Gallimard, 1997.

Lee, Thomas R. *Studies in the Form of Sirach 44–50* (SBLDS 75). Atlanta: Scholars Press, 1986.

Leeuwen, Raymond van. "Proverbs." *NIB* 5 (1997) 1-264.

Lehmann, Gunnar. *Untersuchungen zur späten Eisenzeit in Syrien und Libanon; Stratigraphie und Keramikformen zwischen ca. 720 bis 300 v. Chr.* (Altertumskunde des vorderen Orients 5). Münster: Ugarit-Verlag, 1996.

Lemaire. André. "Abécédaires et exercices d'écolier en épigraphie nord-ouest sémitique." *Journal Asiatique* 266 (1978) 222-235.

Lemaire, André. *Inscriptions hébraïques/introduction, traduction, commentaire* (Littératures anciennes du Proche-Orient 9). Paris: Cerf, 1977.

Lemaire, André. *Les écoles et la formation de la Bible dans l'ancien Israël.* Fribourg, Suisse: Editions universitaires, 1981.

Lerner, M. Bialik. "The External Tractates." *Literature of the Sages* (The Literature of the Jewish People in the Period of the Second Temple and the Talmud 3), ed. Shemuel Safrai. Philadelphia: Fortress Press, 1984, 369-379.

Lerner, M. Bialik. "The Tractate Avot." *Literature of the Sages* (The Literature of the Jewish People in the Period of the Second Temple and the Talmud 3), ed. Shemuel Safrai. Philadelphia: Fortress Press, 1984, 263-282.

Lesko, Leonhard H. "Some Comments on Ancient Egyptian Literacy and Literati." *Studies in Egyptology Presented to Miriam Lichtheim* 2, 2nd ed., ed. Sarah Israelit-Groll. Jerusalem: Magnes, 1990.

Levenson, Jon. *Creation and the Persistence of Evil. The Jewish Drama of Divine Omnipotence.* San Francisco: Harper & Row, 1988.

Levenson, Jon. "The Sources of Torah: Psalm 119 and the Modes of Revelation in Second Temple Judaism." *Ancient Israelite Religion,* ed. Patrick D. Miller, et al. Philadelphia: Fortress, 1987, 559-574.

Lévêque, Jean. *Job et son Dieu. Essai d'exégèse et de théologie biblique* 1. Paris: J. Gabalda, 1970.

Levine, Lee I. *The Ancient Synagogue. The First Thousand Years.* New Haven: Yale University, 2000.

Levine, Lee I. *Jerusalem. Portrait of the City in the Second Temple Period (538 B.C.E.–70 C.E.).* Philadelphia: The Jewish Publication Society, 2002.

Levine, Lee I. "The Jewish Patriarch (Nasi) in Third Century Palestine." *ANRW* 2 19/2. Berlin: Walter de Gruyter, 1979, 649-688.

Levine, Lee I. *Judaism and Hellenism in Antiquity: Conflict or Confluence?* Seattle: University of Washington, 1998.

Levine, Lee I. *The Rabbinic Class of Roman Palestine in Late Antiquity.* New York: Jewish Theological Seminary, 1989.

Levison, Jack. "Is Eve to Blame? A Contextual Analysis of Sirach 25:24." *CBQ* 47 (1985) 617-623.

Lichtheim, Miriam. *Ancient Egyptian Literature* 1 (Berkeley, CA: University of California, 1973); 2 (Berkeley, CA: University of California, 1976); 3 (Berkeley, CA: University of California, 1980).

Lichtheim, Miriam. "Didactic Literature." *Ancient Egyptian Literature. History and Forms,* ed. Antonio Loprieno. Leiden: E. J. Brill, 1996, 243-262.

Lichtheim, Mirian. *Late Egyptian Wisdom Literature in the International Context* (OBO 52). Göttingen: Vandenhoeck & Ruprecht, 1983.

Liddell, H. G., and R. Scott. *Greek-English Lexicon,* 9th ed. with Revised Supplement. Oxford: Oxford University Press, 1996.

Lieberman, Saul. *Greek in Jewish Palestine.* New York: Feldheim, 1965.

Liesen, Jan. *Full of Praise. An Exegetical Study of Sir 39,12-35* (Supplements to the Journal for the Study of Jerusalem). Leiden: Brill, 2000.

Lindenberger, James M. *The Aramaic Proverbs of Ahiqar.* Baltimore: Johns Hopkins University Press, 1983.

Lipiński, Edward. "Royal and State Scribes in Ancient Jerusalem." *Congress Volume Jerusalem, 1986,* ed. J. Emerton (VTSup 40). Leiden: Brill, 1988, 189-199.

Lipschits, Oded, and Joseph Blenkinsopp, eds. *Judah and the Judeans in the Neo-Babylonian Period.* Winona Lake, IN: Eisenbrauns, 2003.

Lohfink, Nobert. *Qoheleth. A Continental Commentary.* Minneapolis: Fortress, 2003.

Lohfink, Norbert. "Qoheleth 5:17-19 — Revelation by Joy." *CBQ* 52 (1990) 625-635.

Long, A. A. *Hellenistic Philosophy. Stoics, Epicureans, Sceptics,* 2nd ed. Berkeley, CA: University of California, 1986.

Long, A. A., and D. N. Sedley. *The Hellenistic Philosophers.* New York: Cambridge University, 1987.

Loprieno, Antonio. "Loyalistic Instructions." *Ancient Egyptian Literature. History and Forms,* ed. Antonio Loprieno. Leiden: E. J. Brill, 1996, 403-414.

Loprieno, Antonio, ed. *Ancient Egyptian Literature. History and Forms.* Leiden: E. J. Brill, 1996.

Loretz, Oswald. *Psalmenstudien: Kolometrie, Strophik und Theologie* (BZAW 309). Berlin: Walter de Gruyter, 2002.

Loretz, Oswald. *Qohelet und der alte Orient. Untersuchungen zu Stil und theologischer Thematik des Buches Qohelet.* Freiburg: University, 1964.

Lüderwitz, G. "What Is the Politeuma?" *Studies in Early Jewish Epigraphy,* ed. J. W. Van Henten and P. W. Van der Horst. Leiden: Brill, 1994, 183-225.

Maag, Victor. *Hiob. Wandlung und Verarbeitung des Problems in Novelle, Dialogdictung und Spätfassungen* (FRLANT 128). Göttingen: Vandenhoeck und Ruprecht, 1982.

Mack, Burton L. *Logos und Sophia: Untersuchungen zur Weisheitstheologie im hellenistischen Judentum* (SUNT 10). Göttingen: Vandenhoeck & Ruprecht, 1973.

Mack, Burton. *Wisdom and the Hebrew Epic: Ben Sira's Hymn in Praise of the Fathers* (Chicago Studies in the History of Judaism). Chicago: University of Chicago, 1985.

Mack-Fisher, Loren. "The Scribe (and Sage) in the Royal Court at Ugarit." *The Sage in Israel and the Ancient Near East,* ed. John G. Gammie and Leo G. Perdue. Winona Lake, IN: Eisenbrauns, 1990, 109-115.

Mack-Fisher, Loren. "A Survey and Reading Guide to the Didactic Literature of Ugarit: A Study on the Sage." *The Sage in Israel and the Ancient Near East,* ed. John G. Gammie and Leo G. Perdue. Winona Lake, IN: Eisenbrauns, 1990, 67-80.

Magness, Jodi. *The Archaeology of Qumran and the Dead Sea Scrolls* (Studies in the Dead Sea Scrolls and Related Literature). Grand Rapids: Eerdmans, 2002.

Maier, Christl. *Die 'fremde Frau' in Proverbien 1–9* (OBO 144). Göttingen: Vandenhoeck & Ruprecht, 1995.

Mantel, Hugo. "The Nature of the Great Synagogue." *World History of the Jewish People* 8, ed. Michael Avi-Yonah and Zvi Barras. New Brunswick: Rutgers University, 1977, 44-52.

Marböck, Johannes. "Der Hohepriester Simon in Sir 50. Ein Beitrag zur Bedeutung von Priestertum und Kult im Sirachbuch." *The Book of Ben Sira in Modern Research,* ed. P. C. Beentjes (BZAW 255). Berlin: Walter de Gruyter, 1997, 215-229.

Marböck, Johannes. "Kohelet und Sirach." *Das Buch Kohelet,* ed. Ludger Schwienhorst-Schönberger (BZAW 254). Berlin: Walter de Gruyter, 1995, 275-301.

Marböck, Johannes. "Structure and Redaction History of the Book of Ben Sira. Review and Prospects." *The Book of Ben Sira in Modern Research,* ed. P. C. Beentjes (BZAW 255). Berlin: Walter de Gruyter, 1997, 62-79.

Marböck, Johannes. *Weisheit im Wandel: Untersuchungen zur Weisheitstheologie bei Ben Sira* (BZAW 272). Berlin: Walter de Gruyter, 1999.

Marrou, H. I. *A History of Education in Antiquity.* New York: Sheed & Ward, 1956.

Martin, Luther H. *Hellenistic Religions,* 2nd ed. New York: Oxford University, 1987.

Martínez, Florentino García. "Qumran Origins and Early History: A Groningen Hypothesis." *Folia orientalia* 25 (1988) 113-136.

Martínez, Florentino García, and Julio Trebolle Barrera. *The People of the Dead Sea Scrolls.* Leiden: Brill, 1995.

Martínez, Florentino García, ed. *Wisdom and Apocalypticism in the Dead Sea Scrolls and in the Biblical Tradition* (BETL 168) Leuven: University Press, 2003.

Martínez, Florentino, García, and Eibert J. C. Tigchelaar, eds. *The Dead Sea Scrolls: Study Edition* 1 & 2. Leiden: Brill, 1997.

Mason, Steve. *Josephus and the New Testament,* 2nd ed. Peabody, MA: Hendrickson Publishers, 2003.

Mattila, S. L. "Ben Sira and the Stoics: A Reexamination of the Evidence." *JBL* 119 (2000) 473-501.

Mazar, Eilat. *Excavations in the South of the Temple Mount: The Ophel of Biblical Jerusalem* 1. Jerusalem: Hebrew University, 1989.

McCann, J. Clinton. "Wisdom's Dilemma: The Book of Job, the Final Form of the Book of Psalms, and the Entire Bible." *Wisdom, You Are My Sister,* ed. Michael L. Barré (CBQ 20). Washington, DC: Biblical Quarterly of America, 19-30.

McCurley, Foster. *Ancient Myths and Biblical Faith. Scriptural Transformation.* Philadelphia: Fortress, 1983.

McDowell, A. G. "Teachers and Students at Deir el-Medina." *Deir el-Medina in the Third Millennium AD. A Tribute to Jac. J. Janssen,* ed. R. J. Demarée and A. Egberts. Leiden: Nederlands Instituut voor het Nabije Oosten, 2000, 217-233.

McKane, William. *Prophets and Wise Men.* London: SCM, 1965.

McNutt, Paula M. *Reconstructing the Society of Ancient Israel* (Library of Ancient Israel). Louisville: Westminster/John Knox, 1999.

Mendelson, Alan. *Philo's Jewish Identity* (BJS 161). Atlanta: Scholars, 1988.

Mendelson, Alan. *Secular Education in Philo of Alexandria.* Cincinnati: Hebrew Union College, 1982.

Menu, Bernadette. "Les carrières des Egyptiens à l'étranger sous les dominations perses: les critères de justification, leur évolution et leurs limites." *Transeuphratène* 9 (1995) 81-90.

Merkelbach, Reinhold. *Isis Regina — Zeus Sarapis: Die griechisch-ägyptische Religion nach den Quellen dargestellt.* Stuttgart: Teubner, 1995.

Meshorer, Ya'akov. *Jewish Coins of the Second Temple Period.* Chicago: Argonaut, 1967.

Mettinger, T. N. G. *State Officials: A Study of the Civil Government Officials of the Israelite Monarchy.* Lund: CWK Gleerup, 1971.

Meyer, Eduard. "Alexander der Grosse und die absolute Monarchie." *Kleine Schriften,* 2nd ed. Halle: M. Niemeyer, 1924, 265-314.

Michalowski, Piotr. "Adapa and the Ritual Process." *Rocznik Orientalistyczny* 41 (1980) 77-82.

Michel, Diethelm. *Untersuchungen zur Eigenart des Buches Qohelet. Mit einem Anhang: Reinhard Lehmann, Bibliographie zu Qohelet* (BZAW 183). Berlin: Walter de Gruyter, 1989.

Middendorp, Theophil. *Die Stellung Jesu Ben Siras zwischen Judentum und Hellenismus.* Leiden: E. J. Brill, 1973.

Milikowsky, Chaim. "Aggadah." *The Oxford Dictionary of the Jewish Religion,* ed. R. J. Zwi Werblowsky and Geoffrey Wigoder. New York: Oxford University Press, 23-24.

Millar, Fergus. "The Background to the Maccabean Revolution: Reflections on Martin Hengel's 'Judaism and Hellenism.'" *JJS* 29 (1978) 1-21.

Millar, Fergus. *The Roman Near East, 31 B.C. to A.D. 337.* Cambridge: Harvard University, 1993.

Miller, Douglas B. *Symbol and Rhetoric in Ecclesiastes: The Place of Hebel in Qohelet's Work* (Academia Biblica 2). Atlanta: Society of Biblical Literature, 2002.

Miller, Stephen G., ed. *Arete: Ancient Writers, Papyri, and Inscriptions on the History and Ideals of Greek Athletics and Games,* 3rd exp. ed. Berkeley, CA: University of California, 2004.

"Mishnah." *The Literature of the Sages* (The Literature of the Jewish People in the Period of the Second Temple and the Talmud 3), ed. Shemuel Safrai. Philadelphia: Fortress Press, 1984.

Mitchell, Thomas N. *Cicero, the Ascending Years.* New Haven: Yale University, 1979.

Mitchell, Thomas N. *Cicero, the Senior Statesman.* New Haven: Yale University, 1991.

Mitsis, Phillip. *Epicurus' Ethical Theory: The Pleasures of Invulnerability.* Ithaca, NY: Cornell University, 1988.

Modrzejewski, J. M. *The Jews of Egypt: From Rameses II to Emperor Hadrian.* Princeton: Princeton University, 1995.

Momigliano, Arnaldo. *Alien Wisdom: The Limits of Hellenization.* Cambridge: Cambridge University, 1975.

Moran, W. L. "Some Considerations of Form and Interpretation in Atra-ḫasis." *Language, Literature, and History. Philological and Historical Studies Presented to Erica Reiner,* ed. Francesca Rochberg-Halton. New Haven: American Oriental Society, 1987, 245-255.

Morenz, Siegfried. *Ägyptische Religion.* Stuttgart: W. Kohlhammer, 1960.

Morgan, Teresa. *Literate Education in the Hellenistic and Roman Worlds* (Cambridge Classical Studies). Cambridge: Cambridge University, 1998.

Mowinckel, Sigmund. "Psalms and Wisdom." *Wisdom in Israel and in the Ancient Near East,* ed. Martin Noth and D. Winton Thomas (VTSup 3). Leiden: Brill, 1955, 205-224.

Mowinckel, Sigmund. "Traditionalism and Personality in Psalms." *HUCA* 23 (1950/51) 205-301.

Müller, Achim. *Proverbien 1–9* (BZAW 291). Berlin: Walter de Gruyter, 2000.

Müller, Hans-Peter. *Babylonien und Israel: historische, religiöse und sprachliche Beziehungen.* Darmstadt: Wissenschaftliche Buchgesellschaft, 1991.

Müller, Hans-Peter. "Der Begriff 'Rätsel' im Alten Testament." *VT* 20 (1970) 465-489.

Müller, Hans-Peter. "Die weisheitliche Lehrerzählung im Alten Testament und seiner Umwelt." *WO* 9 (1977) 77-98.

Müller, Hans-Peter. "Magisch-mantische Weisheit und die Gestalt Daniels." *UF* 1 (1969) 79-94.

Müller, Hans-Peter. "Mantische Weisheit und Apokalyptik." *Congress Volume: Uppsala 1971* (VTSup 22). Leiden: Brill, 1972, 268-293.

Müller, Hans-Peter. "Neige der althebräischen 'Weisheit.' Zum Denken Qohäläts." *ZAW* 90 (1978) 238-264.

Müller, Hans-Peter. "Plausibilitätsverlust herkömmlicher Religion bei Kohelet und den Vorsokratikern." *Gemeinde ohne Tempel Community,* ed. Beate Ego, Armin Lange, und Peter Pilhofer (WUNT 118). Tübingen: Mohr Siebeck, 1999, 99-113.

Müller, Nikolaus. *Die Inschriften der jüdischen Katakombe am Monteverde zu Rom* (Gesellschaft zur Förderung des Wissenschaft des Judentums; Schriften). Leipzig: Gustav Fock, 1919.

Muri, Walter. *Der Arzt im Altertum: griechische und lateinische Quellenstücke von Hippokrates bis Galen* (Tusculum Bücherie). Munich: Heimeran, 1979.

Murphy, Roland. "A Consideration of the Classification 'Wisdom Psalms.'" *VTSup* 9 (1963) 156-167.

Murphy, Roland. "The Faith of Qoheleth." *Word & World* 7 (1987) 253-260.

Murphy, Roland. "On Translating Ecclesiastes." *CBQ* 53 (1991) 573.

Murphy, Roland. "The Sage in Ecclesiastes and Qoheleth the Sage." *The Sage in Israel and the Ancient Near East,* ed. John G. Gammie and Leo G. Perdue. Winona Lake, IN: Eisenbrauns, 1990, 263-271.

Murphy, Roland. "Wisdom and Yahwism." *No Famine in the Land. Studies in Honor of John L. McKenzie,* ed. James W. Flanagan and Anita Weisbrod Robinson. Missoula: Scholars for the Institute of Antiquity and Christianity, Claremont, 1975, 117-126.

Murphy, Roland. "Wisdom's Song: Proverbs 1:20-33." *CBQ* 48 (1986) 456-460.

Murphy, Roland. *Wisdom Literature* (FOTL 13). Grand Rapids: W. B. Eerdmans, 1981.

Murray, Oswyn. "The Greek Symposium in History." *Tria Corda. Scritti in onore di Arnaldo Momigliano,* ed. Emilio Gabba. Como: Edizioni New, 1983.

Murray, Oswyn. "The Symposium as Social Organisation." *The Greek Renaissance of the Eighth Century B.C.: Tradition and Innovation,* ed. Robin Hägg and N. Marinatos. Stockholm: Svenska institutet i Athen, 1983, 195-199.

Murray, Oswyn, ed. *Sympotica. A Symposium on the Symposion.* Oxford: Clarendon, 1994.

Mussies, Gerard. "Greek in Palestine and the Diaspora." *The Jewish People in the First Century,* ed. Shemuel Safrai and Menahem Stern in cooperation with David Flusser and W. C. van Unnik (CRINT 2). Philadelphia: Fortress Press, 1976, 1040-1064.

Nel, Philip J. "Authority in the Wisdom Admonitions." *ZAW* 93 (1981) 418-426.

Nelson, W. David. *Mekhilta De-rabbi Shimon Bar Yohai* (Edward E. Elson Classic). New York: JPS, 2006.

Nestle, Wilhelm. "Der Pessimismus and sein Überwindung bei den Griechen." *Neues Jahrbuch für die klassiche Altertumswissenschaft* 24 (1921) 81-97.

Netzer, Ehud. "A Synagogue from the Hasmonean Period Recently Exposed in the Western Plain of Jericho." *IEJ* 49 (1999) 203-221.

Neusner, Jacob. *Early Rabbinic Judaism.* Leiden: Brill, 1975.

Neusner, Jacob. "The Formation of Rabbinic Judaism: Yavneh (Jamnia) from A.D. 70 to 100." *ANRW* 2 19/2. Berlin: Walter de Gruyter, 1979, 3-42.

Neusner, Jacob. *Introduction to Rabbinic Judaism* (ABRL). New York: Doubleday, 1994.

Neusner, Jacob. *Jerusalem and Athens: The Congruity of Talmudic and Classical Philosophy* (JSJSup 52). Leiden: Brill, 1997.

Neusner, Jacob. *Judaism as Philosophy. The Method and Message of the Mishnah.* Columbia, SC: University of South Carolina, 1991.

Neusner, Jacob. *Judaism. The Evidence of the Mishnah,* 2nd ed. (BJS 129). Atlanta, 1988.

Neusner, Jacob. *Mikhilta Attributed to R. Ishmael. An Introduction to Judaism's First Scriptural Encylopedia.* Atlanta: Scholars for Brown Judaic Studies, 1988.

Neusner, Jacob. *The Mishnah: An Introduction.* London: Jason Aronson Inc., 1989.

Neusner, Jacob. *Torah from Our Sages: Pirke Avot. A New American Translation and Explanation.* Chappaqua, NY: Rossel/Behrman House, 1983.

Neusner, Jacob. *The Tosefta: An Introduction.* Atlanta: Scholars Press, 1992.

Newsom, Carol. "The Book of Job." *NIB* 4 (1996) 317-637.

Newsom, Carol A. "Woman and the Discourse of Patriarchal Wisdom: A Study of Proverbs 1–9." *Gender and Difference in Ancient Israel,* ed. Peggy L. Day. Minneapolis: Fortress, 1989, 142-160.

Nickelsburg, George W. E. "Enochic Wisdom: An Alternative to the Mosaic Torah?" *Hesed Ve-Emet, Studies in Honor of Ernest S. Frerichs,* ed. Jodi Magness and Seymour Gitten (BJS 320). Atlanta: Scholars Press, 1998, 123-132.

Nickelsburg, George W. E. "Stories of Biblical and Early Post-Biblical Times." Jewish Writings of the Second Temple Period. Apocrypha, Pseudepigrapha, Qumran Sectarian Writings, Philo, Josephus (CRINT 2), ed. M. E. Stone. Philadelphia: Fortress Press, 1984, 33-87.

Niehoff, M. R. *Philo on Jewish Identity and Culture.* Tübingen: Mohr Siebeck, 2001.

Nilsson, Martin P. *Geschichte der griechischen Religion* 2, 3rd ed. (HAW 5/2.1-2). Munich: Beck, 1977.

Nilsson, Martin P. *Die hellenistiche Schule.* Munich: C. H. Beck, 1955.

Nordheim, Eckhard von. *Die Lehre der Alten* 1 and 2 (Arbeiten zum Literatur und Geschichte des Hellenistischen Judentum 13). Leiden: Brill, 1980.

Nordheim, Eckhard von. *Die Lehre der Alten* 1: *Das Testament als Literaturgattung im Judentum der Hellenistisch-Römischen Zeit.* Leiden: Brill, 1980.

Nordheim, Eckhard von. *Die Lehre der Alten* 2: *Das Testament als Literaturgattung im Alten Testament und im Alten Vorderen Orient.* Leiden: Brill, 1985.

Nougayrol, Jean. "(Juste) Souffrant." *Ugaritica* 5, ed. C. F. A. Schaeffer (Mission de Ras Shamra 16). Paris: Imprimerie Nationale, 1968, 265-273.

Nougayrol, Jean. *Le palais royal d'Ugarit* 3 (Paris: Imprimerie National, 1955); Vol. 4 (1956); and Vol. 6 (1970).

Nougayrol, Jean. "L'influence babylonienne à Ugarit, d'après les textes en cunéiformes classiques." *Syria* (1962) 28-35.

Nougayrol, Jean. "Tablette bilingue accado-hourite." *Le palais royal d'Ugarit* 3 (Paris: Imprimerie Nationale, 1955, 311-324.

Obbink, Dirk, ed. *Philodemus and Poetry. Poetic Theory and Practice in Lucretius. Philodemus and Horace.* Oxford: Oxford University Press, 1995.

Oded, Bustenay. "Judah and the Exile." *Israelite and Judaean History,* ed. John Hayes and Maxwell Miller. Philadelphia, PA: Westminster, 1977, 435-486.

Oded, Bustenay. "Observations on the Israelite/Judaean Exiles in Mesopotamia during the Eighth-Sixth Centuries B.C.E." *Immigration and Emigration within the Ancient Near East,* ed. Karel van Lerberghe and Antoon Schoors (OLA 65). Leuven: Peeters, 1995, 205-212.

Ogden, Graham. *Qoheleth.* Sheffield: Almond, 1987.

Olivier, J. P. J. "Schools and Wisdom Literature." *Journal of Northwest Semitic Languages* 4 (1975) 49-60.

Oppenheim, A. Leo. *Ancient Mesopotamia: Portrait of a Dead Civilization,* rev. ed., ed. Erica Reiner. Chicago: University of Chicago Press, 1996.

Oppenheim, A. Leo. *The Interpretation of Dreams in the Ancient Near East.* Philadelphia: The American Philosophical Society, 1956.

Oppenheim, A. Leo. "Mantic Dreams in the Ancient Near East." *The Dream and Human Societies,* ed. Gustave Edmund von Grünebaum and Roger Caillois. Berkeley, CA: University of California, 1966.

Oppenheim, A. Leo. "The Position of the Intellectual in Mesopotamian Society." *Daedalus* 104 (1975).

Ostwald, Martin, and J. P. Lynch. *Cambridge Ancient History* 6, 2d. ed. Cambridge: Cambridge University, 1994.

Otto, Eberhard. "Bildung und Ausbildung in Alten Ägypten." *ZÄS* 8 (1956) 41-48.

Otto, Eberhard. *Der Vorwurf an Gott; zur Entstehung der ägyptischen Auseinandersetzungsliteratur* (Vorträge der orientalistischen Tagung im Marburg. Fachgruppe: Ägyptologie). Hildesheim: Gerstenberg, 1951.

Otto, Eberhard. "Monotheistische Tendenzen in der ägyptischen Religion." *Die Welt des Orients* 2/2 Göttingen: Vandenhoeck & Ruprecht, 1955, 99-110.

Otzen, Benedikt. "Old Testament Wisdom Literature and Dualistic Thinking in Late Judaism." *Congress Volume: Edinburgh 1974* (VTSup 28). Leiden: Brill, 1975, 146-157.

Parke, H. W. *Sibyls and Sibylline Prophecy in Classical Antiquity,* ed. B. C. McGing. London: Routledge, 1988.

Parkinson, R. B. "Teachings, Discourses and Tales from the Middle Kingdom." *Middle Kingdom Studies,* ed. Stephen Quirke. New Malden, Surrey: SIA, 1991.

Parpola, Simo. *Letters from Assyrian Scholars to the Kings Esarhaddon and Assurbanipal*

1-2 (Alter Orient und Altes Testament 5). Neukirchen-Vluyn: Neukirchener Verlag, 1970-1983.

Paul, André. "Le Troisième livre des Macchabées." *ANRW* 2. 20/1. Berlin: Walter de Gruyter, 1987, 298-336.

Paul, Shalom. "Deutero-Isaiah and Cuneiform Royal Inscriptions." *JAOS* 88 (1968) 180-186.

Pautrel, Raymond. "Ben Sira et le Stoïcisme." *RSR* 51 (1963) 535-549.

Pedersen, Johannes. "Wisdom and Immortality." *Wisdom in Israel and in the Ancient Near East,* ed. Martin Noth and D. Winton Thomas (VTSup 3). Leiden: Brill, 1955, 238-246.

Pélékidis, Chrysis. *Histoire de l'Éphebie Attique dès Origines à 31 avant Jésus Christ.* Paris: Boccard, 1962.

Perdue, Leo G. "Ben Sirah and the Prophets." *Intertextual Studies in Ben Sira and Tobit: Essays in Honor of Alexander A. Di Lella, O.F.M.,* ed. Jeremy Corley and Vincent Skemp (CBQMS 38). Washington, DC: Catholic Biblical Association of America, 2005, 132-154.

Perdue, Leo G. "Cosmology and the Social Order." *The Sage in Israel and the Ancient Near East.* Winona Lake, IN: Eisenbrauns, 1990, 457-478.

Perdue, Leo G. "The Mantic Sage in Ancient Near Eastern Wisdom." *The Contribution of the Dead Sea Scrolls towards Understanding Prophecy in the Hebrew Bible,* ed. Kristin Troyer and Armin Lange. Leuven: Leuven University Press, forthcoming.

Perdue, Leo G. "Paraenesis and the Death of the Sage." *Paraenesis: Act and Form,* ed. John G. Gammie and Leo G. Perdue. *Semeia* 50 (1990) 81-109.

Perdue, Leo G. "The Riddles of Psalm 49." *JBL* 93 (1974) 533-542.

Perdue, Leo G. "The Testament of David and Egyptian Royal Instructions." *Scripture in Context* 2, ed. William W. Hallo, James M. Moyer, and Leo G. Perdue. Winona Lake, IN: Eisenbrauns, 1983, 79-96.

Perdue, Leo G. "Wisdom and Apocalyptic: The Case of Qoheleth." *Wisdom and Apocalypticism in the Dead Sea Scrolls and in the Biblical Tradition,* ed. Florentino García Martínez (BETL 168). Leuven: University Press, 2003, 231-258.

Perdue, Leo G. *Wisdom and Creation. The Theology of Wisdom Literature.* Nashville, TN: Abingdon, 1994.

Perdue, Leo G. *Wisdom and Cult. A Critical Analysis of the Views of Cult in the Wisdom Literatures of Israel and the Ancient Near East* (SBLDS 30). Missoula, MT: Scholars, 1977.

Perdue, Leo G. *Wisdom in Revolt* (JSOTSup 112). Sheffield: Almond, 1991.

Perdue, Leo G. "Wisdom in the Book of Job." *In Search of Wisdom,* ed. Leo G. Perdue, et al. Louisville: Westminster/John Knox, 1993, 73-80.

Perdue, Leo G., ed. *Scribes, Sages, and Seers* (FRLANT 210). Göttingen: Vandenhoeck & Ruprecht, 2008.

Perdue, Leo G., et al. *Families in Ancient Israel.* Louisville: Westminster/John Knox, 1997.

Peres, Imre. *Griechische Grabinschriften und neutestamentliche Eschatologie* (WUNT 157). Tübingen: Mohr Siebeck, 2003.

Pisani, Giuliano. *Plutarco, L'educazione.* Pordenone: Edizioni Biblioteca dell'Imagine, 1994.

Pohlmann, Karl-Friedrich. "Religion in der Krise — Krise der Religion. Die Zerstörung des Jerusalemer Tempels 587 v. Chr." *Zerstörungen des Jerusalemer Tempels. Geschehen — Wahrnehmung — Bewältigung,* ed. Johannes Hahn. Tübingen: Mohr-Siebeck, 2002, 40-60.

Pomeroy, Susan. *Women in Hellenistic Egypt.* New York: Schocken, 1984.

Pomponio, Francesco, and Ursala Seidl. "Nabû." *Reallexikon der Assyriologie und vorderasiatischen Archäologie* 9. Berlin: Walter de Gruyter, 1998, 16-29.

Pope, Marvin H. *Job,* 3rd ed. (AB 15). Garden City, NY: Doubleday, 1973.

Porten, Bezalel. *Archives from Elephantine. The Life of an Ancient Jewish Military Colony.* Berkeley, CA: University of California, 1968.

Porten, Bezalel, and Ada Yardeni. *Textbook of Aramaic Documents from Ancient Egypt* III. *Literature, Accounts, Lists.* Jerusalem: Hebrew University Press, 1993.

Porter, Stanley E., ed. *Handbook of Classical Rhetoric in the Hellenistic Period, 330 B.C.–A.D. 400.* Leiden: Brill, 1997.

Posener, Georges. *L'enseignement loyaliste: Sagesse égyptienne du Moyen Empire* (Hautes Études Orientales 5). Geneva: Droz, 1976.

Posener, Gerhard. *Littérature et politique dans l'Égypte de la XIIᵉ dynastie* (Bibliothèque de l'École des Hautes Études 307). Paris: Librairie Ancienne Honoré Champion, 1956.

Press, R. "Das Ordal im alten Israel." *ZAW* 10 (1933) 121-140, 227-250.

Price, S. R. F. *Rituals and Power: The Roman Imperial Cult in Asia Minor.* Cambridge: Cambridge University Press, 1984.

Pritchard, J. B., ed. *Ancient Near Eastern Texts,* 3rd ed. Princeton, NJ: Princeton University, 1969.

Quack, J. F. *Die Lehren des Ani: ein neuägyptischer Weisheitstext in seinem kulturellen Umfeld* (OBO 141). Göttingen: Vandenhoeck & Ruprecht, 1994.

Quack, J. F. *Studien zur Lehre für Merikare* (Göttinger Orientforschungen. Reihe 4, Aegypten 23). Wiesbaden: Harrassowitz, 1992.

Rad, Gerhard von. "Job XXXVIII and Ancient Egyptian Wisdom." *Studies in Ancient Israelite Wisdom,* ed. James L. Crenshaw (The Library of Biblical Studies). New York: Ktav, 1976, 267-291.

Rad, Gerhard von. *Theology of the Old Testament* 1 & 2. New York: Harper and Row, 1962, 1965.

Rad, Gerhard von. *Wisdom in Israel.* Nashville: Abingdon, 1972.

Rainey, Anson. "The Scribe at Ugarit: His Position and Influence." *Proceedings of the Israel Academy of Sciences and Humanities* 3 (1969) 126-146.

Ranston, Harry. *Ecclesiastes and the Early Greek Wisdom Literature.* London: Epworth, 1925.

Reese, J. M. *Hellenistic Influence on the Book of Wisdom and Its Consequences* (AnBib 41). Rome: Pontifical Biblical Institute, 1970.

Reese, James M. "Plan and Structure in the Book of Wisdom." *CBQ* 27 (1965) 391-399.

Reiner, Erica. "The Babylonian *Fürstenspiegel* in Practice." *Societies and Languages of the Ancient Near East. Studies in Honour of I. M. Diakonoff.* Warminster, England: Aris & Phillips, 1982, 320-326.

Reiner, Erica. "The Etiological Myth of the Seven Sages." *Or* 30 (1961) 1-11.

Reinink, G. J., and H. L. J. Vanstiphout, eds. *Dispute Poems and Dialogues in the Ancient and Mediaeval Near East. Forms and Types of Literary Debates in Semitic and Related Literatures* (OLA 42). Leuven: Department Oriëntalistiek: Uitgeverij Peeters, 1991.

Reitemeyer, Michael. *Weisheitslehre als Gotteslob. Psalmentheologie im Buch Jesus Sirach* (BBB 127). Berlin: Philo, 2000.

Reiterer, Friedrich V. *Zählsynopse zum Buch Ben Sira* (Fontes et Subsidia ad Bibliam pertinentes 1). Berlin: Walter de Gruyter, 2003.

Rendtorff, Rolff. "Noch einmal: Esra und das "Gesetz." *ZAW* 111 (1999) 228-235.

Reventlow, Henning Graf. *Die Epochen der Bibelauslegung* 1. Munich: C. H. Beck, 1990.

Richardson, Peter. *Building Jewish in the Roman East.* JSJSup 92; Leiden: Brill, 2004.

Richter, Heinz. *Studien zu Hiob* (Theologische Arbeiten 11). Berlin: Evangelische Verlaganstalt, 1955.

Ricoeur, Paul. "Biblical Hermeneutics." *Semeia* 4 (1975) 129-146.

Ricoeur, Paul. "The Narrative Function." *Semeia* 4 (1975) 177-202.

Ringgren, Helmer. *Sprüche*, 2nd ed. (ATD 16). Göttingen: Vandenhoeck & Ruprecht, 1981.

Rist, John M. *Stoic Philosophy.* Cambridge: Cambridge University, 1977.

Rist, John M., ed., *The Stoics.* Berkeley: University of California, 1978.

Robert, André. "Le psaume CXIX et les Sapientiaux." *RB* 48 (1939) 5-20.

Robert, Louis. "Un Corpus des Inscriptions Juives." *REJ* 101 (1937) 73-86.

Robertson, R. G. "Ezekiel the Tragedian." *The Old Testament Pseudepigrapha* 2. *Expansions of the "Old Testament" and Legends, Wisdom and Philosophical Literature, Prayers, Psalms, and Odes, Fragments of Lost Judeo-Hellenistic Works* (ABRL), ed. James H. Charlesworth. New York: Doubleday, 1985, 803-807.

Robins, Gay. *Women in Ancient Egypt.* London: British Museum, 1993.

Robinson, James M. "Jesus as Sophos and Sophia." *Aspects of Wisdom in Judaism and Early Christianity*, ed. Robert L. Wilken (University of Notre Dame Center for the Study of Judaism and Christianity in Antiquity 1). Notre Dame, IN: University of Notre Dame, 1975) 1-16.

Rofé, Alexander. "Revealed Wisdom: From the Bible to Qumran," *Sapiential Perspectives. Wisdom Literature in Light of the Dead Sea Scrolls* (STDJ 51), ed. John J. Collins, et al. Leiden: Brill, 2004.

Römer, W. H. Ph. "Aus einem Schulstreitgespräche." *UF* 20 (1988) 233-245.

Rosengarten, Yvonne. "Le nom et la function de 'sage' dans les practiques religieuses de Sumer et d'Akkad." *RHR* 162 (1962) 133-146.

Rostovtzeff, Mikhail Ivanovich. *The Social & Economic History of the Hellenistic World.* 3 vols. Oxford: At the Clarendon, 1941.

Roth-Gerson, Lea. *The Greek Inscriptions from the Synagogue in Eretz-Israel.* Jerusalem: Yad Izhak Ben Zvi, 1987.

Rowe, Ignacio Márquez. "Scribes, Sages, and Seers in Ugarit." *Scribes, Sages, and Seers* (FRLANT 210). Göttingen, forthcoming.

Rudd, Niall. *The Satires of Horace*, 2nd ed. Berkeley: University of California, 1982.

Rudd, Niall. *Themes in Roman Satire*. Bristol: Bristol Classical, 1998.

Ruffle, Jeffry. "The Teaching of Amenemope and Its Connection with the Book of Proverbs." *TB* 28 (1977) 29-68.

Rüger, Hans-Peter. *Text und Textform im hebräischen Sirach* (BZAW 112). Berlin: Walter de Gruyter, 1970.

Russell, Donald Andrew Frank Moore. "Progymnasmata." *Oxford Classical Dictionary*, 3rd rev. ed., ed. Simon Hornblower and Antony Stallworth. Oxford: Oxford University Press, 2003, 1253.

Russell, Donald Andrew Frank Moore. "Rhetoric, Greek." *Oxford Classical Dictionary*, 3rd rev. ed., ed. Simon Hornblower and Antony Stallworth. Oxford: Oxford University Press, 2003, 1312-1314.

Russell, D. A., and N. G. Wilson, eds. *Menander Rhetor*. Oxford: The Clarendon, 1981.

Russell, D. S. *Divine Disclosure: An Introduction to Jewish Apocalyptic*. Minneapolis: Fortress, 1992.

Russell, D. S. *The Method and Message of Apocalypticism, 200 B.C. to A.D. 100* (OTL). Philadelphia: Westminister, 1964.

Safrai, Shemuel. "Education and the Study of the Torah." *The Jewish People in the First Century*, ed. Shemuel Safrai and Menahem Stern in cooperation with David Flusser and W. C. van Unnik (CRINT 2). Philadelphia: Fortress Press, 1976, 947-948.

Safrai, Shemuel. "Jewish Self Government." *The Jewish People in the First Century* 2, ed. Shemuel Safrai and Menahem Stern in cooperation with David Flusser and W. C. van Unnik (CRINT 2). Philadelphia: Fortress, 1976, 377-392.

Safrai, Shemuel. "The Synagogue." *The Jewish People in the First Century* 2, ed. Shemuel Safrai and Menahem Stern in cooperation with David Flusser and W. C. van Unnik (CRINT 2). Philadelphia: Fortress, 1976, 908-944.

Saldarini, A. J. *The Fathers According to Rabbi Nathan (Abot de Rabbi Nathan) Version B; A Translation and Commentary*. Leiden: E. J. Brill, 1975.

Sander-Hansen, Constintin Emil. *Die Texte der Metternichtstele* (Analecta Aegyptiaca 7). Copenhagen: E. Munksgaard, 1956.

Sanders, E. P. *Judaism: Practice & Belief 63 BCE–66 CE*. London: SCM, 1992.

Sanders, James A. *The Psalms Scroll of Cave 11* (DJD 4). Oxford: Clarendon, 1965.

Sanders, J. T. *Ben Sira and Demotic Wisdom*. Chico, CA: Scholars, 1983.

Sandmel, Samuel. "Philo Judaeus: An Introduction to the Man, His Writings, and His Significance." *Aufstieg und Niedergang* 21/1. 2. Berlin: Walter de Gruyter, 1984, 3-46.

Sarna, Nahum. "Epic Substratum in the Prose of Job." *JBL* 76 (1957) 13-25.

Sauer, Georg. "Gedanken über den thematischen Aufbau des Buches Ben Sira." *Treasures of Wisdom. Studies in Ben Sira and the Book of Wisdom. FS Maurice Gilbert*, ed. Núria Calduch-Benages and Jacques Vermeylen (BETL 143). Leuven: University, 1999, 51-61.

Schaeder, Hans Heinrich. *Ezra der Schreiber*. Tübingen: J. C. B. Mohr, 1940.

Schäfer, Peter. *The History of the Jews in the Greco-Roman World*, rev. ed. with corrections. London: Routledge, 2003.

Schäfer, Peter. *Judeophobia*. Cambridge, MA: Harvard University, 1997.

Scharff, Alexander. *Der historische Abschnitt der Lehre für König Merkiarê* (Sitzungsberichte der Bayerischen Akademie der Wissenschaften 8). Munich: C. H. Beck, 1936.

Schiffmann, Lawrence. "4QMysteries^a: A Preliminary Edition and Translation." *Solving Riddles and Untying Knots: Biblical, Epigraphic, and Semitic Studies in Honor of Jonas C. Greenfield*, ed. Ziony Zivit, Seymour Gitin, and Michael Sokoloff. Winona Lake, IN: Eisenbrauns, 1995, 207-26.

Schiffman, Lawrence H. "4QMysteries^b, a Preliminary Edition." *RevQ* 16 (1993) 203-223.

Schiffman, Lawrence H. "4QMysteries: A Preliminary Translation." *Proceedings of the Eleventh World Congress of Jewish Studies. Division A.* Jerusalem: World Union of Jewish Studies, 1994, 199-206.

Schiffman, Lawrence H. "Halakhic Elements in the Sapiential Texts from Qumran." *Sapiential Perspectives*, 89-100.

Schlott, Adelheid. *Schrift und Schreiber im Alten Ägypten*. Munich: C. H. Beck, 1989.

Schmid, Hansjörg. *Der Tempelturm Etemenanki in Babylon* (Baghdader Forschungen 17). Mainz: Philipp von Zabbern, 1995.

Schmidt, Hans. *Die Psalmen* (HAT 15). Tübingen: J. C. B. Mohr (Paul Siebeck), 1934.

Schnabel, E. J. *Law and Wisdom from Ben Sira to Paul* (WUNT 2/16). Tübingen: Mohr Siebeck, 1985.

Schofield, Malcolm. "Academic Epistemology." *The Cambridge History of Hellenistic Philosophy*. Cambridge: Cambridge University, 1999.

Schoors, Antoon. *The Preacher Sought to Find Pleasing Words. A Study of the Language of Qoheleth* (OLA 41). Leuven: Peeters, 1992.

Schroer, Silvia. *Die Weisheit hat ihr Haus gebaut. Studien zur Gestalt der Sophia in den biblischen Schriften*. Mainz: Matthias-Grünewald Verlag, 1996.

Schubart, Wilhelm. *Einführung in die Papyruskunde*. Berlin: Weidmann, 1918.

Schürer, Emil. *The History of the Jewish People in the Age of Jesus Christ (175 B.C.–135 A.D.)* 1 & 2. Edinburgh: T&T Clark, 1973-1987.

Schwartz, Seth. *Imperialism and Jewish Society. 200 B.C.E. to 640 C.E.* Princeton: Princeton Theological Seminary, 2001.

Scott, R. B. Y. *Proverbs, Ecclesiastes. Introduction, Translation, and Notes* (AB 18). Garden City, NY: Doubleday, 1965.

Scott, R. B. Y. "Wisdom in Creation: The 'Amon of Proverbs VIII 30." *VT* 10 (1960) 213-223.

Sedley, David N. "Academy." *The Oxford Companion to Classical Civilization*, ed. Simon Hornblower and Anthony Spawforth. Oxford: Oxford University, 2003.

Seow, C. L. *Ecclesiastes: A New Translation with Introduction and Commentary* (AB 18C). New York: Doubleday, 1997.

Seow, C. L. "The Social World of Ecclesiastes." *Sages, Scribes, and Seers* (FRLANT 210). Göttingen: Vandenhoeck & Ruprecht, forthcoming.

Shafer, Byron E. ed. *Temples of Ancient Egypt.* Ithaca, NY: Cornell University, 1997.

Sheppard, Gerald T. "The Epilogue to Qoheleth as Theological Commentary." *CBQ* 39 (1977) 182-189.

Sheppard, Gerald. *Wisdom as a Hermeneutical Construct* (BZAW 126). Berlin: Walter de Gruyter, 1980.

Sherwin-White, Susan, and Amélie Kuhrt. *From Samarkhand to Sardis.* Berkeley: University of California, 1993.

Shupak, Nili. *Where Can Wisdom Be Found? The Sage's Language in the Bible and in Ancient Egyptian Literature* (OBO 130). Göttingen: Vandenhoeck & Ruprecht, 1993.

Shutt, R. J. H. "Letter of Aristeas." *The Old Testament Pseudepigrapha* 2. *Expansions of the "Old Testament" and Legends, Wisdom and Philosophical Literature, Prayers, Psalms, and Odes, Fragments of Lost Judeo-Hellenistic Works* (ABRL), ed. James H. Charlesworth. New York: Doubleday, 1985, 7-34.

Silk, Michael S. "Gnome." *Oxford Classical Dictionary,* 3rd rev. ed., ed. Simon Hornblower and Antony Stallworth. Oxford: Oxford University Press, 640, 2003.

Simpson, William Kelly, ed. *The Literature of Ancient Egypt,* new ed. New Haven, CT: Yale University, 1973.

Simpson, William Kelly, ed. *The Literature of Ancient Egypt: An Anthology of Stories, Instructions, Stelae, Autobiographies, and Poetry,* 3rd ed. New Haven, CT: Yale University, 2003.

Sinclair, Daniel. "Halakhah." *The Oxford Dictionary of the Jewish Religion,* ed. R. J. Zwi Werblowsky and Geoffrey Wigoder. New York: Oxford University Press, 1997, 293-294.

Sitzler, Dorothea. *Vorwurf gegen Gott: ein religiöses Motiv im Alten Orient (Ägypten und Mesopotamien)* (Studies in Oriental Religions 32). Wiesbaden: Harrassowitz, 1995.

Six, J. P. "Observations sur les monnaies Phéniciennes." *Numismatic Chronicle* 17 (1877) 221-263.

Sjöberg, A. W. "The Old Babylonian Edubba." *Sumerological Studies in Honor of Thorkild Jacobsen on His Seventieth Birthday* (AS 20). Chicago: University of Chicago, 1975, 159-179.

Ska, J. L. "L'éloge des Pères dans le Siracide (Sir. 44-50) et le canon de l'Ancien Testament." *Treasures of Wisdom. Studies in Ben Sira and the Book of Wisdom. FS Maurice Gilbert,* ed. Núria Calduch-Benages and Jacques Vermeylen (BETL 143). Leuven: Leuven University, 1999, 181-193.

Skehan, Patrick W. "A Single Editor for the Whole Book of Proverbs." *Studies in Israelite Poetry and Wisdom* (CBQMS 1). Washington D.C.: Catholic Biblical Association, 1971, 15-26.

Skehan, Patrick. "Structures in Poems on Wisdom: Proverbs 8 and Sirah 24." *CBQ* 41 (1979) 365-379.

Skehan, Patrick W., and Alexander A. Di Lella. *The Wisdom of Ben Sira. A New Translation with Notes* (AB 39). Garden City, NY: Doubleday, 1987.

Skladny, Udo. *Die ältesten Spruchsammlungen in Israel.* Göttingen: Vandenhoeck & Ruprecht, 1962.

Slater, William J., ed. *Dining in a Classical Context.* Ann Arbor, MI: University of Michigan, 1991.

Sly, Dorothy. *Philo's Alexandria.* London: Routledge, 1996.

Smallwood, E. M. *The Jews under Roman Rule. From Pompey to Diocletian. A Study in Political Relations.* Boston: Brill, 2001.

Smallwood, E. M. *Philonis Alexandrini Legatio ad Gaium,* 2d ed. Leiden: Brill, 1970.

Smend, Rudolf. *Die Weisheit des Jesus Sirach erklärt.* Berlin: Reimer, 1906.

Smith, Duane E. "Wisdom Genres in RS22.439." *Ugaritica* 2, 215-247.

Smith-Christopher, Daniel L. "Reassessing the Historical and Sociological Impact of the Babylonian Exile (597/587-539 B.C.E.)." *Exile: Old Testament, Jewish, and Christian Conceptions,* ed. J. M. Scott. Leiden: Brill, 1997, 7-36.

Smith-Christopher, Daniel L. *The Religion of the Landless: The Social Context of the Babylonian Exile.* Bloomington, IN: Meyer-Stone Books, 1990.

Snaith, J. G. "Biblical Quotations in the Hebrew of Ecclesiasticus." *JTS* 18 (1967) 1-12.

Soden, Wolfram von. "Der grosse Hymnus an Nabû." *ZA* 61 (1971) 44-71.

Speiser, E. A. "The Case of the Obliging Servant." *JCS* 8 (1954) 98-105.

Sperber, Daniel. "Yehudah Ha-Nasi." *The Oxford Dictionary of the Jewish Religion,* ed. R. J. Zwi Werblowsky and Geoffrey Wigoder. Oxford: Oxford, 1997, 739-740.

Spieckermann, Hermann. *Lebenskunst und Gotteslob in Israel. Studien zu Weisheit, Psalter und Theologie* (FAT). Tübingen: Mohr-Siebeck, forthcoming.

Spiegel, Joachim. *Das Werden der altägyptischen Hochkultur.* Heidelberg: F. H. Kerle Verlag, 1953.

Spiegelberg, W. *Die sogenannte demotische Chronik des Pap. 215 der Bibliothèque Nationale zu Paris.* Leipzig: Hinrichs, 1915.

Spittler, R. P. "Testament of Job." *The Old Testament Pseudepigrapha* 1. *Apocalyptic Literature and Testaments (ABRL),* ed. James H. Charlesworth. New York: Doubleday, 1983, 829-868.

Stadelmann, Helge. *Ben Sira als Schriftgelehrter* (WUNT, 2nd series, 6). Tübingen: J. C. B. Mohr, 1980.

Staples, W. E. "Vanity of Vanities." *CJTh* 1 (1955) 141-156.

Stemberger, Günther. "Sages, Scribes, and Seers in Rabbinic Wisdom." *Sages, Scribes, and Seers* (FRLANT 210). Göttingen: Vandenhoeck, forthcoming.

Sterling, Gregory. "Judaism between Jerusalem and Alexandria." *Hellenism in the Land of Israel,* ed. John J. Collins and Gregory E. Sterling (Christianity and Judaism in Antiquity 13). Notre Dame, IN: University of Notre Dame, 2001, appendix, 279-290.

Sterling, Gregory E. "Judaism between Jerusalem and Alexandria." *Judaism in the Land of Israel,* ed. John J. Collins and Gregory E. Sterling. Notre Dame, IN: Notre Dame, 2001, 263-301.

Sterling, Gregory E., ed. *The Ancestral Philosophy: Hellenistic Philosophy in Second Temple Judaism. Essays of David Winston* (BJS 331). Providence, RI: BJS, 2001.

Stern, Ephraim. *Archaeology of the Land of the Bible* 2: *The Assyrian, Babylonian, and Persian Periods, 732-332.* New York: Doubleday, 2001.

Stern, Ephraim. "The Beginning of the Greek Settlement in Palestine in the Light of the

Excavations at Tel Dor." *Recent Excavations in Israel: Studies in Iron Age Archaeology,* ed. Seymour Gitin and William G. Dever (AASOR 49). Winona Lake, IN: Eisenbrauns, 1982, 107-112.

Stern, Ephraim, ed. *The New Encyclopedia of Archaeological Excavations in the Holy Land* 1-4, 2nd ed. Jerusalem: Israel Exploration Society & Carta, 1993.

Stern, Menahem. *Greek and Latin Authors on Jews and Judaism* 1. Jerusalem: Israel Academy of Sciences and Humanities, 1984, 47-52.

Steudel, Annette. "Sapiential Texts." *Qumran Cave 4. Sapiential Texts.* Part 1, ed. Torlief Elgin, et al. (DJD 20). Oxford: Clarendon, 1997, 159-167.

Stone, Michael E. "Ideal Figures and Social Context: Priest and Sage in the Early Second-Temple Age." *Selected Studies in Pseudepigrapha and Apocrypha: With Special Reference to the Armenian Tradition,* ed. Michael E. Stone (VTSup 9). Leiden: E. J. Brill, 1991, 251-270.

Stone, Michael E. *Scriptures, Sects and Visions: A Profile of Judaism from Ezra to the Jewish Revolts.* Cleveland, OH: Collins, 1980, 27-35.

Stowers, Stanley K. "Apostrophe, προσωποποιία, and Paul's Rhetorical Education." *Early Christianity and Classical Culture,* ed. John T. Fitzgerald, Thomas H. Olbricht, and L. Michael White (NovTSup 90). Leiden: Brill, 2003, 351-369.

Stowers, Stanley K. *Letter Writing in Graeco-Roman Antiquity* (Library of Early Christianity). Philadelphia: Westminster, 1986.

Strack, H. L., and Günter Stemberger. *Introduction to the Talmud and Midrash.* Minneapolis: Fortress, 1991.

Strack, H. L., and Günter Stemberger. *Introduction to the Talmud and Midrash,* 2nd ed. Minneapolis: Fortress, 1996.

Stricker, B. H. "De Wijsheid van Anchsjesjonqy." *JEOL* 15 (1933) 11-133.

Strugnell, John, and Daniel J. Harrington. *Qumran Cave 4, 24. Sapiential Texts, Part 2. 4QInstruction (MUSAR L^E MEVN): 4Q415ff. With a re-edition of 1Q26* (DJD 34). Oxford: Clarendon Press, 1999.

Suys, Émile. "Le dialogue du désespéré avec son âme." *Or* 1 (1932) 57-74.

Sweeney, Deborah. "Women's Correspondence from Deir el-Medinah." *Sesto Congresso Internazionale di Egittologia,* Atti 2. Turin: International Association of Egyptologists, 1993, 523-529.

Sweet, Ronald F. G. "The Sage in Akkadian Literature: A Philological Study." *The Sage in Israel and the Ancient Near East,* ed. John G. Gammie and Leo G. Perdue. Winona Lake, IN: Eisenbrauns, 1990, 45-65.

Sweet, Ronald F. G. "The Sage in Mesopotamian Palaces and Royal Courts." *The Sage in Israel and the Ancient Near East,* ed. John G. Gammie and Leo G. Perdue. Winona Lake, IN: Eisenbrauns, 1990, 99-107.

Tanzer, Sarah Jean. *The Sages at Qumran: Wisdom in the Hodayot.* Ph.D. diss. Harvard University, Cambridge, MA, 1987.

Tcherikover, Victor. *Hellenistic Civilization and the Jews.* New York: Athenaeum, 1970.

Tcherikover, Victor. "The Ideology of the Letter of Aristeas." *HThR* 51 (1958) 59-68.

Tcherikover, Victor. "Jewish Apologetic Literature Reconsidered." *Eos* 48 (1956) 169-193.

Tcherikover, Victor A., ed. *Corpus Papyrorum Judaicarum*. Cambridge, MA: Harvard University, 1957-1964.

Terrien, Samuel. "Job." *IB* 3. New York: Abingdon, 1954, 884-892.

Terrien, Samuel. "Quelques remarques sur les affinités de Job avec le Deutéro-Esaïe." *Volume du Congrès Genève 1965* (VTSup 15). Leiden: Brill, 1966, 295-310.

Terrien, Samuel. "Wisdom in the Psalter." *In Search of Wisdom,* ed. Leo G. Perdue, et al. Westminister/John Knox, 1993, 51-72.

Te Velde, Hermann. "Scribes and Literacy in Egypt." *Scripta Signa Vocis: Studies about Scripts, Scriptures, Scribes, and Languages in the Near East, presented to J. H. Hospers,* ed. H. L. J. Vanstiphout, et al. Groningen: E. Forsten, 1986.

Thesleff, Holger, *An Introduction to the Pythagorean Writings of the Hellenistic Period.* Åbo: Åbo Academi, 1961.

Thiers, Christophe. "Civils et militaires dans les temples: Occupation illicite et expulsion." *BIFAO* 95 (1995) 493-516.

Thissen, Heinz-Josef. *Die Lehre des Anchscheschonqi (P.BM 10508)* (Papyrologische Texte und Abhandlungen 32). Bonn: Habelt, 1984.

Thomas, Johannes. *Der Jüdische Phokylides: formgeschichtliche Zugänge zu Pseudo-Phokylides und Vergleich mit der neutestamentlichen Paränese.* Göttingen: Vandenhoeck & Ruprecht, 1992.

Thompson, Reginald Campbell, ed. *Assyrian Medical Texts, from the Originals in the British Museum.* New York: AMS Press, 1982. Reprint.

Tomlinson, Richard Allen. "Temple." *The Oxford Companion to Classical Civilization,* ed. Simon Hornblower and Anthony Spawforth. Oxford: Oxford University, 2003, 705-706.

Tov, Emanuel. "Die griechischen Bibelübersetzungen." *ANRW* 2 20/1. Berlin: Walter de Gruyter, 1987, 121-189.

Towner, W. Sibley. "The Book of Ecclesiastes." *NIB* 5. Nashville, TN: Abingdon Press, 1997, 289-360.

Trebilco, Paul. *The Early Christians in Ephesus from Paul to Ignatius* (WUNT 166). Tübingen: Mohr Siebeck, 2004.

Trible, Phyllis. "Wisdom Builds a Poem: the Architecture of Proverbs 1:20-33." *JBL* 94 (1975) 509-518.

Tripolitis, Antonio. *Religions of the Hellenistic-Roman Age.* Grand Rapids, MI: Eerdmans, 2001.

Tropper, Amran. *Wisdom, Politics, and Historiography — Tractate Avot in the Context of the Graeco-Roman Near East* (Oxford Oriental Monographs). Oxford: Oxford University, 2004.

Trublet, Jacques. "Le corpus sapiential et le Psautier." *La Sagesse biblique de L'Ancien au Nouveau Testaments* (Lectio Divina 160). Paris: Les Editions du Cerf, 1995, 139-174.

Trublet, Jacques, and Jean-Noël. *Approche poétique et théologique des psaumes, Analyses et Méthodes.* Paris: Les Editions du Cerf, 1983.

Tulli, A. "Il Naoforo Vaticano." *Miscellanea gregoriana, raccolta di scritti pubblicati nel I centenario dalla fondazione del Pont. Museo egizio (1839-1939)*. Città del Vaticano: Tip. poliglotta vaticana, 1941, 211-280.

Turcan, Robert. *The Cults of Ancient Rome*. Oxford: Blackwell, 1996.

Turcan, Robert, and Antonio Nevill. *The Cults of the Roman Empire*. Oxford: Blackwell, 1996.

Unger, E. A. *Babylon: Die Heilige Stadt nach der Beschreibung der Babylonier,* 2nd ed. Berlin: Walter de Gruyter, 1970.

Urbach, Ephraim. *The Sages: Their Concepts and Beliefs* 2, 2d ed. Jerusalem: Magnes, 1979.

Valbelle, Dominique. *Les neufs arcs. L'Egyptien et les értangers de la préhistoire à la Conquête d'Alexandre*. Paris: Colin, 1990.

Vanderhooft, David S. *The Neo-Babylonian Empire and Babylon in the Latter Prophets* (HSM 59). Atlanta: Scholars Press, 1999.

VanderKam, James C. *Enoch and the Growth of an Apocalyptic Tradition* (CBQMS 16). Washington, DC: Catholic Biblical Association, 1984.

VanderKam, James C. *From Joshua to Caiaphas*. Minneapolis: Fortress, 2004.

VanderKam, James C. "Mantic Wisdom in the Dead Sea Scrolls." *DSD* 4 (1997), 336-53.

VanderKam, James C. "To What End? Functions of Scriptural Interpretation in Qumran Texts." *Studies in the Hebrew Bible, Qumran, and the Septuagint, Presented to Eugene Ulrich,* ed. Peter W. Flint, Emanuel Tov, and James C. Vanderkam (VTSup 101). Brill: Leiden, 2006.

van Dijk, J. J. A. *La sagesse suméro-accadienne*. Leiden: E. J. Brill, 1953.

Van Leeuwen, Raymond. *Context and Meaning in Proverbs 25–27* (SBLDS 96). Atlanta: Scholars, 1988.

Van Seters, John. "A Date for the 'Admonitions' in the Second Intermediate Period." *JEA* 50 (1964) 13-23.

Van Seters, John. *In Search of History: Historiography in the Ancient World and the History of the Bible*. Winona Lake, IN: Eisenbrauns, 1997.

Vanstiphout, H. L. J. "How Did They Learn Sumerian?" *JCS* 31 (1979) 118-126.

Vanstiphout, H. L. J. "Remarks on 'Supervisor and Scribe' (or Dialogue 4, or Eduba C)." *NABU* 1 (1996) 1-2.

Vatai, F. L. *Intellectuals in Politics in the Greek World from Early Times to the Hellenistic Age*. London: Croom Helm, 1984.

Vawter, Bruce. "Prov. 8:22: Wisdom and Creation." *JBL* 99 (1980) 205-16.

Verbrugghe, Gerald P., and John M. Wickersham. *Berossos and Manetho, Introduced and Translated: Native Traditions in Ancient Mesopotamia and Egypt*. Ann Arbor, MI: University of Michigan, 1996.

Vergot, Joseph. "La notion de dieu dans les livres de sagesse Egyptien." *Les Sagesses du Proche-Orient Ancien* (Bibliothèque des Centres d'Études supérieures spécialisés) Paris: Universitaires de France, 1963, 159-190.

Vermeylen, Jacques. *Job, ses amis et son Dieu: la légende de Job et ses relectures postexiliques* (Studia Biblica 2). Leiden: Brill, 1986.

Vogels, Walter. "The God Who Creates Is the God Who Saves: The Book of Wisdom's Reversal of the Biblical Pattern." *Église et Théologie* 22 (1991) 315-335.

Volten, Aksel. *Zwei altägyptische politische Schriften* (Analecta Ägyptiaca 4). Copenhagen: Einar Munksgaard, 1945.

Volz, Paul. "Ein Beitrag aus den Papyri von Elephantine zu Hiob Kap. 31," *ZAW* 32 (1912) 126-127.

Wacholder, B. Z. *Eupolemus: A Study of Judaeo-Greek Literature.* Cincinnati: Hebrew Union College, 1974.

Waetzoldt, Hartmut. "Der Schreiber als Lehrer in Mesopotamien." *Schreiber, Magister, Lehrer,* ed. J. G. Prinz von Hohenzollern and Max Liedtke. Bad Heilbrunn: Kinkhardt, 1989, 33-50.

Wakemann, Mary K. *God's Battle with the Monster.* Leiden: Brill, 1973.

Walter, N. "'Hellenistiche Eschatologie' im Neuen Testament." *Glaube und Eschatologie,* FS W. G. Kümmel, ed. Erich Grässer and Otto Merk. Tübingen: Mohr-Siebeck, 1985, 335-356.

Walter, Nikolaus. *Der Thoraausleger Aristobulos. Untersuchungen zu seinen Fragmenten und zu pseudepigraphischen Resten der jüdisch-hellenistischen Literatur.* Berlin: Akademie Verlag, 1964.

Wanke, Gunther. "Der Lehrer im alten Israel." *Schreiber, Magister, Lehrer,* ed. Johann Georg Prinz von Hohenzollern and Max Liedtke. Bad Heilbrunn/Obb: Klinkhardt, 1989, 51-59.

Wardy, Bilhah. "Jewish Religion in Pagan Literature during the Late Republic and Early Empire." *ANRW* 2 19/1. Berlin: Walter de Gruyter, 1979, 592-644.

Warren, James. *Epicurus and Democritean Ethics: An Archaeology of Ataraxia.* Cambridge: Cambridge University Press, 2002.

Warren, James. *Facing Death: Epicurus and His Critics.* Oxford: Clarendon, 2004.

Washington, Harold C. *Wealth and Poverty in the Instruction of Amenemope and the Hebrew Proverbs* (SBLDS 142). Atlanta, GA: Scholars Press, 1994.

Waterfield, Robin. *The First Philosophers. The Presocratics and Sophists.* Oxford: Oxford University, 2000.

Watson, Duane F. "Paul and Boasting." *Paul in the Graeco-Roman World,* ed. J. Paul Sampley. Harrisburg: Trinity Press International, 2003, 77-100.

Watts, James W., ed. *Persia and Torah: The Theory of Imperial Authorization of the Pentateuch* (SBLSymS 17). Atlanta: SBL, 2001.

Weigl, Michael. "Compositional Strategies in the Aramaic Sayings of Ahikar: Columns 6-8." *The World of the Aramaeans* III. *Studies in Language and Literature in Honour of Paul-Eugène Dion,* ed. P. Michèle Daviau, John W. Wevers, and Michael Weigl (JSOT 326). Sheffield: Sheffield Academic Press, 2001, 22-82.

Weill, Raymond. "Le livre du 'Désespéré.'" *BIFAO* 45 (1947) 89-154.

Weinfeld, Moshe. *Deuteronomy and the Deuteronomic School.* Oxford: Clarendon Press, 1972.

Weisberg, D. E. *Guild Structure and Political Allegiance in Early Achaemenid Mesopotamia.* Baltimore: Johns Hopkins University, 1967.

Wells, Louise. *The Greek Language of Healing from Homer to New Testament Times* (BZNW 83). Berlin: Walter de Gruyter, 1998.

Wente, Edward. "The Scribes of Ancient Egypt." *CANE* 4 (1995) 2211-2221.

Westermann, Claus. *The Structure of the Book of Job.* Philadelphia: Fortress, 1981.

Westermann, Claus. *What Does the Old Testament Say about God?* Atlanta: John Knox Press, 1979.

Whedbee, J. W. "The Comedy of Job." *Semeia* 7 (1970) 182-200.

White, Hayden. *Metahistory: the Historical Imagination in Nineteenth-Century Europe.* Baltimore: Johns Hopkins University, 1987.

Whiteland, Keith. *The Just King: Monarchical Judicial Authority in Ancient Israel* (JSOTSup 8). Sheffield: JSOT, 1979.

Whybray, Ronald. "Conservatisme et radicalisme dans Qohelet." *Sagesse et religion: [actes du] colloque de Strasbourg, octobre 1976* (Bibliothèque des centres d'études supérieures specialisé d'histoire des religions de Strasbourg). Paris: Les Universitaires de France, 1979, 65-81.

Whybray, Ronald N. *The Intellectual Tradition in the Old Testament* (BZAW 135). Berlin: Walter de Gruyter, 1974.

Whybray, Ronald N. "Proverbs VIII,22-31 and Its Supposed Prototypes." *VT* 15 (1965) 504-14.

Whybray, Ronald N. "Qoheleth, Preacher of Joy." *JSOT* 23 (1982) 87-98.

Whybray, Ronald N. "The Social World of the Wisdom Writers." *The World of Ancient Israel,* ed. R. E. Clements. Cambridge: Cambridge University, 1989, 227-250.

Whybray, Ronald N. *The Succession Narrative: A Study of II Samuel 9–20, I Kings 1 and 2* (SBT, 2nd Series 8). Naperville, IL: Alec R. Allenson, 1968.

Whybray, Ronald N. "The Wisdom Psalms." *Wisdom in Ancient Israel,* ed. John Day, et al. Cambridge: Cambridge University Press, 152-160.

Wicke-Reuter, Ursel. "Ben Sira und die Frühe Stoa. Zum Zusammenhang von Ethik und dem Glauben an eine göttliche Providenz." *Ben Sira's God. Proceedings of the International Ben Sira Conference Durham-Upshaw College 2001,* ed. Renate Egger-Wenzel (BZAW 321). Berlin: Walter de Gruyter, 2002, 268-281.

Wicke-Reuter, Ursel. *Göttliche Providenz und menschliche Verantwortung bei Ben Sira und in der Frühen Stoa* (BZAW 298). Berlin: Walter de Gruyter, 2000.

Wiesmann, H. "Ps. 34 (Vulg. 33)." *Bib* 16 (1935) 416-421.

Wilde, A. de. *Das Buch Hiob* (OTS 22). Leiden: E. J. Brill, 1981.

Wilkinson, Richard H. *The Complete Temples of Ancient Egypt.* London: Thames & Hudson, 2000.

Williams, D. S. "The Date of Ecclesiasticus." *VT* 44 (1994) 563-556.

Williams, David S. "3 Maccabees: A Defense of Diaspora Judaism?" *JSP* 13 (1995) 17-29.

Williams, Ronald J. "Egyptian Wisdom Literature." *AB* 2 (1992), 395-399.

Williams, Ronald J. "Literature as a Medium of Political Propaganda in Ancient Egypt." *The Seed of Wisdom.* Toronto: University of Toronto, 1964.

Williams, Ronald J. "The Sages in Ancient Egypt." *JAOS* 101 (1981) 1-19.

Williams, Ronald J. "Scribal Training in Ancient Egypt." *JAOS* 92 (1972) 214-221.

Williamson, H. G. W. *Israel in the Books of Chronicles.* Cambridge: Cambridge University Press, 1977.

Wilson, G. H. "Shaping the Psalter: A Consideration of Editorial Linkage in the Book of Psalms." *Shape and Shaping of the Psalter,* ed. J. Clinton McCann (JSOTSup 159). Sheffield: JSOT Press, 1993, 42-51, 72-82.

Winston, David. *Logos and Mystical Theology in Philo of Alexandria.* Cincinnati: Hebrew Union College, 1985.

Winston, David. "Review of 'Il libro della sapienza: Struttura e genere letterario.'" *CBQ* 48 (1986) 527.

Winston, David. "The Sage as Mystic in the Wisdom of Solomon." *The Sage in Israel and the Ancient Near East,* ed. John G. Gammie and Leo G. Perdue. Winona Lake, IN: Eisenbrauns, 383-397.

Winston, David. "Theodicy in Ben Sira and Stoic Philosophy." *Of Scholars, Savants, and Their Texts,* ed. Ruth Link-Salinger. New York: Peter Lang, 1989, 239-249.

Winston, David. *The Wisdom of Solomon: A New Translation with Introduction and Commentary* (AB 43). Garden City: Doubleday, 1979.

Winter, Bruce W. *Philo and Paul among the Sophists: Alexandrian and Corinthian Responses to a Julio-Claudian Movement,* 2nd ed. Grand Rapids, MI: W. B. Eerdmans, 2002.

Wischmeyer, Oda. *Die Kultur des Buches Ben Sira* (BZNW 77). Berlin: Walter de Gruyter, 1995.

Wiseman, D. J. "A New Text of the Babylonian Poem of the Righteous Sufferer." *AnSt* 30 (1980) 101-107.

Witherington, Ben, III. *Jesus the Sage: The Pilgrimage of Wisdom.* Minneapolis: Fortress, 2000.

Witt, R. E. *Isis in the Graeco-Roman World.* Ithaca, NY: Cornell University, 1971.

Witte, Markus. *Vom Leiden zur Lehre. Der dritte Redegang (Hiob 21–27) und die Redaktionsgeschichte des Hiobbuches* (BZAW 230). Berlin: Walter de Gruyter, 1994.

Wlosok, Antonie, ed. *Römischer Kaiserkult* (WdF 372). Darmstadt: Wissenschaftliche Buchgesellschaft, 1978.

Wolfson, Harry Austryn. *Introduction to Philo Judaeus,* 2d ed. Oxford: Blackwell Publishers, 1962.

Wolfson, Harry Austryn. *Philo: Foundations of Religious Philosophy in Judaism, Christianity, and Islam* 1 & 2, 2nd ed. Cambridge: Harvard University, 1948.

Woude, A. S. van der. "'Wicked Priest' or 'Wicked Priests'? Reflections on the Identification of the Wicked Priests in the Habakkuk Commentary." *JSS* 33 (1982) 349-359.

Wright, Addison. "The Riddle of the Sphinx: The Structure of the Book of Qoheleth." *CBQ* 30 (1968) 313-334.

Wright, Addison. "The Structure of the Book of Wisdom." *Bib* 48 (1967) 165-184.

Wright, Addison. "The Structure of Wisdom 11–19." *CBQ* 27 (1965) 28-34.

Wright, Benjamin G. "The Discourse of Riches and Poverty in the Book of Ben Sira." *SBLSP.* Atlanta: Scholars Press, 1998, 559-578.

Wright, B. G. *No Small Difference: Sirach's Relationship to Its Hebrew Parent Text* (SCS 26). Atlanta: Scholars Press, 1989.

Yee, Gale A. "An Analysis of Prov. 8:22-31 according to Style and Structure." *ZAW* 94 (1982) 58-66.

Yoder, Christine Roy. *Wisdom as a Woman of Substance: A Socioeconomic Reading of Proverbs 1–9 and 31:10-31* (BZAW 304). Berlin: Walter de Gruyter, 2001.

Žabkar, Louis. "Ba." *LÄ* 1 (1973) 588-598.

Zadok, Ron. *The Jews in Babylonia during the Chaldean and Achaemenid Periods according to the Babylonian Sources.* Haifa: University of Haifa, 1979.

Ziegler, Joseph. *Sapientia Iesu filii Sirach,* ed. Joseph Ziegler (Septuaginta 12/2). Göttingen: Vandenhoeck & Ruprecht, 1965.

Ziegler, Joseph. *Sapientia Salomonis* (Göttingen Septuagint 12/1). Göttingen: Vandenhoeck & Ruprecht, 1962.

Zimmerli, Walther. "Das Buch des Predigers Salomo." *Sprüche/Prediger* (ATD 16). Göttingen: Vandenhoeck & Ruprecht, 1962, 123-351.

Zimmerli, Walther. "Das Buch Kohelet — Traktat oder Sentenzensammlung?" *VT* 24 (1974) 221-230.

Zimmerli, Walther. "The Place and Limit of the Wisdom in the Framework of the Old Testament Theology." *SJTh* 17 (1964) 146-158.

Zimmerli, Walther. "'Unveränderbare Welt' oder 'Gott ist Gott'?" *"Wenn nicht jetzt wann dann?" Aufsätze für Hans-Joachim Kraus zum 65. Geburtstage,* ed. Hans-Georg Geyer, et al. Neukirchen-Vluyn: Neukirchener Verlag, 1983, 103-114.

Index of Modern Authors

Index of Biblical Texts

Index of Nonbiblical Ancient Literature